W9-BNN-589

Schweiz

DEUTSCHLAND

Rhein

Schaffhausen

Bodensee

Basel

Winterthur

Baden

Zürich

St. Gallen

Zürichsee

ÖSTERREICH

Vaduz

LIECHTENSTEIN

Solothurn

Aare

Biel

Bieler See

Luzern

Walensee

Neuchâtel

Schwyz

FRANKREICH

Lac de Neuchâtel

Bern

Vierwaldstätter See

Chur

Davos

Inn

Rhein

Fribourg

Yverdon-les-Bains

Thun

Brienzer See

Interlaken

St. Moritz

Thuner See

Genfer See

Lausanne

Jungfrau 4,158 m

St. Gotthard-Tunnel

A L P E N

Montreux

Rhône

Simplonpass

Locarno

Genf

Zermatt

Lago Maggiore

Lugano

Matterhorn 4,478 m

Lago di Lugano

Mont Blanc 4,807 m

ITALIEN

0   25   50   75 km

0   25   50 mi

DEUTSCHLAND

LIECHTENSTEIN

SCHWEIZ

ÖSTERREICH

Österreich

TSCHECHISCHE REPUBLIK

Donau

NIEDERÖSTERREICH

Schärding

Krems

Donau

St. Pölten

Linz

Melk

Wien

SLOWAKEI

Inn

Braunau

WIENERWALD

OBERÖSTERREICH

Steyr

WIEN

Leitha

DEUTSCHLAND

Bodensee

Salzburg

St. Wolfgang

Bad Ischl

Wiener Neustadt

Eisenstadt

Neusiedler See

Bregenz

Wolfgangsee

Enns

SCHWEIZ

Dornbirn

Zugspitze 2,963 m

Inn

Kitzbühel

Zell am See

SALZBURG

Dachstein 2,995 m

Leoben

Mur

STEIERMARK

BURGENLAND

Vaduz

VORARLBERG

Innsbruck

Salzach

A L P E N

Badgastein

UNGARN

LIECHTENSTEIN

TIROL

Brenner-Paß

Großglockner 3,798 m

Tauern-Tunnel

Gurk

Graz

TIROL

Lienz

Spittal

Wolfsberg

Drau

Wörther See

KÄRNTEN

ITALIEN

Villach

Klagenfurt

Drau

Mur

SLOWENIEN

KROATIEN

0   50   100 km

0   25   50 mi

SEVENTH EDITION

Deutsch heute

GRUNDSTUFE

Jack Moeller
Oakland University

Winnifred R. Adolph
Florida State University

Gisela Hoecherl-Alden
University of Pittsburgh

John F. Lalande II
University of Illinois

In association with

Helmut Liedloff
Southern Illinois University

Constanze Kirmse
Goethe-Institut München

Houghton Mifflin Company Boston New York

Director, Modern Language Programs: E. Kristina Baer
Development Manager: Beth Kramer
Assistant Editor: Angela Schoenherr
Project Editor: Harriet C. Dishman
Senior Production/Design Coordinator: Carol Merrigan
Senior Manufacturing Coordinator: Sally Culler
Marketing Manager: Jay Hu

Cover design by Diana Coe / ko Design Studio
Cover photograph © 1997 by Joachim Schumacher/DAS FOTOARCHIV

Printed in the U.S.A.

Library of Congress Catalog Card Number: 99-71951

ISBN: 0-395-96259-5

123456789-DW-03 02 01 00 99

C O N T E N T S

KAPITEL 3

Was brauchst du?   88

KAPITEL 4

Was studierst du?   126

KAPITEL 5

Servus in Österreich 163

KAPITEL 6

Was hast du vor? 199

KAPITEL 12

Die multikulturelle Gesellschaft   407

Bausteine für Gespräche

Rockfans gegen Ausländerhass   408

Lesestück

Wo ist mein Zuhause?   410

Grammatik und Übungen

Kurzgeschichte

Schlittenfahren – Helga M. Novak   432

REFERENCE SECTION

INTRODUCTION

Deutsch heute: Grundstufe, Seventh Edition is an introductory program in German designed for college students and other adult learners. One goal of *Deutsch heute* is to provide students with a sound basis for learning German as it is used in spoken and written communication today within the context of German-speaking culture. The *Deutsch heute* program offers systematic practice in the four basic language skills of listening, speaking, reading, and writing, along with materials geared to provide a firm foundation in the basic elements of German grammar. *Deutsch heute* also provides activities that guide you in employing your skills in active personal communication and offers you opportunities to experience authentic materials likely to be encountered in a German-speaking country—materials like schedules, menus, and TV listings.

By the end of the course, you will have had the opportunity to master the basic features of the sound and writing systems, become familiar with the communicative functions of the language, role-play various situations with a partner, learn how to get the gist of various types of authentic materials, use actively many basic grammatical structures in everyday conversation and writing as well as understand material that contains grammatical features of lower frequency, use an active vocabulary of approximately 1200 words, and understand a considerable number of additional words.

Another goal of the Seventh Edition of *Deutsch heute* is to introduce you to contemporary life and culture in the three primary German-speaking countries: Germany, Austria, and Switzerland. The dialogues and readings convey important information on everyday life and culture in these countries. The readings are mature in content but simple in structure. Cultural notes (*Land und Leute*) throughout the textbook provide more in-depth information. In combination with the photographs, drawings, and ads included in the Seventh Edition of *Deutsch heute,* the readings help convey to you what life is like in the German-speaking countries today.

A further goal of *Deutsch heute, Seventh Edition* is to have you experience the relationship between culture and language, thereby making you more aware of your own native language and culture.

Organization of the Student Text

The student text contains an introductory chapter **(Einführung)** and twelve regular chapters (*Kapitel*). The *Einführung* is designed to get you speaking and using German for active, personal communication from the very start. It introduces you to the German sound system by means of a short dialogue (*Bausteine für Gespräche*), the German alphabet, and numbers. You will learn to give information about yourself, to spell words, to use numbers in simple arithmetic, to give the day of the week, and to describe the contents of your room by size and color.

Each of the *Kapitel* centers on a cultural theme such as university life, shopping, leisure time, the social position of women, the German economy, Germany since 1945, and Germany as a multicultural society. There are also specific readings on Austria and Switzerland.

A cast of characters (*Personen*) who are students at the *Freie Universität Berlin* and the *Universität Mainz* play a role in the dialogues, some of the readings, and many of the exercises. On page xvii you will learn the names of the characters and a little about them. However, you will come to know them better as you progress through the text. The same characters appear in the workbook and tests so that you will have a sense of familiarity with the activities. A typical chapter is composed of the following sections:

1. *Lernziele* are chapter objectives that summarize the content of each chapter and provide you with learning goals in five basic areas: communication tasks and purposes (*Sprechintentionen*), a reading (*Lesestück*) based on a cultural theme, additional cultural information in English (*Land und Leute*), vocabulary (*Vokabeln*), and grammar (*Grammatik*).

2. *Bausteine für Gespräche* introduce idiomatic and colloquial phrases presented in dialogue format. Each of the dialogues presents a brief episode in the life of two or more of the students who form the cast of characters. A drawing illustrates some aspect of the dialogues and thus provides visual clues to the dialogue situations. English equivalents of the basic dialogues are located in the Reference Section. The equivalents are in colloquial English and not a literal translation of the German. A section called *Brauchbares* (Useful information) follows most dialogues. This section highlights, explains, and sometimes amplifies linguistic features and cultural information from the dialogues. Communication practice and vocabulary development continue in the oral activities that follow, which include *Fragen* (Questions on the dialogues) and partner/group activities offering choices so that you can formulate your own responses. Most chapters contain sections of vocabulary expansion exercises and activities (*Erweiterung des Wortschatzes*). A list of words that you should learn and be able to use (*Vokabeln*) concludes this section.

3. *Lesestücke*, the main cultural readings, present the cultural theme of each *Kapitel*. Each *Lesestück* is preceded by pre-reading activities (*Vorbereitung auf das Lesen*) to give direction to your reading and help you to be successful in second-language reading: *Vor dem Lesen* (Before the reading) activities help to familiarize you with the topic of each reading by letting you discover what you may already know about the topic; *Beim Lesen* (While reading) provides specific questions to answer, words or phrases to look for, or tasks to complete (such as note-taking) as a means of aiding you in structuring your reading experience. The activities in the *Vorbereitung* are in English in *Kapitel 1–4* and in German beginning with *Kapitel 5*. A *Brauchbares* section serves the same function as that section after the dialogues. Readings are then followed by the section *Nach dem Lesen* (After the reading) which contains written and oral exercises, including *Fragen zum*

Lesestück (Questions on the reading), *Erzählen wir* (Let's discuss it), partner/group activities, often a vocabulary-expansion section (*Erweiterung des Wortschatzes*), and a list of words to memorize (*Vokabeln*).

4. *Grammatik und Übungen* (*Grammar and Exercises*) explain grammatical concepts in concise, lucid terms and contain illustrative examples, often with equivalents in English. Grammar is explained in English to ensure immediate comprehension, and basic terms are regularly defined. The German terms for the grammatical features are given in the margin. German structure is often contrasted with English to clarify the structure of both languages. The grammar exercises have German titles and, beginning with *Kapitel 4,* the direction lines are also in German. The direction lines set the scene and clearly state grammatical tasks to make the communicative purpose clearer. The exercises can be completed in writing or orally in class; they can also be used for review and additional practice in combination with the Computer Study Modules and with the audio program for home or language lab study. Included in the grammar exercises are partner/group activities that provide opportunity to use "grammar" in a personal situation.

5. *Wiederholung* (*Review*) activities practice the content, structure, and vocabulary of the chapter in new formats and reintroduce material from earlier chapters.

6. *Grammatik: Zusammenfassung* (*Grammar: Summary*) provides grammatical tables, and, where useful, a brief summary of a grammatical feature introduced in the chapter. This is a reference section that is useful for review.

7. *Land und Leute* (*The Country and Its People*) sections provide more in-depth cultural information about many aspects of the German-speaking countries. The topics of *Land und Leute* are related to the overall chapter theme. Each *Land und Leute* is accompanied by a photo to further illustrate the cultural topic. Activities following the cultural presentation ask you to think about the information in new ways, often as a comparison to your experience in your own culture. For additional information, the Web icon (www) directs you to the **Deutsch heute** Web Site for Web addresses that relate to the cultural topic.

Partner/group activities occur throughout the chapter, in the *Bausteine* and *Lesestück* sections, as well as in the *Grammatik und Übungen* and *Wiederholung.* They are preceded by two facing arrows. ⟳

In one type of partner/group activities, you are requested to respond to questions or statements in a way that reflects your personal opinions, attitudes, or experience. Often, varied responses are listed; these responses represent a variety of attitudes or moods. New vocabulary is marked with a raised degree mark (°). The printed variations do not represent all possible responses, but rather, they are a selection of useful conversational tools covering a range of meanings. You should choose the responses that actually express your own feelings or ideas and invent or recall other expressions from previous chapters.

In a second type of partner/group activity, called *Frage-Ecke,* both you and your partner have a chart. Your chart contains information that your partner wants and your partner's chart contains information that you want. The charts for each partner are printed near each other so when doing this exercise you will, of course, need to look only at your own chart. In addition to the information given in the chart, you are each asked to supply personal information related to the topic of the exercise. Once your partner has answered your question you should ask additional ones to elicit more information. For instance, in *Kapitel 6* your partner tells you what she/he is doing over the weekend. You may then pursue the matter in more detail by asking when, with whom, whether she/he does it often, etc. In this way the exercise leads into a genuine exchange of information.

In the third type of partner/group work you are given a situation that requires communication with a partner but no vocabulary or structures are suggested. Additional words and phrases to express notions such as skepticism, insecurity, and annoyance are found in the Supplementary Expressions of the Reference Section. You may refer to these and to the Supplementary Word Sets to approach more closely what you want to say.

Authentic materials appear at various places throughout the text. "Authentic materials or texts" is a term used to indicate such common printed material as menus, advertisements, classified ads, and television listings. These materials are part of the experience in the daily life of a native German speaker and many of them are also encountered by a visitor to a German-speaking country. You are not expected to understand each word in such a text. Rather you should try to extract only the information that interests you. For example, it is not necessary to read the entire *TV Guide* to find out what program you wish to see on a particular day at a particular time.

To help you learn to deal with such materials a variety of activities are provided that range from questions that help you get essential information and directions that help you guess meaning to opportunities to make use of the material in a role-playing situation. Definitions of all new words are provided in the Vocabulary for Authentic Text Activities in the Reference Section.

Deutsch heute, Seventh Edition is illustrated with numerous photographs, authentic materials, and line drawings. Since many of the photographs and authentic materials are closely related to the cultural notes and themes of the dialogues and core reading selections, they can be effectively used as the basis for many activities. Drawings accompany each set of dialogues and a number of exercises are based on line drawings. Line drawings are also often used to introduce word sets and to demonstrate grammatical concepts and semantic differences explained in the grammar section. Maps of the German-speaking countries are found on the inside cover leaf at the front of the book; a map of Europe is found on the inside cover leaf at the back of the book.

The Reference Section contains these elements:

Bausteine: English Equivalents: The English equivalents printed beside the German version of the dialogues *(Bausteine)* permit you to check your understanding of the conversations. You may also use them to get a general idea of the dialogues before actually working with the German lines.

Supplementary Word Sets: This reference list of supplementary word sets offers you another opportunity to personalize vocabulary. You can consult these word lists, arranged by theme, for any topic in which you have a special interest and for which you may wish to expand your vocabulary. Many of the partner/group activities indicate where these lists may be useful, and they are often correlated with topics presented in the *Erweiterung des Wortschatzes* sections.

Supplementary Expressions: This reference list of supplementary expressions helps you increase the number of things you can say and write during the course of a chapter. The list of expressions is organized according to functions and notions, for example, stalling for time; expressing skepticism, regret, or admiration; asking for favors; and making requests.

Vocabulary for Authentic Text Activities: All words and abbreviations that appear in authentic materials and because of their special nature are not included in the German–English Vocabulary are listed in Vocabulary for Authentic Text Activities. You may consult this section for help if you cannot guess the meaning of a word or phrase and are thus not able to get the gist of the message.

Pronunciation and Writing Guide: This sound-symbol section gives three or four key words and simplified phonetic symbols for each German sound. Each section provides hints on how to pronounce the sound, and where useful, contrasts it with English.

Grammatical Tables: The tables in the Reference Section include the following charts: (1) paradigms for pronouns, articles, adjectives, and nouns; (2) adjectives and adverbs that are irregular in their comparative and superlative forms; (3) lists of prepositions governing the accusative, dative, or genitive case; (4) special verb + preposition combinations; (5) dative verbs; (6) examples of regular and irregular weak verbs, modals, and strong verbs, including stem-changing verbs, in various tenses of the indicative, passive, and subjunctive; and (7) a list of the strong and irregular weak verbs used in the Seventh Edition of **Deutsch heute** with principal parts and English meanings.

German–English Vocabulary: The German–English end vocabulary lists all words used in **Deutsch heute, Seventh Edition** except numbers. Numerals after the English definitions indicate the chapter in which words and phrases are introduced in the *Vokabeln* lists for the *Bausteine für Gespräche* and *Lesestücke.* Recognition vocabulary from readings and exercises not intended for active mastery is also included.

English–German Vocabulary: The English–German end vocabulary contains the words listed in the chapter *Vokabeln* lists. This list of approximately 1200 words constitutes the active vocabulary of a student who has successfully completed the **Deutsch heute** program.

Index: The index indicates the pages on which grammatical features and topics in the *Erweiterung des Wortschatzes* are introduced. References to the cultural notes, called *Land und Leute,* are also included.

Arbeitsheft

The **Arbeitsheft (Workbook/Lab Manual/Video Workbook)** consists of five sections: (1) a workbook with writing exercises coordinated with each chapter of the text; (2) a lab manual that requires you to react orally or in writing to material on the recordings; (3) a video workbook that offers a number of pre- and post-viewing activities for the *Unterwegs!* video; (4) self-tests with an answer key for correction; and (5) proficiency cards, which provide tasks and problem-solving activities for in-class use. Exercises in both the Workbook and the Lab Manual parallel the presentation of content, structure, and vocabulary in the student text. The *Übungen zum Hörverständnis* of the Lab Manual include dialogues and narratives for extra practice in listening comprehension. Many Workbook chapters contain short reading passages based on familiar material to give you extra practice in reading German. The Seventh Edition of the **Deutsch heute Arbeitsheft** contains many communicative exercises that allow you greater freedom of expression, and a number of art- and realia-based exercises.

The proficiency cards supplement the partner activities in the text. The cards are coordinated with each chapter and allow you to synthesize your acquired knowledge of communication tasks and purposes, vocabulary, grammar, and culture in simulations of culturally authentic situations. The proficiency cards offer activities that permit you to be creative and spontaneous in completing a specified communication task. Your instructor will generally refrain from correcting and providing any information or feedback until you have completed the task on the card.

Recordings

The audio recordings that accompany **Deutsch heute, Seventh Edition** were made to provide the best possible models of German speech. Using a cast of native speakers, the recordings provide recorded versions of printed material from the *Einführung,* the *Bausteine,* the *Lesestücke,* exercises from the *Grammatik und Übungen,* indicated by a headphone icon, other exercises called Variation that practice the same grammatical features as their corresponding numbers in the text but appear only in the recordings, and the two short stories in the textbook. In addition, the recordings include the listening comprehension exercises called *Übungen zum Hörverständnis* and the pronunciation sections called *Übungen zur Aussprache* from the Lab Manual. The direction lines of the exercises and activities are in English. The recorded material is indicated by a headphone icon.

Sentences from the *Bausteine* are spoken once at normal speed, then modeled phrase by phrase with pauses for repetition, and finally modeled again with pauses for repetition of complete utterances. The reading selections (*Lesestücke*) are recorded without pauses. The grammar exercises are recorded in three phases: cue, pause for response, and confirmation response. Group/partner activities and activities from the *Erweiterung des Wortschatzes* and *Wiederholung* sections are not on tape. The *Übungen zum Hörverständnis* from the Lab Manual are followed by a pause to allow you to respond in writing. Longer reading passages are read twice. The *Übungen zur Aussprache* are recorded in two phases: cue and pause for response. The recordings are available for student purchase on audio CDs and cassettes.

Video Program

A video program entitled *Unterwegs!* reinforces topics and vocabulary found in **Deutsch heute.** The video was shot on location in the university town of Tübingen. It includes twelve five- to seven-minute episodes, featuring a continuing story line about three young people, two university students, Julian and Sabine, and Sabine's cousin Lisa. Pre-viewing and post-viewing activities in the Video Workbook section of the **Arbeitsheft** guide your viewing of the video material so that you may get the most out of the experience.

Computer Study Modules

Available in both Windows® and Macintosh® platforms, the Computer Study Modules include all the discrete-point exercises from the textbook. You can use this computerized study aid for reinforcement and practice of grammar and vocabulary or as an additional preparation for exams. Your answers will be checked by the program.

CD-ROM

The *Einfach toll!* CD-ROM is a self-study learning tool: you can use it at home or in the language lab to hone your listening skills. The video was shot on location in Mainz, Germany and brings to life scenes of everyday activities in the lives of a number of German young people. The video's eight modules show scenes from school, a birthday party, shopping, a discussion about chores, free time, a café scene, a search for an apartment, and a trip on the Rhine. Each module begins with comprehension activities, then moves to more complex manipulation activities, and concludes with

a creative, freeform activity. Cultural notes within each module provide additional background information on the material presented in the video clips.

Deutsch heute Web Site

The **Deutsch heute** Web Site at www.hmco.com/college, relates specifically to **Deutsch heute** and offers an opportunity for you to test yourself on the grammar and vocabulary from each *Kapitel.* You will also be able to work in a culturally authentic context by completing the Web search activities at the **Deutsch heute** Web Site. The site also lists Web addresses for additional information about the cultural topics in *Land und Leute.*

German Web Resources

The web site, www.hmco.com/college, provides links to existing German sites, maps of the German-speaking world, and transparencies of a general nature that can be downloaded.

Classroom Expressions

Below is a list of common classroom expressions in German (with English equivalents) which the instructor may use. Also provided are common expressions you can use to make comments or requests and ask questions.

Terms of Praise and Disapproval

Gut. Das ist (sehr) gut. Good. That is (very) good.
Schön. Das ist (sehr) schön. Nice. That is (very) nice.
Ausgezeichnet. Excellent.
Wunderbar. Wonderful.
Das ist schon besser. That's better.
Viel besser. Much better.
Nicht schlecht. Not bad.
Richtig. Right.
Natürlich. Of course.
Genau. Exactly.
Sind Sie/Bist du sicher? Are you sure?
Nein, das ist nicht (ganz) richtig. No, that's not (quite) right.
Ein Wort ist nicht richtig. One word isn't right.

Nein, das ist falsch.   No, that's wrong.

Sie haben/Du hast mich nicht verstanden. Ich sage es noch einmal.   You didn't understand me. I'll say it again.

Sie haben/Du hast den Satz (das Wort) nicht verstanden.   You didn't understand the sentence (the word).

Sagen Sie/Sag (Versuchen Sie/Versuch) es noch einmal bitte.   Say (Try) it again please.

General Instructions

Nicht so laut bitte.   Not so loud please.

Würden Sie/Würdet ihr bitte genau zuhören.   Would you please listen carefully.

Stehen Sie/Steht bitte auf.   Stand up please.

Bilden Sie/Bildet einen Kreis.   Form a circle.

Arbeiten Sie/Arbeitet einen Moment mit Partnern.   Work for a minute with partners.

Bringen Sie/Bringt (Bilder) von zu Hause mit.   Bring (pictures) along from home.

(Morgen) haben wir eine Klausur.   (Tomorrow) we're having a test.

Schreiben Sie/Schreibt jetzt bitte.   Please write now.

Lesen Sie/Lest jetzt bitte.   Please read now.

Ich fange (Wir fangen) jetzt an.   I'll (We'll) begin now.

Fangen Sie/Fangt jetzt an.   Begin now.

Hören Sie/Hört bitte auf zu schreiben (lesen).   Please stop writing (reading).

Könnte ich bitte Ihre/eure Aufsätze (Klassenarbeiten, Tests, Übungsarbeiten, Hausaufgaben) haben?   Could I please have your essays (tests, tests, exercises, homework)?

Jeder verbessert seine eigene Arbeit.   Everyone should correct her or his own work (paper).

Verbessern Sie Ihre/Verbessere deine Arbeit bitte.   Please correct your work (paper).

Tauschen Sie mit Ihrem/Tausch mit deinem Nachbarn.   Exchange with your neighbor.

Machen Sie/Macht die Bücher auf (zu).   Open (Shut) your books.

Schlagen Sie/Schlagt Seite (11) in Ihrem/eurem Buch auf.   Turn to page (11) in your book.

Schauen Sie/Schaut beim Sprechen nicht ins Buch.   Don't look at your book while speaking.

Wiederholen Sie/Wiederholt den Satz (den Ausdruck).   Repeat the sentence (the expression).

Noch einmal bitte.   Once again please.

(Etwas) Lauter. (Deutlicher./Langsamer./Schneller.)   (Somewhat) Louder. (Clearer./Slower./Faster.)

Sprechen Sie/Sprich bitte deutlicher.   Please speak more distinctly.

(Jan), Sie/du allein.   (Jan), you alone.

Alle zusammen.   All (everybody) together.

Sprechen Sie/Sprecht mir nach.   Repeat after me.

(Nicht) Nachsprechen bitte.   (Don't) Repeat after me.

Hören Sie/Hört nur zu. Nur zuhören bitte.   Just listen.

Hören Sie/Hört gut zu.   Listen carefully.

Lesen Sie/Lies den Satz (den Absatz) vor.   Read the sentence (the paragraph) aloud.

Jeder liest einen Satz.   Everyone should read one sentence.

Fangen Sie/Fang mit Zeile (17) an.   Begin with line (17).

Nicht auf Seite (19), auf Seite (20).   Not on page (19), on page (20).

Gehen Sie/Geh an die Tafel.   Go to the board.

(Jan), gehen Sie/gehst du bitte an die Tafel?   (Jan), will you please go to the board?

Wer geht an die Tafel?   Who will go to the board?

Schreiben Sie/Schreib den Satz (das Wort) an die Tafel.   Write the sentence (the word) on the board.

Schreiben Sie/Schreibt ab, was an der Tafel steht.   Copy what is on the board.

Wer weiß es (die Antwort)?   Who knows it (the answer)?

Wie sagt man das auf Deutsch (auf Englisch)?   How do you say that in German (in English)?

Auf Deutsch bitte.   In German please.

Verstehen Sie/Verstehst du die Frage (den Satz)?   Do you understand the question (the sentence)?

Ist es (zu) schwer (leicht)?   Is it (too) difficult (easy)?

Sind Sie/Seid ihr fertig?   Are you finished?

Kommen Sie/Komm (morgen) nach der Stunde zu mir.   Come see me (tomorrow) after class.

Jetzt machen wir weiter.   Now let's go on.

Jetzt machen wir was anderes.   Now let's do something different.

Jetzt beginnen wir was Neues.   Now let's begin something new.

Das ist genug für heute.   That's enough for today.

Hat jemand Fragen?   Does anyone have a question?

Haben Sie/Habt ihr Fragen?   Do you have any questions?

Student Responses and Questions

Das verstehe ich nicht. I don't understand that.

Das habe ich nicht verstanden. I didn't understand that.

Ah, ich verstehe. Oh, I understand.

Ich weiß es nicht. I don't know (that).

Wie bitte? *(Said when you don't catch what someone said.)* Pardon./Excuse me?/I'm sorry.

Wie sagt man... auf Deutsch (auf Englisch)? How do you say . . . in German (in English)?

Können Sie den Satz noch einmal sagen bitte? Can you repeat that please?

Kann sie/er den Satz wiederholen bitte? Can she/he repeat the sentence please?

Ich habe kein Papier (Buch). I don't have any paper (a book).

Ich habe keinen Bleistift (Kuli). I don't have a pencil (a pen).

Auf welcher Seite sind wir? Welche Zeile? Which page are we on? Which line?

Wo steht das? Where is that?

Ich habe eine Frage. I have a question.

Was haben wir für morgen (Montag) auf? What do we have due for tomorrow (Monday)?

Sollen wir das schriftlich oder mündlich machen? Should we do that in writing or orally?

Wann schreiben wir die nächste Arbeit? When do we have the next paper (written work)?

Wann schreiben wir den nächsten Test? When do we have the next test?

Für wann (sollen wir das machen)? For when (are we supposed to do that)?

Ist das so richtig? Is that right this way?

(Wann) Können Sie mir helfen? (When) Can you help me?

(Wann) Kann ich mit Ihnen sprechen? (When) Can I see you?

Acknowledgments

The authors and publisher of **Deutsch heute, Seventh Edition,** would like to thank Gabriele Axtmann, Pforzheim, Germany; Simone Berger, Köln, Germany; Winfried Wehrle, Pforzheim, Germany; and Werner Kiausch, Elsfleth, Germany, for their role as native consultants. In this capacity they provided helpful and complete information on a number of cultural topics and questions of language use. They have given generously of their time and we appreciate it.

The authors wish to thank especially Angela Schoenherr, Assistant Editor, who has so ably guided the development of this edition to its conclusion. She has contributed extensively from her experience in pedagogy and was ever watchful for authenticity in language and culture. And finally we thank Angela for her patience and good humor in dealing with the many problems of putting together this text and the ancillaries, not the least of which was to get us to meet our deadlines. For all this we are grateful.

The authors would also like to express their appreciation to the following Houghton Mifflin editorial, art, and design staff and freelancers for their technical and creative contributions to the text: Kristina Baer, Director, for her support and encouragement of the project; Beth Kramer, Development Manager, for overseeing the project and especially for her valuable insights and guidance in developing ideas for this Seventh Edition; Linda Hadley, art editor, for her tireless efforts in finding the appropriate art; Uli Gersiek, layout; Harriet C. Dishman and Caroline Sieg at Elm Street Publications who once again managed the production process well and efficiently; Karen Hohner (copyeditor) for her careful reading and expert marking of the manuscript; and Gertrud Rath-Montgomery and Susanne Van Eyl (proofreaders).

Finally we wish to thank the following people for their thorough and thoughtful review of the Sixth Edition of **Deutsch heute.** Their comments and suggestions were invaluable during the development of the Seventh Edition.

Marlena Bellavia, Central Oregon Community College, Bend, OR

Phillip Campana, Tennessee Technological University, Cookeville, TN

Helga Druxes, Williams College, Williamstown, MA

Harald Hoebusch, University of California, Irvine, CA

Ronald Horwege, Sweet Briar College, Sweet Briar, VA

Hildegard Kural, De Anza College, Cupertino, CA

Manfred Prokop, University of Alberta, Edmonton, Canada

Karin Tarpenning, Oakland Community College, Farmington Hills, MI

Elizabeth Thibault, University of Delaware, Newark, DE

P E R S O N E N
(Cast of Characters)

The following fictional characters appear regularly in the dialogues, some of the readings, many of the exercises and also in the workbook and tests. The characters are all students at either the *Freie Universität Berlin (FUB)* or the *Universität Mainz.*

Gisela Riedholdt (1): First-semester English major with a German minor at *Freie Universität Berlin.* Interested in art. Becomes a good friend of Alex. Lives in the same dormitory as Michael. Her home is in Mainz.

Alex Kaiser (2): Third-semester architectural student. Becomes a good friend of Gisela. Roommate of Uwe. Home is in Hamburg.

David Carpenter (3): American exchange student at *Freie Universität Berlin.* Knows Gisela and her friends.

Uwe Ohrdorf (4): Seventh-semester computer major. Alex and Uwe are roommates. Is a good friend of Claudia.

Claudia Arnold (5): Seventh-semester medical student. Is a good friend of Uwe.

Melanie Beck (6): Fourth-semester German major (previously history). Is a good friend of Michael.

Michael Kroll (7): Third-semester English major. Lives in the same dormitory as Gisela. Plays guitar in a band. Is a good friend of Melanie. Home is in Hamburg.

Monika Berger (8): Lives at home in Mainz and attends the university there. Sister of Stefan and friend of Gisela from school days.

Stefan Berger (9): Lives at home in Mainz and attends the university there. Brother of Monika and friend of Gisela.

Peter Clason (10): American exchange student at *Universität Mainz.* Friends with Monika and Stefan. He knew Monika when she was a German exchange student in the U.S.

Diane (11) and Joan White (12): Two Americans who visit Monika and Stefan Berger in Mainz.

EINFÜHRUNG
(Introduction)

LERNZIELE
(Goals)

Sprechintentionen
(Functions)
Asking for and giving personal
  information: name, age, address,
  telephone number
Introducing oneself
Spelling
Working with numbers
Asking what day it is
Asking about colors

Land und Leute
(The Country and Its People)
Writing German addresses
Registering and studying at a
  German university
Making and receiving telephone
  calls
The telephone system in the
  Federal Republic of Germany

Vokabeln
(Vocabulary)
The alphabet
Numbers
Days of the week
Objects in a student's room
Colors

Grammatik
(Grammar)
Gender of nouns
Indefinite article
Pronouns
Noun-pronoun relationship

Wie heißt du?

*Ein Student und eine
Studentin an der Berliner
Humboldt-Universität.*

BAUSTEINE FÜR GESPRÄCHE

(Building Blocks for Conversation)

The dialogues in this section will help you acquire a stock of idiomatic phrases that will enable you to participate in conversations on everyday topics.

Wie heißt du?

While at the art department to sign up for an excursion to Florence with her art history class, Gisela runs into Alex, who is in the same class but whom she has never really met. After chatting briefly, Gisela and Alex decide to meet before the trip. Then Gisela goes into the office to sign up for the trip to Florence.

Vorm schwarzen Brett

ALEX: Hallo! Ich heiße Alex. Und du?

GISELA: Grüß dich. Ich heiße Gisela.

ALEX: Willst du auch nach Florenz?

GISELA: Ja.

ALEX: Toll! Du, hier ist meine Telefonnummer: 791 20 97. (Sieben, einundneunzig, zwanzig, siebenundneunzig.)

GISELA: Danke – und meine Telefonnummer ist 791 23 44. (Sieben, einundneunzig, dreiundzwanzig, vierundvierzig.)

ALEX: Wie bitte?

GISELA: 791 23 44.

ALEX: O.K. Also, bis bald! Tschüs.

Wie heißen Sie?

Gisela is next in line. She goes into the office to sign up for the excursion to Florence.

Im Büro

FRAU KLUGE: Bitte? Wie heißen Sie?

GISELA: Gisela Riedholt.

FRAU KLUGE: Wie schreibt man das?

GISELA: R-i-e-d-h-o-l-t.

FRAU KLUGE: Und Ihre Adresse?

GISELA: Meine Semesteradresse oder meine Heimatadresse?

FRAU KLUGE: Ihre Semesteradresse, bitte.

GISELA: Lepsiusstraße 27 (siebenundzwanzig), 12163 (zwölf, eins, sechs, drei) Berlin.

FRAU KLUGE: Danke, Frau Riedholt.

GISELA: Bitte.

Brauchbares *(Something useful)*

1. Note that when Alex gives Gisela his telephone number, he begins his sentence with **du (Du, hier ist meine Telefonnummer).** Germans often get the attention of people or introduce a thought by using **Du.** In English one might well say *hey.*
2. How does the address (i.e., the position of the house number, the street name, and the postal code) in Germany differ from where you live?
3. Note that the telephone numbers are stated as double digits. The first two digits in the postal code are generally stated as a single number; each of the remaining digits is spoken individually.
4. **Bitte** has several English equivalents. Name three.
5. **Cognates:** Words in different languages that are related in spelling and meaning and are derived from the same source language are called *cognates.* The words are often pronounced differently. There are hundreds of German–English cognates because the two languages have common roots. Name three cognates in the dialogues.
6. **False cognates:** Some words that look the same in German and English may not have the same meaning. These words are "false" cognates. Note that when Gisela says: **"O.K. Also, bis bald!" also** means *well.* Other meanings of **also** are *therefore, thus, so.* The German word to express the English meaning *also* is **auch.**

    Activities preceded by this symbol give you the opportunity to speak with fellow students about your personal feelings and experiences and to learn how to exchange ideas and negotiate in German, either one on one or as a group. The sentences and expressions to be used by one of the partners or members of a group are in the left column; the responses to be used by the other partner or members of a different group are in the right column. Substitute your own words for those in brackets.

    New vocabulary is indicated by a raised degree mark (°). The definitions of these words are found in the vocabulary lists in the sections called **Vokabeln.** In this chapter the **Vokabeln** section is on pages 18–20. Beginning with *Kapitel 2* the chapters have two **Vokabeln** sections—one in the **Bausteine für Gespräche** section and one in the reading section.

    When you say or write something, you have a purpose in mind. In this sense there is a certain linguistic function or intention you are stating or performing, such as exchanging information (e.g., identifying or asking for information), evaluating (e.g., praising, criticizing), expressing emotions (e.g., pleasure, dissatisfaction), getting something done (e.g., asking for help, giving permission), using social conventions (e.g., greeting, excusing oneself). To help you know when to use the words, phrases, or sentences you are learning, the purpose or function is given in the margin.

Getting acquainted

    1. Wie heißt du?   Get acquainted with members of your class. Introduce yourself to your fellow students and ask what their names are.

Student/Studentin 1 (S1):   *Student/Studentin 2 (S2):*
Ich heiße [Dieter]. Wie heißt du?   Ich heiße [Barbara].

▷ **2. Heißt du Sarah?** See how well you remember the names of at least four fellow students. If you're wrong they will correct you.

Confirming information

Student/Studentin 1 (S1):
Heißt du [Mark Schmidt]?
Du heißt [Monika], nicht°?

Student/Studentin 2 (S2):
Ja°.
Nein°. Ich heiße [Karin].

3. Wie heißen Sie? Ask your instructor for her/his name.

Asking someone's name

Student/Studentin:
Wie heißen Sie?

Herr°/Frau Professor°:
Ich heiße [Lange].

Erweiterung des Wortschatzes

(Vocabulary Expansion)

This vocabulary expansion section contains commonly used words and phrases that supplement those found in the dialogues **(Bausteine für Gespräche)** and in the readings beginning in *Kapitel 1.* You are expected to learn these words so that you will understand them in new contexts and be able to use them to express your own thoughts. The new words and phrases in the **Erweiterung des Wortschatzes** are included in the list of words that appear in the vocabulary sections **(Vokabeln).**

1. The subject pronouns *du* and *Sie*

Wie heißt **du?**
Wie ist **deine** Telefonnumer?

What is your name? (What are *you* called?)
What is *your* telephone number?

Du is equivalent to *you* and is used when addressing a relative, close friend, or person under approximately 15 years of age. In the tenth grade some teachers start to address pupils with **Sie.** Members of groups such as students, athletes, laborers, and soldiers also usually address each other as **du.** It is used when talking to one person and is referred to as the familiar form. The word for *you* used to address more than one friend, relative, etc., will be explained in *Kapitel 1.*

Dein(e) is equivalent to *your.* It is used with a person to whom you say **du.**

Wie heißen **Sie?**
Wie ist **Ihre** Adresse?

What is your name? (What are *you* called?)
What is *your* address?

Sie is also equivalent to *you* but is a more formal form of address, and is used when addressing a stranger or adult with whom the speaker is not on intimate terms. **Sie** is used when speaking to one person or to more than one person.

　　Ihr(e) is equivalent to *your* and is used with a person to whom you say **Sie.** In writing, **Sie** and **Ihr(e)** are capitalized.

　　Dein and **Ihr** modify masculine and neuter nouns. **Deine** and **Ihre** modify feminine nouns. See the section on Gender of nouns on pages 13–14 of this chapter.

LAND UND LEUTE

Go to the
Deutsch heute Web Site at
www.hmco.com/college

Postleitzahlen

In Germany postal codes **(Postleitzahlen)** have five digits and in Austria and Switzerland four. Large cities have several postal codes, each one designating a specific district of that city. German postal codes reveal the geographic location of a town or city. For example, a postal code beginning with 2 indicates a location in northern Germany, e.g., **27765 Hamburg.** A postal code that begins with 8 indicates a location in southern Germany, e.g., **80802 München.**

Stuttgarts Postleitzahlen beginnen alle mit 70–.

Diskussion

Look at the letter in the picture. What, if any, are the differences between the way the address is written and the form in your country? These differences are true for Austria and Switzerland as well as Germany.

2. Das Alphabet

The German alphabet has 26 regular letters and 4 special letters. They are pronounced as follows:

a	ah	**g**	geh	**l**	ell	**q**	kuh	**v**	fau	**ä** äh (a-Umlaut)
b	beh	**h**	hah	**m**	emm	**r**	err	**w**	weh	**ö** öh (o-Umlaut)
c	tseh	**i**	ih	**n**	enn	**s**	ess	**x**	iks	**ü** üh (u-Umlaut)
d	deh	**j**	jot	**o**	oh	**t**	teh	**y**	üppsilon	**ß** ess-tsett
e	eh	**k**	kah	**p**	peh	**u**	uh	**z**	tsett	
f	eff									

Capital letters are indicated by **groß: großes B, großes W.** Lower-case letters are indicated by **klein: kleines b, kleines w.**

Asking for information

 1. Wie schreibt man das? Ask your instructor or a fellow student for her/his name. Then ask how to spell it. (Use the **Sie**-form in speaking with your instructor: **Wie heißen Sie?**)

➤➤ Wie heißt du? *Mark Fischer.*
➤➤ Wie schreibt man das? *Emm-ah-err-kah. Eff-ih-ess-tseh-hah-eh-err.*

2. Abkürzungen. *(Abbreviations.)* Pronounce the following abbreviations and have your partner write them down.

1. Pkw (= Personenkraftwagen, *official word for automobile, e.g., on signs*)

2. VW (= Volkswagen)
3. BMW (= Bayerische Motorenwerke)
4. ADAC (= Allgemeiner Deutscher Automobil-Club)
5. WC (= Wasserklosett; *toilet*)
6. USA (= U.S.A.)
7. DB (= Deutsche Bahn, *German railway*)
8. BASF (*chemical company*)
9. UB (= Universitätsbibliothek)
10. EU (= Europäische Union)

3. Wie schreibt man das? Spell the name of your hometown for your partner. See if she/he can tell where you are from.

Providing information

4. Schreiben Sie das. *(Write that.)* Spell several German words to a partner who will write them down. Then reverse roles. You may use the words listed or choose your own.

tschüs □ danke □ bitte □ Adresse □ Telefonnummer

3. Die Zahlen von 1 bis 1.000

0 = null	10 = zehn	20 = zwanzig	30 = dreißig
1 = eins	11 = elf	21 = einundzwanzig	40 = vierzig
2 = zwei	12 = zwölf	22 = zweiundzwanzig	50 = fünfzig
3 = drei	13 = dreizehn	23 = dreiundzwanzig	60 = sechzig
4 = vier	14 = vierzehn	24 = vierundzwanzig	70 = siebzig
5 = fünf	15 = fünfzehn	25 = fünfundzwanzig	80 = achtzig
6 = sechs	16 = sechzehn	26 = sechsundzwanzig	90 = neunzig
7 = sieben	17 = siebzehn	27 = siebenundzwanzig	100 = hundert
8 = acht	18 = achtzehn	28 = achtundzwanzig	101 = hunderteins
9 = neun	19 = neunzehn	29 = neunundzwanzig	1.000 = tausend

Note the following irregularities:

1. **Eins** *(one)* becomes **ein** when it combines with the twenties, thirties, and so on: **einundzwanzig, einunddreißig.**
2. **Dreißig** *(thirty)* ends in **-ßig** instead of the usual **-zig.**
3. **Vier** *(four)* is pronounced with long [ī], but **vierzehn** *(fourteen)* and **vierzig** *(forty)* are pronounced with short [i].
4. **Sechs** *(six)* is pronounced [şeks], but **sechzehn** *(sixteen)* and **sechzig** *(sixty)* are pronounced [şeç-].
5. **Sieben** *(seven)* ends in **-en,** but the **-en** is dropped in **siebzehn** *(seventeen)* and **siebzig** *(seventy).*
6. **Acht** *(eight)* is pronounced [axt], but the final **t** fuses with initial [ts] in **achtzehn** *(eighteen)* and **achtzig** *(eighty).*
7. Numbers in the twenties, thirties, and so on follow the pattern of the nursery rhyme "four-and-twenty blackbirds":
   24 = **vierundzwanzig** *(four-and-twenty)*
   32 = **zweiunddreißig** *(two-and-thirty)*

8. German uses a period instead of a comma in numbers over 999. German uses a comma instead of a period to indicate decimals.

German	**English**
1.000 g (Gramm)	1,000 g
4,57 m (Meter)	4.57 m

9. Simple arithmetic:
   Addition (**+ = und**): **Fünf und drei ist acht.**
   Subtraction (**− = minus**): **Fünf minus drei ist zwei.**
   Multiplication (**× or · = mal**): **Fünf mal drei ist fünfzehn.**
   Division (**÷ = [geteilt] durch**): **Fünfzehn durch drei ist fünf.**

Using numbers

5. Rechnen. *(Doing arithmetic.)* Find a partner. On a piece of paper each of you *writes* out five simple mathematical problems. Read your five problems to your partner and let her/him solve them; then solve your partner's five problems.

S1:
Wie viel° ist drei und zwei [3 + 2]?
Wie viel ist zehn minus acht [10 − 8]?

S2:
Drei und zwei ist fünf.
Zehn minus acht ist zwei.

LAND UND LEUTE

Go to the
Deutsch heute Web Site at
www.hmco.com/college

Die Universität

The academic year at a German university has two terms: the **Wintersemester,** from mid-October to mid-February; and the **Sommersemester,** from mid-April to mid-July. Students must register each semester. The first time a student registers is called **Immatrikulation;** any subsequent registration is a **Rückmeldung.** Courses taken by the student are listed in an official transcript book **(Studienbuch),** which the student is responsible for, along with certificates signed by a professor to acknowledge the student's presence and success in the seminar **(Seminarscheine).**

German students at public universities do not pay tuition. However, this possibility is being seriously discussed. Not only has the number of university students increased, placing a strain on the facilities and financial resources of the state, but some politicians believe that students will study more seriously and complete their stud-

Studienbescheinigung   UNIVERSITÄT ZU KÖLN

Die mit Hilfe der automatisierten Datenverarbeitung erstellte Bescheinigung ist ohne Unterschrift gültig. Zusätze dürfen nicht angebracht werden ; es sei denn, sie sind von der Hochschule besonders bestätigt.

Frau/Herr:

**Neugebauer
Silvia**
geb. am: **11.08.74**
ist im: **Sommer** semester **1998**
unter der Matrikel-Nr.: **2626454**
eingeschrieben
Angestrebte Abschlußprüfung/Studienfächer im 1. Studiengang:

**1. Staatsprüfung
Allgemeinmedizin   9**

Semesterdauer :
Sommersemester (SS) 1.4. – 30.9., Wintersemester (WS) 1.10. – 31.3.

ies sooner if they must contribute to the cost. In 1998 German students expected to complete their studies in 5.4 years.

German students are required to pay a small administrative fee every time they register and to have health insurance **(Krankenversicherung).** A student ID card **(Studentenausweis)** enables a student to use university facilities such as the library and the cafeteria **(Mensa)** and to get reductions on theater and museum tickets, certain club memberships, and public transportation.

Diskussion

How much do you think a university education should cost?
Compare the German university system with your own.

---

6. Deine Adresse? Deine Telefonnummer? Rollenspiel. *(Role-play.)*

Asking for personal information

Imagine you have a job checking names for the telephone directory. Ask at least three of your fellow students for their names, phone numbers, and addresses. Then get the same information from your instructor. Remember to use **Ihre** with your instructor. Also be sure to say thank you.

S1:
Wie heißt du?
Wie ist deine Telefonnummer?
Wie ist deine Adresse?
Danke.

S2:
[Julia Meier].
[652-9846].
[Park Road zehn].
Bitte.

7. Wie ist die Telefonnummer von ... ?   At the right is part of a page from the Bonn telephone directory. The letters in parentheses indicate districts of Bonn and towns in the greater Bonn area. Note that German telephone books contain titles and professions. For example, **Neubauer, Uwe Dr.** has a doctor title and is probably a Ph.D.; **Neuber, Bruno Dr.** also has a doctor title and is a dentist, as indicated by the word **Zahnarzt; Neubauer, Heinz** is an engineer **(Ing. = Ingenieur).** **Str.** is the abbreviation for **Straße.**

Ask your partner for the addresses and phone numbers of people listed on this page of the telephone book. Exchange roles after three names.

Neubauer Harald
Rosental 25   65 08 02
Neubauer Heinz
Ing.grad. Remposstr. 1   21 67 83
Neubauer Heinz
(Bgo) Kantstr.8   32 38 87
Neubauer Helmut
(Bgo) Tulpenbaumweg 10   32 26 00
Neubauer Hermann
(Bgo) Akazienweg 21   32 38 29
Neubauer Ines
1 Bahnhofstr.99   61 22 25
Neubauer J.
Mohrstr.26   61 45 74
Neubauer Josef
(Dui) Europaring 24   64 22 96
Neubauer Karl
Beuel HeinrichHeineStr.27   47 55 00
Neubauer Klaus
Beuel Geislarstr.124   47 36 77
Neubauer Maria
(Ndk) Langgasse 91   45 00 68
Neubauer Rainer
(Alf) Oberdorf 47   64 06 65
Neubauer Sabine
Friedlandstr.62   67 41 70
Neubauer Uwe Dr.
(Bgo) DechantHeimbachStr.21   31 32 42
Neubauer Wilhelm
(Bgo) EltvillerStr.16   31 68 79
Neubauer Wolf
1 Wolfstr.37   69 14 28
Neubeck Hans Frhr.
von (Bgo) Rotdornweg 83   32 35 13
Neuber Bruno Dr.
Zahnarzt   45 03 05
(Ndk) Provinzialstr.103

LAND UND LEUTE

Go to the
Deutsch heute Web Site at
www.hmco.com/college

Das Telefon

As in all countries, the telecommunication system in Germany has changed dramatically in the last ten years. Before 1995 the telephone system in Germany was a government-owned monopoly, a division of the Federal Post Office **(Bundespost).** Today it is a public corporation—**Deutsche Telekom,** and competition from private companies has been made possible by deregulation. The billing system for phone calls in Germany operates on a message-unit system. In 1998 customers paid 12.1 **Pfennig** for each unit. A unit varies according to the type of call—local **(Ortsgespräch)** or long distance **(Ferngespräch)**— and time of day. Customers pay extra charges for local calls when they exceed the number of units included in the basic rate.

Public telephones in Germany are either coin-operated or card-operated and can be easily spotted because they display the bright pink **Telekom** logo. The telephones operate on a message-unit system that automatically calculates charges for local or long-distance calls. Local calls cost a minimum of 30 Pfennig. Plastic debit cards for a specific amount of telephone charges **(Telefonkarten)** can be purchased at the post office or telephone offices. Despite environmentalists' objections to the non-recyclable telephone cards, they have become very popular because of their varied designs and are traded like American baseball cards.

Every post office maintains public telephones. These are coin- or card-operated, or one can pay for the call at the counter. Calls outside the immediate area require an area code **(Vorwahl)** and incur additional charges. Phone numbers in Germany can vary in length. The following are examples of telephone numbers of two businesses in Munich: 52 60 96 and 2 18 36 75.

Die neuen Telefonzellen sind nicht mehr gelb.

Diskussion

Compare the major characteristics of the German phone system with your own.

Ein Telefongespräch

Ways of talking on the telephone vary from culture to culture. Read through the following informal telephone conversation and see if you can identify any differences between your telephone manners and this conversation. How can you change the English version to make it more idiomatic and appropriate in English? What word in the original German cannot be rendered exactly into English?

—Ingrid Breimann.

—Hier ist Gerda. Kann ich bitte mit Thomas sprechen?

—Hallo, Gerda. Thomas ist nicht zu Hause. Er spielt heute Fußball.

—Ach ja, richtig. Ich rufe am Montag wieder an. Bis dann, Ingrid. Wiederhören.

—Tschüs.

—Ingrid Breimann.

—This is Gerda. Can I speak to Thomas, please?

—Hi, Gerda. Thomas is not at home. He's playing soccer today.

—Oh, that's right. I'll call back on Monday. Till later, Ingrid. Bye.

—Bye.

8. Gespräche. *(Conversations.)*

Asking someone's age

A. Wie alt bist du?°   Find out the ages of four fellow students. Be sure you know their names. Write down the information.

S1:
Wie alt bist du?

S2:
Ich bin [19] Jahre alt.

B. Ich heiße ...   Introduce yourself to the class by giving the information mentioned in the model.

➤ Ich heiße _____ . Ich bin _____ Jahre alt. Meine° Adresse ist _____ .

   Meine Telefonnummer ist _____ .

4. Die Wochentage

Welcher Tag ist heute?	What day is it today?
Heute ist Montag.	Today is Monday.
Dienstag	Tuesday
Mittwoch	Wednesday
Donnerstag	Thursday
Freitag	Friday
Samstag *(in southern Germany)*	Saturday
Sonnabend *(in northern Germany)*	
Sonntag	Sunday

Monday (**Montag**) is considered the first day of the week in German-speaking countries. As a result, calendars begin with **Montag** rather than **Sonntag**. **Sonnabend** is a regional variant for Saturday, especially in northern Germany.

Montag

Dienstag

Mittwoch

Donnerstag

Freitag

Samstag

Sonntag

Notizen

 9. Welcher Tag ist heute? Ask a fellow student what day it is today.

➤ Welcher Tag ist heute? *Heute ist [Mittwoch].*

10. Hat Dennis am° Mittwoch Deutsch? *(Does Dennis have German on Wednesday?)* Say that the following people have German a day later than your friend thinks.

➤ Hat Dennis am Mittwoch Deutsch? *Nein, am Donnerstag.*

1. Hat Claudia am Montag Deutsch?
2. Hat Rebecca am Donnerstag Deutsch?
3. Hat Thomas am Dienstag Deutsch?
4. Hat Kevin am Freitag Deutsch?

5. Gender of nouns°

das Substantiv

Masculine	Neuter	Feminine
the man ← he	the baby ← it the computer ← it the radio ← it the lamp ← it	the woman ← she

Every English noun belongs to one of three genders: masculine, neuter, or feminine. The gender of a singular English noun shows up in the choice of the pronoun that is used to refer back to it.

The English type of gender system is one of natural gender. Nouns referring to male beings are masculine. Nouns referring to female beings are feminine. Nouns referring to young beings (if thought of as still undifferentiated as to sex) are neuter, and all nouns referring to inanimate objects are also neuter. (*Neuter* is the Latin word for *neither*, i.e., neither masculine nor feminine.)

Like English, German generally uses a system of natural gender for nouns that refer to living beings. Unlike English, however, German also makes gender distinctions in nouns that do not refer to living beings. This type of gender system is one of grammatical gender.

Masculine	Neuter	Feminine
der Mann° ← er	das Kind° ← es	die Frau ← sie
der Computer ← er	das Radio° ← es	die Lampe ← sie

In German there are three groups of nouns: masculine (**der**-nouns), neuter (**das**-nouns), and feminine (**die**-nouns). The definite articles **der, das,** and **die** function like the English definite article *the*. Most nouns referring to males are **der**-nouns (**der Mann** = *man*), most nouns referring to females are **die**-nouns (**die Frau** = *woman*), and nouns referring to young beings are **das**-nouns (**das Kind** = *child*). Note that **der Junge**° (= *boy*) is a **der**-noun, but **das Mädchen**° (= *girl*) is a **das**-noun because all words ending in **-chen** are **das**-nouns. Other nouns belong to any one of the three groups: **der Computer, das Radio, die Lampe.**

■ *Signals of gender*

Like English, German signals the gender of a noun in the choice of the pronoun that is used to refer back to it: **er** is masculine, **es** is neuter, and **sie** is feminine. Unlike English, however, German also signals gender in the choice of the definite article that precedes a noun: **der** is masculine, **das** is neuter, and **die** is feminine.

The article is the most powerful signal of gender. You should always learn a German noun together with its definite article, because there is no simple way of predicting the gender of a particular noun.

6. Ein Studentenzimmer *(A student's room)*

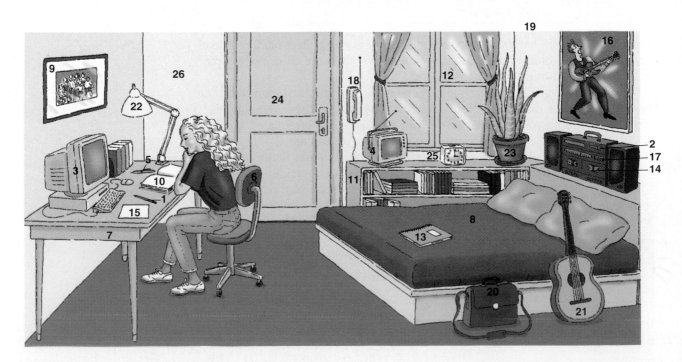

Learn the following nouns:

1. der **Bleistift**
2. der **CD-Spieler** (der **CD-Player**)
3. der **Computer**
4. der **Fernseher**
5. der **Kugel- schreiber** (der **Kuli**)
6. der **Stuhl**
7. der **Tisch**

8. das **Bett**
9. das **Bild**
10. das **Buch**
11. das **Bücherregal**
12. das **Fenster**
13. das **Heft**
14. das **Kassettendeck**
15. das **Papier**
16. das **Poster**
17. das **Radio**
18. das **Telefon**
19. das **Zimmer**

20. die **Büchertasche**
21. die **Gitarre**
22. die **Lampe**
23. die **Pflanze**
24. die **Tür**
25. die **Uhr**
26. die **Wand**

11. Rollenspiel *(role-play):* **Groß oder klein?** Gisela is moving to a new room and Alex plans to help arrange the furniture. He asks whether certain items are large **(groß)** or small **(klein).** Role-play with a partner.

➤➤ Ist das Zimmer groß oder klein? *Das Zimmer ist [groß].*

1. Ist das Fenster groß oder klein?
2. Ist das Bett groß oder klein?
3. Ist der Fernseher groß oder klein?
4. Wie ist der Stuhl?
5. Ist die Pflanze groß oder klein?

6. Wie ist die Uhr?
7. Und die Lampe?
8. Und der Tisch?
9. Und das Bücherregal?
10. Wie ist die Büchertasche?

12. Alt oder neu? Tell your partner whether various things in your room are new **(neu)** or old **(alt).**

> Describing things

➤➤ Computer *Der Computer ist [neu].*

1. Fernseher
2. Bett
3. Lampe
4. CD-Spieler
5. Radio

6. Büchertasche
7. Buch
8. Kugelschreiber
9. Bild
10. Poster

7. The indefinite article *ein*

Im Zimmer ist **ein Tisch** und **eine Lampe.**   In the room there is a table and a lamp.

The German indefinite article **ein** is equivalent to English *a* or *an.*

Masculine	Neuter	Feminine
ein Tisch	ein Bett	eine Lampe

In German the indefinite article has two forms: **ein** for masculine and neuter and **eine** for feminine.

13. Was ist im Zimmer? Tell your partner five things that are in the
Studentenzimmer on p. 14.

⟫ *Im Zimmer ist ein Stuhl, eine Pflanze, ...*

my

14. In meinem° Zimmer. Now tell your partner five things that are in
your room.

⟫ *In meinem Zimmer ist ein Bett, ein Computer, ...*

das Pronomen

8. Pronouns°

Wie alt ist **Alex?**   How old is Alex?
Er ist zweiundzwanzig.   He is twenty-two.

A **pronoun** is a part of speech that designates a person, place, thing, or concept.
It functions as a noun does. A pronoun can be used in place of a noun or a
noun phrase.

9. Noun-pronoun relationship

Der Mann ist groß.	**Er** ist groß.	He is tall.
Der Stuhl ist groß.	**Er** ist groß.	It is large.
Das Kind ist klein.	**Es** ist klein.	She/He is small.
Das Zimmer ist klein.	**Es** ist klein.	It is small.
Die Frau ist groß.	**Sie** ist groß.	She is tall.
Die Lampe ist groß.	**Sie** ist groß.	It is large.

In German the pronouns **er, es,** and **sie** may refer to persons or things. In English the singular pronoun referring to things *(it)* is different from those referring
to persons *(she, he)*.

Note that in referring to people, **groß** means *tall* and **klein** means *short* or
small. In referring to things, **groß** means *large* or *big* and **klein** means *small* or
little.

15. Wie ist das Zimmer? Tanja is seeing your room for the first time since
you made some changes. She's trying to sort out which things are new and
which are old. Respond, using a pronoun instead of the noun.

⟫ *Ist der Tisch neu?   Ja, er ist neu.*

1. Ist der Stuhl alt?
2. Ist die Uhr neu?
3. Ist das Radio alt?
4. Ist die Pflanze neu?
5. Ist die Lampe alt?

6. Ist die Büchertasche neu?
7. Ist das Poster neu?
8. Ist der Computer neu?
9. Ist der Rucksack alt?
10. Ist das Kassettendeck neu?

16. Groß, klein, alt. With your partner look at the pictures of people and
try to decide whether they are tall, short, or old. To get each other's opinions ask
the questions below.

S1: Ist die Frau alt?
S2: Nein, sie ist nicht alt.

S1:
1. Ist das Kind groß?
2. Ist der Mann alt?
3. Ist das Mädchen klein?

S2:
4. Ist der Junge groß?
5. Ist die Frau groß?
6. Ist das Kind klein?

10. Die Farben *(Colors)*

The following sentences should help you remember the colors.

Der Ozean ist **blau.**

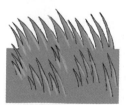

Das Gras ist **grün.**

Die Schokolade ist **braun.**

Die Tomate ist **rot.**

Die Banane ist **gelb.**

Der Asphalt ist **schwarz.**

Die Maus ist **grau.**

Das Papier ist **weiß.**

17. Welche° Farbe? *(What Color?)*   Ask your partner the colors of five items in the student room on page 14. Your partner will then ask you the color of five items.

To ask what color something is one asks:

➤➤ Welche Farbe hat [der Stuhl]?   *What color is [the chair]?*

To answer the question one says:

➤➤ [Der Stuhl] ist [braun].   *[The chair] is [brown].*

Describing things

18. Welche Farbe hat ... ?   Point to an object in the classroom and ask your partner what the color of the item is.

➤➤ Welche Farbe hat [die Wand]?   *[Die Wand] ist [weiß].*

Vokabeln *(Vocabulary)*

The vocabulary sections in each chapter contain the words and phrases that you are expected to learn actively. You should be able to understand them in many contexts and use them to express your own thoughts.

In English, proper nouns like *Monday* or *America* are capitalized, but not common nouns like *address* or *street*. In German, all nouns are capitalized: proper nouns like **Montag** or **Amerika** as well as common nouns like **Adresse** and **Straße.** Unlike English, German does not capitalize proper adjectives.

Compare the following: **amerikanisch**   American
englisch   English
deutsch   German

The German pronoun **Sie** (you *formal*) and the possessive adjective **Ihr** (your *formal*) are capitalized in writing. The pronoun **ich** (I) is not capitalized.

Substantive (Nouns)

die **Adresse** address
das **Bett** bed
das **Bild** picture; photo
der **Bleistift** pencil
das **Buch** book
das **Bücherregal** bookcase
die **Büchertasche** book bag
der **CD-Spieler** (der **CD-Player**)
  CD player
der **Computer** computer
(das) **Deutsch** German
der **Dienstag** Tuesday
der **Donnerstag** Thursday
die **Farbe** color
das **Fenster** window
der **Fernseher** television set
die **Frau** woman; **Frau** Mrs., Ms.
  (*term of address for adult women*)
der **Freitag** Friday
der **Garten** garden
die **Gitarre** guitar
das **Heft** notebook
die **Heimatadresse** home address
der **Herr** gentleman; **Herr** Mr.
  (*term of address*)
das **Jahr** year
der **Junge** boy
das **Kassettendeck** cassette deck
das **Kind** child
der **Kugelschreiber** (der **Kuli,** *collo-quial*) ballpoint pen
die **Lampe** lamp
das **Mädchen** girl

der **Mann** man
der **Mittwoch** Wednesday
der **Montag** Monday
die **Nummer** number
das **Papier** paper
die **Pflanze** plant
das **Poster** poster
der **Professor** (*m.*)/die **Professorin** (*f.*)
  professor
das **Radio** radio
der **Rucksack** backpack
der **Samstag** (*in southern Germany*)
  Saturday
die **Semesteradresse** school
  address
der **Sonnabend** (*in northern
  Germany*) Saturday
der **Sonntag** Sunday
die **Straße** street
der **Student** (*m.*)/die **Studentin** (*f.*)
  student
der **Stuhl** chair
der **Tag** day
das **Telefon** telephone
die **Telefonnummer** telephone
  number
der **Tisch** table
die **Tür** door
die **Uhr** clock, watch
die **Wand** wall
die **Woche** week
die **Zahl** number, numeral
das **Zimmer** room

Verben (Verbs)

bin / ist / sind am / is / are
hast / hat / haben have / has / have

heißen to be named, to be called
schreiben to write

Andere Wörter (Other words)

ach oh
also well
alt old
bitte please; you're welcome (*after
  danke*)
blau blue
braun brown
da there
danke thanks
dann then

das that; the (*neuter*)
dein(e) your (*familiar*)
der the (*masculine*)
die the (*feminine*)
du you (*familiar*)
ein(e) a, an
er he, it
es it
gelb yellow

[geteilt] durch   divided by (in division)

grau   gray

groß   large, big; tall (people)

grün   green

heute   today

ich   I

Ihr(e)   your (formal)

ja   yes

klein   small; short (people)

mal   times (in multiplication)

man   one, people

mein(e)   my

minus   minus (in subtraction)

nein   no

neu   new

nicht? (tag question)   don't you? isn't it?; Du heißt (Sie heißen)

[Monika], nicht?   Your name is [Monika], isn't it?

rot   red

schwarz   black

sie   she, it

Sie   you (formal)

so   so; this way

toll   great, fantastic, terrific

tschüs   so long, good-bye (informal)

und   and; plus (in addition)

von   of

wann   when

weiß   white

welch (-er, -es, -e)   which

wie   how

wie viel   how much

For the numbers 1–1,000, see p. 7.

Besondere Ausdrücke (Special expressions)

am [Freitag]   on [Friday]

Bis bald!   See you later.

Bitte?   May I help you?

Du, ...   Hey, . . . (used to get someone's attention)

Du heißt (Sie heißen) [Mark], nicht?   Your name is [Mark], isn't it?

Grüß dich.   Hello! Hi.

Hallo!   Hello! Hi.

Ich bin 19 Jahre alt.   I'm 19 years old.

Welche Farbe hat ... ?   What color is . . . ?

Welcher Tag ist heute?   What day is today?

(Wie) bitte?   (I beg your) pardon.

Wie alt bist du (sind Sie)?   How old are you?

Wie alt ist ... ?   How old is . . . ?

Wie heißt du (heißen Sie)?   What's your name?

Wie ist deine (Ihre) Adresse?   What's your address?

Wie ist deine (Ihre) Telefonnummer?   What is your telephone number?

Wie ist die Telefonnummer von [Clemens Neumann]?   What is [Clemens Neumann's] telephone number?

Wie schreibt man das?   How do you spell that? (literally: How does one write that?)

Willst du nach [Florenz]?   Are you planning to go to [Florence]?

WIEDERHOLUNG

(Review)

The **Wiederholung** is a review section in which you will have the opportunity to work again with the content, vocabulary, and structures of the current chapter and earlier chapters.

1. Studentenzimmer zu vermieten! *(Student room to rent!)* The ad below advertises a room that is for rent. You don't have to understand every word in order to get the information you need. Read the ad and answer the following questions.

Studentenzimmer
zu vermieten!

Kleines Zimmer, großes Fenster: Fünf Minuten zur Universität.
Bett, Tisch, zwei Stühle, Bücherregal.
DM 575,- im Monat. Kurt Riedl, Schellingstraße 56, 80142 München. Tel.: 34 20 19

1. Ist das Zimmer groß oder klein?
2. Wie ist das Fenster? Groß oder klein?

3. Im Zimmer sind ein _____ , ein _____ , ein _____ und zwei _____ .
4. Wie heißt der Vermieter°?   landlord
5. Wie ist die Adresse?
6. Wie ist die Telefonnummer?

2. Die Galerie. Now that you have a room, you need a place to eat out occasionally. Tell what you know about the Galerie by completing the following sentences.

Die Galerie — Musik-Café, Bar, Restaurant

Der Superbrunch
jeden Sonntag
Live Musik
10-15 Uhr
Preis 20,50 DM pro Person
Schillerstr. 15
Tel. 19 57 93

1. Die Galerie ist ein _____ , eine _____ und ein _____ .
2. Der Superbrunch ist jeden° _____ .   every
3. Die Musik ist _____ .
4. Die Adresse ist _____ .
5. Die Telefonnummer ist _____ .

3. Gespräche *(Conversations)*   Getting acquainted

1. Talk to people whose names you remember. Ask for their telephone numbers and addresses.

2. Introduce yourself to people you don't know.
3. Ask some of the people how to spell their names and be prepared to spell your own for someone else.

4. Zum Schreiben *(To be written)*

1. **Mein Zimmer.**   Identify fifteen items in your room. List them by gender. Then describe five of the items using full sentences.

➤➤ der Stuhl   *Der Stuhl ist braun. Er ist nicht groß.*

2. **Fragen.** *(Questions.)*   While a student at the university in Hamburg in Germany, you are involved in a minor automobile accident. You need to get the name, address, telephone number, and age of the driver of the other vehicle. Write down the questions you would ask to obtain this information.

Guten Tag! Wie geht's?

Sagen diese Frauen „du" zueinander?

BAUSTEINE FÜR GESPRÄCHE

Wie geht's?

In der Bibliothek
PROFESSOR LANGE: Guten Morgen, Frau Riedholt. Wie geht es Ihnen?
GISELA: Guten Morgen, Professor Lange. Gut, danke. Und Ihnen?
PROFESSOR LANGE: Danke, ganz gut.

Im Hörsaal
ALEX: Hallo, Gisela.
GISELA: Grüß dich, Alex. Wie geht's?
ALEX: Ach, nicht so gut.
GISELA: Was ist los? Bist du krank?
ALEX: Nein, ich bin nur furchtbar müde.

Brauchbares

1. **Frau Riedholt:** Adult German women, married and unmarried, are addressed as **Frau.** It is equivalent to English *Ms.* Unmarried women under 18 are usually addressed as **Fräulein.**
2. In the *Einführung* you learned that the German words for *you* are **Sie** or **du.** In the phrases **Wie geht es Ihnen?** and **Und dir?, Ihnen** and **dir** are again different forms of *you.*

| Greeting someone |

⇨ **1. Guten Tag.**   Greet different people in the class. Choose a time of day and greet your partner, who responds appropriately.

S1:
Guten Morgen.
Guten Tag.°
Guten Abend.°

S2:
Morgen.
Tag.
Abend.
Hallo.
Grüß dich.

| Asking people how they are |

⇨ **2. Wie geht's?**   Find a partner and role-play a scene between you and a friend or a professor. Assume you haven't seen your friend or the professor for several days and you run into her/him in the cafeteria **(die Mensa).** Say hello and ask how she/he is.

S1:
Hallo, [Tanja]. Wie geht's?
Guten Tag, Herr/Frau Professor,
   wie geht es Ihnen?

S2:
Gut, danke°. (Und dir?°/Und
   Ihnen?°)

Schüttelkasten

Danke, ganz gut.   **Ich bin müde.**

                                                                    Es geht.°

Nicht so gut.   Schlecht°.   Ich bin krank.

Guten Tag

Adults in German-speaking countries often greet each other with a handshake. When one is first introduced or in a formal situation a handshake is expected. Greetings vary depending on the region and the speakers.

Expressions for greeting each other:

Guten Morgen / Morgen *(informal)*
Guten Tag / Tag *(informal)*
Grüß Gott *(common in southern Germany, Austria)*
Grüezi *(Switzerland)*
Grüß dich *(informal; common in southern Germany, Austria)*
Salut *(informal; Switzerland)*
Servus *(used only between good acquaintances; southern Germany, Austria)*
Guten Abend / 'n'Abend *(informal)*

Go to the
Deutsch heute Web Site at
www.hmco.com/college

Expressions for saying good-bye:

(Auf) Wiedersehen
(Auf) Wiederschauen
Tschüs *(informal)*
Adieu
Ciao *(informal)*
Ade *(informal; southern Germany, Austria)*
Servus *(used only between good acquaintances; southern Germany, Austria)*
Salut *(informal; Switzerland)*
Gute Nacht *(at bedtime)*

Auf Wiedersehen auf dem Hauptbahnhof in Frankfurt.

Diskussion

How do you greet people in English? Make a list of several variations and say when you use them.

Konjugation

Ich gehe
du gehst
er geht
sie geht
es geht

Geht es?

Danke - es geht.

Was machst du gern?

Michael lives in the same dormitory as Gisela.

MICHAEL: Was machst du heute
Abend?

GISELA: Nichts Besonderes. Musik
hören oder so. Vielleicht gehe ich
ins Kino.

MICHAEL: Hmm. Spielst du gern
Schach?

GISELA: Schach? Ja. Aber nicht so
gut.

MICHAEL: Ach komm, wir spielen
zusammen, ja?

GISELA: Na gut! Wann?

MICHAEL: Um sieben?

GISELA: O.K. Bis dann.

das Aerobic;
Aerobic machen

der Fußball; Fußball
spielen

das Schach; Schach
spielen

das Tennis; Tennis
spielen

die Karten; Karten
spielen

das Tischtennis;
Tischtennis spielen

der Basketball;
Basketball spielen

das Computerspiel;
Computerspiel spielen

das Rollerblading;
Rollerblading gehen

der Volleyball; Volleyball spielen   das Gewichtheben;   das Golf; Golf
                                         Gewichte heben   spielen

das Fitnesstraining;   das Videospiel;   das Jogging;
Fitnesstraining machen   Videospiel spielen   joggen

When sample sentences in activities have one or more words in **boldface type,**
you should replace those words in subsequent sentences with the new words
provided.

3. Was spielst du gern?   Find out which activities your partner likes to
do. Then respond to her/his questions. For additional activities and sports, refer
to "Sports and games" in the Supplementary Word Sets in the Reference Section.

Expressing likes and dislikes

S1:
Spielst du | **gern** | Schach?

S2:
Ja. Und du?
Ja. Du auch°, nicht?
Nein. Und du?
Nein. Aber du, nicht?

Schüttelkasten

oft°   viel°
        gut

4. Treibst du gern Sport?   A fellow student asks whether you like to engage in sports. Respond as in the model.

S2:
Treibst du gern Sport°?

Machst du viel Sport?

S1:
Ja. Ich | **schwimme° gern.**
        | wandere° gern.

Nein. Ich mache nicht viel Sport.
Nein. Ich hebe Gewichte.

Asking about personal plans

5. Was machst du? Think about what you are going to do today. Ask a few classmates what they are going to do in their free time. They will ask you in turn.

S1:

Was machst du	heute Morgen°?		S2:	
	heute Nachmittag°?	Ich	arbeite°.
	heute Abend°?		
	am [Montag]?		

SchüttelKasten

spiele Tennis   gehe tanzen°   gehe ins Kino

gehe Rollerblading   mache Fitnesstraining

mache Deutsch°   höre° Musik°   gehe Jogging

Reporting

6. Ich mache das. Report to the class four things you do or don't do. Use **gern, viel, oft, nicht gern, nicht viel, nicht oft.**

➤➤ *Ich spiele [nicht] viel Schach.*

Erweiterung des Wortschatzes

1. Was für ein Mensch sind Sie?

The following adjectives can be used to characterize people. Some of them have English cognates and can be guessed easily.

fleißig	industrious	**nett**	nice
faul	lazy	**freundlich**	friendly
		unfreundlich	unfriendly
froh	happy	**sympathisch**	likeable, agreeable
lustig	cheerful	**unsympathisch**	unpleasant, unappealing
glücklich	happy	**laut**	loud, noisy
traurig	sad	leise quiet	
ruhig	quiet, calm	**intelligent**	intelligent
ernst	serious		
		praktisch	practical
tolerant	tolerant (en)		
kritisch	critical	**sportlich**	athletic
		musikalisch	musical
		unmusikalisch	unmusical

Asking what kind of person someone is and describing someone

1. Frage-Ecke. *(Question corner.)* On the next page are two charts (labeled S1 and S2) with the names and characteristics of several people. Each chart has information that the other doesn't have. Without looking at your partner's chart, ask questions to determine the characteristics of the people on your chart for whom no information is given. Your partner will do the same.

S2: Was für ein Mensch ist Gisela?
S1: Sie ist fleißig und nett.

SI:

Gisela	fleißig	nett
Alex		
Melanie	tolerant	sympathisch
Claudia		
Michael	ernst	musikalisch
Stefan		

S2:

Gisela		
Alex	ruhig	freundlich
Melanie		
Claudia	praktisch	ruhig
Michael		
Stefan	intelligent	sportlich

2. Was für ein Mensch? Ask three students what kind of person they are. Then report on your findings. For additional traits, refer to "Personal qualities and characteristics" in the Supplementary Word Sets in the Reference Section.

Asking and reporting

S1: Was für ein Mensch bist du?
S2: Ich bin lustig.
S1: [Frank] ist lustig.

3. Wie ist diese Person? Characterize each of the persons pictured below, using the adjectives on p. 28. See if your partner agrees.

Expressing agreement and disagreement

Stefan   Dirk   Bettina

Peter   Claudia   Oliver

S1: [Bettina] ist sehr° ernst, nicht?/Ist [Bettina] sehr ernst?
S2: Ja, sehr.
S3: Nein, ich glaube nicht°. Sie° ist sehr lustig.

LAND UND LEUTE

Go to the
Deutsch heute Web Site at
www.hmco.com/college

Fit bleiben

People in German-speaking countries can avail themselves of a wide variety of sports ranging from the traditional biking **(Rad fahren)** to the most recent like inline skating **(Inline-Skating).** Historically, people in German-speaking countries are known for their love of hiking **(wandern)** and walking **(spazieren gehen).** There are well-maintained trails throughout German-speaking countries. Some are simple paths through parks or local scenic spots, while others are part of a vast complex of trails.

Swimming is also a popular activity. In addition to seashore and lakeside beaches, town pools—both indoors and outdoors—provide ample opportunity for swimming. An outdoor pool **(Freibad),** with a nominal admission fee, is generally located on the outskirts of a city. It is often large and surrounded by grassy areas. People come with food and blankets to spend the day picnicking, swimming, and playing volleyball or badminton. In many cities, public indoor pools **(Hallenbäder)** have developed into public spas, offering saunas, hot tubs, massages, swimming lessons, snack bars, hair salons, and exercise machines besides several large swimming and diving pools.

One can find health clubs **(Fitnesscenter)** in most cities. There one can play squash **(Squash)** or work out **(Fitnesstraining),** which includes weightlifting **(Gewichte heben)** and aerobics **(Aerobic).**

„Gesund durch Fitnesstraining" – das glauben viele.

Diskussion

How do you stay fit? Using the vocabulary in the **Land und Leute,** the Supplementary Word Set "Sports and games" in the Reference Section, or another source, describe your fitness routine.

2. Telling time

The following methods are used to express clock time.

Wie viel Uhr ist es?° ⎱
Wie spät ist es?° ⎰ What time is it?

military time

	Method 1	Method 2
1.00 Uhr	Es ist eins.	Es ist eins.
	Es ist ein Uhr.	Es ist ein Uhr.
1.05 Uhr	Es ist fünf (Minuten) nach eins.	Es ist ein Uhr fünf.
1.15 Uhr	Es ist Viertel nach eins.	Es ist ein Uhr fünfzehn.
1.25 Uhr	Es ist fünf (Minuten) vor halb zwei.	Es ist ein Uhr fünfundzwanzig.
1.30 Uhr	Es ist halb zwei.	Es ist ein Uhr dreißig.
1.35 Uhr	Es ist fünf nach halb zwei.	Es ist ein Uhr fünfunddreißig.
1.45 Uhr	Es ist Viertel vor zwei.	Es ist ein Uhr fünfundvierzig.
1.55 Uhr	Es ist fünf (Minuten) vor zwei.	Es ist ein Uhr fünfundfünfzig.
2.00 Uhr	Es ist zwei Uhr.	Es ist zwei Uhr.

Note that German uses a period instead of a colon in time expressions.

German has two ways to indicate clock time. With a few exceptions, they parallel the two ways English indicates clock time.

Method 1 Es ist Viertel nach acht. It's a quarter past eight.
Method 2 Es ist acht Uhr fünfzehn. It's eight-fifteen.

In conversational German, method 1 is used to indicate time. Notice that the **-s** of **eins** is dropped before the word **Uhr.** The expression with **halb** indicates the hour to come, not the preceding hour: **halb zwei = 1.30 Uhr.**

In official time, such as train and plane schedules and concerts, method 2 is used.

Mein Zug fährt um **7.30 Uhr [7 Uhr 30].** My train leaves at 7:30 A.M.
Das Konzert beginnt um **19.30 Uhr [19** The concert begins
  Uhr 30]. at 7:30 P.M.

Official time is indicated on a 24-hour basis.

Um wie viel Uhr spielen wir Tennis? (At) what time are we playing tennis?
Um halb neun. At 8:30.

German uses **um** + a time expression to ask or speak about the specific hour at which something will or did take place.

Wann spielen wir Tennis? *When* are we playing tennis?
Morgen. Um 8.30 Uhr. Tomorrow. At 8:30.

The question word **wann** (*when*) can imply a request for a specific time (e.g., **um 8.30 Uhr**) or a general time (e.g., **morgen**).

4. Wie spät ist es? A friend asks you what time it is. Respond using the times listed below, in German.

Telling time

≫ 2.00 Uhr *Es ist zwei.*

1. 3.00 Uhr   3. 11.45 Uhr   5. 4.55 Uhr
2. 6.15 Uhr   4. 1.20 Uhr   6. 2.30 Uhr

5. Wie viel Uhr ist es?   Below are two sets of clocks. You take set A and your partner takes set B. Do not look at each other's set of clock faces. Take turns asking each other the time on the clock without hands.

A X fragt: **Wie viel Uhr ist es?**

            Wie spät ist es?

    Y sagt: **Es ist. . .**

B X fragt: **Wie viel Uhr ist es?**

            Wie spät ist es?

    Y sagt: **Es ist. . .**

A		B	
1 Y		1 Y	
2 X		2 X	
3	Y "Es ist 22 Uhr 40."	3 X	
4 X		4	Y "Es ist 23 Uhr 55."
5 Y		5 Y	
6 X		6 X	

6. Rollenspiel. *(Role-play.)*   You and a friend have planned to do some things together on Friday, Saturday, and Sunday. Your friend can't remember when you're supposed to do what together, but you can tell her/him by consulting the list below.

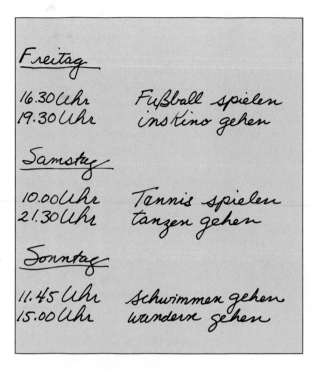

Freitag

16.30 Uhr   Fußball spielen
19.30 Uhr   ins Kino gehen

Samstag

10.00 Uhr   Tennis spielen
21.30 Uhr   tanzen gehen

Sonntag

11.45 Uhr   schwimmen gehen
15.00 Uhr   wandern gehen

S1: Um wie viel Uhr/Wann ... ?
S2: Wir [gehen] um [halb neun] ...

1. gehen wir Freitag ins Kino?
2. gehen wir Samstagabend tanzen?
3. spielen wir am Samstag Tennis?
4. spielen wir Freitag Fußball?
5. gehen wir Sonntag wandern?
6. gehen wir schwimmen?

7. Giselas Terminkalender. *(Appointment calendar.)*
Tell what Gisela's plans are by consulting her
calendar and answering the questions.

1. Welcher Tag ist heute?
2. Wann hat Gisela Deutsch?
3. Um wie viel Uhr ist Gisela in der Bibliothek?
4. Wann spielen Gisela und Alex Tennis?
5. Geht Gisela um 1 Uhr schwimmen?
6. Arbeitet sie um 5 Uhr?
7. Wann geht Gisela ins Kino?

September
9 Donnerstag

7 Uhr
8⁰⁰ 8.10 Deutsch
9⁰⁰
10⁰⁰ Bibliothek
11⁰⁰ Bibliothek
12⁰⁰ Tennis mit Alex
13⁰⁰
14⁰⁰ 14.45 schwimmen
15⁰⁰
16⁰⁰ arbeiten
17⁰⁰ arbeiten
18⁰⁰ arbeiten
19⁰⁰
20⁰⁰ 20.15 Kino mit Martin, Alex und Ute

EINE STUDENTIN IN BERLIN

Vorbereitung auf das Lesen *(Preparation for reading)*

Each chapter of *Deutsch heute* contains a reading section. The readings are designed to broaden your knowledge and familiarity with the culture, customs, history, and current life in Germany, Austria, and Switzerland.

Each reading is accompanied by pre-reading and post-reading activities. In the first pre-reading activity, called **Vor dem Lesen** *(Before reading),* you will be asked to think about what you already know about the reading topic or about what information and vocabulary you would expect to encounter in a reading on the topic at hand. **Vor dem Lesen** may also include a visual (e.g., an ad or photo) for you to interpret as a way to stimulate your thinking about the upcoming reading. In the second pre-reading activity, called **Beim Lesen** *(While reading),* you will find suggestions for things to look for as you work through the text. In the post-reading section, called **Nach dem Lesen** *(After reading),* activities such as **Fragen zum Lesestück** *(Questions about the reading)* help you check your comprehension and express your own views on the reading topic.

In the **Vor dem Lesen, Beim Lesen,** and **Nach dem Lesen** exercises, German words that are new and that you should learn and be able to use are followed by a raised degree mark°. These words and their definitions are listed in the **Vokabeln** section following the reading. Other unfamiliar words are defined in the margin.

The reading in this chapter is a letter Gisela has written to her friends, Monika and Stefan back home in Mainz.

Wohnhäuser in Berlin.

■ *Vor dem Lesen*

1. What would you write about your college or university and your living arrangements in your first letter to friends?
2. Glance at the form of the letter and compare it to that of a personal letter you might write. What is in the first line of the letter? What is the English equivalent of **liebe/lieber?**

■ *Beim Lesen*

1. Circle or make a list of the cognates in the letter.
2. Underline or make a list of the numbers in the letter.

Berlin, den 6. Oktober°

Liebe Monika und lieber Stefan,

wie geht's? Berlin ist interessant, aber sehr groß. Meine neue Adresse ist
5 Lepsiusstraße 27, 12163 Berlin, und meine Telefonnummer ist 030/791 23 44.
Mein Zimmer ist nicht schlecht, vielleicht ein bisschen klein, aber die Universität ist furchtbar groß und hat viele Studenten.
　　Mein Nachbar heißt Michael und kommt aus° Hamburg. Er studiert auch Englisch an der FU°. Am Wochenende spielt er oft Gitarre in einer Blues-
10 band. Sein Freund heißt Alex und studiert Architektur. Beide sind sehr sportlich. Alex ist sehr freundlich, lustig und fleißig und ich glaube, er ist auch sehr intelligent und tolerant. Jedenfalls° ist er furchtbar nett. Michael ist auch sehr sympathisch, aber etwas ernst und ruhig. Vielleicht ist er auch nur etwas schüchtern°. Heute ist Samstag und Alex und Michael arbeiten bis
15 Viertel nach zwei. Ich mache nichts Besonderes, aber heute Nachmittag gehen wir alle drei zusammen schwimmen und später tanzen.

Viele Grüße
eure° Gisela

den 6. Oktober: read as **den sechsten Oktober**

from

FU = Freie Universität Berlin

at any rate

shy

yours

Nach dem Lesen *(After reading)*

1. Fragen zum Lesestück. *(Questions about the reading.)* Answer the following questions about the reading.

1. Wie ist Giselas Adresse? Wie ist die Postleitzahl?
2. Wie ist Giselas Telefonnummer? Wie ist die Vorwahl für Berlin?
3. Wie ist Giselas Zimmer?
4. Wie ist die Universität?
5. Was macht Michael oft am Wochenende?
6. Was machen Gisela und Michael heute?
7. Was für ein Mensch ist Michael?

2. Ergänzen Sie. *(Complete.)* Complete the following sentences using information from the text.

1. Giselas Zimmer ist ein bisschen klein aber _____ .
2. Gisela glaubt, Michael ist _____ .
3. Heute Abend gehen Gisela und Michael _____ .
4. Die Universität _____ .
5. Gisela und Michael studieren _____ .

3. Beschreiben Sie. *(Describe.)*   Give a brief description in German of each of the following items.

1. Berlin
2. Giselas Zimmer
3. Michael

4. Erzählen Sie. *(Tell.)*

1. Using vocabulary from the letter, write down words or phrases that you can use when talking about the following topics in German.
   a. mein Zimmer
   b. meine Universität
   c. ein Freund° oder eine Freundin°
2. Using the words and phrases that you wrote down in 1, have a conversation with another student about the topics. Begin by writing two questions that you can ask your partner.

Vokabeln

Substantive

der **Abend**   evening
das **Aerobic**   aerobics
der **Basketball**   basketball
die **Bibliothek**   library
das **Computerspiel**   computer game
(das) **Deutsch**   German language
(das) **Englisch**   English language (academic subject)
das **Fitnesstraining**   fitness training; **Fitnesstraining machen**   to work out
die **Frage**   question
der **Freund**/die **Freundin**   friend, boyfriend/girlfriend
der **Fußball**   soccer
das **Gewichtheben**   weightlifting; **Gewichte heben**   to lift weights
das **Golf**   golf
das **Jogging**   jogging; **Jogging gehen**   to go jogging
die **Karte**   card; postcard; die **Karten** *(pl.)*   (playing) cards
das **Kino**   movie theater

der **Mensch**   person, human being
die **Minute,** die **Minuten** *(pl.)*   minute
der **Morgen**   morning
die **Musik**   music
der **Nachbar** *(m.)*/die **Nachbarin** *(f.)*   neighbor
der **Nachmittag**   afternoon
die **Nacht**   night
das **Rollerblading**   rollerblading; **Rollerblading gehen**   to go rollerblading
das **Schach**   chess
der **Sport**   sport; **Sport treiben**   to engage in sports
das **Tennis**   tennis
das **Tischtennis**   table tennis, Ping-Pong
die **Universität,** die **Uni** *(colloquial)*   university
das **Videospiel**   video game
das **Viertel**   quarter
der **Volleyball**   volleyball
das **Wochenende**   weekend

Verben

arbeiten   to work; to study
gehen   to go
glauben   to believe

hören   to hear; to listen to
joggen   to jog
kommen   to come

machen to do; to make
schwimmen to swim
sein to be
spielen to play

studieren to study; to attend
   college
tanzen to dance
wandern to hike; to go walking

Andere Wörter

aber but, however
auch also
bis until, till
bisschen: ein bisschen a little
ein(e) a, an
ernst serious
faul lazy
fleißig industrious, hard-working
freundlich friendly
froh happy
furchtbar terrible; very
ganz complete, whole; very; **ganz
   gut** not bad, O.K.
gern gladly, willingly; *used with
   verbs to indicate liking, as in* **Ich
   spiele** *gern* **Tennis.**
glücklich happy
gut good, well; fine
halb half
hallo hello
heute Abend this evening
heute Morgen this morning
heute Nachmittag this afternoon
ihr you (*familiar pl.*)
intelligent smart, intelligent
interessant interesting
krank sick, ill
kritisch critical
laut loud, noisy
lieb- (-er, -e) dear
lustig merry, cheerful
müde tired
musikalisch musical
nach after

natürlich natural
nett nice
nicht not
nichts nothing
nur only
oder or
oft often
praktisch practical
ruhig calm, easy-going, quiet
schlecht bad, badly
sehr very (much)
sein his, its
sie she, they
spät late; **später** later
sportlich athletic
sympathisch likeable, agreeable
tolerant tolerant
traurig sad
um at; **um zehn Uhr** at ten
   o'clock
unfreundlich unfriendly
unglücklich unhappy
unmusikalisch unmusical
unsympathisch unpleasant,
   unappealing
viel much
vielleicht maybe, perhaps
vor before
was what
was für (ein) what kind of (a)
wer who
wir we
zusammen together

Besondere Ausdrücke

am Wochenende on the weekend
Auf Wiedersehen good-bye
bis dann see you then
Es geht. O.K.; Not bad.; All right.
Gute Nacht good night
Guten Abend/Abend good
   evening
Guten Morgen/Morgen good
   morning

Guten Tag / Tag hello
halb half; **halb zwei** one-thirty
Ich glaube nicht. I don't think so.
Ich glaube ja. I think so.
Ich mache Deutsch. I'm doing
   German homework.
in der Bibliothek in the library
ins Kino to the movies
Musik hören listening to music

Na gut! All right.

nicht (wahr)? *(tag question)* don't you? isn't he? isn't that so?, etc.

nichts Besonderes nothing special

O.K. okay, O.K.

um [sieben] Uhr at [seven] o'clock

Um wie viel Uhr? At what time?

Und dir? And you? (How about you?) *(familiar)*

Und Ihnen? And you? (How about you?) *(formal)*

viele Grüße *(closing in a letter)* regards

Viertel nach quarter after

Viertel vor quarter of, quarter to

Was ist los? What's wrong?

Wie geht es Ihnen? How are you?

Wie geht's? How are you? *(literally:* How's it going?*)*

Wie spät ist es? What time is it?

Wie viel Uhr ist es? What time is it?

GRAMMATIK UND ÜBUNGEN

(Grammar and Exercises)

das Subjekt

1. Subject° pronouns

Singular *(sg.)*	Plural *(pl.)*
1. **ich** I	**wir** we
2. **du** you	**ihr** you
(familiar sg.)	*(familiar pl.)*
3. { **er** he, it	
es it	**sie** they
sie she, it	
Sie you *(formal, sg. and pl.)*	

A personal pronoun is said to have "person," which indicates the identity of the subject.

1. First person refers to the one(s) speaking *(I, we).*
2. Second person refers to the one(s) spoken to *(you).*
3. Third person refers to the one(s) or thing(s) spoken about *(he/it/she, they).*

2. The subject pronouns *du, ihr, Sie*

Tag, Julia. ... Was machst **du?**
Tag, Lisa. Tag, Gerd! ... Was macht **ihr?**

In the *Einführung* (p. 5) you learned when to use the familiar form **du. Du** is used to address one person. The familiar form used to address more than one person is **ihr.**

Tag, Herr Wagner. ... Was machen **Sie?**
Tag, Frau Braun. Tag, Fräulein Schneider! ... Was machen **Sie?**

In the *Einführung* (p. 5) you learned when to use the formal form **Sie.** Like the English *you,* **Sie** can be used to address one person or more than one.

3. The meanings and use of *sie* and *Sie*

Glaubt **sie** das?	Does *she* believe that?
Glauben **sie** das?	Do *they* believe that?
Glauben **Sie** das?	Do *you* believe that?

In spoken German, the meanings of **sie** *(she)*, **sie** *(they)*, and **Sie** *(you)* can be distinguished by the corresponding verb forms and by context. In written German, **Sie** *(you)* is always capitalized.

> **sie** + singular verb form = *she*
> **sie** + plural verb form = *they*
> **Sie** + plural verb form = *you* (formal)

1. Ich, du, er.   Give the subject pronouns you would use in the following situations.

> ⟫ You're talking about a female friend.   *sie*
> ⟫ You're talking to a female friend.   *du*

1. You're talking about a male friend.
2. You're talking to a male friend.
3. You're talking about yourself.
4. You're talking about yourself and a friend.
5. You're talking to your parents.
6. You're talking to a clerk in a store.
7. You're talking about your father.
8. You're talking about your sister.
9. You're talking about a child.
10. You're talking to your professor.
11. You're talking about your friends.

4. Present tense of *sein*

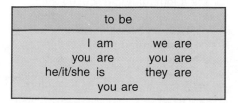

sein	
ich **bin**	wir **sind**
du **bist**	ihr **seid**
er/es/sie **ist**	sie **sind**
Sie **sind**	

to be	
I am	we are
you are	you are
he/it/she is	they are
you are	

The verb **sein**, like its English equivalent *to be,* is irregular in the present tense.

LAND UND LEUTE

Go to the
Deutsch heute Web Site at
www.hmco.com/college

Du vs. *Sie*

Historically speaking, **sie sind** *(they are)* and **Sie sind** *(you are)* are the same form. It was considered polite to address someone in the third-person plural and to capitalize the pronoun in writing.

The development of formal pronouns to address a person was a phenomenon common to most European languages. English used to distinguish singular *thou/thee* from plural *ye/you; thou/thee* was restricted to informal usage, and *ye/you* was used both as informal plural and formal singular and plural. Today only *you* survives as our all-purpose pronoun. In German (as well as in other European languages such as French, Spanish, and Italian) there are still distinctions between the formal and informal pronouns for *you.*

The formal pronoun **Sie** is used for everyday communi-

Sagen diese Studenten "du" oder "Sie" zueinander? (Universität Frankfurt)

cation outside the realm of family and friends. Even neighbors and coworkers address each other as **Sie** (they **siezen**). **Du** (along with its plural form **ihr**) is traditionally a form of address used among relatives or close friends. An older person usually decides on the appropriateness of this form in speaking to someone younger. Most young people address each other with **du** (they **duzen**) nowadays. A step somewhere between **du** and **Sie** is to use a first name and **Sie.** It is often used by an older person to a person who is much younger, for example, when parents meet the friends of their children who are in their late teens or early twenties. The parents usually address them with **Sie,** but use their first names. The friends, of course, say **Herr/Frau ...** and use **Sie.**

Diskussion

Imagine that you are in a German-speaking country. What form of address (**du, Sie,** or **ihr**) would you use when speaking to these people in these situations?

You run into some friends in a shopping mall.
You are introduced to a new business associate in a restaurant.
You are angry at a policeman who is writing out a speeding ticket for you.
You congratulate your best friend on winning the Nobel Prize.
You are asking your parents for money.

2. Was für ein Mensch? At a party you are discussing various people. Describe them by choosing the adjectives.

▶▶ Melanie *Melanie ist intelligent.*

1. Gerd
2. du
3. Monika und Lars
4. Professor Schneider
5. ich
6. wir
7. ihr
8. Ihr Nachbar/Ihre Nachbarin
9. Ihr Partner/Ihre Partnerin
10. Und Sie? Wie sind Sie?

Schüttelkasten

lustig   **sehr ruhig**

laut   fleißig

sehr musikalisch

sympathisch   **nett**

3. So ist sie/er. Your partner will point to a person in one of the photos below and ask you what adjectives you would apply to that person.

Surmising

S1: Was für ein Mensch ist die Frau?
S2: Sie ist intelligent, aber faul.

der Infinitiv

5. Infinitive°

Infinitive	Stem + ending	English equivalents
glauben	glaub + en	*to believe*
heißen	heiß + en	*to be named*
arbeiten	arbeit + en	*to work; to study*
wandern	wander + n	*to hike; to go walking*

The basic form of a verb (the form listed in dictionaries and vocabularies) is the infinitive. German infinitives consist of a stem and the ending **-en** or **-n.**

das Verb

6. The finite verb°

Andrea **arbeitet** viel.　　Andrea *works* a lot.
Arbeitest du viel?　　*Do* you *work* a lot?

The term "finite verb" indicates the form of the verb that agrees with the subject.

das Präsens

7. Present tense° of regular verbs

glauben	
ich glaube	wir glaub**en**
du glaub**st**	ihr glaub**t**
er/es/sie glaub**t**	sie glaub**en**
Sie glaub**en**	

to believe	
I believe	we believe
you believe	you believe
he/it/she believes	they believe
you believe	

In the present tense, most English verbs have two different forms; most German verbs have four different forms.

　　The present tense of regular German verbs is formed by adding the endings **-e, -st, -t,** and **-en** to the infinitive stem. The verb endings change according to the subject. (Note that a few verbs like **wandern** add only **-n** instead of **-en: wir wandern.**) In informal spoken German, the ending **-e** is sometimes dropped from the **ich**-form: **Ich glaub' das nicht.**

Gisela **spielt** gut Tennis.
Frank und Alex **spielen** gut Basketball.

With a singular noun subject **(Gisela)** the verb ending is **-t.** With a plural noun subject **(Frank und Alex)** the verb ending is **-en.**

arbeiten: to work; to study	
ich arbeite	wir arbeiten
du arbeit**est**	ihr arbeit**et**
er/es/sie arbeit**et**	sie arbeiten
Sie arbeiten	

In regular English verbs, the third-person singular ending is usually *-s: she works.* After certain verb stems, however, this ending expands to *-es: she teaches.*

　　German also has verb stems that require an expansion of the ending. If a verb stem ends in **-d** or **-t,** the endings **-st** and **-t** expand to **-est** and **-et.** The other endings are regular.

heißen: to be called, named	
ich heiße	wir heißen
du heiß**t**	ihr heißt
er/es/sie heißt	sie heißen
Sie heißen	

If a verb stem ends in a sibilant **(s, ss, ß, z)**, the **-st** ending contracts to a **-t: du heißt, du tanzt.** The other endings are regular.

4. Heute ist Samstag. Complete the following dialogues by filling in the missing verb endings.

a. Monika und Stefan sind Tinas Freunde. Stefan arbeit_____ in dem Café

an der Uni. Monika arbeit_____ auch dort°. Samstags arbeit_____ Monika   *there*

und Stefan nicht.

MONIKA: Geh_____ du heute joggen?

STEFAN: Nein, ich spiel_____ heute Morgen mit Kevin Tennis. Später

geh_____ wir mit Tina und Peter schwimmen. Und du? Was mach_____ du

heute?

MONIKA: Ich glaub_____ , ich geh_____ joggen. Später lern°_____ ich ein   *study*

bisschen Englisch. Ich schreib_____ nämlich° am Montag eine Klausur°.   *after all/test*

Aber heute Abend geh_____ wir tanzen, nicht wahr?

STEFAN: Ja, Kevin komm_____ um acht.

b. *Gisela und Professor Lange sind in der Bibliothek.*

GISELA: Guten Tag, Professor Lange. Wie geh_____ es Ihnen?

PROFESSOR LANGE: Gut, danke, Frau Riedholt. Was mach_____ Sie denn am

Samstagmorgen in der Bibliothek?

GISELA: Ich schreib_____ die Seminararbeit für Sie, Herr Professor!

PROFESSOR LANGE: Arbeit_____ Sie nicht zu viel, Frau Riedholt! Schönes

Wochenende!

GISELA: Danke, und auf Wiedersehen, Professor Lange.

8. The construction verb + *gern*

Ich spiele **gern** Tennis.	I like to play tennis.
Ich spiele **nicht gern** Golf.	I don't like to play golf.

The most common way of saying in German that you like doing something is to use the appropriate verb + **gern.** To say that you don't like doing something, use **nicht gern.**

Stating preferences

 **5. Was für Musik hörst du gern?**   Ask four fellow students what kind of music they like.

S1: Was für Musik hörst du gern?
S2: Ich höre gern [Jazz].

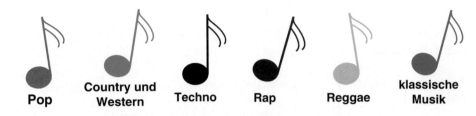

| Jazz | Rock | Pop | Country und Western | Techno | Rap | Reggae | klassische Musik |

 **6. Was machst du?**   State what various people are doing by using the cues in the columns below. Answer in complete sentences.

➤ Jürgen   *Jürgen macht viel Sport. Er geht gern ins Kino.*

1	2	3	4
ich	hören	gern	Sport
Linda und ich (wir)	machen	oft	Volleyball
Christin (sie)	spielen	viel	Musik
du	gehen	gut	ins Kino
Gisela und Alex (sie)			Rollerblading
ihr			
Jürgen (er)			

9. Position of *nicht*

The position of **nicht** is determined by various elements in the sentence.

Herr Wagner *arbeitet* **nicht.**	Mr. Wagner doesn't work.
Mark glaubt *Sophie* **nicht.**	Mark doesn't believe Sophie.
Ich glaube *es* **nicht.**	I don't believe it.
Arbeitest du *heute* **nicht?**	Aren't you working today?

Nicht always follows:

1. the finite verb (e.g., **arbeitet**)
2. nouns used as objects (e.g., **Sophie**)
3. pronouns used as objects (e.g., **es**)
4. specific adverbs of time (e.g., **heute**)

Lukas ist **nicht** *faul.*	Lukas is not lazy.
Das ist **nicht** *Frau Wagner.*	That is not Ms. Wagner.
Wir wandern **nicht** *oft.*	We don't hike much.
Wir gehen heute **nicht** *ins Kino.*	We're not going to the movies today.

Nicht precedes most other kinds of elements:

1. predicate adjectives (a predicate adjective is an adjective that completes the meaning of a linking verb; the most frequently used linking verb is **sein,** *to be:* e.g., Mark ist nicht **faul.**)
2. predicate nouns (a predicate noun is a noun that completes the meaning of a linking verb: e.g., Das ist nicht **Frau Wagner.**)

Sportvereine

Go to the
Deutsch heute Web Site at
www.hmco.com/college

In Germany, Austria, and Switzerland people of all ages engage in sports. For more than 100 years sports clubs **(Sportvereine)** have been an important part of life in German-speaking countries. People who want to participate in competitive sports **(Hochleistungssport)** join a **Sportverein.** School sports are intramural rather than intermural. Athletes are not recruited by schools, and athletic scholarships are uncommon. In Germany alone there are approximately 85,000 **Sportvereine** with 25.9 million registered members. Approximately 2.5 million people work as volunteers in these organizations. The **Sportvereine** sponsor sports for almost every possible athletic interest. Clubs exist for sports as varied as badminton **(Badminton),** track and field **(Leichtathletik)** or water-skiing **(Wasserskilaufen)** and, of course, the world's most popular sport, soccer **(Fußball).** In recent years American football has made inroads in Europe and is represented in the German Sport Association **(Deutscher Sportbund).** The **Deutscher Sportbund** is the umbrella organization of individual clubs and sponsors national campaigns that encourage fitness and participation in sports. There are special activities and clubs for disabled athletes. Most of the **Sportvereine** and sports facilities are subsidized by the 16 federal states and local governments as well as private firms. Even the smallest village has its own **Verein,** which also plays an important part in the social life of the town.

Millions of people participate in running **(Laufen),** swimming **(Schwimmen),** tennis **(Tennis),** and skiing **(Ski-laufen)** competitions every year on the local, national, or international level. Those who win or finish are awarded badges of merit as a sign of personal accomplishment. However, for most people who play sports, the primary purpose is not to win games but to be physically active and to be with people in a social setting.

Fußball is the most popular sport in the German-speaking countries. The German Football Association **(Deutscher Fußball-Bund)** has more than 5.5 million members. More than 75,000 women play soccer. Germany has separate professional soccer leagues **(Bundesliga)** for men and women.

Zwei Fußballvereine spielen gegeneinander. (Weimar)

Diskussion

People in German-speaking countries who want to become professional athletes would probably begin their careers by joining a local **Sportverein.** How does this compare to the career path for a professional athlete in your country?

3. adverbs, including general time adverbs (e.g., nicht **oft,** nicht **sehr,** nicht **gern**)
4. prepositional phrases (e.g., nicht **ins Kino**)

Ich gehe **nicht** *oft ins Kino.*   I don't often go to the movies.

If several of the elements occur in a sentence, **nicht** usually precedes the first one.

7. Wir nicht. Jutta, a new acquaintance, has some questions for you and Hans-Dieter. Answer in the negative.

⟫ Macht ihr viel Sport?   *Nein. Wir machen nicht viel Sport.*

1. Spielt ihr viel Basketball?
2. Spielt ihr oft Tennis?
3. Schwimmt ihr gern?
4. Hört ihr gern Musik?
5. Geht ihr oft ins Kino?
6. Seid ihr sportlich?
7. Tanzt ihr gern?

Finding common likes and dislikes

8. Was machst du gern?   With a partner, try to find two activities you both enjoy doing and two you both dislike doing.

S1: Ich schwimme gern. Schwimmst du auch gern?
S2: Ja, ich schwimme gern./Nein, ich schwimme nicht gern.
     Ich spiele gern Tennis. Spielst du gern Tennis?

Schüttelkasten

Jogging

Basketball   tanzen   arbeiten

Rollerblading gehen   Musik hören

ins Kino gehen   Fitnesstraining machen

10. Present-tense meanings

Linda **arbeitet** gut. = { Linda *works* well. (plain)
Linda *does work* well. (emphatic)
Linda *is working* well. (progressive)

German uses a single verb form to express ideas or actions that may require one of three different forms in English.

Du **gehst** heute Nachmittag schwimmen, nicht?
You*'re going* swimming this afternoon, aren't you?

Ich **mache** das morgen.
I*'ll do* that tomorrow.

German, like English, may use the present tense to express action intended or planned for the future.

9. Wie sagt man das? *(How do you say that?)*   Give the German equivalents of the following sentences.

⟫ Frank does not work well.   *Frank arbeitet nicht gut.*

1. Karla does work a lot.
2. I do believe that.
3. Stefan does play soccer well.
4. You're working tonight, Beatrix.
5. You do that well, Tina.
6. I'm playing tennis today.
7. We're playing basketball today.
8. I believe so.
9. Detlev is going to the movies.
10. I'm going dancing.

11. Informational questions

Wann gehst du schwimmen? ⌃   *When* are you going swimming?
Wer arbeitet heute nachmittag? ⌃   *Who* is working this afternoon?

A question that asks for a particular bit of information is called an informational question. It begins with an interrogative expression such as **wann** *(when)*, **was** *(what)*, **welch(-er, -es, -e)** *(which)*, **wer** *(who)*, **wie** *(how)*, and **was für (ein)** *(what kind of)*. The interrogative is followed by the verb. In an informational question in German, the finite verb is used. In English, a form of the auxiliary verb *to be* or *to do* is often used with a form of the main verb. In German, the voice normally falls at the end of an informational question, just as it does in English.

10. Wer? Was? Wann?   Your partner has a list showing when various people are playing particular games. Ask your partner three questions, one beginning with **wer** *(who)*, one with **was,** and one with **wann.**

Asking informational questions

S1: Wer spielt heute Squash?
S2: Barbara spielt heute Squash.
S1: Wann spielt ihr Volleyball?
S2: Wir spielen um halb sechs Volleyball.
S1: Was spielt Professor Krause?
S2: Er spielt Golf.

Wer?	Wann?	Was?
Barbara	heute	Squash
Anne und Kevin	um drei	Schach
ich	um acht	Fußball
Professor Krause	heute Abend	Golf
wir	um halb sechs	Volleyball

11. Gute Freunde.   Ask your partner about a good friend.

1. Wie heißt deine Freundin/dein Freund?
2. Wie alt ist sie/er?
3. Wie ist ... ?
4. Was macht ... ?

12. Yes/No questions

Gehst du heute schwimmen? ⌄   *Are* you *going* swimming today?
Treiben Sie gern Sport? ⌄   *Do* you *like to play* sports?

A question that can be answered with yes or no begins with the verb. A yes/no question in German uses the finite verb, whereas English often requires a form of the auxiliary verb *to do* or *to be* plus a form of the main verb. In German, the voice normally rises at the end of a yes/no question, just as it does in English.

Confirming or denying

12. Ja oder nein?   Ask your partner three questions based on the cues. Your partner will then ask you the three questions.

arbeiten: heute Abend
S1: Arbeitest du heute Abend?
S2: Ja, ich arbeite heute Abend.
    Nein, ich arbeite heute Abend nicht.

1. schwimmen: gern, oft, gut
2. spielen: gern, gut, oft / Basketball, Golf, Videospiele, Karten
3. schreiben: gern, viel, gut
4. gehen: heute Abend, gern, oft / ins Kino, in die Bibliothek
5. gehen: gern, oft, heute Abend / Jogging, Rollerblading, tanzen
6. hören: oft, gern / Musik, Rock, Rap, klassische Musik
7. heben: oft, gern / Gewichte
8. machen: oft, gern, heute / Fitnesstraining, Aerobic

13. Tag questions

Du hörst gern Musik, **nicht wahr?**   You like to listen to music, *don't you?*
Mark geht heute Abend ins Kino,   Mark is going to the movies
    nicht?   tonight, *isn't he?*

A tag question is literally "tagged on" to the end of a statement. In English the tag equivalent to **nicht wahr?** or **nicht?** depends on the subject of the sentence: *don't you?, aren't you?, isn't he?,* and *doesn't she?,* etc.

13. Nicht?   In a conversation with a friend, ask for confirmation that what you think is correct. Use the tag question **nicht?** or **nicht wahr?**

➤➤ Frau Meier ist sehr nett.   *Frau Meier ist sehr nett, nicht?*
                                Frau Meier ist sehr nett, nicht wahr?

1. Professor Wagner arbeitet viel.
2. Sie und ihr Mann wandern gern.
3. Jürgen ist oft müde.
4. Rita macht viel Sport.
5. Sie schwimmt gut.
6. Sie ist auch sehr intelligent.

14. Wie sagt man das?   You overhear someone on the phone talking with Ina. Translate the questions for Dieter, your German friend.

➤➤ Ina, how are you?   *Ina, wie geht's?*

1. What are you doing, Ina?
2. Are you working?
3. Are you going swimming today?
4. When are you playing tennis, Ina?
5. Does Rudi play well?
6. What kind of person is Rudi?
7. Do you like to play chess?
8. Rudi likes to play, too, doesn't he?
9. You're coming at seven, aren't you?

15. **Ein Interview.**   You are looking for a new roommate. Write five questions you want to ask the person about her/his likes, dislikes, and activities. Then find a partner and conduct an interview.

WIEDERHOLUNG

1. Wer ist Linda?   Read the information on Linda and answer the questions.

Linda ist 19 Jahre alt und Studentin in München. Sie ist sehr fleißig, nett und lustig. Heute ist Donnerstag und Linda macht um 8.50 Uhr° Englisch. Um 10 Uhr spielt sie mit Philipp Tennis und um 13 Uhr geht sie schwimmen. Zusammen mit Philipp, Alex und Gisela geht sie um 19.15 Uhr° ins Kino.

8.50 Uhr: spoken or read **acht Uhr fünfzig**

19.15 Uhr: spoken or read **neunzehn Uhr fünfzehn**

1. Wie alt ist Linda?
2. Wo studiert sie?
3. Was für ein Mensch ist Linda?
4. Welcher Tag ist heute?
5. Um wie viel Uhr macht sie Englisch?
6. Wer spielt mit Linda Tennis? Wann?
7. Wer geht mit Linda ins Kino? Wann?

2. Ja, Veronika.   Confirm Veronika's information about you and your friends.

➤➤ Gabi arbeitet in Basel, nicht wahr?   *Ja, sie arbeitet in Basel.*

1. Du arbeitest in Zürich, nicht?
2. Wolf hört gern Musik, nicht wahr?
3. Renate und Paula spielen gut Rock, nicht?
4. Wir spielen gut Basketball, nicht?
5. Trudi macht viel Sport, nicht wahr?
6. Du und Regina, ihr spielt gern Tennis, nicht?

3. Was machen sie?   Somebody you know slightly is asking about your friends. Construct sentences using the following cues.

➤➤ wie / heißen / der Junge / ?   *Wie heißt der Junge?*

1. er / heißen / Konrad
2. er / studieren / in Berlin / ?
3. nein / er / studieren / in München
4. wie / arbeiten / er / ?
5. er / sein / fleißig
6. was / machen / Martha und er / heute Abend / ?
7. sie / gehen / ins Kino
8. wann / sie / gehen / ins Kino / ?
9. wer / treiben / gern / Sport / ?
10. Martha / spielen / gut / Fußball

4. Ergänzen Sie.   Complete the following exchanges with appropriate words.

1. PROFESSOR: _____ heißen Sie?

   STUDENT: Ich _____ Alex Fischer.

2. HERR WAGNER: Guten Tag, Frau Schneider. Wie _____ es Ihnen?

   FRAU SCHNEIDER: Danke. Es _____ .

3. MARIA: Arbeitest _____ heute nicht?

   VOLKER: Nein, ich _____ heute Tennis.

   MARIA: _____ du viel Sport?

   VOLKER: Ja, _____ spiele gern Volleyball.

4. ALEX: _____ gehst du ins Kino?

   GISELA: _____ 7 Uhr.

5. Wie sagt man das?   Give the German equivalent of the questions you ask Cornelia.

1. Cornelia, how are you?
2. What are you doing?
3. Are you working?
4. Are you going swimming today?
5. Is Michael going also?
6. When are you playing tennis?
7. Does Michael play well?
8. What kind of person is Michael?
9. He likes to play chess, doesn't he?

Was finden diese jungen Leute so lustig? (Universität Mannheim)

6. Wer ist das? Choose one of the persons in the picture on page 50 and invent some facts about the person.

Wie heißt sie/er? Was für ein Mensch ist sie/er? Was macht sie/er gern? Wo studiert sie/er? ???

7. Frage-Ecke. Below are two schedules (labeled S1 and S2) listing some activities for Linda, Philipp, and Alex and Gisela. Each schedule has information the other does not have. First determine who will be S1 and who will be S2. Secondly, you and your partner should then fill in the "ich" column of your respective schedules with your activities for the time periods. Finally, without looking at each other's schedule, ask each other questions to determine the missing activities on your schedule. Be sure to ask your partner what she/he has planned.

S2: Was macht Linda heute Morgen?
S1: Sie macht heute Morgen Deutsch.
S2: Was machen Alex und Gisela Samstag?
S1: Sie spielen Samstag Schach.

S1:

	heute Morgen	heute Abend	Samstag	Sonntag
Linda	Deutsch machen		ins Kino gehen	
Philipp		Musik hören	in die Bibliothek gehen	
Alex und Gisela		tanzen	Schach spielen	
ich				
Partnerin/ Partner				

S2:

	heute Morgen	heute Abend	Samstag	Sonntag
Linda		arbeiten		Karten spielen
Philipp	Deutsch machen			Videospiele spielen
Alex und Gisela	Sport treiben			wandern
ich				
Partnerin/ Partner				

Meeting and greeting people

8. Gespräche.   You meet a fellow classmate on campus. Work out the following dialogue with a partner.

1. Greet her/him.
2. Ask how she/he is.
3. Ask what she/he is doing this afternoon.
4. Tell what you are doing.
5. Ask whether she/he likes to play tennis.
6. Arrange a time to play together tomorrow.

9. Zum Schreiben

1. Think ahead to the weekend and, using complete sentences, write down at least three things you will do and three things you will not do. Use a separate sentence for each thing.
2. Answer the following questions about the form of a personal letter written in German.
   a. Where do you write the city and date for a personal letter?
   b. Look at the punctuation in the city/date line. Where do you find a comma? Where do you find a period?
   c. What is the salutation for a woman? For a man?
   d. How does Gisela close the letter?
   e. Look carefully at the greeting and closing. What punctuation is used after the greeting? After the closing?
3. Using Gisela's letter to Monika and Stefan as a model, write a letter to a friend about your room, your school, and one friend. Before you write the letter, reread Gisela's letter and notice how she uses the words **und, aber, auch, furchtbar,** and **jedenfalls.** Try to use some of these words in your letter. You may also want to review the vocabulary for the names of things in your room that were presented in the *Einführung.*

GRAMMATIK: ZUSAMMENFASSUNG

(Grammar: Summary)

Subject pronouns

Singular		Plural	
1.	**ich** I	**wir** we	
2.	**du** you *(familiar)*	**ihr** you *(familiar)*	
3.	**er** he, it		
	es it	**sie** they	
	sie she, it		
	Sie you *(formal)*		

Present tense of *sein*

sein: to be	
ich **bin**	wir **sind**
du **bist**	ihr **seid**
er/es/sie **ist**	sie **sind**
Sie **sind**	

The verb **sein,** like its English equivalent *to be,* is irregular in the present tense.

Infinitive and infinitive stem

Infinitive	Stem + ending
glauben	glaub + en
wandern	wander + n

The basic form of a verb is the infinitive. Most German infinitives end in **-en;** a few end in **-n,** such as **wandern.** In vocabularies and dictionaries, verbs are listed in their infinitive form.

Present tense of regular verbs

	glauben	arbeiten	heißen
ich	glaub**e**	arbeit**e**	heiß**e**
du	glaub**st**	arbeit**est**	heiß**t**
er/es/sie	glaub**t**	arbeit**et**	heiß**t**
wir	glaub**en**	arbeit**en**	heiß**en**
ihr	glaub**t**	arbeit**et**	heiß**t**
sie	glaub**en**	arbeit**en**	heiß**en**
Sie	glaub**en**	arbeit**en**	heiß**en**

1. German verb endings change, depending on what the subject of the verb is. The verb endings are added to the infinitive stem. There are four basic endings in the present tense of most regular verbs: **-e, -st, -t, en.**
2. If a verb stem ends in **-d** or **-t,** the endings **-st** and **-t** expand to **-est** and **-et.**
3. If a verb stem ends in a sibilant **(s, ss, ß, z),** the **-st** ending contracts to **-t.**

Position of *nicht*

The position of **nicht** is determined by the various elements in the sentence. Because of the great flexibility of **nicht,** its use is best learned by observing its position in sentences you hear and read. Here are several guidelines:

1. **Nicht** always follows the finite verb:

   Bernd arbeitet **nicht.**   Bernd is not working.

2. **Nicht** always follows:

   a. noun objects

   Ich glaube *Bernd* **nicht.**   I don't believe Bernd.

   b. pronouns used as objects

   Ich glaube *es* **nicht.**   I don't believe it.

   c. specific adverbs of time

   Bernd spielt *heute* **nicht.**   Bernd is not playing today.

3. **Nicht** precedes most other elements:

   a. predicate adjectives

   Sebastian ist **nicht** *nett.*   Sebastian isn't nice.

   b. predicate nouns

   Das ist **nicht** *Herr Schmidt.*   That isn't Mr. Schmidt.

   c. adverbs

   Er spielt **nicht** *gut* Tennis.   He doesn't play tennis well.

   d. adverbs of general time

   Er spielt **nicht** *oft* Tennis.   He doesn't play tennis often.

   e. prepositional phrases

   Ute geht **nicht** *ins Kino.*   Ute isn't going to the movies.

4. If several of the elements occur in a sentence, **nicht** usually precedes the first one.

   Ich gehe **nicht** *oft ins Kino.*   I don't often go to the movies.

Informational questions

1	2	3	
Wann	gehen	Sie?	When are you going?
Wo	arbeitest	du?	Where do you work?

In an informational question in German, an interrogative is in first position and the finite verb in second position. Some common interrogatives are **wann, was, welch(-er, -es, -e), wer, wie, was für ein,** and **wo.**

Yes/No questions

1	2	3	
Bist	du	müde?	Are you tired?
Spielt	Andrea	gut?	Does Andrea play well?
Arbeitest	du	heute?	Are you working today?

In a yes/no question in German, the finite verb is in first position.

Wie ist das Wetter?

Das Wetter heute in Freiburg: kalt und nass.

LERNZIELE

Sprechintentionen
Talking about the weather
Inquiring about someone's birthday
Summarizing information
Stating one's nationality

Lesestück
Groß oder klein? Alles ist relativ!

Land und Leute
Berlin
Birthday customs and greetings
Development of the standard
 German language

Vokabeln
Weather expressions
Months and seasons
Suffixes *-er* and *-in*
Names of countries and
 nationalities
The question word *woher*

Grammatik
Simple past tense of *sein*
Present tense of *haben*
Position of the finite verb in
 statements
Nominative case
Plural of nouns
Indefinite article *ein*
Expressing negation by *kein* and
 nicht
Possession with proper names
Possessive adjectives
Demonstrative pronouns *der, das,
 die*

BAUSTEINE FÜR GESPRÄCHE

Wie ist das Wetter?

Im Sommer

FRAU KLUGE: Schönes Wetter, nicht wahr, Professor Lange?

PROFESSOR LANGE: Ja, aber es ist zu heiß und trocken.

FRAU KLUGE: Vielleicht regnet es morgen ja.

PROFESSOR LANGE: Na, hoffentlich!

Im Herbst

MICHAEL: Heute ist es wirklich kalt, nicht?

GISELA: Ja, sehr, und gestern war es noch so schön.

MICHAEL: Jetzt bleibt es bestimmt kalt.

GISELA: Leider.

Im Winter

STEFAN: Was für ein Wetter!

MONIKA: Der Wind ist furchtbar kalt. Ich glaube, es schneit bald.

STEFAN: Wie viel Grad ist es?

MONIKA: Es ist zwei Grad.

Brauchbares

1. In German an adjective that precedes a noun has an ending, e.g., **schön*es* Wetter.** If the adjective does not precede a noun it has no ending (e.g., **Es ist schön**).
2. Note that in German when the subject (e.g., **es**) does not begin the sentence it follows the verb (e.g., **Vielleicht regnet es ja**).
3. **Ja** and **na.** In Professor Lange's statement **Ja, aber es ist zu trocken,** the word **ja** implies agreement, i.e., *yes.* In Frau Kluge's statement **Vielleicht regnet es morgen ja,** the **ja** conveys the meaning of *after all.* The use of little words like **ja** is common in German colloquial speech. Another example is Professor Lange's statement **Na, hoffentlich!** where **na** is equivalent to English *well.*
4. **Was für ein.** Compare the exclamation **Was für ein [Wetter]!**—*What a (weather)!*—to the question **Was für ein [Mensch ist er]?**—*What kind of (person is he)?*
5. German-speaking countries use the Celsius thermometer. Two degrees Celsius = 37 degrees Fahrenheit.

1. Schönes Wetter, nicht? A fellow student comments on the weather. Agree with her/him.

Discussing the weather

S2:
Schönes Wetter, hm?
Gutes
Schlechtes
Furchtbares

S1:
Ja, es ist wirklich | **schön.**
| gut.
| schlecht.
| furchtbar.
| warm°.

2. Das Wetter. Talk about the weather with two or three fellow students. Ask how it is now and then make a prediction about tomorrow. For additional weather expressions, refer to the Supplementary Word Sets in the Reference Section.

Inquiring about the weather

S1:
Wie ist das Wetter heute?

S2:
Es ist **kalt.**

Schüttelkasten

schlecht			heiß°
	nass°		
schön	sonnig°	kühl°	
windig°			schwül°

Vielleicht | **regnet** es morgen.
| schneit es.
| scheint° die Sonne°.

Ja, vielleicht.
Ich glaube nicht.
Hoffentlich nicht.

Predicting the weather

3. Was für ein Wetter! A fellow student is unhappy with the weather. Respond by commenting on the weather yesterday.

Stating displeasure about the weather

S2:
Was für ein | **Wetter!**
| Wind!
| Regen°!
| Schnee°!

S1:
Ja, und gestern war es | **noch schön warm°.**
| auch schlecht.
| auch kalt.
| noch trocken.

4. Was sagen Sie? Make each of the comments below to a partner. After each comment, your partner will respond with an appropriate expression from the list. Your partner should avoid using the same expression each time.

Discussing the weather

Na hoffentlich. □ Leider. □ Vielleicht. □ Jetzt bleibt es so. □ Ja, sehr. □ Vielleicht schneit es bald. □ Vielleicht regnet es ja. □ Nein, noch nicht°.

1. Heute ist es schön warm.
2. Heute ist es wirklich heiß.
3. Es ist zu trocken.
4. Was für ein Wetter!
5. Der Wind ist furchtbar kalt.
6. Schneit es?
7. Jetzt bleibt es bestimmt kalt.

Erweiterung des Wortschatzes

1. Die Monate°

Der Mai war schön, nicht?   May was nice, wasn't it?

All the names of the months are **der**-words.

Januar	Februar	März
April	**Mai**	**Juni**
Juli	August	September
Oktober	**November**	**Dezember**

2. Die Jahreszeiten°

der **Frühling**

der **Sommer**

der **Herbst**

der **Winter**

1. Wie heißen sie?   Answer the following questions about the seasons.

1. Wie heißen die Wintermonate? die Sommermonate?
2. Wie heißen die Herbstmonate? die Frühlingsmonate?

2. Wann ist es ... ?   Tell in what months the following weather conditions occur where you live.

➤➤ Wann ist es oft kalt?   *Im Januar und im Februar.*

1. Wann regnet es viel?
2. Wann schneit es viel?
3. Wann ist es oft heiß / schwül / windig?
4. Wann scheint die Sonne nicht viel?
5. Wann ist es schön warm?
6. Wann ist es sehr trocken?
7. Wann ist der Wind kalt? warm? heiß?
8. Wann ist das Wetter gut – nicht heiß und nicht kalt?

3. Wie ist das Wetter in ... ?   Ask your partner about the weather in one of the four cities below. Your partner will ask you about the weather in one of the other cities. The dates are spoken as **der zehnte Mai, der dritte Januar, der achtundzwanzigste Juli, der zweite Oktober.** Below are forms of the questions and answers you can use.

1. Wie ist das Wetter heute in [Berlin]?
   a. Das Wetter ist heute [schön / schlecht / gut].
   b. Es ist [warm / heiß / kalt / kühl / nass / trocken / sonnig / windig].
   c. Es [regnet / schneit].
   d. Die Sonne scheint heute.
2. Wie viel Grad ist es?
   Es ist [18 Grad]. / Es ist [minus zwei Grad].
3. Welche Jahreszeit ist es [in Berlin]?
4. Wie ist das Wetter [hier / in Vermont] im [Winter / Sommer / Herbst / Frühling]?

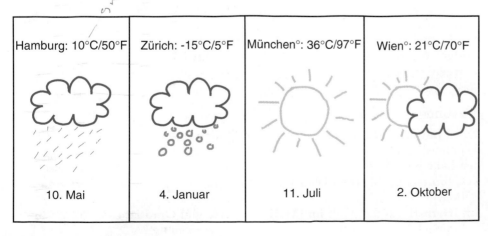

Hamburg: 10°C/50°F   Zürich: -15°C/5°F   München°: 36°C/97°F   Wien°: 21°C/70°F   Munich / Vienna

10. Mai   4. Januar   11. Juli   2. Oktober

⇨ **4. Wann hast du Geburtstag°?** Interview four students to find out the months of their birthdays.

S1:
Wann hast du Geburtstag?

S2:
Ich habe im [Mai] Geburtstag.

Vokabeln

Nouns whose plural forms are commonly used are listed with their plural forms:
die Jahreszeit, -en = die Jahreszeiten.

Substantive

der **Frühling** spring
der **Geburtstag** birthday
der **Grad** degree (*temperature only*)
der **Herbst** autumn, fall
die **Jahreszeit, -en** season
der **Monat, -e** month
der **Regen** rain

der **Schnee** snow
der **Sommer** summer
die **Sonne** sun
das **Wetter** weather
der **Wind** wind
der **Winter** winter
For the months see p. 58.

Verben

bleiben to remain, stay
regnen to rain; **es regnet** it's
  raining
scheinen to shine

schneien to snow; **es schneit** it's
  snowing
war was (*past tense of* **sein**)

Andere Wörter

bald soon
bestimmt certain(ly), for sure
gestern yesterday
heiß hot
hmm hmm
hoffentlich I hope so
jetzt now
kalt cold
kühl cool
leider unfortunately
morgen tomorrow
nass wet

noch still; in addition; **noch nicht**
  not yet
schön nice, beautiful
schwül humid
sonnig sunny
trocken dry
warm warm; **schön warm**
  nice and warm
windig windy
wirklich really
zu too

Besondere Ausdrücke

Es ist [minus] [10] Grad. It's
  [minus] [10] degrees.
Ich habe im [Mai]
  Geburtstag. My birthday is in
  [May].
im [Herbst] in the [fall]; **im [Mai]**
  in [May]

Wann hast du Geburtstag? When
  is your birthday?
Was für ein Wetter! What weather!
Wie ist das Wetter? How's the
  weather?
Wie viel Grad ist es? What's the
  temperature?

GROSS ODER KLEIN?
ALLES IST RELATIV!

Vorbereitung auf das Lesen

■ *Vor dem Lesen*

1. Look at the advertisement below and answer the following questions.
   a. What does the advertisement imply about the winter weather in Germany?
   b. What is the weather like in Florida?
   c. How much does a ticket from Frankfurt to Miami cost? Do you find the price expensive **(teuer),** reasonable **(günstig),** or cheap **(billig)?**

2. Do you think the concept of cold means the same thing to inhabitants of Florida as to those of Toronto, Canada? What temperature do you personally think is cold on a winter day?
3. On a map of the world locate Berlin, the capital of Germany, and Washington, D.C. Which city is farther north?
4. Where do you think winters are colder: Minnesota (U.S.A.), Ontario (Canada), or northern Germany?

5. Where do you think winters are colder: in northern Germany (Hamburg) or in southern Germany (Munich)?
6. In area, Germany is the third largest country of the European Union, after France and Spain. How large do you think Germany is compared to your state or province?
7. Using the map in the front of the book, locate the following cities: Frankfurt am Main, Berlin, Bonn, Dresden, Hamburg, and München.

■ Beim Lesen

1. In the reading you will find data on the number of inhabitants of Germany, Germany's size, and distances within the country. As you are reading, make notes on the relevant facts about Germany.
2. Which words or concepts in the text would you consider to be relative?
3. Circle or make a list of the cognates.

approximately

W ashington ist Amerikas Hauptstadt und liegt circa° 1500 Kilometer weiter südlich als unsere Hauptstadt Berlin. Also ist der Sommer in Amerika auch anders als der Sommer in Deutschland. Ein Amerikaner in Deutschland sagt: „Heute ist es schön warm." Ein Deutscher
5 hört das und denkt: „Warm? Hier? Jetzt? Nein! Furchtbar heiß." Was für Deutsche heiß ist, finden Amerikaner warm, denn das Klima ist in Amerika anders als in Deutschland. In Amerika ist das Wetter oft heiß im Sommer, aber im Winter ist es sehr kalt im Norden und warm im Süden. In Deutsch-

on the other hand
after all

land ist es dagegen° oft kühl im Sommer und nicht so kalt im Winter. Hier
10 beeinflusst nämlich° der Ozean das Klima, und er beeinflusst es mehr im Norden als im Süden und mehr im Westen als im Osten.

Wörter wie „heiß" und „warm" sind also relativ. Auch die Wörter „groß"
at least
und „klein" sind relativ, wenigstens° in der Geographie. Für Deutsche ist Amerika sehr groß. Für Amerikaner ist Deutschland ziemlich klein. Deutsch-
15 land hat etwa zweiundachtzig Millionen Einwohner, Amerika zweihundert-

And yet
siebzig Millionen. Dabei° ist Deutschland nur etwa halb so groß wie Texas (oder Alberta). Von Bonn im Westen nach Dresden im Osten sind es nur etwa fünfhundert Kilometer. Von Hamburg im Norden nach München im

day's journey (by car)
Süden sind es nur achthundert Kilometer. Das ist nur eine Tagesreise°. Von
20 Seattle im Nordwesten nach Miami im Südosten sind es fünf bis sieben

= 3273 miles
Tagesreisen (5267 km)°. In Deutschland haben „groß" und „klein" also andere Dimensionen als in Amerika.

Brauchbares

1. Note the phrase in l. 17–18 **"sind es nur etwa fünfhundert Kilometer"** (*it is only five hundred kilometers*). In German **es** is only a "dummy" subject; the real subject, **fünfhundert Kilometer,** is plural; therefore the verb is plural, i.e., **sind.** With a singular subject the verb would be **ist: Es ist nur ein Kilometer** (*It is only one kilometer*). The equivalent English phrase, *it is,* never changes, whether the real subject is singular or plural.
2. German-speaking countries use kilometers to measure distance. One kilometer (km) equals .62 mile.

Auf der Autobahn sind es nur 72 Kilometer von Augsburg nach Ulm.

Nach dem Lesen

1. Ergänzen Sie.   Using your notes on the size of Germany, complete the following sentences.

1. Deutschland hat _____ Einwohner.

2. Deutschland ist etwa halb so groß wie _____ .

3. Von Bonn nach Dresden sind es etwa _____ Kilometer.

4. Es ist eine Tagesreise von München im Süden nach Hamburg im _____ .

2. Fragen zum Lesestück

1. Wie heißt die deutsche° Hauptstadt?
2. Welche Stadt liegt weiter nördlich° – Berlin oder Washington, D.C.?
3. Was sagt ein Amerikaner in Deutschland im Sommer?
4. Was denkt ein Deutscher?
5. Wie ist das Klima in Amerika?
6. Warum ist der Winter in Deutschland nicht so kalt?
7. Welche Wörter sind relativ?
8. Etwa wie viele Kilometer ist die Tagesreise von Hamburg nach München?
9. Wie viele Kilometer ist für Sie eine Tagesreise?

3. Erzählen wir. *(Let's talk about it.)*

1. Before you can talk about a topic you need to have the appropriate vocabulary. Go back to the text and write down several words in addition to the one provided that you could use when you talk about Germany.

Klima: Sommer, _____ , _____

size

Größe°: Kilometer, _____ , _____

2. Talk briefly about one of the following topics.

Das Wetter in Deutschland.
Deutschland ist klein.

its

4. Deutschland und seine° Nachbarn. Germany is situated in the center of Europe, and it has many neighboring countries. Using the map of Europe on the inside back cover of your book, fill in the missing country names in the paragraph below. Note: Certain names of countries in German are always used with a definite article. Some of these countries are: **die Schweiz** (Switzerland), **die Niederlande** (The Netherlands), and **die Tschechische Republik** (Czech Republic).

center

Deutschland liegt im Zentrum° Europas. Es hat neun Nachbarn: Das Nachbarland im Norden ist _____ ; die Nachbarländer im Süden sind _____ und die _____ ; im Osten liegen _____ und die _____ ; im Westen _____ , _____ , _____ und die _____ .

Über Nacht gab's 60 Zentimeter Neuschnee in Parpan, in der Schweiz.

Erweiterung des Wortschatzes

1. The suffix *-in*

Masculine	der Nachbar
Feminine	die Nachbar**in**
Feminine plural	die Nachbar**innen**

The suffix **-in** added to the singular masculine noun gives the feminine equivalent. The plural of a noun with the suffix **-in** ends in **-nen.**

1. Mann oder Frau?   Give the other form—feminine or masculine—of the words listed below.

➤➤ die Professorin   *der Professor*

1. die Freundin
2. der Student
3. die Amerikanerin
4. der Einwohner

2. Names of countries

Wie groß ist **Deutschland?**   How large is Germany?
Existiert **das romantische Deutschland**   Does romantic Germany still
   noch?   exist?

The names of most countries are neuter; for example **(das) Deutschland** and **(das) Amerika.** Articles are not used with names of countries that are neuter, unless the name is preceded by an adjective.

Die Schweiz ist schön.   Switzerland is beautiful.
Die USA sind groß.   The United States is large.

The names of a few countries are feminine (e.g., **die Schweiz**); some names are used only in the plural (e.g., **die USA**). Articles are always used with names of countries that are feminine or plural.

2. Andere Länder.   Try to guess the English names for the countries listed below.

1. Italien
2. Spanien
3. Griechenland
4. Russland
5. Brasilien
6. Frankreich
7. Norwegen
8. Liechtenstein
9. die Türkei
10. die Niederlande

Go to the
Deutsch heute Web Site at
www.hmco.com/college

Berlin

The origins of the city of Berlin lie in the twelfth century; in its long history Berlin has served as the capital city of many German states and forms of government, including the monarchy of the Hohenzollerns, the Third Reich, and the German Democratic Republic. With the

Der Bundestag hat einen neuen Sitz im Reichstagsgebäude in Berlin.

unification of Germany, Berlin again became the capital of a united Germany. At the end of World War II in 1945, the four Allies divided Germany into four zones of occupation and its capital, Berlin, into four sectors: American, British, French, and Soviet. Currency reforms in the Western zones and then in the Soviet zone in 1948, the blockade of Berlin by the Soviets, and the establishment of western Germany as the **Bundesrepublik Deutschland (BRD)** (Federal Republic of Germany) and of eastern Germany as the **Deutsche Demokratische Republik**

Blick auf die Stadt Berlin aus der neuen Kuppel des Reichstagsgebäudes.

(DDR) (German Democratic Republic) in 1949 led to the separation of Berlin into two parts. The construction of the Berlin Wall **(die Mauer)** in 1961, built by the **DDR** to halt the emigration of several millions of East Germans into West Germany, completed the division of Berlin.

From the end of World War II until the unification of Germany on October 3, 1990, Berlin had a special status under international law. Legally, it belonged neither to the **BRD** nor to the **DDR.** In practice both parts of Berlin were closely connected to their respective systems. Many countries recognized the eastern part of Berlin as the capital of the **DDR.** The **BRD** made Bonn, a medium-sized city on the **Rhein,** its temporary capital.

On November 9, 1989, the wall that divided Berlin was opened. As of October 3, 1990, the date of unification of Germany, Berlin is again one city. It is the largest city in Germany with a population of almost 3.5 million. Article 2 of the **Einigungsvertrag** (Unification Treaty) states that "Berlin is the capital city of Germany." However, Bonn has been assigned a special status as a federal city **(Bundesstadt)** which ensures that it will continue to play an important political role in Germany. The majority of government agencies have moved to Berlin, but they have retained branch offices in Bonn; while those that have remained in Bonn have branches in Berlin. In effect, Bonn is a second seat of government.

Diskussion

Although Berlin has an important historic and emotional significance for many Germans, moving the capital of the Federal Republic of Germany to Berlin became a complicated process. What issues can you imagine could have been discussed while planning the move?

3. Nouns indicating citizenship and nationality

Berlin	der Berliner	die Berlinerin
England	der Engländer	die Engländerin
Spanien	der Spanier	die Spanierin
Norwegen	der Norweger	die Norwegerin
München	der Münchner	die Münchnerin
Kanada	der Kanadier	die Kanadierin
Deutschland	der Deutsche (Deutscher)	die Deutsche

Nouns indicating an inhabitant of a city or a citizen of a country follow several patterns. While you won't be able to predict the exact form, you will always be able to recognize it.

The noun suffix **-er** is added to the name of many cities, states, or countries to indicate a male citizen or inhabitant **(Berliner).** Some nouns take an umlaut **(Engländer).** To indicate a female citizen or inhabitant the additional suffix **-in** is added to the **-er** suffix **(Berlinerin, Engländerin).**

In some instances the **-er/-erin** is added to a modified form of the country **(Kanadier/Kanadierin).** Other countries have still other forms to indicate the citizen or inhabitant **(Deutscher/Deutsche).**

Mark ist **Deutscher.**	Mark is (a) *German.*
Anna ist **Deutsche.**	Anna is (a) *German.*

Note that to state a person's nationality, German uses the noun directly after a form of **sein.** The indefinite article **ein** is not used, whereas in English nouns of nationality may be preceded by an indefinite article.

Ein Berliner und sein Hund.

4. The question word *woher*

Woher kommst du?   Where are you from?
Ich **komme aus** [Frankfurt/   I am from [Frankfurt/
  der Schweiz/den USA].   Switzerland/the U.S.A.].

To ask in German where someone is from, use the interrogative **woher** and a form of the verb **kommen.** To answer such a question, use a form of the verb **kommen** and the preposition **aus.**

3. Frage-Ecke.   Find out where the following people are from and where they live now. Obtain the missing information by asking your partner.

S2: Woher kommt Anton?
S1: Er kommt aus Deutschland.

S2: Was ist Anton?
S1: Er ist Deutscher.

S2: Wo wohnt° Anton?
S1: Er wohnt in München.

S2: Und woher kommst du?
S1: Ich komme aus ...

S1:

	Woher kommt ...?	Was ist ...?	Wo wohnt ... ?
Anton	Deutschland	Deutscher	München
Carmen	Spanien	Spanierin	Barcelona
Kristina			
Herr Heller			
ich			
Partnerin/Partner			

S2:

	Woher kommt ... ?	Was ist ... ?	Wo wohnt ... ?
Anton			
Carmen			
Kristina	Deutschland	Deutsche	Leipzig
Herr Heller	Österreich	Österreicher	Wien
ich			
Partnerin/Partner			

Stating one's nationality

4. Woher kommst du?   Ask five classmates where they are from. Make notes so you can tell others where they are from.

Vokabeln

Substantive

(das) **Amerika** America
der **Amerikaner, -**/die
  Amerikanerin, -nen American
  person
das **Beispiel, -e** example
der **Deutsche** *(m.)*/die **Deutsche**
  (f.)/die **Deutschen** *(pl.)* German
  person
ein **Deutscher** *(m.)*/eine **Deutsche** *(f.)*
  a German person
(das) **Deutschland** Germany
der **Einwohner, -**/die **Einwohnerin,**
  -nen inhabitant
(das) **Europa** Europe
die **Hauptstadt, ¨e** capital
(das) **Kanada** Canada
der **Kanadier,-**/die **Kanadierin,**
  -nen Canadian person
der **Kilometer, -** kilometer

das **Klima** climate
das **Land, ¨er** country, land
die **Million, -en** million
das **Nachbarland, ¨er** neighboring
  country
der **Norden** north
der **Osten** east
(das) **Österreich** Austria
der **Österreicher, -**/die
  Österreicherin, -nen Austrian
  person
der **Ozean** ocean
die **Schweiz** Switzerland
der **Schweizer, -**/die **Schweizerin,**
  -nen Swiss person
die **Stadt, ¨e** city
der **Süden** south
die **USA** *(pl.)* U.S.A.
der **Westen** west

Verben

beeinflussen to influence
denken to think
finden to find; to think
haben to have

liegen to lie; to be situated, be
  located
sagen to say; to tell
wohnen to live, reside

Andere Wörter

alles everything
als than
also therefore, so
andere other
anders different(ly)
deutsch German *(adj.)*
etwa approximately, about
für for
halb half; **halb so groß** half as
  large
hier here
in in
mehr more
nach to *(with cities and neuter*
  countries, e.g., **nach Berlin; nach**
  Deutschland)

nördlich to the north
relativ relative
so ... wie as . . . as
südlich to the south
von from; of
weiter farther, further
wie as
wieder again
wo where
woher where from
ziemlich quite, rather, fairly;
  ziemlich klein rather small

Besondere Ausdrücke

Ich bin [Schweizer/Amerikanerin].
  I am [Swiss/American].
Ich komme aus ...
  I come/am from . . .
nicht so [kalt]   not as [cold]

Woher kommst du?   Where are
  you from?
zum Beispiel (*abbrev.* **z.B.**)   for
  example (*abbrev.* e.g.)

GRAMMATIK UND ÜBUNGEN

1. Simple past tense of *sein*

Present	Heute ist das Wetter gut.	The weather is good today.
Simple past	Gestern war es schlecht.	It was bad yesterday.

The simple past tense of **sein** is **war.**

ich **war**	wir waren
du warst	ihr wart
er/es/sie **war**	sie waren
Sie waren	

I was	we were
you were	you were
he/it/she was	they were
you were	

In the simple past, the **ich-** and **er/es/sie-**forms of **sein** have no verb endings.

1. Wo warst du in den Sommerferien?   Gisela, Michael, and some friends are discussing where they all spent their summer vacation.

≫ Maria / Italien   *Maria war in Italien.*

1. Harald / Dresden
2. ihr / Salzburg
3. Karl und Kristina / Österreich
4. du / Leipzig
5. wir / Zürich

6. Verena / München
7. meine Freunde / Wien
8. Alex / Dänemark
9. Und wo waren Sie in den Sommerferien?

Discussing the weather

▷ **2. Wie war das Wetter?**   Ask a fellow student what the weather was like on four previous days. Record the answers. For additional expressions see "Weather expressions" in the Supplementary Word Sets in the Reference Section.

S1:
Wie war das Wetter [am Samstag]?

Und [am Freitag]?

S2:
Es war [schön].
[Am Samstag] war es [schön].
Es war [kalt].

Schüttelkasten

heiß	sehr kühl		warm
windig	sonnig	furchtbar kalt	schwül

2. Present tense of *haben*

haben: to have	
ich habe	wir haben
du **hast**	ihr habt
er/es/sie **hat**	sie haben
Sie haben	

The verb **haben** is irregular in the **du-** and **er/es/sie-**forms of the present tense.

3. Wann hast du Geburtstag?   Frank and Beate are updating their birthday list. Frank doesn't know the exact dates of their friends' birthdays. Take the role of Beate and tell him in what month the following people's birthdays are. And then give the month of your own birthday.

➤➤ ich / Juli   *Ich habe im Juli Geburtstag.*

1. Petra / Juni
2. du / September
3. Jürgen / Februar
4. ihr / Mai
5. Ulrike und Heinz / Oktober
6. wir / April
7. Und wann haben Sie Geburtstag?

3. Position of the finite verb in statements

1	2	3	4
Der Sommer	ist	in Deutschland	anders.
In Deutschland	ist	**der Sommer**	anders.

In a German statement, the finite verb is always in second position, even when an element other than the subject (for example, an adverb or a prepositional phrase) is in first position. When an element other than the subject is in first position, the subject follows the verb.

4. Hoffentlich ist es schön.   You and Sonja are discussing the weather, hoping it will be nice for an outdoor activity. Agree with her by restating her comments, beginning with the word in parentheses. Follow the model.

➤➤ Es ist heute schön, nicht? (heute)   *Ja. Heute ist es schön.*

1. Es bleibt hoffentlich warm. (hoffentlich)
2. Das Wetter war gestern schlecht, nicht? (gestern)
3. Das Wetter war auch am Mittwoch gut, nicht? (am Mittwoch)
4. Das Wetter bleibt jetzt bestimmt gut, nicht? (jetzt)
5. Die Sonne scheint hoffentlich. (hoffentlich)

LAND UND LEUTE

Go to the
Deutsch heute Web Site at
www.hmco.com/college

Geburtstage

Birthdays are very important to people in German-speaking countries. They seldom forget the birthday of a family member or friend—they write, call, give flowers and/or other gifts. Birthdays are celebrated in different ways. The "birthday child" **(Geburtstagskind)** may have an afternoon coffee party **(Geburtstagskaffee)** with family members and friends or a more extensive birthday party in the evening. At the **Geburtstagskaffee** candles are placed around the edge of a birthday cake **(Geburtstagskuchen)** and blown out by the person whose birthday it is. Although the **Geburtstagskind** is often taken out by family members or friends, he or she usually gives a party or brings a cake to work. Besides giving presents **(Geburtstagsgeschenke)**, it is common to send a birthday card or make a phone call. Common greetings are: **Herzlichen Glückwunsch zum Geburtstag!** *(Happy Birthday!)* or **Alles Gute zum Geburtstag!** *(All the best on your birthday!)*. Often friends or family place ads in newspapers **(Geburtstagsanzeigen),** in which the **Geburtstagskind** is congratulated on her/his birthday.

In Austria and the predominantly Catholic regions of Germany, name days **(Namenstage)** may be celebrated with as much excitement as a birthday. **Namenstage** commemorate the feast day of one's patron saint. Florist shops in these areas typically remind people whose name day is being celebrated.

Herzlichen Glückwunsch zum Geburtstag!

Diskussion

How does the typical celebration of birthdays in German-speaking countries differ from the way you celebrate birthdays, at home or at work?

5. Wer? Was? Wann?   You and Sabrina have been talking to your friends to find out when they are free for a get-together. By consulting your list you are able to tell Sabrina when your various friends are busy and what they are doing. Begin with the time element.

➤➤ *Morgen Abend spielt Ramon Basketball.*

Wer?	Was?	Wann?
Ramon	Basketball spielen	morgen Abend
Michael und Hans	Tennis spielen	am Montag
Anna	ins Kino gehen	heute
Carla	Geburtstag haben	am Sonntag
David und Greta	Volleyball spielen	heute Abend
ich	nicht arbeiten	morgen

6. So ist das Wetter. Tell when your birthday is and what the weather is usually like at that time of year. Make a brief report to a group of four or to the whole class.

> Describing the weather in a particular season

>> *Ich habe im Februar Geburtstag. Im Februar ist es kalt. Es schneit oft und die Sonne scheint nicht viel.*

7. Frage-Ecke. Find out how old the following people are, when their birthdays are, and what the typical weather in that month is. Obtain the missing information from your partner.

S2: Wie alt ist Manfred?
S1: Manfred ist 21 Jahre alt. Wann hat er Geburtstag?
S2: Im Januar.
S1: Wie ist das Wetter im Januar?
S2: Es ist kalt.

S1:

	Wie alt?	Geburtstag	das Wetter
Manfred	21		kalt
Stefanie		Oktober	
Herr Hofer	45		
Frau Vogel		April	nass und kühl
ich			
Partnerin/Partner			

S2:

	Wie alt?	Geburtstag	das Wetter
Manfred		Januar	
Stefanie	30		kühl
Herr Hofer		Juli	heiß und trocken
Frau Vogel	39		
ich			
Partnerin/Partner			

der Nominativ

4. The nominative° case

That woman plays tennis well.
She doesn't play volleyball very well.

English uses word order to signal different grammatical functions (e.g., subject) of nouns or pronouns. In a statement in English the subject precedes the verb.

Die Frau spielt gut Tennis.
Volleyball spielt **sie** aber nicht sehr gut.

German uses a different type of signal to indicate the grammatical function of nouns and pronouns. German uses a signal called *case.* When a noun or pronoun is used as the subject of a sentence, it is in the nominative case.

Masculine	Neuter	Feminine
der	das	die

In the nominative case, the German definite article has three forms. They are all equivalent to "the" in English.

Subject	Predicate noun
Herr Lange ist **Professor.**
Das Mädchen heißt **Gabi Fischer.**
Das ist nicht **der Junge.**

Subject	Predicate noun
Mr. Lange is *a professor.*
The girl's name is *Gabi Fischer.*
That is not *the boy.*

The nominative case is also used for a *predicate noun.* A predicate noun designates a person, concept, or thing that is equated with the subject. A predicate noun completes the meaning of linking verbs such as **sein** and **heißen.** In a negative sentence **nicht** precedes the predicate noun.

8. Wie war das Wetter?   Practice making comments about the weather. Use the cues provided. Make the comments in the past tense.

➤➤ Wetter / schön   *Das Wetter war schön.*

1. Morgen / kalt
2. Tag / warm
3. Wind / warm
4. Sonne / heiß
5. Abend / kalt
6. Tag / nass
7. Sommer / trocken
8. Juli / heiß

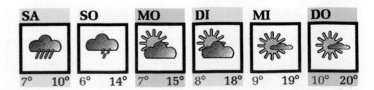

9. Was kostet?   Your partner is moving and wants to sell a few things. Ask how much each item costs. Your partner gives a price. Use a pronoun in your answer.

S1: Was kostet [die Uhr]?
S2: [Sie] kostet 30 Mark.

NUR NICHT
HEUTE

der Plural

5. Plural° forms of German nouns

A thousand years ago English had a variety of ways to signal the plural of nouns. With some nouns it used stem changes: *mann—menn (man, men); fōt—fet (foot, feet);* with other nouns it used endings: *stān—stānas (stone, stones), oxa—oxan (ox, oxen);* and with still other nouns it used no signal at all: *scēap—scēap (sheep, sheep).* Over the centuries the ending *-as* gradually replaced most other plural endings, and its modern development *-(e)s* is now the almost universal signal for the plural of English nouns.

Type	Plural signal	Singular	Plural
1	-	das Fenster	die Fenster
	¨	der Garten	die Gärten
2	-e	der Tisch	die Tische
	¨e	der Stuhl	die Stühle
3	-er	das Kind	die Kinder
	¨er	das Buch	die Bücher
4	-en	die Frau	die Frauen
	-n	die Lampe	die Lampen
	-nen	die Studentin	die Studentinnen
5	-s	das Radio	die Radios

German uses five basic types of signals to mark the plural of nouns: no ending or the endings **-e, -er, -(e)n,** and **-s.** Some of the nouns of types 1, 2, and 3 add umlaut in the plural. Nouns of type 4 that end in **-in** add **-nen** in the plural. German makes no gender distinctions in the plural; the definite article **die** is used with all plural nouns. The indefinite article has no plural form.

When you learn a German noun, you must also learn its plural form because there is no sure way of predicting to which plural-type the noun belongs. You will, however, gradually discover that there is a kind of system to the various types. This "system" depends partly on whether the noun is a **der-, das-,** or **die-** noun, and partly on how many syllables it has.

das Zimmer, - indicates that there is no change in the plural form of the noun: **das Zimmer, die Zimmer**

die Stadt, ¨e indicates that an **-e** is added in the plural, and an umlaut is added to the appropriate vowel: **die Stadt, die Städte**

In the vocabularies of this book, the plural of most nouns is indicated after the singular forms.

Die Kinder sind nett. **Sie** sind nett.
Die Lampen sind alt. **Sie** sind alt.

The personal pronoun **sie** *(they)* may refer to persons or things.

Die deutsche Sprache

Go to the
Deutsch heute Web Site at
www.hmco.com/college

A thousand years ago there was no standard form of the German language. The large central European area from the North Sea and the Baltic Sea to the Alps in the south was inhabited by Germans who lived in many different societies and spoke variations of the German language.

Martin Luther (1483–1546) played an important role in the development and refinement of German. For his Bible translation and other works, Luther used a form of the language spoken in east central Germany; eventually, it became the spoken and written standard for all of Germany as well as Austria and Switzerland. This single standard language is called **Hochdeutsch.** It is used in all domains of public life, including newspapers, radio, TV, and film. Germans consider the German spoken in the area of Hannover, a city in northern Germany, to be the closest to pure **Hochdeutsch,** that is, the most accent free. People from different German-speaking areas can always communicate with each other in **Hochdeutsch.** This way German speakers are linguistically unified despite the fact that local dialects are often incomprehensible to people from different regions within the German-speaking countries. Entire words, intonation, and pronunciation can vary dramatically and may even differ significantly from town to town. (Different ways to say **sprechen** for example, include **schwätzen** and **schnacken.**) Fears in the beginning of the twentieth century that mass media and other developments might cause dialects to die out have not materialized. At the end of the twentieth century, dialects were gaining in prestige and were used to some extent in every German-speaking country. Realizing that local dialects are an important part of popular culture, many writers and singers use their dialects to express themselves artistically and to promote the use of dialects.

In 1996 representatives from German-speaking countries and areas (Austria, Germany, Liechtenstein, Switzerland, Italy, Belgium, Romania, and Hungary) agreed to the first revision of German orthography and punctuation **(Rechtschreibreform)** since 1901. These new spelling rules are intended to modernize and simplify German writing and will become binding in 2005 with a transition period that began in 1998. The new rules have caused a great deal of controversy and raised legal issues about the right of the state to mandate changes in language as well as questions about the evolution of language.

Approximately 100 million people in Germany, Austria, and in parts of Switzerland, Belgium, Italy, Luxembourg, France, and Liechtenstein speak German as their native language. Twenty million people are presently learning German as a foreign language, the vast majority of them in central and eastern Europe.

Seit Martin Luther gibt es eine deutsche Sprache.

Diskussion

The new orthographic rules will allow more freedom in the spelling of foreign words. Many words will look more like German and less like their original language. With that in mind, read this "German" phrase out loud and translate it into English. **Kiep kuhl änd bie peischent!**

10. Der, das, die. State the noun with the definite article and then give the plural with the definite article. Plurals are given with the nouns in the German–English vocabulary list at the end of the book.

⫸ Tisch   *der Tisch / die Tische*

1. Stuhl
2. Buch
3. Bleistift
4. Kugelschreiber
5. Heft
6. Lampe
7. Radio
8. Computer
9. Gitarre
10. Studentin

11. Was ist hier los? *(What's going on here?)*   Talk about the people and things in a small town in Germany. Use the plural.

⫸ Haus / sein / alt   *Die Häuser sind alt.*

1. Garten / sein / klein
2. Straße / sein / alt
3. Nachbar / sein / nett
4. Kind / spielen / gern
5. Frau / arbeiten / viel
6. Mann / arbeiten / auch viel
7. Junge / spielen / gern / Fußball

der unbestimmte Artikel

6. The indefinite article° *ein*

Ist das **ein** Radio oder **eine** Uhr?   Is that *a* radio or *a* clock?

The German indefinite article **ein** is equivalent to English *a* or *an*.

Masculine	Neuter	Feminine
ein Mann	ein Kind	eine Frau

In the nominative case the German indefinite article has two forms: **ein** for masculine and neuter, and **eine** for feminine.

▷⫸ **12. Was ist das?**   Help your partner learn German. Point to a picture and she/he will tell what it is in German.

S1: Was ist das?
S2: Das ist ein Buch.

7. The negative *kein*

Ist das **ein** Radio?
Nein, das ist **kein** Radio.

Is that *a* radio?
No, that's *not a* radio.

Sind die Studenten Amerikaner?
Nein, sie sind **keine** Amerikaner.

Are the students Americans?
No, they are *not* Americans.

The negative form of **ein** is **kein.** It is equivalent to English *not a, not any,* or *no.* It negates a noun that in the positive would be preceded by a form of **ein** (e.g., **ein Radio**) or no article at all (e.g., **Amerikaner**).

Masculine	Neuter	Feminine	Plural
kein Tisch	**kein** Radio	**keine** Uhr	**keine** Radios

In the nominative case **kein** has two forms: **kein** for masculine and neuter, and **keine** for feminine and plural.

13. Das ist es nicht. You are taking your first art course and are showing Jan what you have drawn. He tries to guess what your attempts portray. Tell him his guesses are wrong. Use a form of **kein** in your responses.

≫ Ist das eine Frau?   *Nein, das ist keine Frau.*

1. Ist das ein Kind?   2. Ist das eine Lampe?   3. Ist das ein Bücherregal?

4. Ist das ein Telefon?   5. Ist das ein Computer?   6. Ist das eine Gitarre?

8. *Kein* vs. *nicht*

Ist das **eine** Uhr?	Nein, das ist **keine** Uhr.
Sind sie Amerikaner?	Nein, sie sind **keine** Amerikaner.
Ist das **die** Uhr?	Nein, das ist **nicht die** Uhr.

Kein is used to negate a noun that in an affirmative sentence would be preceded by **ein** or no article at all. **Nicht** is used when negating a noun preceded by a definite article.

14. Nicht oder kein?   Gisela is showing Monika and Stefan pictures she took in Berlin. They are not always sure what they are seeing. Take the role of Gisela and say they are mistaken. Use **nicht** or **kein** before the predicate noun, as appropriate.

>> Ist das Michael?   *Nein, das ist nicht Michael.*
>> Ist das ein Student?   *Nein, das ist kein Student.*

1. Ist das Professor Lange?
2. Ist das ein Nachbar?
3. Ist das die Lepsiusstraße?
4. Ist das eine Studentin?
5. Ist das ein Amerikaner?
6. Ist das die Bibliothek?
7. Ist das Frau Kluge?

9. Showing possession with a proper name

Das ist **Giselas** Buch.	That is *Gisela's* book.
Das ist **Jens'** Kuli.	That is *Jens's* ballpoint pen.

A proper name is a word that designates a specific individual or place (e.g., Ingrid, Berlin). In German as in English, possession and other close relationships are expressed by adding **-s** to the proper names. If the name already ends in a sibilant*, no **-s** is added. In written German, an apostrophe is used only when no **-s** is added (e.g., **Jens' Kuli**).

15. Ist das Gerds Buch?   After a club meeting you and a friend are straightening up. Tell your friend to whom the various things belong. Use the possessive form of the proper name.

>> Gerd / Buch   *Das ist Gerds Buch.*

1. Beate / Kuli
2. Bruno / Lampe
3. Franz / Radio
4. Regina / Heft
5. Thomas / Büchertasche
6. Sylvia / Uhr

---

*For information on sibilants, see *Kapitel 1*, p. 43.

das Possessivpronomen

10. Possessive adjectives°

Mein Zimmer ist groß.	*My* room is large.
Ist **dein** Zimmer groß?	Is *your* room large?
Ist **sein** Zimmer groß?	Is *his* room large?
Ist **ihr** Zimmer groß?	Is *her* room large?
Unser Zimmer ist groß.	*Our* room is large.
Ist **euer** Zimmer groß?	Is *your* room large?
Ist **ihr** Zimmer groß?	Is *their* room large?
Ist **Ihr** Zimmer groß?	Is *your* room large?

German possessive adjectives are equivalent in meaning to the English possessive adjectives, such as *my, his,* and *her.* Context usually makes clear whether **ihr** is the subject pronoun *you,* the adjective *her* or *their,* or the adjective *your.* Note that **Ihr** *(your)* is capitalized, just as the corresponding subject pronoun **Sie** *(you)* is.

der Bleistift	Wo ist ein Bleistift?
	Wo ist **mein** Bleistift?
das Heft	Wo ist ein Heft?
	Wo ist **mein** Heft?
die Uhr	Wo ist eine Uhr?
	Wo ist **meine** Uhr?
die Bücher	Wo sind **meine** Bücher?

Since possessive adjectives have the same forms as **ein,** they are frequently called **ein**-words.

Wo ist **euer** Radio? Wo sind **eure** Bücher?

When **euer** has an ending, the **-e-** preceding the **-r-** is usually omitted.

■ *Negating nouns preceded by possessive adjectives*

Ist das dein Heft?   Nein, das ist **nicht** mein Heft.

Nicht is used to negate a noun that is preceded by a possessive adjective.

16. Wie sagt man das?   Complete the sentences with the German equivalents of the cued words.

➤ _____ Mann arbeitet nicht. *(her)*   *Ihr Mann arbeitet nicht.*

1. _____ Kind heißt Dieter. *(their)*

2. _____ Frau ist lustig. *(his)*

3. Barbara, Frank, was für ein Mensch ist _____ Nachbar? *(your)*

4. Wo sind _____ Kinder, Frau Neumann? *(your)*

5. Ich glaube, das ist _____ Kuli. *(my)*

6. Ist das _____ Uhr, Gisela? *(your)*

17. Ein Brief° von Gisela. Complete Gisela's letter to Monika by filling in the   letter
appropriate possessive pronouns.

Liebe Monika,

ich studiere jetzt in Berlin. _____ Adresse ist Lepsiusstraße 27 und _____ Tele-

fonnummer ist 791 23 44. _____ Zimmer ist klein aber komfortabel. _____

Nachbar heißt Michael und _____ Freund heißt Alex. Alex ist auch _____

Freund. Michael und ich gehen samstags joggen. _____ Samstage zusammen

sind immer schön. _____ Freund heißt Mark, nicht wahr? Wie sind _____

Samstage zusammen? Also ich gehe jetzt joggen und schreibe morgen mehr.

Tschüs,
Gisela

11. Demonstrative pronouns *der, das, die*

Ist Andrea zu Hause?	Is Andrea at home?
Nein, **die** ist nicht zu Hause.	No, *she*'s not at home.
Ist der Computer wirklich neu?	Is the computer really new?
Ja, **der** ist wirklich neu.	Yes, *it*'s really new.
Ist das Bild neu oder alt?	Is the picture new or old?
Ach, **das** ist ziemlich alt.	Oh, *it*'s rather old.
Sind die Berliner freundlich?	Are the Berliners friendly?
Ja, **die** sind freundlich.	Yes, *they*'re friendly.

Der, das, and **die** are often used as demonstrative pronouns to replace nouns. A demonstrative pronoun is used instead of a personal pronoun **(er, es, sie)** when the pronoun is to be emphasized. Demonstrative pronouns usually occur at or near the beginning of a sentence. The English equivalent is usually a personal pronoun *(he, it, she, they)*.

18. Ja, das stimmt. *(Yes, that's right.)*   Tobias is speaking on the phone with Ramona. They're discussing a variety of things and people and agreeing with each other. Use a demonstrative pronoun as the subject.

➤➤ Das Zimmer ist ziemlich klein, nicht?   *Ja, das ist wirklich klein.*

1. Die Musik ist gut, nicht?
2. Der Rucksack ist praktisch, nicht?
3. Der Film war sehr gut, nicht?
4. Das Computerspiel ist lustig, nicht?
5. Professor Müller ist freundlich, nicht?
6. Moritz und Bianca sind furchtbar nett, nicht?

WIEDERHOLUNG

1. Singular, Plural.   Give the singular and plural forms of each noun. Give the appropriate form of the definite article with each noun.

⟫ Einwohner   *der Einwohner, die Einwohner*

1. Mädchen ⠌ₐ.ᵇ   7. Mann
2. Stadt   8. Frau
3. Wort   9. Nachbarin
4. Student   10. Stuhl
5. Tag   11. Kugelschreiber
6. Woche   12. Fenster

2. Am Telefon.   Gisela and Alex are talking on the phone. Complete their conversation from the notes below.

⟫ GISELA: was / du / machen / jetzt / ?   *Was machst du jetzt?*

1. ALEX: ich / hören / Musik
2. GISELA: ihr (du und Michael) / spielen / heute / wieder / Tennis / ?
3. ALEX: nein / Michael / kommen / heute Abend / nicht
4. GISELA: ah / er / arbeiten / wieder
5. ALEX: vielleicht / wir / spielen / morgen
6. GISELA: hoffentlich / es / regnen / morgen / nicht
7. ALEX: ich / glauben / das / nicht
8. GISELA: vielleicht / die Sonne / scheinen
9. ALEX: morgen / Professor Lange / kommen / nicht
10. GISELA: wer / sagen / das / ?

3. Viele Fragen.   Dieter and Lisa have not talked with each other in a while. Dieter has now called Lisa and has a lot of questions. Below is a list of Lisa's answers. You have to finish Dieter's questions.

Dieter	Lisa
⟫ *Wie ist das Wetter?*	Das Wetter ist schön.
1. Regnet _____ ?	Nein, es regnet heute nicht.
2. Scheint _____ ?	Ja, die Sonne scheint.
3. Was _____ ?	Ich höre Musik.
4. Was für _____ ?	Klassische Musik.
5. Wie _____ ?	Der Professor heißt Dr. Becker.
6. Wo _____ ?	Er arbeitet in Berlin.
7. Woher _____ ?	Er kommt aus Wien.
8. Wie alt _____ ?	Professor Becker ist 43.
9. Wer _____ ?	Die Studenten sagen das.
10. Wann _____ ?	Ich schreibe morgen!

4. Und auf Deutsch?   Karoline, your guest from Germany, doesn't understand the conversation of your two American friends. Translate for her.

1. ED: We're playing tennis today, right?
2. KATIE: No, it's too cold. We'll play tomorrow. OK?
3. ED: But it's so nice (out)! The sun's shining and tomorrow it'll rain for sure.
4. KATIE: I don't think so. (Use **das**.)   *Das glaube ich nicht*
5. ED: By the way°, what time are we going to the movies tonight?   **Übrigens**
6. KATIE: At six-thirty. George is coming, too.
7. ED: Really? Isn't he working this evening?   *Wirklich?*
8. KATIE: No, he works on Monday and Tuesday.

5. Geburtstage!   Read the birth announcement and answer the questions. You do not need to understand all the words to get the information required.

1. Wie heißt das Baby?
2. Wie alt ist Emanuel heute?
3. Wie ist Emanuels Adresse?
4. Wie ist seine Telefonnummer?
5. Wie heißen Emanuels Mutter°   mother
   und Vater°?   father
6. Wer ist Franziska?

> Unser Sohn heißt
>
> ## Emanuel Gerhard
>
> und ist am 14. Juli 1995 um 20.13 Uhr auf die Welt gekommen.
> Gewicht: 3000g
> Größe: 50cm
>
> Cornelia und Gerhard Mühlhäuser
> sind die überglücklichen Eltern,
> Franziska ist die überglückliche Schwester.
>
> Schönbichlstraße 14
> 82211 Herrsching am Ammersee
> Telefon: 08152-1538

6. Gespräche   Discussing the weather

1. You are talking to a travel agent. You can't decide where you want to spend your next vacation. Ask about the weather in various places.
2. You are talking to a German friend. She/He wants to know about your first weeks at school. Tell her/him about
   a. a friend or classmate, where she/he is from.
   b. what activities you like to do.
   c. your room and its contents (size, color).

7. Zum Schreiben

1. Imagine you have just arrived in Germany. Write a short paragraph (4–5 sentences) in German about Germany. Before you begin writing, look again at the reading on page 62 to review vocabulary and at the section on word order on page 71. Then make a list (in German) of the things you want to mention in your paragraph, e.g., weather, size, and population. Organize your comments in a paragraph. After you've written your paragraph review each sentence to be sure that each sentence has a subject and a verb and that the verb agrees with the subject. Finally, check the word order of each sentence.
2. Prepare a weather forecast that will tell your fellow students what the weather will be like for the next three days. Two or three sentences per forecast are sufficient. Watch your word order.

> *Am Montag scheint die Sonne. Es bleibt schön.*
> *Am Dienstag kommt der Wind aus dem Osten. Vielleicht regnet es.*
> *Am Mittwoch ist es sehr kalt. Es ist zwei Grad.*

GRAMMATIK: ZUSAMMENFASSUNG

Simple past tense of *sein*

sein: to be	
ich **war**	wir waren
du warst	ihr wart
er/es/sie **war**	sie waren
Sie waren	

Present tense of *haben*

haben: to have	
ich habe	wir haben
du **hast**	ihr habt
er/es/sie **hat**	sie haben
Sie haben	

Position of the finite verb in statements

	1	2	3	4
	Subject	**Verb**	**Adverb**	**Adjective**
Normal	**Der Sommer**	ist	in Deutschland	anders.
	Adverb	**Verb**	**Subject**	**Adjective**
Inverted	In Deutschland	ist	**der Sommer**	anders.

In a German statement, the verb is always in second position. In so-called normal word order, the subject is in first position. In so-called inverted word order, something other than the subject (for example, an adverb, an adjective, or indirect object) is in first position, and the subject follows the verb. Note that both "normal" and "inverted" word order are common in German.

Plural of nouns

Type	Plural signal	Singular	Plural
1	- *(no change)*	das Zimmer	die Zimmer
	¨	der Garten	die G**ä**rten
2	-**e**	das Heft	die Heft**e**
	¨**e**	die Stadt	die St**ä**dt**e**
3	-**er**	das Kind	die Kind**er**
	¨**er**	der Mann	die M**ä**nn**er**
4	-**en**	die Tür	die Tür**en**
	-**n**	die Lampe	die Lampe**n**
	-**nen**	die Studentin	die Studentin**nen**
5	-**s**	das Radio	die Radio**s**

Nominative case of definite articles, indefinite articles, and *kein*

	Masculine	Neuter	Feminine	Plural
Definite article	der ⎫	das ⎫	die ⎫	die ⎫
Indefinite article	ein ⎬ Stuhl	ein ⎬ Radio	eine ⎬ Lampe	— ⎬ Bücher
KEIN	kein ⎭	kein ⎭	keine ⎭	keine ⎭

Kein vs. nicht

Ist das **eine** Uhr?   Nein, das ist **keine** Uhr.
Ist das **die** Uhr?   Nein, das ist **nicht** die Uhr.
Ist das **deine** Uhr?   Nein, das ist **nicht meine** Uhr.

Kein is used to negate a noun that would be preceded by **ein** or no article at all in an affirmative sentence. **Nicht** is used in a negative sentence when the noun is preceded by a definite article **(die)** or a possessive adjective **(meine).** (For positions of **nicht,** see *Kapitel 1,* **Grammatik und Übungen,** section 9.)

Possessive adjectives

■ *Forms and meanings*

Singular		Plural	
ich: **mein**	my	wir: **unser**	our
du: **dein**	your	ihr: **euer**	your
er: **sein**	his, its		
es: **sein**	its	sie: **ihr**	their
sie: **ihr**	her, its		
	Sie: **ihr** your		

■ *Nominative of possessive adjectives*

Masculine	Neuter	Feminine	Plural
ein ⎫	ein ⎫	eine ⎫	— ⎫
mein ⎬ Tisch	**mein** ⎬ Radio	**meine** ⎬ Uhr	**meine** ⎬ Bücher
unser ⎭	**unser** ⎭	**unsere** ⎭	**unsere** ⎭

Demonstrative pronouns and personal pronouns

	Masculine	Neuter	Feminine	Plural
Personal Pronouns	er	es	sie	sie
Demonstrative Pronouns	der	das	die	die

Was brauchst du?

Auch in Wiesbaden hat Schlemmermeyer ein Geschäft.

BAUSTEINE FÜR GESPRÄCHE

Was brauchst du?

DIANE: Sag mal, Stefan, gibt es hier eine Apotheke?
STEFAN: Ja, was brauchst du denn?
DIANE: Ich brauche etwas gegen Kopfschmerzen.
STEFAN: Nimmst du Aspirin? Ich habe eins.

Gehst du heute einkaufen?

MONIKA: Stefan, gehst du heute nicht
einkaufen?
STEFAN: Doch. Warum fragst du?
MONIKA: Wir haben keinen Kaffee mehr.
STEFAN: Ein Pfund ist genug, nicht? Möchtest
du sonst noch etwas?
MONIKA: Ja, bitte ein Brot. Kauf das doch bei
Rischart. Da ist das Brot besser.

Brauchbares

1. The words **mal** in **"Sag mal,"** **denn** in **"Was brauchst du denn?"** and **doch**
   in **"Kauf das doch bei Rischart"** are called *flavoring particles*. They express a
   speaker's attitude about an utterance and do not have exact English equivalents. See pp. 92–93.
2. Stefan says: **Möchtest du sonst noch etwas?** The verb **möchte** does not
   have the characteristic ending **-t** in the **er/es/sie-** form: **er möchte** (*he would
   like*).

▷ **1. Was suchen Sie?** Think of three things you need to buy. A fellow
student or your instructor asks what kind of store you're looking for. Respond.
For names of specialty shops, refer to the Supplementary Word Sets in the Reference Section.

Inquiring about shopping
possibilities

S2:	S1:		
Was suchst° du?	Ich brauche	**Brot.** Gibt es hier	**eine Bäckerei°?**
Was suchen Sie?		Aspirin.	eine Apotheke?
		Wurst°.	eine Metzgerei°?
		Spaghetti°.	einen Supermarkt°?
		einen Kamm°.	eine Drogerie°?

Gesundheit aus
der Apotheke

Expressing needs

2. Geh doch. Your friend needs some things. Tell her/him to go to the store that sells them.

S2:

Ich brauche | **etwas gegen Kopfschmerzen.**
Brot für morgen.
Wurst für heute Abend.
Spaghetti.
ein Heft.
ein Buch über° Schach.

S1:

Geh doch° **in die Apotheke.**

Schüttelkasten

zum Bäcker
           in den Supermarkt
          zum Metzger
ins Kaufhaus°
     in die Buchhandlung°

Inquiring about needs

3. Sonst noch etwas? You've been telling a friend what you need, but there's something you've forgotten. What is it? When she/he asks whether there's anything else you need, say what it is.

S2:
Brauchst du sonst noch etwas?

S1:
Ja, wir haben **kein Brot mehr.**

Schüttelkasten

keine Spaghetti
          kein Bier°
keinen Kaffee
          keine Butter°

4. Rollenspiel. While on vacation in Germany, you develop a splitting headache on Sunday afternoon. You ask the desk clerk in your hotel to direct you to a drugstore. The desk clerk consults the **Notdienst** (*emergency service*) listing in the newspaper and tells you the name, address, and telephone number of a few drugstores open on the weekend. Be sure to note the information you are given.

Notdienste

Von Samstag, 13 Uhr, bis Sonntag, 8.30 Uhr, haben folgende Apotheken Notdienst.

Victoria-Apotheke, Thomas-Mann-Str. 52, Tel. 63 25 06. Flora-Apotheke, Clemens-August-Straße 42, Tel. 22 24 85. Lessing-Apotheke, Beuel, Hermannstr. 72, Tel. 47 56 20. Hardt-Apotheke, Medinghoven, Europaring 42, Tel. 64 38 62. Apotheke am Römerplatz, Bad Godesberg, Rheinstr. 3, Tel. 36 41 04 u. 35 51 68. Martin-Apotheke, Bad Godesberg/Muffendorf, Hopmannstr. 7, Tel. 32 33 06

Von Sonntag, 8.30 Uhr, bis Montag, 8.30 Uhr, haben folgende Apotheken Notdienst.

Einhorn-Apotheke, Poststr. 34, Tel. 65 28 33 u. 63 63 57. Adler-Apotheke, Bonner Talweg/Ecke Weberstr., Tel. 21 05 87. Apotheke im Tannenbusch, Tannenbusch, Paulusplatz 13, Tel. 66 24 56. Kreuz-Apotheke, Oberkassel, Königswinterer Str. 673, Tel. 44 12 11. Engel-Apotheke, Duisdorf, Rochusstr. 192, Tel. 62 26 18. Robert-Koch-Apotheke, Bad Godesberg, Beethovenallee 19, Tel. 35 36 69.

S1: Welche Apotheken sind offen°?
S2: Die Adler-Apotheke, Bonner Talweg/Ecke Weberstraße, Tel. 21 05 87.

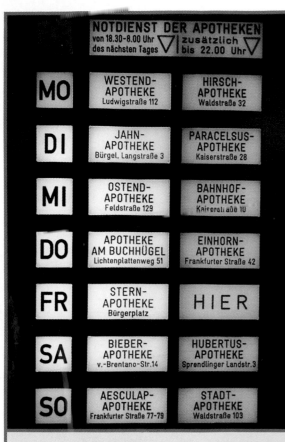

MO	WESTEND-APOTHEKE Ludwigstraße 112	HIRSCH-APOTHEKE Waldstraße 32
DI	JAHN-APOTHEKE Bürgel, Langstraße 3	PARACELSUS-APOTHEKE Kaiserstraße 28
MI	OSTEND-APOTHEKE Feldstraße 129	BAHNHOF-APOTHEKE Kaiserstraße 10
DO	APOTHEKE AM BUCHHÜGEL Lichtenplattenweg 51	EINHORN-APOTHEKE Frankfurter Straße 42
FR	STERN-APOTHEKE Bürgerplatz	HIER
SA	BIEBER-APOTHEKE v.-Brentano-Str.14	HUBERTUS-APOTHEKE Sprendlinger Landstr.3
SO	AESCULAP-APOTHEKE Frankfurter Straße 77-79	STADT-APOTHEKE Waldstraße 103

Sonntags hat die Stadt-Apotheke in Offenbach am Main Notdienst.

Apotheke vs. Drogerie

An **Apotheke** sells both prescription **(rezeptpflichtig)** and nonprescription **(freiverkäuflich)** drugs. In every town and in each section of a large city, one **Apotheke** offers emergency service **(Notdienst)** at night and on Sunday. An **Apotheke** is staffed by a pharmacist **(Apothekerin/Apotheker)**, a university-trained specialist, and several trained assistants.

A **Drogerie** sells a wide variety of toiletries and often herbal and homeopathic remedies as well as many other items (e.g., toys, film, vitamins) found in American drugstores. A **Drogerie** is often found in combination with a natural foods store **(Reformhaus).** The **Drogerie** is gradually being replaced by the larger self-service drugstore **(Drogeriemarkt).** A druggist **(Drogistin/Drogist)** is trained in a three-year apprenticeship.

There are generally fewer over-the-counter drugs in German-speaking countries than in the U.S. Some non-prescription drugs are, nevertheless, **apothekenpflichtig,** that is, to purchase them, one must go to an **Apotheke.** They cannot be found in **Drogerien.** Regulations for particular drugs differ in each country. For example, aspirin is **apothekenpflichtig** in Germany and Austria, but not in Switzerland.

LAND UND LEUTE

www

Go to the *Deutsch heute* Web Site at **www.hmco.com/college**

Dieser Heidelberger Drogeriemarkt hat fast alles – von Postkarten bis Strandkleidung.

Diskussion

How would you explain to a person from a German-speaking country what a drugstore is?

5. **Frage-Ecke.** Find out why various people, including your partner, are going to certain places of business.

S2: Warum° geht Jochen ins Kaufhaus?

because

S1: Er geht ins Kaufhaus, denn° er braucht ein Heft.

S2: Warum gehst du ins Kaufhaus?

S1: Ich gehe ins Kaufhaus, denn ich brauche ein Heft./Ich gehe nicht ins Kaufhaus, denn ich brauche kein Heft.

S1:

	ins Kaufhaus	in die Drogerie	in die Metzgerei	in die Bäckerei	in den Supermarkt
Jochen	ein Heft		Wurst		Brötchen
Monika und Stefan		eine Kassette			
Herr Sommer		einen Kamm		Kuchen	200 Gramm Butter
Partnerin/Partner					

S2:

	ins Kaufhaus	in die Drogerie	in die Metzgerei	in die Bäckerei	in den Supermarkt
Jochen		Bleistifte		sechs Brötchen	
Monika und Stefan	zwei Kulis		250 Gramm Wurst	Brot	Kaffee
Herr Sommer	ein Radio		Salami		
Partnerin/Partner					

Erweiterung des Wortschatzes

1. Flavoring particles

"Flavoring" particles are little words used to express a speaker's attitude about an utterance. They often relate the utterance to something the speaker or the listener has said or thought. Depending on the choice of the flavoring particle and sometimes on the tone of voice, the speaker expresses interest, surprise, impatience, denial, and so on. Because a particle has various shades of meaning that depend on the context, a dictionary can give only the approximate English meaning. With experience you will gain a "feel" for the meaning and use of these words, which are very characteristic of colloquial German. Some of the meanings of the particles are given in the following examples; other meanings will be pointed out later.

■ *Flavoring particle* **mal**

DIANE: Sag **mal,** Stefan, gibt es hier   Tell me Stefan, is there a pharmacy
eine Apotheke?   (around) here?
STEFAN: Frag **mal** Monika.   Ask Monika.

Mal is frequently used with imperatives. It softens the tone of the command.

■ *Flavoring particle* **denn**

STEFAN: Was brauchst du **denn?**   Tell me, what do you need?
DIANE: Aspirin.   Aspirin.

Denn is used frequently in questions to show the personal interest of the
speaker. It softens the speaker's question and makes it less abrupt.

■ *Flavoring particle* **doch**

STEFAN: Kauf das Brot **doch** bei   Be sure and buy the bread at
Rischart.   Rischart's.
Geh **doch** nicht in den Supermarkt.   Definitely don't go to the
                                    supermarket.

The speaker uses **doch** to persuade the listener to do something.

2. *Doch* as a positive response to a negative question

STEFAN: Gehst du heute nicht   Aren't you going shopping today?
einkaufen?
MONIKA: **Doch.**   Yes, I am.

Doch may be used as a positive response to a negative question.

1. Viele Fragen. Your house guest wants to know a lot of things. Respond in
the positive, using **ja** or **doch** as appropriate.

➤➤ Gehst du heute nicht in die Bibliothek?   *Doch.*
➤➤ Gehst du um sieben?   *Ja.*

1. Gibt es hier eine Apotheke?   6. Machen wir heute Abend das
2. Hast du kein Aspirin?   Essen° nicht zusammen?
3. Gehst du nicht in den Supermarkt?   7. Brauchen wir Brot?
4. Kaufst du Wurst?   8. Trinkst° du nicht Kaffee?
5. Ist die Wurst da gut?

3. Lebensmittel

das **Getränk, -e**
1. der **Apfelsaft** ⎫
2. der **Orangensaft** ⎬ der **Saft, ¨e**
3. der **Kaffee** ⎭
4. der **Tee**
5. der **Weißwein, -e** ⎫ der **Wein, -e**
6. der **Rotwein, -e** ⎭
7. das **Bier, -e**
8. die **Milch**
9. das **Mineralwasser**
10. das **Wasser**

das **Gemüse**
11. die **Gurke, -n**
12. die **Karotte, -n**
13. die **Kartoffel, -n**
14. der **Salat, -e**
15. die **Tomate, -n**

das **Obst**
16. der **Apfel, ¨**
17. die **Banane, -n**
18. die **Orange, -n**
19. die **Traube, -n**

das **Fleisch**
20. der **Rinderbraten, -**
21. der **Schinken, -**
22. die **Wurst, ¨e**
23. das **Würstchen, -**

andere Lebensmittel
24. das **Brot, -e**
25. das **Brötchen, -**
26. das **Ei, -er**
27. der **Käse**
28. die **Nudeln** (pl.)
29. der **Fisch, -e**

30. das **Hähnchen, -**
31. die **Butter**
32. die **Margarine**
33. der **Kuchen, -**
34. die **Torte, -n**

2. Was isst du? Interview fellow students to learn what they eat at various meals.

| | Talking about meals and food |

S1:

Was	isst du	**zum Frühstück°?**
	trinkst du	zum Mittagessen°?
		zum Abendessen°?

S2:
Ich esse [zwei Brötchen].
Ich trinke [Orangensaft].

3. Essen und Trinken. Exchange information with your partner about your two favorite foods and drinks in the groups: **Lieblingsgetränke, Lieblingsobst, Lieblingsgemüse, Lieblingsfleisch.**

>> *Meine Lieblingsgetränke sind* ..

Das Brot

LAND UND LEUTE

Bread plays a significant part in the daily nutrition of people in the German-speaking countries. Approximately 200 types of breads are baked in Germany alone. Names, shapes, and recipes vary from region to region. The most popular breads are baked fresh daily in one of the many bakeries (**Bäckereien**) and have a tasty crust. They also tend to have a firmer and often coarser texture than American breads.

A typical breakfast would not be complete without a crisp **Brötchen** or **Semmel,** as rolls are called in many areas. Open-faced sandwiches (**belegte Brote**) are popular for the evening meal and as a light lunch, and are often eaten with a knife and fork. Bread is made from a wide variety of grains, including rye (**Roggen**) and wheat (**Weizen**). Many types of bread are made from several kinds of grain—**Dreikornbrot, Vierkornbrot. Vollkornbrot** is made of unrefined, crushed grain. Bread with sunflower seeds (**Sonnenblumenbrot**) is also very popular. There are bread museums in Ulm, Mollenfelde, and Detmold which often feature **Gebildbrote** (picture breads) in the shape of animals, wreaths, even violins.

Other baked goods are also popular. There are 1200 kinds of **Kleingebäck** (a term used for baked goods like rolls, soft pretzels, bread sticks, etc.). A bakery or pastry shop (**Konditorei**) always has a large selection of cookies (**Kekse**), pastries (**Gebäck**), and cakes (**Kuchen** and **Torten**).

Go to the
Deutsch heute Web Site at
www.hmco.com/college

In dieser Tübinger Bäckerei gibt es über zehn verschiedene Brotsorten.

Diskussion

1. People from German-speaking countries often say that the food they miss the most when they visit the United States is bread. Why do you think that this is the case?
2. How important is bread in your diet? Do you eat a variety of breads?
3. Role-play. With a partner, act out a scene in which you buy products in a **Bäckerei.**

Vokabeln

Starting in *Kapitel 3* vowel changes in the present tense will be noted in parentheses following the infinitive of the verb, e.g., **essen (isst).**

Substantive

das **Abendessen, -**   evening meal
die **Apotheke, -n**   pharmacy
das **Aspirin**   aspirin
der **Bäcker, -**   baker
die **Bäckerei, -en**   bakery
das **Bier, -e**   beer
das **Brot, -e**   bread
die **Buchhandlung, -en**   bookstore
die **Butter**   butter
die **Drogerie, -n**   drugstore
das **Essen, -**   meal; prepared food
das **Frühstück**   breakfast
der **Kaffee**   coffee
der **Kamm, ⸚e**   comb
das **Kaufhaus, ⸚er**   department store
die **Kopfschmerzen** *(pl.)*   headache

die **Lebensmittel** *(pl.)*   food; groceries
der **Liebling, -e**   favorite
das **Lieblingsgetränk, -e**   favorite drink
der **Metzger, -**   butcher
die **Metzgerei, -en**   butcher shop, meat market
das **Mittagessen**   midday meal
das **Pfund, -e**   pound (= 1.1 U.S. pounds; *abbrev.* **Pfd.**)
der **Salat, -e**   lettuce; salad
die **Spaghetti** *(pl.)*   spaghetti
der **Supermarkt, ⸚e**   supermarket
die **Wurst, ⸚e**   sausage, lunch meat
For additional foods, see p. 94.

Verben

brauchen   to need
einkaufen   to shop; **einkaufen gehen**   to go shopping
essen (isst)   to eat
fragen   to ask
kaufen   to buy

möchte (ich möchte, du möchtest, er/sie/es möchte)   would like
nehmen (nimmt)   to take
suchen   to look for
trinken   to drink

Andere Wörter

bei   at; at a place of business **(beim [Metzger]);** at the home of **(bei [Ingrid])**
besser   better
denn   *flavoring particle added to question*
doch   *(after a negative question or statement)* yes [I] am, [I] do; *(flavoring particle)* really; after all
ein paar   a few

etwas   something
gegen   against
genug   enough
kein   not a, not any
mal   *flavoring particle added to an imperative*
offen   open
sonst   otherwise
über   about
warum   why

Besondere Ausdrücke

beim Bäcker   at the baker's (bakery)
beim Metzger   at the butcher's (butcher shop)
es gibt   there is; there are
geh doch   well, then go

in die Apotheke   to the pharmacy
in den Supermarkt   to the supermarket
kein ... mehr   no more . . . ; not . . . any more
Sonst noch etwas?   Anything else?

Was gibt's zum
  [Abendessen]? What's for
  [dinner/supper]?
zum Abendessen   for the evening
  meal, for dinner

zum Bäcker   to the baker's (bakery)
zum Frühstück   for breakfast
zum Metzger   to the butcher's
  (butcher shop)
zum Mittagessen   for the midday
  meal, for lunch

EINKAUFEN AM WOCHENENDE

Vorbereitung auf das Lesen

■ *Vor dem Lesen*

ACHTUNG!

SIE KÖNNEN JETZT STRESSFREIER EINKAUFEN
Ab heute neue Öffnungszeiten

KRONE

Ihr Supermarkt seit 45 Jahren!

Montags bis freitags sind wir von 8 bis 20 Uhr für Sie da,
und jeden Samstag von 8 bis 16 Uhr.

Look at the advertisement for the store **Krone** and answer the following
questions.

1. What kind of a store is **Krone?**
2. How long has **Krone** been in existence?
3. Why is **Krone** running this advertisement?
4. On which day does the store have the shortest business hours?
5. How are the following expressed in German in the ad:
   a. 8 P.M.
   b. every Saturday
6. Where do people in your community go shopping?
7. Where do you do most of your grocery shopping?
8. Are there many specialty shops in your area?
9. The opening times advertised here are typical of Germany. How do these
   times compare with the business hours of stores in your town?
10. Where do you think that shopping is less stressful—in your town or in
    Germany?

■ *Beim Lesen*

In the reading passage you will learn about shopping habits in Germany. As you read, make a list of the places where people go shopping and the things they buy in the various stores.

Es ist Samstag und Monika macht Frühstück. Sie macht es heute besonders schön, denn ihre Freundinnen Diane und Joan aus Amerika sind da. Ihr Bruder° Stefan kommt in die Küche, und Monika sagt: „Du, Stefan, wir haben keinen Kaffee und keine Marmelade mehr. Geh bitte

5 zu Meiers und kauf Kaffee und Marmelade." Stefan nimmt Einkaufstasche und Geld und geht. Nebenan° ist noch ein Tante-Emma-Laden°. Da kaufen° Monika und Stefan manchmal morgens ein. Da kennt man sie. Viele Leute gehen in den Supermarkt, denn da ist es natürlich billiger. Aber bei Meiers ist es viel persönlicher°.

10   Herr Meier sagt: „Guten Morgen, Herr Stamer. Was bekommen Sie denn heute?"

    „Ich brauche Kaffee, ein Pfund."

    „Sonst noch einen Wunsch?"

    „Ja, ich brauche noch Marmelade. Ich nehme zwei Sorten°."

15   „Haben Sie denn Besuch?"

    „Ja, Freundinnen aus Amerika sind da. – Gut, das ist alles für heute." Stefan nimmt noch eine Zeitung und bezahlt.

    „Auf Wiedersehen, Herr Stamer, und schönes Wochenende!"

    „Danke. Auf Wiedersehen."

20   Der Bäcker ist gegenüber°. Da riecht es immer so gut. Stefan kauft Brötchen. Die sind noch ganz warm.

    Das Frühstück ist wirklich sehr gut. Joan und Diane finden die Brötchen und den Kaffee besonders gut.

    Es ist jetzt schon elf Uhr, und Monika sagt: „Wir brauchen noch etwas

25 fürs° Wochenende."

brother

next door / mom-and-pop store
kaufen ein: shop

more personal

kinds

across from there

for the

Einige Leute kaufen immer noch gern im Tante-Emma-Laden ein. (Hannover)

Die Vier gehen zusammen auf den Markt. Sie kaufen Karotten und zwei Kilo Kartoffeln fürs Mittagessen. Der Fischmann ist auch da. Hier kaufen sie frischen Fisch. Den essen sie zum Abendessen. Dann gehen sie auf den Blumenmarkt. Monika kommt oft samstags mit Blumen nach Hause. „Monika,
30 die Blumen bezahle ich aber", sagt Diane.

Auf dem Weg nach Hause gehen sie noch in eine Metzgerei. Dort kaufen sie Fleisch und Wurst. „Habt ihr alles oder braucht ihr auch noch etwas?" fragt Stefan.

„Ich brauche Vitamintabletten", sagt Diane.
35 „Warum Vitamintabletten? Bist du denn krank?" fragt Stefan.

„Nein, ich nehme jeden Tag Vitamintabletten."

„Wirklich? Wir nehmen nur Vitamintabletten, wenn wir krank sind.* Aber gehen wir doch in die Drogerie! Dort bekommen wir Vitamintabletten", sagen Stefan und Monika.
40 „Ist das dann alles?" fragt Stefan.

„Nein, ich brauche noch ein Buch. Wo ist eine Buchhandlung?" fragt Joan.

Brauchbares

1. **Denn** has several meanings. In the dialogue on page 88, **denn** is used as a flavoring particle. Stefan says, **Was brauchst du denn?** In l. 2 above, **denn** is a conjunction and means *for (because):* **denn ihre Freundinnen ... sind da.**
2. L. 6, **"Da kaufen Monika und Stefan manchmal morgens ein":** Note that the verb **einkaufen** is separated into **kaufen** and **ein.** This is called a separable-prefix verb because the prefix **ein** is separated from the verb **kaufen** in the sentence. German has many such verbs and you will learn more about them in *Kapitel 4.*
3. L. 37, **"Aber gehen wir doch in die Drogerie":** **Gehen wir** is the equivalent of *let's go.* The German construction is identical to the present-tense **wir**-form of the verb, but the pronoun **wir** follows the verb.

Nach dem Lesen

1. Wie viele Geschäfte? *(How many stores?)* Compare your list of stores and items with a partner's list. How many stores did you find?

▷ **2. Fragen zum Lesestück**

1. Warum macht Monika das Frühstück besonders schön?
2. Was braucht Monika für das Frühstück?
3. Was für ein Laden ist nebenan?
4. Warum kaufen Monika und Stefan gern bei Meiers?
5. Was braucht Monika für das Wochenende?
6. Wann kauft Monika oft Blumen?
7. Wer bezahlt die Blumen?
8. Was möchte Joan noch kaufen?

---

l. 37: Although Germans are also concerned about health, vitamin pills as a diet supplement do not play the role they do in the United States. Vitamins are regarded more as a natural ingredient of any food.

3. Vokabeln.   In the reading passage, find the phrases you could use in the following situations.

1. You ask a friend if she/he needs something.
2. You ask a friend to buy some coffee for you.
3. You offer to pay for some flowers.
4. You ask if the group has everything.
5. You ask if the group needs something else.

4. Erzählen wir.   How do Monika's and Stefan's shopping habits differ from Joan's and Diane's—or your own? Be prepared to say one or two sentences in class. Use the following topics to get you started.

Supermarkt □ Blumen □ Bäckerei □ Metzgerei

LAND UND LEUTE

Go to the
Deutsch heute Web Site at
www.hmco.com/college

Einkaufen

Traditionally, Germans would do their food shopping in small, neighborhood stores **(Tante-Emma-Läden).** However, their popularity is decreasing rapidly. In 1972 there were 160,400 small stores in the Federal Republic. By 1994 there were only 76,000 and the number is expected to reach 55,000 by the year 2000. These stores are closing at the rate of six to seven per day. Today Germans do most of their food shopping in supermarkets which tend to be smaller than American ones and are located within walking distance of residential areas. Many of the larger department stores **(Kaufhäuser)** also have complete grocery departments **(Lebensmittelabteilungen).** There are also large discount stores **(Einkaufszentren)** on the outskirts of cities which sell not only groceries but a wide variety of items ranging from clothing to electronic equipment, even pre-fabricated houses. Many people go shopping several times a week. Although the supermarkets are self-service stores, fresh foods such as cheeses, meats and cold cuts, bread, and vegetables may be sold by shop assistants at separate counters.

Customers bring their own bags **(Einkaufstaschen)** to the supermarket or buy plastic bags **(Plastiktüten)** or canvas bags at the check-out counter. Customers pack their own groceries and generally pay for their purchases with cash **(Bargeld),** although the use of credit cards **(Kreditkarten)** is becoming more common at larger stores and for on-line shopping.

Diskussion

1. Many people in German-speaking countries can do their routine shopping at stores within walking distance of their home. Compare this situation with one in your area where people must drive to a store. What impact does it have on personal habits, on the design of cities?
2. Why do you think that neighborhood stores are becoming a thing of the past in Germany and other industrialized countries?

Viele Leute kaufen im Supermarkt ein.
(Seewalchen, Österreich)

Erweiterung des Wortschatzes

1. Noun compounds

die **Blumen** + der **Markt** = der **Blumenmarkt**
flowers + market = flower market

kaufen + das **Haus** = das **Kaufhaus**
to buy + building = department store

A characteristic of German is its ability to form noun compounds easily. Where German uses compounds, English often uses separate words. Your vocabulary will increase rapidly if you learn to analyze the component parts of compounds.

der Kopf + **die** Schmerzen = **die** Kopfschmerzen
der Fisch + **der** Mann = **der** Fischmann
das Buch + **die** Handlung = **die** Buchhandlung

The last element of a compound determines its gender.

1. Was bedeutet das? *(What does that mean?)* The compounds listed below are made up of cognates and familiar nouns. Give the English equivalent of each.

1. der Winterabend
2. der Sommertag
3. die Marktfrau
4. der Sonnenschein
5. die Tischlampe
6. die Morgenzeitung
7. die Zimmertür

2. Days of the week and parts of days as adverbs

Noun	Adverb	English equivalent
Montag	**montags**	Mondays
Samstag	**samstags**	Saturdays
Morgen	**morgens**	mornings
Abend	**abends**	evenings

A noun that names a day of the week or a part of a day may be used as an adverb to indicate repetition or habitual action. An **-s** is added to the noun. In German, adverbs are not capitalized.

2. Ein Interview. Interview a partner. Record her/his responses.

Wann isst du mehr – mittags oder abends?
Wann bist du sehr müde – morgens oder abends?
Wann arbeitest du mehr – samstags oder sonntags?
Wann gehst du einkaufen – freitags, samstags oder wann?
Gehst du morgens oder abends einkaufen?

Inquiring about personal habits

3. Units of weight and capacity

1 Kilo(gramm) (kg)	=	1000 Gramm
1 Pfund (Pfd.)	=	500 Gramm
1 Liter (l)		

In the United States a system of weight is used in which a pound consists of 16 ounces. In German-speaking countries the metric system is used: the basic unit of weight is the **Gramm,** and a thousand grams are a **Kilo(gramm).** German speakers also use the older term **Pfund** for half a **Kilo(gramm),** or **500 (fünfhundert) Gramm.** The American *pound* equals **454 Gramm.** The basic unit of capacity in the German-speaking countries is the liter. A liter equals 1.056 quarts.

LAND UND LEUTE

Go to the
Deutsch heute Web Site at
www.hmco.com/college

Der Markt

Many people in the German-speaking countries prefer to buy their groceries at an outdoor market **(Markt)** because of its larger selection of fresh vegetables, fruit, and flowers grown by local farmers. There may also be stands **(Stände)** with bread, fish, sausages, eggs, herbs, and teas. Some markets are held daily, others once or twice a week; still others, like the famous **Viktualienmarkt** in Munich, have become permanent and are open the same hours as regular stores. Smaller cities, like Freiburg, often have a market right in their medieval centers, thus presenting a picturesque image of the past. Large cities, like Berlin or Vienna, offer a more cosmopolitan ambiance with their Turkish, Italian, or Eastern European markets. Hamburg's famous **Fischmarkt** in the St. Pauli harbor district opens very early on Sunday mornings and sells not only fish but a great variety of products that have just arrived from all over the world.

Auf dem Markt gibt es immer frisches Obst und Gemüse.

Diskussion

1. Make a list in German of items that one can buy at an outdoor market.
2. Imagine that you are in Germany. You need to go shopping for the weekend. It's a beautiful Saturday morning and the outdoor market is open. Make a short shopping list and a list of the places where you would buy the items.

4. Units of measurement and quantity

Geben Sie mir zwei **Pfund** Kaffee.	Give me two pounds of coffee.
Ich nehme zwei **Glas** Milch.	I'll take two glasses of milk.
Er kauft zwei **Liter** Milch.	He's buying two liters of milk.
Zwei **Stück** Kuchen bitte.	Two pieces of cake, please.

In German, masculine and neuter nouns expressing measure, weight, or number are in the singular. Note that feminine nouns are in the plural: **Sie trinkt zwei Tassen Kaffee.** *(She drinks two cups of coffee.)*

3. Wie viel brauchen Sie? You're going grocery shopping for an elderly neighbor and are finding out how much of each item she wants you to buy.

≫ Wie viel Kaffee brauchen Sie? (1 Pfd.) *Ich brauche ein Pfund Kaffee.*

1. Wie viel Kartoffeln brauchen Sie? (5 kg)
2. Und wie viel Käse? (200 g)
3. Wie viel Milch brauchen Sie? (2 l)
4. Wie viel Fisch? (2 Pfd.)
5. Und Tee? (100 g)
6. Und wie viel Bananen brauchen Sie? (1 kg)
7. Wie viel Wurst? (150 g)

4. Einkaufen. You and a partner plan to go grocery shopping. You are on a tight budget and are planning to buy only the items advertised at **Preisring-Markt.** You have 50 Marks to spend. Make a list of the items you need, how much of each item you need, and what the cost of each item is. If you need help, see Vocabulary for Authentic Text Activities in the Reference Section.

> Buying groceries

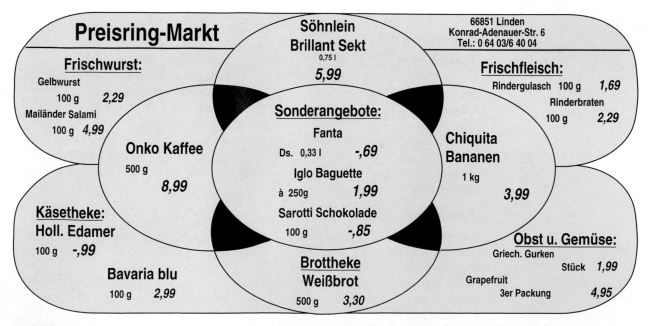

S1: Wir brauchen Kaffee, nicht?	*S2:* Wir brauchen Bananen, nicht?
S2: Ja. Wie viel?	*S1:* Ja. Wie viel?
S1: 500 Gramm.	*S2:* 2 Kilo.
S2: Gut. Wie viel kostet er?	*S1:* Gut. Wie viel macht das?
S1: Acht Mark° neunundneunzig.	*S2:* Sieben Mark achtundneunzig.

Vokabeln

Substantive

der **Besuch, -e** visit; **wir haben Besuch** we have company
die **Blume, -n** flower
die **Einkaufstasche, -n** shopping bag
das **Geld** money
das **Glas, ̈er** glass
das **Gramm** gram (*abbrev.* **g**)
das **Haus, ̈er** house
das **Kilo(gramm)** kilogram (*abbrev.* kg)
die **Küche, -n** kitchen
der **Laden, ̈** store
die **Leute** (*pl.*) people

der **Liter, -** liter (*abbrev.* l = 1.056 U.S. quarts)
die **Mark, -** mark; die **Deutsche Mark (DM)** German currency
der **Markt, ̈e** market
die **Marmelade** marmalade, jam
die **Party, -s** party
das **Stück, -e** piece
die **Tablette, -n** tablet, pill
die **Tasche, -n** bag; pocket
die **Tasse, -n** cup
der **Weg, -e** way
der **Wunsch, ̈e** wish
die **Zeitung, -en** newspaper

Verben

bekommen to receive
bezahlen to pay (for); **sie bezahlt das Essen** she pays for the meal
erklären to explain
finden to find; **Sie finden die Brötchen gut.** They like the rolls.

geben (gibt) to give
kennen to know, be acquainted with
riechen to smell
schließen to close

Andere Wörter

alles everything, all
besonders especially, particularly
billig cheap; **billiger** cheaper
denn (*conj.*) for (because)
dort there
etwas some, somewhat
frisch fresh
immer always
manchmal sometimes

mit with
morgens mornings, every morning
noch ein(e) another
samstags (on) Saturdays
schon already
viele many
wenn (*conj.*) when; whenever; if
zu to

Besondere Ausdrücke

auf dem Weg on the way
auf den Markt to the market
Besuch haben to have company
nach Hause (to go) home
noch etwas something else (in addition)

Schönes Wochenende! Have a nice weekend!
Sonst noch einen Wunsch? Anything else?
Wie viel macht das? How much does that come to?
zu Hause at home

GRAMMATIK UND ÜBUNGEN

1. Verbs with stem-vowel change *e > i*

essen: to eat	
ich esse	wir essen
du **isst**	ihr esst
er/es/sie **isst**	sie essen
Sie essen	

geben: to give	
ich gebe	wir geben
du **gibst**	ihr gebt
er/es/sie **gibt**	sie geben
Sie geben	

nehmen: to take		
ich	nehme	wir nehmen
du	**nimmst**	ihr nehmt
er/es/sie	**nimmt**	sie nehmen
Sie nehmen		

English has only two verbs with stem-vowel changes in the third-person singular, present tense: *say > says (sezz),* and *do > does (duzz).*

German, on the other hand, has a considerable number of verbs with a stem-vowel change in the **du-** and **er/es/sie**-forms. Some verbs with stem vowel **e** change **e** to **i.** The verbs of this type that you know so far are **essen, geben,** and **nehmen.** The stem of **essen** ends in a sibilant; the ending **-st** therefore contracts to a **-t = du isst** (see *Kapitel 1, Grammatik und Übungen,* section 7). **Nehmen** has an additional spelling change: **du nimmst, er/es/sie nimmt.** In the chapter vocabularies in this book, stem-vowel changes are indicated in parentheses: **geben (gibt).**

1. Was geben wir Christin?   Christin needs things for her room at the university. Tell what various friends are giving her. Use the proper form of **geben.**

➤➤ Jürgen / zwei alte Stühle   *Jürgen gibt Christin zwei alte Stühle.*

1. Claudia / zwei Hefte
2. Maria und Volker / ein Radio
3. wir / eine Lampe
4. ihr / eine Uhr
5. Frau Hauff / eine Büchertasche
6. du / ein Buch über Musik
7. ich / zwei Kugelschreiber

Rosina Wachtmeister
Die Zauberflöte
Bilder wie Musik in einer außergewöhnlichen Geschenkedition. Eine geniale Illustration der populärsten Oper aller Zeiten.

➤ DM 39,90

LAND UND LEUTE

Go to the
Deutsch heute Web Site at
www.hmco.com/college

Das Frühstück

Ein qutes Frühstück ist die wichtigste „Mahlzeit am Tag" *(A good breakfast is the most important meal of the day)* is a popular saying in the German-speaking countries. A German breakfast **(Frühstück)** can be quite extensive, especially on weekends or holidays. Usually it consists of a hot beverage, fresh rolls **(Brötchen)** or bread, butter and jam; often there are cold cuts, an egg, cheese or perhaps yogurt, whole grain granola **(Müsli)**, and juice or fruit. Pancakes are not a common breakfast food. Eggs for breakfast are usually soft-boiled **(weich gekocht)**. Scrambled eggs **(Rühreier)** and fried eggs **(Spiegeleier)** are more often served for a light meal either for lunch or in the evening. Traditionally, the main warm meal of the day was eaten at noon **(Mittagessen).** Recently, however, more and more people prefer to eat their warm meal in the evening **(Abendessen).**

Zu einem gemütlichen Frühstück gehören Brötchen, Marmelade, Käse, Eier und Kaffee.

Diskussion

Have a short conversation with a classmate in German in which you plan a meal for a German visitor. Decide which meal you will prepare for the visitor, whether you will serve a German meal or not, and what you will serve.

---

2. Im Café. Complete the conversation among three friends in a café by supplying the appropriate form of the verbs in parentheses.

CLAUDIA: Du, Lars, was _____ du? (nehmen)

LARS: Ich _____ ein Stück Kuchen. (nehmen) Du auch?

CLAUDIA: Nein, aber Ina _____ ein Stück, nicht wahr? (nehmen)

INA: Nein. Kuchen _____ ich nicht so gern. (essen)

CLAUDIA: Was _____ du denn gern? (essen)

INA: Eis. Es _____ hier sehr gutes Eis. (geben)

LARS: Und zu trinken? Was _____ ihr beide? Kaffee oder Tee? (nehmen)

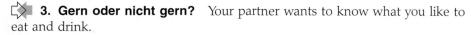 **3. Gern oder nicht gern?** Your partner wants to know what you like to eat and drink.

Answering questions about eating habits

Expressing likes and dislikes

S2:			*S1:*		
Isst du	viel	Brot?	Ja,	viel.	
	gern			gern.	
			Nein,	nicht viel.	
				nicht so gern.	

Schüttelkasten

		Käse			Fleisch
Kuchen			Fisch		
Obst	Gemüse			Wurst	

Trinkst du	viel	Milch?	Ja,	viel.	
	gern			gern.	
			Nein,	nicht viel.	
				nicht so gern.	

Schüttelkasten

		Bier			Tee
Wein			Kaffee		
Saft	Limonade			Mineralwasser	

2. Word order with expressions of time and place

	Time	Place
Sie geht	heute	in die Buchhandlung.

	Place	Time
She's going	to the bookstore	today.

When a German sentence contains both a time expression and a place expression, the time expression precedes the place expression. Note that the sequence of time and place in English is reversed.

4. Wann gehst du? Your friend is trying to guess when you're going to do various errands. Confirm the guesses.

➤➤ Wann gehst du in die Stadt? Heute Morgen?   *Ja, ich gehe heute Morgen in die Stadt.*

1. Wann gehst du in den Supermarkt? Um neun?
2. Wann gehst du in die Buchhandlung? Morgen?
3. Wann gehst du zum Bäcker? Später?
4. Wann gehst du in die Apotheke? Heute Morgen?
5. Wann gehst du ins Kaufhaus? Jetzt?

LAND UND LEUTE

Go to the
Deutsch heute Web Site at
www.hmco.com/college

Währung

C ustomers in German-speaking countries almost always pay cash in stores and restaurants. Only recently have credit cards become popular; checks are used infrequently.

On January 1, 1999 the euro, a single currency **(Währung),** was adopted by eleven European countries, including Germany and Austria. The introduction of a common currency is seen as a major step in the unification of Europe. However, no coins or bills will be issued before January 2002, so people will continue to use the bills **(Scheine)** and coins **(Münzen)** of the national currencies until new **euro** bills and **euro** cents are issued.

Until the introduction of the **euro,** Germany's basic monetary unit has been the **Deutsche Mark (DM),** referred to as the **Mark** when speaking. There are 100 **Pfennig** in a **Mark.** Austria's basic unit has been the **Schilling (öS),** which is divided into 100 **Groschen.** Switzerland's basic unit, the **Franken (sFr)** is also used by Liechtenstein as its basic monetary unit. There are 100 **Rappen (Rp)** in a **Franken.**

In order to make identification of the different denominations clearer, each of the German-speaking countries prints the bills in various colors and their size increases with their value. This system will also be used for the **euro.** For instance, the green DM 20 bill is larger than the blue DM 10 bill; the yellow 200 euro bill is larger than the blue 20 euro bill.

3. Imperatives°

der Imperativ

The imperative forms are used to express commands, offer suggestions and encouragement, give instructions, and try to persuade people. In both German and English, the verb is in the first position.

Infinitive	Imperative		
	du-Form	*ihr*-Form	*Sie*-Form
fragen	frag(e)	fragt	fragen Sie
arbeiten	arbeite	arbeitet	arbeiten Sie
essen	iss	esst	essen Sie
geben	gib	gebt	geben Sie
nehmen	nimm	nehmt	nehmen Sie
sein	sei	seid	seien Sie

■ du-*imperative*

Nadja. { **Frag(e)** Frau List. / **Arbeite** jetzt, bitte. / **Gib** mir bitte das Brot. / **Nimm** doch zwei Aspirin.

Nadja. { *Ask* Mrs. List. / *Work* now, please. / *Give* me the bread, please. / Why don't you *take* two aspirin?

The **du**-imperative consists of the stem of a verb plus **-e,** but the **-e** is often dropped in informal usage: **frage** > **frag.** If the stem of the verb ends in **-d** or **-t,** the **-e** may not be omitted in written German: **arbeite.** If the stem vowel of a verb changes from **e** to **i,** the imperative has this vowel change and never has final **-e: geben** > **gib, essen** > **iss, nehmen** > **nimm.**

■ ihr-*imperative*

Carsten. Peter. { **Fragt** Frau List. / **Gebt** mir bitte das Brot.

Carsten. Peter. { *Ask* Mrs. List. / *Give* me the bread, please.

The **ihr**-imperative is identical with the **ihr**-form of the present tense.

■ Sie-*imperative*

Herr Hahn.
$\left\{\begin{array}{l}\textbf{Fragen Sie} \text{ Frau List.} \\ \textbf{Geben Sie} \text{ mir} \\ \quad \text{bitte das Brot.}\end{array}\right.$
     Mr. Hahn.
$\left\{\begin{array}{l}\textit{Ask} \text{ Mrs. List.} \\ \textit{Give} \text{ me the} \\ \quad \text{bread, please.}\end{array}\right.$

The **Sie**-imperative is identical with the **Sie**-form of the present tense. The pronoun **Sie** is always stated and follows the verb directly. In speech, one differentiates a command from a yes/no question by the inflection of the voice. As in English, the voice rises at the end of a yes/no question and falls at the end of a command.

■ *Imperative of* sein

Fabian, **sei** nicht so nervös!   Fabian, don't *be* so nervous!
Kinder, **seid** jetzt ruhig!   Children, *be* quiet now!
Frau Weibl, **seien Sie** bitte   Mrs. Weibl, please *be*
  so gut und ...   so kind and . . .

Note that the **du**-imperative **(sei)** and **Sie**-imperative **(seien Sie)** are different from the present-tense forms: **du bist, Sie sind.**

Giving directives

5. Auf einer Party: Frau Berg und Julia.   The Bergs have guests. Below are some things Frau Berg says to Sarah and Martin, two people she knows well. She also knows Julia well. How would she say the same things to her?

➤➤ Sarah und Martin, nehmt noch etwas Käse.   *Julia, nimm noch etwas Käse.*

1. Trinkt doch noch ein Glas Wein.
2. Sagt mal, wie findet ihr die Musik?
3. Seid so nett und spielt etwas Gitarre.
4. Esst noch etwas.
5. Kommt, hier sind unsere Fotos von Berlin.
6. Bleibt noch ein bisschen hier.

6. Auf einer Party: Frau Berg und Herr Fromme.   Herr Fromme is an acquaintance but not a personal friend of Frau Berg. Frau Berg uses **Sie** when speaking with him. How would she say the same things to him that she said to Sarah and Martin in exercise 5?

7. Noch eine Party.   At a very large party you hear snatches of conversation. Translate for your German friend who finds it all confusing. Use the **du-** or **ihr-** imperative as appropriate with first names and the **Sie**-imperative with last names.

➤➤ Stay here, Jennifer.   *Bleib hier, Jennifer.*
➤➤ Don't ask, Mr. Lang.   *Fragen Sie nicht, Herr Lang.*

1. Don't work too much, Julia.
2. Say something, Max.
3. Tina and Ute, have another glass of mineral water. (Use **trinken.**)
4. Don't believe that, Mark and Tom.
5. Don't eat so much, Peter.
6. Take aspirin, Michael.

7. Be so kind, Mrs. Schulz, and stay here.
8. Michael, be quiet.
9. Please have some cake, Mrs. Klein. (Use **nehmen.**)

4. Direct object°

das direkte Objekt

Ich höre **Andrea** nebenan.	I hear *Andrea* next door.
Ich schließe die **Tür.**	I shut the *door.*

The direct object is the noun or pronoun that receives or is affected by the action of the verb. The direct object answers the question whom **(Andrea)** or what **(Tür).**

5. Accusative° of the definite articles *der, das, die*

der Akkusativ

	Nominative	Accusative
Masculine	**Der** Kaffee ist billig.	Nehmen Sie **den** Kaffee.
Neuter	**Das** Brot ist frisch.	Nehmen Sie **das** Brot.
Feminine	**Die** Marmelade ist gut.	Nehmen Sie **die** Marmelade.
Plural	**Die** Blumen sind schön.	Nehmen Sie **die** Blumen.

The direct object of a verb is in the accusative case. In the accusative case, the definite article **der** changes to **den.** The articles **das** and **die** (*sg.* and *pl.*) do not show case change in the accusative.

8. Einkaufen gehen. A friend is shopping for things for her/his room. Ask whether she/he intends to buy the things. The things become direct objects in your questions.

➤➤ Die Lampe ist lustig. *Kaufst du die Lampe oder nicht?*

1. Das Radio ist gut.
2. Der Stuhl ist billig.
3. Der Tisch ist schön.
4. Das Bett ist groß.
5. Die Uhr ist billig.
6. Die Blumen sind schön.

6. Word order and case as signals of meaning

Subject	Verb	Direct object
The man	visits	the professor.
The professor	visits	the man.

English usually uses word order to signal the difference between a subject and a direct object. The usual word-order pattern in statements is *subject, verb,* and *direct object.* The two sentences above have very different meanings.

Subject (nom.)	Verb	Direct object (acc.)
Der Mann	besucht	den Professor.

Direct Object (acc.)	Verb	Subject (nom.)
Den Professor	besucht	der Mann.

German generally uses case to signal the difference between a subject and a direct object. The different case forms of the definite article (e.g., **der, den**) signal the grammatical function of the noun. **Der,** in the example above, indicates that the noun **Mann** is in the nominative case and functions as the subject. **Den** indicates that the noun **Professor** is in the accusative case and functions as the direct object. The word-order pattern in statements may be *subject, verb, direct object,* or *direct object, verb, subject.* The two sentences above have the same meaning.

Since German uses cases to signal grammatical function, it can use word order for another purpose: to present information from different perspectives. A speaker may use so-called "normal" word order *(subject, verb, direct object)* or "inverted" word order *(direct object, verb, subject).* The English equivalents vary, depending on context and the meaning the speaker wishes to convey. The sentence **Der Mann besucht den Professor** is equivalent to *The man visits the professor.* The sentence **Den Professor besucht der Mann** is equivalent to saying something like *It's **the professor** the man is visiting.*

Der Professor fragt **die** Studentin etwas.	The professor asks the student something.

When only one noun or noun phrase shows case, it may be difficult at first to distinguish meaning. In the example above, **der Professor** has to be the subject, since the definite article **der** clearly shows nominative case. By the process of elimination, therefore, **die Studentin** has to be the direct object. If **die Studentin** were the subject, the article before **Professor** would be **den.**

Die Frau fragt **das** Mädchen etwas.

Sometimes neither noun contains a signal for case. In an example like the one above, one would usually assume normal word order: *The woman asks the girl something.* Depending on context, however, it is possible to interpret it as inverted word order: *It's **the woman** the girl is asking something.*

Geschäftszeiten

LAND UND LEUTE

For many people in the German-speaking countries, shopping is an integral part of daily life. Going shopping several times a week and walking to a store are very common. Although most food shopping is done in supermarkets, specialty stores **(Fachgeschäfte)** like the bakery, butcher shop, or fruit and vegetable store are still frequently patronized. Some customers enjoy the more personal atmosphere and the convenient location of neighborhood stores.

Business hours for stores are regulated by law in German-speaking countries. In Germany stores may be open from 6:00 A.M. to 8:00 P.M. on weekdays and until 4:00 P.M. on Saturdays; however, on the four Saturdays before Christmas, stores may remain open until 6:00 P.M. Most stores open between 8:30 and 9:30 in the morning, although bakeries and other small stores may open earlier to allow customers to buy fresh **Brötchen** for breakfast or make purchases on the way to work. Many small neighborhood stores close during the early afternoon **(Mittagspause)** for one or two hours from about 1:00 P.M. to 3:00 P.M. Stores are closed on Sundays and holidays.

Go to the
Deutsch heute Web Site at
www.hmco.com/college

Geschäftszeiten

Mo, Di, Mi + Fr	8^{00} – 18^{30} h
Do	8^{00} – 19^{30} h
Sa	8^{30} – 14^{00} h
1. Sa von-April - September	8^{30} – 16^{00} h
1. Sa von Oktober - März	8^{30} – 18^{00} h

CITY APOTHEKE ZUM LÖWEN

Im Winter ist diese Apotheke am Samstag bis 18 Uhr geöffnet.

There are some exceptions to these regulations for businesses in resort areas, for leisure activities, and for the traveling public. If you need to make a late purchase or shop on Sundays, it is often necessary to go to the train station **(Bahnhof)** or find an open gas station **(Tankstelle).** However, even on Sundays you can usually buy fresh flowers for a few hours at a flower shop **(Blumenladen)** and buy a pastry at a pastry shop **(Konditorei).**

These business hours went into effect in 1996 with a new shop closing law **(Ladenschlussgesetz)** and represent a considerable lengthening of the legal shop hours. Owners of large stores and consumers generally support longer store hours, while the unions opposed the new hours because the old law allowed employees to work regular hours and have a full weekend. Owners of small businesses contend that they do not attract enough business to make a profit from longer shopping hours and many small businesses have chosen to close before 8:00 P.M.

Diskussion

Discuss the advantages and disadvantages of a strict shop closing law, and compare the regulations in your community to those in Germany.

9. Wer macht das?   A number of people are having a neighborhood party. What is going on among them? Find out by identifying the subjects of the sentences.

⫸ Die Frau kennt der Nachbar nicht.   *Subject: der Nachbar*

1. Das Kind sucht seine Mutter.
2. Der Junge fragt das Mädchen etwas.
3. Das Mädchen findet der Junge nett.
4. Den Rotwein trinkt der Professor gern.
5. Die Amerikaner kennt die Frau gut.
6. Die Italiener kennen die Frau aber nicht.
7. Den Kuchen essen die Kinder gern.

das Prädikatsnomen

7. Direct object vs. predicate noun°

Predicate noun	Dieter Müller ist **mein Freund**.	Dieter Müller is *my friend*.
Direct object	Kennst du **meinen Freund**?	Do you know *my friend*?

The predicate noun (e.g., **mein Freund**) designates a person, concept, or thing that is equated with the subject (e.g., **Dieter Müller**). A predicate noun completes the meaning of linking verbs such as **sein** and **heißen** and is in the nominative case.

The direct object (e.g., **meinen Freund**) is the noun or pronoun that receives or is related to the action of the verb. The direct-object noun or pronoun is in the accusative case.

Predicate noun	Das ist **nicht** Sabine Meier.
Direct object	Ich kenne Sabine Meier **nicht**.

Nicht precedes a predicate noun and usually follows a noun or pronoun used as a direct object.

10. Ein kleines Interview.   Here are some questions Peter was asked about his German class. Identify the direct object or predicate noun.

1. Sind das alle Studenten?
2. Kennst du die Studenten gut?
3. Ist dein Professor eine Frau oder ein Mann?
4. Ist das dein Deutschbuch?
5. Brauchst du ein Buch aus Deutschland?
6. Hast du Freunde in Deutschland oder Österreich?

WENN'S UM BÜCHER GEHT

Berliner Universitätsbuchhandlung
SPANDAUER STRASSE 2 · 10178 BERLIN
FON (0 30) 2 40 94 31 · FAX (0 30) 2 42 31 13
Internet: http://www.unibuch-berlin.de   E-mail: info@unibuch-berlin.de

EINE DER DREI GROSSEN IN BERLIN
für Hoch-, Fachschulen und Universitäten

11. Was kaufst du? In order to finance your summer trip to Europe you're selling things in your room or apartment. Your partner will decide which items she/he wants and asks the price. After you name the price, she/he decides whether to buy the article.

S2: Was kostet° [der Stuhl]?   cost

S1: [Zwanzig] Mark.

S2: Gut, ich kaufe/nehme [den Stuhl]./ Das ist zu viel. Ich kaufe/nehme [den Stuhl] nicht.

8. Demonstrative pronouns in the accusative case

Wie findest du **den** Kaffee?   How do you like the coffee?
Den finde ich gut.   This is (really) good!

Wie findest du **das** Fleisch?   How do you like the meat?
Das finde ich gut.   That's (really) good!

Wie findest du **die** Torte?   How do you like the cake?
Die finde ich gut.   That is (really) good!

Wie findest du **die** Eier?   How do you like the eggs?
Die finde ich gut.   Those are (really) good!

The accusative forms of the demonstrative pronouns are identical to the accusative forms of the definite articles.

12. Nein, das finde ich nicht. You and Gabi are shopping in a department store. Disagree with all of her opinions.

⟫ Ich finde das Musikheft billig. Du auch?   *Nein, das finde ich nicht billig.*

1. Ich finde das Buch über Schach schlecht. Du auch?
2. Ich finde den Fernseher zu klein. Du auch?
3. Ich finde den Kugelschreiber billig. Du auch?
4. Ich finde die Lampe schön. Du auch?
5. Ich finde das Radio gut. Du auch?
6. Ich finde den Tisch zu groß für das Zimmer. Du auch?
7. Ich finde die Stühle furchtbar. Du auch?
8. Ich finde die Uhr zu groß. Du auch?

9. Accusative of *ein* and *kein*

	Nominative	Accusative
Masculine	Wo ist **ein** Bleistift?	Haben Sie **einen** Bleistift?
	Da ist **kein** Bleistift.	Ich habe **keinen** Bleistift.
Neuter	Wo ist **ein** Heft?	Haben Sie **ein** Heft?
	Da ist **kein** Heft.	Ich habe **kein** Heft.
Feminine	Wo ist **eine** Uhr?	Haben Sie **eine** Uhr?
	Da ist **keine** Uhr.	Ich habe **keine** Uhr.
Plural	Sind das Kulis?	Haben Sie Kulis?
	Das sind **keine** Kulis.	Ich habe **keine** Kulis.

The indefinite article **ein** and the negative **kein** change to **einen** and **keinen** before masculine nouns in the accusative singular. The neuter and feminine indefinite articles and their corresponding negatives do not show case changes in the accusative singular. **Ein** has no plural forms. **Kein,** however, does have a plural form: **keine.**

13. Wer braucht was?   There are a number of new people in your dorm and their rooms are not completely furnished. Tell what each person needs, using the pictures as cues.

➤➤ Peter   *Peter braucht einen Tisch.*

1. Anja
2. Karin
3. Caroline
4. Peter

5. Robin
6. Lisa
7. Florian

➢➢ **14. Ich brauche [keinen Tisch].**   Ask your partner if she/he needs the things in exercise 13. She/He will reply in the negative.

S1: Brauchst du [einen Tisch]?
S2: Nein, ich brauche [keinen Tisch].

10. Accusative of possessive adjectives

	Nominative	Accusative
Masculine	Ist das **mein** Bleistift?	Ja, ich habe **deinen** Bleistift.
Neuter	Ist das **mein** Heft?	Ja, ich habe **dein** Heft.
Feminine	Ist das **meine** Uhr?	Ja, ich habe **deine** Uhr.
Plural	Sind das **meine** Kulis?	Ja, ich habe **deine** Kulis.

The possessive adjectives **(mein, dein, sein, ihr, unser, euer, Ihr)** have the same endings as the indefinite article **ein** in both the nominative and accusative cases.

15. Unsere Freunde.   You're in a café having cake and coffee with Jochen. You talk about your friends. Complete the conversation by supplying appropriate endings to the possessive adjectives.

JOCHEN: Sag' mal, du und Martin arbeitet jetzt bei BMW, nicht?

SIE: Ja, and unser_____ Freund Martin findet sein_____ Arbeit furchtbar. Aber

ich finde mein_____ Arbeit interessant. Freitags bekomme ich mein_____

Geld.

JOCHEN: Du, warum gibt Frank Andrea sein_____ Computer?

SIE: Ich glaube, Andrea gibt Frank ihr_____ Kassettendeck.

JOCHEN: Ach, so. Brauchen wir heute unser_____ Bücher?

SIE: Nein. Du, Jochen, brauchst du dein_____ Kuli?

JOCHEN: Nein. Möchtest du ihn haben? Aber warum isst du dein_____ Kuchen

nicht?

SIE: Die Äpfel sind so sauer! Mein_____ Kuchen ist nicht besonders gut.

16. Was suchst du?   Coming back from a field trip, a number of students are missing items. Tell who is looking for what by completing the sentences with the appropriate possessive adjective.

⟫ Gerd sucht _____ Bleistift.   *Gerd sucht seinen Bleistift.*

1. Monika sucht _____ Buch.

2. Wir suchen _____ Kulis.

3. Katja sucht _____ Radio.

4. Jakob und Dario suchen _____ Bleistift.

5. Sarah sucht _____ Zeitung.

6. Ich suche _____ Deutschbuch.

7. Florian und Julia suchen _____ Bücher.

11. Accusative of *wer* and *was*

Nominative	Accusative
wer tragt?	**Wen** fragt sie?
Was ist los?	**Was** fragst du?

The accusative case form of the interrogative pronoun **wer?** (*who?*) is **wen?** (*whom?*). The accusative and nominative form of **was?** (*what?*) are the same.

17. Wen? Was?   The party is loud and you keep missing the end of your partner's comments. Ask what or whom she/he is talking about. Replace the direct object with **wen?** or **was?** to pose your questions.

➤➤ Ich frage Michael morgen.   *Wen fragst du morgen?*
➤➤ Ich brauche einen neuen Computer.   *Was brauchst du?*

1. Ich kenne Beatrix gut.
2. Ich spiele morgen Golf.
3. Morgen kaufe ich einen neuen Computer.
4. Die Musik finde ich gut.
5. Ich finde Mark lustig.

12. Impersonal expression *es gibt*

Gibt es hier einen Supermarkt?   Is there a supermarket here?
Es gibt heute Butterkuchen.   There's [We're having] butter cake today.

Es gibt is equivalent to English *there is* or *there are*. It is followed by the accusative case.

18. Was gibt es heute zum Abendessen?   Tell what is planned for dinner tonight, and what is not.

➤➤ Fisch – Käse   *Es gibt Fisch, aber keinen Käse.*

1. Brötchen – Kartoffeln
2. Milch – Saft
3. Butter – Margarine
4. Gemüse – Obst
5. Tee – Kaffee
6. Mineralwasser – Wein

die Präposition

13. Prepositions°

Margot kauft die Uhr **für ihren Freund.**   Margot is buying the watch for her friend.

Margot kauft die Uhr **für ihn.**   Margot is buying the watch for him.

A preposition (e.g., **für**—*for*) is used to show the relation of a noun (e.g., **Freund**—*friend*) or pronoun (e.g., **ihn**—*him*) to some other word in the sentence (e.g., **kauft**—*buying*). The noun or pronoun following the preposition is called the object of the preposition.

14. Accusative prepositions

durch	through	Sie geht **durch** die Buchhandlung.
für	for	Sie kauft es **für** das Haus.
gegen	against	Sie hat nichts **gegen** den Mann.
ohne	without	Sie geht **ohne** das Kind.
um	around	Sie geht **um** den Tisch.

The objects of the prepositions **durch, für, gegen, ohne,** and **um** are always in the accusative case.

Er geht **durchs** Zimmer.	durch das = **durchs**
Er braucht eine Batterie **fürs** Auto.	für das = **fürs**
Er geht **ums** Haus.	um das = **ums**

The prepositions **durch, für,** and **um** often contract with the definite article **das** to form **durchs, fürs,** and **ums.** These contractions are common in colloquial German, but are not required.

19. Was machen Anja und David?   Complete the information about Anja and David by filling in the appropriate preposition and adding the correct form of the article or possessive adjective. The gender of unfamiliar nouns is provided in parentheses.

durch □ für □ gegen □ ohne □ um

Anja und David gehen heute _____ d_____ Park (m.) Sie gehen _____

d_____ See° (m.) und sprechen über die Universität. David mag° seinen   lake / likes

Deutschkurs nicht und sagt etwas _____ sein_____ Deutschprofessor. Anja

geht in die Buchhandlung. Sie kauft ein Buch _____ ihr_____ Englischkurs

(m.). Stefan ist auch da. Er fragt Anja and David: „Kommt ihr mit ins Kino?"

Anja und David kommen° nicht mit. Sie arbeiten heute Abend. Stefan geht   **kommen mit:** come along

_____ sein_____ Freunde ins Kino.

15. Accusative of masculine *N*-nouns

Nominative	Accusative
Der Herr sagt etwas.	Hören Sie **den** Herr**n?**
Der Student sagt etwas.	Hören Sie **den** Student**en?**

German has a class of masculine nouns that have signals for case. Not only the article, but the noun itself ends in **-n** or **-en** in the accusative. This class of nouns may be referred to as masculine **N**-nouns or "weak nouns." In the vocabularies of this book, masculine **N**-nouns will be followed by two endings: **der Herr, -n, -en.** The first ending is the singular accusative and the second is the plural ending. The masculine **N**-nouns you know so far are **der Herr, der Junge, der Mensch, der Nachbar,** and **der Student.**

20. Wie sagt man das?   Give the German equivalents of the conversational exchanges below.

1. Do you know the gentleman there, Mrs. Kluge?
   —Yes. He's a neighbor.
2. Why is your neighbor going around the house?
   —Ask Mr. Heidemann.
3. Why is Mr. Leber coming without the children?
   —He's buying books for the children.
4. I have nothing against Mr. Knecht.
   —Who's Mr. Knecht?

16. Accusative of personal pronouns

Nominative		Accusative	
Subject	*Object*	*Subject*	*Object*
Er braucht	**mich.**	*He* needs	*me.*
Ich arbeite für	**ihn.**	*I* work for	*him.*

Pronouns used as direct objects or objects of accusative prepositions are in the accusative case.

Subject pronouns	I	you	he	she	it	we	you	they
Object pronouns	me	you	him	her	it	us	you	them

Some English pronouns have different forms when used as subject or as object.

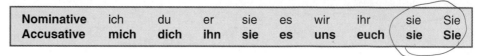

Nominative	ich	du	er	sie	es	wir	ihr	sie	Sie
Accusative	mich	dich	ihn	sie	es	uns	euch	sie	Sie

Some German pronouns also have different forms in the nominative and accusative.

21. Nein danke!   Mark wants to lend you all his things. Say you don't need them. Use a pronoun in each answer.

➤➤ Brauchst du mein Buch über Schach?   *Nein, danke, ich brauche es nicht.*

1. Brauchst du meinen Fußball?
2. Brauchst du mein Musikheft?
3. Brauchst du meinen Kugelschreiber?
4. Brauchst du meine Lampe?
5. Brauchst du meine Stühle?
6. Brauchst du meinen Computer?

22. Wie sagt man das?   Give the German equivalents of the conversational exchanges below.

1. Who is working for us?
   —We're working for you.
2. Are you asking me?
   —Yes, I'm asking you.

3. What do you have against me?
   —I have nothing against you, Mr. Schuhmacher.
4. Do you know Uwe and Barbara?
   —No. I don't know them.

WIEDERHOLUNG

1. Monika geht einkaufen.   Monika needs some things for supper. Tell about her shopping. Restate the sentences below, beginning with the words in italics. Make the necessary changes in word order.

➤➤   Monika braucht Brot *fürs Abendessen.*   *Fürs Abendessen braucht Monika Brot.*

1. Monika geht *heute Morgen* einkaufen.
2. Viele Leute gehen *jetzt* in den Supermarkt.
3. Es ist aber *im Supermarkt* nicht so persönlich.
4. Monika kauft *das Brot* beim Bäcker.
5. Sie geht *dann* auf den Blumenmarkt.
6. Sie kommt oft *samstags* mit Blumen nach Hause.

2. Essen und Trinken.   While having wine and cheese, Laura and Robert talk about eating and drinking. Form sentences, using the cues below.

➤➤   LAURA: wie / du / finden / der Wein / ? *Wie findest du den Wein?*

1. ROBERT: gut // was für Wein / das / sein / ?
2. LAURA: Wein / kommen / aus Kalifornien
3. ROBERT: du / kaufen / der Käse / im Supermarkt / ?
4. LAURA: nein, / ich / kaufen / alles / auf dem Markt
5. LAURA: zum Abendessen / es / geben / Fisch
6. LAURA: du / essen / gern / Fisch / ?
7. ROBERT: nein, / ich / essen / kein Fisch / und / auch / keine Wurst
8. ROBERT: ich / essen / aber / gern / Kuchen
9. LAURA: heute / es / geben / leider / kein Kuchen

3. Beim Frühstück.   Peter is a German exchange student who just arrived last night in New York and is staying with the Schuberts. Harry and Anna Schubert, their two children, Hannah and Frank, and Peter are sitting at the breakfast table. Give the German equivalent of their conversation.

1. MRS. SCHUBERT: Who needs the tea?
2. MR. SCHUBERT: Hannah, give Peter the coffee.
3. HANNAH: Peter doesn't drink coffee.
4. PETER: No, I always drink tea for breakfast.
5. MRS. SCHUBERT: Harry, what are you doing today?
6. MR. SCHUBERT: I'm working in the library. (in the = **in der**)
7. MRS. SCHUBERT: Peter, whom do you know in New York?
8. PETER: I know a professor.
9. FRANK: Peter, are there many cybercafés° in Germany?   **das Internetcafé, -s**
10. PETER: Of course. Why do you ask, Frank?

4. Nicht oder kein?   Answer in the negative, using **nicht** or a form of **kein**.

➤➤ Kauft Erika heute Kartoffeln?   *Nein, sie kauft heute keine Kartoffeln.*

1. Kauft sie Kuchen?
2. Geht sie heute zum Bäcker?
3. Kauft sie das Fleisch im Super-markt?
4. Kauft Gerd heute Käse?
5. Kauft er das Brot beim Bäcker?
6. Kauft er heute Milch?
7. Gibt es hier einen Supermarkt?

5. Frage-Ecke.   Compare the picture of your room with that of your partner.

S1: Mein Zimmer hat [eine Pflanze]. Hast du auch [eine Pflanze]?
S2: Ja, ich habe auch [eine Pflanze]./Nein, aber ich habe Blumen.

S1:   *S2:*

6. Gespräche.   You invite a classmate back to your room or apartment for dinner.

1. She/He makes comments on your room/apartment.
2. Ask her/him what she/he likes to eat.
3. Either you don't have what she/he has mentioned or what you have is not fresh.
4. She/He asks if there is a grocery store nearby.
5. Make a list of what you will buy together for dinner.

7. Zum Schreiben

1. a. Assume that you are one of the two American students, Diane or Joan, who are visiting Monika. (See **Einkaufen am Wochenende** pp. 98–99.) Write a short letter to someone you plan to visit in Austria, in which you tell what you plan to do with your German friends on the second week-end of your visit in Germany. It is O.K., incidentally, to do many of the same things that you did on the first weekend, especially if you enjoyed them.

b. Or assume you are one of the two German students, Monika or Stefan. Write a letter to a friend in which you say you have guests from the U.S.A. and tell what you plan to do with them during the second week (end) of their visit.

   Hinweise (tips): Before you begin your letter turn back to *Kapitel 1* and review the format (opening, closing, etc.) for informal letters. Then make a list of activities you plan to write about, e.g., shopping, playing tennis.

2. Your friend Erik prefers to shop in **Supermärkte,** but your friend Monika prefers **Tante-Emma-Läden.** Write a paragraph in German in which you state your personal preference and your reasons for it.

   Hinweise: Look over the reading (pp. 98–99) and **Land und Leute: Einkaufen** (p. 100) before you begin writing. Think about which things appeal to you in the type of store you prefer. Write down your ideas and then organize them according to their order of importance. Begin your paragraph by stating which type of store you like: **Ich gehe gern [in den Supermarkt]. Da ...**

GRAMMATIK: ZUSAMMENFASSUNG

Verbs with stem-vowel change *e > i*

essen	
ich esse	wir essen
du **isst**	ihr esst
er/es/sie **isst**	sie essen
Sie essen	

geben	
ich gebe	wir geben
du **gibst**	ihr gebt
er/es/sie **gibt**	sie geben
Sie geben	

nehmen	
ich nehme	wir nehmen
du **nimmst**	ihr nehmt
er/es/sie **nimmt**	sie nehmen
Sie nehmen	

Several verbs with the stem vowel **e** (including **essen, geben, nehmen**) change **e > i** in the **du-** and **er/es/sie**-forms of the present tense.

Word order with expressions of time and place

	Time	Place
Monika geht	heute Abend	ins Kino.
Robert war	gestern	nicht hier.

In German, time expressions generally precede place expressions.

The imperative forms

	Infinitive	Imperative	Present
du	sagen	**Sag(e)** etwas, bitte.	Sagst du etwas?
ihr		**Sagt** etwas, bitte.	Sagt ihr etwas?
Sie		**Sagen Sie** etwas, bitte.	Sagen Sie etwas?
du	nehmen	**Nimm** das Brot, bitte.	Nimmst du das Brot?
ihr		**Nehmt** das Brot, bitte.	Nehmt ihr das Brot?
Sie		**Nehmen Sie** das Brot, bitte.	Nehmen Sie das Brot?

■ *Imperative of* **sein**

du	**Sei** nicht so nervös.
ihr	**Seid** ruhig.
Sie	**Seien Sie** so gut.

Accusative case of nouns

Nominative	Accusative
Subject	*Direct Object*
Der Kuchen ist frisch.	Er nimmt **den Kuchen.**
Die Uhr ist schön.	Sie kauft **die Uhr.**

A noun that is used as a direct object of a verb is in the accusative case.

Accusative case of masculine *N*-nouns

Nominative	der Herr	der Junge	der Mensch	der Nachbar	der Student
Accusative	den Herr**n**	den Jung**en**	den Mensch**en**	den Nachbar**n**	den Student**en**

A number of masculine nouns add **-n** or **-en** in the accusative singular.

Accusative case of the definite articles *der, das, die*

	der		das		die		Plural	
Nominative	der	} Käse	das	} Brot	die	} Butter	die	} Eier
Accusative	den		das		die		die	

Accusative case of demonstrative pronouns

Accusative nouns	Accusative pronouns
Ich finde **den Käse** gut.	**Den** finde ich auch gut.
Ich finde **das Brot** trocken.	**Das** finde ich auch trocken.
Ich finde **die Butter** frisch.	**Die** finde ich auch frisch.
Ich finde **die Eier** schlecht.	**Die** finde ich auch schlecht.

Accusative case of *wer* and *was*

Nominative	Accusative
Wer fragt?	**Wen** fragt er?
Was ist los?	**Was** fragst du?

Accusative of *ein, kein,* and possessive adjectives

	Masculine	Neuter	Feminine	Plural
	(der Kuli)	**(das Heft)**	**(die Uhr)**	**(die Kulis)**
Nominative	**ein** **kein** **dein** } Kuli	**ein** **kein** **dein** } Heft	**eine** **keine** **deine** } Uhr	**keine** **deine** } Kulis
Accusative	**einen** **keinen** **deinen** } Kuli	**ein** **kein** **dein** } Heft	**eine** **keine** **deine** } Uhr	**keine** **deine** } Kulis

Kein and the possessive adjectives **(mein, dein, sein, ihr, unser, euer, Ihr)** have the same endings as the indefinite article **ein.**

Accusative case of personal pronouns

Nominative	ich	du	er	es	sie	wir	ihr	sie	Sie
Accusative	**mich**	**dich**	**ihn**	**es**	**sie**	**uns**	**euch**	**sie**	**Sie**

Prepositions with the accusative case

durch	through	Sie geht **durch** das Zimmer. [**durchs** Zimmer]
für	for	Sie kauft die Uhr **für** das Haus. [**fürs** Haus]
gegen	against	Sie hat nichts **gegen** den Mann.
ohne	without	Sie geht **ohne** Herrn Bauer.
um	around	Sie geht **um** das Haus. [**ums** Haus]

Impersonal expression *es gibt*

Es gibt keinen Kaffee mehr.	There is no more coffee.
Gibt es auch keine Brötchen?	Aren't there any rolls, either?

Es gibt is equivalent to English *there is* or *there are*. It is followed by the accusative case.

KAPITEL 4

LERNZIELE

Sprechintentionen
Borrowing and lending things
Talking about student life
Offering explanations/excuses
Describing one's family, nationality, and profession
Talking about personal interests
Inquiring about abilities
Discussing duties and requirements
Inquiring about future plans

Lesestück
Studieren in Deutschland

Land und Leute
Higher education in Germany
The school system in Germany
University admission and financial aid in Germany
Foreign students in Germany
English vs. German terms (education)
Television

Vokabeln
Professions and nationalities
Family members

Grammatik
Werden
Verbs with stem-vowel change *e > ie*
Wissen and *kennen*
Der-words
Modal auxiliaries
Separable-prefix verbs

Was studierst du?

Studenten nach der Vorlesung. (Frankfurt)

BAUSTEINE FÜR GESPRÄCHE

Notizen für die Klausur

GISELA: Hallo, Michael. Kannst du mir bitte deine Notizen leihen?

MICHAEL: Ja, gern.

GISELA: Das ist nett. Für die Klausur muss ich noch viel arbeiten.

MICHAEL: Klar, hier hast du sie. Kannst du sie morgen wieder mitbringen?

Ist das dein Hauptfach?

MICHAEL: Grüß dich. Seit wann gehst du denn in eine Literatur-Vorlesung? Studierst du nicht Geschichte?

MELANIE: Nein, nicht mehr. Ich mache jetzt Germanistik.

MICHAEL: Ah ja? Als Nebenfach?

MELANIE: Nein, als Hauptfach.

MICHAEL: Ach, wirklich? Du, möchtest du nachher Kaffee trinken gehen?

MELANIE: Ich kann leider nicht, muss noch etwas lesen. Morgen habe ich ein Referat und bin nicht besonders gut vorbereitet.

Brauchbares

There are various German equivalents of the English word *study:*

a. **studieren** = *to study a subject,* e.g., **Ich studiere Geschichte** *(I'm majoring in history).* **Studieren** also means to be a student or attend college, e.g., **Ich studiere jetzt** *(I go to college now).*

b. **machen** = *to do homework,* e.g., **Ich mache heute Abend Deutsch** *(I'm going to study German tonight).* **Machen** also means *to major in,* e.g., **Ich mache jetzt Deutsch** *(I'm majoring in German now).*

c. **lernen** = *to study in the sense of doing homework,* e.g., **Ich lerne die Vokabeln** *(I'm studying the vocabulary words).*

Fragen

1. Warum möchte Gisela Michaels Notizen leihen?
2. Warum muss Gisela noch viel lernen?
3. Wann möchte Michael seine Notizen wiederhaben?
4. Warum geht Melanie jetzt in eine Literatur-Vorlesung?
5. Was ist Melanies Hauptfach?
6. Was möchte Michael nachher machen?
7. Warum kann Melanie nicht mitgehen?

LAND UND LEUTE

Go to the
Deutsch heute Web Site at
www.hmco.com/college

Hochschulen

Germany has some 300 institutions of higher learning **(Hochschulen)**. The best known type of institution is the **Universität,** which has a long tradition in German-speaking countries. The oldest university in present-day Germany is the University of Heidelberg, founded in 1386.

Universitäten are both research and teaching institutions. They offer a variety of academic degrees **(Abschlüsse):** the **Diplom** is the first degree for most areas in the sciences, engineering, and other similar fields. Students in humanities generally pursue a **Magister Artium.** All degrees require written and oral examinations as well as an academic dissertation. Students who plan to enter civil service or a profession regulated by the state such as medicine, teaching, or law conclude their studies with the state examination **(Staatsexamen).** With very few exceptions, universities are the only institutions that can confer a doctorate degree. Colleges that specialize in preparing students for careers in art or music are called **Kunsthochschulen** and **Musikhochschulen** respectively.

A newer type of institution of higher learning is the **Fachhochschule** that specializes in fields of study **(Studiengänge)** that are more oriented toward a specific career such as business or engineering. Since their introduction in the 1960's, **Fachhochschulen** have developed into a sound alternative that is fully equivalent to the university. These institutions offer a more structured and limited curriculum than universities, and the course of study can usually be concluded in four and a half years, while most university students expect to spend more than five years to complete their studies.

Professor und Architekturstudentin an der Technischen Hochschule in Frankfurt am Main.

At a university students bear the responsibility for their own progress. There are few exams, papers, and daily assignments, and for many courses there are no exams. At the beginning of the semester students choose classes according to type and subject matter. A **Vorlesung** is a lecture with little discussion, and no exams. An **Übung** is a course that often includes daily assignments, discussion, and a test **(Klausur)** at the end. In a **Seminar,** students write papers and discuss the material. They have to write term papers **(Seminararbeiten)** as well.

After the successful completion of a **Seminar** or **Übung,** students receive a certificate **(Schein),** which includes a grade. A minimum number of **Scheine** is necessary before the student may take the intermediate qualifying exam **(Zwischenprüfung),** which is usually taken after four to six semesters at the university. More **Scheine** are required before a student can write a master's thesis **(Magisterarbeit)** or take examinations for the degree.

Diskussion

Which type of German institution is closest in form to your college or university?

Compare the course types and grading system at a German university to your experience of higher education.

1. Sie brauchen etwas. Sie brauchen etwas. Vielleicht kann eine Kursteilnehmerin/ein Kursteilnehmer es Ihnen leihen. Fragen Sie sie/ihn. (You need something. Perhaps a fellow student can lend it to you. Ask her/him.)

Borrowing objects/lending objects

S1:
Kannst du mir | **deine Notizen** leihen?
     dein Referat
     deine Seminararbeit°
     deinen Kugelschreiber
     deine Disketten°

S2:
Ja, gern.
Klar.
Natürlich.
Tut mir Leid°. Ich brauche
     ihn/es/sie selbst.

2. Hauptfach. Nebenfach. Interviewen Sie vier Studentinnen/Studenten in Ihrem Deutschkurs. Was sind ihre Hauptfächer und Nebenfächer? In den Supplementary Word Sets, Reference Section, finden Sie weitere Studienfächer. (Interview four students in your German class. What are their majors and minors? In the Supplementary Word Sets in the Reference Section, you will find further college majors.)

Discussing college majors and minors

S1:
Was ist dein | **Hauptfach?**
     Nebenfach?

S2:
Ich studiere | **Germanistik.**
Mein | **Nebenfach** ist | **Psychologie°.**

Schüttelkasten

Philosophie°   **Physik°**
Biologie°   Anglistik°   **Kunstgeschichte°**
Informatik°   Mathematik°   Chemie°

3. Was liest du? Was lesen die Studentinnen/Studenten in Ihrem Deutschkurs gern? Fragen Sie sie. (What do the students in your German class like to read? Ask them.)

S1:
Was liest du gern?

S2:
Artikel über | Sport/Musik/Schach.
Bücher über | Psychologie
Krimis°.
Liebesromane°.
Moderne° Literatur.

4. Es tut mir Leid. Ihre Freundin/Ihr Freund möchte später mit Ihnen etwas zusammen machen. Sie können aber nicht. Sagen Sie warum. (Your friend would like to do something together later, but you can't. Say why.)

Offering explanations/ excuses

S2:
Willst du nachher | **Kaffee trinken
     gehen?**
     einkaufen gehen?
     fernsehen°?
     spazieren gehen°?
     ein Video ausleihen?

S1:
Ich kann leider nicht. Ich muss
mein Referat vorbereiten.

Schüttelkasten

Deutsch machen   meine Notizen durcharbeiten°
die Vokabeln lernen   **wieder in die Bibliothek**

LAND UND LEUTE

Go to the
Deutsch heute Web Site at
www.hmco.com/college

See **Land und Leute,
Hochschulen,** p.128.

Das Schulsystem in Deutschland

At the age of six all children go to a **Grundschule** (primary school, grades 1–4). After that they attend either a **Hauptschule, Realschule,** or **Gymnasium,** depending on their ability and the job or career they hope to have. The first two years (grades 5–6) are an orientation period during which the parents and child determine whether the child is in a school suitable to her/his interests and abilities.

Young people preparing to work in the trades or industry (e.g., as a baker or car mechanic) may attend a **Hauptschule** (grades 5–9 or 5–10). After obtaining their certificate **(Hauptschulabschluss),** they enter an apprenticeship program, which includes 3–4 days per week of work training at a business and 8–12 hours per week of study at a vocational school **(Berufsschule)** until at least the age of 18. Approximately one third of the young people follow this path.

Another third of young people, those wanting a job in business, industry, public service, or the health field (e.g., as a bank clerk or nurse) attend a **Realschule** (grades 5–10). The certificate **(Mittlere Reife)** from a **Realschule** is a prerequisite for mid-level positions and permits the students to attend specialized schools **(Berufsfachschule** or **Fachoberschule).** Students who leave the **Gymnasium** after grade 10 also obtain a **Mittlere Reife.**

Young people planning to go to a university or a **Fachhochschule°** attend all grades of a **Gymnasium** (grades 5–13). The certificate of general higher education entrance qualification **(Zeugnis der allgemeinen Hochschulreife),** which is the diploma from a **Gymnasium,** is granted on the basis of grades in courses and the passing of a comprehensive exam **(Abitur).**

Zwei Schülerinnen wissen die Antwort in einem Offenbacher Gymnasium.

In some areas, another type of school, the **Gesamtschule** (comprehensive school), offers secondary instruction for grades 5–10, and in some states the **Gesamtschule** extends to the thirteenth year.

Diskussion

1. Make a chart of the German school system and compare it to the school system where you attended high school.
2. Imagine that you are in Germany and have been asked to make a presentation on the school system in your hometown. How would you compare your school system to the German system? Mention advantages and disadvantages.

Vokabeln

Substantive

die **Anglistik** English studies
(language and literature)
die **Arbeit, -en** work; paper
der **Artikel, -** article
die **Biologie** biology
die **Chemie** chemistry
die **Diskette, -n** disk
das **Fernsehen** television (the
industry); der **Fernseher**
(Einführung) television set
der **Film, -e** film
die **Germanistik** German studies
(language and literature)
die **Geschichte, -n** story; history
das **Hauptfach, ⁻er** major (subject)
die **Informatik** computer science
die **Klausur, -en** test; **eine
Klausur schreiben** to take a test
der **Krimi, -s** mystery (novel or
film)

die **Kunstgeschichte** art history
die **Liebe** love;
der **Liebesroman** romance
(novel)
die **Literatur** literature
die **Mathematik** mathematics; die
Mathe math
das **Nebenfach, ⁻er** minor (subject)
die **Notiz, -en** note
die **Philosophie, -n** philosophy
die **Physik** physics
die **Psychologie** psychology
das **Referat, -e** report
der **Roman, -e** novel
das **Seminar, -e** seminar
die **Seminararbeit, -en** seminar
paper
das **Video, -s** video
die **Vorlesung, -en** lecture

Verben

Separable-prefix verbs are indicated with a raised dot: **durch·arbeiten.** (See
Grammatik und Übungen, section 9, in this chapter.)

aus·leihen to rent (e.g., video); to
check out (e.g., book from library)
bringen to bring
durch·arbeiten to work through;
to study
dürfen (darf) to be permitted to, to
be allowed to; may
fern·sehen (sieht fern) to watch
TV
können (kann) to be able to; can

leihen to lend; to borrow
lernen to learn; to study
lesen (liest) to read
mit·bringen to bring along
müssen (muss) to have to; must
sehen (sieht) to see
sollen (soll) to be supposed to
spazieren gehen to go for a walk
vor·bereiten to prepare
wollen (will) to want to, intend to

Andere Wörter

klar clear; of course, naturally
modern modern
nachher afterwards

nicht mehr no longer, not anymore
seit since (temporal)

Besondere Ausdrücke

Deutsch machen to do/study German (as homework); to study
(subject at the university)
(es) tut mir Leid I'm sorry
ich bin (nicht) gut vorbereitet I am
(not) well prepared

ich kann leider nicht unfortunately,
I can't
**kannst du mir [deine Notizen]
leihen?** can you lend me [your
notes]?
seit wann since when, (for) how long

Go to the
Deutsch heute Web Site at
www.hmco.com/college

N.C. und BAföG

More than 1.9 million students are enrolled in Germany's institutions of higher learning. In the 1960s only 8% of young people pursued academic studies, today one-third does. One of the reasons for this rapid growth is the availability of student aid. In 1971 a law **(Bundesausbildungsförderungsgesetz** or **BAföG)** was passed to give everyone an equal chance to study at the university. Today approximately 50% of students are subsidized through this program which provides half of the aid as a grant and half as a no-interest loan. The basic award is around DM 570 per month. The amount of aid is dependent on the parents' income and other factors. There is no tuition at public universities, so the financial aid is for basic expenses. Students who receive **BAföG** are required to show that they are making satisfactory progress in their studies. The number of semesters that students are eligible for the aid is determined by the program **(Studiengang)** in which they are enrolled, but generally falls between eight and ten semesters. To pay expenses, approximately 59% of students work part-time **(jobben)** either during the semester or during vacation **(Semesterferien).**

This rapid expansion of higher education has led to problems of overcrowding in the universities. University officials are concerned that rooms are used to

Diese Medizinstudenten haben einen Studienplatz bekommen. (Hannover)

180% of their capacity. Students complain about inadequate accessibility of teachers and research materials. Occasionally students engage in strike action to protest what they perceive as the underfunding and overcrowding of universities. In some subject areas, including medicine, law, and psychology, a system called **Numerus clausus (N.C.)** is used to limit the number of students. The subject areas involved may vary from year to year, depending on the enrollment capacity **(Studienplätze).** Places in **N.C.** programs are distributed by a central office mainly on the basis of high school grades **(Noten)** received during the

DURCHSCHNITTLICHE STUDIENDAUER (IN JAHREN)

MEDIZIN	6,5
CHEMIE	6,4
INGENIEURWISSENSCHAFTEN	6,4
LEHRAMT	7,1
GEISTESWISSENSCHAFTEN	6,6
BETRIEBSWIRTSCHAFT	5,9
JURA	6,2

last years of the **Gymnasium** and grades on the final comprehensive examination **(das Abitur).** Students who receive a place at a university which for some reason they do not want to attend, often attempt to trade places with another student. There can be a waiting period of up to five years for admission in some disciplines. The **Regelstudienzeit,** in effect in some states, requires that the students finish their studies within a required number of semesters, on the average 9–10 semesters. Partly because of funding problems and overcrowding, there is now discussion of introducing tuition **(Studiengebühren)** at German universities.

Diskussion

1. What is your opinion of student strikes? For what reasons could you justify a strike?
2. Have a debate on the following subject:

Resolved: Germany should charge tuition for higher education.

Ich studiere an der Uni Mainz
univer sität⊗ mainz
Medizin

STUDIEREN IN DEUTSCHLAND

Vorbereitung auf das Lesen

■ *Vor dem Lesen*

In this reading you will learn some basic information about the German university system and how students live in Germany. Before reading the text answer the following questions about your studies and your college or university.

1. Is your college or university a public or a private institution? What are the entrance requirements?
2. How expensive is your school? How do students pay for their education? Parents, work, scholarship, loan?
3. How is the academic year organized? What do students do on vacation?
4. How many courses are most students taking? How many subject areas are represented by the courses?
5. How long does it take to complete a bachelor's degree?

■ *Beim Lesen*

Take notes on the following topics as you read, and compare a German university to your institution.

	meine Uni	in Deutschland
1. Studienplätze		
2. Studentenjobs		
3. Semesterferien		
4. Examen		

MÖCHTEN SIE IN DEUTSCHLAND STUDIEREN?
INFORMATIONEN FÜR AMERIKANISCHE STUDENTEN

1. Wer kann studieren?

over
of those

in spite of that / space for students / *(Latin)* restricted admissions / that / **vom = von dem:** from the

language test

An deutschen Universitäten studieren heute über° 1,9 Millionen Studenten. Davon° sind 137 000 Ausländer. Es gibt zu wenige Universitäten und die meisten Kurse sind deshalb überfüllt. Deutsche können nur mit dem Abitur studieren, trotzdem° gibt es mehr Studenten als Studienplätze°. Daher haben
5 viele Fächer den N.C., den Numerus clausus°. Junge Leute wissen also, dass° es schwer ist, einen Studienplatz zu finden. Nur mit sehr guten Noten vom° Gymnasium bekommen sie einen Studienplatz. Bevor Amerikaner in Deutschland studieren können, müssen sie in Amerika schon an einer Universität oder einem College Studenten sein. Sie müssen für die deutsche
10 Universität auch eine Sprachprüfung° machen.

2. Wie viel Geld braucht man?

Die Universitäten in Deutschland sind staatlich. Steuern° finanzieren das
Studium. Deshalb gibt es keine Studiengebühren°, aber die Studenten
brauchen Geld für Essen und Wohnen. Leider gibt es nur wenige Studenten-
heime und Studenten müssen oft Zimmer in der Stadt suchen, und die sind
15 oft teuer. Viele Studenten brauchen deshalb Geld vom Staat. Dieses Geld
heißt BAföG°. Nur so kann jeder studieren. Die Hälfte° des Geldes müssen
die Studenten dem Staat später zurückzahlen. Manche Studenten bekommen aber kein BAföG (z.B. wenn ihre Eltern zu viel verdienen) und brauchen
deshalb Jobs. An deutschen Universitäten gibt es aber nicht viele Studenten-
20 jobs und sie müssen andere Jobs finden. Diese Studenten jobben oft auch
im° Semester. Sie studieren dann länger als BAföG-Rezipienten, im Durch-
schnitt° vierzehn Semester. BAföG-Rezipienten studieren dagegen im Durchschnitt nur elf Semester. Zehn Prozent der ausländischen° Studenten
bekommen Stipendien.

taxes
tuition

BAföG: *see p. 132* / half

im = in dem: *here* during the
im Durchschnitt: on the
average / foreign

3. Wann studiert man?

25 Es gibt zwei Semester im Jahr, das Wintersemester (Mitte Oktober oder An-
fang° November bis Mitte oder Ende Februar) und das Sommersemester
(Mitte April oder Anfang Mai bis Mitte oder Ende Juli). Die Semesterferien
sind lang, aber sie sind für die meisten Studenten keine freie Zeit. Viele Studenten müssen in den Ferien jobben oder ein Praktikum° machen. Oft lesen
30 sie in der Bibliothek, schreiben dort ihre Seminararbeiten oder bereiten sich°
auf das nächste Semester vor, denn sie ist in den Semesterferien nicht so
überfüllt.

beginning

internship
themselves

4. Was ist anders?

Studenten studieren ein oder zwei Fächer. Ihre Kurse sind alle in diesen
Fächern. Nehmen° wir zum Beispiel Klaus Brendel aus Aachen. Er studiert
35 Physik und Informatik und möchte Ingenieur werden. Er muss keine Kurse
in Englisch, Geschichte und Biologie machen, denn das hat° er in der Schule
gemacht. In Deutschland führen° Professoren keine Anwesenheitslisten°,
und nur wenige Kurse haben jedes Semester Prüfungen. Dafür° gibt es nach
vier Semestern eine Zwischenprüfung° und dann das große Examen am
40 Ende.

nehmen wir: let's take

hat gemacht: studied / keep /
attendance lists / in place of
that / qualifying exam

Brauchbares

1. l. 3, **Abitur:** In Austria and Switzerland the **Matura** is the equivalent of the
   Abitur.
2. l. 5, **Numerus clausus:** A central computer administers all university admissions—primarily based on grades—for all universities. Leftover slots are assigned by lottery.
3. Note that in dependent clauses—here those beginning with **dass** (l. 5),
   bevor (l. 7), and **wenn** (l. 18)—the finite verb is at the end of the clause, e.g.,
   dass es schwer ist. (See *Kapitel 5,* section 3).
4. l. 22, **vierzehn Semester:** Note that German students measure their progress
   at the university in semesters instead of in years.
5. l. 34, **Nehmen wir:** *let's take.* English imperatives beginning with *let's* can be
   expressed in German with the **wir**-form of the present tense. The pronoun
   wir follows the verb as in **gehen wir:** *let's go.*

Nach dem Lesen

1. Fragen zu dem Lesestück

1. Wie viele Studenten gibt es in Deutschland?
2. Wer kann in Deutschland studieren?
3. Warum haben viele Fächer den Numerus clausus?
4. Was müssen Amerikaner machen, bevor sie in Deutschland studieren dürfen?
5. Wie viel kostet° das Studium in Deutschland?
6. Warum müssen Studenten oft Zimmer in der Stadt suchen?
7. Was ist BAföG?
8. Was machen viele deutsche Studenten in den Ferien?
9. Was studiert Klaus Brendel? Welche Kurse macht er nicht?
10. Wann gibt es Prüfungen an deutschen Universitäten?

2. Was sagt eine Studentin/ein Student aus Deutschland?   How would a German respond to the following statements by an American student? Based on the information in the reading write a logical reply.

1. AMERIKANERIN/AMERIKANER: Morgen haben wir schon wieder eine Prüfung in Mathe!
   DEUTSCHE/DEUTSCHER: _____
2. AMERIKANERIN/AMERIKANER: Die Studiengebühren sind wirklich zu hoch° hier.
   DEUTSCHE/DEUTSCHER: _____
3. AMERIKANERIN/AMERIKANER: Ich wohne sehr gern im Studentenheim.
   DEUTSCHE/DEUTSCHER: _____
4. AMERIKANERIN/AMERIKANER: Ich jobbe 10 Stunden die Woche.
   DEUTSCHE/DEUTSCHER: _____
5. AMERIKANERIN/AMERIKANER: Hoffentlich bin ich in vier Jahren mit dem Studium fertig°.
   DEUTSCHE/DEUTSCHER: _____

3. Was ist das?   Match the descriptions on the right with the terms on the left.

1. BAföG
2. Numerus clausus
3. jobben
4. Studentenheim
5. Abitur

a. die Prüfung und das Diplom am Ende vom Gymnasium
b. Geld für Studenten vom Staat
c. Studentenwohnungen° an der Uni
d. Fächer mit zu wenig Studienplätzen
e. ein anderes Wort für „arbeiten"

student residences

4. Erzählen wir.   Make a list of useful vocabulary and be prepared to talk to a classmate about one of the following topics as it relates to the German university system.

Studenten und Geld ☐ zu viele Studenten ☐ zu viele Prüfungen

Ausländische Studenten

German universities are open to students from other countries. Germany reserves places in its universities for foreigners; even in the **Numerus clausus** disciplines there are spaces available. Recently, Germany has introduced undergraduate and graduate programs in which the language of instruction is English. These programs are attractive to international students and to German students who see their future in an international environment. The programs are offered in subjects ranging from computer science and environmental studies to German studies. Like a German student, a foreigner pays no tuition **(Studiengebühren),** but all students pay thirty to eighty marks in semester fees plus about seventy marks a month for health insurance. A foreign student is not generally allowed to apply for a work permit. To be admitted for study in Germany, an American must usually have had at least two years of college and must pass a language exam.

Go to the
Deutsch heute Web Site at
www.hmco.com/college

To study at a Swiss university, an American needs a bachelor's degree and a working knowledge of the language of instruction, which may be German, French, or Italian. To study in Austria, international students who do not come from the European Union must pay tuition each semester (4000 Schillings) as well as demonstrate proficiency in German and meet general admission standards.

An den deutschen Universitäten studieren auch ausländische Studenten. **(Universität Heidelberg)**

Diskussion

Discuss the advantages and disadvantages of studying abroad. If you choose to attend a German university, would you choose a program which is taught primarily in German or primarily in English? Why?

5. Zur Diskussion

1. Was finden Sie an den deutschen Universitäten gut?
2. Was finden Sie an Ihrer Universität gut?
3. Möchten Sie in Deutschland studieren? Warum (nicht)?

LAND UND LEUTE

Go to the
Deutsch heute Web Site at
www.hmco.com/college

Schule, Hochschule, Klasse, Student

Many words used in English to talk about university studies are not equivalent to the German words which appear to be cognates. In the German-speaking countries a greater distinction is made in words referring to education before college or university and post-secondary education.

- *school:* In German **(die) Schule** refers to an elementary or secondary school. When talking about postsecondary education German speakers use **(die) Universität** or **(die) Hochschule.** The equivalent of *What school do you go to?* is **An welcher Uni studierst du?**
- *high school:* A German equivalent of the U.S. or Canadian *high school* is **(die) Oberschule, (die) höhere Schule,** or **(das) Gymnasium.** A **Hochschule** is a post-secondary school such as a university.
- *student:* In German, **Studentin/Student** refers to someone at a post-secondary institution (i.e., at a **Universität** or **Hochschule**). The word **(die) Schülerin/(der) Schüler** is used for young people in elementary and secondary schools, much as the word *pupil* is used in English.
- *class:* The English word *class* refers to an instructional period or a group of students. The German word **(die) Klasse** refers only to a group of students (e.g., **meine Klasse** = *my class, my classmates*) or a specific grade (e.g., **die zweite Klasse** = *the second grade*). In a **Schule** the word for *class* meaning *instructional period* is **Stunde** (e.g., **die Deutschstunde** = *the German class*). At the university level in German-speaking countries there are several types of classes—**Vorlesung, Übung,** and **Seminar** (see *Land und Leute: Hochschulen,* p. 128). A very general word for a class is **Kurs.** To ask the question *How many students are in your German class?* a German might say: **Wie viele Kursteilnehmer gibt es in Ihrem Deutschkurs?**

Schüler und Schülerinnen in der ersten Klasse.
(München)

Diskussion

Many of the German words related to education look like the English word, but are used differently. Discuss what problems this causes for you learning the German language. You may also want to think about this question: Can you imagine what problems a student learning English would have with English words?

Erweiterung des Wortschatzes

1. Stating one's profession or nationality

Carsten ist Student.   Carsten is a student.
Barbara wird Ingenieurin.   Barbara is going to be an engineer.
Barbara ist Kanadierin.   Barbara is (a) Canadian.
Anton ist Deutscher.   Anton is (a) German.

Herr Becker ist **nicht (kein)** Ingenieur.   Mr. Becker is not an engineer.
Cordula ist **nicht (keine)** Österreicherin;   Cordula is not (an) Austrian;
  sie ist Deutsche.   she's (a) German.

Either **nicht** or **kein** may be used to negate a sentence about someone's profession, nationality, or membership in a group. Remember that no indefinite article (**ein**) is used in the positive statement (see *Kapitel 2*). For names of additional professions, refer to the Supplementary Word Sets in the Reference Section.

1. Neue Freunde.   Auf einem Flug von Toronto nach Frankfurt lernen sich drei junge Leute kennen. Erzählen Sie von ihrem Flug. Geben Sie die Sätze auf Deutsch wieder. (On a flight from Toronto to Frankfurt three young people get acquainted. Tell about their flight. Give the German equivalents of the sentences.)

1. Robert is a Canadian.
2. He is a student.
3. Annette is not a Canadian.
4. She is also not an American; she's a German.
5. She is going to be an engineer.
6. Her brother Christoph lives in Frankfurt; he's a Frankfurter.
7. He is a pharmacist.

2. Persönliche Informationen.   Schreiben Sie eine kurze Autobiographie. Geben Sie an: Name, Nationalität, Adresse und Telefonnummer, Hauptfach, Nebenfach. Was wollen Sie werden? (Write a short autobiography. Give: name, nationality, address and telephone number, college major, minor. What do you want to be?)

> Describing one's nationality and profession

2. Die Familie

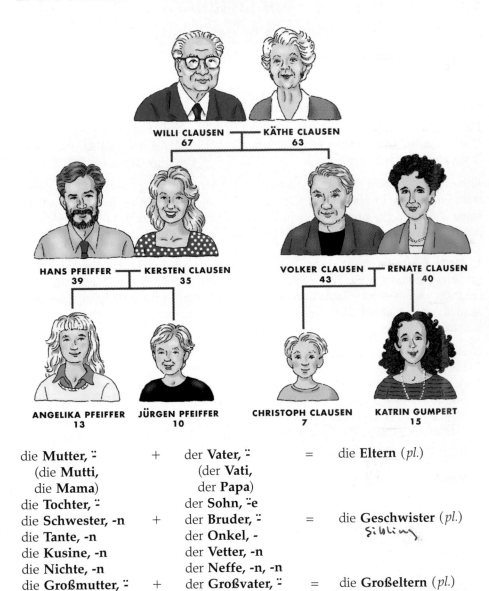

WILLI CLAUSEN — KÄTHE CLAUSEN
67   63

HANS PFEIFFER — KERSTEN CLAUSEN   VOLKER CLAUSEN — RENATE CLAUSEN
39   35   43   40

ANGELIKA PFEIFFER   JÜRGEN PFEIFFER   CHRISTOPH CLAUSEN   KATRIN GUMPERT
13   10   7   15

die **Mutter**, ⸚	+ der **Vater**, ⸚	= die **Eltern** (*pl.*)
(die **Mutti**,	(der **Vati**,	
die **Mama**)	der **Papa**)	
die **Tochter**, ⸚	der **Sohn**, ⸚e	
die **Schwester**, -n	+ der **Bruder**, ⸚	= die **Geschwister** (*pl.*)
		Sibling
die **Tante**, -n	der **Onkel**, -	
die **Kusine**, -n	der **Vetter**, -n	
die **Nichte**, -n	der **Neffe**, -n, -n	
die **Großmutter**, ⸚	+ der **Großvater**, ⸚	= die **Großeltern** (*pl.*)
(die **Oma**, -s)	(der **Opa**, -s)	

Stief-: die **Stiefmutter**; der **Stiefvater**

Refer to the Supplementary Word Sets in the Reference Section for names of additional family members.

3. Der Stammbaum. *(Family tree.)* Lesen Sie über Familie Clausen (Stammbaum oben). Beantworten Sie dann die Fragen. (Read about the Clausen family tree above. Then answer the questions.)

Willi und Käthe Clausen haben eine Tochter, Kersten, und einen Sohn, Volker. Kersten und ihr Mann, Hans Pfeiffer, haben zwei Kinder, Angelika und Jürgen.

Die Kinder haben eine Großmutter, Oma Clausen, und einen Großvater, Opa Clausen. Volker Clausen ist geschieden°. Renate ist seine zweite° Frau. Sie hat eine Tochter, Katrin Gumpert, von ihrem ersten° Mann. Volker ist also Katrins Stiefvater. Renate und Volker haben einen Sohn, Christoph. Angelika Pfeiffer ist seine Kusine, und Jürgen ist sein Vetter. Die Eltern von Angelika und Jürgen sind natürlich seine Tante Kersten und sein Onkel Hans.

divorced / second
first

1. Wie heißt Jürgen Pfeiffers Vetter?
2. Wer ist Angelika Pfeiffers Onkel?
3. Wie heißen die Großeltern von Angelika und Jürgen?
4. Wie heißt Volker Clausens Frau?
5. Wie heißt Volkers Stieftochter?
6. Wie heißt Katrins Halbbruder°?

half brother

⇨ **4. Frage-Ecke.** Ergänzen Sie die fehlenden Informationen. Fragen Sie Ihre Partnerin/Ihren Partner.(Supply the missing information. Ask your partner.)

S2: Wie heißt der Vater von Angelika?
S1: Er heißt Hans Pfeiffer.
S2: Wie alt ist Angelikas Vater?
S1: Er ist 39 Jahre alt.

S1:

	Vater	Mutter	Tante	Onkel	Großvater	Großmutter
Angelika	Hans Pfeiffer 39		Renate Clausen 40		Willie Clausen 67	Käthe Clausen 63
Christoph		Renate Clausen 40		Hans Pfeiffer 39		
ich						
Partnerin/ Partner						

S2:

	Vater	Mutter	Tante	Onkel	Großvater	Großmutter
Angelika		Kersten Clausen 35		Volker Clausen 43		
Christoph	Volker Clausen 43		Kersten Clausen 35		Willie Clausen 67	Käthe Clausen 63
ich						
Partnerin/ Partner						

Vokabeln

Substantive

das **Abitur** diploma from college-track high school [**Gymnasium**]

der **Ausländer, -/**die **Ausländerin, -nen** foreigner

das **Beispiel, -e** example; **zum Beispiel** (*abbrev.* **z.B.**) for example (*abbrev.* e.g.)

die **Eltern** (*pl.*) parents

das **Ende, -n** end, conclusion; **am Ende** at (in) the end

das **Examen, -** comprehensive exam, finals; **Examen machen** to graduate from the university

das **Fach, ̈er** (academic) subject

die **Familie, -n** family

die **Ferien** (*pl.*) vacation; **in den Ferien** on vacation; die **Semesterferien** semester break

das **Gymnasium,** *pl.* **Gymnasien** college-track high school

die **Information, -en** information

der **Ingenieur, -e/**die **Ingenieurin, -nen** engineer

der **Job, -s** job

die **Klasse, -n** class

der **Kurs, -e** course

die **Note, -n** grade; note

das **Picknick, -s** picnic; **Picknick machen** to have a picnic

der **Platz, ̈e** place; seat; space

das **Prozent** percent

die **Prüfung, -en** test, examination

die **Schule, -n** school

das **Semester, -** semester

der **Staat, -en** state, country

das **Stipendium,** *pl.* **Stipendien** scholarship

das **Studentenheim, -e** dormitory

das **Studium** study; studies

die **Zeit, -en** time

For additional family members, see p. 140.

Verben

jobben (*colloq.*) to have a temporary job (e.g., a summer job)

kosten to cost

verdienen to earn

werden (wird) to become

wissen (weiß) to know (a fact)

zahlen to pay

zurück·zahlen to pay back

Andere Wörter

alle all

amerikanisch American

an at; to

daher therefore, for that reason

deshalb therefore, for that reason

dies- (-er, -es, -e) this, these

fertig finished; ready

frei free

hoch high

jed- (-er, -es, -e) each, every; **jeder** everyone

jung young

kanadisch Canadian

lang long; **länger** longer

manch- (-er, -es, -e) many a (*sg.*); some (*pl.*)

meist- most; **die meisten (Leute)** most of (the people)

privat private

schwer hard, difficult; heavy

staatlich public, government owned

teuer expensive

wenig little; **ein wenig** a little; **wenige** few

wenn (*conj.*) if; when, whenever

zurück back, in return

zu viel too much

Ein Schachspiel im Park.

Der erste Schultag.

GRAMMATIK UND ÜBUNGEN

1. Present tense° of *werden*

das Präsens

werden: to become	
ich werde	wir werden
du **wirst**	ihr werdet
er/es/sie **wird**	sie werden
Sie werden	
du-*imperative:* werde	

Werden is irregular in the **du-** and **er/es/sie-**forms in the present tense.

1. Sie werden anders.   Einige Leute werden anders. Sagen Sie wie. (Some people are changing. Say how.)

 Erik / leider / müde   *Erik wird leider müde.*

1. ich / auch / müde
2. Petra / besser / in Mathe
3. die Kinder / groß
4. du / leider / faul

5. wir / tolerant
6. ihr / sehr / froh
7. Hans und Karin / besser / in Deutsch
8. und Sie? / besser / in Deutsch

2. Verbs with stem-vowel change *e* > *ie*

sehen: to see	
ich sehe	wir sehen
du **siehst**	ihr seht
er/es/sie **sieht**	sie sehen
Sie sehen	
du-imperative: **sieh**	

lesen: to read	
ich lese	wir lesen
du **liest**	ihr lest
er/es/sie **liest**	sie lesen
Sie lesen	
du-imperative: **lies**	

Several verbs with the stem-vowel **e** change the **e** to **ie** in the **du-** and **er/es/sie-**forms of the present tense and in the **du-**imperative. Since the stem of **lesen** ends in a sibilant, the **du-**form ending contracts from **-st** to **-t** (see *Kapitel 1, Grammatik und Übungen,* section 7).

Talking about personal interests

2. Lesen und sehen. Was für Filme sehen die Leute gern? Was lesen sie gern? (What kind of films do the following people like to see? What do they like to read?)

➤➤ Erik / ernste Filme   *Erik sieht gern ernste Filme.*

1. Ingrid / lustige Filme
2. Gabi und Jürgen / amerikanische Filme
3. du / Schwarzweißfilme / ?
4. Christine / Bücher / über Sport
5. Detlev / Bücher / über Musik
6. du / Bücher / über Politik / ?
7. ihr / Bücher / über Geschichte / ?

3. Filme und Bücher. Interviewen Sie drei Studentinnen/Studenten in Ihrem Deutschkurs. Was für Filme sehen sie gern? Was für Bücher lesen sie gern? Berichten Sie darüber. Benutzen Sie auch Wörter aus dem Anhang: Supplementary Word Sets, „Film and Literature". (Interview three students in your German class. What kind of films do they like to see? What kind of books do they like to read? Report on your findings. Also use words from the reference section.)

S1: Was für Filme siehst du gern?
S2: [Tom]: Ich sehe gern [alte Filme, Krimis, Horrorfilme, Dokumentarfilme, Science-Fiction-Filme].
S1: Was für Bücher liest du gern?
S3: [Linda]: Ich lese gern [Biographien, Liebesromane, Horrorgeschichten, historische Romane, Krimis, Science-Fiction, Bücher über Politik/Musik, moderne Literatur].
S1: [Tom] sieht gern [alte Filme]. [Linda] liest gern [Biographien].

3. Present tense of *wissen*

wissen: to know	
ich **weiß**	wir wissen
du **weißt**	ihr wisst
er/es/sie **weiß**	sie wissen
Sie wissen	

Wissen is irregular in the singular forms of the present tense. Note that the **du-**form ending contracts from **-st** to **-t**.

4. Die Universität Heidelberg.   David ist Amerikaner und möchte etwas über die Universität Heidelberg wissen. Er spricht mit Barbara und Karin. Karin studiert da. Ergänzen Sie ihren Dialog mit den passenden Formen von **wissen.** (David is an American and would like to know something about Heidelberg University. He is speaking with Barbara and Karin. Karin studies there. Complete their dialogue with the appropriate forms of **wissen.**)

DAVID: Du Barbara. Was _____ du über die Universität Heidelberg?

BARBARA: Nicht viel. Aber ich glaube, Karin _____ viel darüber.

KARIN: Na, alle Leute _____, dass° Heidelberg die älteste° Universität Deutsch-   that / oldest
lands ist.

BARBARA: So? Das _____ wir alle? _____ du denn, wie alt?

KARIN: Natürlich. Im Jahre 1986 war sie 600 Jahre alt.

DAVID: Das ist ja wirklich alt.

4. *Wissen* and *kennen*

Kennst du Martin?	Do you *know* Martin?
Weißt du, wo er wohnt?	Do you *know* where he lives?
Nein, aber ich **weiß** seine Telefonnummer.	No, but I *know* his telephone number.
Sie **kennt** Professor Schmidt gut.	She *knows* Professor Schmidt well.

There are two German equivalents for the English *to know:* **wissen** and **kennen. Wissen** means *to know something as a fact.* **Kennen** means *to be acquainted with a person, place, or thing.*

Kennen was used as a verb in Middle English and is still used in Scottish. The noun *ken* means perception or understanding: "That is beyond my ken."

„Wer viel weiß, will noch mehr wissen."

BROCK HAUS
DIE ENZYKLOPÄDIE
IN 24 BÄNDEN

Brockhaus. Die Enzyklopädie.
Das Wissen der Welt – neuester Stand.

5. Die Stadt Heidelberg. Jetzt möchte David etwas über die Stadt Heidelberg wissen. Ergänzen Sie ihren Dialog mit den passenden Formen von **wissen** oder **kennen**. (Now David would like to know something about the town of Heidelberg. Complete their dialogue with the appropriate forms of **wissen** or **kennen**.)

DAVID: _____ ihr Heidelberg gut?

BARBARA: Ja, wir _____ die Stadt ganz gut.

DAVID: Dann _____ du, wo die Bibliothek ist.

KARIN: Natürlich _____ wir das. Du, David, ich _____ein Buch über Heidelberg.

DAVID: _____ du, wo man das Buch kaufen kann?

KARIN: Ja, in jeder Buchhandlung.

DAVID: _____ du den Autor?

KARIN: Ja, den _____ wir alle. Das ist unser Professor.

5. *Der-*words

Diese Klausur ist schwer.	*This* test is hard.
Jede Klausur ist schwer.	*Every* test is hard.
Welche Klausur hast du?	*Which* test do you have?
Manche Klausuren sind nicht schwer.	*Some* tests are not hard.
Solche Klausuren sind nicht interessant.	*Those kinds* of tests aren't interesting.

In the singular, **so ein** is usually used instead of **solcher: So eine Uhr ist sehr teuer.** *That kind of/such a watch/clock is very expensive.*

	Masculine *der*	Neuter *das*	Feminine *die*	Plural *die*
Nominative	dies**er**	dies**es**	dies**e**	dies**e**
Accusative	dies**en**	dies**es**	dies**e**	dies**e**

The words **dieser, jeder, welcher?, mancher,** and **solcher** are called **der**-words because they follow the same pattern in the nominative and accusative cases as the definite articles. **Jeder** is used in the singular only. **Welcher?** is an interrogative adjective, used at the beginning of a question. **Solcher** and **mancher** are used almost exclusively in the plural.

Der Stuhl **(da)** ist neu.   *That* chair is new.

The equivalent of *that (those)* is expressed by the definite article **(der, das, die)**. **Da** is often added for clarity.

6. Wie findest du diese Stadt? Beate ist Österreicherin und ihr Freund Mark ist Kanadier. Beate zeigt Mark einige Bilder. Geben Sie die richtige Form von den Wörtern in Klammern. (Beate is an Austrian and her friend Mark a Canadian. Beate is showing Mark some pictures. Give the correct form of the words in parentheses.)

BEATE: Kennst du _____ Stadt? (dieser)

MARK: Nein. Ich kenne viele Städte in Österreich, aber _____ nicht. (dieser)

BEATE: _____ Städte kennst du schon? (welcher)

MARK: Salzburg, zum Beispiel.

BEATE: Siehst du _____ Haus? (dieser) Da wohne ich.

MARK: Sind im Fenster immer _____ Blumen? (solcher)

BEATE: Ja, schön, nicht?

MARK: Hat _____ Haus _____ Garten? (jeder, so ein)

BEATE: Nein, das ist für viele Leute zu viel Arbeit. Aber mein Vater arbeitet gern im Garten.

6. Modal auxiliaries°

das Modalverb

Ich **muss** jetzt arbeiten.	I *have to* work now.
Erika **kann** es machen.	Erika *can* do it.
Ich **darf** nichts sagen.	I *am* not *allowed* to say anything.

Both English and German have a group of verbs called *modal auxiliaries*. Modal auxiliary verbs **(muss, kann, darf)** indicate an attitude about an action; they do not express the action itself. In German, the verb that expresses the action is in the infinitive form **(arbeiten, machen, sagen)** and is in last position.

Modals are irregular in the present-tense singular. They have no endings in the **ich-** and **er/es/sie-**forms, and five of the six modals show stem-vowel change, e.g., **können > kann.**

können: can, to be able to, to know how to do	
ich **kann** es erklären	wir **können** es erklären
du **kannst** es erklären	ihr **könnt** es erklären
er/es/sie **kann** es erklären	sie **können** es erklären
Sie **können** es erklären	

7. Was können diese Leute? Was können diese Leute tun? Erzählen Sie. (What can these people do? Tell [about it].)

≫ Mark schwimmt gut.   *Mark kann gut schwimmen.*

1. Karla spielt gut Tennis.
2. Wir machen Spaghetti.
3. Ich erkläre die Geschichte.
4. Du tanzt gut.
5. Herr Professor, Sie schreiben schön.
6. Karin und Peter tanzen wunderbar.
7. Ihr schwimmt gut.

8. Was kannst du? Interviewen Sie einige Studentinnen/Studenten in Ihrem Deutschkurs. Was können sie machen oder nicht machen? (Interview several students in your German class. What can they do or not do?)

Inquiring about abilities

S1: Kannst du Gitarre spielen?

S2: Ja, ich kann Gitarre spielen./Nein, ich kann nicht Gitarre spielen.

1. gut schwimmen
2. Golf spielen
3. gut tanzen
4. gut Geschichten erzählen
5. Schach spielen
6. im Sommer viel Geld verdienen

wollen: to want, wish; to intend to	
ich **will** arbeiten	wir **wollen** arbeiten
du **willst** arbeiten	ihr **wollt** arbeiten
er/es/sie **will** arbeiten	sie **wollen** arbeiten
Sie **wollen** arbeiten	

9. Was wollen diese Leute? Was wollen diese Leute tun oder nicht tun? (What do these people intend to do or not do?)

➤➤ Erich geht einkaufen. *Erich will einkaufen gehen.*

1. Beatrice macht Musik.
2. Du gehst heute Abend tanzen, nicht?
3. Erich trinkt Kaffee.
4. Ich bezahle das Essen.
5. Die Kinder essen Kuchen.
6. Ihr macht Mathe.
7. Frau Kaiser studiert Geschichte.

Making plans

10. Willst du? Sie und Ihre Partnerin/Ihr Partner machen für heute Abend oder morgen Pläne. Was wollen Sie machen? Was sagt Ihre Partnerin/Ihr Partner? (You and your partner are making plans for this evening. What do you want to do? What does your partner say?)

S1:

Willst du	**morgen**	**ins Kino** gehen?	Ja,	**gern.**
	heute Abend	joggen		vielleicht.
	am Samstag	tanzen		Nein, ich kann nicht.

S2:

Schüttelkasten

Deutsch machen   fernsehen   **Musik hören**

spazieren gehen

zusammen für die Klausur arbeiten

Rollerblading gehen   **einkaufen gehen**   **im Internet surfen**

sollen: to be supposed to	
ich **soll** morgen gehen	wir **sollen** morgen gehen
du **sollst** morgen gehen	ihr **sollt** morgen gehen
er/es/sie **soll** morgen gehen	sie **sollen** morgen gehen
Sie **sollen** morgen gehen	

11. Wir planen eine Party. Sie und ihre Freunde planen eine Party. Was soll jede Person mitbringen, kaufen oder machen? (You and your friends are planning a party. What should everyone bring, buy, or do?)

➤➤ Gabi und Moritz: Musik mitbringen   *Gabi und Moritz sollen Musik mitbringen.*

1. wir: Käse kaufen
2. du: Salat machen
3. ich: Brot kaufen
4. Corinna: Wein mitbringen
5. ihr: Bier kaufen

müssen: must, to have to	
ich **muss** jetzt arbeiten	wir **müssen** jetzt arbeiten
du **musst** jetzt arbeiten	ihr **müsst** jetzt arbeiten
er/es/sie **muss** jetzt arbeiten	sie **müssen** jetzt arbeiten
Sie **müssen** jetzt arbeiten	

12. Was müssen diese Leute tun?   Sagen Sie, was diese Leute tun müssen. Ergänzen Sie die Dialoge mit der richtigen Form von **müssen**. (Say what these people have to do. Complete the dialogues with the correct form of **müssen**.)

1. BEATRIX: Was _____ du morgen machen?

   LIANE: Ich _____ eine Klausur schreiben.

   BEATRIX: Dann _____ du jetzt lernen, nicht?

2. NADJA: _____ ihr heute Abend wieder in die Bibliothek?

   STEFFI UND NILS: Ja, wir _____ noch zwei Kapitel durcharbeiten.

3. MARKUS: Was _____ Karin, Carsten und Beate am Wochenende machen?

   ROBERT: Karin _____ ein Buch über Psychologie lesen. Und Carsten und Beate _____ Referate vorbereiten.

> Discussing duties and requirements

Deutsch	Engl.	Mathe	Physik	Chemie	Kunst
Datum/Note	Datum/Note	Datum/Note	Datum/Note	Datum/Note	Datum/Note

13. Was musst du machen?   Was muss Ihre Partnerin/Ihr Partner heute, morgen oder am Wochenende machen? Fragen Sie sie/ihn. (What does your partner have to do today, tomorrow, or on the weekend? Ask her/him.)

S1:

Was musst du | **heute** machen?

morgen
am Wochenende

S2:

Heute muss ich | am Computer arbeiten.

Morgen
Am Wochenende

Schüttelkasten

ein Referat vorbereiten	arbeiten	einen Artikel schreiben
ein Buch für Geschichte lesen	in die Bibliothek gehen	
viele E-Mails schreiben		Deutsch machen

dürfen: may, to be permitted to	
ich **darf** es sagen	wir **dürfen** es sagen
du **darfst** es sagen	ihr **dürft** es sagen
er/es/sie **darf** es sagen	sie **dürfen** es sagen
Sie **dürfen** es sagen	

14. Viele Regeln. *(Lots of rules.)*   Dirk ist in einem neuen Studentenheim. Es gibt viele Regeln. Sehen Sie die Bilder an und beschreiben Sie die Regeln. Nehmen Sie ein logisches Modalverb. (Dirk is in a new dormitory. There are lots of rules. Look at the pictures and describe the rules. Use a logical modal verb.)

smoke

➤➤ nicht rauchen
➤➤ *Hier darf man nicht rauchen°.*

von 11:30 bis 13:00 Uhr

von 22 bis 6 Uhr

Trinkwasser

von ... bis ... essen   von ... bis ... nicht schwimmen   Wasser trinken

16-20 Uhr

heute Abend

Ruhe

von ... bis ... lernen   ... Musik hören/tanzen gehen   immer ruhig sein

7. *Mögen* and the *möchte*-forms

mögen: to like	
ich **mag** keine Tomaten	wir **mögen** Erik nicht
du **magst** keine Eier	ihr **mögt** Melanie nicht
er/es/sie **mag** kein Bier	sie **mögen** Schmidts nicht
Sie **mögen** keinen Kaffee	

Mögen Sie Frau Lenz?   Nein, ich **mag** sie nicht.

The modal **mögen** is often used to express a fondness or dislike for someone or something. With this meaning it usually does not take a dependent infinitive.

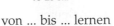 **15. Was für Musik magst du?**   Sagen Sie, was für Musik Sie mögen. Fragen Sie dann Ihre Partnerin/Ihren Partner. (Tell what kind of music you like. Then ask your partner.)

S1: Ich mag Hardrock. Was für Musik magst du?
S2: Ich mag Reggae.

SchüttelKasten

| Techno | Rap | **Rock** | klassische Musik | **Blues** | Jazz | **Country** |

ich **möchte** gehen	wir **möchten** gehen
du **möchtest** gehen	ihr **möchtet** gehen
er/es/sie **möchte** gehen	sie **möchten** gehen
Sie **möchten** gehen	

Möchte is a different form of the modal **mögen.** The meaning of **mögen** is *to like;* the meaning of **möchte** is *would like (to).*

16. Ja, das möchten wir. Was möchten Sie und Ihre Freundinnen/Freunde später machen? Erzählen Sie. (What would you and your friends like to do later? Tell about it.)

➤➤ Dirk: heute Abend ins Kino gehen *Dirk möchte heute Abend ins Kino gehen.*

1. wir: heute Nachmittag einkaufen gehen
2. du: mehr arbeiten
3. ihr: bestimmt hier bleiben
4. Gabi: im Café essen
5. Lotte und Erika: Musik hören
6. ich: ein interessantes Buch lesen
7. Rolf: am Wochenende wandern

17. Was möchtet ihr machen? Fragen Sie drei Studentinnen/Studenten, was sie tun möchten. (Ask three students what they would like to do.)

Inquiring about future plans

S1: Was möchtest du | **am Wochenende**
heute Abend
im Sommer machen?
S2: Ich möchte [einkaufen gehen].

SchüttelKasten

| fernsehen | einen Krimi lesen | **tanzen gehen** | **jogging gehen** |
| **im Internet surfen** | **wandern** | Rollerblading gehen | Fitnesstraining machen |

8. Omission of the dependent infinitive with modals

Ich **kann** das nicht.   = Ich **kann** das nicht **machen.**
Ich **muss** in die Bibliothek.   = Ich **muss** in die Bibliothek **gehen.**
Das **darfst** du nicht.   = Das **darfst** du nicht **tun.**

Modals may occur without a dependent infinitive if a verb of motion (e.g., **gehen**) or the idea of *to do* (**machen, tun**) is clearly understood from the context.

Ich **kann** Deutsch.   I can speak German. (I know German.)

Können is used to say that someone knows how to speak a language.

18. In die Bibliothek? Nein.   Christin und Mark studieren an der Universität Hamburg. Christin ist Deutsche, Mark ist Amerikaner. Sie trinken im Café Kaffee. Geben Sie ihr Gespräch auf Englisch wieder. (Christin and Mark go to the University of Hamburg. Christin is German and Mark American. They're drinking coffee in a café. Give the English equivalent of their conversation in German.)

1. CHRISTIN: Willst du jetzt nach Hause?
2. MARK: Nein, ich muss noch in die Bibliothek.
3. CHRISTIN: Was willst du da?
4. MARK: Ich muss Shakespeare lesen. Musst du auch in die Uni?
5. CHRISTIN: Nein, was soll ich denn da? Heute ist Sonntag!
6. MARK: Sag mal, kannst du gut Englisch?
7. CHRISTIN: Ja, ich kann aber auch Französisch.
8. MARK: Darf hier jeder in die Bibliothek?
9. CHRISTIN: Ja, wer° will, der° darf.

whoever / (that person)

19. Wie sagt man das?

1. Can you work this afternoon?
   No, I have to go home.
2. May I pay (for) the coffee?
   No, you may not. [Add **das.**] Du darfst das nicht.
3. Dirk wants to go to the movies tonight.
   What would he like to see? Was möchte er sehen?
4. Barbara intends to study German.
   Good. She already knows German well.
5. It's supposed to rain tomorrow.
   Really? That can't be. Vierdich.

▷ **20. Frage-Ecke.**   Ergänzen Sie die fehlenden Informationen. Fragen Sie Ihre Partnerin/Ihren Partner. (Supply the missing information. Ask your partner.)

S2: Was müssen Kai und Sabine machen?
S1: Sie müssen Mathe machen.

S1:

	müssen	dürfen	wollen	sollen	können
Martina		Kaffee trinken	tanzen gehen	einen Job suchen	
Kai und Sabine	Mathe machen			Blumen mitbringen	
Dominik		keine Eier essen	viel Geld verdienen		
Stefans Schwester	in die Bibliothek		fernsehen		gut Tennis spielen
ich					
Partnerin/ Partner					

S2:

	müssen	dürfen	wollen	sollen	können
Martina	jobben				gut tanzen
Kai und Sabine		Kuchen essen	ins Kino gehen		das Essen bezahlen
Dominik	in die Vorlesung gehen			sein Referat vorbereiten	gut Englisch
Stefans Schwester		Milch trinken		lesen	
ich					
Partnerin/ Partner					

9. Separable-prefix verbs°

das trennbare Verb

to get up	I get up early
to throw away	Don't throw away all those papers!

English has a large number of two-word verbs, such as *to get up, to throw away.* These two-word verbs consist of a verb, such as *get*, and a particle, such as *up.*

einkaufen	Monika **kauft** morgens **ein.**
mitbringen	**Bringen** Sie bitte Blumen **mit!**

German has a large number of "separable-prefix verbs" that function like certain English two-word verbs. Examples are **durcharbeiten, einkaufen, fernsehen, mitbringen, vorbereiten,** and **zurückzahlen.** In present-tense statements and questions, and in imperative forms, the separable prefix (**durch-, ein-, fern-, mit-, vor-, zurück-**) is in the last position.

Monika möchte Blumen **mit**bringen.

In the infinitive form, the prefix is attached to the base form of the verb.

Basic verb	Erik **sieht** gern lustige Filme. Erik likes to see amusing films.
Separable-prefix verb	Erik **sieht** gern **fern.** Erik likes to watch TV.

The meaning of a separable-prefix verb, such as **fernsehen,** is often different from the sum of the meanings of its parts: **sehen** *(see),* **fern** *(far off).*

Ute will nicht **fern'**sehen.   Elfi sieht nicht **fern'.**

In spoken German, the stress falls on the prefix of separable-prefix verbs. In vocabulary lists in this textbook, separable-prefixes are indicated by a raised dot between the prefix and the verb: **durch·arbeiten, fern·sehen, ein·kaufen, mit·bringen, vor·bereiten, zurück·zahlen.**

21. Michaels Tagesplan. Michael erzählt Uwe von seinen Plänen für heute. (Michael is telling Uwe about his plans for today.)

➤➤ heute Nachmittag einkaufen *Ich kaufe heute Nachmittag ein.*

> 1. Großmutter Blumen mitbringen
> 2. meine Notizen durcharbeiten
> 3. mein Referat vorbereiten
> 4. heute Nachmittag spazieren gehen
> 5. heute Abend fernsehen

22. Fernsehprogramme. Sehen Sie die Fernsehprogramme von ZDF und SAT 1 auf Seite 155 an. Beantworten Sie die Fragen. (Look at the listings for the TV channels ZDF and SAT 1 on page 155. Answer the questions.)

tip / **Schlagen nach:** refer to / see

(TV) channels / (TV) programs

news programs

Hinweis°: Schlagen° Sie nach: Siehe° Reference Section, Vocabulary for Authentic Text Activities, *Kapitel 5,* Fernsehprogramm.

1. In den Programmen° gibt es auch amerikanische Sendungen°. Welche sind das?
2. Es gibt auch viele englische Wörter. Welche sind das?
3. Welches Programm hat mehr Sendungen für Kinder?
4. In Deutschland heißen die Nachrichtensendungen° „Tagesschau" und „heute". Wie viele Nachrichtensendungen gibt es in den zwei Programmen? Wann kommen sie?
5. Wo und wann gibt es Sportsendungen?
6. Wo und wann kann man eine Fitness-Sendung ansehen?

23. Fernsehen. Suchen Sie für jede Kategorie von Fernsehsendungen eine Sendung auf Seite 155 oder eine Sendung im amerikanischen Fernsehen. Geben Sie die Zeit an. (For every category of TV programs find a program on page 155 or a program from American TV. Give the time.)

Hinweis: Sehen Sie nach: „TV programs" in Supplementary Word Sets, Reference Section.

Seifenoper	Nachrichten
Fernsehserie	Spielfilm
Musiksendung	Sportsendung

24. Deine Lieblingssendung. Interviewen Sie drei Studentinnen/Studenten in Ihrem Deutschkurs. Wie oft sehen sie fern? Welche Sendungen mögen sie? Welche mögen sie nicht? Warum? Was ist ihre Lieblingssendung? (Interview three students in your German class. How often do they watch TV? Which programs do they like? Which don't they like? Why? What is their favorite program?)

S1:
Wie oft siehst du fern?
Welche Sendungen magst du?
Was ist deine Lieblingssendung?

S2:
Einmal [zweimal, dreimal] die Woche.
Ich sehe gern [...]. Es ist lustig.
Meine Lieblingssendung ist [...].

Samstag, 4. März

ZDF

8.00 Nachbarn in Europa.
9.00 heute.
9.03 Morgenmagazin
Sport extra.
9.45 fit forever.
10.00 heute.
10.03 Globus. Natur und
Umwelt.
10.30 Info Arbeit und Beruf.
11.30 Kinderprogramm.
11.30 Anne auf Green Gables.
Kinderfilm (ab 4).
11.55 Geschichten von der Straße
(ab 4).
12.15 Benjamin Blümchen.
Zeichentrickserie (ab 4).
12.40 Neue Abenteuer mit Black
Beauty (ab 6).
12.55 Presseschau.
13.00 heute.
13.05 Mittagsmagazin.
13.25 Die fliegenden Ärzte.
14.02 Gesundheits-Tips.
14.07 Fußball.
15.40 X-Base .
Computer Future Club.
16.10 Diese Woche.
Schlagzeilen und Bilder.
16.30 Videofashion!
Internationale
Modetrends.
16.58 heute.
17.03 SOKO 5113. Krimiserie.
17.53 Sport heute.
18.00 Die Schwarzwaldklinik.
18.55 Vorschau.
19.00 heute.
19.20 Wetter.
19.25 Frauenarzt.
Familienserie.
20.15 Jede Menge Leben.
Neue Serie.
Happy Birthday,
Dorothee.
21.15 Die volkstümliche
Hitparade.
Die Hits des Monats.
21.45 heute-journal.
22.00 Die Sport-Reportage.
22.50 Willemsens Woche.
Talkshow mit Roger
Willemsen. Live aus
Hamburg.
23.20 Rob Roberts.
US-Polit-Thriller (1992)
mit Tim Robbins.
1.10 heute nacht.
Magazin mit Nina Ruge.

SAT 1

6.00 Deutschland heute
morgen.
6.40 White Fang. Serie.
7.05 Kinderprogramm.
7.05 Grimmy (ab 6).
7.30 James Bond (ab 8).
7.55 Silverhawks (ab 10).
8.20 Conan (ab 8).
8.50 Die Abenteuer des jungen Indiana Jones.
9.45 Games World. Die
Videowelt der Spiele.
10.15 jump ran.
Basketball.
11.05 Falcon Crest.
US-Familiensaga.
12.05 Unter der Sonne
Kaliforniens.
Serie.
13.05 Loving - Wege der
Liebe.
US-Familienserie.
13.30 Reiter gegen Sitting
Bull. Der US-Western
„Cavalry Scout" mit
Rod Cameron.
14.50 Das große
Wunschkonzert.
Stars der Volksmusik.
16.14 Glücksrad.
Gameshow aus Berlin.
17.00 SAT 1 Newsmagazin.
Nachrichten.
18.00 ran-SAT 1– Fußball.
19.30 Riskier' was!
Das trickreiche Quiz.
20.00 Der Bergdoktor.
Dt. Familienserie:
Schwester Namenlos.
21.00 Wolffs Revier.
Dt. Krimiserie (1994).
22.00 Chicago Hope.
Krankenhausserie.
23.00 News & Stories.
Chaos Navigation in
Russland.
0.05 Klute.
US-Thriller (1970) mit
Jane Fonda.

LAND UND LEUTE

Go to the
Deutsch heute Web Site at
www.hmco.com/college

Fernsehen

Germany has both public **(öffentlich-rechtlich)** and private **(privat)** television which is designated as **das duale System.** The public channels are run as nonprofit public corporations and supervised by broadcasting councils. Their programming is financed primarily by fees collected from owners of televisions and radios. These fees are approximately twenty marks monthly. Each community has access to two national public channels and at least one regional channel. These are referred to respectively as **ARD (Arbeitsgemeinschaft der öffentlich-rechtlichen Rundfunkanstalten Deutschlands)** or **Erstes Programm, ZDF (Zweites Deutsches Fernsehen)** or **Zweites Programm,** and **Drittes Programm (Regionalprogramm).** The **ARD** includes both television and radio. Commercials on these channels are usually shown in two to three clusters per evening and are restricted to a maximum of twenty minutes per workday. There are no commercials after 8 P.M. or on Sundays or holidays. The private stations, which are available through subscription via cable, have become strong competitors to the public TV stations. The major cable stations are **RTL, SAT 1, SAT 2,** and **3 SAT.** Viewers find them attractive because they offer more light entertainment and feature films than the public stations, whose schedule consists of around 44% informational programs. More and more Germans are opting for TV via satellite instead of cable.

Dieser Fernsehbericht handelt von Wölfen.

Statistically, the average German watches television a little over three hours a day. Popular programs on German TV include news shows **(Nachrichten),** game shows, sports **(Sportsendungen),** movies **(Spielfilme),** and series **(Serien)** such as situation comedies or detective shows **(Krimis)**—many of which are coproductions with Swiss and Austrian television or imported from the United States. Most movies and sitcoms are American made with dubbed voices; many game shows are based on American models. American and other foreign films are usually with dubbed voices rather than subtitles. For many programs, stereo broadcasting makes it possible to hear the soundtrack either in German or in the original. People who live close to a border sometimes receive broadcasts from a neighboring country.

Diskussion

Gerd Bacher, a former Director-General of the public broadcasting system in Austria **(Österreichischer Rundfunk),** made the following statement: **„Öffentlich-rechtlicher Rundfunk braucht Geld, um Programm zu machen. Privatfernsehen braucht Programm, um Geld zu machen."** What do you think he meant by this statement? What is the role of public broadcasting in your community? In your life?

WIEDERHOLUNG

1. Andrea muss zu Hause bleiben.   Andrea möchte ins Kino gehen, aber sie muss leider zu Hause bleiben. Sagen Sie warum. (Andrea would like to go to the movies but unfortunately she has to stay home. Tell why.)

1. Andrea / (möchte) / gehen / heute Abend / ins Kino
2. sie / müssen / lernen / aber / noch viel
3. sie / können / lesen / ihre Notizen / nicht mehr
4. sie / müssen / schreiben / morgen / eine Klausur
5. sie / müssen / vorbereiten / auch noch / ein Referat
6. sie / wollen / studieren / später / in Kanada

2. Mach das.   Sagen Sie Thomas, was er heute Morgen alles machen muss. Benutzen Sie den **du**-Imperativ. (Tell Thomas all the things he has to do this morning. Use the **du**-imperative form.)

⫸ aufstehen / jetzt   *Steh jetzt auf.*

1. essen / Ei / zum Frühstück
2. gehen / einkaufen / dann
3. kaufen / alles / bei Meiers
4. kommen / gleich / nach Hause
5. vorbereiten / dein Referat
6. durcharbeiten / deine Notizen

3. Wer arbeitet für wen?   Sie und Ihre Freundinnen und Freunde arbeiten für Familienmitglieder. Wer arbeitet für wen? Benutzen Sie die passenden Possessivpronomen. (You and your friends work for members of your families. Who works for whom? Use the appropriate possessive adjectives.)

⫸ Annette / Großmutter   *Annette arbeitet für ihre Großmutter.*

1. Felix / Tante
2. ich / Vater
3. du / Mutter / ?
4. Jürgen / Onkel
5. Karin und Sonja / Schwester
6. wir / Eltern
7. ihr / Großvater / ?

4. Wie sagt man das?   Übersetzen Sie das Gespräch zwischen Julia und Christine. (Translate the conversation between Julia and Christine.)

CHRISTINE: Julia, may I ask something?
JULIA: Yes, what would you like to know?
CHRISTINE: What are you reading?
JULIA: I'm reading a book. It's called *Hello, Austria*.
CHRISTINE: Do you have to work this evening?
JULIA: No, I don't think so.
CHRISTINE: Do you want to go to the movies?
JULIA: Can you lend me money?
CHRISTINE: Certainly. But I would like to pay for you.

1.   2.   3.   4.

5.   6.   7.   8.

5. Bildgeschichte.   Erzählen Sie, was Daniel heute alles macht. Schreiben Sie einen oder zwei Sätze zu jedem Bild. (Tell everything Daniel is doing today. Write one or two sentences for each picture.)

6. Rollenspiel

1. Ihre Freundin/Ihr Freund macht einen Kurs, der Sie interessiert. Fragen Sie sie/ihn, was man alles für den Kurs machen muss. (Your friend is taking a course that interests you. Ask her/him what you have to do for the course.)
2. Letzte Woche waren Sie nicht im Deutschkurs, denn Sie waren krank. Sie fragen drei andere Studentinnen/Studenten, ob sie Ihnen ihre Notizen leihen können. Alle sagen nein und erklären Ihnen, warum sie das nicht können. (Last week you weren't in German class because you were ill. You ask three other students whether they can lend you their notes. They all say no and explain why they can't.)
3. Sie und Ihre Mitbewohnerin/Ihr Mitbewohner unterhalten sich über den Abend – was können, sollen, wollen, Sie machen. Am Ende gehen Sie Kaffee trinken und hören Musik. (You and your roommate are talking about the evening—what you can, should, or want to do. You end up going to have coffee and listening to music.)

Großeltern, Eltern und Enkelkinder (grandchildren).

7. Zum Schreiben

1. Choose one of the people in the photo above and make up a profile about that person. Give the person a name and describe her/him:

   a. age
   b. relationship to others in the photo
   c. nationality
   d. profession (see Reference Section: Supplementary Word Sets)
   e. what the person likes to do in her/his free time
   f. what the person likes to eat and drink

   You may find it helpful to review the *Vokabeln* sections in this and prior chapters and to write a few key words next to the points mentioned in a–f before you begin writing.

2. Describe in German a typical Friday at your college or university. Before you begin your description think about what you want to mention, e.g., your classes, where you eat, your shopping habits, and your plans for the evening.

Hinweise: After you have written your description(s), check over your work, paying particular attention to the following:

- Check that each sentence has a subject and a verb and that the verb agrees with the subject.
- Check the word order of each sentence.
- Be sure you have used correct punctuation and capitalization.
- Watch for the position of the prefix in separable-prefix verbs.
- If you have used a modal auxiliary, be sure the dependent infinitive is at the end of the sentence.

GRAMMATIK: ZUSAMMENFASSUNG

Present tense of *werden*

werden	
ich werde	wir werden
du **wirst**	ihr werdet
er/es/sie **wird**	sie werden
Sie werden	

Verbs with stem-vowel change *e > ie*

sehen	
ich sehe	wir sehen
du **siehst**	ihr seht
er/es/sie **sieht**	sie sehen
Sie sehen	
du-*imperative:* **sieh**	

lesen	
ich lese	wir lesen
du **liest**	ihr lest
er/es/sie **liest**	sie lesen
Sie lesen	
du-*imperative:* **lies**	

Present tense of *wissen*

wissen	
ich **weiß**	wir wissen
du **weißt**	ihr wisst
er/es/sie **weiß**	sie wissen
Sie wissen	

Der-words

	Masculine	Neuter	Feminine	Plural
	der	*das*	*die*	*die*
Nominative	dies**er** Mann	dies**es** Kind	dies**e** Frau	dies**e** Leute
Accusative	dies**en** Mann	dies**es** Kind	dies**e** Frau	dies**e** Leute

Der-words follow the same pattern in the nominative and accusative as the definite articles.

Meanings and uses of *der*-words

dies- (-er, -es, -e)	this; these *(pl.)*
jed- (-er, -es, -e)	each, every *(used in the singular only)*
manch- (-er, -es, -e)	many a, several, some *(used mainly in the plural)*
solch- (-er, -es, -e)	that kind of (those kinds of), such *(used mainly in the plural; in the singular* **so ein** *usually replaces* **solch-***)*
welch- (-er, -es, -e)	which *(interrogative adjective)*

Modal auxiliaries

■ *Present tense*

	dürfen	**können**	**müssen**	**sollen**	**wollen**	**mögen**	**(möchte)**
ich	darf	kann	muss	soll	will	mag	(möchte)
du	darfst	kannst	musst	sollst	willst	magst	(möchtest)
er/es/sie	darf	kann	muss	soll	will	mag	(möchte)
wir	dürfen	können	müssen	sollen	wollen	mögen	(möchten)
ihr	dürft	könnt	müsst	sollt	wollt	mögt	(möchtet)
sie	dürfen	können	müssen	sollen	wollen	mögen	(möchten)
Sie	dürfen	können	müssen	sollen	wollen	mögen	(möchten)

German modals are irregular in that they lack endings in the **ich-** and **er/es/sie-** forms, and most modals show stem-vowel changes.

Stefanie muss jetzt **gehen.**   Stefanie has to leave now.

Modal auxiliaries in German are often used with dependent infinitives. The infinitive is in last position.

■ *Meanings*

Infinitive	Meaning	Examples	English equivalents
dürfen	permission	Ich **darf** arbeiten.	I'm allowed to work.
können	ability	Ich **kann** arbeiten.	I can (am able to) work.
mögen	liking	Ich **mag** es nicht.	I don't like it.
müssen	compulsion	Ich **muss** arbeiten.	I must (have to) work.
sollen	obligation	Ich **soll** arbeiten.	I'm supposed to work.
wollen	wishing, wanting, intention	Ich **will** arbeiten.	I want (intend) to work.

Ich **mag** Paul nicht.   I don't like Paul.
Mögen Sie Tee?   Do you like tea?
Möchten Sie Tee oder Kaffee?   Would you like tea or coffee?

Möchte is a different form of the modal **mögen.** The meaning of **mögen** is *to like;* the meaning of **möchte** is *would like (to).*

Separable-prefix verbs

mitbringen	**Bring** Blumen **mit!**	Bring flowers.
fernsehen	**Siehst** du jetzt **fern?**	Are you going to watch TV now?

Many German verbs begin with prefixes such as **mit** or **fern.** Some prefixes are "separable," that is, they are separated from the base form of the verb in the imperative (e.g., **bring ... mit**) and in the present tense (e.g., **siehst ... fern**). The prefix generally comes at the end of the sentence. Most prefixes are either prepositions (e.g., **mit**) or adverbs (e.g., **fern**).

The separable-prefix verbs you have had are **durcharbeiten, einkaufen, fernsehen, mitbringen, vorbereiten,** and **zurückzahlen.**

Warum **kauft** Stefan heute **ein**?   Warum will Stefan heute **einkaufen?**
Bringt er Blumen **mit**?   Kann er Blumen **mitbringen?**

The separable prefix is attached to the base form of the verb (e.g., **einkaufen, mitbringen**) when the verb is used as an infinitive.

Servus in Österreich

*Dieses schöne Haus im
Salzkammergut ist heute
eine Jugendherberge.*

BAUSTEINE FÜR GESPRÄCHE

Fährst du morgen zur Uni?

UWE: Fährst du morgen mit dem Auto zur Uni?

CLAUDIA: Ja. Willst du mitfahren?

UWE: Ja, gern. Ich hab' so viele Bücher für die Bibliothek. Kannst du mich vielleicht abholen?

CLAUDIA: Ja, kein Problem. Ich komme dann um halb neun bei dir vorbei. Geht
das?

UWE: Ja, klar. Ich warte dann unten.

Fragen

1. Wer fährt mit dem Auto zur Uni?
2. Warum möchte Uwe mitfahren?
3. Wann holt Claudia Uwe ab?
4. Wo wartet Uwe?

In den Ferien

MICHAEL: Was machst du in den Ferien?

MELANIE: Ich fahre nach Österreich.

MICHAEL: Fährst du allein?

MELANIE: Nein, ich fahre mit meiner
Freundin. Die kennt Österreich ziemlich gut.

MICHAEL: Fahrt ihr mit dem Auto?

MELANIE: Nein, mit der Bahn. Wir wollen vor
allem wandern.

MICHAEL: Und wo übernachtet ihr?

MELANIE: In Wien schlafen wir bei Freunden.
Und sonst zelten wir.

Brauchbares

1. The chapter title **Servus in Österreich** is equivalent to *Hello in Austria.*
   Servus is a common greeting in Austria among young people and good
   friends, that is, those with whom one would use **du.** Austrians find the use of
   this greeting with people one doesn't know very well, especially by non-
   Austrians, close to insulting.

Fragen

1. Wohin° fährt Melanie in den Ferien?
2. Warum ist es gut, dass Melanies Freundin mitfährt?
3. Wie kommen Melanie und ihre Freundin nach Österreich?
4. Wo schlafen sie in Wien?
5. Wo schlafen sie, wenn sie nicht in Wien sind?

Jugendherbergen

I n German-speaking countries young people can stay inexpensively at a youth hostel (**Jugendherberge**). Germany alone has over 780 **Jugendherbergen;** Austria and Switzerland have over 120 each. Originally established in the early twentieth century, **Jugendherbergen** were located no more than a day's hike apart. They are found not only near vacation spots and national parks, but also in cities and towns. The appearance of **Jugendherbergen** varies greatly. Some are found in modern buildings while others are in small country houses or even in old fortresses. All serve a simple, cafeteria-style breakfast and provide bedding, if needed. Many have curfews and some even require their guests to help with various chores.

Traveling to other European countries is very popular among German students, particularly since there are special railway fares for young people through the age of 26 (**BahnCard Junior).** (North Americans in that age group can also obtain reduced fares.)

Jugendherberge in Salzburg.

Diskussion

Plan a trip through a German-speaking country in which you stay at **Jugendherbergen.**

---

1. Kann ich mitfahren?   Ihr Auto ist kaputt. Vielleicht können Sie morgen mit einer Studentin/einem Studenten aus Ihrem Deutschkurs mitfahren. Fragen Sie sie/ihn.

Discussing transportation

S1:			*S2:*		
Fährst du mit dem Auto zur	**Uni?**		Ja, willst du mitfahren?		
	Arbeit?		Nein,	**mein Auto ist kaputt°.**	
				ich nehme den Bus°.	
				ich gehe immer zu Fuß°.	
				ich laufe°.	
				ich fahre mit dem Rad°.	
Wann	**gehst** du zur	**Uni?**	Um	**acht.** Ist das zu	**früh°?**
	fährst	Arbeit?		halb neun.	spät?
Wann kommst du wieder nach Hause?			Um vier. Soll ich auf dich warten?		
			Gegen° sechs.		

Discussing travel plans

2. Was machst du in den Ferien?   Ihre Partnerin/Ihr Partner möchte wissen, was Sie in den Sommerferien machen. Sagen Sie es ihr/ihm.

S2:
Hast du schon Pläne° für die Ferien?

S1:
Ja,
| ich fahre nach Österreich.
| ich möchte | **wandern.**
| | zelten.
| | viel schwimmen.
| | Wasserski fahren°,
| | schlafen°.
| | Ski laufen°.

Nein, ich habe keine.
Ich muss arbeiten.
Nein, die Ferien sind zu kurz°.

3. Rollenspiel.   Erzählen Sie Ihrer Freundin/Ihrem Freund von Ihren Plänen für morgen. Fragen Sie sie/ihn dann, was für Pläne sie/er hat.

Erweiterung des Wortschatzes

1. *Wo?* and *wohin?*

Wo ist Dieter?
Where is Dieter?

Wohin geht Erika?
Where is Erika going?

English *where* has two meanings: *in what place* and *to what place.* German has two words for *where* that correspond to these two meanings: **wo** (*in what place,* i.e., position) and **wohin** (*to what place,* i.e., direction).

1. Wie bitte?   You don't understand what Nicole is saying. Ask her to repeat her statements.

➤➤ Cornelia fährt zur Uni.   *Wohin fährt Cornelia?*
➤➤ Erik arbeitet im Supermarkt.   *Wo arbeitet Erik?*

1. Dieter fährt in die Schweiz.
2. Tanja arbeitet beim Bäcker.
3. Bärbel fährt nach Österreich.
4. Schmidts wandern in Österreich.
5. Fischers kaufen immer im Supermarkt ein.
6. Mark geht nach Hause.

In vielen Wiener Kaffeehäusern kann man auch draußen sitzen.

LAND UND LEUTE

Go to the
Deutsch heute Web Site at
www.hmco.com/college

Das Kaffeehaus

The **Kaffeehaus** was first introduced to the German-speaking areas in the seventeenth century. The Viennese **Kaffeehäuser** in the late nineteenth and early twentieth centuries were especially famous as gathering places for artists, writers, and even revolutionaries like Leon Trotsky. Today, **Cafés** are still popular meeting places throughout the German-speaking countries and often provide newspapers and magazines for their customers. People from all walks of life, business people, students and artists, enjoy taking a break for coffee and perhaps a piece of cake. In addition to **Kaffee** and a wide variety of **Kuchen** and **Torten,** many **Cafés** offer a small selection of meals (hot and cold), ice cream treats, and beverages.

A cup of coffee costs around 25–30 **Schilling** in Austria, 3–4 **Franken** in Switzerland, and 3–4 **Mark** in Germany, and there are no free refills. In most Viennese **Kaffeehäuser** coffee is served with a small glass of water on a small wooden or silver tray. A spoon is placed upside down across the top of the water glass. Coffee with **Schlagobers** *(whipped cream)* is a favorite in Vienna.

Cafés are usually not open evenings, but they are open six or seven days per week. The day on which a **Café** or restaurant is closed is called its **Ruhetag.** Most **Cafés** have a sign posted in a prominent place indicating their **Ruhetag.**

Diskussion

Historical research: Coffee was introduced to Europe by the Turks in the seventeenth century. Find out something about the relationship between the Ottoman Empire and Austria or how coffee came to Europe.

2. Wie fährt man? Man fährt ...

mit dem Fahrrad/Rad

mit dem Auto/mit dem Wagen

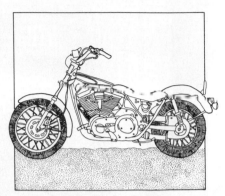

mit dem Motorrad

mit dem Bus

mit der Straßenbahn

mit der U-Bahn

mit der Bahn/mit dem Zug

mit dem Schiff

Das Flugzeug. (Man fliegt.)

Talking about transportation

2. Wie fahren Sie? Answer the following questions. For additional transportation terms, refer to the Supplementary Word Sets in the Reference Section.

1. Haben Sie ein Fahrrad? einen Wagen? ein Motorrad?
2. Ist es/er neu oder alt?
3. Wie fahren Sie zur Uni? Mit dem Bus? Mit dem Auto? Mit dem Rad? Mit der U-Bahn?
4. Fliegen Sie gern? viel?

Öffentliche Verkehrsmittel°

public transportation

LAND UND LEUTE

Go to the
Deutsch heute Web Site at
www.hmco.com/college

Public transportation is efficient and much utilized by the people in German-speaking countries. Buses, streetcars, subways, and trains are owned either by the federal or local government. While the popularity of the car continues to grow, governments subsidize public transportation because public transportation is better for the environment **(umweltfreundlich)** and ensures that everyone has access to transportation. Reduced rates are available for senior citizens **(Seniorenkarten)** and for students at all levels **(Schüler-/Studentenkarten).** In towns, villages, and suburbs there is convenient bus and sometimes streetcar **(Straßenbahn)** service. Major cities have a subway **(Untergrundbahn or U-Bahn)** and/or a modern commuter rail system **(Schnellbahn/Stadtbahn or S-Bahn).** The German, Austrian, and Swiss post offices provide extensive bus service between towns. If needed, even ferries are included in the public transportation network, such as the ferry on the Alster Lake **(Alsterfähre)** in Hamburg.

Die Wiener Straßenbahn ist eine praktische Alternative zum Auto.

Trains are still a major part of the transportation system in German-speaking countries for both long and short distance travel. Larger cities have more than one train station **(Bahnhof),** but the main train station **(Hauptbahnhof)** is usually a prominent building located in the center of town. In addition to transportation facilities, larger train stations may also have a variety of restaurants and shops to serve the traveling public. To commute, people often use short-distance trains **(Nahverkehrszüge).** Fast, comfortable **Inter-City Express (ICE)** trains run hourly between major cities. This system is being supplemented with the **Interregio-Züge,** which depart every two hours. The slightly slower "through" trains **(D-Züge)** also make long distance runs, but stop more frequently than the **ICE** trains. A network of trains known as the **Euro-City Express** connects the major cities throughout Europe. By 2005 it is expected that the **Transrapid,** a magnetic elevated train **(Magnetbahn),** will cover the 280 km distance between Berlin and Hamburg in an hour.

Diskussion

Discuss your experience with public transportation. Consider these questions: Does your community have an extensive public transportation system? To what extent do you think that providing transportation is a responsibility of the government?

Vokabeln

Substantive

das **Auto, -s** automobile, car
die **Bahn, -en** train; railroad
der **Bus, -se** bus
das **Fahrrad, ̈-er** bicycle
das **Flugzeug, -e** airplane
der **Fuß, ̈-e** foot
das **Motorrad, ̈-er** motorcycle
der **Plan, ̈-e** plan
das **Problem, -e** problem
das **Rad, ̈-er** (*short for* **Fahrrad**)
   bike, bicycle; **ich fahre Rad** I ride
   a bike

das **Schiff, -e** ship
der **Ski, -er** (**Ski** *is pronounced*
   Schi) ski
die **Straßenbahn, -en** streetcar
die **U-Bahn, -en** subway
der **Wagen, -** car
der **Wasserski, -er** water ski
der **Zug, ̈-e** train

Verben

ab·holen to pick up
fahren (fährt) to drive, to travel;
   mit (dem Auto) fahren to go by
   (car)
fliegen to fly
laufen (läuft) to run; to go on foot;
   to walk
mit·fahren (fährt mit) to drive
   (go) along
schlafen (schläft) to sleep

Ski laufen (läuft Ski) to ski
übernachten to spend the night/to
   stay (*in a hotel or with friends*)
vorbei·kommen to come by
warten (auf + *acc.*) to wait (for)
Wasserski fahren (fährt
   Wasserski) to water ski
zelten to camp in a tent

Andere Wörter

allein alone
dir (*dat.*) (to *or* for) you
früh early
kaputt broken; exhausted (*slang*)

kurz short, brief
unten downstairs; below
wem (*dat.* of **wer**) (to *or* for) whom
wohin where (to)

Besondere Ausdrücke

bei dir at your place
bei mir vorbeikommen to come
   by my place
gegen [sechs] around, about
   [6 o'clock]

Geht das? Is that OK?
mit (dem Auto) by (car)
vor allem above all
zu Fuß on foot; **Ich gehe immer**
   zu Fuß. I always walk.

Die Wiener Oper ist in der ganzen Welt berühmt.

Kulturstadt Wien

LAND UND LEUTE

Go to the
Deutsch heute Web Site at
www.hmco.com/college

Austria has a very rich and diverse cultural tradition. The university of Vienna **(Wien),** founded in 1365, is the oldest university in the present German-speaking world. In the late eighteenth and early nineteenth centuries, Vienna was the center of a musical culture associated with such names as Haydn, Mozart, Beethoven, and Schubert. In the second half of the nineteenth century the **Operette** reached its prime with composers like Johann Strauss the Younger and Franz Lehár. At the end of the 19th century (referred to in French as **Fin de Siècle**), Vienna was a major intellectual and artistic center of Europe. Two important names of that time are Sigmund Freud, who established psychoanalysis, and Gustav Mahler, who continued the city's great musical tradition. Today, Vienna continues to attract well-known Austrian artists, performers, and writers, as well as creative people from Eastern European countries.

Diskussion

1. Choose a famous Austrian. In a few sentences describe the life and achievements of the person to your classmates without mentioning the person's name. See if your classmates can guess the identity of the person.
2. Organize your own Austrian Music Festival. Bring a tape or CD of music by an Austrian composer or a composer who worked in Vienna.

 # ÖSTERREICH: EIN PORTRÄT

Vorbereitung auf das Lesen

In diesem Text lernen Sie einiges° über Österreich.   some things

■ *Vor dem Lesen*

Sehen° Sie sich die Landkarte° von Österreich am Anfang° des Buches an und lesen Sie die folgende° Information. Dann beantworten Sie die Fragen.

Sehen Sie sich an: look at / map / beginning / following

size / **qkm = Quadrat-
kilometer:** square
kilometers (32,375 sq. miles)
larger / New Brunswick,
Canada / low plain /
population

type of government /
federation / federal states

- **Größe°:** 83.855 qkm°
  etwa so groß wie Maine (86.027 qkm)
  etwas größer° als Neubraunschweig° (72.000 qkm)
- **Topographie:** Im Osten Tiefebene°, im Western und in der Mitte hohe Berge.
- **Bevölkerung°:** 8 Millionen Einwohner
- **Regierungsform°:** Bundesstaat° mit 9 Bundesländern°
  parlamentarische Demokratie
- **Hauptstadt:** Wien (1, 5 Millionen Einwohner)
- **8 Nachbarn:** Italien (I)*, Fürstentum Liechtenstein (FL), die Schweiz (CH),
  Deutschland (D), die Tschechische Republik (ČZ), die Slowakei
  (SK), Ungarn (H), Slowenien (SLO)

1. Welche anderen parlamentarischen Demokratien kennen Sie?
2. Österreich ist ein Land mit vielen Bergen. Das Gebirge heißt die Alpen. Was
   kann man in den Bergen machen? Machen Sie gern Urlaub in den Bergen?
3. Welche berühmten Österreicher kennen Sie?
4. Haben Sie schon ein Österreich-Bild? Was wissen Sie schon über Österreich?
5. Die Österreicher sagen, Österreich liegt im Herzen von Europa. Warum sagen
   sie das?

who

6. Herr Obermaier, der° in diesem Text über Österreich spricht, kommt aus
   Graz. Suchen Sie Graz auf der Landkarte von Österreich.

Beim Lesen

1. Herr Obermaier erwähnt einige berühmte Österreicher. Machen Sie eine
   Liste von ihnen.

relationships

2. Was erfahren Sie im Text über Österreichs Beziehungen° zu anderen Ländern?

kommt mit: comes along

Andreas Obermaier aus Graz besucht seine amerikanische Kusine
Sandra Heller. Sie ist Deutschprofessorin. Er kommt° mit in ihren
Deutschkurs und spricht mit den Studenten über Österreich.

meine ... Herren: ladies and
gentlemen

homeland

Guten Tag, meine° sehr verehrten Damen und Herren,
5   vielen Dank, dass ich heute als Gast in Ihrem Deutschkurs über mein
Heimatland° sprechen darf.

Österreich liegt in Mitteleuropa und ist nur etwa so groß wie Maine, ein
bisschen größer als die kanadische Provinz Neubraunschweig. Heute leben
ungefähr acht Millionen Menschen dort. Die meisten Menschen, 1, 5 Millio-
10   nen, leben in Wien, der Hauptstadt. Seit 1995 gehört Österreich auch zur Europäischen Union.

Nehmen wir: let's take

Wahrscheinlich kennen Sie die meisten Österreich-Klischees schon. Sie sind
nicht nur wahr, sondern meistens auch positiv. Nehmen° wir zum Beispiel
das Klischee „Österreich – das Land der Musik". Musik war und ist sehr
15   wichtig für uns Österreicher. Viele weltberühmte Komponisten wie Haydn,
Mozart und Schubert waren Österreicher, und bis heute gibt es jedes Jahr

numerous

zahlreiche° Musikfeste.

---

*The abbreviations in parentheses are the international symbols used on automobile
stickers.

Ein anderes Klischee ist „Österreich – das Land der Kultur" – auch das ist wahr, denn es kommen doch relativ viele bekannte Schriftsteller, Künstler
20 und Wissenschaftler aus unserer kleinen Alpenrepublik. Franz Werfel, Gustav Klimt und Sigmund Freud sind auch in Ihrem Land bekannt.

Was assoziieren° Sie noch mit Österreich? Sport, vor allem Wintersport. Dass Österreichs Skiläuferinnen und Skiläufer in den Olympischen Winterspielen immer wieder Medaillien° gewinnen ist kein Klischee, sondern die
25 Wahrheit°.

associate

medals / truth

Ein letztes Klischee ist „das gemütliche Österreich". Überall gibt es Cafés, in denen man gemütlich sitzen, Kaffee trinken und gute Torten essen kann. Dort trifft man seine Freunde oder liest die Zeitung und bleibt so lange, wie man will.

30 Wenn das Ihr Österreich-Bild ist, dann sind Sie nicht allein! Die meisten Leute denken an Österreichs Geschichte und Kultur. Doch, meine Damen und Herren, vergessen Sie dabei° nicht, dass Österreichs Lage° in Mitteleuropa politisch und wirtschaftlich für das Land wichtig ist. Während° des Kalten Krieges hat Österreich versucht°, politisch, kulturell und wirtschaftlich
35 neutral zu sein. Deshalb hat dieses kleine Land seit dem Zweiten Weltkrieg nicht nur 2,1 Millionen Flüchtlinge° aufgenommen°, sondern ist auch Sitz° wichtiger° internationaler Organisationen wie der UNO* und OPEC**. Österreich ist heute eines der reichsten° Industrieländer der Welt und exportiert seine Produkte in die ganze Welt.

in this connection / location
during
tried

refugees / **hat aufgenommen:** accepted / seat of important *(genitive case)* / richest

40 Wussten° Sie zum Beispiel, dass es neben° Hewlett Packard und General Motors 350 amerikanische Firmen in Österreich gibt? Neben den klassischen Musikfesten finden° jedes Jahr interessante Avantgarde-Feste statt, und an den Universitäten arbeiten innovative Wissenschaftler mit der neuesten Technologie.

Wussten Sie: did you know / besides
finden statt: take place

45 Und das, meine Damen und Herren, war mein Kurzporträt von Österreich. Ich hoffe, es° hat Ihnen gefallen. Vielen Dank für Ihre Aufmerksamkeit°. Ich bin jetzt gern bereit Ihre Fragen zu beantworten.

es … gefallen: you liked it / attention

Brauchbares

1. l.4. To start a speech German speakers generally begin with **Meine Damen und Herren** *(ladies and gentlemen).* **Meine sehr verehrten Damen und Herren** which Andreas Obermeier uses is very formal, something like *Most honored ladies and gentlemen.*
2. l.15–16. Three famous Austrian composers are mentioned: **Franz Josef Haydn** (1732–1809), friend of Mozart and inspiration for Beethoven, composed over 100 symphonies, 50 piano sonatas, and numerous operas, masses, and songs.
   Wolfgang Amadeus Mozart (1756–1791) is considered one of the greatest composers of all time. He was a child prodigy who began composing before he was five, at the age of six gave concerts throughout Europe, and by

United Nations (Organization)

**Organization of Petroleum Exporting Countries*

the age of 13 had written concertos, sonatas, symphonies, and a German operetta and an Italian opera. In his short life time he composed over 600 works—18 masses, 41 symphonies, 28 piano concertos, 8 well-known operas, and many chamber works.

Franz Schubert (1797–1828) wrote his first composition at the age of 13 and his first symphony at 16. In one year at the age of 18 he wrote 140 songs. In his short life time Schubert wrote 998 works which include 9 symphonies, 7 masses, many piano pieces, and 606 songs.

3. l.20. The writer **Franz Werfel** (1890–1945) fled from Nazi-occupied Austria to France and then on to the United States. His work consists of poetry, dramas, and novels. He is best known in the United States for his novels *The Forty Days of Musa Dagh* (1934), which tells of the struggle of the Armenians against the Turks in World War I, and the *Song of Bernadette* (1942), which is about the saint from Lourdes.

The painter **Gustav Klimt** (1862–1918) was the most famous painter of Art Nouveau in Vienna. He is best known for his portraits and landscapes. Some of his works are in the Museum of Modern Art, New York City.

The psychiatrist **Sigmund Freud** (1856–1939) is known as the founder of psychoanalysis. When in 1938 the Nazis occupied Austria and made it part of Germany, Freud fled to England where he died the next year.

4. l.31. **doch:** You already know **doch** as a flavoring particle and as a positive response to a negative statement or question (see *Kapitel 3*). **Doch** is also a conjunction which means *nevertheless, still, however,* as in the line **Doch, meine Damen und Herren, vergessen Sie dabei nicht ...**

5. l.34. **hat versucht** *(tried);* l.36, **hat aufgenommen** *(accepted);* and l.46, **hat gefallen** *(liked):* German has several past tenses. One of them is called the present perfect tense and is made up of a form of **haben** and a participle. This past tense will be practiced in *Kapitel 6.*

6. l.38–39, **exportiert seine Produkte:** Exports make up 29.5% of Austria's gross domestic product. In comparison, in the United States exports make up 8.5% of its GDP and in Canada it is 34.9% of the GDP.

7. l.46, **gefallen** means *to like:* You have already met other words meaning to like—**mögen** and **gern. Mögen** usually expresses stronger feelings than **gefallen:**
Deine Freunde **gefallen** mir nicht. (I don't like your friends = I don't care for them.)
Deine Freunde **mag** ich nicht. (I don't like your friends = I dislike them.)
Gern is used with verbs: Ich koche **gern.** (I like to cook.)

Nach dem Lesen

1. Fragen zum Lesestück

1. Warum kommt Herr Obermaier in den Deutschkurs?
2. Ist Österreich größer oder kleiner als Ihr Bundesland/Ihre Provinz?
3. Was sind einige der weltbekannten Klischees über Österreich?
4. In welcher Sportart ist Österreich besonders erfolgreich°?
5. Möchten Sie in ein österreichisches Café gehen? Warum (nicht)?
6. Warum ist die geographische Lage Österreichs politisch und wirtschaftlich wichtig?
7. Welche internationalen Organisationen haben Büros° in Österreich?

successful

offices

8. Warum kann man sagen, dass Österreich ein Land der Kontraste ist?
9. Herr Obermaier erwähnt° einige berühmte Österreicher. Welche kennen Sie?   *mentions*
10. Stellen° Sie Herrn Obermaier eine Frage.   **Stellen … Frage:** ask a question

2. Vokabeln. Welches Wort oder welche Wendung° passt° zu welchem Thema? Ordnen° Sie das Wort zu dem Thema°, dann suchen Sie noch zwei Wörter oder Wendungen im Text zu den Themen.   *phrase / fits*   *match / topic*

Wörter/Wendungen: neutral □ Mozart □ Industrieland
Themen: Wirtschaft □ Außenpolitik° □ Musik   *foreign policy*

3. Erzählen wir. Sprechen Sie mit einer Partnerin/einem Partner über eines der folgenden Themen:

Warum ich Österreich besuchen will.
Wichtiges° über Österreich.   *important things*
Ich möchte in Österreich arbeiten.

Wien – Schloss Schönbrunn, die Sommerresidenz der Habsburger Kaiser.

LAND UND LEUTE

Go to the *Deutsch heute* Web Site at **www.hmco.com/college**

Die Habsburger

A very significant period in Austria's history is the era under the rule of the House of Habsburg. In 1273 Rudolf von Habsburg was the first member of the Habsburg family to be elected emperor of the Holy Roman Empire **(Heiliges Römisches Reich),** which existed from 962 until 1806. In the first 400 years of Habsburg rule, the empire expanded greatly. The expansion was due to wars and to a successful **Heiratspolitik,** which deliberately aimed at advantageous marriages with the ruling European houses. The success of Napoleon's wars at the beginning of the nineteenth century led to the end of the empire in 1806. Members of the House of Habsburg continued to rule the Austro-Hungarian Empire until 1918, however, when Austria was declared a republic.

Diskussion

Find a map of early twentieth century Europe and compare it to a current map. Which modern countries were part of the Austro-Hungarian Empire before World War I?

Vokabeln

Substantive

die **Alpen** (*pl.*) Alps
der **Berg, -e** mountain
der **Brief, -e** letter
das **Café, -s** café
die **Dame, -n** lady
der **Dank** thanks; **vielen Dank** many thanks
das **Fest, -e** festival; party
die **Firma,** *pl.* **Firmen,** company
der **Gast, ¨e** guest
das **Handy, -s** cellular phone
das **Klischee, -s** cliché
der **Komponist, -en, -en**/die **Komponistin, -nen** composer
der **Krieg, -e** war; der **Weltkrieg** world war

der **Künstler, -**/die **Künstlerin, -nen** artist
die **Landkarte, -n** map
das **Porträt, -s** portrait
das **Produkt, -e** product
der **Regenschirm, -e** umbrella
der **Schriftsteller, -**/die **Schriftstellerin, -nen** writer
der **Skiläufer, -**/die **Skiläuferin, -nen** skier
das **Taschenbuch, ¨er** paperback book
die **Welt, -en** world
die **Wirtschaft** economy
der **Wissenschaftler, -**/die **Wissenschaftlerin, -nen** scientist

Verben

beantworten to answer (a question, a letter)
besuchen to visit; to attend (e.g., a lecture, school)
gefallen (gefällt) (+ *dat.*) to please, be pleasing to; **es gefällt mir** I like it
gehören (+ *dat.*) to belong to
gewinnen to win

hoffen to hope
leben to live
schenken to give (as a gift)
sitzen to sit
sprechen (spricht) to speak
treffen (trifft) to meet
vergessen (vergisst) to forget
versuchen to try

Andere Wörter

bekannt known, famous
bereit ready, prepared; willing
berühmt famous
bevor (*conj.*) before
dass (*conj.*) that
doch (*conj.*) nevertheless, still, however
gemütlich comfortable, informal
hoh- (-er, -es, -e) high (the form of **hoch** used before nouns, as in **hohe Berge** high mountains)
lange (*adv.*) for a long time
letzt- (-er, -es, -e) last
meistens mostly

obwohl (*conj.*) although
österreichisch Austrian (*adj.*)
reich rich
sondern (*conj.*) but (on the contrary)
überall everywhere
ungefähr approximately
wahr true; **nicht wahr?** isn't that true?
wahrscheinlich probably
weil (*conj.*) because
wichtig important
wirtschaftlich economical

Besondere Ausdrücke

immer wieder again and again

nicht nur ... sondern auch not only . . . but also

Neutralität

Go to the
Deutsch heute Web Site at
www.hmco.com/college

World War II ended in 1945, but because of the East-West conflict, Austria's sovereignty was not restored until 1955. The Soviet Union finally agreed to a peace treaty after Austria declared its policy of permanent neutrality **(immerwährende Neutralität).** Therefore, during the Cold War, Austria was neither a member of NATO nor of the Warsaw Pact. From the end of World War II until the end of the Cold War approximately 45 years later, Austria granted temporary or permanent asylum to about two million people from more than thirty countries. In fact, its decision to allow East German refugees to enter through its border with Hungary in 1989 was a contributing factor to the fall of the government of East Germany.

UNO-Gebäude in Wien.

Until the end of World War I in 1918, Austria included lands that today are part of eastern European countries—the Czech Republic, Romania, Hungary, and the former Yugoslavia. Because of these ties, Austria served as an important link between eastern and western Europe during the Cold War, and it continues to play an important and special role in Europe today. Austria joined the European Union **(Europäische Union)** in 1995 but has not surrendered its neutrality. It is an active member of the United Nations and serves as the site of many international congresses and conferences. Vienna ranks among the leading convention cities in the world.

Diskussion

Both Switzerland and Austria are neutral nations that are active in international organizations. Do you think that the policy of neutrality is a good one for a nation? How important do you think that international organizations such as the United Nations or the Red Cross are?

GRAMMATIK UND ÜBUNGEN

1. Verbs with stem-vowel change *a* > *ä*

fahren: to drive	
ich fahre	wir fahren
du **fährst**	ihr fahrt
er/es/sie **fährt**	sie fahren
Sie fahren	
du-*imperative:* fahr(e)	

laufen: to run; to go on foot, walk	
ich laufe	wir laufen
du **läufst**	ihr lauft
er/es/sie **läuft**	sie laufen
Sie laufen	
du-*imperative:* lauf(e)	

Some verbs with stem-vowel **a** or **au** change **a** to **ä** in the **du-** and **er/es/sie-**forms of the present tense. The verbs you know with this change are **fahren, schlafen,** and **laufen.**

1. Zwei Gespräche.   (a) Ute fährt wieder nach Salzburg. Ergänzen Sie die Sätze mit der passenden Form von **fahren.**

KAI: Sag mal, Ute, _____ du übers Wochenende nach Salzburg?

UTE: Ja. Ich glaube schon.

KAI: _____ Katja mit?

UTE: Nein. Ich _____ allein. Katja und Tina _____ nach Wien. Aber so viel Zeit

habe ich nicht.

KAI: Also dann, gute Reise.

(b) Kais ganze Familie joggt gern. Ergänzen Sie die Sätze mit der passenden Form von **laufen.**

UTE: Du, Kai, _____ du jeden Morgen?

KAI: Nicht jeden Morgen, aber ich _____ viel. Mutti _____ aber jeden Morgen.

UTE: Deine Schwester Beatrix _____ auch viel, nicht?

KAI: Ja. Mein Vater und sie _____ vierzig Minuten nach der Arbeit. Morgens

haben sie keine Zeit. Du und Erik, ihr _____ auch gern, nicht?

UTE: Ja, aber wir _____ nur am Wochenende.

lake
befindet sich: is located
ad / reference section
meaning

2. Restop Altea.   Mondsee ist eine Stadt und auch ein See°. Restop Altea Motel befindet° sich in Mondsee. Was wissen Sie über das Motel? Lesen Sie die Anzeige° für das Motel und beantworten Sie die Fragen. Im Anhang° finden Sie die Bedeutung° der neuen Wörter (Vocabulary for Authentic Text Activities).

RESTOP

ALTEA
M O T E L

MONDSEE
Tel. 0 62 32/28 76–28 79, Telex 63 33 57 altea
Telefax 06 2 32/28 76/5

DER MONDSEE LIEGT IHNEN ZU FÜSSEN

Idealer Ausgangspunkt für jung und alt in äußerst ruhiger Lage. Das ist unser Motel mit 46 Komfortzimmern, erreichbar von beiden Fahrtrichtungen der A-1-Autobahn. In unserem Panorama-Restaurant überraschen wir Sie mit kulinarischen Spezialitäten. Hoteleigener Badestrand!

Es lädt Sie ein:
Der Mondsee:	zum Segeln, Surfen, Wasserschilaufen und zu Schiffsrundfahrten.
Die Bergwelt:	zum Bergwandern und Bergsteigen.
Mondsee:	zum Besuch von Kulturstätten und Veranstaltungen.
Die Umgebung:	zum Tennisspielen, zum Golfen auf zwei Plätzen mit neun bzw. 18 Löchern, zu Ausflugsfahrten ins Salzkammergut.
Unser Haus:	mit dem Weekend-Hit, zahle 2 Nächte und bleibe 3!

Gute Erholung und viel Vergnügen!

1. Welche Autobahn fährt nach Mondsee?
2. Wie viele Zimmer hat das Motel?
3. Was für Sport kann man treiben?
4. Was ist der Weekend-Hit?
5. Warum schläft man in diesem Motel gut?

Making plans for the weekend

3. Rollenspiel. Sie möchten ein Wochenende in Mondsee verbringen°. Versuchen Sie, Ihre Partnerin/Ihren Partner zu überreden° mitzukommen. Sagen Sie ihr/ihm, was man da alles machen kann. Hier sind einige Vorschläge°.

spend
persuade
suggestions

S1: Fahren wir nach Mondsee? Komm doch mit! □ Wir kommen ganz leicht° nach Mondsee. □ Ich möchte gern auf dem See° segeln°. □ Kannst du surfen? □ Und ich möchte auch gerne gut essen. □ Wir können ins Salzkammergut fahren.

easily
lake / sail

S2: Hast du denn ein Auto? □ Ich kann nicht segeln. □ Kann man da auch gut wandern? □ Gibt es in Mondsee einen Golfplatz? □ Ist das nicht zu teuer? □ Ich möchte vor allem meine Ruhe° haben.

peace and quiet

der Hauptsatz / die
koordinierende Konjunktion

2. Independent clauses° and coordinating conjunctions°

Wir wollen am Wochenende zelten. Es soll regnen.
Wir wollen am Wochenende zelten, **aber** es soll regnen.

An independent (or main) clause can stand alone as a complete sentence. Two
(or more) independent clauses may be connected by a coordinating conjunction
(e.g., **aber**). Because coordinating conjunctions are merely connectors and not
part of either clause, they do not affect word order. Thus the subject comes before the verb. The coordinating conjunctions you know are **aber, denn, oder,
sondern,** and **und.**

Erika kommt morgen, **aber** Christel kommt am Montag.

In written German, the coordinating conjunctions **aber, denn,** and **sondern** are
generally preceded by a comma.

Erika kommt morgen **und** Christel kommt am Montag.

The conjunctions **und** and **oder** are generally not preceded by a comma, although writers may choose to use one for clarity.

4. Erika und Sabine.   Sagen Sie, was Sabine und Erika diese Woche machen.
Verbinden Sie jedes Satzpaar° mit einer koordinierenden Konjunktion.

pair of sentences

>> Die Studentin heißt Erika. Ihre   *Die Studentin heißt Erika und*
Freundin heißt Sabine. (und)   *ihre Freundin heißt Sabine.*

1. Erika wohnt bei einer Familie. Sabine wohnt bei ihren Eltern. (aber)
2. Erika arbeitet zu Hause. Sabine muss in die Bibliothek gehen. (aber)
3. Erika arbeitet schwer. Am Mittwoch hat sie eine Klausur. (denn)
4. Sabine hat ihre Klausur nicht am Mittwoch. Sie hat sie am Freitag. (sondern)
5. Was machen die Mädchen in den Ferien? Wissen sie es nicht? (oder)

■ Sondern *and* aber

Paul fährt morgen nicht mit dem   Paul isn't going by car tomorrow,
  Auto, **sondern** geht zu Fuß.   *but (rather)* is walking.

Sondern is a coordinating conjunction that expresses a contrast or contradic-
tion. It connects two ideas that are mutually exclusive. It is used only after a
negative clause and is equivalent to *but, on the contrary, instead, rather.* When the
subject is the same in both clauses, it is not repeated. This is also true of a verb
that is the same; it is not repeated.

Cordelia tanzt nicht nur viel,   Cordelia not only dances a lot,
  sondern auch gut.   *but* also well.

The German construction **nicht nur . . . sondern auch** is equivalent to *not
only . . . but also.*

Er fährt nicht mit dem Auto, **aber**   He isn't going by car, *but* his father
  sein Vater fährt mit dem Auto.   is.

Aber as a coordinating conjunction is equivalent to *but* or *nevertheless.* It may be
used after either positive or negative clauses.

5. Was macht Annette? Erzählen Sie, was Annette heute alles macht. Ergänzen Sie die Sätze mit **aber** oder **sondern.**

⟫ Annette spielt heute nicht Fußball, _____ Tennis.
Annette spielt heute nicht Fußball, sondern Tennis.

1. Sie spielt Tennis nicht gut, _____ sie spielt es sehr gern.

2. Sie geht nicht zur Vorlesung, _____ in die Bibliothek.

3. Im Café bestellt sie Bier, _____ sie trinkt Eriks Kaffee.

4. Sie möchte den Kaffee bezahlen, _____ sie hat kein Geld.

5. Sie fährt nicht mit dem Bus nach Hause, _____ geht zu Fuß.

> Showing connections and relationships

6. Meine Freunde. Ihre Freundinnen und Freunde haben viel zu tun. Sagen Sie, was sie machen. Benutzen Sie **nicht nur… sondern auch.**

⟫ Karola studiert Musik. Sie studiert auch Sport.
Karola studiert nicht nur Musik, sondern auch Sport.

1. Adrian lernt Deutsch. Er lernt auch Spanisch.
2. Sabine arbeitet im Café. Sie arbeitet auch im Supermarkt.
3. Bettina besucht° einen Tanzkurs. Sie besucht auch einen Karatekurs.   attends
4. Bernd spielt Fußball und Hockey. Er spielt auch Tennis.
5. Jan macht Informatik. Er macht auch Geschichte und Mathematik.

3. Dependent clauses° and subordinating conjunctions°

> der Nebenatz / die subordinierende Konjunktion

Independent Clause	Conjunction	Dependent Clause
Rita sagt,	**dass**	sie nach Österreich **fährt.**
Sie übernachtet bei Freunden,	**wenn**	sie zu Hause **sind.**

A dependent (subordinate) clause is a clause that cannot stand alone; it must be combined with an independent clause to express a complete idea. Two signals distinguish a dependent clause from an independent clause: (1) it is introduced by a subordinating conjunction **(dass, wenn)** and (2) the finite verb **(fährt, sind)** is at the end. In writing, a dependent clause is separated from the independent clause by a comma. A few common subordinating conjunctions are: **dass,** *that;* **obwohl,** *although;* **weil,** *because;* **wenn,** *if; when.*

7. Österreicher fahren in die Ferien. Wie und wo verbringen° viele Österreicher die Ferien? Verbinden Sie die Sätze mit den Konjunktionen in Klammern.   spend

⟫ In den Ferien fahren viele Österreicher nach Ungarn. Alles ist da billiger … (weil)
In den Ferien fahren viele Österreicher nach Ungarn, weil da alles billiger ist.

1. Die Österreicher finden es auch gut. Ungarn ist nicht so weit. (dass)
2. Sie können nicht vor Mitte Juli fahren. Die Sommerferien beginnen erst dann. (weil)
3. Nach Prag fahren sie auch oft. Die Ferien sind kurz. (wenn)

4. Viele Musikfans bleiben in Österreich. Im Sommer sind in Bregenz und Salzburg die Festspiele. (wenn)
5. In den Winterferien fahren viele Österreicher nach Italien. Das Skilaufen ist dort billiger. (weil)
6. Es ist gut für die Österreicher. Ihr Land liegt in Mitteleuropa. (dass)

■ *Dependent clauses and separable-prefix verbs*

Statement	Monika **kauft** gern im Supermarkt **ein.**
Dependent clause	Monika sagt, **dass** sie gern im Supermarkt **einkauft.**

In a dependent clause, the separable prefix is attached to the base form of the verb, which is in final position.

Reporting on actions

8. Was sagt Gabi? Sagen Sie Mark, was Gabi über ihre Pläne sagt. Beginnen Sie jeden Satz mit: **Gabi sagt, dass…**

➤➤ Sie kauft in der Stadt ein. *Gabi sagt, dass sie in der Stadt einkauft.*

1. Renate kommt mit. *mitkommen*
2. Renate kommt um neun bei ihr vorbei. *kommt*
3. Sie kaufen auf dem Markt ein.
4. Sie bereitet dann zu Hause ein Referat vor.
5. Renate bringt ein paar Bücher mit.
6. Sie bringt die Bücher am Freitag zurück.

■ *Dependent clauses and modal auxiliaries*

Statement	Rita **möchte** in die Schweiz fahren.
Dependent clause	Rita sagt, **dass** sie in die Schweiz fahren **möchte.**

In a dependent clause, the modal auxiliary is the finite verb and therefore is in final position, after the dependent infinitive.

9. Andreas sagt das. Andreas sagt, was er alles tun möchte und tun muss. Sagen Sie einem Freund, was Andreas sagt.

➤➤ Ich soll meine Seminararbeit zu Ende schreiben. *Andreas sagt, dass er seine Seminararbeit zu Ende schreiben soll.*

1. Ich muss meine E-Mails durchlesen.
2. Ich soll einen Brief° an meine Großeltern schreiben.
3. Ich will mit dem Computer arbeiten.
4. Ich möchte ein bisschen im Internet surfen.
5. Ich möchte heute Abend ein bisschen fernsehen.

Giving reasons

10. Freizeit. Ihre Partnerin/Ihr Partner fragt, warum Sie nicht dies und das in Ihrer Freizeit und in den Ferien machen. Beginnen Sie Ihre Antwort mit **weil.** Unten finden Sie einige mögliche Antworten.

S2: Warum gehst du nicht ins Kino?
S1: Weil ich kein Geld habe.

S2:

1. Warum gehst du nicht Rollerblading?
2. Warum gehst du nicht mit Freunden ins Café?
3. Warum gehst du nicht tanzen?
4. Warum joggst du nicht?
5. Warum liest du nicht einen Krimi?
6. Warum machst du nicht Ferien in Österreich?
7. Warum spielst du nicht Golf?
8. Warum spielst du nicht mit uns Karten?
9. Warum bist du immer so müde?

S1:

Ich will zu Hause bleiben.
Ich muss eine Seminararbeit schreiben.
Ich will allein sein.
Ich muss arbeiten.
Ich will in die Bibliothek gehen.
Ich habe kein Geld.
Ich habe keine Zeit.
Ich kann nicht tanzen.
Das interessiert mich nicht.
Ich kann nicht schlafen.

■ *Dependent clauses beginning a sentence*

	1	2	
	Paul	**fährt**	mit dem Bus.
1		2	
Weil sein Auto kaputt ist,		**fährt**	er mit dem Bus.

In a statement, the finite verb is in second position. If a sentence begins with a dependent clause, the entire clause is considered a single element, and the finite verb of the independent clause is in second position, followed by the subject.

11. Eine Radtour durch die Schweiz.   Gerhard und Fabian planen eine Radtour° durch die Schweiz. Verbinden Sie jedes Satzpaar°. Beginnen Sie den neuen Satz mit der angegebenen° Konjunktion.

> (wenn) Das Wetter ist gut. Gerhard   *Wenn das Wetter gut ist, wollen*
> und Fabian wollen in die Schweiz.   *Gerhard und Fabian in die Schweiz.*

bicycle trip / pair of sentences
cued

1. (weil) Sie haben wenig Geld. Sie fahren mit dem Rad.
2. (wenn) Sie fahren mit dem Rad. Sie sehen mehr vom Land.
3. (wenn) Es ist nicht zu kalt. Sie zelten.
4. (wenn) Das Wetter ist sehr schlecht. Sie schlafen bei Freunden.
5. (obwohl) Sie haben wenig Geld. Sie können vier Wochen bleiben.
6. (weil) Sie haben nur vier Wochen Ferien. Sie müssen im August wieder zu Hause sein.

der Dativ

4. Dative case

Nominative	**Der** Mann heißt Falk.
Accusative	Kennst du **den** Mann?
Dative	Ich gebe **dem** Mann meine Zeitung.

In addition to nominative and accusative, German has a case called *dative.*

Masculine	Neuter	Feminine	Plural
de**m** Mann	de**m** Kind	de**r** Frau	de**n** Freunden
dies**em** Mann	dies**em** Kind	dies**er** Frau	dies**en** Freunden
ein**em** Mann	ein**em** Kind	ein**er** Frau	kein**en** Freunden
ihr**em** Mann	unser**em** Kind	sein**er** Frau	mein**en** Freunden

The definite and indefinite articles, **der-**words, and **ein-**words change their form in the dative case. Nouns add an **-n** in the dative plural, unless the plural already ends in **-n** or **-s: meine Freunde > meinen Freunden;** but **die Frauen > den Frauen, die Autos > den Autos.**

5. Masculine N-nouns in the dative

Nominative	der Herr	der Student
Accusative	den Her**rn**	den Student**en**
Dative	dem Her**rn**	dem Student**en**

Masculine **N-**nouns, which add **-n** or **-en** in the accusative, also add **-n** or **-en** in the dative singular. The masculine **N-**nouns you know so far are: **der Herr, der Junge, der Komponist, der Mensch, der Nachbar, der Name, der Student,** and **der Tourist.**

6. Dative of *wer?*

Nominative	**Wer** sagt das?	*Who* says that?
Dative	**Wem** sagen Sie das?	*To whom* are you saying that?

The dative form of the interrogative **wer?** *(who?)* is **wem?** *([to] whom?).*

7. Dative verbs

Das Haus **gehört meinen** Eltern.	The house belongs to my parents.
Kerstin **glaubt ihrer** Schwester nicht.	Kerstin doesn't believe her sister.

Most German verbs take objects in the accusative. However, a few verbs take objects in the dative. The dative object is usually a person. Such verbs can be classified as "dative verbs." The dative verbs you've learned so far are **glauben, gefallen,** and **gehören.** A more complete list of dative verbs is found in section 17 of the Grammatical Tables in the Reference Section.

Daniela **glaubt ihrem** Freund Erik.   Daniela believes her friend Erik.
Erik **glaubt es** nicht.   Erik doesn't believe it.

The verb **glauben** always takes personal objects (e.g., **ihrem Freund**) in the dative case. However, impersonal objects (e.g., **es**) after **glauben** are in the accusative case.

12. Wem gehört das?   Sie und Carsten kommen von einer Bustour nach Berlin zurück. Alle Passagiere sind schon fort°. Sie sind noch im Bus und sehen einige Dinge°. Carsten fragt, wem die Dinge gehören. Sie wissen es.

gone
things

⨠ das Poster (dein Freund Uwe)
    Wem gehört das Poster?   *Das Poster gehört deinem Freund Uwe.*

1. der Regenschirm°   2. das Handy°   3. der Rucksack
(dein Professor)   (deine Professorin)   (die Amerikanerin)

4. die Landkarte°   5. das Taschenbuch°   6. die Zeitung
(der Engländer)   (deine Freundin Cornelia)   (der Busfahrer)

Das Bild **gefällt mir.**   *I like* the picture.
Mir gefällt es nicht, dass Mark so wenig liest.   *I don't like* (the fact) that
    Mark reads so little.

Gefallen is equivalent to English *like.* When using the verb **gefallen,** what one likes is the subject and thus in the nominative case. The person who likes something is in the dative. Note that sentences with **gefallen** often begin with the dative.

means / **geben wieder:** render

13. **Was bedeutet° das?** Geben° Sie die Sätze auf Englisch wieder.

1. Wie gefällt deinem Freund Mark Hamburg?
2. Ihm gefällt es sehr.
3. Was gefällt deinem Freund nicht so gut?
4. Ihm gefällt es nicht, dass es so viel regnet.
5. Es gefällt Mark auch nicht, dass es so viele Autos gibt.

8. Dative personal pronouns

Singular						
Nominative	ich	du	er	es	sie	Sie
Accusative	mich	dich	ihn	es	sie	Sie
Dative	**mir**	**dir**	**ihm**	**ihm**	**ihr**	**Ihnen**

Plural				
Nominative	wir	ihr	sie	Sie
Accusative	uns	euch	sie	Sie
Dative	**uns**	**euch**	**ihnen**	**Ihnen**

Dative personal pronouns have different forms from the accusative pronouns, except for **uns** and **euch.**

roommate / **räumen auf:** are straightening up

14. **Was denkt Sabine?** Sabine ist Ihre Mitbewohnerin°. Sie räumen° Ihre Wohnung auf. Fragen Sie, wem die Dinge gehören und ob sie Sabine gefallen. Antworten Sie immer mit einem logischen Personalpronomen.

⟫ Gehört der Regenschirm deinem Vater? (ja)   *Ja, der Regenschirm gehört ihm.*
⟫ Gefällt dir das Poster? (nein)   *Nein, das Poster gefällt mir nicht.*

1. Gehört der Rucksack deiner Schwester? (ja)
2. Gehört dir das Video? (nein)
3. Gefällt dir das Video? (ja)
4. Gehören die Disketten deinen Kusinen? (ja)
5. Gehört die Einkaufstasche deiner Mutter? (ja)
6. Gehören die CDs deinem Bruder? (ja)
7. Gefallen dir die CDs? (nein)

das indirekte Objekt

9. Indirect object°

	Indirect object	Direct object
Katrin schenkt	ihrem Freund	einen CD-Spieler.
Katrin is giving	her friend	a CD-player.

In both English and German some verbs take two objects, which are traditionally called the direct object (e.g., **CD-Spieler**—*CD player*) and the indirect object (e.g., **Freund**—*friend*). The indirect object is usually a person and answers the question *to whom* or *for whom* the direct object is intended. Some verbs that can take both direct and indirect objects are **bringen, erklären, geben, kaufen, leihen, sagen, schenken°,** and **schreiben.**

10. Signals for indirect object and direct object

	Indirect (dative) object	Direct (accusative) object
Katrin schenkt	ihren Eltern	einen CD-Spieler.
Katrin is giving	her parents	a CD player.

English signals the indirect object by putting it before the direct object or by using the preposition *to* or *for*, e.g., Katrin is giving a CD player *to* her parents. To determine in English whether a noun or pronoun is an indirect object, add *to* or *for* before it.

German uses case to signal the difference between a direct object and an indirect object. The direct object is in the accusative, and the indirect object is in the dative. Since the case signals are clear, **German never uses a preposition to signal the indirect object.**

15. Geburtstage. Einige Leute haben diesen Monat Geburtstag. Theresa und David diskutieren, was sie den Leuten schenken. Bestimmen° Sie das indirekte Objekt (Dativ) und das direkte Objekt (Akkusativ). Übersetzen° Sie die Sätze.

> identify
> translate

≫ DAVID: Wem schenkst du die Blumen?

indirect object: Wem

direct object: die Blumen

English equivalent: To whom are you giving the flowers?

1. THERESA: Diese Blumen bringe ich meiner Großmutter.
2. THERESA: Was kaufst du deiner Freundin?
3. DAVID: Meiner Freundin möchte ich ein T-Shirt schenken.
4. THERESA: Ich schreibe meinem Bruder einen Brief.
5. THERESA: Leider kann ich Christian nichts schenken. Ich habe kein Geld mehr.
6. DAVID: Das muss ich meinem Freund erklären.

16. Was macht Dieter? Wem kauft, leiht, gibt, schenkt Dieter etwas? Ergänzen Sie die Sätze mit der Dativform der Wörter° in Klammern.

> of the words

≫ Dieter kauft _____ neue Weingläser. (seine Eltern) *Dieter kauft seinen Eltern neue Weingläser.*

1. Er leiht _____ sein neues Fahrrad. (ich)

2. _____ bringt er Blumen mit. (seine Großmutter)

3. Er leiht _____ seinen neuen Roman. (sein Freund Erik)

4. Will er _____ seinen Rucksack leihen? (du)

5. Er schenkt _____ seinen alten Computer. (sein Bruder)

6. Dieter gibt _____ ein interessantes Video. (wir)

11. Word order of direct and indirect objects

	Indirect object	Direct-object noun
Katrin leiht	*ihrem Freund*	**ihr Fahrrad.**
Katrin leiht	*ihm*	**ihr Fahrrad.**

The direct (accusative) object determines the order of objects. If the direct object is a noun, it usually follows the indirect (dative) object.

	Direct-object personal pronoun	Indirect object
Katrin leiht	**es**	*ihrem Freund.*
Katrin leiht	**es**	*ihm.*

If the direct (accusative) object is a personal pronoun, it always precedes the indirect (dative) object. Note that a pronoun, whether accusative or dative, always precedes a noun.

17. Kleine Gespräche. Ergänzen Sie die kleinen Gespräche mit den angegebenen° Wörtern. Achten° Sie auf die richtige Wortfolge°.

cued / pay attention / word order

≫ PAUL: Schenkst du _____ _____ ? (den kleinen Tisch/Michaels Schwester)
Schenkst du Michaels Schwester den kleinen Tisch?

≫ HEIKE: Ja, ich schenke _____ _____ . (ihn/Michaels Schwester)
Ja, ich schenke ihn Michaels Schwester.

1. PAUL: Schenkst du _____ _____ ? (deine Gitarre/Michael)

   HEIKE: Ja, ich schenke _____ _____ . (sie/ihm)

2. MUTTI: Schenkst du _____ _____ zum Geburtstag? (diesen CD-Spieler/Christine)

   STEFFI: Ja, ich schenke _____ _____ . (ihn/Christine)

3. VATI: Schreibst du _____ oft _____ ? (E-Mails/deinen Freunden)

   DIRK: Ja, ich schreibe _____ _____ . (viele E-Mails/ihnen)

4. LIANE: Willst du _____ _____ leihen? (deinen Rucksack/mir)

   UTE: Ja. Ich leihe _____ _____ gern. (ihn/dir)

18. Frage-Ecke. Sie und einige Freundinnen und Freunde haben im Lotto° gewonnen°. Mit dem Geld kaufen Sie Ihren Freunden und Familienmitgliedern° schöne Geschenke°. Wer bekommt was?

lottery / won
members of your family / presents

S1: Was schenkt Ralf seinen Eltern?
S2: Er schenkt ihnen zwei Wochen in Wien.

S1:

	Eltern	Schwester	Bruder	Melanie
Karsten	einen Porsche	einen Computer		
Stefanie	Winterferien in Spanien			einen Fernseher
Ralf		eine Gitarre	ein Fahrrad	
ich				
Partnerin/ Partner				

S2:

	Eltern	Schwester	Bruder	Melanie
Karsten			neue Skier	einen schönen Ring
Stefanie		einen CD-Spieler	ein Kassettendeck	
Ralf	zwei Wochen in Wien			eine Uhr
ich				
Partnerin/ Partner				

19. Wie sagt man das?

1. What are you giving your mother for her birthday?
   —I'm giving her flowers and a book.
2. Whom are you writing the card to?
   —[To] my cousin Martin.
3. Are you lending your friend money? He wants to buy his parents flowers.
   —No. I don't lend him money any more.
4. Is that motorcycle new? Does it belong to you?
   —No, to my sister.

20. Geburtstagsgeschenke. Sie wissen nicht mehr, was Sie Ihren Familienmitgliedern und Verwandten° zum Geburtstag schenken sollen. Fragen Sie vier Studentinnen/Studenten in Ihrem Deutschkurs, was sie gern schenken. — relatives

S1: Was schenkst du [deiner Mutter] zum Geburtstag?
S2: Ich schenke [ihr] [ein Buch].
S1: Vater □ Bruder □ Schwester □ Großmutter □ Großvater □ Eltern
S2: Uhr □ Blumen □ Liebesroman □ Krimi □ Tasche □ Rucksack □ Fernseher □ Regenschirm

12. Dative prepositions

aus	out of	Gerd geht früh **aus** dem Haus.
	(to come) from *[cities and countries]*	Anna kommt **aus** Österreich.
außer	besides, except for	Wer ist **außer** den Studenten hier?
bei	with *(at the home of)*	Nils wohnt **bei** seiner Tante.
	at *(a place of business)*	Lisa arbeitet **bei** Siemens.
	near *(in the proximity of)*	Die Bäckerei ist **bei** der Universität.
mit	with	Elsa fährt **mit** ihrem Freund zur Uni.
	by means of *(transportation)*	Fährst du **mit** dem Auto zur Uni?
nach	to *(with cities and countries used without an article)*	Rita fährt im Sommer **nach** Österreich.
	after	Arno kommt **nach** dem Essen.
seit	since *(time)*	Petra ist **seit** Mittwoch in Wien.
von	from	Was hören Sie **von** Ihrem Freund Paul?
	of	Österreich ist ein Land **von** 8.000.000 Einwohnern.
	by	Die Oper ist **von** Mozart.
zu	to *(with people and some places)*	Wir gehen gern **zu** unseren Nachbarn.
		Wann fährst du **zur** Uni?
	for *(in certain expressions)*	Was gibt's **zum** Abendessen?

The prepositions **aus, außer, bei, mit, nach, seit, von,** and **zu** are always followed by the dative. Some common translations are provided in the chart above.

■ *bei*

In addition to the meanings listed above, **bei** has many uses that are hard to translate exactly. It is used, in a general way, to indicate a situation: **beim Lesen** *(while reading)*, **bei der Arbeit** *(at work)*, **bei diesem Wetter** *(in weather like this).*

■ *bei/mit*

Sarah wohnt **bei** ihren Eltern.　　Sarah lives *with* her parents.
Sarah fährt morgen **mit** ihren Eltern.　　Sarah's driving *with* her parents tomorrow.

One meaning of both **bei** and **mit** is *with.* However, they are not interchangeable. **Bei** indicates location. **Bei ihren Eltern** means at the home of her parents. **Mit** expresses the idea of doing something together **(mit ihren Eltern).**

■ *nach/zu*

Schmidts fahren morgen **nach** Salzburg.　　The Schmidts are going *to* Salzburg tomorrow.
Ich muss **zum** Bäcker.　　I have to go *to* the bakery.

One meaning of both **zu** and **nach** is *to*. **Zu** is used to show movement toward people and many locations. **Nach** is used with cities and countries without an article.

■ *seit*

Tanja ist **seit** Montag in Hamburg.	Tanja has been in Hamburg *since* Monday.
Jürgen wohnt **seit** drei Wochen in Wien.	Jürgen has been living in Vienna *for* three weeks.

Seit plus the present tense is used to express an action or condition that started in the past but is still continuing in the present. Note that English uses the present perfect tense (e.g., *has been living*) with *since* or *for* to express the same idea.

■ *Contractions*

Brot kaufen wir nur **beim** Bäcker.	bei dem = **beim**
Jürgen kommt jetzt **vom** Markt.	von dem = **vom**
Monika geht **zum** Supermarkt.	zu dem = **zum**
Kerstin geht **zur** Uni.	zu der = **zur**

The prepositions **bei, von,** and **zu** often contract with the definite article **dem,** and **zu** also contracts with the definite article **der.** While contractions are generally optional, they are required in certain common phrases such as:

zum Frühstück/Mittagessen/ Abendessen	beim Arzt°	doctor
zum Beispiel	zum Arzt gehen	
zum Geburtstag	zum Bäcker gehen	
beim Bäcker	zur Uni/Schule gehen	
	vom Arzt kommen	

Contractions are not used when the noun is stressed or modified: **Gehen Sie immer noch zu dem Bäcker in der Bahnhofstraße?** (*Do you still go to the baker on Bahnhofstraße?*)

Österreich ist ein Alpenland: Blick von Salzburg auf die Alpen.

Discussing ideas for
birthday presents

21. Christine in Wien.   Daniela erzählt von ihrer Freundin Christine. Ergänzen Sie die Sätze mit den passenden Präpositionen und Artikeln und Possessiv-pronomen.

Christine kommt _aus_ d_er_ Schweiz. _Seit_ ein _em_ Jahr wohnt sie _Bei_ ein _er_ Familie in Wien. Sie will Musikerin werden und geht jeden Tag _zum_ Konservatorium (das). Zwei Tage in der Woche muss sie jobben. Sie arbeitet _bei_ ein _em_ Bäcker. Nächsten Sommer macht sie _mit_ ihr _er_ Freundin Petra eine Radtour. Sie fahren _nach_ Salzburg zu den Fest-spielen°. Ich höre nicht sehr oft _auf_ Christine, denn sie hat wenig Zeit. Aber _von_ ihr _em_ Bruder bekomme ich manchmal E-Mails. Im September möchte ich _nach_ Wien fahren und Christine besuchen.

famous festival of music and theater

trip / ad / **bietet an:** offers

understand / **sehen Sie nach:** look up

22. Eine Reise° nach Budapest.   Die Anzeige° bietet° eine Reise von Wien nach Budapest an. Beantworten Sie die Fragen. Wenn Sie etwas nicht verste-hen°, sehen° Sie im Anhang nach (Vocabulary for Authentic Text Activities).

fährt ab: leaves
treffen sich: meet
lasts

1. Um wie viel Uhr fährt der Bus von Wien ab°?
2. Wo treffen° sich die Touristen in Wien?
3. Wie lange dauert° die Rückfahrt von Budapest nach Wien?
4. Was kostet die Reise nach Budapest?
5. Wie viel mehr kostet ein Einbettzimmer?

23. Rollenspiel. Sie und Ihre Partnerin/Ihr Partner sind in Wien und finden in der Zeitung die Anzeige auf Seite 192. Sie möchten für ein paar Tage nach Budapest fahren und gehen zu einem Reisebüro°. Da haben Sie viele Fragen: Wie viel kostet die Reise? Was bekommt man alles für den Preis? Wie viele Tage ist man in Budapest? Welche Tage?

Making plans for a vacation

travel agency

24. Verkehrsmittel. Fragen Sie Ihre Partnerin/Ihren Partner, wie man am besten° von Ort° zu Ort fahren kann. Benutzen° Sie den Plan.

am besten: best of all / place / use

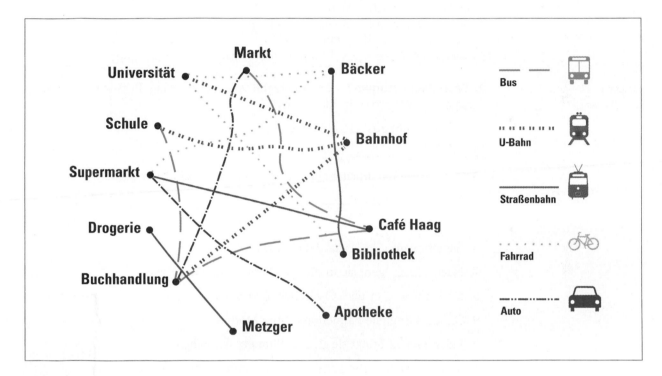

S1: Wie komme ich am besten von der Uni zur Bibliothek?
S2: Am besten fährst du mit dem Fahrrad.

1. Wie komme ich am besten von der Schule zum Bahnhof°?
2. Wie komme ich am besten vom Markt zum Café Haag?
3. Wie komme ich am besten vom Metzger zur Drogerie?
4. Wie komme ich am besten von der Buchhandlung zum Markt?
5. Wie komme ich am besten von der Uni zum Bäcker?

train station

25. Was wissen Sie von Katrin? Sagen Sie auf Deutsch, was Sie über Katrin wissen.

1. Mondays Katrin does not go out of the house.
2. Tuesdays she sleeps at her girlfriend's.
3. Wednesdays she goes to the university early.
4. For breakfast she eats nothing except a roll.
5. She goes [*fahren*] to the university by streetcar.
6. I believe her friend Karoline is from Frankfurt.
7. She has been living here for a year.

WIEDERHOLUNG

trip
cued

1. Eine Reise° nach Österreich.   Erzählen Sie von Davids Reise nach Österreich. Benutzen Sie die angegebenen° Wörter.

1. David / sein / Amerikaner
2. er / fliegen / nach / Wien
3. er / sprechen / mit / einige / Studenten
4. sie / erzählen / von / diese Universität
5. nach / zwei Tage / David / fahren / mit / Zug / nach / Salzburg

complete
parentheses

2. Was macht Monika?   Sandra erzählt von Monikas Tag. Ergänzen° Sie die Sätze mit den Wörtern in Klammern°.

1. Monika geht aus _____ . (das Haus)

2. Sie geht zu _____ . (der Bäcker)

3. _____ Andrea arbeitet bei _____ . (ihre Freundin / der Bäcker)

4. Monika arbeitet für _____ . (ihr Onkel)

5. Sie erklärt _____ auch viel über Computer. (er)

6. Sie fährt mit _____ zur Arbeit. (das Fahrrad)

7. Nach _____ geht sie in die Buchhandlung. (die Arbeit)

8. Sie kauft _____ über Österreich. (ein Buch)

9. _____ bringt sie Blumen mit. (ihre Mutter)

10. Jeden Freitag bringt sie _____ Blumen. (sie, *sing.*)

11. Morgen schenkt sie _____ das Buch zum Geburtstag. (ihr Vater)

12. Nächstes Jahr fährt sie mit _____ nach Österreich. (ihre Freunde)

13. Das sagt sie _____ heute am Telefon. (sie, *pl.*)

setzt sich: sits down

3. Jetzt weiß er es.   In einem Café setzt° sich Dieter Meier an Karen Müllers Tisch. Nach zehn Minuten weiß Dieter einiges über Karen. Sagen Sie, was Dieter alles weiß. Beginnen Sie jeden Satz mit **Er weiß, dass...**

KAREN: Ich bin Österreicherin.
DIETER: Kommst du aus Wien?
KAREN: Nein, aus Salzburg.
DIETER: Wohnst du in einem Studentenheim?
KAREN: Nein, bei einer Familie.
DIETER: Was studierst du denn?

economics

KAREN: Wirtschaftswissenschaft° ist mein Hauptfach und Englisch mein Nebenfach. Ich möchte in Amerika arbeiten.
DIETER: Warst du schon in Amerika?
KAREN: Leider noch nicht.

4. Wie sagt man das?

1. VERENA: Would you like to go to Austria this summer?
2. CARINA: Yes. Gladly. Do you want to go by car or by train?
3. VERENA: By bike. If the weather stays nice.

4. EIN FREUND: Can you lend me your German book?
5. SIE: Of course, I can give it to you.
6. EIN FREUND: And can you also explain the dative° to me?   dative = **der Dativ**
7. SIE: Do we have enough time?

5. Wo soll ich studieren?

Ihre Partnerin/Ihr Partner möchte in Europa studieren. Sie/Er weiß aber nicht, ob sie/er in Deutschland oder Österreich studieren soll. Wählen° Sie ein Land und erzählen Sie von dem Land. Hier sind einige Fragen.   choose

Wie groß ist das Land?	Hat es viele Berge?
Wie viele Einwohner hat es?	Hat es viel Industrie?
Wie viele Nachbarn hat es?	Wie heißt die Hauptstadt?

6. Zum Schreiben

Sie studieren in Wien und möchten Ihre Freundin/Ihren Freund überreden° auch in Wien zu studieren. In einem kurzen Brief schreiben Sie ihr/ihm von den Vorteilen°.   persuade

   advantages

Wien, den 30. Dezember 2000

Liebe [Barbara],/Lieber [Paul],
ich bin ...

...

Viele Grüße
deine [Jennifer]/dein [David]

After you have finished your letter, check the following carefully:

- Subject and verb agreement
- Word order and punctuation in sentences with conjunctions
- Genders and cases of all nouns and pronouns
- Case used with each preposition

GRAMMATIK: ZUSAMMENFASSUNG

Verbs with stem-vowel change *a* > *ä*

fahren	
ich fahre	wir fahren
du **fährst**	ihr fahrt
er/es/sie **fährt**	sie fahren
Sie fahren	
du-*imperative:* fahr(e)	

laufen	
ich laufe	wir laufen
du **läufst**	ihr lauft
er/es/sie **läuft**	sie laufen
Sie laufen	
du-*imperative:* lauf(e)	

Independent clauses and coordinating conjunctions

Erik **kommt** morgen, aber Christl **muss** morgen arbeiten.

In independent (main) clauses the finite verb **(kommt, muss)** is in second posi-tion. A coordinating conjunction **(aber)** does not affect word order. The five common coordinating conjunctions are **aber, denn, oder, sondern,** and **und.**

Dependent clauses and subordinating conjunctions

Ich weiß, dass Frank morgen **kommt.**
      dass Petra morgen **mitkommt.**
      dass Helmut nicht **kommen kann.**

In dependent (subordinate) clauses:

1. The finite verb **(kommt)** is in final position.
2. The separable prefix **(mit)** is attached to the base form of the verb **(kommt)** in final position.
3. The modal auxiliary **(kann)** is a finite verb and therefore is in final position, after the infinitive **(kommen).**

Some common subordinating conjunctions are **dass, obwohl, weil,** and **wenn.**

Wenn du mit dem Rad fährst, **siehst** du mehr vom Land.

When a dependent clause begins a sentence, it is followed directly by the finite verb **(siehst)** of the independent clause.

Dative case

■ *Articles,* **der-** *and* **ein-***words in the dative case*

	Masculine	Neuter	Feminine	Plural
Nominative	der Mann	das Kind	die Frau	die Freunde
Accusative	den Mann	das Kind	die Frau	die Freunde
Dative	**dem** Mann	**dem** Kind	**der** Frau	**den** Freunden
	diesem Mann	**diesem** Kind	**dieser** Frau	**diesen** Freunden
	einem Mann	**einem** Kind	**einer** Frau	**keinen** Freunden
	ihrem Mann	**unserem** Kind	**seiner** Frau	**meinen** Freunden

■ *Nouns in the dative plural*

Nominative	die Männer	die Frauen	die Radios
Dative	den Männer**n**	den Frauen	den Radios

Nouns in the dative plural add **-n** unless the plural already ends in **-n** or **-s**.

■ *Masculine* N-*nouns in the dative case*

Nominative	der Herr	der Mensch
Accusative	den Herrn	den Menschen
Dative	**dem** Herrn	**dem** Menschen

For the masculine **N**-nouns used in this book, see the Grammatical Tables in the Reference Section.

■ *Dative of* **wer**

Nominative	wer
Accusative	wen
Dative	**wem**

Dative personal pronouns

	Singular					
Nominative	ich	du	er	es	sie	Sie
Accusative	mich	dich	ihn	es	sie	Sie
Dative	**mir**	**dir**	**ihm**	**ihm**	**ihr**	**Ihnen**

	Plural			
Nominative	wir	ihr	sie	Sie
Accusative	uns	euch	sie	Sie
Dative	**uns**	**euch**	**ihnen**	**Ihnen**

Word order of direct and indirect objects

	Indirect object	Direct-object noun
Katrin schenkt	*ihrer Schwester*	**den Rucksack.**
Katrin schenkt	*ihr*	**den Rucksack.**

The direct (accusative) object determines the order of objects. If the direct object is a noun, it follows the indirect (dative) object.

	Direct-object pronoun	Indirect object
Katrin schenkt	**ihn**	*ihrer Schwester.*
Katrin schenkt	**ihn**	*ihr.*

If the direct (accusative) object is a personal pronoun, it precedes the indirect (dative) object.

Dative verbs

Das Fahrrad **gehört** meinem Bruder.
Ich **glaube** dir nicht.

Most German verbs take objects in the accusative. A few verbs take objects in the dative. The dative object is usually a person. For convenience such verbs can be classified as "dative verbs."

For dative verbs used in this book, see the Grammatical Tables in the Reference Section.

Dative prepositions

aus	out of; from (= *is a native of*)
außer	besides, except for
bei	with *(at the home of);* at *(a place of business);* near *(in the proximity of);* while *or* during *(indicates a situation)*
mit	with; by means of *(transportation)*
nach	to *(with cities, and countries used without an article);* after
seit	since, for *(referring to time)*
von	from; of; by *(the person doing something)*
zu	to *(with people and some places);* for *(in certain expressions)*

Contractions of dative prepositions

bei dem	=	**beim**
von dem	=	**vom**
zu dem	=	**zum**
zu der	=	**zur**

KAPITEL 6

Was hast du vor?

*Diese jungen Leute
wollen ins Kino gehen.*

BAUSTEINE FÜR GESPRÄCHE

Was habt ihr vor?

UWE: Sagt mal, was macht ihr am Wochenende?

MELANIE: Keine Ahnung.

MICHAEL: Ich habe am Freitag Probe mit der Band. Am Samstag spielen wir in der Musikfabrik.

UWE: Du, Melanie, da können wir doch zusammen hingehen, oder?

MELANIE: Gute Idee. Das ist super. Vielleicht geht auch Alex mit?

MICHAEL: Der kann nicht. Er muss fürs Examen arbeiten.

UWE: Also, Melanie, ich hole dich um acht ab. In Ordnung?

Fragen

1. Was hat Michael am Wochenende vor?
2. Wohin möchte Uwe gehen?
3. Warum kann Alex nicht mitgehen?
4. Wann holt Uwe Melanie ab?

Es hat geschmeckt.

ALEX: Wo warst du gestern Abend?

GISELA: Warum?

ALEX: Ich habe bei dir angerufen, aber da war niemand da. Ich wollte mit dir ins Kino gehen.

GISELA: Gestern war ich mit Claudia im Café an der Uni. Sie hat mich eingeladen.

ALEX: Ah, das Café ist gut. Die haben tolle Salate.

GISELA: Ja, genau, wir haben Fischsalat gegessen.

ALEX: Hör auf, ich kriege gleich Hunger!

Fragen

1. Warum hat Alex bei Gisela angerufen?
2. Warum war Gisela nicht zu Hause?
3. Wie findet Alex das Café an der Uni?
4. Was haben Gisela und Claudia gegessen?

Brauchbares

1. To say they can go there Uwe uses the verb **hingehen. Hin** is used with verbs and adverbs to show direction away from the speaker. **Hin** is practiced in *Kapitel 7.*

2. To ask whether Melanie agrees with him, Uwe ends one sentence with **"oder?"** and the other with **"In Ordnung?"** These two phrases are common in German conversation. **Oder?** is equivalent to *Or don't you agree?* and **In Ordnung?** is equivalent to *Is that all right with you?*

3. Alex says, **"Ich wollte ... ins Kino gehen."** **Wollte** is the simple past tense form of the modal **wollen** and will be practiced in *Kapitel 10*.

4. Gisela uses the verb **einladen** to say Claudia treated her. The basic meaning of **einladen** is *to invite*.

1. Was machst du in der Freizeit?   Fragen Sie Ihre Partnerin/Ihren Partner, was sie/er in ihrer/seiner Freizeit macht. Benutzen Sie auch Wörter aus dem Anhang° (Supplementary Word Sets, „Hobbies" und „Sports and games").

Discussing leisure-time activities

reference section

S1:	*S2:*
Was sind deine Hobbys?	**Radfahren.**

SchüttelKasten

Musik hören/machen

Science Fiction lesen

Fotografieren°   **Kochen°**

Im Internet surfen°

Rollerblading gehen

Joggen   Skilaufen/Wasserskifahren

Was hast du am Wochenende vor?	Ich gehe	**schwimmen.** Ski laufen/Wasserskifahren. windsurfen°. tanzen.
	Ich will	**viel lesen.** faulenzen°. arbeiten. Fußball/Tennis im Fernsehen sehen.

2. Hast du Hunger oder Durst?   In einer Gruppe von vier stellen° Sie einander Fragen. Finden° Sie heraus, ob die anderen Studenten Hunger oder Durst haben.

stellen ... Fragen: ask each other questions/ **finden heraus:** find out

S1:	*S2:*
Hast du Hunger?	Ja, großen Hunger. Nein, ich habe keinen Hunger. Nein, ich habe schon gegessen°.
Hast du Durst?	Ja, großen Durst. Nein, ich habe keinen Durst. Nein, danke. Ich habe eben° eine Cola° getrunken°.

LAND UND LEUTE

Go to the
Deutsch heute Web Site at
www.hmco.com/college

Freizeit

Although the Germans have a reputation for being industrious, they are also known as the world champions in leisure time **(Freizeitweltmeister).** The work week in Germany ranges from 35.5 hours a week to 39. In 1998 Germans worked an average of 1573 hours in the year. In contrast American workers worked 1903 hours. Germany ranks second among the industrialized nations in paid vacation time **(Urlaub)** and Finland ranks first. The United States and Japan bring up the rear in paid vacation time.

Segeln ist ein beliebter Sport in Deutschland.

Germans spend much of their free time taking vacation trips abroad. Germans make around 20 million trips into foreign countries and spend more than 75 billion marks abroad. The most popular European destinations for Germans are Spain, Italy, and Austria. Outside of Europe the favorite destinations are the United States and Canada. About one-third of the vacation trips are taken in Germany.

Diskussion

Below is a chart with the average number of paid vacation days (not including paid holidays) and the average work week for some member nations of the European Union. These statistics apply to industrial workers.

Country	Paid vacation days	Work week (hours)
Germany	30	37
Austria	26.5	38.4
Finland	37.5	40
France	25	39
Great Britain	25	38.8

1. Compare the vacation days for these countries with the number of days employees receive in your area.
2. Most European nations have more paid vacation days than in the United States. Do you think that so much vacation time is a good policy? Make a plan of how you would spend six weeks of vacation time. You do not have to take all six weeks at the same time.

3. Gegessen und getrunken. Was haben Sie gestern gegessen und getrunken? Beantworten Sie die Fragen erst selbst° und fragen Sie dann Ihre Partnerin/Ihren Partner. Erzählen Sie den anderen Studenten, was sie/er gesagt hat.

yourself

Talking about food and dining out

1. Wo hast du gestern zu Abend gegessen?

zu Hause ☐ im Café an der Uni ☐ in ...

2. Was hast du gegessen?

Steak° und Pommes frites° ☐ Spaghetti ☐ Wurst und Brot ☐ Pizza°

3. Was hast du getrunken?

eine Cola ☐ ein Wasser

4. Hat es geschmeckt?

Danke, gut. ☐ Ganz toll. ☐ Nicht besonders. ☐ Nein, leider nicht.

4. Ein Rollenspiel. Sie haben Ihre Partnerin/Ihren Partner zu einem Essen im Café an der Uni eingeladen. Diskutieren Sie, was Sie bestellen° wollen. Beginnen Sie mit den folgenden Sätzen. Eine Übersetzung° der Speisekarte° finden Sie im Anhang (Vocabulary for Authentic Text Activities).

order
translation/menu

S1: Was isst du?
S2: Ich nehme Wurstsalat mit Brot.
S1: Und was trinkst du?
S2: Ich trinke einen Apfelsaft. Und was isst du?
usw.°

usw. (= und so weiter): etc. (and so on)

Café an der Uni

Getränke

Große Tasse Kaffee mit Sahne		4,20
Große Tasse Schokolade mit Sahne		4,20
Große Tasse frisch gebrühter Tee		4,20
Cappuccino		4,50
Espresso		3,30
Schweppes Sodawasser	0,2l	3,80
Schweppes Bitter Lemon	0,2l	3,80
Schweppes Ginger Ale	0,2l	3,80
Apfelsaft	0,25l	3,20
Coca-Cola	0,25l	3,20
Fanta	0,25l	3,20
Johannisbeersaft	0,2l	4,00
Pils vom Fass	0,3l	3,80
Export vom Fass	0,3l	3,50

Kuchen und Gebäck

Bitte treffen Sie an unserer Schauvitrine Ihre Wahl und bestellen Sie bei Ihrer Bedienung!

Torten	4,20
Kuchen	3,80
Croissant	2,50
Portion Schlagsahne	1,50

Eis

Kleines Eis (drei Kugeln nach Wahl)	6,00
mit Sahne	6,60
Großes Eis (fünf Kugeln nach Wahl)	7,80
mit Sahne	8,40
Eiskaffee	6,20

Toasts

„Hawaii" mit Schinken, Käse und Ananas	8,20
„Spezial" mit Schinken, Käse und Pilzen	8,90
„Farmer"-Toast mit Truthahnbrust und Spiegelei	10,20

Kalte Speisen

Baguette „Café an der Uni"	8,20
Baguette mit Thunfisch und Ei	8,20
Wurstsalat mit Brot	7,50
Käsebrot, Emmentaler oder Camembert	6,20
Wurstbrot, Salami, Bierschinken oder Leberwurst	6,20

Salate

Griechischer Salat mit Brot	12,00
Salatschüssel mit frischen Saisonsalaten, Ei, Dressing und Brot	11,50
Große Salatplatte mit Schinken, Käse, Pepperoni, Oliven, frischen Salaten und Brot	14,80

Warme Gerichte

Gebackener Camembert mit Preiselbeeren, Salatbeilage und Brot	9,70
Spaghetti „Bolognese"	9,80
Tortellini in Sahnesauce mit Salat	12,50
Pizza mit Schinken, Käse, Salami, Oliven, Pepperoni und Champignons	10,50
Schnitzel Wiener Art mit Kartoffelsalat	12,50

Geöffnet:
Montag bis Freitag 8 - 22 Uhr
Samstag und Feiertage 9 - 22 Uhr

Alle Preise sind Inklusivpreise und enthalten Bedienungsgeld und Mehrwertsteuer.

LAND UND LEUTE

Go to the
Deutsch heute Web Site at
www.hmco.com/college

Essen zu Hause und als Gast

Although a growing number of Germans eat their main hot meal in the evening **(Abendessen)**, many Germans still eat their main meal at noon **(Mittagessen).** It may consist of up to three courses: appetizer **(Vorspeise)**, entrée **(Hauptgericht** or **Hauptspeise),** and dessert **(Nachtisch** or **Dessert),** which is usually fruit, pudding, or ice cream. Cakes and pastries are served at afternoon coffee time **(Kaffee).**

Before a meal, it is customary to say **Guten Appetit** or **Mahlzeit,** and others may wish you the same by responding **Danke, gleichfalls.** Even in a restaurant, when sharing a table with a stranger who has asked if it is all right to sit at the table by saying **Ist hier noch frei?,** one wishes the stranger **Guten Appetit** when the meal arrives.

Abendessen bei einer Familie in Ostdorf bei Balingen.

Most restaurants post their menus outside. After the meal, one pays the server. A service charge **(Bedienung)** is included in the bill. However, it is customary to add a tip **(Trinkgeld)** by rounding off the bill for small amounts (e.g., 8 marks instead of 7,20) and giving a 5 to 10 percent tip for larger amounts.

When people are invited to a friend's house for dinner or for **Kaffee,** it is customary to bring a small gift. Most often the guest will bring a small bouquet, a box of chocolates, or a bottle of wine.

Diskussion

Imagine that your German E-mail pen pal is coming to visit. Explain to her/him what kind of eating habits to expect in your area and how they might be different from those in Germany.

Fachinger: ein Mineralwasser.

Vokabeln

Beginning in *Kapitel 6* the past participles of strong verbs (see p. 222) will be listed after the infinitive, e.g., **einladen, eingeladen.**

Substantive

die **Ahnung**   hunch; idea; **keine Ahnung!**   no idea!
die **Band, -s**   (musical) band
die **Cola, -s**   cola drink
der **Durst**   thirst; **Durst haben**   to be thirsty
die **Freizeit**   free time
das **Hobby, -s**   hobby
der **Hunger**   hunger; **Hunger haben**   to be hungry

die **Idee, -n**   idea
das **Internet** internet; **im Internet surfen**   to surf the internet
die **Pizza, -s**   pizza
die **Pommes frites** *(pl.)*   French fries
die **Probe, -n**   rehearsal
das **Steak, -s**   steak

Verben

an·rufen, angerufen   to phone; **bei [dir] anrufen**   to call [you] at home
auf·hören   to stop (an activity)
ein·laden (lädt ein), eingeladen   to invite; to treat
essen: gegessen
faulenzen   to lounge around, be idle
fotografieren   to photograph
kochen   to cook
kriegen   to get

mit·gehen, ist mitgegangen   to go along
schmecken (+ *dat.*)   to taste; **der Käse schmeckt mir**   the cheese tastes good; **hat es geschmeckt?**   did it taste good?
trinken: getrunken
vor·haben   to intend, have in mind
windsurfen gehen   to go windsurfing; **surfen**   to surf

Andere Wörter

eben   just
genau   exact(ly); **genau!**   that's right
gleich   immediately; in a minute; same; similar

niemand   no one
super   super, great

Besondere Ausdrücke

ein Wasser   a bottle/glass of mineral water
gestern Abend   last night
in Ordnung?   is that all right (with you)?

oder?   or don't you agree?
zu Abend essen   to have (eat) dinner

FREIZEITPLÄNE

Vorbereitung auf das Lesen

■ *Vor dem Lesen**

am liebsten: most of all

1. Was machen Sie am liebsten° in Ihrer Freizeit?

   Radfahren ☐ Joggen ☐ Fernsehen ☐ am Computer arbeiten° ☐ Lesen ☐ Wandern oder Spazierengehen ☐ mit Freunden zusammen sein ☐ ins Kino, Theater° oder Konzert° gehen ☐ im Internet surfen ☐ Faulenzen

expressions / answer / use

   Sie können diese Wörter und Wendungen° in Ihrer Antwort° benutzen°:

   Am liebsten ...
   In meiner Freizeit ...
   Meistens ...

zur Entspannung: for relaxation
survey

   Zur Entspannung° ...

2. Machen Sie eine Umfrage° unter den Studentinnen/Studenten.

   ➤➤ *Was machst du am liebsten in deiner Freizeit?*

ads

3. Sehen Sie die Anzeigen° an und beantworten Sie die Fragen.
   a. Welche Band spielt im Olympiastadion?
   b. Wo kann man ein amerikanisches Musical sehen?
   c. Wo kann man die Theaterkarten° von 10 bis 18 Uhr kaufen?
   d. Wann endet das Musical? Kann man nach dem Musical in die Oly-Disco gehen?
   e. Wann schließt die Disco am Samstag?
   f. Wer geht in diese Disco?

possibilities

   g. Welche von den drei Möglichkeiten° gefallen Ihnen?

Staatstheater am Gärtnerplatz
Telefon 2 01 67 67
Vorverkauf im Theater
Mo.-Fr. 10-18 Uhr, Sa. 10-13 Uhr
Maximilianstr. 11-13
Mo.-Fr. 10-13, 15.30-17.30, Sa. 10-13 Uhr
Der Fiedler auf dem Dach (Anatevka)
Musical Jerry Bock
Beginn: 19.30   Ende: 22.45 Uhr

---

*Remember, words appearing with a raised degree mark but no definition in the margin are new "active" words that you should learn and be able to use. These words and their definitions appear in the **Vokabeln** section that most closely follows the exercise.

Dieser junge Mann geht in seiner Freizeit gern Rollerblading.

■ Beim Lesen

Was machen die Leute im Text in ihrer Freizeit? Machen Sie eine Liste.

Peter Bosch ist Reporter bei einer Studentenzeitung und macht Straßeninterviews für die Zeitung. Seine Frage: „Was hast du letztes Wochenende in deiner Freizeit gemacht?"

Silke, 25 Jahre:

„Freizeit? Ich habe schon ewig keine richtige Freizeit mehr gehabt. Ich
5 studiere Englisch und bekomme BAföG, da möchte ich natürlich so schnell wie möglich mit dem Studium fertig werden. Doch am Sonntagabend hat die Jule Neigel Band im Olympiastadion gespielt; die musste° ich hören,   had to denn ihre Musik gefällt mir. Samstagmorgen bin ich einkaufen gegangen. Ich habe nämlich letzten Monat gejobbt, und mit dem Geld habe ich einen Rock
10 und eine Bluse gekauft. Den Rest vom Wochenende war ich die meiste Zeit zu Hause und habe gelernt, denn ich habe bald mein Examen. Da bleibt leider nicht viel Zeit für Hobbys."

Stefan, 19 Jahre:

„Ich habe seit zwei Monaten meinen Führerschein und fahre gern mit meinem Auto spazieren. Letzten Samstag bin ich sehr früh aufgestanden. Ich
15 bin zu meinen Großeltern gefahren und habe sie besucht. Sie wohnen etwa hundertfünfzig Kilometer nördlich von München.

Ich höre gern Rockmusik. Am Samstag sind meine Freunde und ich tanzen gegangen. Die Oly-Disco finde ich besonders toll. Mein Auto ist

Die Jule Neigel Band.

natürlich zu Hause geblieben, denn ich habe Bier getrunken. Ins Kino gehe
20 ich nicht so gern. Das finde ich so passiv, denn man kann dort nicht mit
Freunden sprechen. Eine Disco ist da schon viel besser, oder eine Kneipe."

Evi, 31 Jahre:

"Viele Leute sagen, Deutsche arbeiten zu viel und sind sehr fleißig. Ich
denke auch manchmal, ich arbeite zu viel. Ich bin Ärztin und muss oft viele
Stunden im Krankenhaus sein. Letztes Wochenende habe ich aber frei
25 gehabt. Ich habe am Samstag zuerst mit meinem Bruder Tennis gespielt,
dann bin ich mit meinem Freund Rad gefahren. Ich treibe gern Sport. Und
außerdem ist Sport gesund. Am Abend hat meine Familie Geburtstag
gefeiert, denn meine Großmutter ist 83 Jahre alt geworden! Am Sonntag sind
mein Freund und ich ins Staatstheater am Gärtnerplatz gegangen. Wir haben
30 das Musical ,Der Fiedler auf dem Dach' gesehen. Mich hat das Stück interessiert, aber mein Freund hat es etwas langweilig gefunden. Ich gehe in
meiner Freizeit gern aus. Manchmal bin ich aber ganz einfach auch gern zu
Hause, sehe fern, höre Radio, lese ein Buch oder tue nichts."

Brauchbares

1. In l. 7 Silke says, **"Die musste ich hören." Musste** is the simple past tense
of **müssen,** which will be practiced in *Kapitel 10.*
2. To an American it might seem that Stefan is getting his driver's license rather
late. Reasons for this are found in **Land und Leute: Führerschein,** p. 210.

Nach dem Lesen

1. Fragen zum Lesestück

1. Lesen Sie Ihre Liste von den Freizeitbeschäftigungen° im Text. Was machen Sie in Ihrer Freizeit? — free-time activities
2. Was studiert Silke?
3. Was macht Silke am Sonntag?
4. Warum hat Silke nicht viel Zeit für ihre Hobbys?
5. Wie alt ist Stefan?
6. Wie lange hat Stefan schon seinen Führerschein?
7. Warum geht Stefan gern in eine Disco oder Kneipe?
8. Warum bleibt Stefans Auto zu Hause?
9. Was ist Evis Beruf°? — profession
10. Wann hat Evi frei gehabt?
11. Mit wem geht Evi ins Theater?
12. Welches Musical spielt im Staatstheater?
13. Was macht Evi gern zu Hause?
14. Mit wem (Silke, Stefan oder Evi) möchten Sie gern ein Wochenende verbringen°? Warum? — spend (time)

2. Wer hätte das sagen können°?   Silke, Stefan oder Evi?

hätte sagen können: could have said

1. Ich habe wenig Freizeit. _____

2. Ich spreche gern mit meinen Freunden. _____

3. Ich studiere in München. _____

4. Ich fahre gern spazieren. _____

5. Ins Kino gehen gefällt mir nicht. _____

6. Ich muss oft lernen. _____

7. Ich muss viele Stunden arbeiten. _____

8. Ich habe neue Kleidung° gekauft. _____

9. Meine Großmutter ist 83 Jahre alt. _____

10. Ich höre gern Rockmusik. _____

11. Ich spiele gern Tennis. _____

3. Erzählen wir.   Besprechen° Sie eins der folgenden Themen° in einer Gruppe von drei Studenten.

discuss / **eins ... Themen:** one of the following topics

- Was ich in meiner Freizeit mache
- Warum ich keine Freizeit habe

LAND UND LEUTE

Go to the
Deutsch heute Web Site at
www.hmco.com/college

Der Führerschein

The minimum age for a driver's license in the German-speaking countries is eighteen (though exceptions are sometimes made for people as young as sixteen who need a car to make a living). To obtain a license one must attend a private driving school **(Fahrschule).** (Driver education courses are not offered in school.) In Germany a driving course consists of 18 hours of theoretical study and a minimum of 35 hours of practical driving lessons **(Fahrstunden)** as well as approximately 10 additional hours of special practice **(Sonderausbildung),** e.g., freeway **(Autobahn)** and night-time driving **(Nachtfahren).** At the end, every student must pass a theoretical test with a perfect

Fahrschule Hahn ist nur eine der vielen Hamburger Fahrschulen.

score, and a driving test. The **Führerschein** is then issued temporarily for two years, after which time the driver can obtain it for life, if her/his driving record shows no entries for drunken driving or other at-fault violations. The total cost of the driving lessons plus the 250 mark test fee **(Prüfungsgebühr)** is around 3000 marks. The failure rate is 1 in 4.

The member nations of the European Union have agreed to standards for driver's licenses that will apply in all member countries. Drivers receive an EU license and national driver's licenses of member nations are valid throughout the European Union.

Diskussion

Countries have different laws and regulations about driving. Comment on the following laws found in German-speaking countries in comparison to regulations in your country or state.

1. Germany has no speed limit on most sections of the **Autobahnen.**
2. Switzerland has a law prohibiting speaking on a hand-held phone while driving.
3. In Germany truck traffic is forbidden on Sundays and holidays as well as Saturdays at the height of the vacation season.
4. Switzerland and Austria charge a fee for using **Autobahnen.** There is no fee in Germany.

Erweiterung des Wortschatzes

1. Infinitives used as nouns

Mein Hobby ist **Wandern.**   My hobby is *hiking.*
Frühmorgens ist **das Joggen** toll. *Jogging* early in the morning is great.

German infinitives may be used as nouns. An infinitive used as a noun is always neuter. The English equivalent is often a gerund, that is, the *-ing* form of a verb used as a noun.

1. In Deutschland. Die folgenden Meinungen° hört man in Deutschland oft. Wie   opinions
sagt man das auf Englisch?

1. Laufen ist schön.
2. Natürlichkeit in Essen und Trinken gefällt den Deutschen.
3. Es gehört zum Einkaufen am Wochenende, dass man Blumen mitbringt.
4. Schwimmen ist ein schöner Sport.
5. Skilaufen ist toll.

2. Tagträume°. In diesen Situationen gehen° die Deutschen Tagträumen nach: daydreams / **gehen nach:**
                                                                                  indulge in

bei der Arbeit	51%
beim Spaziergang°	49%
in der Badewanne°	44%
beim Autofahren	26%
beim Fernsehen	19%
beim Essen	12%

walk
bathtub

1. Wo gehen die Deutschen am meisten Tagträumen nach? Wo am wenigsten?
2. Wann haben Sie Tagträume? Warum?
3. Was träumen Sie?

Arbeiten soll Spaß machen. Lesen auch.

EXTRA-HEFT
Mit 100 neuen
Super-Singles

AMICA im Mai. Ab 16.4. am Kiosk.

articles of clothing

2. Kleidungsstücke°

1. der **Anzug, ̈e**	11. das **Hemd, -en**
2. der **Badeanzug, ̈e**	12. das **Jackett, -s**
3. der **Handschuh, -e**	13. das **Kleid, -er**
4. der **Hut, ̈e**	14. das **Polohemd, -en**
5. der **Pulli, -s**	15. das **T-Shirt, -s**
6. der **(Regen)mantel, ̈**	16. die **Badehose, -n**
7. der **(Regen)schirm, -e**	17. die **Bluse, -n**
8. der **Rock, ̈e**	18. die **(Hand)tasche, -n**
9. der **Schuh, -e**	19. die **Hose, -n**
10. der **Stiefel, -**	20. die **Jacke, -n**
	21. die **Jeans** (*pl.*)
	22. die **Krawatte, -n**
	23. die **Mütze, -n**
	24. die **Shorts (die kurzen Hosen)**
	25. die **Socke, -n**
	26. die **(Sonnen)brille, -n**
	27. die **Strumpfhose, -n**

For additional articles of clothing see the Supplementary Word Sets on clothing in the Reference Section.

3. Was tragen die Leute? Beschreiben° Sie, was eine der Personen auf den Bildern trägt oder auf einem Bild, das Sie mitgebracht haben. Ihre Partnerin/Ihr Partner soll Ihnen sagen, wen Sie beschrieben haben, und beschreibt Ihnen dann eine andere Person.

S1: Diese Frau trägt einen Rock, eine ...
S2: Das ist ...

Herr und Frau Bosch kaufen ihrem Sohn Martin ein Mountainbike.

Herr König und seine Kinder Kerstin und Markus gehen spazieren.

Discussing clothes

4. Was tragen Sie? Beantworten Sie die Fragen erst selbst und fragen Sie dann Ihre Partnerin/Ihren Partner. Denken Sie daran **du** mit Ihrer Partnerin/Ihrem Partner zu benutzen°.

use

1. Was tragen Sie im Winter? Im Sommer?
2. Was tragen Sie, wenn Sie in die Vorlesung gehen?
3. Was tragen Sie, wenn Sie tanzen gehen?
4. Was möchten Sie zum Geburtstag haben?
5. Welche Farben tragen Sie gern?

Expressing opinions and likes and dislikes

several/members of the class

5. Wie gefällt es dir? Fragen Sie mehrere° Kursteilnehmer°, wie sie die Kleidungsstücke finden. Sie können dazu ein Bild aus diesem Buch nehmen oder Bilder von zu Hause mitbringen.

S1:
Was hältst° du von [dem Kleid]?

S2:
[Das] muss furchtbar teuer sein. Was kostet [es]?
[Das] ist schön/toll/praktisch.
[Das] sieht° billig aus.
[Das] ist nichts Besonderes.

wählen aus: choose

6. Wer ist das? Wählen° Sie zusammen mit einer Partnerin/einem Partner eine Studentin/einen Studenten aus Ihrem Deutschkurs aus und beschreiben Sie, was sie/er trägt. Die anderen Studenten sollen herausfinden, wen Sie beschreiben.

Vokabeln

Substantive

die **Antwort, -en** answer
der **Arzt, ⸚e**/die **Ärztin, -nen** doctor, physician
die **Bluse, -n** blouse
die **Disco, -s** (also **Disko**) dance club
der **Führerschein, -e** driver's license
das **Interview, -s** interview
die **Karte, -n** ticket; die **Theaterkarte, -n** theater ticket
die **Kleidung** clothing
die **Kneipe, -n** bar, pub
das **Konzert, -e** concert; **ins Konzert gehen** to go to a concert
das **Krankenhaus, ⸚er** hospital
For additional articles of clothing see p. 212.

das **Mountainbike, -s** mountain bike
das **Musical, -s** musical
der **Reporter, -**/die **Reporterin, -nen** reporter
der **Rest, -e** rest, remaining part
der **Rock, ⸚e** skirt
die **Rockmusik** rock (music)
die **Sache, -n** thing; matter; **Sachen** (*pl.*) clothes
das **Stück, -e** piece (of music); **Theaterstück** play (theater)
die **Stunde, -n** hour
das **Theater, -** theater; **ins Theater gehen** to go to the theater
das **Thema,** *pl.* **Themen** topic

Verben

auf·stehen, ist aufgestanden to get up; to stand up

aus·gehen, ist ausgegangen to go out

aus·sehen (sieht aus), ausgesehen to look like, seem

beschreiben, beschrieben to describe

bleiben: ist geblieben

fahren: ist gefahren

feiern to celebrate

gebrauchen to use

gehen: ist gegangen

halten (hält), gehalten to hold; **halten von** to think of, have an opinion

interessieren to interest

Rad fahren (fährt Rad), ist Rad gefahren to ride a bicycle; **ich fahre Rad** ride a bike

sehen: gesehen

spazieren fahren (fährt spazieren), ist spazieren gefahren to go for a drive

tragen (trägt), getragen to wear; to carry

tun (tut), getan to do

werden: ist geworden to become; **es wird kalt** it's getting cold

Andere Wörter

außerdem besides, in addition, as well

einfach simple; simply

ewig forever; eternally

frei: frei haben to be off from work; **frei sein** to be unoccupied

gesund healthy

langweilig boring

möglich possible

passiv passive

richtig correct, right; proper

schnell fast, quickly

zuerst first, first of all, at first

Besondere Ausdrücke

am Computer arbeiten to work at the computer

GRAMMATIK UND ÜBUNGEN

1. The present perfect tense°

das Perfekt

Ich **habe** mit Karin **gesprochen.**
I *have spoken* with Karin.
I *spoke* with Karin.

Sie **ist** nach Hause **gegangen.**
She *has gone* home.
She *went* home.

German has several past tenses. One of them is the present perfect tense, which is commonly used in conversation to refer to past actions or states.

The present perfect tense is made up of the present tense of the auxiliary **haben** or **sein** and the past participle of the verb. In independent clauses, the past participle is the last element. (For dependent clauses see section 10.)

LAND UND LEUTE

Go to the
Deutsch heute Web Site at
www.hmco.com/college

Das Theater

Theater in the German-speaking countries has a long tradition. The present system of theaters with resident staffs goes back to the eighteenth century. Many theaters were founded then by local rulers to provide entertainment for the court. Today there are more than 500 theaters in the German-speaking countries. In Germany, most of the theaters are repertory theaters under the jurisdiction of city governments **(Stadttheater),** some are under the jurisdiction of an individual state **(Staatstheater),** and some are private theaters **(Privattheater).**

In addition to the repertory theaters there are also many experimental theaters **(Freie Theatergruppen).** Some of the private theaters are small stages run in conjunction with a pub **(Kneipe** or **Wirtschaft)** which helps to finance the theater. Many theaters receive government subsidies for their productions. The repertory **(Spielplan)** of German-speaking theaters usually includes a variety of German and foreign plays. The top three playwrights performed in German-speaking theaters are Shakespeare, Goethe, and Brecht. The American author Neil Simon ranks tenth.

Auch Theater machen Werbung.

Diskussion

Imagine that you are a member of a group trying to open a new theater in your community. What kind of financing could you get? Where would you locate the theater? What authors would you produce?

---

das Partizip Perfekt / das
regelmäßige schwache Verb

2. Past participles° of regular weak verbs°

Infinitive	Past participle	Present perfect tense
spielen	ge + spiel + t	Tania **hat** gestern nicht **gespielt.**
arbeiten	ge + arbeit + et	Sie **hat gearbeitet.**

German verbs may be classified as weak or strong according to the way in which they form their past tenses. A German weak verb is a verb whose infinitive stem **(spiel-, arbeit-)** remains unchanged in the past tense forms.

In German, the past participle of a weak verb is formed by adding **-t** to the unchanged infinitive stem. The **-t** expands to **-et** in verbs whose stem ends in **-d** or **-t (arbeiten > gearbeitet),** and in some verbs whose stem ends in **-m** or **-n** **(regnen > geregnet)**. Most weak verbs also add the prefix **ge-** in the past participle. In English, the past participle of corresponding verbs (called "regular" verbs) is formed by adding **-ed** to the stem, e.g., *play > played, work > worked*.

3. Auxiliary *haben* with past participles

ich **habe** etwas **gefragt**	wir **haben** etwas **gefragt**
du **hast** etwas **gefragt**	ihr **habt** etwas **gefragt**
er/es/sie **hat** etwas **gefragt**	sie **haben** etwas **gefragt**
Sie **haben** etwas **gefragt**	

The chart above shows how the present perfect tense of a weak verb is formed, using the auxiliary **haben.**

1. Wir haben es schon gehört. Ihre Freundin/Ihr Freund möchte anderen ein paar Neuigkeiten° erzählen. Sagen Sie Ihrer Freundin/Ihrem Freund, dass diese Leute die Neuigkeiten schon gehört haben.

news

⋙ Frau Fischer   *Frau Fischer hat es schon gehört.*

1. Klaus
2. ich
3. Professor Weber
4. unsere Freunde
5. wir
6. Karin

2. Am Wochenende.   Sabine erzählt vom Wochenende. Ergänzen Sie die Sätze. Benutzen Sie das Perfekt.

⋙ Am Wochenende war sehr viel los. Am Freitagabend _____ Robert und ich Tennis _____ . (spielen)   *Am Freitagabend haben Robert und ich Tennis gespielt.*

1. Du _____ mich _____ , was am Wochenende los war. (fragen)

2. Also, Bettina _____ am Samstag wieder _____ . (jobben)

3. Ich _____ heute Morgen für meine Matheklausur _____ , aber am Nachmittag nur _____ . (lernen/faulenzen)

4. Am Sonntag _____ wir den Geburtstag meiner Mutter _____ . (feiern)

5. Meine Schwester _____ ihr wirklich schöne Blumen _____ . (schenken)

6. Vati _____ das ganze Essen _____ . (kochen)

7. _____ es wirklich gut _____ ? (schmecken)

8. Leider _____ es _____ . (regnen)

9. Aber es war eigentlich O.K. Wir _____ Karten _____ . (spielen)

das unregelmäßige
schwache Verb

4. Past participles of irregular weak verbs°

Infinitive	Past participle	Present perfect tense
bringen	ge + brach + t	Wer **hat** die Blumen **gebracht?**
denken	ge + dach + t	Jens **hat** an den Wein **gedacht.**
kennen	ge + kann + t	Sie **hat** Thomas gut **gekannt.**
wissen	ge + wuss + t	Wir **haben** es **gewusst.**

A few weak verbs, including **bringen, denken, kennen,** and **wissen,** are irregular. They are called irregular weak verbs because the past participle has the prefix **ge-** and the ending **-t,** but the verb also undergoes a stem change. The past participles of irregular weak verbs are noted in the vocabularies as follows: **denken, gedacht.**

3. Alles vorbereiten.   Gerd und seine Freunde bereiten eine Party vor. Geben Sie die folgenden Sätze im Perfekt wieder.

>> Gerd denkt an Christine.   *Gerd hat an Christine gedacht.*

wine shop

1. Christine denkt an den Wein.
2. Gerd kennt das Weingeschäft°.
3. Kennst du das Geschäft?
4. Klaus kennt es nicht.
5. Klaus weiß die Telefonnummer nicht.
6. Gerd weiß die Telefonnummer.
7. Wer bringt die Pizza?
8. Was bringst du?

denken aus: think up

4. Was wollen Sie sagen?   Denken° Sie sich mit einer Partnerin/einem Partner eine Geschichte aus. Benutzen Sie zehn schwache Verben. Erzählen Sie im Perfekt.

arbeiten □ brauchen □ bringen □ denken □ faulenzen □ feiern □ fragen □ glauben □ hören □ jobben □ kaufen □ kennen □ kochen □ kosten □ kriegen □ leben □ lernen □ machen □ regnen □ sagen □ schenken □ schmecken □ schneien □ spielen □ suchen □ tanzen □ wandern □ warten □ wissen □ wohnen □ zahlen □ zelten

5. Use of the present perfect tense

In English, the present perfect tense and the simple past tense have different meanings.

Where are you going?
Gerd has invited me to dinner (and I'm going this evening).

The present perfect tense (e.g., *has invited*) in English refers to a period of time that continues into the present and is thus still uncompleted.

What did you do today?
Gerd invited me to dinner (and I went).

The simple past tense (e.g., *invited*) in English, on the other hand, refers to a period of time that is completed at the moment of speaking.

Gerd hat mich zum Essen eingeladen.   { Gerd has invited me to dinner.
                                            { Gerd invited me to dinner.

In German, the present perfect tense (e.g., **hat eingeladen**) refers to all actions or states in the past, whereas in English the simple past tense is used for completed actions and the present perfect tense for uncompleted actions. Context usually makes the meaning clear.

    In German, the present perfect tense is most frequently used in conversation to refer to past actions or states, and is therefore often referred to as the "conversational past." German also has a simple past tense (see *Kapitel 10*) that is used to narrate connected events in the past, and which is, therefore, frequently called the "narrative past."

 **5. Ich hab' das nicht gewusst.**   Beantworten Sie die folgenden Fragen erst selbst und fragen Sie dann eine Partnerin/einen Partner. Denken Sie daran **du** zu benutzen.

> Talking about the past

1. Wo hast du als Kind gewohnt?
2. Wie viele Bücher hast du für deine Kurse gekauft?
3. Wie viel haben die Bücher gekostet?
4. Hast du dieses Semester schon viel Deutsch gelernt?
5. Bis wann hast du gestern Abend gearbeitet?
6. Wie hat das Essen gestern Abend geschmeckt?
7. Was hast du letzte Woche in deiner Freizeit gemacht?

6. Wie sagt man das?   Geben Sie die folgenden Kurzdialoge auf Deutsch wieder und benutzen Sie das Perfekt.

≫ What did Erik say?   *Was hat Erik gesagt?*
    —I didn't hear it.   *—Ich habe es nicht gehört.*

1. Christel bought a jacket.
    —What did it cost?
2. Why didn't the men work yesterday?
    —It rained.
3. Why didn't Barbara buy the purse?
    —She didn't have any money.
4. Markus cooked the dinner last night.
    —Really? I didn't know that.
5. Who brought the wine?
    —I don't know. I didn't ask.

■ **Kreativität gefragt.**

■ **Heute schon geklickt ?**

EUROCERT
DIN EN ISO 9002
ZQM07796-00

mediadesign
akademie

LAND UND LEUTE

Go to the
Deutsch heute Web Site at
www.hmco.com/college

Feiertage

Germans enjoy a minimum of eleven legal, paid holidays per year. These holidays are days off in addition to vacation time. In some states, such as Bavaria, the people have fifteen holidays. With the exception of some transportation facilities, some restaurants and recreational facilities, businesses in Germany must be closed on legal holidays.

Germany celebrates both secular and religious holidays. Among the secular holidays are New Year's Eve **(Silvester),** New Year's Day **(Neujahr),** and **Tag der Arbeit** on May 1, which is celebrated in honor of workers. The newest holiday is the national holiday, **Tag der deutschen Einheit** (Day of Unity), celebrated on October 3 to commemorate the unification of East and West Germany in 1990.

The following Christian holidays are observed throughout the country: Good Friday **(Karfreitag);** Easter **(Ostern**—both **Ostersonntag** and **Ostermontag);** Ascension Day **(Christi Himmelfahrt),** the sixth Thursday after Easter; Pentecost **(Pfingsten),** the seventh Sunday and Monday after Easter; Christmas Eve **(Heiligabend),** and December 25 and 26 **(erster Weihnachtstag** and **zweiter Weihnachtstag).** Four other Christian holidays are observed in some states, but not all.

Diskussion

1. Many countries around the world have a holiday to honor workers on May 1. Do some historical research and find out why this is a popular date for this holiday. Hint: An important event in the history of the union movement in the United States took place in May.
2. Do you think that it is a good idea for businesses to be closed on holidays? Why or why not?

Prost Neujahr! – Feuerwerk in Mittenwald.

KONEN
reduziert

SONDERANGEBOTE
DAMEN

T-Shirts
schmale und weite Formen, diverse Farben.
19.–

Jeans
Markenfabrikate, Blue- und Color-Denim.
ab 69.–

Blazer
1/2-und 1/1 Arm, Cardigan-form, Polyester/Viskose, sommerliche Farben.
149.–

Popeline-Mäntel
in extralang und Swinger-mäntel in vielen Farben.
198.–

YOUNG FASHION-Kleider
frech, Baumwoll-Single oder Viskose.
ab 69.–

SONDERANGEBOTE
HERREN

Halbarm Hemden
reine Baumwolle, Unis und viele klassische Streifen.
39.–

Sportswear-Hosen
Baumwolle und Baumwolle/Leinen, bügelfrei und pflegeleicht.
79.–

Sportive Overjackets
maritime Farben.
179.–

Business-Anzüge
modern Dessins, vorwiegend aus Cool Wool, ein- und zweireihige Formen.
398.–

Das große Münchener Modehaus für Damen, Herren und Kinder • Sendlinger Straße

KONEN
Donnerstag bis 20.30 Uhr

7. Einkaufen bei Konen. Konen ist ein Kleidergeschäft° in München. Sehen Sie sich die Anzeige an und beantworten Sie die folgenden Fragen. clothing store

1. Welche englischen Wörter finden Sie?
2. Wann schließt Konen am Donnerstag?
3. Für wen gibt es Sonderangebote°? specials
4. Finden Sie die Jeans teuer?

8. **Rollenspiel.** Sie treffen eine Freundin/einen Freund (Ihre Partnerin/Ihren Partner). Sie/Er hat heute neue Sachen an. Die Sachen gefallen Ihnen gut und Sie möchten wissen, wo Ihre Partnerin/Ihr Partner die Sachen gekauft hat, wie viel sie gekostet haben und was für Kleidungsstücke° man in dem Geschäft kaufen kann. Ihre Partnerin/Ihr Partner sagt Ihnen, wo sie/er die Sachen gekauft hat (vielleicht bei Konen?). Benutzen Sie das folgende Muster° für Ihr Gespräch. Zusätzliche° Wörter finden Sie im Anhang (Supplementary Word Sets).

clothes

model
additional

S1: Du, das T-Shirt ist toll!
S2: Der Mantel gefällt mir auch.
S1: Wie viel hat er gekostet?
S2: Hundertachtundneunzig Mark.
S1: Hast du sonst noch etwas gekauft?
S2: Ja, [...].
S1: Wo hast du die Sachen gekauft?
S2: Bei Konen.

das starke Verb

6. Past participles of strong verbs°

Infinitive	Past participle	Present perfect tense
sehen	ge + seh + en	Ich **habe** es **gesehen.**
finden	ge + fund + en	Ich **habe** es **gefunden.**
nehmen	ge + nomm + en	Ich **habe** es nicht **genommen.**

The past participle of a strong verb ends in **-en.** (Note the exception **getan.**) Most strong verbs also add the **ge-** prefix in the past participle. Many strong verbs have a stem vowel of the past participle **(gefunden)** that is different from that of the infinitive, and some verbs also have a change in the consonants **(genommen).** Past participles of strong verbs are noted in the vocabularies as follows: **schreiben, geschrieben.**

For a list of strong verbs, see #23 of the Grammatical Tables in the Reference Section.

Infinitive	Past participle
halten	gehalten
schlafen	geschlafen
tragen	getragen
tun	getan

9. **Pizza machen.** Ute und Michaela sprechen über Peter. Ergänzen Sie die Sätze im Perfekt.

➤➤ UTE: Warum _____ Peter heute so lange _____ ? (schlafen)
Warum hat Peter heute so lange geschlafen?

1. MICHAELA: Er _____ heute nicht viel _____ . (tun)

2. Er _____ nur eine Pizza _____ . (machen)

3. UTE: Was _____ die Freunde von seinem Plan _____ ? (halten)

4. MICHAELA: Sie _____ auch eine Pizza _____ . (machen)

5. Dann _____ sie die Pizzas zu den Nachbarn _____ . (tragen)

6. UTE: Was _____ die Nachbarn dann _____ ? (tun)

7. MICHAELA: Sie _____ die Pizza natürlich _____ . (essen)

   Sie _____ gut _____ . (schmecken)

Infinitive	Past participle
geben	gegeben
lesen	gelesen
sehen	gesehen
essen	gegessen
liegen	gelegen
sitzen	gesessen

10. Ein Abend bei mir. Sie haben Klaus gestern Abend eingeladen. Erzählen Sie, was Sie gemacht haben. Benutzen Sie das Perfekt.

➤➤ Ein Buch über die Schweiz liegt da.   *Ein Buch über die Schweiz hat da gelegen.*

1. Was machst du mit dem Buch?
2. Ich gebe es Klaus.
3. Zuerst liest er das Buch.
4. Dann essen wir ein Wurstbrot.
5. Ich esse auch einen Apfel.
6. Später sehen wir einen Film im Fernsehen.

Infinitive	Past participle
helfen	geholfen
nehmen	genommen
sprechen	gesprochen
treffen	getroffen
finden	gefunden
trinken	getrunken
leihen	geliehen
schreiben	geschrieben

11. Was haben sie getan? Geben Sie die folgenden Kurzdialoge im Perfekt wieder.

➤➤ Nehmen Paul und Manuel den Zug?   *Haben Paul und Manuel den Zug genommen?*

   —Nein, ich leihe ihnen mein Auto.   *—Nein, ich habe ihnen mein Auto geliehen.*

1. Trinken Sie Kaffee?
   —Nein, ich nehme Tee.
2. Schreibst du die Karte?
   —Nein, ich finde sie nicht.
3. Sprechen Gerd und Susi Englisch mit euch?
   —Ja, wir finden das toll.

decide

exaggerate

⇨ **12. Mein Tag war langweilig/interessant.**   Sprechen Sie mit einer Partnerin/einem Partner oder in einer Gruppe darüber, was Sie in den letzten 24 Stunden gemacht haben. Benutzen Sie die Fragen. Dann entscheiden° Sie, welche Person den interessantesten und welche Person den langweiligsten Tag hatte. Wenn Sie Ihren Tag interessanter machen wollen, übertreiben° Sie ruhig ein bisschen! Erzählen Sie dann den anderen Studenten im Deutschkurs, was Sie gemacht haben.

S1:   *S2:*
Hast du gut geschlafen?   Ja.
                          Nein, ich habe die ganze Nacht getanzt.

1. Bis wann hast du geschlafen?
2. Was hast du zum Frühstück gegessen?
3. Was hast du zum Frühstück getrunken?
4. Was für Kleidung hast du getragen?
5. Was hast du gelesen?
6. Wen hast du heute in der Uni gesehen?
7. Mit wem hast du heute gesprochen?

das trennbare Verb

7. Separable-prefix verbs° in the present perfect tense

Infinitive	Past participle	Present perfect tense
anrufen	an + **ge** + rufen	Kirstin **hat** gestern **angerufen**.
einkaufen	ein + **ge** + kauft	Ingrid **hat** heute **eingekauft**.

The prefix **ge-** of the past participle comes between the separable prefix and the stem of the participle. Some separable-prefix verbs are weak; others are strong. In spoken German the separable prefix receives stress: **an'gerufen.** A list of some separable-prefix verbs you have encountered follows.

Infinitive	Past participle
aufhören	aufgehört
anrufen	angerufen
aussehen	ausgesehen
einkaufen	eingekauft
einladen	eingeladen
fernsehen	ferngesehen
vorhaben	vorgehabt

13. Studentenleben.   Geben Sie die folgenden Kurzdialoge im Perfekt wieder.

⟫ Lädt Klaus für Samstag einige   *Hat Klaus für Samstag einige Freunde*
Freunde ein?   *eingeladen?*
—Natürlich. Er lädt alle seine   *—Natürlich. Er hat alle seine Freunde*
Freunde ein.   *eingeladen.*

1. Kauft er auch Wein ein?
   —Na klar. Er kauft auch Käse, Wurst und Brot ein.
2. Bringen seine Freunde etwas mit?
   —Natürlich. Sie bringen viel mit.

3. Lädt Klaus auch Evi ein?
   —Ja, aber sie hat etwas vor.
4. Wann hörst du mit deiner Arbeit auf?
   —Um acht. Dann rufe ich Sigrid an.

14. Wer hat was gemacht? Sagen Sie, was die Leute auf den Bildern gestern in ihrer Freizeit gemacht haben. Denken° Sie sich Namen für die Personen aus.

denken aus: think up

Vokabeln: am Computer arbeiten □ einen Brief schreiben □ fernsehen □ im Supermarkt einkaufen □ Spaghetti kochen □ viel schlafen □ Zeitung lesen

≫ *(Tina) hat die Zeitung gelesen.*

 1.
 2.

 3.
 4.
 5.
6.

8. Past participles without the *ge-* prefix

■ *Verbs ending in* **-ieren**

Infinitive	Past participle	Present perfect tense
studieren	studiert	Dirk **hat** in München **studiert.**
interessieren	interessiert	Der Film **hat** mich nicht **interessiert.**

Verbs ending in **-ieren** do not have the prefix **ge-** in the past participle. They are always weak verbs whose participle ends in **-t.** These verbs are generally based on words borrowed from French and Latin; they are often similar to English verbs.

15. Worüber hat man diskutiert?   Ergänzen Sie die Kurzdialoge im Perfekt.

➤➤ DIRK: Wo _____ du _____ , Katja? (studieren) *Wo hast du studiert, Katja?*

KATJA: Ich _____ in München _____ . (studieren) *Ich habe in München studiert.*

1. JÖRN: Mit wem _____ Gerd so lange _____ ? (telefonieren)

   KEVIN: Mit Laura. Er _____ ihr zum Geburtstag _____ . (gratulieren)

2. UTE: Dirk _____ mit seinem Freund über ein Problem _____ . (diskutieren)

   BETTINA: Schön. Aber warum _____ sie so lange _____ ? (diskutieren)

3. UTE: Die Professoren _____ wieder für mehr Mathematik _____ .

   plead   (plädieren°)

   CARSTEN: Die Studenten _____ wieder gegen diesen Plan _____ , nicht

   wahr? (protestieren)

das untrennbare Verb   ■ *Verbs with inseparable prefixes°*

Infinitive	Past participle	Present perfect tense
beantworten	beantwortet	Du **hast** meine Frage nicht **beantwortet.**
bekommen	bekommen	Ich **habe** nichts **bekommen.**
besuchen	besucht	Paul **hat** seine Tante **besucht.**
bezahlen	bezahlt	Wer **hat** das **bezahlt?**
erklären	erklärt	Ich **habe** es schon **erklärt.**
erzählen	erzählt	Erik **hat** es **erzählt.**
gefallen	gefallen	**Hat** es dir **gefallen?**
gehören	gehört	Wem **hat** diese alte Uhr **gehört?**
gewinnen	gewonnen	Wer **hat** das Fußballspiel **gewonnen?**
vergessen	vergessen	Ich **habe** seinen Namen **vergessen.**
versuchen	versucht	**Hast** du wirklich alles **versucht?**

Some prefixes are never separated from the verb stem. These prefixes are **be-, emp-, ent-, er-, ge-, ver-,** and **zer-.** Inseparable-prefix verbs do not add the prefix **ge-** in the past participle. Some inseparable-prefix verbs are weak; others are strong.

An inseparable prefix is not stressed in spoken German: **bekom′men.**

trip

16. Petras Reise° in die Schweiz.   Petra hat eine Reise in die Schweiz gemacht. Erzählen Sie von ihrer Reise und geben Sie jeden Satz im Perfekt wieder.

➤➤ Petra erzählt von ihren Ferien.   *Petra hat von ihren Ferien erzählt.*

1. Sie bezahlt die Reise selbst.
2. Die Schweiz gefällt Petra sehr.
3. Sie besucht da Freunde.
4. Sie bekommt da auch guten Käse.
5. Ein Schweizer erklärt ihr vieles.
6. Er erzählt viel Lustiges.

9. Auxiliary *sein* with past participles

ich	**bin gekommen**	wir	**sind gekommen**
du	**bist gekommen**	ihr	**seid gekommen**
er/es/sie	**ist gekommen**	sie	**sind gekommen**
	Sie **sind gekommen**		

Some verbs use **sein** instead of **haben** as an auxiliary in the present perfect.

Warum **ist** Silke so früh **aufgestanden?**	Why did Silke get up so early?
Sie **ist** nach Freiburg **gefahren.**	She drove to Freiburg.

Verbs that require **sein** must meet two conditions. They must:

1. be intransitive verbs (verbs without a direct object) and
2. indicate a change in condition (e.g., **aufstehen**) or motion to or from a place (e.g., **fahren**).

Infinitive		Past participle
aufstehen		aufgestanden
fahren		gefahren
fliegen	ist	geflogen
gehen		gegangen
kommen		gekommen

Infinitive		Past participle
laufen		gelaufen
schwimmen		geschwommen
wandern	ist	gewandert
werden		geworden

Wer **ist** wieder so lange bei Helmut **geblieben?**	Who stayed so late at Helmut's again?
Ich **bin** es nicht **gewesen.**	It wasn't I.

The verbs **bleiben** and **sein** require **sein** as an auxiliary in the present perfect tense, even though they do not indicate a change in condition or motion to or from a place.

Wie **war** der Kaffee?	How was the coffee?
Der Kuchen **war** gut.	The cake was good.

The simple past tense of **sein (war)** is used more commonly than the present perfect tense of **sein (ist gewesen),** even in conversation.

Deutsche Bahn **DB**

Lieber clever gefahren
als dumm gelaufen.

Das StadtTicket.

17. So war es. Ergänzen Sie die Kurzdialoge im Perfekt.

⏩ JÖRG: Sag mal, Bettina, _____ du mit dem Auto _____ ? (fahren) *Sag mal, Bettina, bist du mit dem Auto gefahren?*

⏩ BETTINA: Nein, ich _____ _____ . (fliegen) *Nein, ich bin geflogen.*

1. LIANE: _____ du nach Österreich _____ , Tim? (fahren)

   TIM: Nein, ich _____ auch in den Ferien zu Hause _____ . (bleiben)

2. HERR LEHMANN: _____ Müllers auch schwimmen _____ ? (gehen)

   FRAU LEHMANN: Ja, aber sie _____ erst später _____ . (kommen)

3. MUTTI: Warum _____ ihr nicht schwimmen _____ ? (gehen)

   KINDER: Es _____ zu kalt _____ . (werden)

4. INA: _____ du auch in den Ferien jeden Tag so früh _____ ? (aufstehen)

   STEFFI: Ja, ich _____ im Park mit meinem Hund _____ . (laufen)

about

18. Frage-Ecke. Sprechen Sie mit Ihrer Partnerin/Ihrem Partner darüber°, was Evi, Dirk, Stefan, Silke, Sie und Ihre Partnerin/Ihr Partner am Wochenende gemacht haben.

S1: Was hat Evi gemacht?
S2: Evi ist spazieren gegangen und hat einen Roman gelesen.

S1:

	Evi	Dirk	Stefan	Silke	ich	Partnerin/Partner
im Restaurant essen				X		
spazieren gehen						
fernsehen						
Rad fahren		X				
faulenzen		X				
in die Kneipe gehen						
einen Roman lesen				X		
mit Freunden telefonieren						

Ruf doch mal an!

Die Telefon-Information für Österreich-Reisende

So einfach ist es, zu Hause anzurufen: Von allen öffentlichen Telefonen. Ausgenommen sind Ortsmünztelefone.

S2:

	Evi	Dirk	Stefan	Silke	ich	Partnerin/Partner
im Restaurant essen						
spazieren gehen	X					
fernsehen			X			
Rad fahren						
faulenzen						
in die Kneipe gehen			X			
einen Roman lesen	X					
mit Freunden telefonieren			X			

19. Was haben Sie gemacht?   Sprechen Sie mit Ihrer Partnerin/Ihrem Partner darüber, was Sie beide gemacht haben. Benutzen Sie die Fragen oder denken° Sie sich Ihre eigenen Fragen aus.

Talking about past activities

denken ... aus: think up your own questions

- Wann bist du gestern aufgestanden? Am Sonntag?
- Wohin bist du nach dem Frühstück gegangen? Oder bist du [zu Hause/im Studentenheim] geblieben?
- Wo hast du gestern Abend gegessen?
- Was hast du gestern Abend getrunken?
- Wann bist du heute zur Uni gefahren?
- Wie viele Vorlesungen hast du gehabt?
- Wann bist du gestern wieder nach Hause gegangen?
- Was hast du im Fernsehen gesehen?
- Was hast du letzte Woche gekauft?
- Wann bist du am Samstag ins Bett gegangen?

10. Dependent clauses in the present perfect tense

Silke erzählt, dass sie gestern einen guten Film gesehen **hat.**
Sie sagt, dass sie mit Freunden ins Kino gegangen **ist.**

In a dependent clause, the present-tense form of the auxiliary verb **haben** or **sein** follows the past participle and is the last element in the clause.

20. Neugierig *(curious).*   Ihre Freundin/Ihr Freund möchte viel über Nicole wissen. Beantworten Sie ihre/seine Fragen mit den Sätzen in Klammern. Beginnen Sie jeden Satz mit **weil.**

≫ Warum hat Nicole im Sommer keine Reise° gemacht? (Sie hat bei einer Computerfirma gearbeitet.)
Weil sie bei einer Computerfirma gearbeitet hat.

trip

1. Warum hat Nicole in den Ferien gearbeitet? (Sie hat das Geld fürs Studium gebraucht.)
2. Warum hat sie so viel Geld gebraucht? (Alles ist so teuer geworden.)
3. Warum ist sie in die Buchhandlung gegangen? (Sie hat ein Buch gesucht.)

language

4. Warum hat sie dieses Buch gekauft? (Es hat ihr gefallen.)
5. Warum hat sie Deutsch gelernt? (Sie hat die Sprache° interessant gefunden.)
6. Warum ist sie noch nicht nach Deutschland gefahren? (Sie hat nicht genug Geld gehabt.)

21. Bildgeschichte. Erzählen Sie, was Steffi am Montag gemacht hat. Schreiben Sie zu jedem Bild einen oder zwei Sätze im Perfekt.

1.

2.

3.

4.

5.

6.

7.

WIEDERHOLUNG

help

1. Das gefällt ihnen nicht. Sie suchen Geschenke für Ihre Freundinnen/ Freunde. Sandra möchte Ihnen helfen° Bücher, CDs und Videos für sie auszusuchen. Beantworten Sie ihre Fragen mit *nein*.

➤ Liest Kevin gern klassische Literatur? *Nein, klassische Literatur gefällt ihm nicht.*

➤ Liest Claudia gern Krimis? *Nein, Krimis gefallen ihr nicht.*

1. Hört Anna gern klassische Musik?
2. Hört Benjamin gern Rockmusik?
3. Sieht Marion gern Actionfilme?
4. Sehen Hans und Lisa gern Dokumentarfilme?
5. Liest Alex gern Romane?
6. Und du: Hörst du gern Jazz?
   Liest du gern Liebesromane?
   Siehst du gern alte Filme?

Go to the
Deutsch heute Web Site at
www.hmco.com/college

Der deutsche Film

Going to the movies is a favorite pastime of people in the German-speaking countries. Movies were invented over 100 years ago. Some of the earliest film premieres were in Germany. In Berlin in 1885 Max and Emil Skladanowsky produced a seven-minute film which is still in existence. The German movie industry flourished during the era of silent films and early "talkies" (1919–1932). Directors like Fritz Lang, F. W. Murnau, and F. W. Pabst were considered among the finest in the world, and the German use of the "moving camera" influenced many directors.

During the Nazi era (1933–1945), many great German and Austrian filmmakers emigrated to the United States and other countries. Some of them never returned; this loss led to a period of mediocrity in German filmmaking that lasted until the mid-sixties. At that point a generation of young filmmakers began to introduce the New German Cinema **(Neuer deutscher Film).** Many of those directors are now famous, including the late Rainer Werner Fassbinder, Werner Herzog, Wim Wenders, and Wolfgang Petersen. Since then other directors such as Margarethe von Trotta, Volker Schlöndorff, Doris Dörrie, and Percy Adlon have gained international recognition. However, 80% of the films shown in German movie theaters today are American, with dubbed voices.

Einer von Wim Wenders Filmen ist „Der amerikanische Freund".

Diskussion

Many people from German-speaking countries or of German heritage have been successful in the American movie industry. See if you can find information about one of the following people: Marlene Dietrich, Billy Wilder, Nastassja Kinski, Leonardo DiCaprio, Wolfgang Petersen, Fritz Lang.

missing

2. Frank hat Freunde zum Essen eingeladen.   Erzählen Sie über Frank und ergänzen Sie die fehlenden° Präpositionen.

1. Frank lebt _____ zwei Monaten in Bremen.

2. Er arbeitet _____ einer amerikanischen Firma.

3. _____ Samstag hat er einige Freunde _____ Essen eingeladen.

4. Am Wochenende kommen seine Freunde oft _____ ihm.

5. Sie sind _____ zwölf gekommen.

6. Frank hat _____ seine Freunde einen Fisch gegrillt.

7. _____ dem Wein trinken sie eine ganze Flasche.

8. Der Wein kommt _____ Italien.

9. _____ dem Essen gehen sie _____ einem Fußballspiel.

3. Pizza oder Spaghetti?   Beschreiben Sie, wie Renate ein Essen für ihre Freunde vorbereitet hat. Benutzen Sie das Perfekt und die folgenden Wörter.

1. Renate / einladen / am Samstag / Freunde / zum Essen
2. sie / machen / eine Pizza
3. sie / haben / keinen Käse // und / ihre Freundin Monika / laufen / zu / Supermarkt
4. die Pizza / aussehen / ein bisschen schwarz
5. dann / sie / kochen / Spaghetti

4. Wie sagt man das?

1. —Why did you come by bus?
   —My car is broken down.
   —I'm sorry.
2. —Did you like Denmark?
   —Yes. We hiked a lot.
   —Did you camp (in a tent)?
   —No. It rained too much. We slept at friends' (houses).
3. —Would you like a piece (of) cake?
   —Gladly. I'm hungry.
   —How does it taste?
   —Very good.

5. Fragen über die Uni.   Was hat David über das Studium in Deutschland herausgefunden? Verbinden Sie die Sätze mit den Konjunktionen in Klammern.

1. David hat viele Fragen. (weil) Er möchte in Deutschland studieren.
2. Er studiert vielleicht vier Semester dort. (wenn) Die Uni ist nicht zu teuer.
3. Nicole sagt ... (dass) Es kostet nichts.
4. Dann studiert er. (wenn) Er kann einen Studentenjob finden.
5. Nicole sagt ... (dass) Es gibt leider wenige Studentenjobs.

▷ **6. Rollenspiel.**   Ihre Partnerin/Ihr Partner ist gestern Abend mit einer Freundin/einem Freund ausgegangen. Fragen Sie sie/ihn, was sie gemacht haben.

7. Zum Schreiben

1. Jürg und Anja sprechen über verschiedene° Themen. Wählen° Sie eins von den Themen und schreiben Sie ein Gespräch zwischen Jürg und Anja.   various/choose

   das Wetter □ Einkaufen □ die Vorlesung □ eine Seminararbeit vorbereiten □ das Essen □ das Wochenende □ Ferien

2. Schreiben Sie eine Woche lang ein Tagebuch° auf Deutsch. Schreiben Sie auf, was Sie jeden Tag gemacht haben. Sie können die folgenden Verben benutzen: diary

   aufstehen □ arbeiten □ besuchen □ fernsehen □ kaufen □ gehen □ spielen □ sprechen (mit) □ lernen

3. Stellen° Sie sich vor, dass Sie ein Jahr lang an einer Universität in Deutschland studieren. Schreiben Sie einen Brief an eine Freundin oder einen Freund in Deutschland und beschreiben Sie die letzten paar Wochen. Mögliche Themen sind: das Wetter, die Kurse, Leute, die° Sie jetzt kennen, Freizeitaktivitäten wie Sport, Fernsehen, Musik, Konzerte, Kneipen, Filme.   **stellen vor:** imagine

whom

4. **Ein Werbespot°.** Nehmen Sie die **Konen-Anzeige** auf S. 221 und schreiben Sie einen Radio-Werbespot. Hier sind einige Wörter, die Sie benutzen können.   short ad

   heute bei Konen ... □ Popeline-Mäntel ... □ gut einkaufen ... □ jeden Donnerstag bis 20.30 geöffnet°   **öffnen:** to open

Hinweise: After you have completed the writing assignment, check over your work, paying particular attention to the following:

- agreement between subject and verb
- gender and case of all nouns and pronouns (see all chapters, especially *Einführung, Kapitel 3, 5*)
- choice of prepositions and correct case used with the prepositions (see *Kapitel 3* and *5*)
- choice of auxiliary verb in the present perfect tense (see this chapter)
- word order in sentences with dependent and independent clauses (see *Kapitel 5*)
- word order in sentences with the present perfect tense (see this chapter)

Hier gibt es Sachen für den Neuen Mann. (Stuttgart)

GRAMMATIK: ZUSAMMENFASSUNG

The present perfect tense

Hast du gestern Abend **ferngesehen?**   Did you watch TV last night?
Nein, ich **bin** ins Kino **gegangen.**   No, I went to the movies.

The German present perfect tense, like the English present perfect, is a compound tense. It is made up of the present tense of the auxiliary **haben** or **sein** and the past participle. In independent clauses, the past participle is in final position. (For dependent clauses, see below.)

Past participles of regular weak verbs

Infinitive	Past participle	Present perfect tense
sagen	ge + sag + t	Er **hat** es **gesagt.**
arbeiten	ge + arbeit + et	Sie **hat** schwer **gearbeitet.**
baden°	ge + bad + et	Er **hat** gestern nicht **gebadet.**
regnen	ge + regn + et	Es **hat** gestern **geregnet.**

to bathe

The past participle of a weak verb is formed by adding **-t** to the unchanged infinitive stem. The **-t** expands to **-et** in verbs like **arbeiten, baden,** and **regnen.** In the past participle, most weak verbs also have the prefix **ge-.**

Past participles of irregular weak verbs

Infinitive	Past participle	Present perfect tense
bringen	ge + brach + t	Wer **hat** das **gebracht?**
denken	ge + dach + t	Sie **hat** nicht an die Zeit **gedacht.**
kennen	ge + kann + t	Sie **hat** deinen Freund gut **gekannt.**
wissen	ge + wuss + t	Sie **hat** es **gewusst.**

A few weak verbs are irregular. The past participle has the prefix **ge-** and the ending **-t;** there is also a change in the stem vowel and in the consonants of several verbs.

Past participles of strong verbs

Infinitive	Past participle	Present perfect tense
nehmen	ge + nomm + en	Ich **habe** das Brot **genommen.**
essen	ge + gess + en	Ich **habe** heute wenig **gegessen.**
tun	ge + ta + n	Ich **habe** das nicht **getan.**

The past participle of a strong verb ends in **-en.** (Note the exception **getan.**) Most strong verbs also add the **ge-** prefix in the past participle. Many strong verbs have a stem vowel of the past participle that is different from that of the infinitive, and some verbs also have a change in the consonants.

For a list of strong verbs, see #23 of the Grammatical Tables in the Reference Section.

Past participles of separable-prefix verbs

Infinitive	Past participle	Present perfect tense
aufhören	auf + **ge** + hört	Lisa **hat** mit der Arbeit **aufgehört.**
anrufen	an + **ge** + rufen	Gerd **hat** sie **angerufen.**

The prefix **ge-** of the past participle comes between the separable prefix and the stem of the participle. Some separable-prefix verbs are weak (e.g., **aufhören**); others are strong (e.g., **anrufen**).

Past participles without the *ge-* prefix

■ *Verbs ending in* **-ieren**

Present tense	Present perfect tense
Jutta **studiert** in Heidelberg.	Jutta **hat** in Heidelberg **studiert.**
Jens **repariert** sein Auto.	Jens **hat** sein Auto **repariert.**

Verbs ending in **-ieren** do not have the prefix **ge-** in the past participle. They are always weak verbs whose participle ends in **-t.** These verbs are generally based on words borrowed from French and Latin; they are often similar to English verbs.

■ *Verbs with inseparable prefixes*

Present tense	Present perfect tense
Birgit **erzählt** von ihrer Arbeit.	Sie **hat** von ihrer Arbeit **erzählt.**
Sie **bekommt** einen neuen Computer.	Sie **hat** einen neuen Computer **bekommen.**

Some prefixes are never separated from the verb stem. These prefixes are **be-, emp-, ent-, er-, ge-, ver-,** and **zer-.** Inseparable-prefix verbs do not add the prefix **ge-** in the past participle. Some inseparable-prefix verbs are weak (e.g., **erzählen**); others are strong (e.g., **bekommen**).

Musiker proben.

Use of the auxiliary *haben*

Christine **hat** heute schwer **gearbeitet.**	Christine worked hard today.
Sie **hat** ein Referat **geschrieben.**	She wrote a report.

Haben is used to form the present perfect tense of most verbs.

Use of the auxiliary *sein*

Schmidts **sind** spät nach Hause **gekommen.**	The Schmidts came home late.
Sie **sind** dann spät **aufgestanden.**	Then they got up late.

The auxiliary **sein** is used to form the present perfect tense of intransitive verbs (i.e., verbs that do not have a direct object) when these verbs denote a change in condition (e.g., **aufstehen**) or motion to or from a place (e.g., **kommen**).

Warum **bist** du so lange **geblieben?**	Why did you stay so long?
Es ist so schön **gewesen.**	It was so nice.

The intransitive verbs **bleiben** and **sein** require the auxiliary **sein,** even though they do not indicate a change in condition or motion to or from a place.

Verbs using the auxiliary *sein*

You have already encountered some verbs that take the auxiliary **sein** in the present perfect tense. They are shown in the table below.

Infinitive	Auxiliary	Past participle
aufstehen	ist	aufgestanden
bleiben	ist	geblieben
fahren	ist	gefahren
fliegen	ist	geflogen
gehen	ist	gegangen
kommen	ist	gekommen
laufen	ist	gelaufen
schwimmen	ist	geschwommen
sein	ist	gewesen
wandern	ist	gewandert
werden	ist	geworden

Use of the present perfect tense in dependent clauses

Klaus sagt, dass David ihm eine Karte geschrieben **hat.**
Er sagt, dass David nach Österreich gefahren **ist.**

In a dependent clause, the auxiliary **haben** or **sein** follows the past participle and is the last element in the clause, because it is the finite verb.

Andere Länder — andere Sitten

Ein Straßencafé in Frankfurt am Main.

BAUSTEINE FÜR GESPRÄCHE

Was machst du nach dem Kurs?

PETER: Was machst du nach dem Kurs? Gehst du in die Bibliothek?

MONIKA: Nein, ich treffe Anna im Altstadtcafé.

PETER: In der Fußgängerzone?

MONIKA: Ja, gehst du mit?

PETER: Nein, danke, ins Altstadtcafé gehe ich nicht so gern. Da ist immer so schlechte Luft. Alles ist voll Rauch.

MONIKA: Gehst du vielleicht mit in einen Biergarten? Im Waldgarten sitzt man schön draußen.

PETER: Aber du, ich bin pleite.

MONIKA: Macht nichts. Ich lade dich ein.

Fragen

1. Wen trifft Monika? Wann? Wo?
2. Wo ist das Altstadtcafé?
3. Wohin geht Peter nicht so gern? Warum nicht?
4. Warum findet Peter einen Biergarten bestimmt besser?
5. Leiht Monika Peter Geld? Warum (nicht)?

Vorbereitungen für ein Fest

MONIKA: Sag, willst du nicht endlich mal das Wohnzimmer aufräumen? Da liegen überall deine Bücher herum.

STEFAN: Muss das sein?

MONIKA: Klar, wir müssen das Essen vorbereiten und den Tisch decken. In einer Stunde kommen die Leute.

STEFAN: Was? Schon in einer Stunde? Du meine Güte! Und wir müssen noch Staub saugen, Staub wischen, abwaschen, abtrocknen, die Küche sieht aus wie …

MONIKA: Jetzt red nicht lange, sondern mach schnell. Ich helf' dir ja.

Fragen

1. Warum soll Stefan das Wohnzimmer aufräumen?
2. Wann kommen die Gäste?
3. Was müssen Monika und Stefan noch machen?

Brauchbares

1. In the first conversation Monika says, **"Gehst du vielleicht mit in einen Biergarten?"** In the German construction expressing *to go along somewhere,* the **mit** precedes the place one is going to.

2. When Peter objects to the Altstadtcafé, Monika suggests a beer garden. Outdoor cafés and restaurants are very common in German-speaking countries. Even restaurants at rest stops on the **Autobahn** have patios so patrons can eat outside. The moderate climate of the summers lends itself to pleasant outdoor dining.
3. Monika's last sentence is **"Ich helf' dir ja."** In colloquial German the ending **e** is often dropped from the verb in the **ich**-form. **Ja** is a flavoring particle here.

Fußgängerzonen

Most people in German-speaking countries live in urban areas. Three-fourths of the German population live in cities, and two-thirds live in cities with a population of more than 100,000.

LAND UND LEUTE

Go to the
Deutsch heute Web Site at
www.hmco.com/college

In der Heidelberger Fußgängerzone kann man gemütlich einkaufen.

The physical layout of cities in the German-speaking countries is generally different from that of cities in the United States. The concept of building large suburbs and shopping malls around a city is uncommon in most of Europe. A city **(Großstadt)** or town **(Stadt)** in German-speaking countries has a center containing office buildings as well as apartment buildings, stores, and places for cultural events. Many downtown areas have been converted to traffic-free pedestrian zones **(Fußgängerzonen)**. A typical pedestrian zone has large department stores as well as small specialty stores and street vendors, restaurants, and outdoor cafés. The streets are often lined with flowers, bushes, and trees and sometimes lead into small squares, where people can rest on benches. The downtown shopping areas are used not only by people who live in the city, but also by people who live in the outskirts or in nearby villages.

Diskussion

Describe the shopping area and downtown where you live. Using the information in the cultural note, compare your shopping and downtown areas to those in German-speaking countries. Do you see any major advantages or disadvantages to having a city center as is common in German-speaking countries?

fellow student
various

Making plans

⇨ **1. Was machst du?**   Eine Kursteilnehmerin/ein Kursteilnehmer° möchte etwas machen und fragt, was Ihre Pläne zu verschiedenen° Zeiten sind.

S1:

Was machst du | **nach dem Seminar?**
| nach der Vorlesung?
| heute Nachmittag?
| am Wochenende?

S2:

Ich gehe | **in einen Biergarten.**
| in die Bibliothek.
| ins Café.
| ein Video ausleihen.
| nach Hause.

Ich treffe [Michael] | **im Café.**
| in einem Biergarten.
| in der Bibliothek.

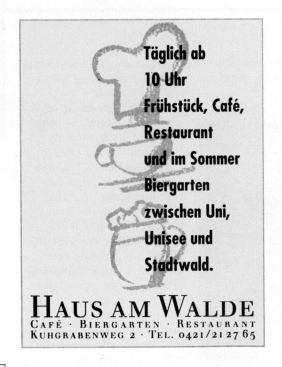

Täglich ab
10 Uhr
Frühstück, Café,
Restaurant
und im Sommer
Biergarten
zwischen Uni,
Unisee und
Stadtwald.

HAUS AM WALDE
CAFÉ · BIERGARTEN · RESTAURANT
KUHGRABENWEG 2 · TEL. 0421/21 27 65

Preparing for a party

⇨ **2. Ein Fest.**   Ein Freund/eine Freundin hat Sie zu einem Fest eingeladen. Fragen Sie, was geplant ist und was Sie mitbringen sollen.

S1:

Was macht ihr auf
   dem Fest?

Was soll ich zu dem
   Fest mitbringen?

S2:

Wir | **tanzen.**
| hören Musik.
| essen viel.
| reden viel.
| schauen° ein Video an.

Bring doch | **die Bilder von deiner Ferienreise° mit.**
| etwas zu | **essen**
| | trinken
| ein paar | **Flaschen° Cola**
| | CDs
| | Videos

Erweiterung des Wortschatzes

Hausarbeit

die Spülmaschine einräumen

den Tisch decken

Geschirr spülen

abtrocknen

das Bad putzen

die Spülmaschine ausräumen

die Küche sauber machen

Staub wischen

Staub saugen

die Wäsche waschen

1. Hausarbeit. Fragen Sie mehrere Kursteilnehmer und finden Sie heraus, welche Hausarbeiten sie zu Hause machen und welche sie nicht machen. Benutzen Sie die Bilder. Weitere Wörter finden Sie im Anhang (Supplementary Word Sets).

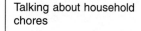

Talking about household chores

S1: Welche Arbeiten machst du zu Hause?
S2: Ich räume die Spülmaschine ein.
S1: Welche Arbeiten machst du nicht?
S2: Ich sauge nicht Staub.

Diese Studenten aus Hannover feiern ein Fest.

stellen auf: draw up

Scheduling chores

2. Frage-Ecke. Sie und Ihre Partnerin/Ihr Partner stellen° den Plan für die Hausarbeit am Wochenende auf. Sagen Sie, was Julia, Lukas, Alex, Lena, Sie und Ihre Partnerin/Ihr Partner am Freitag und Samstag machen.

S1: Was macht Julia am Freitag?
S2: Sie kocht das Abendessen.
S1:

	Freitag	Samstag
Julia		das Wohnzimmer aufräumen
Lukas	das Abendessen kochen	
Alex		die Küche sauber machen
Lena	abwaschen	
ich		
Partnerin/		

S2:

	Freitag	Samstag
Julia	das Abendessen kochen	
Lukas		Staub saugen
Alex	das Bad putzen	
Lena		Geschirr spülen
ich		
Partnerin/ Partner		

Vokabeln

Substantive

das **Bad, ¨er**   bath; bathroom
der **Biergarten, ¨**   beer garden
die **Ferienreise, -n**   vacation trip
das **Fest, -e**   party; celebration; feast; **auf dem Fest**   at the party; **ein Fest geben**   to give a party
die **Flasche, -n**   bottle; **eine Flasche Mineralwasser**   a bottle of mineral water
die **Fußgängerzone, -n**   pedestrian zone
das **Geschirr**   dishes

die **Hausarbeit**   housework; chore
die **Luft**   air
der **Rauch**   smoke
die **Reise, -n**   trip, journey
die **Spülmaschine, -n**   dishwasher
der **Staub**   dust
die **Vorbereitung, -en**   preparation
der **Wald, ¨er**   forest
die **Wäsche**   laundry
das **Wohnzimmer, -**   living room

Verben

ab·trocknen to dry dishes; to wipe dry

ab·waschen (wäscht ab), abgewaschen to do dishes

an·schauen to look at, watch (e.g., ein Video)

auf·räumen to straighten up (a room)

aus·räumen to unload (dishwasher); to clear away

decken to cover; **den Tisch decken** to set the table

ein·räumen to load (dishwasher); **ich räume die Spülmaschine ein** I load the dishwasher; **ich räume das Geschirr in die Spülmaschine ein** I put the dishes in the dishwasher

helfen (hilft), geholfen (+ *dat.*) to help; **hilf mir** help me

putzen to clean

reden to talk

sitzen: gesessen

spülen to rinse; to wash; **Geschirr spülen** to wash dishes

Staub saugen to vacuum; **ich sauge Staub** I vacuum; **ich habe Staub gesaugt** I vacuumed

Staub wischen to dust; **ich wische Staub** I'm dusting; **ich habe Staub gewischt** I dusted

treffen (trifft), getroffen to meet

waschen (wäscht), gewaschen to wash

Andere Wörter

draußen outside

endlich finally

herum around; **herum·liegen** to be lying around

lieber preferably, rather; **ich sitze lieber draußen** I prefer to sit outside

pleite broke, out of money

sauber clean; **sauber machen** to clean

voll full

Besondere Ausdrücke

Du meine Güte! Good Heavens!

Er geht mit in einen Biergarten. He is going along to a beer garden.

Mach schnell! Hurry up!

Macht nichts! Doesn't matter!

EIN AUSTAUSCHSTUDENT IN DEUTSCHLAND

Vorbereitung auf das Lesen

■ *Vor dem Lesen*

1. Viele Leute sprechen gern über ihre Zeit im Ausland. Mögliche Themen sind das Essen oder die Reise selbst°, z.B. der Flug°. Welche anderen Themen können Sie nennen°?

   itself / flight
   name

2. Denken° Sie an ein Land – Kanada, Deutschland, die USA. Was assoziieren Sie mit diesem Land? Was ist typisch oder stereotyp für das Land?

   Denken Sie an: think of

■ *Beim Lesen*

which

1. Machen Sie eine Liste von den Themen, über die° Monika und Peter sprechen.

observations

2. Welche Bemerkungen° von Peter und Monika finden Sie stereotyp?

Der Austauschstudent Peter Clason studiert seit einem Jahr an der Universität Mainz. Er sitzt mit Monika in einer Studentenkneipe. Monika ist ein Jahr in Amerika gewesen. Mit ihr kann man deshalb gut über die Unterschiede zwischen Deutschland und Amerika reden. Monika fragt:
5 „Du, Peter, sag mal, was ist für dich hier in Deutschland eigentlich anders? Was hast du beobachtet?"

first / ride
since then
larger

in general
missed

apart / therefore
interrupted

first of all

finally
event / for a longer time

PETER: Vieles ist ja genauso wie in Amerika. Aber vieles ist doch auch anders. Da war zum Beispiel meine erste° Fahrt° auf der Autobahn. Furchtbar, sag' ich dir. Die fahren wie die Wilden, hab' ich gedacht. Seitdem° fahr' ich
10 richtig gern mit dem Zug. Außerdem hat fast jede größere° Stadt einen Bahnhof und es gibt genug Züge. Sie sind sauber. Sie fahren pünktlich ab und sie kommen pünktlich an. Überhaupt° funktioniert alles.

MONIKA: Ja, das habe ich in Amerika vermisst° – die öffentlichen Verkehrsmittel. Es gibt zwar Busse, aber die fahren nicht so oft. Alles ist auch so weit
15 auseinander°. Deswegen° braucht man wirklich ein Auto. – Aber Peter, es tut mir Leid, ich habe dich unterbrochen°. Was ist sonst noch anders in Deutschland?

PETER: Also mit den Bussen hast du ja Recht. Was noch? Vielleicht die Parks in jeder Stadt, die vielen Blumen in den Fenstern, auf den Märkten, in den
20 Restaurants. Und dann das Essen. Erstens° ist das Essen selbst anders – anderes Brot und Bier, mehr Wurst und so. Dann wie man isst – wie man Messer und Gabel benutzt, meine ich. Und schließlich° hab' ich auch gefunden, dass das Essen mehr ein Ereignis° ist. Man sitzt länger° am Tisch und spricht miteinander.

25 MONIKA: Ja, da hast du auch wieder Recht. Aber ich weiß nicht, ob das in allen Familien so ist. In vielen Familien arbeiten beide Eltern. Da bleibt auch nicht mehr so viel Zeit fürs Reden.

PETER: Ach ja, und noch etwas. Alles ist so sauber in Deutschland, aber manchmal gehen die Deutschen ein bisschen zu weit. Ich habe einmal im

rubber boots
telephone booth

30 Dezember eine Frau in Gummistiefeln° gesehen. Sie hat eine öffentliche Telefonzelle° geputzt. Das, liebe Monika, kann wohl nur in Deutschland passieren! Aber nun mal zu dir. Was hast du denn in Amerika so beobachtet?

really

MONIKA: Einige Sachen haben mir ausgesprochen° gut gefallen. Zum Beispiel
35 kann man in Amerika auch abends und am ganzen Wochenende einkaufen gehen. Das finde ich toll. Und ich finde die Amerikaner unglaublich freundlich. In den Geschäften und Restaurants waren alle

on the one hand / helpful
on the other hand / less
friendliness
appears

einerseits° sehr hilfsbereit°...

PETER: Und, andererseits°, was hat dir weniger° gefallen?

40 MONIKA: Na ja, also sei mir bitte nicht böse, aber diese Freundlichkeit° erscheint° mir manchmal doch auch sehr oberflächlich. Einmal war ich zum Beispiel beim Arzt, und die Krankenschwester hat „Monika" zu mir gesagt und nicht „Miss" oder „Ms. Berger". Sie hat mich doch gar nicht gekannt! Wir benutzen den Vornamen nur unter guten Freunden.

simply
everyday life

45 PETER: Das sehen wir eben° anders. Ein nettes Lächeln und ein freundliches Wort im Alltag° machen das Leben eben einfacher.

Im Münchener Hauptbahnhof.

Brauchbares

1. l.9, **"Die fahren wie die Wilden ... ":** On much of the **Autobahn** there is no speed limit **(die Geschwindigkeitsbegrenzung** or **das Tempolimit).** Although environmentalists keep advocating a speed limit of 100 km per hour everywhere, polls show that 80% of the German population opposes limits of any kind.

2. l.21, **"Dann wie man isst ... ":** If only a fork or spoon is needed, the other hand rests on the table next to the plate. If both a knife and fork are used, the knife is held in the right hand all during the meal. Open-faced sandwiches are common and eaten with a knife and fork.

3. l.41–42, **"Einmal war ich zum Beispiel beim Arzt ... ":** Another example of American "friendliness" that would be rare in German culture is the supermarket cashier who greets the customer with a "Hi, how are you?", perhaps makes an additional comment, and then says, "Have a good day."

4. l.44, **"Wir benutzen den Vornamen nur unter guten Freunden.":** Adult Germans use **du** and first names only with close friends. Although students use first names and **du** with each other immediately, it is still prudent in most situations for a foreign visitor to let a German-speaking person propose the use of the familiar **du.**

5. In l.45 Peter says, **"Das sehen wir eben anders.":** Eben is a flavoring particle that can be used by a speaker in a discussion in a final or closing statement to imply that she/he has no desire or need to discuss the point further. In other contexts it is used to support or strengthen a previous statement or idea or even to express strong agreement with what someone has said.

Die Deutschen in Amerika

German immigration in the New World began on an organized basis in 1683 when 33 Germans from Krefeld arrived in Philadelphia on the ship Concord. They were looking for religious and political freedom and came to Pennsylvania through the auspices of William Penn and a German named Franz Daniel Pastorius. The settlers called the community they built Germantown, which in 1854 became a part of Philadelphia. Seven million German emigrants have come to the U.S.A. Between 1820 and 1920 alone, more than six million German immigrants arrived, many of them farmers and artisans.

Today approximately 58 million Americans, out of a total population of 270 million, claim German ancestry. The states with the largest German ancestry are: Wisconsin (52% of the total population claim full or part German ancestry); South Dakota and North Dakota (47% each); Nebraska and Iowa (46% each); Minnesota (43%); Kansas (35%); and Indiana, Montana, Ohio, and Pennsylvania (33% each).

Das Pastorius-Haus in Germantown.

Diskussion

Do some historical research. The following famous Americans all have roots in a German-speaking country. How many of the names do you know? Look up information about a name that you do not know or add another name to the list.

Hannah Arendt, John Jacob Astor, Maximilian Berlitz, Wernher von Braun, Walter Chrysler, Albert Einstein, Karen Louise Erdrich, Milton S. Hershey, Paul Hindemith, Henry Kissinger, Franz Daniel Pastorius, Margarethe Meyer Schurz, Levi Strauss, John Sutter

Nach dem Lesen

1. Fragen zum Lesestück

1. Über welche Themen haben Monika und Peter gesprochen?
2. Wie fahren die Deutschen auf der Autobahn?
3. Mit welchem Verkehrsmittel fährt Peter gern?
4. Wie sind die Züge in Deutschland?
5. Warum ist Monika in Amerika nicht gern mit dem Bus gefahren?
6. Peter findet, dass die Deutschen vielleicht zu sauber sind. Warum glaubt er das?

7. Wie ist das Einkaufen anders in Amerika?

8. Was hat Monika bei dem amerikanischen Arzt nicht gefallen?

9. Findet Peter, dass die Amerikaner zu freundlich sind?

2. Vokabeln sammeln. *(Gathering vocabulary.)* Suchen Sie Wörter und Wendungen° im Text zu den folgenden Themen:

expressions

das Essen

Verkehrsmittel

3. Positives und Negatives. Peter und Monika machen Notizen über ihre Erlebnisse° im Ausland. Was steht° auf den Listen?

*experiences / **steht**: stands, here: is*

	Positives	Negatives
Peter über Deutschland		
Monika über Amerika		

4. Zur Diskussion. Sind Amerikaner freundlich oder zu freundlich? Geben Sie Beispiele, warum Ausländer sagen, dass Amerikaner freundlich sind. Geben Sie Beispiele, wann Amerikaner vielleicht oberflächlich sind.

5. Erzählen wir. Sprechen Sie über eines der folgenden° Themen. Was ist in Deutschland anders als hier? Was ist genauso wie bei Ihnen?

following

Autofahren	Fernsehen
Blumen	Freundlichkeit
Essen	Vornamen
Einkaufen	Züge

Erweiterung des Wortschatzes

1. Die Möbel und Küchengeräte°

kitchen appliances

das Wohnzimmer
1. der **Couchtisch, -e**
2. der **Schreibtisch, -e**
3. der **Sessel, -**
4. das **Sofa, -s**
5. der **Teppich, -e**

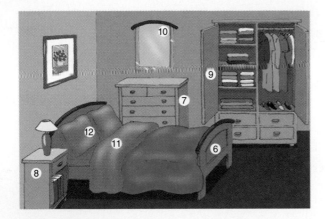

das Schlafzimmer

6. das **Bett, -en**
7. die **Kommode, -n**
8. der **Nachttisch, -e**
9. der **Schrank, ⸚e**
10. der **Spiegel, -**

11. die **Bettdecke, -n**
12. das **Kissen, -**

die Küche

13. der **Herd, -e**
14. der **Kühlschrank, ⸚e**
15. die **Spülmaschine, -n**

ziehen um: are moving

1. Was steht wo?   Sie ziehen um°. Machen Sie eine Liste und schreiben Sie auf, was in jedes Zimmer kommt.

die Küche	das Wohnzimmer	das Esszimmer°	das Schlafzimmer

2. Frage-Ecke.   Ihre Partnerin/Ihr Partner und verschiedene andere Leute haben einige neue Möbel und andere neue Sachen in ihren Wohnungen°. Finden Sie heraus, was sie haben und in welchen Zimmern die Sachen sind.

S2: Was ist neu in der Küche und im Esszimmer von Herrn Becker?
S1: In der Küche ist der Herd und im Esszimmer der Tisch neu.

S1:

	in der Küche	im Wohnzimmer	im Esszimmer	im Schlafzimmer
Herr Becker	Herd		Tisch	
Frau Hauff		Sofa	4 Stühle	
Andrea	Geschirr			Schreibtisch
Jens		Bücherregal		Kommode
ich				
Partnerin/ Partner				

S2:

	in der Küche	im Wohnzimmer	im Esszimmer	im Schlafzimmer
Herr Becker		Pflanze		Schrank
Frau Hauff	Kühlschrank			Nachttisch
Andrea		Sessel	Teppich	
Jens	Spülmaschine		Bild von den Großeltern	
ich				
Partnerin/ Partner				

Freunde *vs.* Bekannte

Germans do not use the word **Freund/Freundin** as freely as Americans use *friend.* A **Freund/Freundin** is a person with whom one is on intimate terms, a person who is often called "a very good friend" by Americans. Germans tend to have fewer **Freunde** and a larger circle of acquaintances **(Bekannte).** Even acquaintances of years' standing, e.g., neighbors and co-workers, do not necessarily become **Freunde.**

Most teenagers and young adults in German-speaking countries spend their free time with a group of friends, rather than with one friend or a date. This is true for single men and women as well as for many couples in that age group. While an American college student might say "I'm going on a date," a German student is more likely to say **Ich treffe mich mit meinen Freunden** *(I'm meeting with my friends).*

Studenten an der Berliner Humboldt-Universität machen eine Pause.

Diskussion

What is a good friend? Make a list of five qualities that you expect to find in a "good friend." Find the German equivalents of the words and compare your list with the lists of other students. Can you make any distinctions between the qualities you expect from "good friends" **(Freunde)** and "friends" **(Bekannte)?** Would your list of characteristics be any different?

3. Meine Wohnung. Beschreiben Sie Ihrer Partnerin/Ihrem Partner ein Zimmer in Ihrem Haus oder in Ihrer Wohnung. Sprechen Sie auch über Details wie Farbe und Größe von den Sachen in Ihrem Zimmer und ob sie alt oder neu sind.

≫ *Im Schlafzimmer habe ich ein Bett, einen Schreibtisch, ein Bücherregal und eine Lampe. Der Schreibtisch ist modern und groß. Das Bücherregal ist...*

2. The verbs *legen/liegen, stellen/stehen, setzen/sitzen, hängen, stecken*

Wohin? **Wo?**

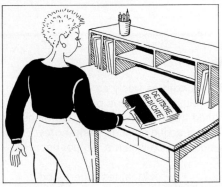

Lisa **legt** das Buch auf den Schreibtisch.

Das Buch **liegt** auf dem Schreibtisch.

Herr Schumann **stellt** die Lampe in die Ecke°.

Die Lampe **steht** in der Ecke.

Anna **setzt** die Katze° auf den Boden°.

Die Katze **sitzt** auf dem Boden.

Felix **hängt** das Poster an die Wand.

Das Poster **hängt** an der Wand.

Jessica **steckt** die Zeitung in die Tasche.

Die Zeitung **steckt** in der Tasche.

In English, the all-purpose verb for movement to a position is *to put,* and the all-purpose verb for the resulting position is *to be.* German uses several verbs to express the meanings *put* and *be.*

Position			
to put		*to be*	
legen, gelegt	*to lay*	liegen, gelegen	*to be lying*
stellen, gestellt	*to place upright*	stehen, gestanden	*to be standing*
setzen, gesetzt	*to set*	sitzen, gesessen	*to be sitting*
stecken, gesteckt	*to stick (into)*	stecken, gesteckt	*to be inserted (in)*
hängen, gehängt	*to hang*	hängen, gehangen	*to be hanging*

The German verbs expressing *to put* all take direct objects and are weak.

Ich **habe** das Buch auf den Tisch **gelegt.**

The German verbs expressing position *(be)* do not take direct objects and, except for **stecken,** are strong.

Das Buch **hat** auf dem Tisch **gelegen.**

4. Wir räumen auf. Sie räumen zusammen mit Elisabeth Ihr Zimmer auf. Beschreiben Sie, was Sie tun. Benutzen Sie passende Verben aus der Tabelle.

➤➤ Elisabeth _____ das Buch auf den Tisch. *Elisabeth legt das Buch auf den Tisch.*

1. Ich _____ das Poster an die Wand.

2. Elisabeth _____ den Sessel in die Ecke.

3. Die Lampe muss über dem Tisch _____ .

4. Die Hefte _____ auf der Kommode.

5. Ich _____ das Geld in die Tasche.

6. Der Fernseher _____ unter dem Fenster.

7. Ich _____ die Schuhe in den Schrank.

8. Der Mantel _____ schon in dem Schrank.

9. Der Regenschirm _____ auch in dem Schrank.

10. Die Katze _____ auf dem Schreibtisch.

11. Elisabeth _____ die Katze auf den Boden.

12. Die Bücher müssen in dem Bücherregal _____ .

13. Ich _____ die Vase° auf das Bücherregal.

Häuser und Wohnungen

LAND UND LEUTE

Most people in German-speaking countries live in apartments, either rented **(Mietwohnung)** or owned **(Eigentumswohnung).** Inhabitants of **Mietwohnungen** share the cleaning of the stairway, attic, and basement, unless the owner has hired a superintendent **(Hausmeisterin/Hausmeister).**

Only 41% of the people in western Germany and 27% in eastern Germany own a single family home **(Einfamilienhaus)**—compared to more than 80% of the people in the U.S. Even though the federal government, cities, and counties have tried to make it easier and more affordable to become a homeowner, land remains limited and expensive; construction materials and wages remain costly; planning, licensing, and building codes are complex; and mortgages still require very large down payments.

Go to the
Deutsch heute Web Site at
www.hmco.com/college

Einfamilienhaus in Bielefeld.

A typical house has stucco-coated walls and a tile or slate roof. Normally there is a full basement **(der Keller)** that is used primarily for storage or as a work area. The first floor **(erster Stock** or **erste Etage)** is what is usually considered the second story in American homes. The ground floor is called **das Erdgeschoss** or **Parterre.** Privacy is assured not only by closed doors but also by window curtains **(Gardinen)** and drapes **(Vorhänge).** Many homes and apartments are equipped with outdoor shutters **(Rolläden)** that unfold vertically over the windows.

In addition to the modern houses, each region of Germany has its own traditional architecture. **Fachwerkhäuser** (half-timbered houses) lend charming character to many town centers.

Diskussion

Research project: What differences do you find between German homes and North American homes?

Wegweiser für Wohneigentum
Der Trend geht wieder zum Eigenheim mit *Gartenzwergen.*

Vokabeln

Substantive

die **Angst, ⸚e** fear
das **Ausland** (*no pl.*) foreign countries; **im Ausland** abroad
der **Austauschstudent, -en, -en**/die **Austauschstudentin, -nen** exchange student
die **Autobahn, -en** freeway, expressway
der **Bahnhof, ⸚e** train station
der **Boden, ⸚** floor
die **Ecke, -n** corner
das **Esszimmer, -** dining room
die **Gabel, -n** fork
der **Hund, -e** dog
die **Katze, -n** cat
die **Krankenschwester, -n** nurse
das **Leben, -** life

der **Löffel, -** spoon
das **Messer, -** knife
die **Möbel** (*pl.*) furniture; das **Möbelstück** piece of furniture
der **Park, -s** park
das **Restaurant, -s** restaurant
das **Schlafzimmer, -** bedroom
der **Unterschied, -e** difference
die **Vase, -n** vase
das **Verkehrsmittel, -** means of transportation
der **Videorecorder, -** VCR
der **Vorname, -n, -n** first name
die **Wohnung, -en** dwelling, apartment
For items of furniture and kitchen appliances see pp. 247–248.

Verben

ab·fahren (fährt ab), ist abgefahren to depart (by vehicle)
an·kommen, ist angekommen (in + *dat.*) to arrive (in)
benutzen to use
beobachten to observe
hängen to hang (something), put
hängen, gehangen to be hanging
lächeln to smile
legen to lay, put (horizontal)

meinen to mean; to think, have an opinion; **was meinst du?** what do you think?
passieren, ist passiert (+ *dat.*) to happen; **was ist dir passiert?** what happened to you?
setzen to set, put
stecken to stick, put into, insert
stehen, gestanden to stand; to be located
stellen to place, put (upright)

Andere Wörter

beide both
böse (**auf** + *acc.*) angry (at)
eigentlich actually
einander one another, each other; **miteinander** with each other
fast almost
genauso exactly the same
nächst (-er, -es, -e) next
ob (*conj.*) whether, if

oberflächlich superficial
öffentlich public
pünktlich punctual
selbst oneself, myself, itself, etc.
unglaublich unbelievable
unter (+ *acc. or dat.*) under; among
weit far
zwar it's true; to be sure; indeed
zwischen (+ *acc. or dat.*) between

Besondere Ausdrücke

gar nicht not at all
Recht haben to be right; **Du hast Recht.** You're right.

sei [mir] nicht böse don't be mad [at me]
was noch? what else?

GRAMMATIK UND ÜBUNGEN

1. *Hin* and *her*

Meine Tante wohnt nicht hier, sondern in Hamburg.	My aunt doesn't live here, but rather in Hamburg.
Wir fahren einmal im Jahr **hin.**	Once a year we go *there*.
Und zweimal im Jahr kommt sie **her.**	And twice a year she comes *here*.

Hin and **her** are used to show direction. **Hin** shows motion away from the speaker, and **her** shows motion toward the speaker. **Hin** and **her** occupy last position in the sentence.

Er war letztes Jahr in Europa. Er möchte wieder **dorthin.**	He was in Europe last year. He wants to go there again.
Kommen Sie mal **herauf.**	Come on up here.

Hin and **her** may be combined with several parts of speech, including adverbs, prepositions, and verbs.

Woher kommen Sie?	**Wo** kommen Sie **her?**	Where are you from?
Wohin fahren Sie?	**Wo** fahren Sie **hin?**	Where are you going?

In spoken German, **hin** and **her** are often separated from **wo. Hin** and **her** occupy last position in the sentence.

1. Ilse und Axel.   Stellen Sie Fragen über Ilse und Axel. Benutzen Sie **wo, wohin** oder **woher.**

⟫ Ilse und Axel wohnen bei München.   *Wo wohnen sie?*
⟫ Sie fahren jeden Morgen nach München.   *Wohin fahren sie? / Wo fahren sie hin?*

1. Sie arbeiten in einer Buchhandlung.
2. Sie gehen am Samstag in den Supermarkt.
3. Die Blumen kommen vom Markt.
4. Sie fahren am Sonntag in die Berge.
5. Sie wandern gern in den Bergen.
6. Nach der Wanderung° gehen sie in ein Restaurant.   hike
7. Sie essen gern im Restaurant.
8. Nach dem Essen fahren sie wieder nach Hause.
9. In den Ferien fahren sie in die Schweiz.
10. Axel kommt aus der Schweiz.

PRIVATE GESUNDHEITSVORSORGE

Man sollte schon **wissen**, **wohin** die Reise geht.

Was ist alles in diesem Wohnzimmer?

die Präposition mit Dativ oder Akkusativ

2. Two-way prepositions°

Dative: **wo?**

Ilse arbeitet **in der Küche.**
Ilse is working *in the kitchen.*

Accusative: **wohin?**

Axel kommt **in die Küche.**
Axel comes *into the kitchen.*

German has nine prepositions that take either the dative or the accusative. The dative is used when position *(place where)* is indicated, answering the question **wo?** (e.g., **in der Küche**). The accusative is used when a change of location *(place to which)* is indicated, answering the question **wohin?** (e.g., **in die Küche**).

In their basic meanings, the two-way prepositions are "spatial," referring to positions in space (dative) or movements through space (accusative). To distinguish place *where* from place *to which,* German uses different cases; English sometimes uses different prepositions (e.g., *in* vs. *into*).

Preposition	Meaning	*Wo?* (Preposition + dative)	*Wohin?* (Preposition + accusative)
an	on *(vertical surfaces)*	Das Bild hängt **an der** Wand.	Sabine hängt das Bild **an die** Wand.
	at *(the side of)*	Ute steht **am (an dem)** Fenster.	
	to		Benno geht **ans (an das)** Fenster.
auf	on top of *(horizontal surfaces)*	Kurts Buch liegt **auf dem** Tisch.	Sabine legt ihr Buch **auf den** Tisch.
	to		Ich gehe **auf den** Markt.
hinter	behind/in back of	Inge arbeitet **hinter dem** Haus.	Nils geht **hinter das** Haus.
in	in, inside (of)	Paula arbeitet **im (in dem)** Wohnzimmer.	
	into		Jürgen geht **ins (in das)** Wohnzimmer.
	to		Wir gehen **ins (in das)** Kino.
neben	beside, next to	Ritas Stuhl steht **neben dem** Fenster.	Jan stellt seinen Stuhl **neben das** Fenster.
über	over, above	Eine Lampe hängt **über dem** Tisch.	Hugo hängt eine andere Lampe **über den** Tisch.
	across *(direction)*		Ich gehe **über die** Straße.
unter	under	Ein Schuh steht **unter dem** Bett.	Kurt stellt den anderen Schuh **unter das** Bett.
vor	in front of	Ilses Auto steht **vor dem** Haus.	Armin fährt sein Auto **vor das** Haus.
zwischen	between	Die Seminararbeit liegt **zwischen den** Büchern.	Judith legt die Seminararbeit **zwischen die** Bücher.

3. Prepositional contractions

Er geht **ans** Fenster.	an das = **ans**
Er steht **am** Fenster.	an dem = **am**
Sie geht **ins** Zimmer.	in das = **ins**
Sie ist **im** Zimmer.	in dem = **im**

The prepositions **an** and **in** often contract with **das** and **dem**. Other possible contractions are **aufs, hinters, hinterm, übers, überm, unters, unterm, vors,** and **vorm.**

2. Was ist wo? Sehen Sie sich das Bild an und ergänzen Sie die Sätze mit passenden Präpositionen, Artikeln und Substantiven.

➤➤ Der Hund liegt _____ . *Der Hund liegt unter dem Tisch.*

1. Der Stuhl steht _____ .
5. Das Bild hängt _____ .

2. Die Vase steht _____ .
6. Die Katze sitzt _____ .

3. Die Bücher stehen _____ .
7. Der Sessel steht _____ .

4. Der Tisch steht _____ .
8. Die Lampe hängt _____ .

3. Das habe ich gemacht. Erzählen Sie, was Sie mit einigen Sachen in Ihrem Zimmer gemacht haben.

➤➤ Ich habe das Bild _____ Wand gehängt. *Ich habe das Bild an die Wand gehängt.*

1. Ich habe den Stuhl _____ Tisch gestellt.

2. Ich habe die Vase _____ Bücherregal gestellt.

3. Ich habe die Bücher _____ Bücherregal gestellt.

4. Ich habe den Tisch _____ Bücherregal gestellt.

5. Ich habe die Lampe _____ Tisch gehängt.

6. Ich habe den Sessel _____ Bücherregal und _____ Tür gestellt.

7. Der Hund ist _____ Tisch gegangen.

8. Die Katze ist _____ Sessel gegangen.

4. Aufräumen. Sie und Ihr Bruder erwarten einen Gast und räumen das Haus auf. Beantworten Sie seine Fragen.

➤➤ Wohin stell' ich das Radio? (auf / Nachttisch). *Auf den Nachttisch.*

1. Wohin stell' ich die Bücher? (in / Bücherregal)
2. Wo sind meine Schuhe? (unter / Bett)
3. Wohin soll ich sie stellen? (in / Schrank)
4. Wo hängt meine Jacke? (hinter / Tür)
5. Wohin stell' ich diesen Sessel? (an / Fenster)
6. Wo soll die Vase stehen? (auf / Tisch)
7. Wohin leg' ich die Zeitung? (auf / Schreibtisch)
8. Wohin tue ich diese Wäsche? (in / Kommode)
9. Wohin soll ich das Poster hängen? (an / Wand)
10. Wo ist das neue Video? (in / Videorecorder°)

4. *An* and *auf* = on

Der Spiegel hängt **an der Wand.**	The mirror is hanging on the wall.
Mein Buch liegt **auf dem Schreibtisch.**	My book is lying on the desk.

An and **auf** can both be equivalent to *on.* **An** = *on (the side of)* is used in reference to vertical surfaces. **Auf** = *on (top of)* is used in reference to horizontal surfaces.

5. *An, auf,* and *in* = to

Veronika geht **an** die Tür.	Veronika goes to the door.
Bernd geht **auf** den Markt.	Bernd goes to the market.
Lore geht **in** die Stadt.	Lore goes to town.

The prepositions **an, auf,** and **in** can be equivalent to the English preposition *to.*

5. Julia hat endlich ein Zimmer. Julia richtet° ihr neues Zimmer ein.   *is arranging*
Ergänzen Sie die Sätze mit den fehlenden Präpositionen **an** oder **auf.**

➤➤ Julia stellt den Schreibtisch _____ Fenster.
Julia stellt den Schreibtisch ans Fenster.

1. Den Stuhl stellt Julia _____ Schreibtisch.

2. Sie hängt das Bild _____ Wand.

3. Sie legt die Bücher _____ Schreibtisch.

4. Der Schirm hängt _____ Tür. Das gefällt ihr nicht und sie legt ihn _____
   Schrank.

5. _____ Stuhl liegt ihr Mantel. Den hängt sie _____ Tür.

6. Die Blumen stellt sie _____ Bücherregal.

7. Und jetzt geht sie _____ Markt und kauft ein.

LAND UND LEUTE

Go to the
Deutsch heute Web Site at
www.hmco.com/college

Geschlossene Türen

An American visiting a business or a home in a German-speaking country will be struck by the fact that inside doors are mostly closed. Doors to offices in American businesses, public buildings, and universities tend to be open. An open door in a German, Austrian, or Swiss firm, however, might bother the employee. Open doors imply lack of privacy. If the door has a glass pane it is usually of milk glass so that one can't see through it.

Doors also tend to be shut in private homes. When one enters a typical German home there is an entrance hall **(die Diele/der Flur).** From this hall, doors lead into the living room, kitchen, bathroom, and bedrooms. These doors remain closed so that a visitor cannot look into the rooms.

The people in German-speaking countries take their privacy seriously. They feel their privacy is violated if they can be seen or if outside noise disturbs them in their homes. Therefore, while Americans tend to solve noise problems by sound-proofing, most people in German-speaking countries observe regulations that require a quiet time around mid-day **(Ruhezeit)** and after 10 P.M. During these hours, people try not to engage in activities that might disturb the neighbors. In a country like Germany that is half the size of Texas but with a population

Zimmertüren bleiben meistens geschlossen.

of 82 million and where most people live in apartment houses, the need to preserve privacy is understandable.

Diskussion

Germany is one of the most densely populated countries in Europe. It has approximately 226 inhabitants per square kilometer or 589 per square mile. The close proximity of living conditions has an effect on ideas of privacy and influences housing patterns. Find out the density of population in your country and state and discuss ideas of privacy in your culture. You may want to consider the following issues: the differences between living in an apartment, single-family home, or dormitory room; times and levels of noise that you consider acceptable; how you define your private space, the role of doors, your relationship with neighbors.

6. Am Wochenende. Susan ist ein Jahr lang als Austauschstudentin in Deutschland. Sie wohnt mit Erika zusammen. Erzählen Sie, was Susan am Wochenende macht. Benutzen Sie die Wörter.

➤➤ Susan / gehen / auf / Markt
Susan geht auf den Markt.

1. auf / Markt / sie / kaufen / Blumen / für / ihr Zimmer
2. dann / sie / gehen / in / Buchhandlung
3. Erika / arbeiten / in / Buchhandlung
4. Susan / müssen / in / Drogerie
5. in / Drogerie / sie / wollen / kaufen / Kamm
6. sie / gehen / dann / in / Café
7. in / Café / sie / treffen / Erika
8. sie / sitzen / an / Tisch / in / Ecke

6. Special meanings of prepositions

In addition to their basic meanings, prepositions have special meanings when combined with specific verbs (e.g., **denken an,** *to think of*) or with certain nouns (e.g., **Angst vor,** *fear of*). Each combination should be learned as a unit, because it cannot be predicted which preposition is associated with a particular verb or noun. The prepositions **durch, für, gegen, ohne, um** and **aus, außer, bei, mit, nach, seit, von, zu** take the accusative and dative respectively. The case of the noun following two-way prepositions must be learned. When **über** means *about/concerning,* it is always followed by the accusative case. A few combinations are given below.

denken an (+ *acc.*)
Ich **denke** oft **an** meine Freunde.

to think of/about
I often *think of* my friends.

schreiben an (+ *acc.*)
Martina **schreibt an** ihren Vater.

to write to
Martina *is writing to* her father.

studieren an/auf (+ *dat.*)
Mark **studiert an/auf** der Universität München.

to study at
Mark is *studying at* the University of Munich.

warten auf (+ *acc.*)
Wir **warten auf** den Bus.

to wait for
We're *waiting for* the bus.

helfen bei
Hilf mir bitte **bei** meiner Arbeit.

to help with
Please *help* me *with* my work.

fahren mit
Wir **fahren mit** dem Auto nach Ulm.

to go by (means of)
We're *going* to Ulm *by* car.

reden/sprechen über (+ *acc.*)
Meine Eltern **sprechen** oft **über** das Wetter.

to talk/speak about
My parents often *talk about* the weather.

reden/sprechen von
Kevin **redet** wieder **von** seinem Porsche.

to talk/speak about/of
Kevin *is talking about* his Porsche again.

schreiben über (+ *acc.*)
Anna schreibt über ihre Arbeit.

to write about
Anna *is writing about* her work.

halten von
Sarah **hält** nicht viel **von** dem Plan.

to think of, have an opinion of
Sarah doesn't *think* much *of* the plan.

Angst haben vor (+ *dat.*)
Tobias **hat Angst vorm** Fliegen.

to be afraid of
Tobias *is afraid of* flying.

7. Mein Bruder. Ihr Freund Lukas erzählt Ihnen von seinem Bruder. Geben Sie die Sätze auf Englisch wieder. Achten° Sie besonders auf die Verben und Präpositionen.

pay attention

1. Mein Bruder geht auf die Universität.
2. Oft schreibt er Briefe an mich und meine Eltern.
3. Ich denke oft an ihn, weil er mir immer bei meinen Hausaufgaben° geholfen hat.

homework

4. Wie oft haben wir stundenlang über Politik, Sport und Frauen gesprochen!
5. In seinem letzten Brief hat er mir von seiner Freundin Cornelia erzählt.
6. Soll ich ihm auch von meiner Freundin erzählen?

8. Was macht Dennis am Samstag? Erzählen Sie, was Dennis am Samstag macht. Benutzen Sie die Wortverbindungen° mit einem passenden Verb. Variieren Sie die Verben so viel wie möglich. Sie können auch erzählen, was er nicht macht.

phrases

➤➤ in die Bibliothek *Dennis geht in die Bibliothek.*

1. in der Bibliothek
2. auf dem Markt
3. mit dem Auto
4. in die Berge
5. in einem Café
6. auf der Autobahn
7. über Musik
8. im Restaurant

9. Ein Jahr in Deutschland. Geben Sie die Sätze über Peters Jahr in Deutschland auf Deutsch wieder.

1. Peter lives behind a supermarket.
2. There are parks in every city.
3. In the restaurants there are flowers on every table.
4. Peter goes to the university by bus.
5. He doesn't like to drive on the freeway.
6. One can buy aspirin only in the pharmacy.
7. After a meal his friends sit at the table a long time. (*Word order:* long time / table)
8. They talk about sports, books, and their seminar reports.

7. Time expressions° in the dative

der Zeitausdruck

Am Montag bleibt Karla immer zu Hause.	On Monday Karla always stays home.
Philipp kommt **in** einer Woche.	Philipp's coming in a week.
Ich lese gern **am** Abend.	I like to read in the evening.
Marcel arbeitet **vor** dem Essen.	Marcel works before dinner.
Laura war **vor** einer Woche hier.	Laura was here a week ago.

With time expressions, **an, in,** and **vor** take the dative case. The use of **am** + a day may mean *on that one day* or *on all such days*.

10. Wann machst du das?   Ein Freund von Ihnen denkt, dass er weiß, wann Sie was machen. Korrigieren Sie ihn und benutzen Sie dazu die Zeitausdrücke im Dativ.

≫ Du arbeitest nur am Morgen, nicht? (Abend)   *Nein, nur am Abend.*

1. Frank kommt in fünf Minuten, nicht? (zwanzig Minuten)
2. Sollen wir vor dem Seminar Kaffee trinken gehen? (Vorlesung)
3. Du gehst am Donnerstag schwimmen, nicht? (Wochenende)
4. Du fährst am Samstagnachmittag nach Hause, nicht? (Sonntagabend)
5. Rita kommt in zwei Wochen, nicht? (eine Woche)
6. Du musst die Arbeit vor dem Wintersemester fertig haben, nicht? (Sommersemester)
7. Im Sommer fährst du in die Berge, nicht? (Herbst)
8. Du gehst nur einmal im Monat in die Bibliothek, nicht? (Woche)

8. Time expressions in the accusative

| Definite point | Martin kommt **nächsten Sonntag.** | Martin is coming next Sunday. |
| Duration | Er bleibt **einen Tag.** | He's staying (for) one day. |

Nouns expressing a definite point of time or a duration of time are in the accusative, and do not use a preposition.

11. Wann und wie lange?   Eine Pianistin kommt und Michael möchte gern wissen, wie lange sie bleibt. Ergänzen Sie die Sätze.

≫ Wann war die Pianistin in Hamburg?—Sie war *letzten Mittwoch* in Hamburg. *(last Wednesday)*

1. Wann kommt sie zu uns? — Sie kommt _____ zu uns. *(this weekend)*
2. Wie lange bleibt sie? — Sie bleibt _____ . *(a day)*
3. Wie oft übt° sie? — Sie übt _____ . *(every morning)*   practice
4. Wann fährt sie wieder weg°? — Sie fährt _____ wieder weg. *(next Monday)*   away
5. Wann kommt sie wieder? — Sie kommt _____ wieder. *(next year)*
6. Wie lange bleibt sie dann? — Dann bleibt sie _____ . *(a month)*

12. Pläne.   Sprechen Sie mit Ihrer Partnerin/Ihrem Partner darüber, was Sie am Wochenende oder in den Ferien machen wollen.

S2: Was machst du [am Wochenende]?
S1: Ich will [nichts tun].

Times: am Wochenende □ am Mittwoch □ nach dem Abendessen □ im Sommer □ in den Ferien

Activities: ins Kino gehen □ mit Freunden kochen □ lesen □ ein Video anschauen □ Freunde treffen □ tanzen gehen □ eine Wanderung machen □ im Internet surfen □ Fitnesstraining machen

das **da**-Kompositum

9. *Da*-compounds°

Erzählt Bianca **von ihrem Freund?**	Ja, sie erzählt viel **von ihm.**
Erzählt Bianca **von ihrer Arbeit?**	Ja, sie erzählt viel **davon.**

In German, pronouns used after prepositions normally refer only to persons **(Freund).** To refer to things and ideas **(Arbeit),** a **da**-compound consisting of **da** + a preposition is generally used: **dadurch, dafür, damit,** etc. **Da-** expands to **dar-** when the preposition begins with a vowel: **darauf, darin, darüber.**

13. Was hält Monika von Amerika?   Monika und Peter sind in den USA.
Monikas Freund Alex fragt, was sie in den USA macht und wie es ihr gefällt. Beantworten Sie Alex' Fragen mit „ja" und benutzen Sie ein **da**-Kompositum oder eine Präposition mit einem Pronomen.

⮞ Gefällt es Monika bei ihren amerikanischen Freunden?
   Ja, es gefällt Monika bei ihnen.
⮞ Hat sie Hunger auf deutsches Brot?
   Ja, sie hat Hunger darauf.

1. Redet sie gern mit Peter?
2. Reden sie oft über kulturelle Unterschiede?
3. Hilft sie Peter oft mit seinem Deutsch?
4. Geht sie gern mit ihren Freunden essen?
5. Denkt Monika oft an zu Hause?
6. Erzählt sie gern von ihrem Leben in Deutschland?
7. Fährt sie oft mit dem Fahrrad?
8. Erzählt sie oft von ihren Freunden?

das **wo**-Kompositum

10. *Wo*-compounds°

Von wem spricht Bianca?	Sie spricht **von ihrem Freund.**
Wovon (Von was) spricht Bianca?	Sie spricht **von ihrer Arbeit.**

The interrogative pronouns **wen** and **wem** are used with a preposition to refer only to persons. The interrogative pronoun **was** refers to things and ideas. As an object of a preposition, **was** may be replaced by a **wo**-compound consisting of **wo** + a preposition: **wofür, wodurch, womit,** etc. **Wo-** expands to **wor-** when the preposition begins with a vowel: **worauf, worin, worüber.** A preposition + **was (von was, für was)** is colloquial.

Matthias wohnt seit September in München.	**Seit wann** wohnt er in München?

Wo-compounds are not used to inquire about time. To inquire about time, **wann, seit wann,** or **wie lange** is used.

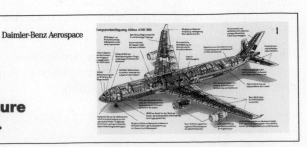

— Daimler-Benz Aerospace

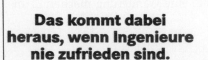

Das kommt dabei heraus, wenn Ingenieure nie zufrieden sind.

14. Wie bitte? Rolf nuschelt°, weil er müde ist. Sie hören nicht genau, über wen oder worüber er spricht. Fragen Sie ihn, was er gesagt hat. Benutzen Sie ein **wo**-Kompositum oder eine Präposition mit Pronomen und ersetzen° Sie die fett gedruckten° Ausdrücke.

mumbles

replace
fett gedruckt: *boldfaced*

➤➤ Klaus hat die Arbeit **mit dem Kugelschreiber** geschrieben.

Womit hat er sie geschrieben?

➤➤ Er hat sie **mit Annette** geschrieben.

Mit wem hat er sie geschrieben?

1. Susanne hat **von ihrer Vorlesung** erzählt.

_____ hat sie erzählt?

2. Sie hat auch **von Professor Weiß** erzählt.

_____ hat sie erzählt?

3. Udo arbeitet **für Frau Schneider.**

_____ arbeitet er?

4. Sabine ist **mit Gerd** essen gegangen.

_____ ist sie essen gegangen?

5. Beim Essen hat sie **von ihrer Arbeit** erzählt.

_____ hat sie beim Essen erzählt?

6. Nachher hat sie **mit Udo** Tennis gespielt.

_____ hat sie nachher Tennis gespielt?

7. Sie hat nur **über das Tennisspiel** geredet.

_____ hat sie geredet?

8. Sie denkt nur **an Tennis.**

_____ denkt sie nur?

9. Sie wohnt jetzt wieder **bei ihren Eltern.**

_____ wohnt sie jetzt wieder?

10. Sie denkt nicht mehr **an eine eigene° Wohnung.**

_____ denkt sie nicht mehr?

her own

🗨 **15. So bin ich.** Ihre Partnerin/Ihr Partner möchte Sie besser kennen lernen° und fragt Sie nach Ihren Interessen und wie Sie auf Dinge reagieren. Ergänzen Sie° die Sätze und bereiten Sie sich auf die Konversation vor°. Ihre Partnerin/Ihr Partner erzählt dann einer dritten Person, was Sie gesagt haben.

kennen lernen: *get to know*
complete / **bereiten ... vor:**
prepare yourself for the conversation

Getting to know someone better

S2: Woran denkst du oft?
S1: Ich denke oft an die Sommerferien.
S2: [Rita/Thomas] denkt oft an die Sommerferien.

1. Ich denke oft an _____ .

2. Ich spreche gern über _____ .

3. Ich weiß viel/wenig über _____ .

4. Ich halte nicht viel von _____ .

5. Ich rede oft mit _____ .

6. Ich schreibe oft an _____ .

7. Ich habe oft Probleme mit _____ .

8. Ich muss oft über _____ lächeln.

11. Indirect questions

Direct question	Indirect question
Wann kommt Paul nach Hause? When is Paul coming home?	Weißt du, **wann Paul nach Hause kommt?** Do you know *when Paul is coming home?*
Kommt er vor sechs? Is he coming before six?	Ich möchte wissen, **ob er vor sechs kommt.** I'd like to know *whether (if) he's coming before six.*

An indirect question (e.g., **wann Paul nach Hause kommt; ob er vor sechs kommt**) is a dependent clause. It begins with a question word **(wann)** or, if there is no question word, with the subordinating conjunction **ob.** The finite verb **(kommt)** is therefore in final position.

An indirect question is introduced by an introductory clause such as:

Weißt du, ... ?
Ich möchte wissen, ...
Kannst du mir sagen, ... ?
Ich weiß nicht, ...

■ *Indirect informational questions*

Direct informational question	Wann fährt Birgit zur Uni?
Indirect informational question	Ich weiß nicht, wann Birgit zur Uni fährt.

Indirect informational questions are introduced by the same question words that are used in direct informational questions (**wer, was, wann, wie lange, warum,** etc.). The question word functions as a subordinating conjunction.

16. Lia hat einen neuen Freund.   Barbara and Gerd sprechen über Lias neuen Freund. Führen° Sie das Gespräch nach dem folgenden Muster° weiter.

führen weiter: continue / model

➤➤   BARBARA: Wie heißt er?   GERD: *Ich weiß nicht, wie er heißt.*

1. Was macht er?
2. Wie lange kennt sie ihn schon?
3. Wo wohnt er?
4. Wie alt ist er?
5. Wo arbeitet er?
6. Warum findet sie ihn so toll?
7. Wann sieht sie ihn wieder?

■ *Indirect yes/no questions*

Yes/No question	Fährt Birgit heute zur Uni? Is Birgit driving to the university today?
Indirect question	Weißt du, **ob** Birgit heute zur Uni fährt? Do you know *if/whether* Birgit is driving to the university today?

Indirect yes/no questions are introduced by the subordinating conjunction **ob. Ob** has the meaning of *if* or *whether* and is used with main clauses such as **Sie fragt, ob ...** and **Ich weiß nicht, ob ...**

■ *ob* vs. *wenn*

Paul fragt Birgit, **ob** sie zur Uni fährt.	Paul is asking Birgit *if/whether* she's driving to the university.
Er möchte mitfahren, **wenn** sie zur Uni fährt.	He would like to go along, *if* she's driving to the university.

Both **wenn** and **ob** are equivalent to English *if*. However, they are not interchangeable. **Wenn** begins a clause that states the condition under which some event may or may not take place. **Ob** begins an indirect yes/no question.

17. Ob Birgit zur Uni fährt?   Gerd möchte mit Birgit zur Uni fahren und fragt Paul, ob er ihre Pläne kennt. Setzen° Sie **ob** oder **wenn** in die Lücken° ein.

setzen ein: insert / blanks

1. GERD: Weißt du, _____ Birgit morgen zur Uni fährt?

2. PAUL: Ich glaube, sie fährt, _____ ihr Auto wieder läuft.

3. GERD: Ich muss sie dann fragen, _____ das Auto wieder in Ordnung ist.

4. PAUL: Ich weiß aber nicht, _____ sie um acht Uhr oder erst° um neun fährt.

only

Weißt du, _____ sie manchmal mit dem Rad in die Uni fährt?

5. GERD: Nein, und ich frage mich, warum sie immer mit dem Auto fährt,

besonders _____ sie immer lange suchen muss, bis sie endlich parken kann.

6. PAUL: Ich habe sie mal gefragt, _____ wir vielleicht zusammen mit dem Rad

fahren sollen, aber ich denke, das macht sie erst°, _____ ihr Auto total kaputt

not till

ist.

SIEMENS

Wissen Sie eigentlich, was für ein Handy zu Ihnen paßt?

Siemens. Communication unlimited.

WIEDERHOLUNG

experiences

1. Das hat Mark in Deutschland beobachtet.   Erzählen Sie von Marks Erfahrungen° in Deutschland. Benutzen Sie die folgenden Wörter.

1. Mark / fahren / nicht gern / auf / Autobahn
2. Leute / fahren / wie die Wilden

Sesame Street

3. viele Kinder / sehen / im Fernsehen / *Sesamstraße*°
4. die vielen Blumen und Parks / gefallen / er
5. viele Leute / trinken / an / Sonntag / um vier / Kaffee
6. man / benutzen / Messer und Gabel / anders
7. man / sitzen / nach / Essen / lange / an / Tisch

vacation

2. Ferien.   Ergänzen Sie die folgenden Sätze über Urlaub° in Deutschland, Österreich und der Schweiz mit den passenden Präpositionen.

1. Im Sommer kommen viele Ausländer _____ Deutschland. (an, nach, zu)

2. Manche kommen _____ ihre Kinder. (mit, ohne, von)

3. Sie fahren natürlich _____ der Autobahn. (an, über, auf)

4. Junge Leute wandern gern _____ Freunden. (bei, ohne, mit)

some

5. Einige° fahren _____ dem Fahrrad. (bei, an, mit)

6. Viele Kanadier fahren gern _____ Salzburg. (zu, auf, nach)

7. Sie fahren auch gern _____ die Schweiz. (an, in, nach)

8. _____ den Märkten kann man schöne Sachen kaufen. (auf, an, in)

9. Zu Hause erzählen die Kanadier dann _____ ihrer Reise. (über, von, um)

3. Etwas über Musik.   Beantworten Sie die folgenden Fragen. Benutzen Sie entweder ein Pronomen oder ein **da**-Kompositum für Ihre Antwort.

≫ Hast du gestern mit deiner Freundin gegessen? (Ja)
   Ja, ich habe gestern mit ihr gegessen.
≫ Habt ihr viel über Musik geredet? (Ja)
   Ja, wir haben viel darüber geredet.

works

1. Kennst du viele Werke° von Schönberg? (Ja)
2. Hältst du viel von seiner Musik? (Nein)

kennen lernen: meet

3. Möchtest du Frau Professor Koepke kennen lernen°? (Ja)
4. Sie weiß viel über Schönberg, nicht? (Ja)

Liest sie: Is she lecturing

5. Liest° sie dieses Semester über seine Musik? (Ja)
6. Meinst du, ich kann die Vorlesung verstehen? (Nein)

4. Wie sagt man das?   Erik Schulz studiert an der Universität Zürich.
Erzählen Sie auf Deutsch ein bisschen, was er dort macht.

1. Erik Schulz goes to the University of Zürich.
2. In the summer he works for his neighbor.
3. On the weekend he goes with his girlfriend Karin to the mountains.
4. They like to hike.
5. Afterwards they are hungry and thirsty.
6. Then they go to a café, where they have coffee and cake. (Use **trinken** and
   essen.)

5. Wer weiß das?   Stellen Sie den anderen Studentinnen und Studenten
die folgenden Fragen. Schreiben Sie auf,° wer die Antworten weiß und wer sie
nicht weiß.

⟫ *Mark weiß, wie die Hauptstadt der° Schweiz heißt.*
⟫ *Tom weiß nicht, wo Mozart gelebt hat.*

Fragen:

1. Wie heißt die Hauptstadt der Schweiz?
2. Wo hat Mozart gelebt?
3. In welchem Land liegt Konstanz?
4. In welchen Ländern machen die Deutschen gern Ferien?
5. Was trinken die Deutschen gern?
6. Wie viele Sprachen spricht man in der Schweiz?
7. Wie viele Nachbarländer hat Österreich?

6. Zur Diskussion.   Sie sprechen mit einer/einem neuen Bekannten aus
Österreich über Kultur und Sitten° in den USA. Diskutieren Sie über die folgenden Ansichten°. Benutzen Sie dazu die Wörter und Ausdrücke, die hier aufgelistet sind. Vergleichen° Sie Ihre Reaktionen mit den Reaktionen von den anderen
Kursteilnehmern.

Redemittel°

Richtig. □ Genau. □ Natürlich. □ Eben. □ Du hast Recht. □ Wirklich? □ Meinst
du? □ Ja, vielleicht. □ Vielleicht hast du Recht. □ Das finde ich gar nicht. □ Was
hast du gegen [Freundlichkeit]? □ Ich sehe das ganz anders. □ Das siehst du
nicht richtig.

Amerikaner sind zu freundlich. Das kann nicht echt° sein.
Das amerikanische Fernsehen ist toll.
Rock ist besser als klassische Musik.
Die Amerikaner gehen zu wenig zu Fuß.
Die Amerikaner essen zu viele Hamburger und Pommes frites.

7. Zum Schreiben

1. Wählen Sie eines der folgenden Themen und schreiben Sie dazu auf Deutsch
   mehrere Sätze über Deutschland und Ihr Land.

   Blumen □ Wetter □ Autofahren □ Fernsehen □ Essen □ Universität □
   Einkaufen

Discussing cultural
differences

schreiben auf: write down

of the

customs

views

compare

speech acts

genuine

Stellen ... vor: imagine

2. Stellen Sie sich vor°, Sie sind Monika Berger. Schreiben Sie Ihrer Freundin Kerstin einen Brief über den amerikanischen Austauschstudenten Peter Clason. Schreiben Sie darüber:

a. wo Sie Peter getroffen haben
b. wie Peter aussieht
c. woher er kommt
d. worüber Sie und Peter geredet haben
e. was Sie und Peter am Wochenende machen

Hinweise: Before beginning the writing assignments, make notes of the points you want to mention. Try to use two-way prepositions and some of the verbs that require special prepositions. Pay close attention to the case used with two-way prepositions.

For a list of other things to pay attention to when writing or reviewing your writing, see *Hinweise,* p. 233.

GRAMMATIK: ZUSAMMENFASSUNG

Hin and *her*

Komm bitte **her.**	Please come here.
Fall nicht **hin!**	Don't fall down.

Hin and **her** are used to show direction. **Hin** indicates motion in a direction away from the speaker, and **her** shows motion toward the speaker. **Hin** and **her** function as separable prefixes and therefore occupy final position in a sentence.

Komm mal **herunter!**	Come on down here.
Wann gehen wir wieder **dorthin?**	When are we going there again?

In addition to verbs, **hin** and **her** may be combined with other parts of speech such as adverbs (e.g., **dorthin**) and prepositions (e.g., **herunter**).

Two-way prepositions and their English equivalents

an	at; on; to
auf	on, on top of; to
hinter	behind, in back of
in	in, inside (of); into; to
neben	beside, next to
über	over, above; across; about
unter	under; among
vor	in front of; before; ago
zwischen	between

Nine prepositions take either the dative or the accusative. The dative is used for the meaning *place where,* in answer to the question **wo?** The accusative is used for the meaning *place to which,* in answer to the question **wohin?** The English equivalents of these prepositions may vary, depending on the object with which they are used. For example, English equivalents of **an der Ecke** and **an der Wand** are *at the corner* and *on the wall.*

Prepositional contractions

am	= an dem	**im**	= in dem
ans	= an das	**ins**	= in das

The prepositions **an** and **in** may contract with **das** and **dem.** Other possible contractions are **aufs, hinters, hinterm, übers, überm, unters, unterm, vors,** and **vorm.**

Special meanings of prepositions

Prepositions have special meanings when combined with specific verbs (e.g., **denken an**) or with certain nouns (e.g., **Angst vor**).

denken an (+ *acc.*)	to think of/about
schreiben an (+ *acc.*)	to write to
studieren an/auf (+ *dat.*)	to study at
warten auf (+ *acc.*)	to wait for
helfen bei	to help with
fahren mit	to go by (means of)
reden/sprechen über (+ *acc.*)	to talk/speak about
reden/sprechen von	to talk/speak about/of
schreiben über (+ *acc.*)	to write about
halten von	to think of, have an opinion of
Angst haben vor (+ *dat.*)	to be afraid of

Time expressions in the dative

am Montag	on Monday, Mondays
am Abend	in the evening, evenings
in der Woche	during the week
in einem Jahr	in a year
vor dem Essen	before the meal
vor einem Jahr	a year ago

In expressions of time, the prepositions **an, in,** and **vor** are followed by the dative case.

Time expressions in the accusative

Definite point	Katrin kommt **nächsten Freitag.**	Katrin is coming *next Friday.*
Duration	Sie bleibt **einen Tag.**	She's staying *(for) one day.*

Nouns expressing a definite point in time or a duration of time are in the accusative. No preposition is used in these expressions. Note that words such as **nächst** and **letzt** have endings like the endings for **dies: diesen / nächsten / letzten Monat; dieses / nächstes / letztes Jahr.**

*Da-*compounds

Spricht Sabrina gern **von ihrem Freund?**   Ja, sie spricht gern **von ihm.**
Spricht Sabrina oft **von der Arbeit?**   Ja, sie spricht oft **davon.**

In German, pronouns after prepositions normally refer only to persons. German uses a **da-**compound, consisting of **da** + preposition, to refer to things or ideas.

*Wo-*compounds

Von wem spricht Sabrina?   Sie spricht **von ihrem Freund.**
Wovon (Von was) spricht Sabrina?   Sie spricht **von der Arbeit.**

The interrogative pronoun **wen** or **wem** is used with a preposition to refer to persons. The interrogative pronoun **was** refers to things and ideas. As an object of a preposition, **was** may be replaced by a **wo-**compound consisting of **wo** + a preposition. A preposition + **was** is colloquial: **von was.**

Patrick wohnt seit September in   **Seit wann** wohnt er in München?
  München.

Wo-compounds are not used to inquire about time. To inquire about time, **wann, seit wann,** or **wie lange** is used.

Indirect questions

Weißt du, **warum** Petra heute nicht kommt?   Do you know *why* Petra
                                                   isn't coming today?

Ich weiß auch nicht, **ob** sie morgen kommt.   I also don't know *if/whether*
                                                   she's coming tomorrow.

An indirect question is a dependent clause. The finite verb is therefore in last position. An indirect question is introduced by an introductory clause such as: **Weißt du, ... ?; Ich möchte wissen, ... ; Kannst du mir sagen, ... ?; Ich weiß nicht, ...**

  An indirect informational question begins with the same question words that are used in direct informational questions (**warum, wann, wer, was, wie lange,** etc.).

  An indirect yes/no question begins with **ob. Ob** can always be translated as *whether.*

Produzentin bei einem
Berliner Jazz-Sender.

Berufstätige Frauen

BAUSTEINE FÜR GESPRÄCHE

Ein Ferienjob

PERSONALCHEFIN: Herr Ohrdorf, Sie studieren jetzt im achten Semester Informatik und wollen zwei Monate bei uns arbeiten.

UWE: Ja, richtig.

PERSONALCHEFIN: Wie ich sehe, haben Sie schon als Informatiker gearbeitet.

UWE: Ja, ich habe letztes Jahr auch einen Ferienjob gehabt und da habe ich ganz gute praktische Erfahrungen gesammelt.

PERSONALCHEFIN: Und was wollen Sie später damit machen?

UWE: Ich möchte eine Stelle bei einer Bank, eine Aufgabe mit viel Verantwortung, hoffe ich.

Fragen*

1. Was studiert Uwe? Warum?
2. Was für einen Ferienjob hat er schon einmal gehabt?
3. Wie hat der Job ihn auf die neue Stelle vorbereitet?
4. Wo möchte er später eine Stelle finden?
5. Was erwartet° er von dieser Stelle?

Der Computer ist nur die Maschine. Erst die Software ist das Werkzeug, das den Computer zum Arbeitsgerät macht.

Wir führen Programme für die meisten Einsatzgebiete eines Personalcomputers.

HANNES KELLER COMPUTERZENTRUM **AG**
EIDMATTSTRASSE 36
8032 ZURICH
TELEFON 01 69 36 33

---

* Reminder: Words appearing with a raised degree mark but no definition in the margin are new "active" words that you should learn and be able to use. These words and their definitions appear in the **Vokabeln** section that most closely follows the exercise.

1. Eine neue Stelle. Sie und Ihre Partnerin/Ihr Partner führen° ein Vorstellungsgespräch°. Die Bewerberin/der Bewerber° sollte vor dem Interview überlegen°, was sie/er weiß.

conduct
job interview / applicant
think about

S1 (Personalchefin/Personalchef):
Können Sie   mit **dem Computer** arbeiten?
               Textverarbeitungsprogramme

S2 (Bewerberin/Bewerber):
Ja. Sehr gut.
Nein, tut mir Leid.

Talking about one's
qualifications for a job

Haben Sie schon praktische Erfahrung
als Informatikerin/Informatiker?

Ja, │ **ich habe bei einer**
    │ **kleinen Firma**
    │ **gearbeitet.**
    │ ich habe letztes Jahr
    │ einen Ferienjob
    │ gehabt.

Warum wollen Sie die Stelle
wechseln°?

Ich möchte │ **neue Erfah-**
           │ **rungen**
           │ **sammeln.**
           │ mehr Verant-
           │ wortung
           │ bekommen.
           │ mehr ver-
           │ dienen.

2. Wo möchten Sie lieber arbeiten – in einem Büro oder im Freien°?
Beantworten Sie die folgenden Fragen erst selbst und vergleichen° Sie dann Ihre Antworten mit denen der anderen Kursteilnehmer.

outdoors
compare

1. Was studierst du?
2. Arbeitest du lieber allein oder mit anderen zusammen?
3. Wo möchtest du lieber arbeiten? In einem Büro oder im Freien?
4. Wie soll die Arbeit sein? Interessant? Leicht°? Schwer?

Ärztin in ihrer Praxis in Hannover.

additional

Talking about future goals

3. Berufe°.   Fragen Sie vier andere Kursteilnehmerinnen/Kursteilnehmer, was sie werden möchten und warum. Zusätzliche° Vokabeln zum Thema Berufe finden Sie im Anhang (Supplementary Word Sets).

S1: Was möchtest du werden?
S2: Ich möchte [Ingenieurin/Ingenieur] werden.
S1: Ich [arbeite gern mit Maschinen°].

1. Wie wichtig ist dir das Geld? Ein sicherer° Arbeitsplatz?
2. Kannst du mit dem Computer arbeiten?
3. Kannst du mit Textverarbeitungsprogrammen arbeiten?
4. Tippst° du deine Arbeiten selbst?

der **Lehrer**/die **Lehrerin**

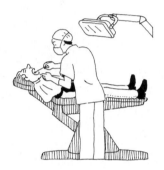

der **Zahnarzt**/die **Zahnärztin**

die **Architektin**/der **Architekt**

der **Rechtsanwalt**/
die **Rechtsanwältin**

der **Musiker**/die **Musikerin**

die **Politikerin**/der **Politiker**

der **Informatiker**/
die **Informatikerin**

die **Journalistin**/
der **Journalist**

die **Ärztin**/der **Arzt**

die **Geschäftsfrau**/
der **Geschäftsmann**

ОК

Zwei Filmregisseurinnen

Two of Germany's leading film directors are women—Margarethe von Trotta (b. 1942) and Doris Dörrie (b. 1955). Von Trotta's stature as a director was given additional recognition during the 45th **Internationale Filmfestspiele** in Berlin **(die Berlinale)** in 1995, which celebrated the 100th anniversary of the movies. Her movie, *Das Versprechen* (The Promise), opened the festival. Although von Trotta now resides in Italy, her films are "German" with German themes. The plot of *Das Versprechen* is an East German–West German love story that culminates in the night of the fall of the Berlin Wall on November 9, 1989. Many of her movies make political statements.

Dörrie's *Keiner liebt mich* was also a box office hit in 1995. Dörrie had made a name for herself with her early movie *Männer,* a clever and amusing story that nevertheless is critical of traditional gender roles. She has continued to fulfill the promise of *Männer* with many well-received movies since, especially with her hit movie from 1998, *Bin ich schön?*

Doris Dörrie, Filmregisseurin.

Margarethe von Trotta, Filmregisseurin.

Diskussion

Have a film evening. Check at a local video store, library, or school resource, and borrow a German film to view with some friends.

job opportunities

4. Stellenangebote°.   Sehen Sie die Stellenangebote an und beantworten Sie die Fragen. Wenn Sie Hilfe brauchen, sehen Sie im Anhang nach (Vocabulary for Authentic Text Activities).

1. Welche Stellen sind für eine Studentin/einen Studenten praktisch?
2. Welche Stelle ist nicht in Deutschland?
3. Welche Stellen sind nur für eine Frau? Für eine Frau oder einen Mann? Woher wissen Sie das? Was halten Sie davon?

Kindermädchen
f. 3jhr. Zwillingsmädchen von italienischer Familie auf dem Lande gesucht. Separates Zimmer mit Bad. Bewerbung mit Lebenslauf, Foto und Zeugnissen an **G. Vrafino, 10034 Boschetto-Chivasso (Turin)**

Studentenjob
Taxifahrer/in auch als Festfahrer/Aushilfen. Gute Konditionen, Ausbildung im Schnellkurs.

☎ **4484770, 17-19 U.**

Wir suchen im Raum Südosten eine/n
tüchtige/n u. aufgeschlossene/n
Elektroinstallateur/in
Muß selbständig arbeiten können.
Elektro Hiering, ☎ 6116659

Wir suchen für unser Fotofachlabor eine/n
Fotolaborant/in
ganz- od. halbtags, auf Wunsch
Schichtdienst. ☎ **47 20 91**

Exportfirma sucht ab sofort eine/n
Sekretär/in
mit Sprachkenntnissen in Italienisch u.
Englisch. Zuschr. u. ✉ ZS9800194

Vokabeln

Substantive

der **Arbeitsplatz, ⸚e**   job, position; workplace

der **Architekt, -en, -en**/die **Architektin, -nen**   architect

die **Aufgabe, -n**   assignment; task, set of duties; die **Hausaufgaben** homework

die **Bank, -en**   bank

der **Beruf, -e**   profession, occupation

der **Chef, -s**/die **Chefin, -nen**   boss

die **Erfahrung, -en**   experience

das **Geschäft, -e**   store; business

die **Geschäftsfrau, -en** businesswoman/der **Geschäftsmann, leute** businessman, businesspeople

der **Informatiker, -**/die **Informatikerin, -nen** computer specialist

der **Journalist, -en, -en**/die **Journalistin, -nen**   journalist

der **Lehrer, -**/die **Lehrerin, -nen** teacher

die **Maschine, -n**   machine

der **Musiker, -**/die **Musikerin, -nen**   musician

der **Personalchef, -s**/die **Personalchefin, -nen**   head of the human resources (personnel) department

der **Politiker, -**/die **Politikerin, -nen**   politician

der **Rechtsanwalt, -anwälte**/die **Rechtsanwältin, -nen**   lawyer, attorney

die **Stelle, -n**   position, job; place

die **Verantwortung**   responsibility

das **Textverarbeitungsprogramm,
-e** word processing program; **mit
Textverarbeitungsprogrammen
arbeiten** to do word processing

der **Zahnarzt, ⁻e**/die **Zahnärztin,
-nen** dentist

Verben

erwarten to expect
sammeln to collect
tippen to type; **er tippt seine
Arbeiten** he types his papers

verdienen to earn
wechseln to change

Andere Wörter

best- (-er, -es, -e) best
leicht light; easy

sicher safe; secure; certain(ly)

Besondere Ausdrücke

bei einer Firma arbeiten to work
for a company; **bei [Siemens]
arbeiten** to work for [Siemens]

mit dem Computer arbeiten to do
work (on) a computer

ZWEI FRAUENPORTRÄTS

Vorbereitung auf das Lesen

■ *Vor dem Lesen*

1. Machen Sie eine Liste von berühmten Frauen. Nennen Sie mindestens° eine   at least
   Naturwissenschaftlerin und eine Dichterin°. Welche berühmten deutschen   poet
   Frauen kennen Sie?
2. In der deutschen Verfassung° steht: „Männer und Frauen sind gleich-
   berechtigt°." Was verstehen° Sie persönlich unter „gleichberechtigt"?
      Welche der folgenden Ideen sind wichtig für die Gleichberechtigung°?
   Welche nicht?
   a. Männer und Frauen sind gleich.
   b. Männer und Frauen sollen das gleiche Gehalt° für die gleiche Arbeit   salary
      bekommen.
   c. Männer sollen bei der Hausarbeit helfen.
   d. Frauen müssen berufstätig° sein.
   e. Gleichberechtigung ist nur für Frauen.

■ *Beim Lesen*

Dieser Text beschreibt zwei deutsche Frauen. Eine ist berufstätig, die andere ist
Hausfrau°. Machen Sie Notizen zu diesen Fragen:

1. In welchen Punkten° sind die Frauen gleich?
2. In welchen Punkten sind sie ungleich? Denken Sie dabei an ihr Alter°, ihre   age
   Arbeit, ihre Familie.

I n der deutschen Verfassung heißt es: „Männer und Frauen sind gleichberechtigt." (ARTIKEL 3,2) Die Verfassung ist also klar und eindeutig°. Da
gibt es kein Wenn und Aber. Aber die Wirklichkeit ist etwas kompli-
zierter. Hier sind zwei Beispiele von zeitgenössischen° Frauen in Deutsch-
5 land.

GISELA ANTON – **Ehefrau°, Mutter, Physikerin, Privatdozentin°**

Dr. Gisela Anton ist Privatdozentin für Physik an der Universität Bonn und
hat 1994 für ihre Forschung° den Leibniz-Preis° gewonnen. Dr. Antons Stelle
besteht allerdings nicht nur aus° Schreibtischarbeit. Das Erfolgsrezept° der
Wissenschaftlerin ist Spaß an der Arbeit. „Das ist ganz wichtig. Die Motiva-
10 tion gehört dazu. Die Physik ist schon ein hartes Studium. Aber wenn man
Motivation hat, und es macht Freude, das wird schon laufen°."

Die 40-jährige° Physikerin hat drei Kinder. Ihr Mann ist auch Physiker,
aber nicht an der Universität. Er arbeitet in der Industrie. Zum Glück
wohnen Frau Antons Eltern im gleichen Haus. Tagsüber° passen sie auf die
15 Kinder auf. Trotzdem ist ihre Doppelrolle als Wissenschaftlerin und Mutter
für Gisela Anton nicht einfach. „Ich arbeite ca.° 45 Stunden in der Woche im
Institut und abends und am Wochenende zu Hause. Auch wenn ich am
Kochtopf° stehe, geht mir die Physik durch den Kopf°."

Oft aber geben Frauen ihren Beruf für ihre Familie auf, um Hausfrau und
20 Mutter zu° sein. Unser nächstes Beispiel illustriert so einen Fall°.

HELGA KRAUSS – **Ehefrau, Hausfrau, Krankenschwester, Mutter**

„In der Zeitung habe ich gelesen: Eine Hausfrau arbeitet 75 Stunden in der
Woche", sagt die 58-jährige Hausfrau Helga Krauß. „Das ist sicher richtig,
denn man hat ja nicht nur den Haushalt – die Kinder, das Kochen, das
Putzen, das Waschen, den Mann, den Garten – die meisten Frauen meiner
25 Generation helfen ihren Männern auch oft im Geschäft." Helga Krauß ist
gelernte° Krankenschwester. Ihr Mann ist Arzt. Sie haben vier Kinder. Wegen
der Kinder ist sie zu Hause geblieben und hat ihren Beruf als Krankenschwester aufgegeben. „Heute mache ich zum Beispiel die Buchhaltung° für
die Praxis° meines Mannes. Außerdem bin ich nicht nur Hausfrau und Mut-
30 ter, sondern auch Großmutter. Meine Tochter und auch meine Schwie-
gertochter° sind beide berufstätig. Und tagsüber passe ich auf die Kinder auf.
Die beiden jungen Frauen haben lange nach einem Kindergartenplatz für
ihre Kinder gesucht. Sie haben jedoch keinen gefunden, denn sie sind verheiratet. Kindergartenplätze gibt es fast nur für alleinstehende° Mütter und
35 sehr wenige für verheiratete Mütter mit berufstätigen Männern."

Im Beruf gibt es also eine Entwicklung° zu mehr Gleichberechtigung. Das ist
gar keine Frage. Vor der Frauenbewegung° der 70er-Jahre waren weniger
Frauen in akademischen° Berufen. Und sobald sie Kinder bekamen°, haben

---

Margin glossary:

unambiguous

contemporary

wife / lecturer (not on tenure track)

research / prize
besteht aus: consists of / recipe for success

das ... laufen: it'll work
40-year-old

during the day

ca. = circa: approximately

am Kochtopf: at the stove / head

um ... zu: in order to / case

trained

bookkeeping
practice

daughter-in-law

single

development
women's movement
professional / **Kinder bekamen:** had children

die Frauen oft ihren Beruf aufgegeben. Ein Beispiel dafür ist Helga Krauß.
40 Heute aber wollen immer mehr Frauen im Beruf bleiben oder wieder in den Beruf zurückgehen, wenn die Kinder ein bisschen älter° sind. Für Gisela Anton ist es immer klar gewesen, dass sie auch als Mutter weiter an der Universität arbeitet. Sie ist jedoch trotz ihres Erfolges keine Professorin, sondern Privatdozentin. An den deutschen Universitäten gibt es noch sehr wenig
45 wirkliche Gleichberechtigung. Zwar sind über 43% aller Studierenden° Frauen, aber nur 5,5% sind Professorinnen. Frauen werden nicht so schnell zu Professorinnen wie ihre männlichen° Kollegen.

Konkret heißt das: Frauen sind heute zwar in der Wahl° eines Berufes frei und gleichberechtigt, doch wenn sie Familie haben, ist ihre Freiheit oft illu-
50 sorisch°. Sie haben fast immer mehr Arbeit als ihre Kollegen und Ehemänner°. Denn die Statistik zeigt, dass nur jeder dritte Mann seiner Frau regelmäßig° im Haushalt und mit den Kindern hilft.

older / students / male / choice / illusory / husbands / regularly

Brauchbares

1. l. 1, **Verfassung:** The general word for *constitution* is **Verfassung.** Germany's constitution is called **"Das Grundgesetz."**
2. l. 7, **Leibniz-Preis:** The prize is named in honor of Gottfried Wilhelm Leibniz or Leibnitz (1646–1716), a German philosopher and mathematician. He developed the infinitesimal calculus (1675–76) independently of Newton, and published his work three years before Newton.
3. l. 34, **Kindergartenplätze:** In Germany only 79% of children over the age of 3 are in publicly financed daycare facilities, compared to 100% in France, 95% in Belgium, and 92% in Italy. In Germany only 3% of children under the age of 3 are in daycare facilities. In Denmark it is 48% and in France 20%.

Nach dem Lesen

1. Fragen zum Lesestück

1. Beschreiben Sie Gisela Anton: ihren Beruf, ihre Familie, ihre Arbeit zu Hause.
2. Welche Bedeutung° hat der Leibniz-Preis für Gisela Anton? — *significance*
3. Warum ist es ein Glück, dass Giselas Eltern im gleichen Haus wohnen?
4. Woran denkt Gisela beim Kochen?
5. Warum geben manche Frauen ihren Beruf auf?
6. Beschreiben Sie Helga Krauß: ihren Beruf, ihre Familie, ihre Arbeit zu Hause.
7. Wie steht es mit der Gleichberechtigung an vielen deutschen Universitäten?
8. Warum ist die Freiheit der Berufswahl° für Frauen oft illusorisch? — *choice of occupation*
9. Wie hat die Frauenbewegung das Leben der Frauen in Deutschland verändert°? — *changed*

2. Was machen Gisela Anton und Helga Krauß?
Suchen Sie die Stellen im Text, die° die Arbeit der beiden Frauen beschreiben. Dann beschreiben Sie ihre Arbeit: — *which*

1. Was machen die zwei Frauen tagsüber?
2. Welche Arbeit finden Sie interessanter°? Warum? — *more interesting*
3. Welche Arbeit finden Sie schwerer°? Warum? — *more difficult*
4. Hat die eine Frau mehr Arbeit als die andere?

3. Probleme der Frauen. Suchen Sie Informationen im Text zum Thema Kinder und der Doppelrolle der Frau. Beantworten Sie dann die Fragen:

1. Was bedeutet im Text Doppelrolle?
2. Welche Probleme haben berufstätige Frauen in Deutschland?

4. Erzählen wir. Sprechen Sie etwa eine Minute über eines der folgenden Themen:

Die Doppelrolle der Frau
Die Arbeit von Frauen heute
Eine Frau, die° ich kenne

whom

Erweiterung des Wortschatzes

1. Word families

arbeiten	*to work*
die **Arbeit**	*the work*
der **Arbeiter**/die **Arbeiterin**	*the worker*

Like English, German has many words that belong to families and are derived from a common root.

related

meaning / **fett gedruckt:** boldfaced

1. Noch ein Wort. Ergänzen Sie die Sätze mit einem sinnverwandten° Wort und geben Sie dann die Bedeutung° aller fett gedruckten° Wörter wieder.

1. München hat 1,3 Millionen **Einwohner.** Viele Münchner _____ in kleinen

   Wohnungen.

2. Der **Koch** und die **Köchin** in diesem Restaurant benutzen nie ein

   Kochbuch, aber sie _____ sehr gut.

3. Auf unserer **Wanderung** haben wir viele **Wanderer** getroffen. Der **Wander-**

   weg war schön. Wir _____ wirklich gern.

4. —Ich muss jetzt zum **Flughafen.**

   —Wann geht dein **Flugzeug?**

   —Ich _____ um 10 Uhr 30.

5. In dieser **Bäckerei backen** sie gutes Brot. Ich finde, der _____ macht auch

   guten Kuchen.

2. Noun suffixes *-heit* and *-keit*

die **Freiheit**	*freedom*	die **Wirklichkeit**	*reality*
frei	*free*	**wirklich**	*really*

Nouns ending in **-heit** and **-keit** are feminine nouns. Many nouns of this type are related to adjectives. The suffix **-keit** is used with adjectives ending in **-ig** or **-lich.**

2. Dieses Wetter! Erganzen Sie Sandras Aussagen° über das Wetter. Benutzen Sie ein Substantiv, das auf **-heit** endet und das mit dem fett gedruckten Adjektiv verwandt ist.

comments

1. Der Garten ist sehr **trocken.** Wie lange dauert° diese _____ noch?

lasts

2. Dieses Wetter ist nicht **gesund.** Es ist nicht gut für die _____ .

3. Ich werde ganz **krank.** Hoffentlich ist es keine ernste _____ .

4. Aber die Natur ist immer **schön.** Mir gefällt ihre _____ .

5. In der Natur lebt man **frei.** Da ist die _____ groß.

3. Was für ein Mensch ist Dirk? Erzählen Sie, was für ein Mensch Dirk ist. Benutzen Sie ein Substantiv, das auf **-keit** endet und das mit dem fett gedruckten Adjektiv verwandt ist.

1. Für Dirk muss alles **natürlich** sein. Auch bei Mädchen findet er _____ besonders schön.

2. Dirk ist besonders **freundlich.** Die Mädchen mögen seine _____ .

3. Er findet es **wichtig,** dass man sehr nett ist. Es ist für ihn von großer _____ .

Vokabeln

Substantive

der **Erfolg, -e** success
die **Freiheit** freedom
die **Freude, -n** pleasure; **Freude machen** to give pleasure
die **Gleichberechtigung** equal rights
das **Glück** luck; **zum Glück** fortunately
die **Hausfrau, -en** housewife
der **Haushalt** household; **den Haushalt machen** to take care of the house
die **Industrie, -n** industry
der **Kindergarten, ⁚** nursery school; kindergarten

der **Kollege, -n, -n**/die **Kollegin, -nen** colleague
der **Physiker, -**/die **Physikerin, -nen** physicist
der **Punkt, -e** point
der **Spaß, ⁚e** enjoyment; fun; joke; **an der Arbeit Spaß haben** to enjoy one's work; **das macht Spaß** that is fun; **viel Spaß** have fun; **er hat nur Spaß gemacht** he was only joking
die **Verfassung, -en** constitution
die **Wirklichkeit** reality
die **Wissenschaft, -en** science

Verben

auf·geben (gibt auf), aufgegeben to give up
auf·passen to watch out; **aufpassen auf** + _acc._ to take care of

lehren to teach
nennen, genannt to name
verstehen, verstanden to understand
zeigen to show

Andere Wörter

allerdings   to be sure; it is true
berufstätig   employed
dritt- (-er, -es, -e)   third
gleichberechtigt   having equal
  rights
hart   hard; difficult
jedoch *(coord. conj. or adv.)*   however
kompliziert   complicated

schlank   slender
sobald *(subord. conj.)*   as soon as
trotz *(+ gen.)*   in spite of
trotzdem   nevertheless
verheiratet   married
wegen *(+ gen.)*   on account of,
  because of

Besondere Ausdrücke

das heißt   that means
es heißt   it says

immer mehr   more and more

GRAMMATIK UND ÜBUNGEN

der Genitiv

1. Genitive case°

■ *Showing possession and close relationships*

Ich habe mit dem Sohn **des
  Bäckers** gesprochen.
Das ist die Frage **eines Kindes.**
Die Farbe **der Wände** gefällt mir.

I talked to *the baker's* son.

That is *a child's* question.
I like the color *of the walls.*

English shows possession or other close relationships by adding 's to a noun or
by using a phrase with *of.* English generally uses the 's form only for persons.
For things and ideas, English uses the *of*-construction.

German uses the genitive case to show possession or other close relationships. The genitive is used for things and ideas as well as for persons. The genitive generally follows the noun it modifies **(die Frage eines Kindes).**

die Freundin **von meinem Bruder** (meines Bruders)
zwei **von ihren Freunden** (ihrer Freunde)
ein Freund **von Thomas** (Thomas' Freund)

In spoken German the genitive of possession is frequently replaced by **von** +
dative.

ein Freund **von mir**
ein Freund **von Nicole**

Von + *dative* is also used in phrases similar to the English *of mine, of Nicole,* etc.

■ *Masculine and neuter nouns*

Hast du den Namen **des Kindes**
  verstanden?
Das ist die Meinung **meines
  Professors.**

Did you understand *the child's*
  name?
That is *my professor's* opinion.

Masculine and neuter nouns of one syllable generally add **-es** in the genitive;
nouns of two or more syllables add **-s.** The corresponding articles, **der-** words,
and **ein-**words end in **-es** in the genitive.

Gleichberechtigung: Wichtige Daten

LAND UND LEUTE

A few milestones in the progress of women toward equality:

1901   German universities begin to admit women.

1918   German women receive the right to vote and to be elected to parliament.

1949   The Basic Law of the Federal Republic **(Grundgesetz)** guarantees the right of a person to decide on her or his role in society.

1955   The Federal Labor Court **(Bundesarbeitsgericht)** states that there should be no discrimination on the basis of gender in compensation for work performed.

Go to the
Deutsch heute Web Site at
www.hmco.com/college

1977   Women and men are judged by law to be equal in a marriage. Either can take the surname of the other, or a combination of both names. A divorce may now be granted on the principle of irreconcilability rather than guilt, and all pension rights that the spouses accrued during marriage are equally divided.

1979   Women are entitled to a six-month leave to care for a newborn child. By 1990 the leave-time had increased to 12 months and was available to women or men.

1980   The law prohibits gender discrimination in hiring practices, wages, working conditions, opportunities for advancement, and termination policies.

1986   Years spent raising children are included in the calculation of retirement pensions.

1991   Women have the option of keeping their maiden names. Children may have the name of either parent.

1993   Either parent may stay home to care for a child until the child turns three years old.

Vielleicht haben diese Frauen Erziehungsurlaub genommen.

Diskussion

Historical research. Compare the milestones in the progress of German women with important milestones in your country's policies concerning women.

◼ Masculine **N**-nouns

Die Frau **des Herrn** da kommt aus Österreich.	The wife *of the man* there is from Austria.
Haben Sie die Frage **des Jungen** verstanden?	Did you understand *the boy's* question?

Masculine nouns that add **-n** or **-en** in the accusative and dative singular also add **-n** or **-en** in the genitive. A few masculine nouns add **-ns: des Namens.**

For a list of masculine **N**-nouns, see Reference Section, Grammatical Tables, #9.

1. Wie sagt man das?   Geben Sie die Wortverbindungen auf Deutsch wieder. Benutzen Sie den Genitiv.

1. the man's plan
2. the color of the house
3. the car of the year
4. the child's bicycle
5. the boy's story
6. Mr. Schmidt's car
7. the name of the country
8. the color of the shirt

◼ Feminine and plural nouns

Die Farbe **der Bluse** gefällt mir.	I like the color *of the blouse.*
Schmidts sind Freunde **meiner Eltern.**	Schmidts are friends *of my parents.*

Feminine and plural nouns do not add a genitive ending. The corresponding articles, **der**-words, and **ein-**words end in **-er** in the genitive.

is moving / **Ihre Nähe:** near where you live

2. Hast du die Adresse?   Ihre Freundin/Ihr Freund zieht° in Ihre Nähe° und braucht einige Adressen. Helfen Sie ihr/ihm.

➤➤   Kennst du eine Apotheke?   *Hier ist die Adresse einer Apotheke.*

1. Kennst du eine Bäckerei?	4. Gibt es hier eine Buchhandlung?
2. Und eine Metzgerei?	5. Wo ist die Bibliothek?
3. Wo ist eine Drogerie?	

◼ The interrogative pronoun wessen?

Wessen CD-Spieler ist das?	*Whose* CD player is that?
Wessen CDs sind das?	*Whose* CD's are those?

The question word to ask for nouns or pronouns in the genitive is **wessen.** It is the genitive form of **wer** and is equivalent to English *whose.*

◼ Possessive adjectives

Theresa ist die Freundin **meines Bruders.**	Theresa is *my brother's* girlfriend.
Hast du die Telefonnummer **seiner Freundin?**	Do you have *his girlfriend's* telephone number?

Possessive adjectives take the case of the noun they modify. Even though a possessive adjective already shows possession (**mein** = my, **sein** = his), it must itself be in the genitive case when the noun it goes with is in the genitive (**meines Bruders** = of my brother); **die Freundin meines Bruders** shows *two* possessive relationships.

3. Wessen Telefonnummer ist das? Beantworten Sie die folgenden Fragen und benutzen Sie den Genitiv. Lesen Sie das Beispiel.

>> meine Eltern *Wessen Telefonnummer ist das?*
>>   *Das ist die Telefonnummer meiner Eltern.*

1. meine Tante   4. seine Schwester
2. sein Bruder   5. ihre Großeltern
3. ihr Freund Mark   6. unser Nachbar

4. Eine Fußballmannschaft° plant ihr Jahresfest. Alle sprechen gleichzeitig°. Wiederholen Sie die Sätze mit der Genitivform der Wörter in Klammern.

soccer team
at the same time

>> KEVIN: Der Termin° des Festes ist   *Der Termin der Party ist*
>>   nächsten Samstag. (die Party) *nächsten Samstag.*

date

1. MARTIN: Wie ist die Adresse des Biergartens? (das Café)
2. DOMINIK: Kennst du die Ideen seiner Freundin? (unser Nachbar)
3. STEFAN: Wie heißt die Freundin deines Bruders? (deine Schwester)
4. ALEX: Kennst du den Namen dieser Firma? (dieses Geschäft)
5. MARIO: Das ist die Telefonnummer meines Vetters. (meine Kusine)
6. PATRICK: Ich hole dich mit dem Auto meines Vaters ab. (meine Mutter)

5. Wer ist das? Wählen Sie eine Partnerin/einen Partner und stellen Sie sich gegenseitig Fragen° über Ihre Familien. Lesen Sie das Beispiel.

stellen ... Fragen: ask each other questions

1. Wo wohnt der Freund deiner Schwester?
2. Wo wohnt die Freundin deines Bruders?
3. Wie ist die Telefonnummer deines Freundes? deiner Freundin?
4. Hast du die Adresse deiner Tante? deines Onkels? deiner Großeltern?
5. Was für ein Auto hat der Freund deiner Schwester? die Freundin deines Bruders?
6. Wie heißen die Bekannten° deiner Eltern?

| Discussing friends and family |

aquaintances

2. Genitive of time

| Indefinite past | **Eines Tages** hat mir Melanie alles erklärt. | *One day* Melanie explained everything to me. |
| Indefinite future | **Eines Tages** mache ich das vielleicht. | *Someday* maybe I'll do that. |

Nouns expressing an indefinite point in time are in the genitive.

Go to the
Deutsch heute Web Site at
www.hmco.com/college

Diese Frau hat Recht auf sechs Wochen Schwangerschaftsurlaub.

Familienpolitik

In Germany federal policy concerning women **(Frauenpolitik)** and families **(Familienpolitik)** covers a number of areas in the lives of women, men, and children. One aim is to help both women and men reconcile their professional and personal lives. In recent years opportunities for flexible work hours, **(Gleitzeit)** part-time work **(Teilzeitbeschäftigung)** with full benefits, or sharing jobs have improved. Many single mothers receive financial aid, and every woman has the right to a maternity leave of six weeks preceding and eight weeks after the birth of the child while receiving her full salary **(Mutterschutz),** the cost of which is shared by the government and her employer. Another benefit is the child-rearing leave **(Erziehungsurlaub),** which allows either parent to stay home until the child turns three. During that time the parent on leave receives DM 600 monthly **(Erziehungsgeld)** for the first six months. After that the amount depends on the parents' income and is paid for up to two years. Up to three years of time spent rearing a child or caring for a sick member of the family can be applied towards the person's pension claim. Mothers-to-be receive a "family benefit" **(Familiengeld)** of DM 1,000, of which the mother receives DM 500 six weeks before the birth of the child and an additional DM 500 after the birth.

Diskussion

Many of the benefits that are available to mothers and families in Germany are expensive for both the government and businesses. To what extent do you think that the benefits for families are worth the high cost?

3. Prepositions with the genitive

(an)statt	*instead of*	Kommt Anna **(an)statt** ihrer Schwester?
trotz	*in spite of*	**Trotz** des Wetters fahren wir in die Berge.
während	*during*	**Während** des Sommers bleiben wir nicht in Hamburg.
wegen	*on account of*	**Wegen** des Wetters gehen wir nicht schwimmen.

The prepositions **anstatt** or **statt, trotz, während,** and **wegen** require the genitive case.

wegen **dem Wetter** (des Wetters)
trotz **dem Regen** (des Regens)

In colloquial usage many people use the prepositions **statt, trotz, wegen,** and sometimes **während** with the dative.

trotz **ihm**
wegen **dir**

In colloquial usage dative pronouns are frequently used with the prepositions: **statt ihr, trotz ihm, wegen mir.**

6. Eine Wanderung.   Die Firma, bei der° Ihr Vater arbeitet, macht manchmal eine Wanderung. Ihre Freundin/Ihr Freund fragt Sie, wie die letzte Wanderung war. Beantworten Sie die Fragen mit den Wörtern in Klammern.   **which**

⟫ Bist du auch mitgegangen?   *Ja, trotz des Wetters.*
   (ja, trotz / das Wetter)

1. Warum ist dein Bruder zu Hause geblieben? (wegen / seine Arbeit)
2. Ist deine Schwester mitgegangen? (ja, statt / mein Bruder)
3. Sind viele Leute gekommen? (nein, wegen / das Wetter)
4. Wann macht ihr Pläne für die nächste Wanderung? (während / diese Woche)
5. Warum gehen die Leute eigentlich wandern? (wegen / das Café)

4. Adjectives°

das Adjektiv

◼ *Predicate adjectives*

Die CD ist **toll.**
Der Wein wird sicher **gut.**
Das Wetter bleibt jetzt **schön.**

Predicate adjectives are adjectives that follow the verbs **sein, werden,** or **bleiben** and modify the subject. Predicate adjectives do not take endings.

◼ *Attributive adjectives*

Das ist eine **tolle** CD.
Das ist ein **guter** Wein.
Wir haben jetzt **schönes** Wetter.

Attributive adjectives are adjectives that precede the nouns they modify. Attributive adjectives have endings.

Hier gibt es deutsches und türkisches Essen.

5. Preceded adjectives

■ *Adjectives preceded by a definite article or* **der**-*word*

	Masculine	Neuter	Feminine	Plural
Nom.	der alte Mann	das kleine Kind	die junge Frau	die guten Freunde
Acc.	den alten Mann	das kleine Kind	die junge Frau	die guten Freunde
Dat.	dem alten Mann	dem kleinen Kind	der jungen Frau	den guten Freunden
Gen.	des alten Mannes	des kleinen Kindes	der jungen Frau	der guten Freunde

	M.	N.	F.	Pl.
Nom.	e	e	e	en
Acc.	en	e	e	en
Dat.	en	en	en	en
Gen.	en	en	en	en

Definite articles and **der**-words indicate gender and/or case. Therefore, attributive adjectives do not have to. Their endings are simply **-e** or **-en.**

Diese Handschuhe sind **teuer.**   Willst du diese **teuren** Handschuhe wirklich kaufen?

Adjectives ending in **-er** may omit the **-e** when the adjective takes an ending.

schauen sich um: look around

7. Neue Sachen.   Viktoria und Anna schauen sich im Warenhaus um°. Sie sehen viele schöne Sachen, aber sie kaufen nichts. Ergänzen Sie die Sätze mit den passenden Endungen im Nominativ oder Akkusativ.

1. VIKTORIA: Sag' mal, Anna, wie findest du dies＿＿＿ rot＿＿＿ Pulli?

2. ANNA: Ganz gut, aber d＿＿＿ blau＿＿＿ Pulli hier gefällt mir besser.

3. VIKTORIA: Vielleicht kaufe ich dies＿＿＿ kurz＿＿＿ Rock.

4. ANNA: Der Rock gefällt mir auch. Willst du lieber d＿＿＿ braun＿＿＿ oder

    d＿＿＿ schwarz＿＿＿ ?

5. VIKTORIA: Ich weiß nicht. Vielleicht kaufe ich anstatt des Rocks dies＿＿＿

    toll＿＿＿ Hose.

great

6. ANNA: Gute Idee. Du, schau mal! D＿＿＿ weiß＿＿＿ Hemd da ist Klasse°.

    Es passt gut zu der Hose.

7. VIKTORIA: Meinst du? Ja, doch. Gut, ich kaufe auch d＿＿＿ weiß＿＿＿

    Hemd. Aber Moment mal, ich kann ja gar nichts kaufen. Ich habe ja gar kein

    Geld.

Describing things

▷ **8. Woher hast du das?**   Fragen Sie vier Kursteilnehmerinnen/Kursteilnehmer, woher sie bestimmte Dinge haben (z.B. ein Kleidungsstück, eine Tasche). Beschreiben Sie die Dinge genau (Farbe, Größe usw.).

S1:
Woher hast du/haben Sie [die schöne
   braune Büchertasche]?

S2:
[Die] habe ich [von meiner Mutter].
[Die] habe ich [in einem kleinen
   Geschäft gekauft].

9. Wie sind diese Orte°?   Verena und Mario sprechen über ihre tägliche Rou-   places
tine. Geben Sie die Sätze mit einem passenden Adjektiv wieder.

➤➤ Mario isst gern in dem Café   *Mario isst gern in dem billigen Café*
   an der Uni.   *an der Uni.*

Schüttelkasten

alt	modern	schön		groß
gut			**laut**	
			neu	
ruhig	billig			
klein				**gemütlich**

1. Verena isst lieber in dem Biergarten im Wald.
2. Abends sitzen die beiden gern in der Kneipe an der Uni.
3. Nachmittags arbeitet Verena in der Buchhandlung am Markt.
4. Mario arbeitet in dem Musikgeschäft in der Altstadt.
5. Abends laufen sie zusammen in dem Park im Stadtzentrum.

10. Viele Fragen.   Peter hat viele Fragen. Ergänzen Sie die Sätze mit den
passenden Endungen für Adjektive im Plural.

1. Warum trägst du immer noch dies_____ alt_____ Schuhe?

2. D_____ neu_____ Schuhe finde ich viel schöner.

3. Wann hast du dies_____ toll_____ Hemden bekommen?

4. Wer hat dies_____ warm_____ Handschuhe gekauft?

5. Was hältst du von dies_____ neu_____ CDs?

6. Was hältst du von dies_____ viel_____ Fragen?

11. Hier ist alles klein.   Erzählen Sie die Geschichte noch einmal mit dem
Adjektiv **klein** vor jedem Substantiv. Achten° Sie auf die richtigen Endungen.   pay attention

➤➤ Das Haus steht in der Sonnenstraße.
   Das kleine Haus steht in der kleinen Sonnenstraße.

Der Junge wohnt in dem Haus. Hinter dem Haus ist der Garten. In dem Garten
steht die Bank°. Auf der Bank sitzt der Junge. Unter der Bank liegt der Ball von   bench
dem Jungen. Er will mit dem Ball spielen. Er nimmt den Ball in die Hand und
kickt ihn durch das Fenster. Peng! Da ist das Fenster kaputt.

■ *Adjectives preceded by an indefinite article or* **ein**-*word*

	Masculine	Neuter	Feminine	Plural
Nom.	ein alt**er** Mann	ein klein**es** Kind	eine jung**e** Frau	meine gut**en** Freunde
Acc.	einen alt**en** Mann	ein klein**es** Kind	eine jung**e** Frau	meine gut**en** Freunde
Dat.	elnem alt**en** Mann	einem klein**en** Kind	einer jung**en** Frau	meinen gut**en** Freunden
Gen.	eines alt**en** Mannes	eines klein**en** Kindes	einer jung**en** Frau	meiner gut**en** Freunde

	M.	N.	F.	Pl.
Nom.	er	es	e	en
Acc.	en	es	e	en
Dat.	en	en	en	en
Gen.	en	en	en	en

Adjectives preceded by an indefinite article or an **ein**-word have the same endings as those preceded by **der**-words (**-e** or **-en**), except when the **ein**-word itself has no ending. These are **-er** for masculine nominative and **-es** for neuter nominative and accusative. Since in these instances **ein** does not indicate the gender of the noun, the adjective has to take on that function. Note the following table.

Nom.	ein alt**er** Mann	ein klein**es** Kind
Acc.	—	ein klein**es** Kind

Stimmen zu: agree

12. Du hast Recht.   Regina sagt einige Dinge über den Kurs. Stimmen° Sie zu und benutzen Sie Adjektive im Nominativ für Ihre Antworten.

≫ Professor Schmidts Musikvorlesung   *Ja, das war wirklich eine trockene*
war trocken, nicht?   *Vorlesung.*

1. Das Buch ist auch trocken, nicht?
2. Aber das Bier nachher war gut, nicht?
3. Die Klausur in Deutsch war lang und schwer, nicht?
4. Professor Langes Seminar ist interessant, nicht?
5. Eriks Referat war ziemlich kurz, nicht?
6. Das Referat war auch ziemlich schlecht, nicht?
7. Professor Memmels Kurs ist leicht, nicht?

13. Frage-Ecke.   Sie und Ihre Partnerin/Ihr Partner sprechen über Geburtstagsgeschenke. Finden Sie erst heraus, was Ihre Freunde ihrer Familie und ihren Freunden schenken. Fragen Sie dann Ihre Partnerin/Ihren Partner, was sie/er ihrer/seiner Familie und ihren/seinen Freunden schenken möchte.

S2: Was möchte Gerhard seinen Eltern schenken?
S1: Er möchte seinen Eltern einen teuren Videorecorder schenken.

S1:

	Eltern	Schwester	Bruder	Freundin/ Freund
Gerhard	ein teurer Videorecorder	eine blaue Bluse		
Susi			ein neues Fahrrad	eine heiße CD
Anna		eine kleine Katze	ein australischer Hut	
ich				
Partnerin/ Partner				

S2:

	Eltern	Schwester	Bruder	Freundin/ Freund
Gerhard			ein neuer Krimi	ein schönes Bild
Susi	ein neuer Computer	ein roter Mantel		
Anna	ein guter CD-Spieler			ein gutes Buch
ich				
Partnerin/ Partner				

14. Ich habe gewonnen.   Sie haben im Lotto gewonnen. Sagen Sie Ihrer Partnerin/Ihrem Partner, was Sie sich kaufen. Ihre Partnerin/Ihr Partner kann Ihnen vorschlagen°, was Sie ihr/ihm kaufen sollen. Benutzen Sie die Bilder und passende Adjektive.   suggest

S1: Ich kaufe mir einen neuen teuren CD-Spieler. Was kann ich dir kaufen?
S2: Du kannst mir ein neues Radio kaufen.

15. Alles ist neu. In Andreas Leben hat sich viel verändert. Fragen Sie sie nach Details.

⟫ Ich hab' ein neues Auto.   *Erzähl mal von deinem neuen Auto.*

1. Ich hab' eine neue Freundin.
2. Ich hab' einen neuen Kassettenrecorder.
3. Ich hab' ein neues Fahrrad.
4. Ich hab' eine neue Wohnung.
5. Ich hab' neue Freunde.
6. Ich hab' einen neuen Deutschprofessor.
7. Ich hab' neue Vorlesungen.

16. Träume. In einer Gruppe von vier Personen sprechen Sie über Ihre Träume. Eine Person beginnt und erzählt, wovon sie/er träumt° oder was sie/er haben möchte, und fragt dann die nächste Person.

dreams

Stating wants/desires

S1: Ich träume von [einem schönen Wochenende]. Wovon träumst du?
S2: Ich träume von [einem tollen Motorrad].

Träume: Reise □ Auto □ Frau □ Haus □ Mann □ Motorrad □ Wochenende

Adjektive: schnell □ klein □ reich □ schön □ interessant □ weiß □ groß □ toll □ lang

6. Unpreceded adjectives

	Masculine	Neuter	Feminine	Plural
Nom.	guter Wein	gutes Brot	gute Wurst	gute Brötchen
Acc.	guten Wein	gutes Brot	gute Wurst	gute Brötchen
Dat.	gutem Wein	gutem Brot	guter Wurst	guten Brötchen
Gen.	guten Weines	guten Brotes	guter Wurst	guter Brötchen

	M.	N.	F.	Pl.
Nom.	er	es	e	e
Acc.	en	es	e	e
Dat.	em	em	er	en
Gen.	en	en	er	er

Adjectives not preceded by a definite article, a **der**-word, an indefinite article, or an **ein**-word must indicate the gender and/or case of the noun. They have the same endings as **der**-words, with the exception of the masculine and neuter genitive.

 17. Peter isst gern. Geben Sie die Sätze mit der richtigen Form der Adjektive in Klammern wieder.

⟫ Brötchen schmecken gut. (frisch)   *Frische Brötchen schmecken gut.*

1. Bier schmeckt auch gut. (deutsch)
2. Ich trinke gern Wein. (trocken)
3. Blumen auf dem Tisch gefallen mir. (frisch)
4. In vielen Städten kann man Fisch kaufen. (frisch)
5. Ich koche gern mit Wein. (deutsch)
6. Ich habe Hunger. (groß)

7. Zum Mittagessen esse ich gern Steak. (amerikanisch)
8. Zum Abendessen esse ich gern Wurst. (deutsch)

18. Ein Geburtstagsfest.   Sie und Ihre Partnerin/Ihr Partner planen ein Geburtstagsfest für eine Freundin. Diskutieren Sie darüber, was es zu essen geben soll, und schließen Sie dann einen Kompromiss°.

schließen ... Kompromiss: come to a compromise

S1: Ich möchte ungarischen Käse servieren.
S2: Ich möchte lieber holländischen Käse servieren.

Schüttelkasten

der Tee

der Wein   der Fisch   das Brot

das Bier

die Salami   **der Kaffee**

das Steak

der Kuchen

der Käse   **die Orangen**

Adjektive: italienisch □ türkisch □ englisch □ ungarisch □ brasilianisch □ französisch □ amerikanisch □ deutsch □ holländisch □ spanisch

19. Welche Wünsche haben Sie?   Sehen Sie sich zusammen mit Ihrer Partnerin/Ihrem Partner die folgende Tabelle an. Beantworten Sie die folgenden Fragen dazu. Sprechen Sie dann mit Ihrer Partnerin/Ihrem Partner über Ihre eigenen Wünsche.

Stating wants/desires

Umfrage: Welche Wünsche sind Ihnen besonders wichtig?

glückliches Familienleben 89%
Sicherheit und Ordnung im öffentlichen Leben 84%
persönliche Sicherheit 82%
Liebe und Partnerschaft 78%
das Leben genießen° 74%
Geld und Wohlstand° 60%
beruflicher Erfolg 57%
Urlaub° und reisen 57%
viele Freizeitaktivitäten 51%
Regierungswechsel° in Berlin 46%
neue Wohnung/neues Haus 16%

enjoy
affluence

vacation

change of government

1. Welche Wünsche sind den Deutschen am wichtigsten?
2. An welcher Stelle stehen
   a. Liebe° und Partnerschaft?
   b. Erfolg im Beruf?
   c. Freizeit?
3. Was ist Ihnen wichtig? Stellen° Sie Ihre eigene Liste von Wünschen auf.
4. Vergleichen Sie Ihre Liste mit der Liste Ihrer Partnerin/Ihres Partners. Was ist Ihnen wichtiger als Ihrer Partnerin/Ihrem Partner und was ist Ihnen nicht so wichtig? Erklären Sie warum.

love

Stellen auf: draw up

7. Ordinal numbers

1. erst-	6. sechst-	21. einundzwanzigst-
2. zweit-	7. siebt-	32. zweiunddreißigst-
3. dritt-	8. acht-	100. hundertst-
		1000. tausendst-

An ordinal number is a number indicating the position of something in a sequence (e.g., the first, the second). In German, the ordinal numbers are formed by adding **-t** to numbers 1–19 and **-st** to numbers beyond 19. Exceptions are **erst-, dritt-, siebt-,** and **acht-.**

Die neue Wohnung ist im **dritten** Stock.
Am **siebten** Mai habe ich Geburtstag.

The ordinals take adjective endings.

das Datum

8. Dates°

Der Wievielte ist heute?	What is the date today?
Heute ist **der 1. (erste)** März.	Today is March first.
Den Wievielten haben wir heute?	What is the date today?
Heute haben wir **den 1. (ersten)** März.	Today is March first.

In German, there are two ways to express dates. Dates are expressed with ordinal numbers preceded by the masculine form of the definite article referring to the noun **Tag.** A period after a number indicates that it is an ordinal. The day always precedes the month.

Hamburg, **den 2. März 1996.**

Dates in letter headings or news releases are always in the accusative.

Asking for personal information

20. Zwei Tage später.   Frank vergisst immer, wann seine Freunde Geburtstag haben. Ihr Geburtstag ist immer zwei Tage später als er denkt. Beantworten Sie seine Fragen.

>> Hat Inge am neunten Mai Geburtstag?   *Nein, am elften.*

1. Hat Gisela am dreizehnten Juli Geburtstag?
2. Hat Willi am ersten Januar Geburtstag?
3. Hat Uwe am zweiten März Geburtstag?
4. Hat Elke am sechsten November Geburtstag?
5. Hat Claudia am achtundzwanzigsten April Geburtstag?
6. Hat Gerd am fünfundzwanzigsten Dezember Geburtstag?

21. Zwei Fragen.   Fragen Sie vier Kursteilnehmerinnen/Kurtsteilnehmer, wann sie Geburtstag haben und in welchem Semester sie studieren.

S1: Wann hast du Geburtstag?
S2: Am [siebten Juni].
S1: In welchem Semester/Jahr bist du?
S2: [Im zweiten.]

WIEDERHOLUNG

1. Vorbereitungen. Bilden Sie Sätze und beschreiben Sie, wie Sie das Haus aufräumen, bevor Ihre Gäste kommen.

1. du / wollen / einräumen / Spülmaschine / jetzt / ?
2. ich / müssen / sauber machen / Küche / nachher
3. du / möchten / aufräumen / Wohnzimmer / ?
4. wer / sollen / sauber machen / Badezimmer / ?
5. nachher / ich / wollen / noch / Staub saugen
6. du / können / Staub wischen

2. Ein Amerikaner in Deutschland. Ergänzen Sie die Sätze mit den passenden Adjektivendungen.

Ein amerikanisch_____ Student studiert an einer deutsch_____ Universität. Er

wohn in einem schön_____ , hell_____° Zimmer bei einer nett_____ Fami-   bright

lie. In seinem Zimmer gibt es alles – ein bequem_____° Bett, eine groß_____   comfortable

Kommode, einen modern_____ Schreibtisch, Platz für viel_____ Bücher auf

einem groß_____ Bücherregal – aber keinen Fernseher. Im ganz_____ Haus

ist kein Fernseher. Im Wohnzimmer steht neben dem grün_____ Sofa eine

toll_____ Stereoanlage°, in seinem Zimmer hat er ein klein_____ Radio, aber   stereo system

das ganz_____ Haus hat nicht einen einzig°_____ Fernseher. Das   single

gibt es!°   **Das gibt es!:** There is such a
             thing!

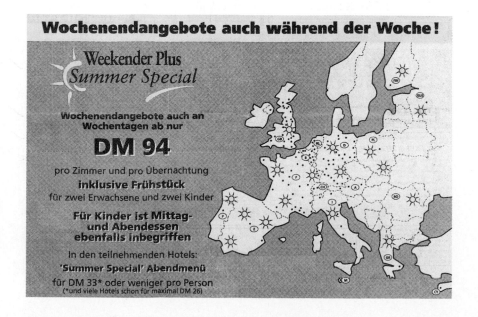

LAND UND LEUTE

Go to the
Deutsch heute Web Site at
www.hmco.com/college

Berufstätige Frauen

The report on progress toward equality in the professional life of men and women is a mixed one. The number of German women with positions of responsibility in business and public life has risen in the past years. Among these some names stand out. Rita Süßmuth became President of the **Bundestag** in 1988, a position she held until a change of government in 1998. In 1994 Jutta Limbach became the President of the Federal Constitutional Court **(Bundesverfassungsgericht).** Erika Emmerich is President of the Automobile Industry Association **(Verband der deutschen Autoindustrie).** But women still have a long way to go to achieve true equality with their male counterparts.

In the cabinet of the government formed in 1998 five of the fifteen members are women. Of the 669 representatives elected in 1998 to the **Bundestag,** 30.3% are women. This is better than the 26% representation in the previous **Bundestag.** But the fact that a little more than 52% of all eligible voters are women highlights the inadequacy of the current representation.

The statistics from the business world are mixed. Although 55% of women between the ages of 15 and 65 work, half of that number work in the service industry (clerical workers, health workers and sales clerks). Women are still paid less than men in many positions. Female wage earners average 25% less pay than men and at times as much as 40% less than men. In white-collar jobs men earn on the average more than 2000 marks per month more than women. Women are more likely to be underemployed than men. Only 6% of the working women are self-employed. In civil service, 32% of federal employees are women and 9% of university professors are women.

German women do not lack educational opportunities or qualifications. In 1997 around 41% of the graduates from institutions of higher learning were women, as were 42% of apprentices. But the challenge of family and career has not been solved. The German government views the inflexible working hours of companies and the lack of part-time jobs with benefits as a major impediment to combining family and career. Jutta Limbach has stated that for women between the ages of

In der Bundesregierung sind fünf Ministerinnen. Andrea Fischer, Edelgard Bulmahn, Heidemarie Wieczorek-Zeul, Christine Bergman, Herta Däubler-Gmelin.

20–30 the **"Frauenfrage"** (women's question) is a **"Kinderfrage"** (children's question). Under 2% of fathers take advantage of the **Erziehungsurlaub,** the leave that permits either parent to take care of a child until her or his third birthday. Thus, childrearing remains primarily the woman's responsibility.

Diskussion

Using information from this note and other information in the text, compare the position of women in Germany with the position of women in your country.

3. Eine Schweizerin in Deutschland.   Erzählen Sie, wo Susanne studiert und was sie in den Sommerferien macht. Benutzen Sie die Wörter in Klammern.

1. Susanne studiert an _____ . (die Universität Tübingen)

2. Sie wohnt in _____ . (ein großes Studentenheim)

3. Sie denkt oft an _____ . (ihre Freunde zu Hause)

4. Sie kommt aus _____ . (die Schweiz)

5. In _____ fährt sie nach Hause. (die Sommerferien)

6. Sie arbeitet bei _____ . (ihre Tante)

7. Sie fährt mit _____ zur Arbeit. (der Bus)

8. Am Sonntag macht sie mit _____ eine kleine Wanderung. (ihr guter Freund)

9. Nach _____ gehen sie in ein Café. (die Wanderung)

10. Leider hat sie _____ . (kein Geld)

11. Ihr Freund muss _____ etwas Geld leihen. (sie)

12. Nachher gehen sie auf _____ . (ein Fest)

4. Wie sagt man das?

1. —My friend Karin is studying at the University of Tübingen.
   —Does she live with a family?
   —Yes. The family is nice, and she likes her large room.
2. What's the date today?
   —It's February 28.
   —Oh oh. Karin's birthday was yesterday.
3. Awful weather today, isn't it?
   —Yes, but I'm going hiking, in spite of the weather.

5. Letzte Woche. Erzählen Sie, was diese Leute letzte Woche gemacht haben.

⟫ Stefanie macht Hausarbeit. *Stefanie hat Hausarbeit gemacht.*

1. Sie räumt ihr Schlafzimmer auf.
2. Gerd wäscht jeden Tag ab.
3. Stefanie trocknet manchmal ab.
4. Ich kaufe ein.
5. Ich fahre mit dem Fahrrad auf den Markt.
6. Gerd kocht am Wochenende.
7. Stefanie putzt das Badezimmer.

6. Was weißt du über Karin Meier? Ihre Freundin/Ihr Freund erzählt Ihnen von Karin Meier, die° vor einigen Jahren aus Ihrer Stadt weggezogen° ist. Wiederholen Sie, wie man sagt, was man von Beruf ist (Kapitel 4, Erweiterung des Wortschatzes). Geben Sie dann die Sätze auf Deutsch wieder.

who / moved away

1. Karin is a doctor.
2. Her husband is a lawyer.
3. Karin's brother Max is a teacher.
4. Her sister Lisa is a student.
5. Lisa would like to become an engineer.

▷⟫ **7. Was meinst du?** Beantworten Sie die folgenden Fragen und finden Sie dann heraus, wie Ihre Partnerin/Ihr Partner sie beantwortet hat. Sie können Ihrer Partnerin/Ihrem Partner auch noch mehr Fragen stellen.

1. Wer macht den Haushalt bei dir zu Hause?
2. Welchen Beruf hat deine Mutter? Was macht sie da? (Hausfrau ist auch ein Beruf.)
3. Wie gleichberechtigt sind Männer und Frauen hier in diesem Land? In der Wirtschaft? Zu Hause?
4. Wer war die erste berufstätige Frau in Ihrer Familie? (Großmutter? Mutter? Tante?)
5. Wann sitzt die erste Frau auf dem Präsidentenstuhl in den USA?

8. Zum Schreiben
1. Schreiben Sie eine kurze Biographie von Gisela Anton oder Helga Krauß. Denken Sie sich etwas über ihr Leben aus°, was Sie nicht im Text gelesen haben. Hier sind einige Möglichkeiten.

denken Sie sich aus: invent

- wo sie ihren Mann kennen gelernt hat
- was ihr an ihrem Mann besonders gefallen hat
- inwiefern° sie mit ihrem Leben zufrieden° ist und inwiefern nicht
- was sie in ihrer Freizeit gern macht

to what extent / satisfied

single

2. Im Lesestück steht etwas über alleinstehende° Mütter. Glauben Sie, dass es schwer ist, eine alleinstehende Mutter oder ein alleinstehender Vater zu sein? Erklären Sie auf Deutsch, warum das schwer ist oder warum nicht. Hier sind einige Stichwörter°:

cues

- Zeit
- Geld

discipline

- Disziplin°

3. Beschreiben Sie eine Frau, die Ihr Leben beeinflusst hat, und wodurch° sie es   by what means
   beeinflusst hat.

Hinweise: Before beginning your German paragraph, make notes for each point you wish to include. Try to make your account more graphic and descriptive by using attributive adjectives. After you have finished writing, check the case endings of each adjective. Also pay particular attention to the case used with each preposition. For other things to watch for in your writing, refer to p. 233.

GRAMMATIK: ZUSAMMENFASSUNG

Forms of the genitive

■ *Forms of articles, **der**-words, and **ein**-words*

	Masculine	**Neuter**	**Feminine**	**Plural**
Definite article	de**s** Mann**es**	de**s** Kind**es**	de**r** Frau	de**r** Freunde
***Der**-words*	dies**es** Mann**es**	dies**es** Kind**es**	dies**er** Frau	dies**er** Freunde
Indefinite article	ein**es** Mann**es**	ein**es** Kind**es**	ein**er** Frau	—
***Ein**-words*	ihr**es** Mann**es**	unser**es** Kind**es**	sein**er** Frau	mein**er** Freunde

■ *Forms of nouns*

Masculine/Neuter	**Feminine/Plural**
der Name **des Mannes**	der Name **der Frau**
ein Freund **des Mädchens**	ein Freund **der Kinder**

Masculine and neuter nouns of one syllable generally add **-es** in the genitive; masculine and neuter nouns of two or more syllables add **-s**. Feminine and plural nouns do not add a genitive ending.

■ *Forms of masculine **N**-nouns*

Nom.	der Herr	der Student
Acc.	den Herr**n**	den Student**en**
Dat.	dem Herr**n**	dem Student**en**
Gen.	des Herr**n**	des Student**en**

■ *The interrogative pronoun **wessen?***

Nom.	wer?
Acc.	wen?
Dat.	wem?
Gen.	wessen?

Uses of the genitive

■ *Possession and other relationships*

das Buch **meines Freundes**	my friend's book
die Mutter **meines Freundes**	my friend's mother
die Farbe **der Blumen**	the color of the flowers

■ *Prepositions*

(an)statt	*instead of*	Kommt Erika **(an)statt** ihrer Freundin?
trotz	*in spite of*	**Trotz** des Wetters wandern wir.
während	*during*	**Während** der Ferien wandern wir.
wegen	*on account of*	**Wegen** des Wetters bleiben sie zu Hause.

■ *Genitive of time*

Indefinite past	**Eines Tages** hat mir Julia alles erklärt.	*One day* Julia explained everything to me.
Indefinite future	**Eines Tages** mache ich das vielleicht.	*Someday* maybe I'll do that.

Adjectives

■ *Adjectives preceded by a definite article or **der**-word*

	Masculine	Neuter	Feminine	Plural
Nom.	der alt**e** Mann	das klein**e** Kind	die jung**e** Frau	die gut**en** Freunde
Acc.	den alt**en** Mann	das klein**e** Kind	die jung**e** Frau	die gut**en** Freunde
Dat.	dem alt**en** Mann	dem klein**en** Kind	der jung**en** Frau	den gut**en** Freunden
Gen.	des alt**en** Mannes	des klein**en** Kindes	der jung**en** Frau	der gut**en** Freunde

	M.	N.	F.	Pl.
Nom.	e	e	e	en
Acc.	en	e	e	en
Dat.	en	en	en	en
Gen.	en	en	en	en

■ *Adjectives preceded by an indefinite article or **ein**-word*

	Masculine	Neuter	Feminine	Plural
Nom.	ein alt**er** Mann	ein klein**es** Kind	eine jung**e** Frau	meine gut**en** Freunde
Acc.	einen alt**en** Mann	ein klein**es** Kind	eine jung**e** Frau	meine gut**en** Freunde
Dat.	einem alt**en** Mann	einem klein**en** Kind	einer jung**en** Frau	meinen gut**en** Freunden
Gen.	eines alt**en** Mannes	eines klein**en** Kindes	einer jung**en** Frau	meiner gut**en** Freunde

	M.	N.	F.	Pl.
Nom.	er	es	e	en
Acc.	en	es	e	en
Dat.	en	en	en	en
Gen.	en	en	en	en

■ *Unpreceded adjectives*

	Masculine	Neuter	Feminine	Plural
Nom.	guter Wein	gutes Brot	gute Wurst	gute Brötchen
Acc.	guten Wein	gutes Brot	gute Wurst	gute Brötchen
Dat.	gutem Wein	gutem Brot	guter Wurst	guten Brötchen
Gen.	guten Weines	guten Brotes	guter Wurst	guter Brötchen

	M.	N.	F.	Pl.
Nom.	er	es	e	e
Acc.	en	es	e	e
Dat.	em	em	er	en
Gen.	en	en	er	er

Ordinal numbers

1. erst-	6. sechst-	21. einundzwanzigst-
2. zweit-	7. siebt-	32. zweiunddreißigst-
3. dritt-	8. acht-	100. hundertst-
		1000. tausendst-

The ordinals (numbers indicating position in a sequence) are formed by adding
-t to the numbers 1–19 and -st to numbers beyond 19. Exceptions are **erst-,
dritt-, siebt-,** and **acht-.**

Dies ist mein **drittes** Semester.   This is my third semester.

The ordinals take adjective endings.

KAPITEL 9

LERNZIELE

Grüezi in der Schweiz

Die Baseler Straßenbahn wünscht schöne Ferien.

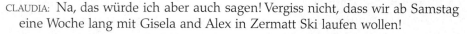
BAUSTEINE FÜR GESPRÄCHE

Hast du dich erkältet?

CLAUDIA: Hallo, Uwe! Was ist los? Du hustest ja füchterlich.

UWE: Ja, ich habe mich erkältet. Der Hals tut mir furchtbar weh.

CLAUDIA: Hast du auch Fieber?

UWE: Ja, ein bisschen – 38.

CLAUDIA: Du Armer! Du siehst auch ganz blass aus!

UWE: Ich fühle mich auch wirklich krank. Vielleicht gehe ich lieber zum Arzt.

CLAUDIA: Na, das würde ich aber auch sagen! Vergiss nicht, dass wir ab Samstag eine Woche lang mit Gisela and Alex in Zermatt Ski laufen wollen!

Fragen

1. Beschreiben Sie Uwes Krankheit.
2. Warum ist es besser, dass er zum Arzt geht?
3. Mit wem wollen Uwe und Claudia Ski laufen gehen?

(Drei Tage später)

Wie fühlst du dich heute?

CLAUDIA: Wie fühlst du dich heute? Bist du gestern zum Arzt gegangen?

UWE: Ja, ich war in der Uni-Klinik. Die Ärztin hat mir was verschrieben und es geht mir jetzt schon wesentlich besser. Das Fieber ist weg.

CLAUDIA: Willst du immer noch am Samstag mit in die Schweiz fahren?

UWE: Aber klar doch! Den Urlaub haben wir doch schon seit Monaten geplant.

CLAUDIA: Das Wetter soll nächste Woche toll sein. Vergiss nicht deine Sonnen-brille mitzubringen.

Fragen

1. Warum geht es Uwe nach drei Tagen besser?
2. Wie soll das Wetter nächste Woche in den Alpen sein?

Kapellbrücke mit Wasserturm (1333) in Luzern.

Brauchbares

1. In Uwe's two sentences, **"ich habe mich erkältet"** and **"Ich fühle mich auch wirklich krank"** note that in German there is the pronoun **mich.** These pronouns are reflexive pronouns and the verbs that use them are called reflexive verbs. The English equivalents of these two verbs have no reflexive pronouns. For more discussion of reflexive verbs see p. 318.

2. Uwe's temperature of 38°C = 100.4°F. Normal body temperature is 37°C.

3. Claudia's exclamation, **"Na, das würde ich aber auch sagen!"** is the equivalent of Engish *I would also say so.* **Würde** is the equivalent of the English *would*-construction. Like *would,* **würde** is used to express polite requests, hypothetical situations, or wishes. **Würde** is derived from the verb **werden,** and it is the subjunctive form.

4. Zermatt is considered by many to be Switzerland's best all-round ski resort. At 1620 meters (5,250 ft.) it is dominated by the Matterhorn (4477 m or 14,691 ft.), one of the world's most photographed and recognized mountains. All three of Zermatt's ski areas are above 3100 m (10,200 ft.) and are open from late November to early May, giving it the longest winter season in the Alps. Zermatt can only be reached by rail; no cars are allowed.

5. Uwe speaks about **Urlaub. Urlaub** is used to express the idea of being or going on vacation (British English: *on holidays*). **Ferien** is used when speaking about a break from study or work: **Sommerferien** (*university break*).

Inquiring about someone's health

1. Was hast du?   Ihre Partnerin/Ihr Partner sieht blass aus. Fragen Sie, was mit ihr/ihm los ist.

S1:
Du siehst blass aus. Was hast du°?

S2:
Mir geht es nicht gut°.
Ich fühle mich nicht wohl°.
Mir ist schlecht°.
Ich habe | **Kopfschmerzen.**
            | Zahnschmerzen°.
            | Magenschmerzen°.
            | Rückenschmerzen°.
Ich bin erkältet.

2. Geht es dir besser?   Fragen Sie eine Freundin/einen Freund nach° ihrer/seiner Erkältung.

S1:
Was macht deine Erkältung°?

S2:
Es geht mir | **besser.**
               | schon besser.
               | schlechter°.
Ich fühle mich | **krank.**
                  | schwach°.
                  | schwächer als gestern.

▷ **3. Wie fühlst du dich?**   Fragen Sie eine Kursteilnehmerin/einen Kursteilnehmer, wie sie/er sich fühlt.

1. Was machst du, wenn du Fieber hast?
2. Was machst du, wenn du dich erkältet hast?
3. Wie oft gehst du zum Zahnarzt?

Erweiterung des Wortschatzes

1. Der Körper°

1. der **Hals, ¨e**
2. der **Arm, -e**
3. die **Hand, ¨e**
4. der **Finger, -**
5. der **Bauch**, *pl.* **Bäuche**
6. das **Bein, -e**
7. das **Knie, -**
8. der **Fuß, ¨e**
9. der **Rücken, -**

2. Der Kopf

1. das **Haar, -e**
2. das **Ohr, -en**
3. das **Auge, -n**
4. die **Nase, -n**   das **Gesicht, -er**
5. der **Mund, ¨er**
6. die **Lippe, -n**
7. das **Kinn, -e**

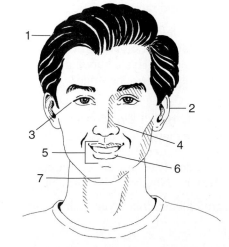

soccer team
lost
team member

1. Jeder ist verletzt. Alexanders Fußballmannschaft° hat nicht nur das Fußballspiel verloren°, sondern sich auch verletzt. Fragen Sie Ihre Partnerin/Ihren Partner, wo jedes Mannschaftsmitglied° verletzt ist.

S1: Wo ist Nummer 1 verletzt?
S2: Der Arm tut ihm weh.°

wählen aus: choose
guess

2. Wer ist es? Sehen Sie sich alle Studenten in Ihrem Deutschkurs an und wählen Sie eine/einen aus°. Ihre Partnerin/Ihr Partner wird Ihnen Fragen stellen und raten°, wen sie sich ausgesucht haben.

S2: Ist sie/er groß oder klein?
    Hat Sie/er blonde/schwarze/braune/rote Haare?
    Sind die Haare kurz/lang?
    Trägt sie/er eine Brille?

help/thief

3. Hilfe°! Ein Dieb°! Als Sie im Park waren und gelesen haben, haben Sie gesehen, wie jemand mit Ihrem Fahrrad weggefahren ist. Beschreiben Sie den Dieb der Polizei (= Ihrer Partnerin/Ihrem Partner). Ihre Partnerin/Ihr Partner wird den Dieb aus dieser Gruppe von vier bekannten Fahrraddieben heraussuchen°. Nützliche° Wörter sind:

pick out/useful

groß/klein; schlank/dick°; attraktiv/unattraktiv; wenig/viel

Haare: blond°, dunkel°, lang/kurz, hellbraun°
Nase: groß/klein, dünn°, lang
Mund: groß/klein
Brille?

S1: Der Mann ist groß, schlank, ...

Vokabeln

Adjectives and adverbs that add umlauts in the comparative and superlative are indicated as follows: **arm(ä).**

Substantive

die **Erkältung**   cold *(illness)*
das **Fieber**   fever
das **Gesicht, -er**   face
der **Hals, ˈe**   throat, neck
die **Klinik, -en**   clinic
der **Kopf, ˈe**   head
der **Körper, -**   body
die **Krankheit, -en**   illness
der **Magen, -**   stomach; die
 Magenschmerzen *(pl.)*
 stomachache

der **Rücken, -**   back; die
 Rückenschmerzen   back pain
der **Schmerz, -en**   pain
der **Urlaub**   vacation; **in/im/**
 auf Urlaub   on vacation; **in**
 Urlaub fahren   to go on vacation
der **Zahn, ˈe**   tooth; die
 Zahnschmerzen *(pl.)*   toothache
For additional parts of the body, see
 page 307.

Verben

sich erkälten   to catch a cold;
 erkältet: ich bin erkältet   I have
 a cold
sich fühlen   to feel *(ill, well, etc.)*
husten   to cough
verletzen   to injure, hurt; **ich habe**
 mir den Arm verletzt   I've
 injured/hurt my arm; **ich habe**
 mich verletzt   I hurt myself

verschreiben, verschrieben   to
 prescribe
weh·tun (+ *dat.*)   to hurt; **Die Füße**
 tun mir weh.   My feet hurt.
würde (*subjunctive of*
 werden)   would; **ich würde das**
 auch sagen   I would also say that

Andere Wörter

ab   from a certain point on; away
(from); **ab heute**   from today
arm (ä)   poor
blass   pale; **ganz blass**   pretty pale
blond   blond
dick   fat; thick
dunkel   dark
dünn   thin
fürchterlich   horrible, horribly
hell   light; bright; **hellbraun**   light
brown

schade   that's too bad, a pity, a
shame
schlecht   bad; **schlechter**   worse
schwach   weak; **schwächer**   weaker
weg   away; off; gone
wesentlich   essential, substantial, in
the main
wohl   well

Besondere Ausdrücke

du Armer   you poor fellow
Mir geht es (nicht) gut.   I am (not)
well.
Mir ist schlecht.   I feel nauseated.

Was hast du?   What is wrong with
you? What's the matter?
Was macht deine Erkältung?
How's your cold?

EIN BRIEF AUS DER SCHWEIZ

Vorbereitung auf das Lesen

■ *Vor dem Lesen**

1. Viele Leute haben Brieffreunde°. Was schreibt man einer Brieffreundin oder
einem Brieffreund im ersten Brief?
2. Was möchten Sie Ihren Brieffreunden über Ihre Stadt oder Ihr Land
erzählen? Nennen Sie zwei Dinge°.
3. Welche Stichwörter° assoziieren Sie mit der Schweiz?
4. Sehen Sie sich die Landkarte von der Schweiz am Anfang° des Buches an
und lesen Sie die folgende Information.

key words

*size / **qkm** =
Quadratkilometer: square
kilometers / Nova Scotia
population / **ca.** (abbrev. for
circa): approximately
type of government / federal
state / cantons*

- **Größe°:** 41.288 qkm°; etwa halb so groß wie Österreich (83.855 qkm) oder
Maine (86.027 qkm) etwas kleiner als Neuschottland° (52.841 qkm)
- **Bevölkerung°:** ca.° 7 Millionen Einwohner
- **Topographie:** $\frac{2}{3}$ des Landes sind hohe Berge
- **Regierungsform°:** Bundesstaat° mit 26 Kantonen°, parlamentarische
Demokratie
- **Hauptstadt:** Bern
- **5 Nachbarn:** Frankreich (F)**, Deutschland (D), Österreich (A), Fürstentum
Liechtenstein (FL), Italien (I)

---

*Remember, words that appear with a raised degree mark (°) but for which no definition is
given in the margin are active words you should learn and be able to use. These words and
their definitions are listed in the **Vokabeln** section that most closely follows the exercise.

**The abbreviations in parentheses are the international symbols used on automobile
stickers.

a. Ist Ihr Land oder Bundesland° größer° oder kleiner° als die Schweiz?

state, province / larger / smaller

b. Ist die Schweiz größer als Österreich oder nur halb so groß?

c. Hat die Schweiz mehr Einwohner als Österreich oder weniger°?

fewer

d. Wie heißen die Nachbarn der Schweiz?

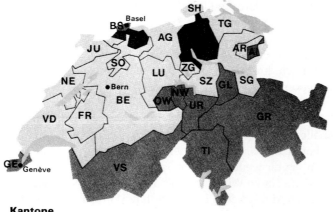

Kantone

ZH	Zürich	FR	Freiburg	AG	Aargau
BE	Bern	SO	Solothurn	TG	Thurgau
LU	Luzern	BS	Basel-Stadt	TI	Tessin
UR	Uri	BL	Basel-Land	VD	Waadt
SZ	Schwyz	SH	Schaffhausen	VS	Wallis
OW	Obwalden	AR	Appenzell A.-Rh.	NE	Neuenburg
NW	Nidwalden	AI	Appenzell I.-Rh.	GE	Genf
GL	Glarus	SG	St. Gallen	JU	Jura
ZG	Zug	GR	Graubünden		

■ *Beim Lesen*

Beantworten Sie diese Fragen:

1. Schreibt Claudia „du" oder „Sie" in ihrem Brief an Thomas?
2. Welche Fragen stellt° Claudia an Thomas?
3. Machen Sie Stichwörter zu Claudias wichtigen Themen.

V iele Schweizer sind nach Amerika ausgewandert. Deswegen gibt es in Amerika auch einige Orte mit Schweizer Namen. Einige amerikanische und Schweizer Städte haben Partnerschaften° und organisieren Brieffreundschaften° mit dem Ziel junge Amerikaner und

partnership

pen pals (correspondence friendship)

5 Schweizer zusammenzubringen. Thomas Wild aus New Glarus in Wisconsin und Claudia Handschin aus Glarus in der Schweiz möchten eine Brieffreundschaft beginnen. In ihrem ersten Brief an Thomas beschreibt Claudia ihr Land:

Lieber Thomas,

10 mein Name ist Claudia Handschin und ich bin 22 Jahre alt. Ich studiere Chemie in Basel, aber ich komme aus Glarus. Ich interessiere mich für Amerika. Da unsere zwei Städte eine Partnerschaft haben, habe ich deine Adresse und ein bisschen Information über dich bekommen. Deine Urgroßeltern° sind voriges° Jahrhundert von Glarus nach Amerika ausgewan

great-grandparents / last

15 dert, nicht wahr? Du studierst Deutsch, nicht wahr? Sprichst du auch Deutsch zu Hause oder sprechen nur die älteren Leute in New Glarus noch Deutsch? Hast du Verwandte hier in Glarus?

65% aller° Schweizer sprechen Deutsch. Deutsch ist jedoch nur eine von
den offiziellen Sprachen unseres Landes. Italienisch, Französisch und Rätoro-
20 manisch° sind die anderen. Deswegen hat unser Land auch offiziell keinen
deutschen, französischen oder italienischen Namen, sondern einen lateini-
schen: "Confoederatio Helvetica". Das heißt auf deutsch, "Schweizerische
Eidgenossenschaft°". Unsere kleine Schweiz hat nämlich 26 autonome Kantone, und Bern ist die Hauptstadt.

25   Glarus liegt in der deutschen Schweiz. Wir sprechen zu Hause Schweizerdeutsch. Das ist ein deutscher Dialekt, aber er ist dem Hochdeutschen°
nicht sehr ähnlich. Im Kindergarten sprechen wir noch Dialekt, und erst in
der Schule lernen wir Hochdeutsch. So sagen wir zum Beispiel zu einem
Bekannten: "Grüezi! Woane gaasch?" für "Grüß dich! Wohin gehst du?"
30 Außer in der Schule sprechen wir Hochdeutsch noch mit Ausländern, unter
mehr formellen Umständen° und oft im Radio und Fernsehen. Wenn wir
schreiben, benutzen wir selten Dialekt.

Was kann ich dir weiter von der Schweiz erzählen? Du weißt wohl, dass
die Schweiz eine starke Wirtschaft hat. Aber du weißt vielleicht nicht, dass
35 unser kleines Land fast keine Rohstoffe hat. Wir müssen Rohstoffe und
Lebensmittel importieren. Um die bezahlen zu können, müssen wir auf den
Weltmärkten konkurrieren können. Das können wir nur durch Qualität. Wir
Schweizer machen alles sehr präzis: Maschinen, Instrumente, chemische
Produkte und Apparate. Diese Qualitätsprodukte sind zusammen mit dem
40 Tourismus die Basis für die starke Wirtschaft der Schweiz. Eine starke
Wirtschaft ist wiederum° die Basis für unseren hohen Lebensstandard, und
sie macht auch die Neutralität der Schweiz möglich. Die Schweiz ist politisch
neutral. Doch sie kann nur dann neutral bleiben, wenn sie wirtschaftlich
stark ist. Viele junge Leute finden, dass unser Land Mitglied der EU werden
45 soll. Sonst könnte° die Wirtschaft schwächer werden. Schließlich werden
Welt und Wirtschaft immer internationaler. Konservativere und ältere Leute
argumentieren dagegen. Für sie ist die Mitgliedschaft° in der EU das Ende
der Schweizer Neutralität. Wie wir aus zwei Weltkriegen wissen, ist Neutralität eine gute Politik. Neutralität hat in der Schweiz auch eine lange Tradi-
50 tion: Unser Land ist seit fast fünfhundert Jahren neutral. Die jungen Leute
fürchten aber, die Schweiz bleibt zwar neutral, aber auch isoliert von der
Welt. Wer weiß, was richtig ist?

So, lieber Thomas, für heute ist das alles aus der Schweiz. Bitte schreibe
mir bald etwas über Amerika. Ich freue mich schon auf deinen Brief!

55 Liebe Grüße

deine Claudia

Margin glosses:

of all

Rhaeto-Romanic

Confederation

High German

circumstances

in turn

could

membership

Brauchbares

1. Nouns ending in **-schaft** designate a group or condition. English equivalents often end in *-ship*: **Partnerschaft** (l. 3), *partnership;* **Brieffreundschaft** (l. 4), *pen pals (correspondence friendship);* **Mitgliedschaft** (l. 47), *membership.* Note also **Eidgenossenschaft** (l. 23), *confederation.* Nouns ending in **-schaft** are feminine and their plural ending is **-en.**
2. l.36–37, **"auf den Weltmärkten konkurrieren":** Exports make up 27% of the gross domestic product of Switzerland.
3. **"unser hoher Lebensstandard"** (l. 41): In per capita income (1998) Switzerland, with $24,881, ranks just behind the U.S. with $26,977. (Comparable countries are: Japan, $21,930; Canada, $21,916; Austria, $21,322; and Germany, $20,370.)
4. The verb **könnte** in l. 45 is a subjunctive form of **können** and is equivalent to English *could.* Subjunctive is treated in *Kapitel 11.*

Nach dem Lesen

1. Fragen zum Lesestück

1. Warum schreibt Claudia Handschin an Thomas?
2. Warum interessiert sich Thomas wohl für die Schweiz?
3. Welcher Prozentsatz° von Schweizern spricht Deutsch?   percentage
4. Warum ist der offizielle Name der Schweiz ein lateinischer Name?
5. Wann lernen die Kinder Hochdeutsch?
6. Warum schreibt Claudia den Brief auf Hochdeutsch?
7. Was importieren und was exportieren die Schweizer?
8. Was ist die Basis für die starke Wirtschaft der Schweiz?
9. Wie lange ist die Schweiz schon neutral?

2. Claudia Handschin.   Ergänzen° Sie die fehlende° Information über Claudia,   complete / missing
und dann schreiben Sie einen kurzen Absatz° über sie.   paragraph

Alter° _____   age

Wohnort _____

Universität _____

Hauptfach _____

3. Die Schweizer Neutralität.   Suchen Sie im Text die Stellen über Wirtschaft
und Neutralität. Dann sagen Sie, wer laut° Claudia die folgenden Bemerkungen°   according to / comments
machen könnte° – ein junger Schweizer oder ein älterer, konservativer   could
Schweizer.

1. Wir dürfen nicht Mitglied der EU werden. Da verlieren° wir unsere   lose
   Neutralität.
2. Unsere Wirtschaft wird schwächer, wenn wir nicht Mitglied der EU werden.
3. Wir wollen uns nicht von der Welt isolieren.
4. Wir brauchen eine starke Wirtschaft, um neutral zu bleiben.
5. Wir wissen aus der Geschichte, dass Neutralität das Beste für uns ist.

LAND UND LEUTE

Go to the
Deutsch heute Web Site at
www.hmco.com/college

Die viersprachige Schweiz

Invasions by different ethnic tribes over a period of many hundred years shaped Switzerland's linguistic character. Today there are four national languages, each one spoken in a specific region or regional pocket. 65% of the population speak German, about 19% speak French, over 10% speak Italian. The fourth national language, Rhaeto-Romanic (**Rätoromanisch**) is in danger of dying out since less than 1% of the population speaks it. Experts predict that it may be extinct by the year 2005. In a more conscious effort to preserve the language, the Swiss voted in a constitutional referendum in 1996 to elevate Rhaeto-Romanic to the status of an official language (**Amtssprache**) of the Swiss Confederation. However, German, French, and Italian are the primary **Amtssprachen** used to conduct business and political affairs. Every Swiss can learn these languages at school, and usually gains at least a passive understanding of them. Each of the four national languages has many dialects; Rhaeto-Romanic alone has five dialects, Swiss German has many more. Although High German (**Hochdeutsch**) is taught in the schools, many Swiss resist speaking it. **Hochdeutsch** is referred to as written German (**Schriftdeutsch**). The primary spoken language of German-speaking Swiss is the dialect called **Schwyzerdütsch.**

Considering the small size—the longest North-South distance is 137 miles (220 km) and the longest East-West distance is 216 miles (348 km)—and considering the multitude of languages and dialects, Switzerland is linguistically and culturally a highly diversified country. Only in a political sense do the Swiss see themselves as a unity.

Schweizer Postautodienst
Service des cars postaux suisses
Servizio degli autopostali svizzeri
Servetsch d'autos da posta svizzer

Deutsch, Französisch, Italienisch und Rätoromanisch sind die vier Sprachen der Schweiz.

Diskussion

Switzerland has established a long history of linguistic and cultural diversity while maintaining political unity. Quickly write down three things (concepts or institutions) that you think are important for the political unity of a country. Compare your list with your classmates. How important does the class think that a common language is for political unity?

Erweiterung des Wortschatzes

1. Adjectives used as nouns

Herr Schmidt ist **ein Bekannter** von mir.	Mr. Schmidt is *an acquaintance* of mine.
Frau Schneider ist **eine Bekannte** von mir.	Ms. Schneider is *an acquaintance* of mine.
Thomas hat **keine Verwandten** mehr in der Schweiz.	Thomas has *no relatives* in Switzerland any more.

Many adjectives can be used as nouns. They retain the adjective endings as though a noun were still there: **ein Deutscher (Mann), eine Deutsche (Frau).** In writing, adjectives used as nouns are capitalized.

1. Ein guter Bekannter. Sie sind mit einer Freundin/einem Freund auf einer Party. Dort sind auch einige Austauschstudenten aus Deutschland. Die zwei Studenten sprechen über eine andere Person. Ihre Freundin/Ihr Freund spricht kein Deutsch. Übersetzen° Sie die Kommentare für sie/ihn.

translate

1. Kennst du den großen Blonden dort?
2. Er ist ein guter Bekannter von mir.
3. Er ist Arzt. Er ist immer sehr freundlich zu den Kranken.
4. Seine Tochter ist drei Jahre alt. Die Kleine ist wirklich süß°.

sweet, nice

5. Er lebt in den USA, aber er ist Deutscher.
6. Hier leben viele Deutsche.

Das Gute daran ist, dass es billig ist.	*The good [thing]* about it is that it is cheap.
Hast du **etwas Neues** gehört?	Have you heard *anything new?*
Ja, aber **nichts Gutes.**	Yes, but *nothing good.*

Adjectives expressing abstractions (**das Gute,** the good; **das Schöne,** the beautiful) are neuter nouns. They frequently follow words such as **etwas, nichts, viel,** and **wenig,** and take the ending **-es (etwas Schönes).** Note that **anderes** is not capitalized in the expression **etwas anderes.**

2. Wie war das Wochenende? Auf derselben° Party sprechen ein Deutscher und ein Amerikaner über ihr Wochenende. Sie übersetzen noch einmal für Ihre Freundin/Ihren Freund.

the same

1. ANDREA: Hast du am Wochenende etwas Schönes gemacht?
2. MICHAEL: Nein. Ich habe nichts Besonderes gemacht.
3. ANDREA: Dann erzähle ich dir etwas Interessantes.
4. Ich habe einen neuen deutschen Film gesehen. Und das Beste war: mein Freund hat mich eingeladen.
5. MICHAEL: War der Film auf Deutsch?
6. ANDREA: Ja! Das war ja das Gute daran!
7. Und ich habe sogar fast alles verstanden.
8. MICHAEL: Ach, schön für dich. Aber so etwas Langweiliges wie dieses Wochenende habe ich lange nicht gehabt. Können wir jetzt von etwas anderem reden?

LAND UND LEUTE

Go to the
Deutsch heute Web Site at
www.hmco.com/college

Die Schweiz: Ein Lied im Dialekt

How much the German Swiss dialect **(Schwyzerdütsch)** differs from High German **(Hochdeutsch)** can be seen in comparing a song by the Swiss singer Mani Matter with a High German version. The title of the song is *Heidi* and is in the dialect spoken in Bern, the capital of Switzerland.

Heidi
Är wont a dr glyche gass
und i bin mit dir i d'klass
so ischs cho, das mir grad beidi
ds härz a di verlore hei.
    Heidi, mir wei di beidi,
    beidi, Heidi, hei di gärn.

The High German translation is:

Er wohnt in der gleichen Gasse*
und ich bin mit dir in der Klasse.
So ist es, dass, wir gerade
beide
das Herz** an dich verloren**
haben.
    Heidi, wir wollen dich beide,
    beide, Heidi, haben dich gern.

Der Berner Kabarettist Mani Matter (1936–1972).

    ———
  *street
  **heart/lost

Diskussion

Compare the two versions of the song. Which differences do you observe that would indicate different grammar endings or pronunciation in Swiss German than in High German?

2. The adjectives *viel* and *wenig*

Wir haben **wenig** Geld, aber **viel** Zeit.

We have *little* money but *lots of* time.

When used as adjectives, **viel** and **wenig** usually have no endings in the singular.

Dieter hat **viele** Freunde.
Das kann man von **vielen** Menschen sagen.

Dieter has *lots* of friends.
You can say that about *many* people.

In the plural, **viel** and **wenig** take regular adjective endings.

3. Viel oder wenig? Suchen Sie sich passende° Wörter aus und fragen Sie Ihre Partnerin/Ihren Partner danach. Benutzen Sie folgende Fragewörter: wie viel?/wie viele? warum? welche?

appropriate

Freunde □ Freundinnen □ Kurse dieses Semester □ CDs □ Kassetten □ Freizeit □ Geld □ Kreditkarten □ Videos □ Uhren

Vokabeln

Substantive

der **Anfang, ⸚e** beginning
der **Apparat, -e** apparatus, appliance
der/die **Bekannte** (*noun declined like adj.*) acquaintance
der **Brieffreund, -e**/die **Brieffreundin, -nen** pen pal
der **Dialekt, -e** dialect
das **Ding, -e** thing
der **Gruß, ⸚e** greeting; **viele/liebe Grüße** (*closing of a letter*) best regards
das **Instrument, -e** instrument

das **Jahrhundert, -e** century
die **Kreditkarte, -n** credit card
der **Lebensstandard** standard of living
das **Mitglied, -er** member
der **Ort, -e** place (geographical)
die **Qualität, -en** quality
der **Rohstoff, -e** raw material
die **Situation, -en** situation
die **Sprache, -n** language
der/die **Verwandte** (*noun declined like adj.*) relative
das **Ziel, -e** goal

Verben

auf·wachen, ist aufgewacht to wake up
aus·wandern, ist ausgewandert to emigrate
beginnen, begonnen to begin
sich **freuen (auf** + *acc.*) to look forward to; sich **freuen (über** + *acc.*) to be pleased (about/with)
fürchten to fear; sich **fürchten (vor** + *dat.*) to be afraid of

(sich) interessieren (für) to be interested (in)
verstehen, verstanden to understand
wünschen (du wünschst) to wish; **was wünschst du dir zum Geburtstag?** what do you want for your birthday?

Andere Wörter

ähnlich (+ *dat.*) similar	**langsam** slow
alt: älter older	**neutral** neutral
da (*sub. conj.*) since, because	**schließlich** finally, after all
deswegen therefore, for that reason	**Schweizer** (*adj.*) Swiss
erst (adj.) first; **erst** (adv.) not until, only, just	**selten** seldom
falsch wrong, false	**stark: stärker** stronger

Besondere Ausdrücke

auf [Deutsch]   in [German]

[sie] schreibt an [ihn] + *acc.*   [she] to write to someone; **sie schreibt einen Brief an ihn**   she writes a letter to him (Also: **sie schreibt ihm einen Brief.**)

[sie] stellt Fragen an [ihn]   [she] asks questions of [him] (Also: **sie stellt ihm Fragen.**)

um ... zu (+ *infinitive*)   (in order) to; **um neutral zu bleiben**   in order to remain neutral

GRAMMATIK UND ÜBUNGEN

1. Reflexive constructions

Accusative	Ich habe **mich** gewaschen.	I washed *(myself)*.
Dative	Kaufst du **dir** einen neuen Farbfernseher?	Are you buying (yourself) a new color TV?

A reflexive pronoun indicates the same person or thing as the subject. A reflexive pronoun may be in either the accusative or the dative case, depending on its function in the sentence.

das Reflexivpronomen

2. Forms of reflexive pronouns°

	ich	du	er/es/sie	wir	ihr	sie	Sie
Accusative	mich	dich	**sich**	uns	euch	**sich**	**sich**
Dative	mir	dir	**sich**	uns	euch	**sich**	**sich**

Reflexive pronouns differ from personal pronouns only in the **er/es/sie, sie** (*pl.*), and **Sie** forms, which are all **sich.**

■ *Use of accusative reflexive pronouns*

Direct object	Ich habe **mich** schnell gewaschen.	I washed *(myself)* in a hurry.
Object of preposition	Max erzählt etwas über **sich.**	Max is telling something about *himself.*

A reflexive pronoun is in the accusative case when it functions as a direct object or as the object of a preposition that requires the accusative.

Schweizer Geschichte

Go to the
Deutsch heute Web Site at
www.hmco.com/college

Switzerland's roots reach back more than 2,000 years, when a Celtic people called the Helvetians lived in the area that is now Switzerland. Over the course of several hundred years, the Alemanni, the Burgundians, and the Franks settled there as well. The Holy Roman Empire came into existence in A.D. 962. Most of this area became part of it in A.D. 1033. In the 13th century, the Habsburg family, the ruling house of Austria (1282–1918) and rulers of the Empire, gained control over these regions. The cantons **(Kantone)** Schwyz, Uri, and Unterwalden started the Swiss Confederation (1291) and fought for their independence. August 1 is now a national holiday celebrating the alliance of the three cantons. Between 1315 and 1388 Switzerland defeated Austria in three different wars and finally gained independence from the Holy Roman Empire in 1499. The period of greatest expansion came to an end in the 16th century. From that point on the Swiss Confederation began to embrace a policy of neutrality which was internationally recognized by the Congress of Vienna in 1815. Switzerland never participated in World War I or World War II. During the Nazi era in Germany, Switzerland accepted approximately 30,000 refugees, but it also turned a similar number away. In 1996 it became known that Swiss banks had done business with the Nazi party and that the banks had either lost track of the accounts of many German Jews or had plundered the accounts. Consequently, the Swiss banks set up a fund to aid Holocaust survivers. As the result of litigation in the United States, Swiss banks were ordered in 1998 to pay some $1.25 billion to Holocaust survivors or heirs of victims who had deposited money in Swiss banks.

Ein Beispiel für Schweizer Architektur aus dem Kanton Schwyz.

Today Switzerland is composed of 26 cantons, three of which are divided into half-cantons. It remains independent and neutral, although the possibility of joining the European Union is being explored. It has an army to defend these principles, if necessary. Military service is compulsory for all men. After completing their service, soldiers take home their rifles and uniforms for they are still obligated to spend several weeks at regular intervals retraining. They remain members of the armed forces and on inactive status.

Diskussion

Wilhelm (William) Tell is the national hero of Switzerland and the inspiration for works of music and literature. See what you can find out about this figure and why he represents an important event in Swiss history.

Wanderer mit Blick auf das Matterhorn (4,477 Meter).

had
form

1. Sie fühlen sich heute besser.   Sie und Ihre Freunde hatten° denselben Virus. Jeder fühlt sich heute besser. Bilden° Sie Sätze und benutzen Sie das passende Reflexivpronomen im Akkusativ.

➤➤ *Veronika fühlt sich heute besser.*

1. Gabi und Rolf   4. wir
2. du   5. Philipp
3. ich   6. ihr

■ *Use of dative reflexive pronouns*

Indirect object	Kaufst du **dir** einen neuen Computer?	Are you going to buy *yourself* a new computer?
Dative verb	Ich kann **mir** nicht helfen.	I can't help *myself.*
Object of preposition	Sprichst du von **dir?**	Are you talking about *yourself?*

A reflexive pronoun is in the dative case when it functions as an indirect object, the object of a dative verb, or the object of a preposition that requires the dative case.

2. Was wünschen sie sich aus der Schweiz? Frau Schmidt fährt zu einer Konferenz in die Schweiz und bringt ihrer Familie und ihren Freunden Souvenirs mit. Bevor sie in die Schweiz gereist ist, hat sie alle gefragt, was sie sich wünschen°. Frau Schmidts Nachbarin spricht mit ihrer Tochter über ihre Wünsche. Ergänzen Sie den Text mit den richtigen Formen von **wünschen** und den Reflexivpronomen im Dativ.

Frau Schmidts Tochter Margot _____ _____ eine Wolljacke. Ihr Mann _____

_____ eine Schweizer Armbanduhr°. Oliver, ihr Sohn, _____ _____ ein Buch   wristwatch

über die Schweiz. Ihre Eltern _____ _____ Schweizer Schokolade. Ich _____

_____ einen schönen Fotokalender. Was hast du _____ _____ ? Letztes Jahr

hast du _____ von Frau Schmidt eine CD von einer Schweizer Techno-Gruppe

_____ , nicht wahr? Du und dein Bruder – _____ ihr _____ wieder CDs?

Hoffentlich bekommen wir alles, was wir _____ _____ .

3. Was wünschen sie sich? Stefan und seine Freunde sprechen darüber, was sie sich zum Geburtstag wünschen. Sehen Sie sich die Bilder an und fragen Sie Ihre Partnerin/Ihren Partner, was die einzelnen° Personen sich wünschen. Dann fragen Sie Ihre Partnerin/Ihren Partner, was sie/er sich wünscht.

Discussing wishes

individual

| Stefan | Michaela | Sabine | die Eltern | Claudia | mein Bruder Dirk |

ein neues Fahrrad □ einen besseren Fotoapparat □ eine teure Lederjacke □
neue Schuhe □ ein Handy □ eine schicke° Sonnenbrille   chic

S1: Was wünscht sich Stefan?
S2: Stefan wünscht sich eine teure Lederjacke.

S1: die Eltern? Claudia? mein Bruder Dirk? Partnerin/Partner?
S2: Stefan? Michaela? Sabine? Partnerin/Partner?

3. Verbs of personal care and hygiene

Wann badest du?
Ich bade abends.

Wann duschst du?
Ich dusche morgens.

Wann putzt du dir die Zähne?
Ich putze mir morgens die Zähne.

Wann rasierst du dich?
Ich rasiere mich morgens.

Wann schminkst du dich?
Ich schminke mich morgens.

Wann ziehst du dich an?
Ich ziehe mich morgens an.

Wann kämmst du dich?
Ich kämme mich morgens.

Wann ziehst du dich aus?
Ich ziehe mich abends aus.

Wann wäschst du dir Gesicht und
Hände?
Ich wasche mir abends Gesicht
und Hände.

■ *Verben*

sich an·ziehen, angezogen   to get dressed; **ich ziehe mich an**   I get dressed
sich aus·ziehen, ausgezogen   to get undressed; **ich ziehe mich aus**   I get
  undressed
baden   to take a bath; **ich bade**   I take a bath
(sich) duschen   to shower; **ich dusche (mich)**   I take a shower (**Duschen** can
  be used with or without the reflexive pronoun; the meaning is the same.)

sich kämmen   to comb; **ich kämme mich**   I comb my hair; **ich kämme mir die Haare**   I comb my hair

putzen   to clean; **ich putze mir die Zähne**   I brush/clean my teeth

sich rasieren   to shave; **ich rasiere mich**   I shave

sich schminken   to put on make-up; **ich schminke mich**   I put on make-up; **ich schminke mir die Lippen/Augen**   I put on lipstick/eye make-up

sich waschen (wäscht), gewaschen   to wash; **ich wasche mich**   I wash myself; **ich wasche mir die Hände**   I wash my hands

⇨ **4. Wann machst du das?**   Fragen Sie Ihre Partnerin/Ihren Partner nach ihrer/seiner täglichen Routine.

> Describing one's daily routine

S1:		*S2:*	
Wann	**wachst du auf°?**	**Um (sieben).**	
	stehst du auf?	Morgens.	
	duschst du?	Abends.	
	ziehst du dich an?	Vor/Nach dem Frühstück.	
	putzt du dir die Zähne?	Vorm Schlafengehen.	
	kämmst du dir die Haare?	Vor/Nach dem Essen.	
	wäschst du dir die Hände?	Nach einer schmutzigen° Arbeit.	dirty
	ziehst du dich aus?	[Drei]mal° am Tag.	times
	badest du?		
	gehst du schlafen?		

4. Reflexive verbs in German vs. English

Setz dich.	Sit down.
Fühlst du **dich** nicht wohl?	Don't you feel well?
Hast du **dich** gestern **erkältet?**	Did you catch a cold yesterday?
Hast du **dich** zu leicht **angezogen?**	Did you dress too lightly?
Mark hat **sich** heute nicht **rasiert.**	Mark didn't shave today.
Ich **freue mich** auf deinen Brief.	I'm looking forward to your letter.
Anna **interessiert sich** für Musik.	Anna is interested in music.

In German, some verbs regularly have a reflexive pronoun as part of the verb pattern. The English equivalents of these verbs do not have reflexive pronouns. In general, the reflexive construction is used more frequently in German than in English. In the vocabularies of this book, reflexive verbs are listed with the pronoun **sich: sich fühlen.**

5. Wie sagt man das?

1. Do you feel better today, Mr. Meier?
   —No, I don't feel well.
2. How did Astrid catch cold?
   —I don't know. Did she catch cold again?
3. Lotte, why haven't you dressed yet?
   —It's still early. I'll get dressed later.
4. Please sit down, Erna.
   —Thanks, I'll sit on this chair.
5. Are you interested in old films?
   —Yes, I'm looking forward to Casablanca on TV. (*on* = **im**)

LAND UND LEUTE

Go to the
Deutsch heute Web Site at
www.hmco.com/college

Die politischen Institutionen der Schweiz

Although politicial life in Switzerland is essentially based in the cantons (comparable to states in the U.S. and provinces in Canada), federal affairs are represented by several constitutional bodies.

Swiss citizens who are 18 years and older have the right to vote for the National Council **(Nationalrat).** Each citizen can vote for a party and a candidate. Elections for the Council of States **(Ständerat)** vary according to cantonal law. The National Council and the Council of States form the Federal Assembly **(Bundesversammlung),** which elects a cabinet of Federal Ministers **(Bundesrat)** and the Federal President **(Bundespräsident/Bundespräsidentin).** Although the President is the head of state, his/her duties are largely ceremonial and he/she does not hold special power within the government.

The Federal Assembly decides on new or amended laws. However, if within three months of such a decision, 50,000 signatures are collected from voters, the law must be put to the Swiss people for a vote. The law then only takes effect if the majority vote in favor. Some selected recent referenda: (1) In 1992 voters approved Switzerland joining the International Monetary Fund and the World Bank. (2) In 1993 voters approved a rise in the price of gasoline and the introduction of a value-

Der Nationalrat tagt in Bern.

added tax to replace the sales tax. They rejected an initiative to ban ads for alcohol and tobacco products. (3) In 1994 the people approved a referendum for an outright ban in 10 years on all heavy trucks traveling through Switzerland to other European countries. Such vehicles will have to be hauled by rail. No new major highways may be built. (4) In 1996 the voters rejected a referendum that would have drastically limited immigration to Switzerland and ultimately denied asylum to refugees and illegal immigrants.

Despite its long democratic tradition, it was not until 1971 that a referendum gave women the right to vote in federal elections and to hold federal office. In 1981 a referendum was passed that bars discrimination against women under canton as well as federal law.

Diskussion

Look at the issues recently decided by referendum in Switzerland. Do you believe that it is a good idea for voters to decide on such issues directly and on a regular basis? Which issue would you suggest for a national referendum in your country?

5. Definite article with parts of the body

Ich habe **mir die** Hände gewaschen. I washed *my* hands.
Hast du **dir die** Zähne geputzt? Did you brush *your* teeth?

In referring to parts of the body, German uses a definite article (e.g., **die**) and a reflexive pronoun (e.g., **mir**) where English uses a possessive adjective (e.g., *my*).

Ich muss **mir die** Schuhe anziehen. I have to put on *my* shoes.

In German the definite article is also often used with clothing.

6. Schon fertig. Sagen Sie, was Sie gemacht haben.

≫ Gesicht waschen *Ich habe mir das Gesicht gewaschen.*

1. Hände waschen   4. Zähne putzen
2. Haare waschen   5. saubere Jeans anziehen
3. Haare kämmen   6. ein sauberes Hemd anziehen

7. Was sagen Sie? Beantworten Sie die Fragen erst selbst und vergleichen° Sie dann Ihre Antworten mit den Antworten Ihrer Kursteilnehmer/innen.

compare

1. Wann duschst oder badest du?
2. Wäschst du dir abends oder morgens die Haare?
3. Mit was für einem Shampoo wäschst du dir die Haare?
4. Wann putzt du dir die Zähne?
5. Mit welcher Zahnpasta° putzt du dir die Zähne?

toothpaste

6. Ziehst du dir die Schuhe aus, wenn du fernsiehst?
7. Ziehst du dir alte Sachen an, wenn du abends nach Hause kommst?

6. Infinitives with *zu*

Infinitives with *zu*	Ich brauche heute nicht **zu** arbeiten.	I don't have to [need to] work today.
Modals and infinitive	Musst du morgen arbeiten?	Do you have to work tomorrow?

In English, dependent infinitives used with most verbs are preceded by *to*. In German, dependent infinitives used with most verbs are preceded by **zu.** Dependent infinitives used with modals are not preceded by **zu.**

Du brauchst nicht mit**zu**kommen. You don't need to come along.
Wir haben vor übers Wochenende We're planning to stay here over
  da**zu**bleiben.   the weekend.

When a separable-prefix verb is in the infinitive form, the **zu** comes between the prefix and the base form of the verb.

  Infinitive phrases need not be set off by commas although writers may choose to use a comma for clarity.

  Some verbs you know that can be followed by **zu** + an infinitive are **aufhören, beginnen, brauchen, lernen, scheinen, vergessen,** and **vorhaben.**

passed

8. Das haben wir vor. Dieter hat gerade sein Examen an der Universität be-standen°. Sie und Ihre Freunde feiern sein Examen mit einer Party. Erzählen Sie noch einmal, was Sie gemacht haben, und verbinden Sie dieses Mal die beiden Sätze.

⟫ Wir laden 20 Gäste ein. Das haben wir vor.
   Wir haben vor 20 Gäste einzuladen.

1. Ich bereite das Essen vor. Das muss ich noch.
2. Ich koche Spaghetti. Das habe ich vor.
3. Dieter geht einkaufen. Das will Dieter.
4. Er kauft eine besonders gute Torte. Das hat er vor.
5. Ich räume (nicht) auf. Das brauche ich nicht. (In your answer, omit the **nicht** in parentheses.)
6. Dieter macht alles. Das muss Dieter.
7. Er putzt das Bad (nicht). Das braucht er nicht. (In your answer, omit the **nicht** in parentheses.)

Talking about household chores

9. Hausarbeit. Sie und Ihre Freundin/Ihr Freund sprechen über die Hausarbeit, die Sie machen.

einkaufen □ kochen □ das Bett machen □ [bei der Hausarbeit] helfen □ Geschirr spülen □ abtrocknen □ aufräumen □ [die Küche] sauber machen □ Fenster putzen □ [die Wäsche/das Auto] waschen □ [im Garten] arbeiten □ die Spülmaschine ein- und ausräumen □ Staub saugen

S1:
Ich muss [jeden Tag] [abwaschen], und du?

S2:
Ja, ich muss auch [Geschirr spülen]. Ich brauche nicht [Geschirr zu spülen].

■ *Expressions requiring infinitives with* **zu**

Es ist schön frühmorgens zu joggen.
Aber es ist schwer früh aufzustehen.

It's nice to jog early in the morning.
But it's hard to get up early.

Infinitives with **zu** are used after a number of expressions, such as **es ist schön, es ist schwer, es macht Spaß, es ist leicht,** and **es ist Zeit.**

10. Nicole studiert in Zürich. Erzählen Sie, was Nicole in Zürich macht.

⟫ *Es ist schwer früh aufzustehen.*

1. Sie steht früh auf.
2. Sie fährt mit dem Zug.
3. Sie versteht die Vorlesungen.
4. Sie sitzt mit Freunden im Biergarten.
5. Sie findet einen Studentenjob.
6. Sie geht mit Freunden Rollerblading.

Schüttelkasten

Es ist schwer   **Es ist gut**
        Es macht Spaß
            Es ist nicht leicht   Es ist schön

11. Es macht Spaß ...   Sie und Ihre Partnerin/Ihr Partner wollen sich besser kennen lernen: Erzählen Sie einander, was Sie gut, schlecht, schwer und leicht finden und was Ihnen Spaß macht.

S1: Es ist schön [am Sonntag nichts zu tun].
S2: Es ist schwer [zu schlafen].

Es macht Spaß ...	Es ist leicht ...
Es ist schön ...	Es ist gut ...
Es ist schwer ...	Ich habe keine Zeit ...

7. The construction *um ... zu* + infinitive

Die Schweiz muss wirtschaftlich stark sein, **um** neutral **zu** bleiben.	Switzerland has to remain economically strong *in order to* remain neutral.

The German construction **um ... zu** + infinitive is equivalent to the English construction *(in order) to* + infinitive.

12. Was meinen Sie?   Ergänzen Sie die Sätze und vergleichen Sie dann Ihre Sätze mit den Sätzen von Ihrer Partnerin/Ihrem Partner.

➤➤ *Um gesund zu bleiben, [muss man viel Sport treiben].*

Um schöne Ferien zu haben, ...	Um glücklich zu sein, ...
Um gute Noten zu bekommen, ...	Um reich zu werden, ...
Um ein gutes Examen zu machen, ...	[Um ... zu ... ...,]
Um viele Freunde zu haben, ...	

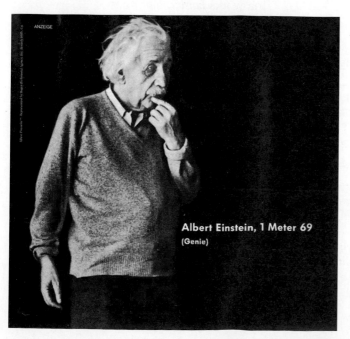

Albert Einstein, 1 Meter 69
(Genie)

Man muß nicht groß sein, um groß zu sein.

8. Comparison of adjectives and adverbs

■ *Comparison of equality*

Die Schweiz ist halb **so groß wie** Österreich.	Switzerland is half *as large as* Austria.
Erik schwimmt nicht **so** gut **wie** Klaus.	Erik doesn't swim *as* well *as* Klaus does.
Diese Reise ist genau**so** schön **wie** die letzte.	This trip is just *as* nice *as* the last one.

The construction **so ... wie** is used to express the equality of a person, thing, or activity to another. It is equivalent to English *as . . . as.*

13. Katja kann das auch.   Sie finden, dass Katja genauso gut ist wie Ihre Freunde.

➤➤ Franz ist intelligent.   *Katja ist genauso intelligent wie er.*

1. Klaus ist freundlich.
2. Martha arbeitet viel.
3. Frank spielt gut Gitarre.
4. Rita kann schnell schwimmen.
5. Christian kann gut kochen.
6. David spricht gut Französich.

der Komparativ

■ *Comparative forms°*

Base form	klein	Österreich ist **klein.**	Austria is *small.*
Comparative	kleiner	Die Schweiz ist noch **kleiner.**	Switzerland is even *smaller.*

The comparative of an adjective or adverb is formed by adding **-er** to the base form.

Ina arbeitet **schwerer als** Kai.	Ina works *harder than* Kai.
Ina ist **fleißiger als** Kai.	Ina is *more industrious than* Kai.

The comparative form plus **als** is used to compare people, things, or activities. **Als** is equivalent to English *than.*

Base form	dunkel	teuer
Comparative	**dunkler**	**teurer**

Adjectives ending in **-el** drop the final **-e** of the base form before adding **-er.** Adjectives ending in **-er** may follow the same pattern.

Base form	groß	Hamburg ist **groß.**
Comparative	größer	Hamburg ist **größer** als Bremen.

Many common one-syllable words with stem vowel **a, o,** or **u** add an umlaut in the comparative form, including **alt, dumm, jung, kalt, kurz, lang, oft, rot,** and **warm.** Adjectives and adverbs of this type are indicated in the vocabularies of this book as follows: **kalt (ä).**

14. Wie ist die neue Wohnung? Ihre Freundin/Ihr Freund möchte wissen, wie Ihre neue Wohnung Ihnen gefällt. Die Wohnung ist das Gegenteil° von dem, was Ihre Freundin/Ihr Freund denkt.

opposite

Making comparisons

➤➤ Ist deine neue Wohnung kleiner als die alte? *Nein, sie ist größer.*

1. Ist sie billiger als die alte Wohnung?
2. Ist die Küche größer als die alte?
3. Ist diese Wohnung neuer als die andere?
4. Ist die neue Wohnung wärmer als die andere?
5. Ist der Weg zur Uni länger als vorher°?
6. Also musst du für die Vorlesungen nicht früher aufstehen?

previously

Base form	gern	gut	hoch	viel
Comparative	**lieber**	**besser**	**höher**	**mehr**

A few adjectives and adverbs have irregular comparative forms.

Jörg sieht **gern** fern.	Jörg likes to watch TV.
Karin liest **lieber.**	Karin prefers [likes more] to read.

The English equivalent of **lieber** is *to prefer,* or *preferably,* or *rather* with a verb.

15. In einem Möbelgeschäft. Sie und eine Freundin/ein Freund sehen sich verschiedene Möbel an und vergleichen sie.

➤➤ Die Kommode ist groß. *Aber diese Kommode ist größer.*

1. Der Couchtisch ist billig.
2. Das Sofa kostet viel.
3. Der Teppich sieht gut aus.
4. Der Sessel ist teuer.
5. Der Schrank ist hoch.
6. Die Preise° sind hoch.

prices

16. Was machst du lieber? Ihre Partnerin/Ihr Partner fragt Sie, welche Aktivitäten Sie lieber als andere machen.

Stating preferences

S2: Was machst du lieber? **Joggen oder Rad fahren?**
Zeitungen oder Bücher lesen?
Klassische Musik oder Rock hören?
Das Badezimmer sauber machen oder
das Wohnzimmer aufräumen?
Staub wischen oder Staub saugen?
Gartenarbeit oder Hausarbeit?
Ins Kino oder zu einer Party gehen?
Italienisch oder chinesisch essen gehen?

S1: Ich fahre lieber Rad.

■ *Preceded comparative adjectives*

Das ist kein besser**er** Plan.	That's not a better plan.
Hast du eine besser**e** Idee?	Do you have a better idea?

Comparative adjectives that precede nouns take adjective endings.

dissatisfied

17. Unzufrieden°.   Stefanie ist mit allem unzufrieden und will alles besser haben. Ergänzen Sie die Sätze mit einer passenden Komparativform.

⟫ Stefanie hat eine schöne Wohnung, aber sie möchte eine _____ haben.
Stefanie hat eine schöne Wohnung, aber sie möchte eine schönere haben.

1. Sie hat ein großes Auto, aber sie möchte ein _____ haben.

2. Sie kauft immer teure Kleider, aber sie wünscht sich noch _____ .

3. Sie isst oft in guten Restaurants, aber sie möchte in _____ essen.

4. Sie hat einen schnellen Computer, aber sie kauft sich bald einen _____ .

5. Sie macht schöne Ferien, aber sie wünscht sich _____ .

6. Stefanie hat einen guten Job, aber sie braucht bestimmt einen _____ .

der Superlativ

■ *Superlative forms°*

Base form	alt	Trier ist sehr **alt**.	Trier is very *old*.
Superlative	ältest-	Es ist die **älteste** Stadt in Deutschland.	It is the *oldest* city in Germany.

The superlative of an adjective is formed by adding **-st** to the base form. The **-st** is expanded to **-est** if the adjective stem ends in **-d, -t,** or a sibilant. The superlative of **groß** is an exception: **größt-.** The words that add umlaut in the comparative also add umlaut in the superlative. Superlative adjectives that precede nouns take adjective endings.

18. Was weißt du über Deutschland?   Ihre Freundin/Ihr Freund spricht mit Ihnen über Deutschland. Erklären Sie ihr/ihm, dass die Orte° die ältesten, größten usw. sind.

places

⟫ Trier ist eine alte Stadt, nicht?   *Ja, Trier ist die älteste Stadt Deutschlands.*

1. Die Universität Heidelberg ist eine alte Universität, nicht?
2. Bayern ist ein großes Land, nicht?
3. Bremen ist ein kleines Land, nicht?
4. Berlin ist sicher eine sehr große Stadt.
5. Der Rhein ist bestimmt ein langer Fluss°.

river

| Im Winter arbeitet Frau Greif **am schwersten.** | In the winter Mrs. Greif works *(the) hardest.* |
| Im Winter sind die Tage **am kürzesten.** | In the winter the days are *(the) shortest.* |

The superlative of adverbs (e.g., **am schwersten**) and predicate adjectives (e.g., **am kürzesten**) is formed by inserting the word **am** in front of the adverb or adjective and adding the ending **-(e)sten** to it. The construction **am** + superlative is used when it answers the question **wie?** (*how?*) as in: **Wie arbeitet Frau Greif im Winter? Sie arbeitet am schwersten.**

19. Alles ist am größten.   Claudia spricht im Superlativ. Wenn jemand etwas sagt, wiederholt sie es und sagt es ist am größten, am kältesten, am langsamsten usw. Stellen Sie sich vor, Sie sind Claudia.

⟫ Im Sommer sind die Tage lang.   *Im Sommer sind die Tage am längsten.*

1. Im Herbst sind die Farben interessant.
2. Im Frühling sind die Blumen schön.
3. Im Winter sind die Tage kalt.
4. Regina fährt langsam.
5. Hans-Jürgen arbeitet schwer.
6. Ingrid und Thomas tanzen schön.

| Lukas ist der jüngste Sohn, und Fabian ist **der älteste (Sohn).** | Lukas is the youngest son and Fabian is *the oldest (son).* |

The superlative of attributive adjectives (with a following noun expressed or understood) is formed by inserting **der/das/die** in front of the adjective and adding the appropriate ending to the superlative form of the adjective.

> 1. Im Juni sind die Rosen **am schönsten.**
> 2. Diese Rose ist **die schönste.**
>   Diese Rosen sind **die schönsten.**

The above chart shows the two patterns of superlative predicate adjectives. The adjectives preceded by **der/das/die** have **-e** in the singular and **-en** in the plural.

20. Die schönsten, neuesten Sachen. Wie Claudia, findet auch Peter alles am besten. Stellen Sie sich vor, Sie sind Peter.

➤➤ Diese Schuhe sind sehr billig. *Diese Schuhe sind die billigsten.*

1. Diese Blumen sind sehr schön.
2. Dieses Auto ist sehr teuer.
3. Diese Jacke ist sehr warm.
4. Dieses T-Shirt ist toll.

5. Dieser CD-Spieler ist billig.
6. Dieses Kassettendeck ist ziemlich teuer.

Base form	gern	gut	hoch	viel
Comparative	lieber	besser	höher	mehr
Superlative	liebst-	best-	höchst-	meist-

The adjectives and adverbs that are irregular in the comparative are also irregular in the superlative. Irregular forms are indicated in the vocabularies of this book as follows: **gern (lieber, liebst-).**

21. Was sind das alles für Leute in diesem Sportclub? Beantworten Sie die Fragen über den Sportclub im Superlativ.

➤➤ Frank spielt lieber Tennis als Basketball. Und Fußball?
Fußball spielt er am liebsten.

1. Peter spielt aber besser als Frank. Und Georg?
2. Inge treibt mehr Sport als ihr Bruder. Und ihre Schwester?
3. Gudrun schlägt° den Ball höher als Lisa. Und Karoline?
4. Julians Tennisschuhe kosten mehr als Ullis Schuhe. Und Marks Schuhe?
5. David joggt lieber morgens als mittags. Und abends?
6. Nach dem Sport hören sie lieber Reggae als klassische Musik. Und Rockmusik?

hits

Discussing personal information

 22. Was meinst du? Beantworten Sie die Fragen erst selbst und vergleichen Sie dann Ihre Antworten mit den Antworten Ihrer Partnerin/Ihres Partners.

1. Was trinkst du am liebsten?
2. Was isst du am liebsten?
3. An welchem Tag gehst du am spätesten ins Bett?
4. Welche Sprache sprichst du am besten?
5. Was studierst du am liebsten?
6. Wer arbeitet in deiner Familie am schwersten?
7. Welchen Sport treibst du am liebsten?
8. Welcher Politiker spricht am besten?
9. Welche Stadt ist die schönste?
10. Wer ist der beste Profi-Basketballspieler? Der beste Tennisspieler? Der beste Golfspieler?

 23. Was wissen Sie schon über diese Länder? Sehen Sie mit Ihrer Partnerin/Ihrem Partner zusammen die Tabelle und die Karte von Europa am Ende Ihres Buches an. Vergleichen Sie die Länder und benutzen Sie Ausdrücke wie **groß, so groß wie, größer als, am größten.** Nützliche Adjektive sind auch **klein, viel** und **wenig.**

Land	Größe (qkm)	Einwohner
Deutschland	357.048	82.000.000
Italien	301.278	57.200.000
Österreich	83.855	8.000.000
Portugal	92.075	9.900.000
die Schweiz	41.288	7.000.000
Spanien	504.750	39.200.000

S1: Ich denke, Italien ist kleiner als Deutschland.

S2: Ja, das stimmt. Es hat auch weniger Einwohner als Deutschland. Aber Italien hat mehr Einwohner als Portugal und es ist auch größer als Portugal.

S1: Ja, Portugal ist klein, es ist auch kleiner als Spanien ... etc.

WIEDERHOLUNG

1. Erik fühlt sich nicht wohl.   Annette denkt, dass Erik krank aussieht. Geben Sie die Sätze auf Deutsch wieder.

ANNETTE: Why did you get up so late?
ERIK: I don't feel well.
ANNETTE: Do you have a fever?
ERIK: No. I caught a cold. My throat hurts.
ANNETTE: You look pale. Maybe it's better if you go to the doctor.
ERIK: You're right. I do feel weak.

2. So beginnt mein Tag.   Beschreiben Sie, wie Ihr Tag anfängt°. Benutzen Sie die folgenden Wörter und Wortverbindungen.   begins

aufstehen ☐ baden oder duschen ☐ sich anziehen ☐ tragen ☐ etwas trinken und essen ☐ sich die Zähne putzen ☐ sich die Haare kämmen

3. In der Schweiz ist es anders.   Verbinden Sie die Sätze mit einer passenden Konjunktion aus der Liste.

aber ☐ da ☐ dass ☐ denn ☐ ob ☐ oder ☐ und ☐ weil ☐ wenn

≫ Diane Miller studiert in der Schweiz. Sie möchte mehr Deutsch lernen.
   Diane Miller studiert in der Schweiz, denn sie möchte mehr Deutsch lernen.

1. Sie geht mit ihrer Freundin Nicole. Ihre Freundin geht einkaufen.
2. Diane ist erstaunt°. Nicole geht jede Woche dreimal einkaufen.   surprised
3. Sie nimmt eine Einkaufstasche mit. Sie geht zum Supermarkt.
4. Nicole kauft fast alles im Supermarkt. Die Sachen sind da oft billiger.
5. Sie kauft Tabletten in der Apotheke. Sie kauft einen Kamm in der Drogerie.
6. Beim Bäcker kauft sie frischen Kuchen. Sie kauft kein Brot.
7. Diane ist erstaunt. Nicole geht in so viele Geschäfte.

4. Bei Beckers in Zürich.   Robert, ein amerikanischer Student, wohnt bei Familie Becker in Zürich. Im folgenden Dialog laden Anja Becker und ihre Freundin Bianca Robert ein, mit ihnen eine Reise nach Österreich zu machen. Ergänzen Sie den Text mit den passenden Possessivpronomen.

1. ANJA: Komm, Robert, wir machen gerade _____ Ferienpläne. Wir fahren nach

    Österreich zu _____ Freunden. Du kommst doch mit, oder?

2. ROBERT: Ja, gern. Wie lange bleibt ihr denn bei _____ Freunden?

3. BIANCA: Eine Woche. Du kannst _____ Arbeit mitnehmen.

4. ROBERT: Ja, das muss ich. Ich muss _____ Referat vorbereiten.

5. ANJA: Das Schöne ist, dass Vater gesagt hat, wir können _____ Auto nehmen.

6. ROBERT: Das finde ich sehr nett von _____ Vater, Anja.

7. BIANCA: Ja, das ist toll! Ich wollte schon _____ Schwester fragen, ob sie uns

    _____ Wagen gibt.

8. ANJA: Na, den brauchen wir jetzt nicht. Ich glaube, _____ Reise wird super!

5. Mein Bruder.   Sebastian spricht über seinen Bruder. Er benutzt in seinen Sätzen Wörter, die miteinander verwandt° sind. Manche Wörter sind neu für Sie, aber vielleicht können Sie ihre Bedeutung° erraten°, weil Sie das verwandte Wort kennen. Geben Sie die Sätze auf Englisch wieder.

related
meaning / guess

1. Ich habe meinem Bruder geholfen. Er hat meine Hilfe gebraucht.
2. Er ist Student. Er studiert in Leipzig. Mit dem Studium ist er erst in vier Jahren fertig.
3. Weil er Geld braucht, will er sein Motorboot verkaufen. Dann will er sich ein Motorrad kaufen.
4. Motorrad fährt er sehr gern. Aber der Fahrschulkurs war teuer. Die Fahrschule hat er letztes Jahr besucht.
5. Im Sommer will er dann durch Deutschland reisen. Die Reise wird bestimmt ganz toll.
6. Wenn das Wetter gut ist, will er zelten. Sein Zelt ist klein und praktisch.

6. Wie sagt man das?

1. Dietmar is taller than his brother.
    —Yes, but still shorter than his father.
2. I work best in the mornings.
    —Really? I prefer to work evenings.
3. Today is the coldest day of the year.
    —Yes, and it isn't getting warmer.
4. Do you like to work with younger people?
    —Yes. But I like to work with older people most of all.

7. Eine Wohnung im Tessin. Eine Schweizer Familie wohnt in Zürich. Sie möchte eine Wohnung im Tessin, einem wärmeren Teil der Schweiz an der italienischen Grenze, haben. In einer Zeitung finden sie drei Anzeigen°, eine auf Französisch, eine auf Deutsch und eine auf Italienisch. Lesen Sie die deutsche Anzeige und beantworten Sie die Fragen. Worterklärungen finden Sie im Anhang (Vocabulary for Authentic Text Activities).

ads

1. An welchem See° liegt die Wohnung?
lake
2. Wie groß ist die Wohnung?
3. Wo hat man Platz für Boot° und Auto?
boat
4. Was kann man in seiner Freizeit machen?
5. Wie teuer ist die Wohnung?
6. Was nimmt der Verkäufer° in Zahlung?
seller
7. Wie kann man den Eigentümer° erreichen°?
owner / reach

Westschweiz (inkl. Wallis) EL

Occasion unique à Yverdon

Une villa de maitre, début XIXe, comprenant propriété attenante de 16 317 m², ainsi qu'une ferme à rénover. Situation dominante avec vue imprenable sur la ville et sur le lac de Neuchâtel, à 2 minutes en voiture du centre ville.
Pour plus de renseignements, écrire sous chiffre 22-120-5843, Est Vaudois, 1820 Montreux.
ELX977 855M

Tessin EE

Bootsgarage am Luganersee

in **Maroggia**, direkt am See, 3½-Zimmer-Wohnung inkl. Bootsgarage mit Aufzug, Parkplatz in Einstellhalle, Lift, Anteil an Aussenbad, Hallenbad, Sauna, Pergola mit Cheminée. Fr. 720 000.–. Nehme Ferrari oder Porsche in Zahlung.
Tel. (045) 21 71 77
  (045) 51 25 43
Fax (045) 21 67 07
EEX977 676L

Pian San Giacomo/ San Bernardino GR, 1000 s/m

Vendo

Chalet

composto da:
1 appartamento con grande soggiorno, camino, 3 camere, servizi, grande terrazza
1 appartamento con soggiorno, camera, servizi legnaia, lavanderia, riscaldamento elettrico
Grazioso giardino con tavolo in granito, posteggi, tranquillità, soleggiato, vista aperta, completamente arredato.
5 min. dalle piste di S. Bernardino, 40 min. di autostrada N 13 da Lugano o Locarno.
Prezzo Fr. 395 000.–. Tel. sera (091) 54 20 21.
EKX977 509G

---

8. Rollenspiel. Sie sind Ärztin/Arzt. Ihre Partnerin/Ihr Partner ist Ihre Patientin/Ihr Patient. Sie/Er sagt Ihnen, dass sie/er sich nicht wohl fühlt, und beschreibt viele verschiedene Symptome. Sie glauben, dass die Patientin/der Patient gestresst ist, und sagen ihr/ihm, sie/er soll die tägliche Routine ändern.

9. Zum Schreiben. Sie haben hier drei mögliche Themen. Wählen Sie sich eins aus° und schreiben Sie.

wählen aus: select

1. Stellen Sie sich vor°, Sie sind Thomas, an den Claudia den Brief über die Schweiz auf Seite 311–312 geschrieben hat. Antworten Sie auf Claudias Brief. Vergessen Sie nicht die folgenden Informationen:

stellen vor: pretend

- Danken Sie Claudia für den Brief.
- Schreiben Sie etwas über sich selbst, ähnlich wie Claudia es im ersten Abschnitt° ihres Briefes getan hat.

paragraph

- Beantworten Sie Claudias Fragen.
- Schreiben Sie ein bisschen über Ihre Stadt, Ihren Staat oder Ihre Provinz, z.B., wo liegt sie/er, welche Städte, was ist besonders?
- Erklären Sie ihr, warum sie gern oder ungern dort leben.
- Bitten° Sie sie zurückzuschreiben.

request

- Erklären Sie ihr, dass Sie sich auf Ihre Antwort freuen.

2. In ihrem Brief hat Claudia ein bisschen über sich selbst geschrieben. Wie ist Claudia? Denken Sie sich noch ein bisschen mehr über sie aus°, zum Beispiel über ihre Familie und was sie gern tut.

denken aus: make up

internship

roommate

3. Sie machen bald ein Praktikum° bei einer Schweizer Firma in Zürich. Sie sollen in Zürich mit einer anderen Praktikantin/einem anderen Praktikanten zusammen wohnen. Sie haben gerade einen Brief von Ihrer neuen Mitbewohnerin°/Ihrem Mitbewohner bekommen. Antworten Sie auf ihren/seinen Brief. Schreiben Sie in Ihrem Brief das folgende:

- Beschreiben Sie sich selbst (wie Sie aussehen, wie Sie sind).
- Sagen Sie, was Sie studieren.
- Erzählen Sie, was Sie gern in Ihrer Freizeit tun.
- Fragen Sie über Zürich und das Leben dort.
- Beschreiben Sie auch Ihre Morgenroutine.

Hinweise: As you write your letter, remember to use **du**-forms and to give your letter the proper German heading, salutation, and closing.

After you have written your letter, or description, review it, paying particular attention to the following:

- subject-verb agreement
- word order
- case used with prepositions
- adjective endings
- reflexive pronouns

GRAMMATIK: ZUSAMMENFASSUNG

Reflexive constructions

■ *Forms of reflexive pronouns*

	ich	du	er/es/sie	wir	ihr	sie	Sie
Accusative reflexive	mich	dich	sich	uns	euch	sich	sich
Dative reflexive	mir	dir	sich	uns	euch	sich	sich

Use of reflexive constructions

■ *Accusative reflexive pronouns*

Direct object	Ich habe **mich** gewaschen.	I washed *(myself)*.
Object of preposition	Hast du das für **dich** gemacht?	Did you do that for *yourself?*

■ *Dative reflexive pronouns*

Indirect object	Hast du **dir** ein neues Auto gekauft?	Did you buy *yourself* a new car?
Dative verb	Ich kann **mir** nicht helfen.	I can't help *myself.*
Object of preposition	Spricht Edith von **sich** selbst?	Is Edith talking about *herself?*

■ *Reflexive vs. personal pronouns*

Reflexive	Max hat das für **sich** gemacht.	Ich kann **mir** nicht helfen.
	Max did it for *himself.*	I can't help *myself.*
Personal	Max hat das für **ihn** gemacht.	Max kann **mir** nicht helfen.
	Max did it for *him.*	Max can't help *me.*

Definite articles with parts of the body

Ich habe **mir die** Hände gewaschen.

I washed *my* hands.

Sophia hat **sich die** Haare gekämmt.

Sophia combed *her* hair.

In referring to parts of the body, German often uses a definite article and a dative pronoun. English uses a possessive adjective.

Infinitives with *zu*

Theo versucht alles **zu** verstehen.
Er kann alles verstehen.

Theo tries to understand everything.
He can understand everything.

Dependent infinitives used with most verbs are preceded by **zu.** Dependent infinitives used with modals are not preceded by **zu.**

Hannah hat keine Zeit die Arbeit **zu** machen.

Hannah has no time to do the work.

Es war schwer die Vorlesung **zu** verstehen.

It was difficult to understand the lecture.

Infinitives with **zu** are also used after a large number of expressions like **sie hat keine Zeit** and **es ist schwer.** While a comma is not required to set off an infinitive phrase, a writer may choose to use a comma for the sake of clarity.

Es ist schwer so früh auf**zu**stehen.
Es ist Zeit jetzt auf**zu**hören.

When a separable prefix is in the infinitive form, the **zu** comes between the prefix and the base form of the verb.

The construction *um ... zu* + infinitive

Amerikaner kommen oft nach Deutschland, **um** dort **zu** studieren.

Americans often come to Germany *in order to* study there.

The German construction **um ... zu** + infinitive is equivalent to the English construction *(in order) to* + infinitive.

Comparison of adjectives and adverbs

■ *Forms of the comparative and superlative*

Base form	klein	*small*	schön	*beautiful*
Comparative	**kleiner**	*smaller*	**schöner**	***more beautiful***
Superlative	**kleinst-**	*smallest*	**schönst-**	*most beautiful*

German forms the comparative by adding the suffix **-er** to the base form. It forms the superlative by adding the suffix **-st** to the base form. The ending **-est** is added to words ending in **-d (gesündest-), -t (leichtest-),** or a sibilant **(kürzest-).** An exception is **größt-.**

Base form	alt	groß	jung
Comparative	**älter**	**größer**	**jünger**
Superlative	**ältest-**	**größt-**	**jüngst-**

Many one-syllable adjectives and adverbs with stem vowel **a, o,** or **u** add an umlaut in the comparative and the superlative.

Base form	gern	gut	hoch	viel
Comparative	**lieber**	**besser**	**höher**	**mehr**
Superlative	**liebst-**	**best-**	**höchst-**	**meist-**

A few adjectives and adverbs are irregular in the comparative and superlative forms.

■ *Special constructions and uses*

Bernd ist nicht **so groß wie** Jens.
Es ist heute **so kalt wie** gestern.

Bernd is not *as tall as* Jens.
Today it is just *as cold as* yesterday.

In German the construction **so ... wie** is used to make comparisons of equality. It is equivalent to English *as . . . as.*

Erika ist **größer als** ihre Mutter.
Es ist **kälter als** gestern.

Erika is *taller than* her mother.
It is *colder than* yesterday.

The comparative form of an adjective or adverb is used to make comparisons of inequality. **Als** is equivalent to English *than.*

Verena singt **am schönsten.**
Im Frühling ist das Wetter hier **am schönsten.**
Die kleinsten Blumen sind **die schönsten.**

Verena sings *the best.*
The weather here is *nicest* in the spring.
The smallest flowers are *the prettiest* (flowers).

The pattern **am** + superlative with the ending **-en** is used for adverbs (as in the first example above), and for predicate adjectives (as in the second example). The superlative of attributive adjectives, with a following noun that is expressed or understood, is preceded by the article **der/das/die** (as in the third example). The superlative form of the adjective therefore has an ending.

LERNZIELE

Sprechintentionen
Talking about cultural events
Making and responding to an invitation
Asking about cultural interests
Asking someone about her/his past

Lesestück
Deutschland: 1945 bis heute

Vokabeln
The suffix *-ung*
Immer + comparative
City names used as adjectives
Dates

Land und Leute
Bertolt Brecht
Two German states
After unification
Germany: The government

Grammatik
Simple past tense
Past perfect tense
Conjunctions *als, wenn,* and *wann*

Deutschland: 1945 bis heute

Berlin: Die größte Baustelle Europas.

BAUSTEINE FÜR GESPRÄCHE

Wie war's?

MICHAEL: Wo warst du gestern Abend?

GISELA: Ich war mit Alex im Theater, im Berliner Ensemble.

MICHAEL: Ah, und was gab es? Wie war es?

GISELA: Man spielte ein Brecht-Stück, *Leben des Galilei.* Es war sehr interessant.

MICHAEL: Hattet ihr gute Plätze?

GISELA: Ja, wir hatten ganz prima Plätze. Wir hatten sogar Studentenkarten. Die kosteten nur zehn Mark, und wir konnten wirklich gut sehen.

MICHAEL: Würdest du das Stück empfehlen?

GISELA: Ja, unbedingt. Ich wollte es zuerst gar nicht sehen, aber dann fand ich es absolut toll.

MICHAEL: In der Zeitung stand ja eine gute Kritik.

GISELA: Naja, und danach gingen wir noch in die Wunder-Bar, tranken etwas und unterhielten uns lange über das Stück.

MICHAEL: Du, ich habe Karten für die Oper nächste Woche. Hättest du Lust mitzugehen?

Fragen

1. Wo war Gisela gestern Abend?
2. Mit wem war sie dort?
3. Was haben sie gesehen?
4. Was für Karten hatten sie?
5. Wie war das Stück?
6. Was würde Michael gern tun?

Brauchbares

1. When Michael asks, **"Würdest du das Stück empfehlen?"** he is using a common German construction that consists of a form of **würde** and the infinitive of a verb. It is equivalent to *would* + a verb in English. This **würde**-construction will be practiced in *Kapitel 11.*
2. Note that to say something is written or printed somewhere, e.g., in a newspaper or sentence, German uses the verb **stehen.** Thus Michael says, **"In der Zeitung stand ja eine gute Kritik."**
3. In Michael's question, **"Hättest du Lust mitzugehen?"** **hättest** is the subjunctive form of **haben.** The subjunctive is used to make a statement more polite and will be presented in *Kapitel 11.*

1. Wo warst du?   Ihre Partnerin/Ihr Partner ist gestern Abend ausgegangen. Finden Sie heraus, wo sie/er war und wie der Abend war.

Talking about cultural events

S1:

Wo warst du gestern Abend?

Was gab es?

Hattet ihr gute Plätze?

S2:

Im Theater.
Im Konzert.
Im Kino.
In der Oper°.

Die Dreigroschenoper
  [*The Threepenny Opera*].
Goethes *Faust.*
Ende gut, alles gut.
Die Zauberflöte [*The Magic Flute*].
Fidelio.
Lohengrin.
Beethovens *Neunte.*
Schumanns *Klavierkonzert°.*

Ja, wir bekamen sogar Studentenkarten.
Ja, und die kosteten nur [zwanzig] Mark.
Ja, wir konnten wirklich gut [sehen/hören].
Ja, wir hatten ganz prima Plätze.
Leider nein, die guten waren zu teuer.

2. Hast du Lust?   Laden Sie Ihre Partnerin/Ihren Partner ein, mit Ihnen zusammen auszugehen. Der Partner/die Partnerin kann ja oder nein sagen.

Making and responding to an invitation

S1:

Hast du Lust **in die Oper** zu gehen?

ins | Musical
Theater
Konzert
Popkonzert°
Open-Air-Konzert°
Kino

S2:

Ja, gern.
In welche?/In welches?
Oh ja, das interessiert mich sehr.
Wenn du mich einlädst, schon.
Nein, ich habe leider keine Zeit.
Nein, ich habe wirklich keine Lust.

3. Gehst du mit?   In einer Gruppe von drei bis vier Studenten sprechen Sie darüber, was Sie am Wochenende machen wollen. Wollen Sie z.B. ins Theater, in die Oper, in ein Konzert oder in ein Musical gehen? Wenn Sie sich entschieden° haben, besprechen° Sie auch, wie viel Geld Sie für die Karten ausgeben° wollen und was Sie danach° tun wollen. Benutzen Sie die folgenden Ausdrücke.

decided / discuss
spend / afterwards

Ich möchte ins [...].
Ich würde lieber [...].
Das ist [...].

⬦ **4. Interview.**   Fragen Sie Ihre Partnerin/Ihren Partner, was ihr/ihm gefällt. Schreiben Sie die Antworten auf und erzählen Sie den anderen Kursteilnehmerinnen/Kursteilnehmern, was Sie herausgefunden haben.

Fragen Sie Ihre Partnerin/Ihren Partner,

1. ob sie/er oft ins Theater geht.
2. was für Theaterstücke sie/er gern sieht.
3. ob sie/er lieber ins Kino geht.
4. wie oft sie/er ins Kino geht – einmal in der Woche, zweimal im Monat, usw.
5. welche neuen Filme sie/er gut findet.
6. ob sie/er manchmal in die Oper geht.
7. welche Opern sie/er kennt.
8. ob sie/er oft ins Konzert geht.
9. was für Musik sie/er gern hört.
10. welche Rockbands sie/er gut findet.
11. welche Fernsehsendungen° sie/er gut findet.

Erweiterung des Wortschatzes

The suffix -ung

wandern	to hike	die Wanderung, -en	*hike*
wohnen	to live	die Wohnung, -en	*dwelling, apartment*

The suffix **-ung** may be added to a verb stem (e.g., **wander-, wohn-**) to form a noun. All nouns ending in **-ung** are feminine.

form

1. Eine Einladung.   Katja erzählt von einer Party bei Rolf Braun. Bilden° Sie Substantive mit der Endung **-ung** aus den fett gedruckten Verben und ergänzen Sie die Sätze. Geben Sie dann das englische Äquivalent für die Substantive wieder.

1. Rolf Braun hat mich für Samstagabend **eingeladen.** Habt ihr auch eine

   _____ bekommen?

2. Ja, aber Mark hat sich vor einer Woche **erkältet** und seine _____ wird einfach nicht besser.

3. Vielleicht hast du Glück. Du weißt, Rolf **sammelt** schon seit Jahren Automodelle und er möchte uns seine _____ zeigen.

4. Und er **beschreibt** jedes Modell sehr genau. Solche _____ finde ich langweilig.

5. Du, er **erzählt** oft Anekdoten von den Modellen. Seine _____ sind immer interessant.

6. **Meinst** du? Ich habe eigentlich eine andere _____.

Bertolt Brecht.

Bertolt Brecht

LAND UND LEUTE

Go to the
Deutsch heute Web Site at
www.hmco.com/college

Bertolt Brecht (1898–1956) is one of the most important figures of the twentieth-century theater. His dramatic theories have influenced many playwrights and theater directors throughout the world. As a young playwright during the twenties, Brecht took the German theater by storm with *The Threepenny Opera (Die Dreigroschenoper);* it shocked and fascinated audiences with its depiction of London's criminal underworld and the social and political forces underlying it. Brecht's critical focus on society and his dramatic theories revolutionized the German stage and made him a celebrity.

As an outspoken opponent of National Socialism, however, Bertolt Brecht had to flee Germany in 1933. He lived temporarily in several European countries until he settled down in California. Like many other German emigrants, he found refuge in the United States until the end of World War II and the end of the National Socialist regime. Brecht wrote some of his major plays in exile: *Mutter Courage und ihre Kinder* (1941), *Der gute Mensch von Sezuan* (1942), *Leben des Galilei* (1943).

In 1947, after he had been called before the House Committee on Un-American Activities, he moved back to Europe and eventually chose the German Democratic Republic as his home. With his wife, Helene Weigel, he founded the *Berliner Ensemble,* a theater in former East Berlin that continues to perform Brecht's plays and tries to put his theories into practice.

Diskussion

During the Third Reich many Germans, like Brecht, left Germany. This choice is often called **"äußere Emigration"** in contrast to **"innere Emmigration"** which refers to writers, artists, and intellectual figures who remained in Germany but were unable to publish their work during the Third Reich. Imagine that you are a major novelist living in a dictatorship. Which path would you choose? Which factors would you have to consider in making the decision?

Das Berliner Ensemble spielt Der gute Mensch von Sezuan. *(Bertolt-Brecht-Platz)*

Vokabeln

Beginning with the **Vokabeln** of *Kapitel 10,* the simple past tense of irregular weak and strong verbs (e.g., **empfahl**) is given.

Substantive

die **Bar, -s**   bar, pub; nightclub
die **Hausaufgabe, -n**   homework; **Hausaufgaben machen**   to do homework
das **Klavier, -e**   piano; das **Klavierkonzert**   piano concerto
die **Kritik**   criticism; review
die **Lust**   desire; pleasure; **Lust haben** (+ **zu** + *infinitive*)   to be in the mood, feel like; **ich habe keine Lust das zu tun**   I don't feel like doing that

das **Open-Air-Konzert, -e**   outdoor concert
die **Oper, -n**   opera; **in die Oper gehen**   to go to the opera
das **Popkonzert, -e**   pop concert
die **Rockband, -s**   rock band
die **Sendung, -en**   radio or TV program; die **Fernsehsendung, -en**   TV program

Verben

empfehlen (empfiehlt), empfahl, empfohlen   to recommend

sich unterhalten (unterhält), unterhielt, unterhalten   to talk; **sich unterhalten über** (+ *acc.*) to talk about

Andere Wörter

absolut   absolutely, completely
danach   afterwards
prima   fantastic, great (**prima** *takes no adj. endings*)

sogar   even
unbedingt   without reservation, absolutely

Besondere Ausdrücke

es stand in der Zeitung   it said in the newspaper

was gab es?   what was playing? what was offered?

BURGTHEATER

SPIELZEIT

PREMIEREN   PLÄNE

BERLINER ENSEMBLE

Bertolt Brecht
LEBEN DES GALILEI

DEUTSCHLAND: 1945 BIS HEUTE

Vorbereitung auf das Lesen

■ *Vor dem Lesen*

1. Sie lesen hier über Deutschlands Geschichte zwischen 1945 und heute. Was wissen Sie schon über diese Zeit?
2. Machen Sie eine Liste von Daten, Wörtern oder Namen zu den folgenden Themen. Versuchen Sie mindestens° drei Stichwörter° für jeden Punkt aufzuschreiben°.   *at least / key words*
   a. der Zweite Weltkrieg
   b. Berlin
   c. der Kalte Krieg
   d. die Europäische Union (EU)
3. Berichten Sie einer kleinen Gruppe, was Sie aufgelistet haben.

■ *Beim Lesen*

Machen Sie Notizen von allen Ereignissen°, die° mit dem Kalten Krieg zu tun haben.   *events / that*

Über vier Jahrzehnte° lang gab es praktisch° zwei deutsche Haupt-städte: Bonn und Ost-Berlin. Theoretisch blieb Berlin jedoch immer die Hauptstadt. Als 1994 die letzten alliierten° Soldaten die Stadt verließen, war Berlin erst seit vier Jahren wieder die offizielle Hauptstadt von

5 Deutschland, aber Bonn war noch immer der Sitz° der Regierung. 1945 hat-ten die Alliierten die ehemalige° Hauptstadt des Dritten Reiches° in vier Sektoren aufgeteilt und kontrollierten Berlin bis zur Wiedervereinigung. Wenn die Hauptstadt und Deutschland geteilt waren – so argumentierte man – konnte das Land nie wieder stark genug werden um einen neuen

10 Krieg anzufangen.

    Europa hatte Angst vor einem starken Deutschland, denn es war im 20. Jahrhundert für zwei Weltkriege verantwortlich gewesen. Deutsche Soldaten hatten zwischen 1938 und 1944 außer der Schweiz alle Nachbarländer zu-mindest° eine Zeitlang° besetzt°. Außerdem hatten die Nationalsozialisten   *at least / a while / occupied*

15 nicht nur im eigenen Land, sondern auch in allen besetzten Nachbarländern systematisch die jüdische° Bevölkerung° verfolgt° und in Konzentra-tionslager° gebracht. Im Holocaust starben über sechs Millionen Juden°. Außer den Juden verfolgten die Nationalsozialisten auch noch Zigeuner°, Be-hinderte°, Homosexuelle sowie° ihre politischen Gegner° – die Kommunis-   *Jewish / population / persecuted / concentration camps / Jews / gypsies / the handicapped / as well as / opponents*

20 ten, Sozialisten und Sozialdemokraten.

    Nach dem Ende des Krieges wurden die Spannungen° zwischen den Russen und den drei westlichen Siegermächten° (England, Frankreich und den USA) immer stärker. Sie kulminierten schließlich 1948 in der Berliner Blockade. Die Russen wollten die westlichen Soldaten zwingen Berlin zu ver-   *tensions / victorious powers*

25 lassen und blockierten die Straßen von und nach Berlin. Unter der Führung° Amerikas organisierten die westlichen Alliierten die Berliner Luftbrücke°. Ein Jahr lang versorgten° die Flugzeuge die Stadt mit allem, was die Leute zum   *leadership / airlift / provided*

decades / for all practical purposes
allied
seat
*former / **das Dritte Reich:** the Third Reich*

Während der Luftbrücke 1948 landet in Berlin alle paar Minuten ein Flugzeug.

raisins / coal

Leben brauchten – von Rosinen° bis Kohle°. Und deshalb nannten die
Berliner die Flugzeuge der Luftbrücke „Rosinenbomber". Doch als die Blo-
30 ckade 1949 zu Ende war, gab es zwei souveräne deutsche Staaten: die Bundesrepublik Deutschland (BRD) mit der provisorischen Hauptstadt Bonn und
die Deutsche Demokratische Republik (DDR) mit der Hauptstadt Ost-Berlin.
Der Kalte Krieg hatte begonnen. Die neuen Fronten waren der Ostblock und
der Westblock. Die neue Grenze hieß „der Eiserne Vorhang°". Nicht alle Ost-

der Eiserne Vorhang: the
Iron Curtain

now

35 deutschen waren für den Kommunismus. Da es dem Westen auch wirtschaftlich besser ging als dem Osten, versuchten viele Ostdeutsche nun° ihr
Land zu verlassen. Um den Exodus zu beenden baute die DDR-Regierung
1961 die Mauer. Mit den Worten: „Ich bin ein Berliner!" demonstrierte der
Präsident John F. Kennedy die Solidarität des Westens mit den Berlinern, als
40 er 1963 die geteilte Stadt besuchte.
    In dieser Zeit war die Angst vor dem Kommunismus größer als die Angst
vor einem starken Deutschland. Ein wirtschaftlich und politisch starkes West-
europa sollte vor dem Kommunismus schützen. Besonders Westdeutschland
wollte nach dem Krieg wirtschaftlich, politisch und kulturell mit seinen
45 Nachbarn zusammenarbeiten, um wieder ein Teil Europas zu werden. Es
wollte seinen Nachbarn zeigen, dass es wirklich für den Frieden war. So ent-

was established / community

stand° die Europäische Gemeinschaft° (EG) und ihre ersten Mitglieder waren
außer Deutschland noch Belgien, Frankreich, Italien, Luxemburg und die
Niederlande. In den nächsten Jahrzehnten bekam die EG immer mehr Mit-
50 glieder. Heute heißt die Organisation die Europäische Union (EU) und zu ihr
gehören auch Dänemark, Finnland, Griechenland, Großbritannien, Irland,
Österreich, Portugal, Schweden und Spanien.
    Ende der 80er-Jahre gab es in der wirtschaftlichen Union der Ostblock-
staaten (COMECON) wirtschaftliche und politische Reformen. In der DDR,

55 besonders in Leipzig, kam es 1989 zu großen, friedlichen° Demonstrationen.   peaceful
Die Menschen wollten mehr individuelle Freiheit und am 9. November 1989
musste die Regierung der DDR die Mauer öffnen. Endlich war das verhasste°   hated
Symbol des Kalten Krieges gefallen.
    Seit dem 3. Oktober 1990 sind West- und Ostdeutschland wieder ein
60 Land. Mit ihren 82 Millionen Einwohnern ist die neue Bundesrepublik jetzt
der größte Staat in der EU. Das vereinte° Berlin ist mit über drei Millionen   unified
Einwohnern die größte deutsche Stadt. Der Kalte Krieg war endgültig° vor-   definitely
bei, als 1994, nach 49 Jahren, die Alliierten Berlin offiziell verließen.

Brauchbares

1. l. 6, **das Dritte Reich:** Hitler declared that he would build a third empire,
   successor to the Holy Roman Empire (962–1806) and the Empire (1871–
   1918) established under William I of Prussia. William I was proclaimed Emperor of Germany in 1871.
2. l. 14, **Nationalsozialisten:** National Socialists (Nazis) were members of the
   party of the **Nationalsozialistische Deutsche Arbeiterpartei** that ruled
   Germany under Adolf Hitler from 1933 to 1945. The policies of the party
   were anti-democratic, extremely nationalistic, imperialistic, and virulently
   anti-Semitic.
3. l. 20, **Sozialdemokraten:** Social Democrats were members of the labor-
   oriented Social Democratic party **(Sozialdemokratische Partei Deutschlands).** The party was outlawed by Hitler.
4. l. 23, **immer stärker:** For more information on the construction **immer +**
   comparative, see p. 350.
5. l. 26, **Berliner Luftbrücke:** During the blockade of Berlin **(Berliner Blockade)** the Allies supplied over 2 million West Berliners with food and fuel by
   a round-the-clock air lift. There were 277,264 flights made at 3.5-minute intervals. By the end of the lift in 1949, 8,000 tons of goods (2/3 of it coal) were
   flown in daily. A monument commemorating the U.S. and British airmen
   who died during the airlift stands at Tempelhof Field, the airport in former
   West Berlin that was the main terminal of the airlift.
6. l. 33, **Ostblock:** The eastern block was made up of nations under communist
   domination and the influence of the Soviet Union. COMECON (Council for
   Mutual Economic Assistance) was founded in 1949 but was only active between the years 1956–1991. COMECON was controlled by the heads of state
   and was a vehicle for organizing industrial production and coordinating economic policy.
7. l. 34, **der Eiserne Vorhang:** The Iron Curtain was the name for the political
   and ideological barrier that prevented understanding between the Soviet bloc
   and western Europe after World War II. The expression became current after it
   was used by Winston Churchill in a speech at Fulton, Missouri, in 1946.
8. l. 38, **Worten:** The German word **Wort** has two plurals. The plural form,
   Worte, is used for words in context. The other plural, **Wörter,** is used for
   words not in a particular context as in a dictionary or list.

Nach dem Lesen

1. Fragen zum Lesestück

1. Wie viele Jahre gab es zwei deutsche Hauptstädte?
2. Warum teilten die Alliierten Berlin auf?
3. Gebrauchen Sie eine Landkarte und machen Sie eine Liste von den Ländern, die° Deutschland im Zweiten Weltkrieg besetzt hat.

which

4. Die Nazis verfolgten viele Gruppen. Nennen Sie diese Gruppen.
5. Welche Gruppe verfolgten die Nazis am konsequentesten?
6. Was ist im Holocaust passiert?
7. Warum blockierten die Russen im Jahre 1948 Berlin?
8. Was nannten die Berliner „Rosinenbomber"? Warum?
9. Zwischen welchen Jahren gab es zwei deutsche Staaten?
10. Was wollte John F. Kennedy zeigen, als er sagte: „Ich bin ein Berliner"?
11. Warum wollte Deutschland Mitglied der Europäischen Gemeinschaft werden?
12. Wer waren die ersten Mitglieder der westlichen Wirtschaftsunion?
13. Warum demonstrierten viele Menschen 1989 in der DDR?
14. Mit welchem Wort beschreibt das Lesestück die Revolution in Leipzig?

2. Der Kalte Krieg

scene

compare

1. Viele Historiker sagen, dass Deutschland ein wichtiger Schauplatz° des Kalten Krieges war. Beim Lesen des Textes haben Sie Notizen zum Thema Kalter Krieg gemacht. Vergleichen° Sie Ihre Notizen mit der folgenden Liste. Was haben Sie aufgeschrieben, was nicht auf dieser Liste steht?

events / **ordnen ein:** arrange
geben an: give

2. Ordnen° Sie die folgenden Ereignisse° chronologisch ein, und geben° Sie ein Jahr oder eine Zeit an.

Chronologie	Jahr	Ereignis
_____	_____	der Zweite Weltkrieg
_____	_____	Gründung° der BRD und der DDR
_____	_____	die alliierten Truppen verlassen Berlin
_____	_____	Bau° der Mauer
_____	_____	Aufteilung° Berlins
_____	_____	Vereinigung Deutschlands
_____	_____	Fall der Mauer
_____	_____	die Luftbrücke
_____	_____	Reformen in den Ostblockländern
_____	_____	Demonstrationen in Leipzig
_____	_____	Gründung einer Wirtschaftsunion im Westen

establishment

construction

division

Zwei deutsche Staaten

LAND UND LEUTE

Two German states existed from 1949–1990. In the later years of the separation, West Germany (The Federal Republic of Germany/**Die Bundesrepublik Deutschland**) referred to this situation as "two states, but one nation" **(zwei Staaten, eine Nation),** and its constitution assumed a future reunification. East Germany (The German Democratic Republic/**Die Deutsche Demokratische Republik**), in contrast, was increasingly dedicated to building an independent, separate country. While West Germany developed a market economy, East Germany followed an economic system of central planning. While the citizens of East Germany liked the fact that there was no unemployment, that government subsidies kept rents and prices of food staples low, and that the government provided health care and a pension system, they found that the political system restricted individual freedom, and the scarcity of non-staple consumer goods was a daily irritant.

The construction of the Berlin Wall **(Mauerbau)** in 1961 was the most dramatic attempt to stop the wave of people leaving East Germany. In addition, the gradual build-up of the border system of fences, dogs, and minefields between the two states had made the border practically impenetrable.

In the early seventies, Willy Brandt, Chancellor of the Federal Republic of Germany, made the first open overtures to East Germany (part of his **Ostpolitik**) and thereby laid the groundwork for cooperation with East Germany. In the course of the years the climate between the two countries improved. At first retirees **(Rentner)** and later others from East Germany were allowed to visit West Germany, permanent representations similar to embassies **(ständige Vertretungen)** were established, and West Germans living in border areas were allowed to travel more freely across the border **(grenznaher Verkehr)**.

In 1989, the overall political climate in eastern European countries began to change. Hungary was the first to open the Iron Curtain by taking down the barbed wire and letting vacationing East Germans cross into Austria. A democratic movement spread throughout the Warsaw Pact countries, of which East Germany was a member. Throughout East Germany there were large demonstrations and in November 1989, the government opened the Berlin Wall and subsequently resigned. The freedom movement culminated in free elections in March 1990.

Go to the
Deutsch heute Web Site at
www.hmco.com/college

Diskussion

In both the East and the West the Germans expressed their feelings about the divided state. During the protests in East Germany, the people marched carrying banners with slogans, while in the West, people had covered the Berlin Wall with graffiti.
Explain the meaning of the following slogans from that time.

August 1961: Bau der Berliner Mauer.

1. Wir sind ein Volk°.
2. Auf die Dauer° fällt die Mauer.
3. Wende° ohne Umkehr°.
4. Privilegien° weg! Wir sind das Volk!

people
auf die Dauer: in the long run / change (revolution of 1989) / turning back / perks provided to the functionaries of the ruling party

3. Erzählen wir. Erklären Sie in einfachen Worten die folgenden Ereignisse oder Daten. Ihr Publikum spricht nur wenig Deutsch.

der Holocaust
die Luftbrücke
der 3. Oktober 1990
die EU

Erweiterung des Wortschatzes

1. *Immer* + comparative

Seit dem Krieg ist der Lebensstandard der Deutschen **immer mehr** gestiegen.

Since the war, the living standard of the Germans has risen *more and more.*

The construction **immer** + comparative indicates an increase in the quantity, quality, or degree expressed by the adjective or adverb. In English, the comparative is repeated (e.g., *more and more*).

1. Wie geht es den Deutschen heute?   Frau Weiß, die während des Krieges eine junge Frau war, erzählt Ihnen und Ihrem Freund, wie sich das Leben in Deutschland seit dem Ende des Krieges verändert hat. Ihr Freund versteht kein Deutsch, also übersetzen° Sie die Aussagen° von Frau Weiß ins Englische.

translate / statements

1. Der Lebensstandard der Deutschen wird immer höher.
2. Die Wohnungen werden immer größer.
3. Sie tragen immer bessere Kleidung.
4. Die Arbeitszeit wird immer kürzer.
5. Die Ferien werden immer länger.
6. Immer weniger Leute bleiben während der Ferien zu Hause.
7. Das Leben wird immer schöner.
8. Immer mehr Ausländer wollen in Deutschland einwandern°.

immigrate

2. City names used as adjectives

1948 organisierten die Alliierten die **Berliner** Luftbrücke.
Das Café Demel ist ein sehr bekanntes **Wiener** Kaffeehaus.

In 1948 the Allies organized the *Berlin* airlift.
The café Demel is a very well-known *Viennese* coffee house.

Names of cities used as adjectives end in **-er.** The **-er** ending is never declined, i.e., no additional adjective endings are used to indicate gender or case.

3. Dates

1945 teilten die Alliierten Berlin in vier Sektoren auf.
Im Jahre 1963 besuchte Präsident Kennedy Berlin.

In 1945 the Allies divided Berlin into four sectors.
In 1963 President Kennedy visited Berlin.

In dates that contain only the year, German uses either the year by itself (e.g., **1945**) or the phrase **im Jahr(e) 1945.** English uses the phrase *in* + the year (e.g., *in 1945*).

Vokabeln

Substantive

die **Brücke, -n** bridge
die **Bundesrepublik Deutschland** Federal Republic of Germany (*the name of West Germany from 1949 to 1990; today the official name for all of Germany*)
die **Demonstration, -en** demonstration
der **Flughafen, ⁻** airport
der **Frieden** peace
die **Gefahr, -en** danger

die **Grenze, -n** border, boundary; limit
die **Mauer, -n** wall
der **Präsident, -en, -en**/die **Präsidentin, -nen** president
die **Regierung, -en** government
der **Soldat, -en, -en**/die **Soldatin, -nen** soldier
der **Teil, -e** part
die **Wiedervereinigung** reunification

Verben

an·fangen (fängt an), fing an, angefangen to begin
auf·schreiben, schrieb auf, aufgeschrieben to write down
bauen to build
berichten to report
fallen (fällt), fiel, ist gefallen to fall
öffnen to open
schützen to protect

sterben (stirbt), starb, ist gestorben to die
teilen to divide; **auf·teilen (in + acc.)** to split up (into)
verlassen (verlässt), verließ, verlassen to leave, abandon
zerstören to destroy
zwingen, zwang, gezwungen to force, compel

Andere Wörter

als (*sub. conj.*) when
eigen own
nie never
noch immer still
politisch political(ly)

verantwortlich (für) responsible (for)
vorbei over; gone
westlich Western

Besondere Ausdrücke

zu Ende over, finished

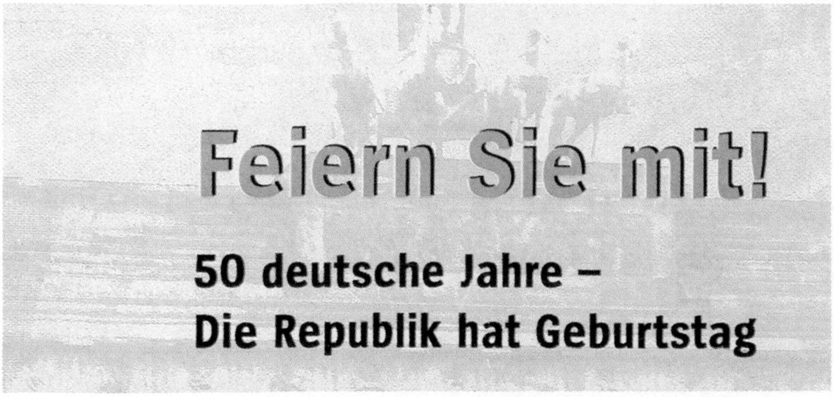

Feiern Sie mit!
**50 deutsche Jahre –
Die Republik hat Geburtstag**

Nach der Vereinigung

When the Berlin Wall fell (9 November 1989), few observers believed that East and West Germany would be unified less than a year later. Unification came about in two major stages. In July 1990, economic union occurred when the **Deutsche Mark** became the common currency of East and West Germany. On 3 October 1990, political unification was completed and the districts of former East Germany were regrouped into five new states **(Länder)**, referred to as **FNL (Fünf Neue Länder): Mecklenburg-Vorpommern, Brandenburg, Sachsen-Anhalt, Sachsen,** and **Thüringen.** Berlin also acquired the full status of a **Bundesland.** The first all-German elections followed in December 1990. For the most part, unification meant that West German laws applied in the new states.

Economic unification revealed that the economy of East Germany, the strongest in Eastern Europe and supporting the highest living standard in that area, was by western standards in a shambles. Unemployment grew rapidly. To facilitate the conversion to a market economy, the German government established a trustee agency **(Treuhandanstalt).** It broke up the state-owned combines **(Kombinate)** and helped establish 30,000 private businesses, arranging for new or restructured ownership. West Germans have been paying a surtax to finance these changes. So far, unification has cost Germans hundreds of billions of marks, resulting in a substantial budget deficit.

Neues Einkaufszentrum am Potsdamerplatz in Berlin.

Unification also called for coordination of social and governmental services in the east and west. Generally, for former East Germans, it meant fewer social benefits and government services than before unification. At the same time consumer prices rose substantially.

In addition to these political and economic considerations, the two parts of Germany were faced with the necessity of adjusting to each other on a personal level. The social division was reflected in the terms **"Ossis"** (eastern Germans) and **"Wessis"** (western Germans). **Wessis** accused the **Ossis** of being lazy while the **Ossis** perceived the **Wessis** as arrogant and unfriendly.

Diskussion

Even some ten years after unification, one still hears of the **"Mauer im Kopf."** What do you think that the **Mauer im Kopf** is? What is your interpretation of this expression?

GRAMMATIK UND ÜBUNGEN

1. The simple past tense° vs. the present perfect tense

das Präteritum

The simple past tense, like the present perfect (see *Kapitel 6*), is used to refer to events in the past. However, the simple past and the present perfect are used in different circumstances.

■ *Uses of the simple past*

Als ich zehn Jahre alt **war, wohnten** wir in Berlin. Da **stand** die Mauer noch. Die Leute aus Ostberlin **konnten** nicht zu uns in den Westen kommen. Das **verstand** ich nicht.	When I *was* ten years old, we *lived* in Berlin. The wall *was* still *standing* then. The people from East Berlin *could*n't come to us in the West. I *did*n't *understand* that.

The simple past tense (e.g., **wohnten, stand**) is often called the narrative past because it narrates a series of connected events in the past. It is used more frequently in formal writing—literature, newspaper articles, recipes, directions, etc.

■ *Uses of the present perfect tense*

MONIKA: **Hast** du gestern Abend **ferngesehen?**	*Did* you *watch* TV last night?
DIETER: Nein, ich **habe** ein paar Briefe **geschrieben.**	No, I *wrote* a few letters.

The present perfect tense (e.g., **hat ferngesehen, hat geschrieben**) is also called the conversational past because it is used in conversational contexts and in informal writing such as personal letters, diaries, and notes, all of which are actually a form of written "conversation."

Note that English always uses the simple past (e.g., *did you watch, wrote*) when referring to an action completed in the past.

■ *Uses of* **sein, haben,** *and modals in the simple past*

MONIKA: Jürgen **konnte** am Freitag nicht kommen.
DIETER: **War** er krank oder **hatte** er keine Zeit?
MONIKA: Er **war** leider krank.

The simple past tense forms of **sein (war), haben (hatte),** and the modals (e.g., **konnte**) are used more frequently than the present perfect tense, even in conversation.

**Haus der Geschichte
der Bundesrepublik Deutschland**

Dienstag bis Sonntag 9.00 - 19.00 Uhr, Eintritt frei.

Museumsmeile Adenauerallee 250 53113 Bonn
Tel.: 02 28/91 65-0 Fax: 02 28/91 65-3 02 www.hdg.de

2. *Sein* and *haben* in the simple past tense

sein		haben	
ich war	wir war**en**	ich hatte	wir hatt**en**
du war**st**	ihr war**t**	du hatte**st**	ihr hatte**t**
er/es/sie war	sie war**en**	er/es/sie hatte	sie hatt**en**
Sie war**en**		Sie hatt**en**	

You learned in *Kapitel 2* that the simple past tense of **sein** is **war.** The simple past tense of **haben** is **hatte.** In the simple past, all forms except the **ich-** and **er/es/sie-**forms add verb endings.

1. Noch einmal.   Wiederholen Sie die Kurzgespräche noch einmal im Präteritum.

⟫ Wie ist das neue Musical?   *Wie war das neue Musical?*
   —Ach, es ist nichts Besonderes.   *—Ach, es war nichts Besonderes.*

1. Bist du in den Ferien zu Hause?
   —Nein, ich bin bei meinem Onkel.
2. Seid ihr heute in der Bibliothek?
   —Ja, wir sind den ganzen Tag da.
3. Ist das Buch interessant?
   —Nein, es ist furchtbar langweilig.

excursion

2. In den Bergen.   Erzählen Sie Ihrer Freundin, warum Sie und einige andere Leute nicht zu einem Ausflug° in die Berge mitgekommen sind.

⟫ Dennis _____ viel Arbeit.   *Dennis hatte viel Arbeit.*

1. Irma _____ eine Erkältung.

2. Ich _____ eigentlich keine Zeit.

3. Wir _____ Besuch aus England.

4. Simon _____ keine guten Wanderschuhe.

5. Nils und Anke _____ eine Vorlesung.

6. Markus _____ Angst.

3. Modals in the simple past

Infinitive	Past stem	Tense marker	Simple past	English equivalent
dürfen	durf-	-te	**durfte**	was allowed to
können	konn-	-te	**konnte**	was able to
mögen	moch-	-te	**mochte**	liked
müssen	muss-	-te	**musste**	had to
sollen	soll-	-te	**sollte**	was supposed to
wollen	woll-	-te	**wollte**	wanted to

In the simple past tense, most modals undergo a stem change. The past tense marker **-te** is added to the simple past stem. Note that the past stem has no umlaut.

können	
ich konnte	wir konnte**n**
du konnte**st**	ihr konnte**t**
er/es/sie konnte	sie konnte**n**
Sie konnte**n**	

In the simple past, all forms except the **ich-** and **er/es/sie-**forms add verb endings to the **-te** tense marker.

3. Auf einem Geburtstagsfest. Sie und Ihre Freunde organisierten ein Fest. Erzählen Sie, was passierte. Benutzen Sie die Modalverben im Präteritum.

≫ Ich will meine Freunde einladen. *Ich wollte meine Freunde einladen.*

1. Klaus kann die CDs nicht mitbringen.
2. Katja muss noch abwaschen.
3. Frank will abtrocknen.
4. Michael soll das Wohnzimmer sauber machen.
5. Die Gäste sollen in zwei Stunden kommen.
6. Wir müssen daher schnell aufräumen.
7. Jens kann leider nicht lange bleiben.

1949–1999

50 Jahre
Bundesrepublik Deutschland

⬜▷ **4. Frage-Ecke.**   Letzte Woche hatten Sie, Ihre Partnerin/Ihr Partner und einige andere Leute viel zu tun. Finden Sie heraus, wer was tun konnte, wollte, sollte und musste.

S1: Was wollte Adrian tun?
S2: Er wollte mehr Sport treiben.

S1:

	konnte	wollte	sollte	musste
Bettina		mit ihrer Diät beginnen	ein Referat schreiben	
Adrian	seine Arbeit fertig machen			die Garage aufräumen
Frau Müller	sich mit Freunden unterhalten	eine kurze Reise nach Paris machen		
Herr Meier			seinem Sohn bei der Arbeit helfen	sich einen neuen Computer kaufen
ich				
Partnerin/ Partner				

S2:

	konnte	wollte	sollte	musste
Bettina	jeden Tag genug schlafen			die Fenster putzen
Adrian		mehr Sport treiben	seine Großeltern besuchen	
Frau Müller			mit ihren Freunden Golf spielen	Babysitting bei ihrer Tochter machen
Herr Meier	jeden Tag spazieren gehen	einen neuen Krimi lesen		
ich				
Partnerin/ Partner				

5. Meine Kindheit.   Vergleichen Sie Ihre Kindheit mit der Kindheit Ihrer Partnerin/Ihres Partners. Beantworten Sie erst die folgenden Fragen für sich selbst. Dann fragen Sie Ihre Partnerin/Ihren Partner. Schließlich erzählen Sie Ihren Kursteilnehmerinnen/Kursteilnehmern von Ihrer eigenen Kindheit und der Ihrer Partnerin/Ihres Partners.

Asking someone about her/his past

1. Musstest du deinen Eltern viel helfen?
2. Durftest du viel fernsehen?
3. Musstest du sonntags Hausaufgaben machen?
4. Wie lange durftest du abends ausbleiben?
5. Um wie viel Uhr musstest du ins Bett gehen?
6. Konntest du machen, was du wolltest?
7. Was durftest du nicht machen?
8. Was wolltest du werden, als du ein Kind warst?

4. Regular weak verbs in the simple past

Infinitive	Stem	Tense marker	Simple past
machen	mach-	-te	machte
sagen	sag-	-te	sagte
reden	red-	-ete	redete
arbeiten	arbeit-	-ete	arbeitete
regnen	regn-	-ete	regnete

In the simple past tense, regular weak verbs add the past-tense marker **-te** to the infinitive stem. Regular weak verbs with a stem ending in **-d (reden)** or **-t (arbeiten)** and verbs like **regnen** and **öffnen** insert an **-e** before the tense marker. The addition of the **-e** ensures that the **-t,** as a signal of the past, is audible. This is parallel to the insertion of the extra **-e** in the present tense (**er arbeitet;** past tense **er arbeitete**).

machen	
ich machte	wir machten
du machte**st**	ihr machtet
er/es/sie machte	sie machten
Sie machten	

reden	
ich redete	wir redeten
du redete**st**	ihr redetet
er/es/sie redete	sie redeten
Sie redeten	

In the simple past, all forms except the **ich-** and **er/es/sie-**forms add verb endings to the **-te** tense marker.

6. So war es früher.   Erzählen Sie, was Sie und Ihr Freund Michael vor einigen Jahren gemacht haben. Benutzen Sie das Präteritum.

➤➤ Ich arbeite in einem Supermarkt.   *Ich arbeitete in einem Supermarkt.*

1. Ich verdiene natürlich sehr wenig.
2. Mein Freund Michael lernt nicht genug Mathe.
3. Aber er baut die besten Flugzeugmodelle.
4. Er sammelt viele davon.
5. Sein Vater kritisiert° ihn oft.
6. Die beiden reden nicht wirklich miteinander.
7. Michael und ich machen nicht genug Hausaufgaben°.
8. Wir hören zu viel Rockmusik.

7. Wir fahren zelten.   Erzählen Sie im Präteritum, wie Ihr Wochenende auf
dem Campingplatz war.

➤➤ Am Samstag regnet es nicht.   *Am Samstag regnete es nicht.*

1. Gerd arbeitet nur bis 12 Uhr.
2. Gerd und Klaus machen eine Wanderung.
3. Sie zelten in den Bergen.
4. Susi und Alex warten am Campingplatz auf ihre Freunde.
5. Alle baden im See°.
6. Am Abend öffnen sie eine Flasche Bier.
7. Sie reden über dies und das.
8. Sie machen schon Pläne für die nächste Wanderung.

5. Irregular weak verbs in the simple past

Infinitive	Past stem	Tense marker	Simple past	Examples
bringen	brach-	-te	**brachte**	Peter brachte die Blumen nach Hause.
denken	dach-	-te	**dachte**	Jutta dachte an ihre Arbeit.
kennen	kann-	-te	**kannte**	Wir kannten ihre Chefin.
nennen	nann-	-te	**nannte**	Sie nannten das Kind nach dem Vater.
wissen	wuss-	-te	**wusste**	Du wusstest das schon, nicht?

German has a few weak verbs that have a stem vowel change in the simple
past. (For this reason they are called *irregular* weak verbs.) The verbs **bringen**
and **denken** also have a consonant change. The tense marker **-te** is added to the
simple past stem. Several of the most common irregular weak verbs are listed in
the chart above.

bringen	
ich brachte	wir brachten
du brachte**st**	ihr brachtet
er/es/sie brachte	sie brachten
Sie brachten	

In the simple past, all forms except the **ich-** and **er/es/sie-**forms add verb endings to the **-te** tense marker.

8. Vor Jahren.   So haben viele Leute vor zwanzig Jahren die Rolle der Frauen gesehen. Berichten Sie von den Meinungen im Präteritum.

➤➤ Viele Leute haben wenig über die Emanzipation gewusst.
   Viele Leute wussten wenig über die Emanzipation.

1. Sie haben nur typische Rollen von Mann und Frau gekannt.
2. Viele Frauen haben aber anders gedacht.
3. Sie haben andere Ideen gehabt.
4. Die Kinder haben so wie die Eltern gedacht.
5. Wir haben auch die Probleme gekannt.
6. Die Frau hat oft nur die Hausarbeit gekannt.
7. Sie haben berufstätige Frauen „Rabenmütter°" genannt.   unfit mothers

9. Eine Reise in die USA.   Letztes Jahr war Bettina in den USA. Erzählen Sie von ihrer Reise und benutzen Sie das Präteritum.

1. Last summer Bettina made a trip to the U.S.A.
2. She traveled to Boston. [use **reisen**]
3. She thought Boston was [use **sein**] great.
4. She could speak English well.
5. She wanted to study at a university there.
6. The semester cost a lot of money.
7. At a party, she talked with a German student. [use **reden**]
8. They talked about life in America. [use **reden**]
9. He knew a lot about Boston.
10. Bettina had many questions.

6. Separable-prefix verbs in the simple past

Present	Simple past
Wolf **kauft** für seine Freunde **ein.**	Wolf **kaufte** für seine Freunde **ein.**
Er **bringt** für alle etwas zu trinken **mit.**	Er **brachte** für alle etwas zu trinken **mit.**

In the simple past, as in the present, the separable prefix is separated from the base form of the verb and is in final position.

10. Eine Party. Erzählen Sie, wie Ihre Freunde eine Party vorbereiteten. Bilden Sie Sätze im Präteritum.

➤➤ Lilo / aufräumen / die Wohnung   *Lilo räumte die Wohnung auf.*

1. Ralf / einkaufen
2. er / mitbringen / vom Markt / Blumen
3. Lilo und Theo / zurückzahlen / es / ihm
4. Theo / vorbereiten / das Essen
5. erst um sechs / sie / aufhören / zu arbeiten

7. Strong verbs in the simple past

Infinitive	Simple past stem	Examples
sprechen	sprach	Adrian sprach mit Bettina.
gehen	ging	Bettina ging ins Theater.

A strong verb undergoes a stem change in the simple past. The tense marker **-te** is not added to a strong verb in the simple past tense.

sprechen		
ich sprach	wir sprach**en**	
du sprach**st**	ihr sprach**t**	
er/es/sie sprach	sie sprach**en**	
Sie sprach**en**		

In the simple past, all forms except the **ich-** and **er/es/sie-**forms add verb endings to the simple past stem. The stem change of strong verbs cannot always be predicted, but you will probably not have trouble guessing the infinitive form and thus the meaning of most of the verbs. While there are thousands of weak verbs, the number of strong verbs in German is fortunately relatively small. This book uses approximately 60 strong verbs. The list of these verbs is found in the Grammatical Tables in the Reference Section. In the vocabularies of this book, the simple past stem is printed after the infinitive, followed by the past participle: **liegen, lag, gelegen.**

strange / experience   **11. Alexanders merkwürdiges° Erlebnis°.**   Lesen Sie die folgende Anekdote und setzen Sie alle fett gedruckten Verben ins Präteritum. Benutzen Sie die Liste mit dem Präteritum der Verben am Ende des Textes.

Heute **gehe** ich in der Fußgängerzone einkaufen. Plötzlich **steht** ein Mann vor mir, **sieht** mir in die Augen und **sagt:** „Hallo, Stefan. Wie geht's denn?" „Na, gut, danke", **antworte** ich und **weiß** nicht, was ich im Moment noch sagen **soll,** denn ich **weiß** seinen Namen nicht. Er **will,** dass wir zusammen essen gehen, **empfiehlt** ein gutes Lokal und wir **gehen** hin. Das Essen **ist** gut und wir **trinken** eine Flasche Wein dazu. Beim Essen **spricht** er über dies und das. Ich **sage** sehr wenig. „Du kennst mich nicht mehr", **sagt** er. „Doch", **sage** ich, aber es ist nicht wahr. Nach dem Essen **sagt** er: „Ich rufe dich in einer Woche an. Vielleicht können wir uns wieder treffen." „Das wäre schön", **antworte** ich. Ich

Deutschland: die Regierung

LAND UND LEUTE

I n the Federal Republic of Germany each state **(Bundesland)** has a constitution. However, the central government is strong.

National elections to the House of Representatives **(der Bundestag)** take place every four years. All German citizens over 18 have a "first vote" **(Erststimme)** and a "second vote" **(Zweitstimme),** which permits them to vote for a particular candidate as well as for a political party. The representative one votes for need not belong to the party one votes for. The constitution **(Grundgesetz)** of the Federal Republic stipulates that a political party has to have a minimum of 5% of all the votes cast to be represented in the **Bundestag.**

The **Bundestag** is the only federal body elected directly by the people. The Federal Council **(Bundesrat)** represents the federal states **(Bundesländer)** and is made up of members of the state governments or their representatives. The President **(Bundespräsident/ Bundespräsidentin)** is elected by the Federal Convention (comparable to the U.S. Electoral College). The President's tasks are mainly ceremonial in nature.

The head of the government in the Federal Republic of Germany is the Federal Chancellor **(Bundeskanzler/Bundeskanzlerin),** who is nominated by the President and elected by the **Bundestag.**

Go to the
Deutsch heute Web Site at
www.hmco.com/college

Eröffnungsfeier des Bundestags im Berliner Reichstagsgebäude.

Diskussion

Compare the government of Germany to your own. Which institutions are similar to ones in your country, which aspects are different?

---

gebe ihm die Hand und **sage:** „Also, mein Lieber, bis bald." Du, Ute, etwas verstehe ich nicht. Warum hat er immer Stefan zu mir gesagt? „Ja, das ist ja wirklich merkwürdig, Alexander", **antwortet** Ute.

antwortete ☐ empfahl ☐ gab ☐ ging ☐ lud ein ☐ sagte ☐ sah ☐ sollte ☐ sprach ☐ stand ☐ trank ☐ war ☐ wollte ☐ wusste

12. Berlin. Lesen Sie die Information über die Teilung° und Wiedervereinigung von Berlin (Zeile 1–10, Seite 345). Merken Sie sich° jedes Verb im Präteritum und schreiben Sie auf ein Blatt° Papier das englische Äquivalent. Dann geben Sie die Infinitivform auf Deutsch.

■ *Verbs with past-tense vowel long* ā *and short* ă

Infinitive	Simple past stem *(ā)*
empfehlen	empfahl
essen	aß
geben	gab
kommen	kam
lesen	las
liegen	lag
nehmen	nahm
sehen	sah
sitzen	saß
sprechen	sprach
treffen	traf
tun	tat

Infinitive	Simple past stem *(ă)*
finden	fand
helfen	half
stehen	stand
trinken	trank

13. Die Sommerarbeit. Peggy, eine Amerikanerin, hat ihrer deutschen Freundin Marga einen Brief über ihren Sommerjob bei einer deutschen Firma geschrieben. Lesen Sie den Brief und beantworten Sie die Fragen.

Samstag, den 1. Oktober

Liebe Marga,

du wolltest etwas über meinen Sommerjob wissen. Also, ich kam am 5. Juni in München an. Viele Menschen waren auf dem Flughafen. Zuerst verstand ich nur wenig. Aber die Deutschen waren sehr nett, vor allem meine Chefin Frau Volke. Sie half mir auch sehr bei der Arbeit. Ich fand die Arbeit dann viel leichter. Um 10 Uhr morgens machten wir immer Pause und tranken Kaffee. Manchmal waren unsere Gespräche so interessant, dass wir nicht pünktlich wieder an die Arbeit gingen. Aber Frau Volke sagte nichts. Wie du siehst, kann ich jetzt viel mehr Deutsch. Schreib bald.

Herzliche Grüße°

deine *Peggy*

1. Wann kam Peggy in München an?
2. Was sah sie auf dem Flughafen?
3. Wer war besonders nett?
4. Warum fand Peggy die Arbeit im Büro leicht?
5. Was machte man um 10 Uhr morgens?
6. Warum ging man manchmal im Büro nicht wieder pünktlich an die Arbeit?

■ *Verbs with past-tense vowel* **ie, u,** *and* **i**

Infinitive	Simple past stem *(ie)*
bleiben	blieb
fallen	fiel
gefallen	gefiel
halten	hielt
laufen	lief
schlafen	schlief
schreiben	schrieb
verlassen	verließ

Infinitive	Simple past stem *(u or i)*
fahren	fuhr
tragen	trug
gehen	ging

14. Die Reise nach Frankfurt. Jürgen hat seinem Freund Rainer einen Brief über seine Reise nach Frankfurt geschrieben. Lesen Sie den Brief und beantworten Sie die Fragen.

Dienstag, den 10. Juli

Lieber Rainer,

du wolltest wissen, was ich letzte Woche gemacht habe. Nun, ich fuhr mit dem Zug nach Frankfurt. Meine Freundin Julia fuhr natürlich mit. Es war heiß und wir trugen Shorts. Wir liefen ein bisschen in der Fußgängerzone herum und gingen schließlich ins Kino. Wir blieben nur eine halbe Stunde. Der Film gefiel uns nämlich nicht. Dann gingen wir ein Glas Apfelwein trinken. Am Abend fuhren wir dann wieder nach Hause. Julia schrieb Briefe, aber ich habe den ganzen Weg geschlafen.

Herzliche Grüße

dein

Jürgen

1. Wie war das Wetter?
2. Wohin fuhren Jürgen und Julia?
3. Was für Hosen trugen sie?
4. Wo liefen sie ein bisschen herum?
5. Warum blieben sie nur eine halbe Stunde im Kino?
6. Was machten sie nach dem Kino?
7. Was tat Julia auf der Rückreise° nach Hause?   return trip
8. Was tat Jürgen?

15. Eine Nacht im Leben von Herrn Zittermann.   Lesen Sie die Anekdote und beantworten Sie die Fragen. Dann schreiben Sie ein Ende für die Geschichte.

suddenly / light / motionless

flashlight / firmly

Herr Zittermann war allein im Haus. Er lag im Bett, aber er schlief noch nicht. Er hatte die Augen offen. Plötzlich° sah er unter der Tür Licht°. Starr° blieb er liegen. Was war los? Er bekam Angst. Er stand auf und nahm seine große Taschenlampe°, die natürlich auf dem Nachttisch lag. Fest° hielt er die Taschen-lampe in der Hand. Er ging zur Tür und sah ...

1. Wo lag Herr Zittermann?
2. Wie viele Leute waren im Haus?
3. Schlief Herr Zittermann?
4. Was sah er plötzlich?
5. Was war seine Reaktion?
6. Was lag auf dem Nachttisch?
7. Wohin ging er?

accident

16. Ein Unfall° in der Herzogstraße.   Sie sind Journalistin/Journalist und schreiben über einen Unfall. Benutzen Sie die Bilder und Wortverbindungen und schreiben Sie Ihren Artikel. Leider haben Sie nicht alle Informationen und müssen die Geschichte selber zu Ende schreiben.

➤ ein blauer Wagen / schnell um die Ecke / fahren
Ein blauer Wagen fuhr schnell um die Ecke.

1. eine alte Frau / über die Straße / laufen   2. sie / nicht / das Auto / sehen

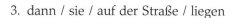

3. dann / sie / auf der Straße / liegen

4. ein Fußgänger / zu der Frau / kommen

5. er / die Frau / zu einer Bank° / tragen   bench

6. Wie ging die Geschichte weiter?

■ *Past tense of* **werden**

Infinitive	Simple past stem
werden	wurde

17. Berufe.   Sie waren auf einem Schultreffen°. Erzählen Sie, was Ihre   class reunion
Klassenkameradinnen und Klassenkameraden von Beruf wurden. Benutzen Sie
das Präteritum von **werden.**

≫ Erika / Ingenieurin   *Erika wurde Ingenieurin.*

1. du / Lehrer
2. Inge / Geschäftsfrau
3. wir / Journalisten
4. Sebastian / Apotheker
5. Steffi und Franziska / Ärztinnen
6. Gerd / Rechstanwalt
7. Karen / Informatikerin

das Plusquamperfekt

8. Past perfect tense°

Thomas **war** noch nie in Köln **gewesen.**	Thomas *had* never *been* in Cologne.
Er **hatte** noch nie den Rhein **gesehen.**	He *had* never *seen* the Rhine.

The English past perfect tense consists of the auxiliary *had* and the past participle of the verb. The German past perfect tense consists of the simple past of **haben** (e.g., **hatte**) or **sein** (e.g., **war**) and the past participle of the verb. Verbs that use a form of **haben** in the present perfect tense also use a form of **haben** in the past perfect; those that use a form of **sein** in the present perfect also use a form of **sein** in the past perfect.

9. Use of the past perfect tense

Edith konnte am Montag nicht anfangen, weil sie am Sonntag krank **geworden war.**	Edith couldn't begin on Monday, because she *had gotten* sick on Sunday.

The past perfect tense is used to report an event or action that took place before another event or action that was itself in the past. The following time-tense line will help you visualize the sequence of tenses.

2nd point earlier in past	1st point in past time	Present time	Future time
Past perfect	Present perfect or simple past		

18. Der Fall der Mauer. Herr Pabst hat immer in Ostdeutschland gewohnt und spricht über den Fall der Berliner Mauer. Geben Sie das englische Äquivalent seiner Aussagen wieder.

erlauben: to permit

citizens

after

1. Zuerst konnte niemand glauben, dass die DDR das Reisen nach Westdeutschland erlaubt° hatte.
2. Als die Mauer gefallen war, fuhren unglaublich viele DDR-Bürger° in den Westen.
3. Nachdem° sie diese Reise gemacht hatten, kamen die meisten wieder nach Hause zurück.
4. Sie hatten ein Stück vom Westen gesehen und wollten dann einfach wieder zu Hause sein.
5. Wer nie selbst in der Bundesrepublik gewesen war, kannte sie doch ein wenig aus dem Fernsehen.
6. Viele gingen aber zurück, weil sie eine andere Idee vom Westen gehabt hatten.

10. Uses of *als, wenn,* and *wann*

Als, wenn, and **wann** are all equivalent to English *when,* but they are not interchangeable in German.

Als Paula gestern in Hamburg war, ging sie ins Theater.	When Paula was in Hamburg yesterday, she went to the theater.
Als Paula ein Teenager war, ging sie gern ins Theater.	When Paula was a teenager, she liked to go to the theater.

Als is used to introduce a clause concerned with a single event in the past or with a block of continuous time in the past.

Wenn Renate in Hamburg ist, geht sie ins Theater.	When Renate is in Hamburg, she goes to the theater.
Wenn Erik in Hamburg war, ging er jeden Tag ins Theater.	When (whenever) Erik was in Hamburg, he went (would go) to the theater every day.

Wenn is used to introduce a clause concerned with events or possibilities in present or future time. **Wenn** is also used to introduce a clause concerned with repeated events *(whenever)* in past time.

Wann gehen wir ins Kino?	When are we going to the movies?
Ich habe keine Ahnung, **wann** wir ins Kino gehen.	I have no idea when we're going to the movies.

Wann is used only for questions. It is used to introduce both direct and indirect questions.

19. Wann ...? Ein Freund stellt Ihnen viele Fragen, die Sie nicht beantworten können. Antworten Sie mit indirekten Fragen. Benutzen Sie die folgenden Sätze, wenn Sie antworten.

Redemittel°: Ich weiß nicht ☐ Ich frage mich auch ☐ Ich möchte auch wissen ☐ Ich habe keine Ahnung ☐

speech acts

⟫ Wann schreiben wir die nächste Deutschklausur?   *Ich weiß nicht, wann wir die nächste Deutschklausur schreiben.*

1. Wann müssen wir die nächste Hausaufgabe abgeben°?   turn in
2. Wann macht die Bibliothek am Samstag zu?
3. Wann kommen unsere Pizzas?
4. Wann ruft Stefan an?
5. Wann können wir Pause machen°?   **Pause machen:** take a break

An der Universität Freiburg machen Studenten eine Pause.

20. Bernd und der Fall der Mauer. Erzählen Sie, was Bernd nach dem Fall der Mauer getan hat. Verbinden Sie die Sätze mit **als, wenn** oder **wann**.

≫ Die Mauer stand noch. Bernd wohnte in Dresden.
Als die Mauer noch stand, wohnte Bernd in Dresden.

1. Seine Tante schrieb ihm aus Köln. Er wurde immer ganz traurig.
2. Die Mauer fiel. Ein großes Chaos begann.
3. Die Tante fragte Bernd am Telefon: „Wann kommen die Eltern?"

news
curious

4. Auch Bernd setzte sich ins Auto. Er hörte die Nachricht°.
5. Er fuhr dann nach Köln. Er war sehr neugierig°.
6. Seine Tante hat ihm gesagt: „Die Eltern kommen in Köln an. Wir haben dann ein großes Fest." (*Do not change the introductory sentence:* Seine Tante hat ihm gesagt.)

WIEDERHOLUNG

1. Eine Reise nach Paris. Lesen Sie den Bericht von Kristinas Reise nach Paris und beantworten Sie die Fragen.

dreamed
immediately
railroad

Kristina wohnte in Leipzig. Sie war Ingenieurin. Sie wollte immer gern Paris sehen. Aber als es noch die Grenze in Deutschland gab, konnte sie natürlich nicht nach Frankreich reisen. Sie fuhr in alle Länder von Osteuropa und kam sogar bis nach China. Doch in Wirklichkeit träumte° sie immer von Paris. Als dann die Grenze fiel, konnte sie es kaum glauben. Sofort° kaufte sie sich eine Fahrkarte für die Eisenbahn° und machte die lange Reise nach Paris. Die Stadt fand sie ganz toll, aber unglaublich teuer. Solche Preise kannte sie nicht! Da war sie dann ganz froh, dass sie wieder nach Hause fahren konnte. Aber – sie hatte Paris gesehen!

1. Was war Kristina von Beruf?
2. Wovon träumte sie immer?
3. In welche Länder konnte sie früher nur reisen?
4. Wohin fuhr sie, als die Grenze fiel?
5. Wie fand sie die Stadt?
6. Warum war sie froh, wieder nach Hause zu fahren?

2. Zwei kurze Gespräche. Ergänzen Sie die Kurzgespräche. Benutzen Sie die richtige Form der Verben aus der Liste in jedem Satz.

aufstehen □ stehen □ verstehen

most of the time

MANUEL: Sonntags _____ ich immer sehr spät _____. Meistens° _____ dann das Mittagessen schon auf dem Tisch.

STEFFI: Also wirklich, ich kann nicht _____, wie man so lange schlafen kann.

ankommen □ bekommen □ kommen

ELISABETH: Wann sind Sie denn in München _____?

THERESA: Vor einer Stunde. Ich bin dieses Mal mit dem Zug _____, nicht mit

dem Flugzeug.

ELISABETH: Ah, also haben Sie meinen Brief noch früh genug _____.

3. Erzählen Sie von gestern.   Was haben Sie gestern Morgen gemacht? Be- | add
nutzen Sie passende Wörter und Wortverbindungen aus der Liste. Wenn Sie
wollen, können Sie auch noch andere Aktivitäten hinzufügen°.   add

aufstehen □ baden □ sich die Haare kämmen □ sich anziehen □ Kaffee kochen
□ ein Stück Toast essen □ Kaffee trinken □ Zeitung lesen □ sich die Zähne
putzen □ in die Vorlesung gehen

4. Was bedeutet das?   Bilden Sie neue Substantive aus den folgenden
Wörtern und geben Sie die englischen Äquivalente wieder.

1. die Bilder + das Buch
2. die Farb(e) + der Fernseher
3. die Blumen + das Geschäft
4. die Kinder + der Garten
5. die Geschicht(e) + s + der Lehrer
6. das Hotel + der Gast

7. der Abend + das Kleid
8. das Haus + das Tier
9. der Brief + der Freund
10. die Sonne + n + die Brille

5. Ferienpläne.   Sprechen Sie mit Ihrer Partnerin/Ihrem Partner über
Dinge, die Sie in Ihren Ferien machen wollten, und warum. Erklären Sie auch,
was Sie machen konnten. Denken Sie daran: In einer Konversation benutzt man
das Perfekt, außer für die Verben **sein** und **haben** und Modalverben.

⟫ *Ich wollte jeden Tag mit Jürgen Tennis spielen.*
  Aber er ist selten gekommen, und so habe ich wenig gespielt.

Themen: reisen □ [Tennis] spielen □ nach [Europa] fliegen □ [einem Freund]
helfen □ eine Arbeit suchen □ [Freunde] besuchen □ einen Film sehen □ [ein
Buch] lesen □ spät aufstehen □ schwimmen □ einkaufen gehen

6. Zum Schreiben

1. Wählen Sie einen Satz, der° mit **als** beginnt, und einen, der mit **wenn** be- | that
   ginnt. Schreiben Sie dann einen kurzen Absatz° zu jedem Satz. Denken Sie | paragraph
   daran, dass Sie das Präteritum benutzen müssen, wenn Sie ihren Absatz mit
   als beginnen.

   ■ Als ich vier Jahre alt war, ...
   ■ Als ich noch in die Schule ging, ...
   ■ Als ich das letzte Mal auf einem Fest war, ...
   ■ Als ich ...
   ■ Wenn ich [müde/glücklich/deprimiert°/nervös/böse] bin, ... | depressed
   ■ Wenn ich Hausarbeit machen muss, ...
   ■ Wenn ich ...

2. Schreiben Sie die Geschichte über Herrn Zittermann in Übung 15 auf Seite 364 zu Ende.

Hinweise: After you have written your paragraph or story ending, check the following:

- Choice of past tenses
- Form of the past tenses
- Use of **als, wenn, wann**

GRAMMATIK: ZUSAMMENFASSUNG

Sein, haben, and *werden* in the simple past

Infinitive	Simple past
sein	war
haben	hatte

sein			
ich war		wir waren	
du warst		ihr wart	
er/es/sie war		sie waren	
	Sie waren		

haben			
ich hatte		wir hatten	
du hattest		ihr hattet	
er/es/sie hatte		sie hatten	
	Sie hatten		

werden			
ich wurde		wir wurden	
du wurdest		ihr wurdet	
er/es/sie wurde		sie wurden	
	Sie wurden		

Modals in the simple past

Infinitive	Simple past
dürfen	durfte
können	konnte
mögen	mochte
müssen	musste
sollen	sollte
wollen	wollte

Simple past of regular weak verbs

Infinitive	Stem	Tense marker	Simple past
glauben	glaub-	-te	glaubte
spielen	spiel-	-te	spielte
baden	bad-	-ete	badete
arbeiten	arbeit-	-ete	arbeitete
regnen	regn-	-ete	regnete

Irregular weak verbs in the simple past

Infinitive	Simple past
bringen	brachte
denken	dachte
kennen	kannte
nennen	nannte
wissen	wusste

In the simple past tense, modals, weak verbs, and irregular weak verbs have the past-tense marker **-te.** In verbs with a stem ending in **-d** or **-t,** and in some verbs ending in **-n** or **-m,** the tense marker **-te** expands to **-ete.** Like **hatte,** all forms except the **ich-** and **er/es/sie-**forms add endings to the past-tense marker **-te.**

Simple past of strong verbs

Infinitive	Simple past
gehen	ging
sehen	sah
schreiben	schrieb

Strong verbs undergo a stem vowel change in the simple past. Like **sein,** they do not take the past-tense marker **-te.** The **ich-** and **er/es/sie-**forms have no verb endings.

Selected strong verbs

Below is a table of selected strong verbs. For a more complete list see the Grammatical Tables, #23, in the Reference Section.

Infinitive	Simple past stem	Infinitive	Simple past stem
anfangen	fing an	liegen	lag
anziehen	zog an	nehmen	nahm
bleiben	blieb	schlafen	schlief
empfehlen	empfahl	schreiben	schrieb
essen	aß	sehen	sah
fahren	fuhr	sein	war
fallen	fiel	sitzen	saß
finden	fand	sprechen	sprach
geben	gab	stehen	stand
gefallen	gefiel	tragen	trug
gehen	ging	treffen	traf
halten	hielt	trinken	trank
helfen	half	tun	tat
kommen	kam	verlassen	verließ
laufen	lief	werden	wurde
lesen	las		

Separable-prefix verbs in the simple past

Present tense	Simple past
Sie **kauft** immer im Supermarkt **ein**.	Sie **kaufte** immer im Supermarkt **ein**.
Er **kommt** immer **mit**.	Er **kam** immer **mit**.

In the simple past tense, as in the present tense, the separable prefix is separated from the base form of the verb and is in final position.

Past perfect tense

Ich **hatte** vor zwei Tagen
  angefangen zu arbeiten.
Gerd **war** am Montag **angekommen**.

I *had started* working two days
  before.
Gerd *had arrived* on Monday.

The German past perfect is a compound tense that consists of the simple past of either **haben** or **sein** plus the past participle of the main verb. It is used to report an event or action that took place before another past event or action.

Uses of *als*, *wenn*, and *wann* meaning *when*

Als, wenn, wann are used as follows:

1. **als**—a single event in past time

   Als Katrin Dieter gestern sah,
     sprachen sie über Politik.

   When Katrin saw Dieter yesterday,
     they talked about politics.

2. **als**—a block of continuous time in the past

   Als Katrin jung war, sprach sie
     gern über Politik.

   When Katrin was young, she
     liked to talk about politics.

3. **wenn**—repeated events (*whenever*) in past time

   Früher **wenn** sie Dieter sah,
     redete sie immer über
     Politik.

   In the past, *when* (whenever) she used
     to see Dieter, she always spoke
     about politics.

4. **wenn**—present or future time

   Wenn wir in München sind,
     gehen wir ins Konzert.

   When (whenever) we are in Munich,
     we go to a concert.

5. **wann**—introduces direct questions

   Wann beginnt das Konzert?

   When does the concert begin?

6. **wann**—introduces indirect questions

   Ich weiß nicht, **wann** das
     Konzert beginnt.

   I don't know *when* the concert
     begins.

Wirtschaft und Beruf

Das BMW-Gebäude in Berlin.

BAUSTEINE FÜR GESPRÄCHE

Stellenanzeigen

ALEX: Na, was gibt's Neues in der Zeitung?

UWE: Ich weiß nicht. Ich hab' bis jetzt nur die Anzeigen durchgesehen.

ALEX: Welche? Die Heiratsanzeigen?

UWE: Quatsch. Die Stellenanzeigen! Ich suche Arbeit. Ich hätte gern einen interessanten Job, wo man gut verdient.

ALEX: Ja, das wäre toll. Du suchst ja schon eine ganze Weile. Viel Glück!

Ein Termin

UWE: Guten Tag. Ohrdorf ist mein Name, Uwe Ohrdorf. Ich würde gern Frau Dr. Ziegler sprechen. Ich habe einen Termin bei ihr.

SEKRETÄRIN: Guten Tag, Herr Ohrdorf. Ja bitte, gehen Sie doch gleich hinein. Sie erwartet Sie schon.

Brauchbares

1. Besides looking at **Stellenanzeigen** in the newspaper, Uwe can search **das Internet,** where thousands of jobs are listed.

2. In **Ein Termin** Uwe says, **"Ich würde gern Frau Dr. Ziegler sprechen."** All forms of formal social address begin with **Frau** or **Herr.** Titles such as **Doktor** or **Professor** follow. The family name comes last.

3. Note in the same sentence that to request to speak to someone officially, the construction in German is **sprechen** + direct object. In English one might say *I would like to speak with* or *to Dr. Ziegler.*

Deutsche Lieblings-
arbeitgeber: Mercedes,
BMW und Lufthansa

Traumkonzerne der Jungmanager

Wo deutsche Hochschulabsolventen am liebsten arbeiten würden

BMW	60%
Mercedes-Benz	59%
The Boston Consulting Group	55%
Lufthansa	52%
McKinsey & Company	52%
Siemens	52%
Bosch	50%
Audi	48%

FOCUS-Magazin

Fragen

1. Warum weiß Uwe nicht, was in der Zeitung steht?
2. Was für einen Job sucht er?
3. Wen möchte Uwe sprechen?
4. Warum soll Uwe gleich hineingehen?

1. Die Zeitung. Fragen Sie drei Kursteilnehmerinnen/Kursteilnehmer, welche Zeitung sie lesen und warum sie die Zeitung lesen. Notieren Sie sich die Antworten und berichten Sie den anderen Studentinnen/Studenten, was Sie herausgefunden haben.

S1:
Welche Zeitung liest du?
Warum liest du Zeitung – wofür
  interessierst du dich?

S2:
Ich lese [*Die Zeit*].
Für | **Politik.**

Schüttelkasten

Wirtschaft	**Musik**	
Sport	Theater Literatur	Comics

2. Was ist wichtig? Fragen Sie vier Kursteilnehmerinnen/Kursteilnehmer, was sie in ihrem Beruf wichtig finden. Hier sind einige Möglichkeiten.

sicherer Arbeitsplatz   gut verdienen
den Menschen helfen   Teilzeitarbeit
interessante oder leichte Arbeit   viel Freizeit
nicht [den ganzen Tag] im Büro sitzen   nette Kollegen

3. Rollenspiel: Im Büro. Wählen° Sie eine der folgenden Rollen und führen Sie ein sinnvolles° Gespräch. Vergessen Sie nicht, sich zu grüßen°. Hier sind einige Sprechhilfen°.

choose
meaningful / greet
aids for conversation

Frau/Herr Richter:
Ich würde gern Frau/Herrn
  Dr. Schulze sprechen.

Ich habe einen Termin für ... Uhr.

Ich bin ganz sicher, dass ich den
  Termin heute habe.

Sekretärin/Sekretär:
Es tut mir Leid.
  Sie/Er ist im Moment beschäftigt°.
  Sie/Er telefoniert gerade. Haben
  Sie einen Termin mit ihr/ihm?

Um ... Uhr hat sie/er einen
  Termin. Sind Sie sicher, dass der
  Termin für heute/ ... Uhr war?

Gehen Sie bitte gleich hinein.
  Sie/Er erwartet Sie.

acquaintances

look up

placed

4. **Heiraten/Bekanntschaften°.** Im Dialog auf S. 374 hat Alex gefragt, ob Uwe die Heiratsanzeigen liest. Sehen Sie sich die Heiratsanzeigen an und beantworten Sie die folgenden Fragen. Unbekannte Vokabeln können Sie im Anhang nachschlagen° (Vocabulary for Authentic Text Activities).

Heiraten/Bekanntschaften

SOS! Wo finde ich eine treue, lustige Partnerin bis 35 J. zum Verlieben, bin 40 J., schlank, jugendl. Erscheinung, etwas schüchtern, reiselustig, selbständig u. Tierliebhaber. Bildzuschr. u. Nr. 764/G an diese Zeitung.

2 junggebliebene Freundinnen, verwitwet, 60 u. 65 J., suchen 2 nette Herrn. mögl. mit Auto, die mit ihnen Tanzen, Schwimmen und gemeinsame. nette Stunden verbringen. Zuschr. mögl. mit Bild unt. Nr. 2/835083/G-Z.

ER, 28 J., 189 cm. schlank. sucht nette SIE, meine Hobbys sind Bodybuilding. Motorrad fahren. Kino u. Essen gehen. Bitte schreibe mir an WT 1/167

Wo ist der liebenswerte, gebildete Mann, großzügig im Denken und Handeln. kein Opatyp. ca. 180 groß? Eine attraktive, symp. Sie. mit Herz. Hirn und Niveau, 47 J., schlk., 167 groß. würde Ihn gerne kennenlernen. Freundl. Zuschr. m. Tel.-Ang. unt. Nr. 2/835181/G-S.

Elfi ist von Beruf Küchenhilfe und ist **21 J.** alt. Sie hat blonde Haare, geht gerne schwimmen und spazieren. Wenn Du sie kennenlernen möchtest, dann schreibe unter AA 2154.

1. Wie alt sind die Leute, die die Anzeigen aufgegeben° haben?
2. Wie alt sollen die Partnerinnen/Partner sein?
3. Wer möchte mit der Antwort zusammen ein Bild haben?
4. Was bedeutet „Opatyp"?
5. In welchen Anzeigen ist das Aussehen wichtig?
6. Was für Menschen finden Sie sympathisch?

Vokabeln

Substantive

die **Anzeige, -n** announcement; ad
die **Comics** *(pl.)* comics
die **Heirat** marriage
der **Moment, -e** moment; **im Moment** at the moment
die **Politik** politics; political science
der **Quatsch** nonsense; **Quatsch!** nonsense!

die **Teilzeitarbeit** part-time work
der **Termin, -e** appointment; **einen Termin bei (jemandem) haben** to have an appointment with (someone)
die **Weile** while; **eine ganze Weile** a long time

Verben

beschäftigen to occupy, keep busy; **beschäftigt sein** to be busy; **sich beschäftigen (mit)** to be occupied (with)
durch·sehen (sieht durch), sah durch, durchgesehen to look through; to glance over; to examine

haben: hätte would have
heiraten to marry, get married
sein: wäre would be
telefonieren (mit jemandem) to telephone (someone)
werden: würde would

Andere Wörter

hinein   in (*as in* **hineingehen**   to
go in)

Besondere Ausdrücke

Viel Glück!   Good luck!

Was gibt's Neues?   What's new?

Das soziale Netz

The foundations of German social legislation were laid during the time that Otto von Bismarck (1815–1898) was chancellor. Statutory health insurance **(Krankenversicherung)**, workers compensation **(Unfall- und Invalidenversicherung)**, and retirement benefits **(Rentenversicherung)** were introduced at that time. The costs were to be shared by the employer, the employee, and the state. Retirement age was set at 65.

In Germany today these kinds of insurance are still statutory. All employed people below a certain income must belong to a **Krankenkasse,** which takes care of basic health costs. There is also unemployment insurance **(Arbeitslosenversicherung)** and insurance for long-term nursing care **(Pflegeversicherung).** The entire social "safety net" **(soziales Netz)** includes further benefits such as **Kindergeld,** a monthly payment to parents to offset child-rearing expenses, low-income rent allowances **(Wohngeld),** compensation for the victims of war, financial aid for students, subsidized child care, and others. The state also provides social welfare **(Sozialhilfe)** for those in need.

These benefits come at a cost to the taxpayer. The benefits make up 42.3% of the gross pay and the income tax rate varies from a low of 25.9% to a high of 53% (1999). The U.S.A. rates go from 15% to 39.6%.

Go to the
Deutsch heute Web Site at
www.hmco.com/college

Das Arbeitsamt kann helfen, wenn man eine Stelle sucht.

Diskussion

Make a list of the social benefits in Germany which have been mentioned in this chapter and in *Kapitel 8* (**Familienpolitik,** p. 288). What are the equivalent benefits in your country?

PROBLEME MIT DER WIRTSCHAFT

Vorbereitung auf das Lesen*

Dieser Text kommt aus einem Artikel der *Süddeutschen Zeitung.* Er beschreibt die Sorgen° eines Angestellten° in der Zeit wirtschaftlicher Probleme.

■ Vor dem Lesen

kreuzen an: check off

Lesen Sie die folgende Liste und kreuzen Sie für jedes Wort eine oder mehr der drei Kategorien an°:

in general

	Wirtschaft allgemein°	Firma	Mitarbeiter
Angst			
Familienprobleme			
Arbeitssuche			
Depression			
mehr Freizeit			
Finanzprobleme			
Profit			
Kündigung°			
Streiks°			
Inflation			
Sorgen			
sinkende Produktion			
Kosten sparen			
weniger Arbeitsplätze			
teure Rohstoffe			
Konkurrenz°			

dismissal

competition

---

*Reminder: Words appearing with a raised degree mark but with no definition in the margin are new "active" words that you should learn and be able to use. These words and their definitions appear in the **Vokabeln** section that most closely follows the exercise.

■ *Beim Lesen*

Dieser Text zeigt die Konsequenzen wirtschaftlicher Probleme für das Leben von Mitarbeitern. Was für Probleme haben die Wirtschaft und die Firma? Was für Probleme haben die Mitarbeiter? Beim Lesen machen Sie zwei Listen:

Probleme	
Wirtschaft/Firma	Mitarbeiter

Heute ist Montag und ich bin wieder im Büro. Wie immer, wenn ich weg war, liegen Berge von Post auf meinem Schreibtisch. Letzte Woche war ich auf einer Geschäftsreise in San Francisco. Jetzt muss ich erst einmal° alles durcharbeiten. Dazwischen° klingelt immer wieder das
5 Telefon. Wie soll ich denn da den Postberg nur vom Tisch kriegen? Diesmal ist es das Büro des Personalchefs. Seine Assistentin fragt: „Herr Gartner, hätten Sie in einer halben Stunde Zeit? Herr Sundmann möchte Sie sprechen." „Ja, kein Problem, wenn's nicht zu lange dauert", antworte ich und merke, dass ich blass werde. Schließlich weiß ich ja, was das heißt. Jetzt bin ich
10 dran. Ich versuche, klar zu denken und nicht in Panik zu geraten°.

   Herr Sundmann ist unser Personalchef. Wenn er anruft, oder seine Assistentin, dann weiß jeder in der Firma, was das heißt. In drei Jahren haben dreihundertfünfzig Mitarbeiter ihre Stelle verloren. Die Büros links und rechts von mir sind eins nach dem anderen leer geworden. Die Krise betrifft° natür-
15 lich nicht nur uns allein. Heute gibt es mehr Streiks als früher. Neue Technologie und Veränderungen° auf dem Markt betreffen° heute die ganze deutsche Wirtschaft. Wie die meisten deutschen Firmen, so lebt auch unsere vom Außenhandel. Deutschland muss viele Rohstoffe importieren. Früher hatte Deutschland eine niedrige Inflationsrate. Da konnten unsere Kunden
20 mit stabilen Preisen rechnen°. Heute wird jedoch alles immer teurer. Aber jetzt gibt es auch immer mehr Länder, die die gleichen Waren billiger herstellen. Mit ihnen kann Deutschland immer weniger konkurrieren. Das haben wir hier in unserer Firma gemerkt. Also weiß ich, dass der Besuch beim Personalchef in diesen Tagen Kündigung° bedeutet. Beim Gespräch mit
25 ihm wird es auch vor allem um Geld gehen°. Ich muss mich gut darauf vorbereiten. Susanna, meine Exkollegin, hat dies alles vor einem halben Jahr durchgemacht. Sie ist immer noch arbeitslos und meist zu Hause, wenn ich sie anrufe.

erst einmal: first of all / in between

to get into

affects

changes / affect

rechnen mit: count on

dismissal
um ... gehen: revolve around money

Münchener gehen zur Arbeit.

Oh je!: Oh dear!

the more fortunate one

severance pay

(job) application

related to one's job or career

Oh je!° Warum muss mir das jetzt passieren? Wenn ich etwas jünger
30 wäre, dann fände ich sicher leichter eine neue Stelle. Aber mit fünfund-
vierzig? Es würde mir auch nichts ausmachen, weniger zu verdienen. Wer
weiß, vielleicht bin ich am Ende der Glücklichere°? Vielleicht finde ich
schnell eine neue Stelle, und ich bekomme ja auch meine Abfindung° von
der Firma. Da ich zwölf Jahre lang hier gearbeitet habe, müsste meine
35 Abfindung ein Jahresgehalt sein. Aber mein jetziges hohes Gehalt ist bei der
Bewerbung° sicher ein Problem. Und wenn ich in einem Jahr keine neue
Stelle finden kann, muss ich vielleicht meine Wohnung verkaufen. Aber Moment mal! Wäre es denn wirklich das Ende der Welt? Ich hätte doch auch
mehr Zeit für die Kinder und meine Hobbys! Ich könnte endlich Bücher
40 lesen oder die Wohnung renovieren. Alles Dinge, die ich immer schon
machen wollte, für die ich aber früher nie Zeit hatte. Aber würde ich diese
Dinge wirklich alle tun? Hätte ich wirklich Freude daran? Ich glaube nicht,
denn ich mache mir jetzt schon große Sorgen um meine berufliche° Zukunft.
Unsichere Zeiten zur Zeit!

Brauchbares

1. l. 15, **Streiks:** In the over 50 years of its existence the Federal Republic of
   Germany has had relatively few labor strikes. Employer- and union-
   representatives of the major industries usually meet once a year to modify
   existing industry-wide work agreements **(Tarifverträge).** If they cannot agree,
   both parties accept an independent negotiator. It is only in exceptional cases
   that unions organize strikes, for which they need the votes of 75% of their
   members.

2. l. 18, **Außenhandel:** Germany exports one-third of its industrial output. The
   most important German exports are machinery, automobiles, chemical products, and electronics. In 1995 Germany, with exports of $524 billion (10.4% of

total exports on the international market), was in second place worldwide. The U.S.A. led with exports of $585 billion (11.6%). In 1997 Germany exported goods in the amount of DM 886.8 billion. Germany's principal trading partners are France, the Netherlands, the United Kingdom, Italy, and the U.S.A.

3. l. 21–22, **Waren billiger herstellen:** Of the industrial nations of the world, Germany has had the highest hourly labor costs for several years. In 1997 hourly labor costs for production workers averaged $28.28, compared to $18.24 for workers in the U.S.A. In 1998 the cost of fringe benefits was 42.3% of the gross pay. These costs were shared by the worker and management, which means that a German employer pays 20–25% above the basic wages.

Nach dem Lesen

1. Fragen zum Lesestück

1. Warum war Herr Gartner in San Francisco?
2. Was liegt auf seinem Schreibtisch?
3. Wer ruft Herrn Gartner an?
4. Warum wird Herr Gartner blass?
5. Wer ist Herr Sundmann?
6. Wie viele Leute haben schon ihre Stelle in der Firma verloren?
7. Wovon lebt die deutsche Wirtschaft?
8. Warum ist die deutsche Wirtschaft in einer Krise? Geben Sie mindestens zwei Gründe° an.
9. Wie hoch könnte Herrn Gartners Abfindung sein?
10. Was wird das Thema sein, wenn Herr Gartner mit dem Personalchef spricht?
11. Was für Probleme sieht Herr Gartner bei der Bewerbung um eine neue Stelle?
12. Wofür hätte Herr Gartner Zeit, wenn er arbeitslos° würde?
13. Wie sieht Herr Gartner seine Zukunft?

2. Unsichere Zukunft.   In diesem Text gibt es viele Stellen, wo der Mitarbeiter über seine Zukunft nachdenkt°. Suchen Sie fünf Stellen im Text mit den Wörtern: **vielleicht, könnte, müsste, würde.** Benutzen Sie jeden Ausdruck in einem Satz°.

thinks about

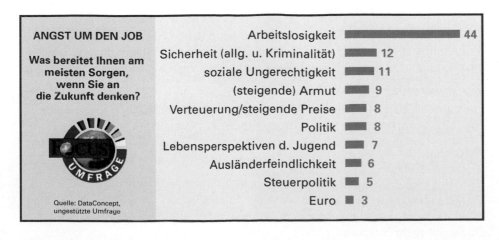

ANGST UM DEN JOB

Was bereitet Ihnen am meisten Sorgen, wenn Sie an die Zukunft denken?

Quelle: DataConcept, ungestützte Umfrage

Arbeitslosigkeit	44
Sicherheit (allg. u. Kriminalität)	12
soziale Ungerechtigkeit	11
(steigende) Armut	9
Verteuerung/steigende Preise	8
Politik	8
Lebensperspektiven d. Jugend	7
Ausländerfeindlichkeit	6
Steuerpolitik	5
Euro	3

LAND UND LEUTE

Go to the
Deutsch heute Web Site at
www.hmco.com/college

Die Mitbestimmung

Democratic codetermination **(Mitbestimmung)** is a right guaranteed by law in Germany. **Mitbestimmung** gives workers the right and the responsibility to participate in important decisions about their company. Employees of the company have representatives on special councils. These councils ensure that wage agreements, laws, and regulations are carried out. They also participate in decisions about work shifts, overtime, personnel changes, continuing education, and other internal policies.

Was wollen diese Metallarbeiter?

For companies with more than 2,000 employees, the law requires that an equal number of representatives of shareholders and of employees sit on the board of directors **(Aufsichtsrat).** In Austria, the ratio of employees to shareholders on the board is 1:3. Switzerland does not require **Mitbestimmung;** however, some companies have internal councils that function like those in German companies.

Diskussion

Group project: Contact your local chamber of commerce or a state or provincial agency and find out if there are any German, Austrian, or Swiss companies in your region.

3. Zum Schreiben.   Lesen Sie die folgenden Sätze zur Situation der Wirtschaft, der Firma und der Mitarbeiter. Verbinden° Sie Sätze der verschiedenen° Gruppen und zeigen Sie Zusammenhänge°. Viele Variationen sind möglich.

combine
various / connections

Konjunktionen: weil ☐ aber ☐ denn ☐ und
Adverbien: deshalb ☐ später ☐ dann ☐ leider ☐ in einem Jahr

⋙ *Weil die Inflation höher ist, kann die Firma keine stabilen Preise garantieren.*

Wirtschaft
1. Die Wirtschaft ist in einer Krise.
2. Viele Länder stellen die Waren billiger her.
3. Die Rohstoffe werden teurer.
4. Die Inflation ist höher.
5. Es gibt mehr Streiks.

Firma

1. Die Firma verkauft nicht mehr so viele Waren.
2. Die Firma kann keine stabilen Preise garantieren.
3. Die Firma reduziert ihr Personal.
4. Die Firma muss/will sparen.
5. Die Firma macht weniger Profit.

Mitarbeiter

1. Der Mitarbeiter verliert seine Stelle.
2. Der Mitarbeiter hat mehr Zeit für seine Kinder.
3. Der Mitarbeiter muss eine neue Stelle suchen.
4. Der Mitarbeiter hat Angst vor der Zukunft.

4. Erzählen wir. Benutzen Sie die Notizen, die Sie sich beim Lesen gemacht haben, und sprechen Sie über ein Thema:

1. Stellen Sie sich vor°, Sie verlieren vielleicht Ihre Stelle. Was sagen Sie zu Ihrer Familie oder Ihren Freunden? Versuchen Sie eine Minute zu sprechen.   **stellen ... vor:** imagine
2. Sprechen Sie kurz über die deutsche Wirtschaft.

Erweiterung des Wortschatzes

The suffix *-lich*

der Beruf	occupation	**beruflich**	career-related
der Freund	friend	**freundlich**	friendly
fragen	to ask	**fraglich**	questionable
krank	ill, sick	**kränklich**	sickly

German adjectives and adverbs may be formed from some nouns or verbs by adding the suffix **-lich.** The suffix **-lich** may also be added to other adjectives. Some stem vowels are umlauted: **ä, ö,** and **ü.** The English equivalent is often an adjective or adverb ending in *-ly,* e.g., *sick* and *sickly.*

1. Politische Reden°. Gestern Abend hat der Wirtschaftsminister an der Universität eine Rede gehalten. Heute Abend soll die Rede im Fernsehen kommen. Anna und Gerd sprechen über die Rede. Geben Sie die fett gedruckten Wörter auf Englisch wieder. Welche Verben, Substantive oder Adjektive sind mit den fett gedruckten Wörtern verwandt?   speeches

ANNA: Wie war es gestern Abend?

GERD: Ich fand die Rede inhaltlich° sehr interessant, aber Sarah sagt, der Minister hat über viele politisch unkluge° Dinge gesprochen.   in regard to the content / unwise

ANNA: Dass Sarah das gesagt hat, ist wirklich **unglaublich. Schließlich** ist ihr Vater der Assistent des Ministers. Hat sie das wirklich **öffentlich** gesagt?

GERD: Nein, sie hat mir das privat gesagt. Wusstest du eigentlich, dass Hans-Jürgen gestern Abend schließlich doch noch gekommen ist?

ANNA: Ja, aber es ist **fraglich,** ob er heute Abend kommt. Wir wollten doch nach der Sendung die Rede diskutieren, nicht wahr?

GERD: Ja und ich freue mich schon darauf. Gestern Abend war jeder so **freundlich.**

ANNA: Das ist **natürlich verständlich.** Wir sind alle Politologiestudenten° und haben die gleichen Interessen.   political science students

Vokabeln

Substantive

der/die **Angestellte** *(noun decl. like adj.)* salaried employee, white-collar worker

der **Außenhandel** foreign trade

das **Gehalt, ̈er** salary

der **Grund, ̈e** reason

der **Handel** trade

der **Kunde, -n, -n**/die **Kundin, -nen** customer, client

der **Mitarbeiter, -**/die **Mitarbeiterin, -nen** employee

die **Post** mail; post office

der **Preis, -e** price

der **Satz, ̈e** sentence

die **Sorge, -n** care, worry; **sich Sorgen machen (um)** to worry (about)

der **Streik, -s** strike

die **Ware, -n** wares, merchandise, goods

die **Zukunft** future

Verben

antworten (+ *dat.*) to answer (*as in* **ich antworte der Frau**); **antworten auf** (+ *acc.*) to answer (*as in* **ich antworte auf die Frage**)

aus·machen to matter; **es macht mir nichts aus** it doesn't matter to me

bedeuten to mean; **Was bedeutet das?** What does that mean?

dauern to last; to require time

finden: fände would find

her·stellen to produce; to manufacture

klingeln to ring

konkurrieren to compete

können: könnte would be able to

merken to notice; to realize

müssen: müsste would have to

sparen to save

verkaufen to sell

verlieren, verlor, verloren to lose

sich vor·bereiten (**auf** + *acc.*) to prepare oneself (for)

wollen: wollte would want

Andere Wörter

arbeitslos unemployed, out of work

diesmal this time

leer empty

links on/to the left

niedrig low

rechts on/to the right

unsicher insecure; unsafe

Besondere Ausdrücke

[ich bin] dran it is [my] turn

Moment mal! Just a minute!

wie immer as always

zur Zeit at the moment

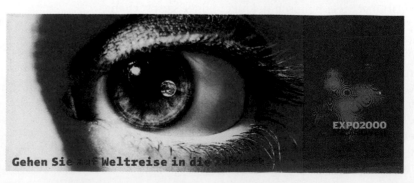

EXPO2000

Gehen Sie auf Weltreise in die Zukunft

Die Europäische Union

The European Union **(Europäische Union)** strives for economic and political union of its member countries. Since its beginning as the European Community **(Europäische Gemeinschaft)**, it has made considerable progress in creating a single market without internal borders. Goods, services, and capital can move freely without custom regulations within the EU. Citizens of EU countries can, without restrictions, travel, live, and work anywhere within the EU.

The European Union now stretches from the Arctic Circle to the island of Crete in the Mediterranean. Over 374.5 million people live in the EU. The gross domestic products **(Bruttosozialprodukt)** of the EU and the U.S.A. are the two largest in the world.

In spite of its successes, many problems and goals remain. Working hours, wages, and extended benefits are issues that need to be resolved. The goal of a political confederation of states with common foreign and defense policies and common laws seems to be even more difficult to obtain.

Go to the
Deutsch heute Web Site at
www.hmco.com/college

Diskussion

Citizens of the European Union have certain rights in common. These rights are called single market rights. Often the rights guaranteed by the European Commission in regard to job qualifications or residence conflict with the regulations of an individual member state. One of the most common areas of conflict concerns vehicles. For instance, a problem resolved by the Commission concerned a

Alle fünf Jahre findet eine Europawahl statt.

ban on trailers towed by motorcycles in Denmark. Danish legislation (Traffic Law §70) applied this prohibition to foreign-registered as well as Danish-registered motorcycles. The Commission considered the prohibition incompatible with the principle of free movement of goods in the single market (Article 30 of the EC Treaty). Following the Commission's intervention, the Danish legislation in question has been modified to permit motorcycles in Denmark to tow trailers. The move has been warmly welcomed by motorcycle enthusiasts in both Denmark and other member states.

Do you agree with the way in which the conflict was resolved?

GRAMMATIK UND ÜBUNGEN

der Konjunktiv

1. Subjunctive mood° vs. indicative mood

Indicative	Kerstin kommt heute nicht.	*Kerstin is not coming today.*
	Vielleicht kommt sie morgen.	*Perhaps she'll come tomorrow.*

In *Kapitel 1–10* you have primarily been using verbs in sentences that make statements and ask questions dealing with "real" situations. Verb forms of this type are said to be in the indicative mood. The indicative is used in statements that are factual *(Kerstin is not coming today)* or likely *(Perhaps she'll come tomorrow)*.

Subjunctive	Ich **würde** das nicht **tun.**	I *would* not *do* that.
	Ich **täte** das nicht.	
	Hätte Stefan das **getan?**	*Would* Stefan *have done* that?

When we talk about "unreal" situations we may use verbs in the subjunctive mood. The subjunctive is used in statements that are hypothetical, potential, unlikely, or contrary to fact. When a speaker says "I wouldn't do that," she/he means "I wouldn't do that if I were you (or she, he, or someone else)," because she/he thinks it is not a good idea. When the speaker asks "Would Stefan have done that?", she/he is postulating a hypothetical situation.

Wishes	Ich **möchte** eine Tasse Kaffee.	I *would like* a cup of coffee.
Polite requests	**Würden** Sie das bitte **tun?**	*Would* you *do* that, please?

The subjunctive is also used to express wishes and polite requests. You have been using **möchte** to express wishes since *Kapitel 3*. **Möchte** *(would like)* is the subjunctive form of **mögen** *(to like)*.

German has two ways to express the subjunctive mood. One way is to use the **würde**-construction (Ich **würde** das nicht **tun**). The other way is to use the subjunctive form of the main verb (Ich **täte** das nicht). The meaning of both ways is the same (I *would* not *do* that). In conversational German the **würde**-construction is used much more frequently than the subjunctive form of main verbs, with the exception of a few verbs that are commonly used in the subjunctive (**hätte, wäre,** and the modals).

Present-time	Wenn ich nur Zeit **hätte.**	If only I *had* time.
Past-time	Wenn ich nur Zeit **gehabt hätte.**	If only I *had had (would have had)* time.

Subjunctive forms express two time categories: present time, which also can refer to the future *(if only I had time now or in the future)*, and past time *(if only I had had time in the past)*.

2. The *würde*-construction°

Ich **würde** das nicht **machen.**   I *would*n't *do* that.
Max **würde** uns bestimmt **helfen.**   Max *would* certainly *help* us.

To talk about "unreal" situations in the present, German often uses a **würde**-construction. English uses a *would*-construction.

ich **würde** es **machen**	wir **würden** es **machen**
du **würdest** es **machen**	ihr **würdet** es **machen**
er/es/sie **würde** es **machen**	sie **würden** es **machen**
Sie **würden** es **machen**	

The **würde**-construction consists of a form of **würde** plus an infinitive. **Würde** is the subjunctive form of **werden.** It is formed by adding an umlaut to **wurde,** the simple past of **werden.**

1. Freizeit.   Was würden die folgenden Leute tun, wenn sie nächste Woche frei hätten?

⋙ Jens   sein Referat fertig schreiben   *Jens würde sein Referat fertig schreiben.*

1. Christoph — viel im Internet surfen
2. ich — faulenzen
3. Liane und Ina — jeden Tag ins Kino gehen
4. du — öfter ins Fitnesscenter gehen
5. mein Onkel Mark — Rollerblading lernen
6. meine Eltern — eine kleine Reise machen

3. Uses of the *würde*-construction

Hypothetical statements	Ich **würde** ihm **helfen.**	I *would help* him.
Wishes	Wenn er mir nur helfen **würde.**	If only he *would help* me.
Polite requests	**Würden** Sie mir bitte **helfen?**	*Would* you please *help* me?

The **würde**-construction is used in hypothetical statements, in wishes, and in polite requests.

2. Monika würde das auch gern tun.   Was würde Monika auch gern tun? Benutzen Sie die **würde**-Konstruktion und **gern.**

⋙ Christine arbeitet in einer großen Firma.   *Monika würde auch gern in einer großen Firma arbeiten.*

1. Christine verdient viel.
2. Sie macht oft Geschäftsreisen.
3. Sie fährt dreimal im Jahr in Urlaub.
4. Sie kauft sich eine größere Wohnung.
5. Am Wochenende macht sie Fitnesstraining.

Inquiring about someone's wishes

➪ **3. Was würden Sie gern machen?** Beantworten Sie die folgenden Fragen erst selbst und vergleichen Sie Ihre Antworten dann mit den Antworten von zwei anderen Kursteilnehmerinnen/Kursteilnehmern.

class (session)

➤➤ Was würdest du nach dem Deutschkurs° am liebsten machen?
Ich würde am liebsten nach Hause gehen/einen Kaffee trinken/schlafen.

1. Was würdest du heute Abend gern machen?
2. Was würdest du am Freitagabend am liebsten machen?
3. Was würdest du im Sommer gern machen?
4. Was würdest du nach dem Studium gern machen?
5. Von wem würdest du am liebsten einen Brief, eine E-Mail oder einen Anruf bekommen?

der Konjunktiv der Gegenwart

4. Present-time subjunctive° of the main verb

Wenn Alex besser Golf **spielte,** würden wir mit ihm spielen.	If Alex *played* better golf, we'd play with him.
Wenn ich das **könnte**, würde ich es tun.	If I *could* (do that), I would (do it).
Wenn sie müde **wäre**, würde sie ins Bett gehen.	If she *were* (colloquial: *was*) tired, she would go to bed.

Notice that in English the subjunctive forms of main verbs are often identical with the past tense (e.g., *played, could, were* [colloquial: *was*]). In German the same principle applies. For weak verbs, the present-time subjunctive is identical to the simple past tense (e.g., **spielte**); for modals and strong verbs, the subjunctive is based on the simple-past tense form of the verb (e.g., **konnte > könnte, war > wäre**). German uses the present-time subjunctive to express subjunctive for present and future time.

5. Present-time subjunctive of the main verb vs. the *würde*-construction

Present-time subjunctive	*Würde*-construction
Wenn er nur besser **spielte**.	Wenn er nur besser **spielen würde**.
Wenn sie nur etwas **täte**.	Wenn sie nur etwas **tun würde**.
Wenn er nur **ginge**.	Wenn er nur **gehen würde**.

In present-time either the **würde**-construction or the subjunctive form of the main verb can be used. However, for the verbs **sein, haben,** and the modals, the present-time subjunctive is generally used instead of the **würde**-construction.

dream

Eine Million im Lotto – was nun?
CDs für eine Million wäre mein Traum.°
(Chrissi, 24)

6. Present-time subjunctive of *sein* and *haben*

sein	
ich wäre	wir wären
du wärest	ihr wäret
er/es/sie wäre	sie wären
Sie wären	

haben	
ich hätte	wir hätten
du hättest	ihr hättet
er/es/sie hätte	sie hätten
Sie hätten	

The verbs **haben** and **sein** are more commonly used in their subjunctive forms, **wäre** and **hätte,** than as part of the **würde**-construction. Notice that the subjunctive of **haben** is identical to the simple past tense (i.e., **hatte**) except that an umlaut has been added.

In strong verbs like **sein** the endings **-est** and **-et** often contract to **-st** and **-t: wärest > wärst, wäret > wärt.** Note that the endings above are used on all verbs in the subjunctive.

4. Wären alle froh darüber?   Manche Politiker möchten auf allen Autobahnen ein Tempolimit°. Sagen Sie, was die folgenden Leute davon halten.   speed limit

≫ Robert / sicher froh   *Robert wäre sicher froh.*

1. Christine / unglücklich
2. du / sicher auch unglücklich
3. Corinna und Rafael / dagegen
4. wir / dafür
5. ihr / hoffentlich dafür
6. die Grünen / glücklich
7. ich / sehr froh

5. Was hättest du lieber?   Sagen Sie, was für eine Stelle Sie lieber hätten.

≫ Was hättest du lieber? Eine Stelle mit einem guten Gehalt oder viel Freizeit?   *Ich hätte lieber eine Stelle mit viel Freizeit.*

1. mit viel Verantwortung oder wenig Verantwortung?
2. in einer großen Firma oder in einer kleinen Firma?
3. mit netten Kollegen oder mit einem netten Chef?
4. in der Nähe° einer Großstadt oder in einer Kleinstadt?   vicinity
5. mit vielen Geschäftsreisen oder ohne Geschäftsreisen?

6. Hättest du Lust?   Entscheiden° Sie erst selbst, was Sie in Ihrer Freizeit   decide
machen wollen. Dann fragen Sie drei Kursteilnehmerinnen/Kursteilnehmer, was sie gern machen möchten.

S1:

Hättest du Lust | **Rollerblading zu gehen?**
ins Kino zu gehen?
eine Party zu geben?
eine Radtour zu machen?
Musik zu hören?
ein Video auszuleihen?
Russisch zu lernen?
einkaufen zu gehen?

S2:

Das wäre schön.
Wenn ich nur Geld hätte.
Das würde ich gern machen.
Das würde Spaß machen.
Wenn ich nur Zeit hätte.
Dazu hätte ich keine Lust.

Go to the
Deutsch heute Web Site at
www.hmco.com/college

Berufliche Ausbildung

Despite high income-tax rates and high labor costs, Germany has a very productive economy. Experts attribute this in large measure to the fact that Germany has a well-trained labor force.

Most young people who finish the **Hauptschule** (*see* **Das Schulsystem in Deutschland**, p. 130) or have a **Mittlere Reife** enter an apprenticeship (**Ausbildung**) program. There are approximately 400 such **Ausbildungsberufe**. An **Ausbildung** generally lasts three years. During this time the trainees (**Auszubildende**, also called **Lehrlinge**) work three to four days a week in a company and attend vocational school (**Berufsschule**) one to two days a week. Large companies have special workshops and staffs for trainees; in small businesses trainees often learn directly from the boss. **Auszubildende** receive benefits and a salary that increases every year. At the end of their **Ausbildung** trainees take exams both at the workplace and the **Berufsschule**. By passing the exam a woman becomes a journeywoman (**Gesellin**) and a man becomes a journeyman (**Geselle**). After five more years of work and additional schooling a **Geselle/Gesellin** may become a **Meister/Meisterin**. People who achieve the status of **Meister/Meisterin** have demonstrated on the basis of rigorous testing that they possess all the knowledge and skills necessary to operate a business. Only people who have passed the **Meisterprüfung** are allowed to train **Auszubildende** (**Azubis**).

Eine Wissenschaftlerin mit einer Auszubildenden im European Space Operations Center in Darmstadt.

Diskussion

1. Imagine that you would like to open a cabinetry business and perhaps teach young people carpentry. Compare what you would need to do to achieve your goal in Germany with your own country.
2. In Germany one needs apprenticeship training to become a mechanic, a hairdresser or a graphic artist. Compare this situation to that in your own country.

Expressing wishes

7. Wenn ich nur ... Sagen Sie Ihrer Partnerin/Ihrem Partner, was Sie sich wünschen, und fragen Sie sie/ihn dann, was ihre/seine Wünsche sind. Hier sind einige Möglichkeiten.

1. Wenn ich nur [...] hätte.

   mehr Geld □ Zeit □ mehr Freunde □ weniger Probleme □ Arbeit □ keine Hausaufgaben □ ein besseres Auto □ mehr Energie

2. Wenn ich nur [...] wäre.

   toleranter □ fleißiger □ ruhiger □ nicht so müde □ nicht so faul □ älter □ berühmt

7. Conditional sentences°

der Konditionalsatz

A conditional sentence contains two clauses: the condition (**wenn**-clause) and the conclusion. The **wenn**-clause states the conditions under which some event may or may not take place.

■ *Conditions of fact*

Wenn ich Zeit **habe, komme** ich **mit.**

If I *have* time (maybe I will, maybe I won't), I'll *come* along.

Conditions of fact are conditions that can be fulfilled. Indicative verb forms are used in conditions of fact.

■ *Conditions contrary to fact*

Wenn ich Zeit **hätte, würde** ich **mitkommen.**
Wenn ich Zeit **hätte, käme** ich mit.

If I *had* time [but I don't], I *would come along.*

A sentence with a condition contrary to fact indicates a situation that will not take place. The speaker only speculates on how some things could or would be under certain conditions (if the speaker had time, for example).

To talk about the present, a speaker uses present-time subjunctive of the main verb (e.g., **hätte**) in the condition clause (**wenn**-clause) and in the conclusion a **würde**-construction (e.g., **würde mitkommen**) or the present-time subjunctive of the main verb (e.g., **käme**). Formal written German tends to avoid the **würde**-construction in the **wenn**-clause. Subjunctive forms of strong and weak verbs are discussed under headings 9–11 in this section.

8. Frage-Ecke. Fragen Sie Ihre Partnerin/Ihren Partner und finden Sie heraus, was die folgenden Leute tun würden, wenn sie arbeitslos oder krank wären oder wenn sie mehr Zeit und viel Geld hätten.

S1: Was würde Frau Müller machen, wenn sie mehr Zeit hätte?
S2: Wenn sie mehr Zeit hätte, (dann) würde sie öfter Tennis spielen.

S1:

	arbeitslos wäre	krank wäre	mehr Zeit hätte	viel Geld hätte
Frau Müller	Zeitung lesen		öfter Tennis spielen	in die Schweiz reisen
Herr Schäfer		viel schlafen		
Susanne und Moritz	spazieren gehen		Auto fahren	
ich				
Partnerin/Partner				

S2:

	arbeitslos wäre	krank wäre	mehr Zeit hätte	viel Geld hätte
Frau Müller		zum Arzt gehen		
Herr Schäfer	eine neue Stelle suchen		seine Freunde besuchen	ein neues Auto kaufen
Susanne und Moritz		nichts essen		ihr Haus renovieren
ich				
Partnerin/Partner				

9. Was wäre, wenn ... ? Beantworten Sie die folgenden Fragen erst selbst. Fragen Sie dann Ihre Partnerin/Ihren Partner, was sie/er tun würde. Berichten Sie den Kursteilnehmerinnen/Kursteilnehmern, was Sie herausgefunden haben.

Was würdest du tun,
1. wenn du 10 Jahre älter wärest?
2. wenn du sehr reich wärest?
3. wenn du Deutschlehrerin/Deutschlehrer wärest?
4. wenn du Präsidentin/Präsident der USA wärest?
5. wenn du kein Geld fürs Studium hättest?
6. wenn deine Freunde keine Zeit für dich hätten?
7. wenn du morgen frei hättest?
8. wenn du kein Auto hättest?
9. wenn dein Fernseher kaputt wäre?
10. wenn du morgen krank wärest?
11. wenn wir morgen 30°C hätten?

S1: Was würdest du tun, wenn du 10 Jahre älter wärest?
S2: Ich würde ein Haus kaufen/ein Buch schreiben/heiraten.

8. Modals in present-time subjunctive

Infinitive		Simple past	Present-time subjunctive
dürfen		durfte	**dürfte**
können		konnte	**könnte**
mögen	er/es/sie	mochte	**möchte**
müssen		musste	**müsste**
sollen		sollte	**sollte**
wollen		wollte	**wollte**

The present-time subjunctive of modals is identical to the simple-past tense except that the modals that have an umlaut in the infinitive also have an umlaut in the subjunctive.

Müsstest du die Arbeit allein machen?   *Would* you *have* to do the work alone?

Like **sein (wäre)** and **haben (hätte),** the modals are generally used in their subjunctive form rather than as infinitives with the **würde-**construction.

Dürfte ich auch mitkommen?	*Might* I come along, too?
Könntest du noch etwas bleiben?	*Could* you stay a while?
Müsste sie vor allen Leuten sprechen?	*Would* she *have to* speak in front of all the people?
Möchten Sie in einer Stunde essen?	*Would* you *like to* eat in an hour?
Solltet ihr jetzt nicht gehen?	*Should*n't you be going now?

The subjunctive forms of the modals are frequently used to express polite requests or wishes.

Ich wollte, ich hätte Zeit.	*I wish* I had time.
Ich wollte, sie käme bald.	*I wish* she would come soon.

The expression **ich wollte** is used frequently to introduce wishes. Note that the verb **wollte** is subjunctive. Thus, strictly, **ich wollte** is equivalent to *I would wish.*

10. Etwas höflicher°, bitte!   Sie und einige Freunde möchten heute Abend ausgehen. Sie haben einige Fragen. Sie wollen höflich sein und benutzen deshalb den Konjunktiv für die Modalverben.

more politely

➤➤ Können wir das Restaurant allein finden?   *Können wir das Restaurant allein finden?*

1. Können wir nicht bald gehen?
2. Du musst noch abwaschen.
3. Kann ich dir helfen?
4. Dürfen Susi und Christiane mitkommen?
5. Sollen wir Gerd nicht auch einladen?
6. Darf ich für euch alle etwas zu trinken kaufen?
7. Kannst du für das Essen zahlen?

11. Wenn es nur anders wäre.   Sie wünschen sich, dass vieles in Ihrem Studentenheim anders wäre. Erzählen Sie einer Freundin/einem Freund davon.

⟫   Klaus kocht immer Spaghetti.   *Ich wollte, Klaus würde nicht immer Spaghetti kochen.*

⟫   Michael macht das Zimmer nicht sauber   *Ich wollte, Michael würde das Zimmer sauber machen.*

1. Martin spielt den ganzen Tag Computerspiele.
2. Christoph hört immer Musik.
3. Bernd redet so viel.
4. Wolfgang kommt immer zu spät.
5. Stefan schließt die Tür nicht.

12. Ich wollte, ich könnte ...   Ergänzen Sie die Sätze. Finden Sie dann heraus, was Ihre Partnerin/Ihr Partner geschrieben hat und was sie/er gern tun würde.

1. Ich wollte, ich könnte _____ .

2. Wenn ich Zeit hätte, _____ .

3. Wenn meine Eltern viel Geld hätten, _____ .

4. Ich sollte _____ .

5. Ich würde gern _____ .

13. Was ist dir im Leben am wichtigsten?   Finden Sie heraus, was drei bis vier Lebensziele von Ihrer Partnerin/Ihrem Partner sind.

S1: Was ist dir im Leben wichtig?
S2: Ich möchte vor allem [einen guten Job haben].
     Dann möchte ich [einen Sinn° im Leben finden].
     Drittens möchte ich [gesund sein].

Lebensziele:
heiraten und Kinder haben
viel Geld verdienen
gesund sein
schöne Dinge haben wie ein tolles Auto, teure Kleidung
ein schönes/großes Haus haben
einen guten Job haben
Glück haben
Spaß und Freude am Leben haben
einen Sinn im Leben finden
anderen Menschen helfen

KÖNNTEN WIR NICHT BALD GEHEN?

9. Present-time subjunctive of strong verbs

Infinitive		Simple past	+ umlaut for a, o, u	+ subjunctive ending	Present-time subjunctive
kommen	er/es/sie {	kam	käm	-e	käme
bleiben		blieb	blieb	-e	bliebe

kommen	
ich **käme**	wir **kämen**
du **kämest**	ihr **kämet**
er/es/sie **käme**	sie **kämen**
Sie **kämen**	

The present-time subjunctive of strong verbs is formed by adding subjunctive endings to the simple-past stem of the verb. An umlaut is added to the stem vowels **a**, **o**, or **u**. For a list of subjunctive forms of strong verbs, see #23 of the Grammatical Tables in the Reference Section. Although the **würde**-construction and the subjunctive form of the main verb are equivalent in meaning, the **würde**-construction is more common in spoken German.

14. An einem langweiligen Arbeitstag. Hier sind einige Gedanken°, die Frau Müller hat, wenn sie sich im Büro langweilt°. Die Verben in diesen Sätzen sind im Konjunktiv. Suchen Sie den passenden englischen Satz auf der rechten Seite.

thoughts
langweilt sich: is bored

⟫ Das ginge. *That would work.*

1. Das täte ich gern.
2. Wir kämen gern zu der Konferenz.
3. Frau Lange ginge sicher mit zum Chef.
4. So etwas gäbe es bei mir nicht.
5. Das wäre ein gutes Geschäft.
6. Und wenn die Sekretärin krank würde?

a. That would be a good deal.
b. Such a thing would never happen with me.
c. And (what) if the secretary would get sick?
d. I would do that gladly.
e. We would be glad to come to the conference.
f. Frau Lange would certainly come along to [see] the boss.

15. Ferienträume°. Frank träumt von den Ferien und was er machen könnte, wenn alles anders wäre. Ergänzen Sie Franks Sätze und benutzen Sie den Konjunktiv des Hauptverbs° für den ersten Teil des Satzes und die **würde**-Konstruktion für das Ende.

vacation dreams

main verb

⟫ Leider habe ich kein Auto, aber wenn _____ . (in die Schweiz fahren)
Leider habe ich kein Auto, aber wenn ich ein Auto hätte, dann würde ich in die Schweiz fahren.

1. Es gibt keinen Schnee, aber wenn _____ . (Ski laufen)

2. Leider habe ich kein Geld, aber wenn _____ . (nach Hawaii fliegen)

3. Es ist nicht warm genug, aber wenn _____ . (zelten)

4. Dieses Buch ist nicht interessant, aber wenn _____ . (lesen)

5. Ich habe keine Lust, aber wenn _____ . (mir ein Video ausleihen)

10. Present-time subjunctive of regular weak verbs

Infinitive		Simple past	Present-time subjunctive
spielen		spielte	**spielte**
kaufen	er/es/sie	kaufte	**kaufte**
arbeiten		arbeitete	**arbeitete**
baden		badete	**badete**

The present-time subjunctive forms of regular weak verbs are identical to the simple-past forms.

16. Wenn Corinna das nur machte!   Corinna spielt in einer kleinen Band Gitarre. Ihre Freunde haben sie zum Wochenende eingeladen. Ergänzen Sie die Sätze und benutzen Sie den Konjunktiv des Verbs in Klammern. Übersetzen Sie dann die Sätze für einen der Gäste, der° kein Deutsch spricht.

who

➤➤ Wenn Nils nicht so oft _____ (telefonieren), könnte Corinna uns anrufen. *Wenn Nils nicht so oft telefonierte, könnte Corinna uns anrufen. (If Nils wouldn't telephone so often, Corinna would be able to call us.)*

1. Wenn Corinna uns _____ (besuchen), dann könnte sie nicht arbeiten.

2. Wenn ihre Freunde mitkämen, _____ (brauchen) sie nicht allein zu spielen.

joined in

3. Wenn ihre Freunde _____ (mitmachen°), könnten wir die Nachbarn

    einladen.

play with (them)

4. Wenn Nils eine Gitarre _____ (kaufen), müsste er auch mitspielen°.

5. Wenn die Gitarre nicht so viel _____ (kosten), könnten wir sie ihm kaufen.

11. Present-time subjunctive of irregular weak verbs

Infinitive		Simple past	Present-time subjunctive
bringen		brachte	brächte
denken	er/es/sie	dachte	dächte
wissen		wusste	wüsste

The present-time subjunctive forms of irregular weak verbs are like the simple-past forms, but with an umlaut added.

17. Ein Picknick.   Stefan spricht mit seiner Schwester Monika über seine Pläne für ein Picknick. Übersetzen Sie, was er sagt, ins Englische.

STEFAN: Hättest du Zeit mitzukommen?
MONIKA: Ich dächte schon.
STEFAN: Ich wüsste nicht, wen wir sonst einladen sollten.
MONIKA: Vielleicht Onkel Max und Tante Gabi.
STEFAN: Vielleicht könnten wir alle zusammen fahren?
MONIKA: Schön. Das könnten wir.
STEFAN: Wenn ich nur wüsste, wo die beiden sind!
MONIKA: Was meinst du, was brächte Onkel Max mit?

herring

STEFAN: Heringe°, wie immer. Ich brächte etwas zu trinken mit.

12. Past-time subjunctive°

Wenn sie das **gewusst hätte, hätte** sie mir **geholfen.**	If she *had known* that, she *would have helped* me.
Wenn sie das **gewusst hätte, wäre** sie nicht **mitgekommen.**	If she *had known* that, she *would not have come* along.

The past-time subjunctive consists of the subjunctive forms **hätte** or **wäre** + past participle. The past-time subjunctive is used to express hypothetical statements, wishes, and contrary-to-fact conditions in past time.

18. Wenn sie das gewusst hätte ...   Sagen Sie, was Beate gemacht oder nicht gemacht hätte, wenn sie gewusst hätte, dass das Wetter am Wochenende schön ist.

➤ Sie ist übers Wochenende nicht weggefahren.
➤ Sie ist zu Hause geblieben.

Wenn sie das gewusst hätte, wäre sie übers Wochenende weggefahren.
Wenn sie das gewusst hätte, wäre sie nicht zu Hause geblieben.

1. Sie ist nicht an den See° gefahren.   lake
2. Sie hat ihre Freunde nicht zum Picknick eingeladen.
3. Sie hat nicht gezeltet.
4. Sie ist nicht schwimmen gegangen.
5. Sie ist ins Kino gegangen.
6. Sie hat so viel geschlafen.

19. Sie hätten es anders gemacht.   Alle sind unzufrieden damit, was sie gestern gemacht haben. Ergänzen Sie die Sätze und sagen Sie, was die Leute lieber gemacht hätten.

➤ Karin ist schwimmen gegangen, aber _____ (lieber ins Theater gegangen).
➤ Marc hat gearbeitet, aber _____ (lieber geschlafen).

Karin ist schwimmen gegangen, aber sie wäre lieber ins Theater gegangen.
Marc hat gearbeitet, aber er hätte lieber geschlafen.

1. Ich habe in der Mensa° gegessen, aber _____ (lieber in einem eleganten   university cafeteria

   Restaurant gegessen).

2. Katarina hat an einem Referat gearbeitet, aber _____ (lieber im Garten gear-

   beitet).

3. Heike und Lars haben Tennis gespielt, aber _____ (lieber gewandert).

4. Klaus hat ferngesehen, aber _____ (lieber ins Kino gegangen).

5. Corinna hat klassische Musik gehört, aber _____ (lieber Hardrock gehört).

6. Dirk hat sich aufs Examen vorbereitet, aber _____ (lieber eine Radtour

   gemacht).

20. Eine schwere Woche. Ihre Kursteilnehmerinnen/Kursteilnehmer beschweren sich° über die schwere Woche, die° sie gehabt haben. Suchen Sie sich einen Tag aus und fragen Sie sie, was sie an dem Tag gemacht haben. Fragen Sie dann, was sie lieber gemacht hätten. Dann sagen Sie, was Sie lieber gemacht hätten. Hier sind einige Sprechhilfen°.

S1: Was hast du am Mittwoch gemacht?
S2: Am Mittwoch habe ich den Chef zum Flughafen gebracht.
S1: Was hättest du lieber gemacht?
S2: Ich wäre lieber auf eine Party gegangen. Und du, was hast du ...?

1. Am Montagabend bin ich lange [im Büro/in der Bibliothek] geblieben.
2. Am Dienstag bin ich zu [einem Kunden/Freund] nach [Frankfurt] gefahren.
3. Am Mittwoch habe ich [den Chef/meine Mutter] zum Flughafen gebracht.
4. Am Donnerstag habe ich den ganzen Tag am Computer gearbeitet.
5. Am Freitag bin ich mit meinen [Kollegen/Freunden] essen gegangen.
6. Am Samstag habe ich [meine Wohnung/mein Zimmer] aufgeräumt.
7. Am Sonntag habe ich alle neuen Zeitschriften durchgesehen.

Stichwörter:

ins Kino gehen   zu meiner Freundin fahren

meinen Freund besuchen   auf eine Party gehen

ein gutes Buch lesen   mir ein Video ausleihen

im Garten sitzen   im Internet surfen

in der Sonne liegen   faulenzen

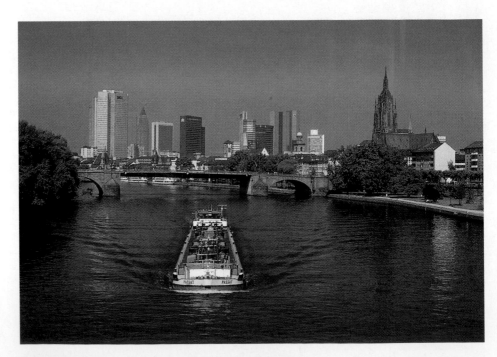

Frankfurt am Main ist das deutsche Bankzentrum.

WIEDERHOLUNG

1. Was sagen Sie?   Sagen Sie, was Sie unter bestimmten Bedingungen° tun würden. Fragen Sie dann Ihre Partnerin/Ihren Partner.

unter ... Bedingungen: under certain circumstances

Was würdest du tun, ...

1. wenn du viel Geld bekämest?
2. wenn heute Sonntag wäre?
3. wenn du heute Geburtstag hättest?
4. wenn du jetzt zwei Wochen Ferien hättest?
5. wenn du das teure Essen im Restaurant nicht bezahlen könntest?
6. wenn Freunde dich zu einem Fest nicht einladen würden?

2. Meine Freundin Sandra.   Erzählen Sie von Ihrer Freundin Sandra und setzen Sie die fehlenden° Präpositionen in die Lücken° ein.

missing / blanks

1. Habe ich dir _____ meiner Freundin Sandra erzählt?

2. Mit 19 Jahren hat sie _____ dem Studium angefangen.

3. Jetzt arbeitet sie _____ Siemens.

4. Sie arbeitet den ganzen Tag _____ Computer.

5. Sie und ihre Kollegen bereiten sich _____ eine Konferenz vor.

6. Sie erzählt ihrem Freund _____ ihrer Arbeit.

7. In ihrer Freizeit schreibt sie einen Roman. Sie spricht gern mit Mark _____ ihr Projekt.

3. Was möchten Sie?   Erzählen Sie, was Sie möchten. Ergänzen Sie die Sätze mit den Adjektiven in Klammern oder anderen passenden Akjektiven. Achten Sie auf die richtigen Adjektivendungen.

1. Wenn ich Geld hätte, würde ich mir ein _____ **Auto** kaufen. (klein, groß, billig, teuer)

2. Ich wollte, man würde mich zu einem _____ **Fest** einladen. (nett, toll, klein, laut, interessant)

3. Ich möchte einen _____ **Pulli** kaufen. (warm, blau, leicht, toll)

4. Ich würde gern mal einen _____ **Film** sehen. (toll, interessant, schön, modern, klassisch, gut)

5. Ich möchte eine _____ **Reise** nach Deutschland machen. (lang, kurz, billig)

6. Ich möchte einen Computer haben, aber es müsste ein _____ **Computer** sein. (billig, teuer, klein, einfach, groß, schnell, anwenderfreundlich°)

user-friendly

4. Was hat er gemacht?   Lesen Sie, was Michael gestern gemacht hat. Beantworten Sie dann die Fragen dazu.

Michael ging morgens für eine Stunde zu einer Vorlesung. Nachmittags saß er in der Bibliothek und arbeitete. Den Abend hatte er frei. Er ging mit Freunden in eine Kneipe. Da war die Musik live. Es war eine Volksliedgruppe°. Alle Studenten sangen mit. Das hat viel Spaß gemacht.

folk song group

1. Wohin ging Michael morgens?
2. Was machte er nachmittags?
3. Wohin ging er abends?
4. Warum gingen Michael und seine Freunde in die Kneipe?
5. Wer sang mit?

5. Wie sagt man das?

1. I have nothing planned for the weekend. (*use* **vorhaben;** for = **am**)
   —Would you like to go hiking?
2. Could it be that Erik is ill?
   —I don't know. You could ask him.
3. Would you like to go for a walk?
   —Gladly. I could go this afternoon.
4. Could you help me, please?
   —I wish I had (the) time.
5. Would you like to watch TV?
   —No. I don't feel like it.

6. Deutsch als Berufssprache.   Viele Studentinnen/Studenten lernen Deutsch, um bessere Qualifikationen für den Arbeitsmarkt zu haben. Aber es gibt auch andere Gründe Deutsch zu lernen. Hier sind fünf Gründe Deutsch zu lernen. Welcher ist für Sie der wichtigste Grund? Welche anderen Gründe gibt es Deutsch zu lernen? Besprechen Sie Ihre Antworten mit Ihrer Partnerin/Ihrem Partner.

1. *Wichtige Verkehrssprache in Europa und in der Welt.*   100 Millionen Europäer haben Deutsch als Muttersprache. In Osteuropa lernen mehr Schüler Deutsch als Englisch. In Japan lernen 68% der Schüler Deutsch.

trading partner / non-European

2. *Mit Deutschen ins Geschäft kommen.*   Deutschland ist der wichtigste Handelspartner° für fast alle europäischen Länder und viele außereuropäische° Länder.

advantages

3. *Vorteile° im Tourismus.*   Besucher aus deutschsprachigen Ländern sind in vielen Ländern die größte und wichtigste Touristengruppe.

4. *Kultursprache Deutsch.*   Deutsch ist die Sprache Goethes, Nietzsches und Kafkas, von Mozart, Bach und Beethoven, von Freud und Einstein.

advances / occupy
research

5. *Wissenschaftliche Fortschritte°.*   Deutschsprachige Publikationen belegen° den zweiten Platz in der Forschung°. Deutschsprachige Wissenschaftler haben mehr als 78 Nobelpreise gewonnen.

wählen aus: choose
paragraph

7. Zum Schreiben.   Wählen Sie ein Thema aus° und schreiben Sie einen kurzen Abschnitt°.

differences
guideline

1. Schreiben Sie einen Abschnitt auf Deutsch über die wirtschaftlichen Unterschiede° zwischen Ihrem Land und Deutschland. Benutzen Sie die Fragen als Hilfestellung°.

- In welchem Land spielt der Außenhandel eine größere Rolle? Warum?
- Welches Land hat mehr Rohstoffe?
- Welche Produkte exportieren diese Länder vor allem?
- In welchem Land sehen die Chancen für eine gesunde Wirtschaft besser aus? Warum?

2. Wie wäre es, wenn Sie einen Tag mit einer berühmten Person verbringen°   spend time
   könnten? Die Person kann heute leben oder eine historische Persönlichkeit
   sein. Schreiben Sie einen kurzen Abschnitt über den Tag und benutzen Sie
   die Fragen als Hilfestellung°.   guideline

   - Was würden Sie machen?
   - Worüber würden Sie sprechen?
   - Warum möchten Sie den Tag mit diesem Menschen verbringen?

Hinweise:

1. Use the subjunctive when expressing hypothetical statements, suppositions, wishes.
2. In expressing hypothetical situations or giving reasons for your comments, you will be using dependent clauses. Be sure to watch the position of the verbs.

GRAMMATIK: ZUSAMMENFASSUNG

Subjunctive mood

Indicative	Ich **komme** nicht zur Party.	I'm not *coming* to the party.
	Was **hast** du **gemacht?**	What *did* you *do?*
	Kannst du mir **helfen?**	*Can* you *help* me?
Subjunctive	Ich **käme** nicht zur Party.	I *would*n't *come* to the party.
	Was **hättest** du **gemacht?**	What *would* you *have done?*
	Könntest du mir **helfen?**	*Could* you *help* me?

In both English and German, the indicative mood is used to talk about "real" conditions or factual situations. The subjunctive mood is used to talk about "unreal," hypothetical, uncertain, or unlikely events as well as to express wishes and polite requests.

Present-time subjunctive	Wenn ich heute (oder morgen) nur mehr Zeit **hätte.**	If only I *had (would have)* more time today (or tomorrow).
Past-time subjunctive	Wenn ich gestern nur mehr Zeit **gehabt hätte.**	If only I *had had (would have had)* more time yesterday.

Subjunctive forms express two time categories: present time (which can refer to the future as well) and past time.

The *würde*-construction

■ *Forms*

ich **würde** es **machen**	wir **würden** es **machen**
du **würdest** es **machen**	ihr **würdet** es **machen**
er/es/sie **würde** es **machen**	sie **würden** es **machen**
Sie **würden** es **machen**	

The **würde**-construction consists of a form of **würde** + infinitive. **Würde** is the subjunctive form of **werden**. It is formed by adding an umlaut to **wurde**, the simple past of **werden**.

■ *Uses*

Hypothetical statement	Ich **würde** das nicht **machen**.	I *would* not *do* that.
Wishes	Wenn er mir nur **helfen würde**.	If only he *would help* me.
Polite requests	**Würdest** du mir bitte **helfen**?	*Would* you please *help* me?

To talk about "unreal" situations or hypothetical statements in the present, to express wishes, and to make polite requests, German may use a **würde** construction. The **würde**-construction is the most common way to express subjunctive mood in conversational German.

Present-time subjunctive of main verbs

Ich **täte** das nicht. ⎫
Ich **würde** das nicht **tun**. ⎭   I *would*n't *do* that.

The subjunctive form of the main verb (e.g., **täte**) and the **würde**-construction (e.g., **würde tun**) are equivalent in meaning. However, the **würde**-construction is more common in conversation for most verbs.

Present-time subjunctive of *sein* and *haben*

sein	
ich **wäre**	wir **wären**
du **wärest**	ihr **wäret**
er/es/sie **wäre**	sie **wären**
Sie **wären**	

haben	
ich **hätte**	wir **hätten**
du **hättest**	ihr **hättet**
er/es/sie **hätte**	sie **hätten**
Sie **hätten**	

The verbs **haben** and **sein** are more commonly used in their subjunctive forms, **wäre** and **hätte**, than in the **würde**-construction.

Eine Million im Lotto – was nun?
Meine Familie könnte ein Auto gebrauchen. Ich selbst habe keine großen Träume.
(Miroslav, 21)

Modals in present-time subjunctive

Infinitive	Simple past	Present-time subjunctive
dürfen	durfte	**dürfte**
können	konnte	**könnte**
mögen	mochte	**möchte**
müssen	musste	**müsste**
sollen	sollte	**sollte**
wollen	wollte	**wollte**

The modals are generally used in their subjunctive form rather than as infinitives with the **würde-**construction.

Present-time subjunctive of strong verbs

Infinitive	Simple past	Present-time subjunctive
bleiben	blieb	**bliebe**
geben	gab	**gäbe**
gehen	ging	**ginge**
kommen	kam	**käme**
tun	tat	**täte**

The present-time subjunctive forms of strong verbs are formed by adding subjunctive endings to the simple-past stem. An umlaut is added to the stem vowels **a, o,** and **u.**

Subjunctive verb endings

ich	käm**e**	wir	käm**en**
du	käm**est**	ihr	käm**et**
er/es/sie	käm**e**	sie	käm**en**
	Sie	käm**en**	

The subjunctive endings above are used for all verbs. The subjunctive verb endings **-est** and **-et** often contract to **-st** and **-t: kämest > kämst, kämet > kämt.**

Present-time subjunctive of regular weak verbs

Infinitive	Simple past	Present-time subjunctive
kaufen	kaufte	**kaufte**
arbeiten	arbeitete	**arbeitete**

The present-time subjunctive forms of weak verbs are identical to the simple-past forms.

Present-time subjunctive of irregular weak verbs

Infinitive	Simple past	Present-time subjunctive
bringen	brachte	**brächte**
denken	dachte	**dächte**
wissen	wusste	**wüsste**

Past-time subjunctive

Wenn ich Zeit **gehabt hätte, wäre** ich **gekommen.**	If I *had had* time, I *would have come.*
Wenn sie hier **gewesen wäre, hätte** ich sie **gesehen.**	If she *had been* here, I *would have seen* her.

The past-time subjunctive consists of the subjunctive forms **hätte** or **wäre** + a past participle. A **würde-**construction exists in past-time, but it is not commonly used: **Ich würde es nicht getan haben.**

Uses of the *würde*-construction and the subjunctive of the main verb

■ *Hypothetical statements*

Ich **würde** das nicht **tun.** Ich **täte** das nicht.	I *would*n't *do* that [if I were you].
Ich **hätte** das auch **getan.**	I *would have done* that too.

■ *Wishes*

Wenn Inge das nur **tun würde.** Wenn Inge das nur **täte.**	If only Inge *would do* that.
Wenn Gabi das nur **getan hätte.**	If only Gabi *had done* that.

■ *Polite requests*

Würden Sie das für mich **tun?** **Täten** Sie das für mich?	*Would* you *do* that for me?
Könnten Sie das für mich **tun?**	*Could* you *do* that for me?

■ *Conditions contrary to fact*

Present time	
Wenn ich Zeit **hätte, käme** ich. Wenn ich Zeit **hätte, würde** ich **kommen.**	If I *had* time [but I don't], I *would come.*

Past time	
Wenn ich Zeit **gehabt hätte, wäre** ich **gekommen.**	If I *had had* time [but I didn't], I *would have come.*

Contrary-to-fact sentences consist of two clauses: the condition (**wenn-**clause) and the conclusion. Conditions contrary to fact cannot be fulfilled. Conditions contrary to fact are expressed in the subjunctive mood.

The *würde*-construction vs. present-time subjunctive of the main verb

Wenn Jutta nicht so fleißig
 wäre, hätte sie mehr Freizeit
 und **könnte** ein Hobby **haben.**

If Jutta *were* not so diligent,
 she *would have* more time and
 could have a hobby.

In conversational German the **würde**-construction is frequently used instead of the subjunctive of the main verb. However, the subjunctive of the main verb is preferred to the **würde**-construction for **sein (wäre), haben (hätte),** and the modals, e.g., **könnte.**

Wenn Gerd täglich Zeitung **läse,**
 würde er alles besser verstehen.

If Gerd *read* the newspaper daily,
 he would understand everything
 better.

Formal written German tends to avoid the **würde**-construction in the **wenn-**clause.

EINE KURZGESCHICHTE

Franz Hohler was born in 1943 in Biel, Switzerland. He is a well-known and popular cabaret artist who appears regularly in one-person shows in Switzerland and Germany. He is also a singer/songwriter **(Liedermacher)** *with a number of CD's to his credit and an author of plays for the stage, TV, and radio and of stories for children and adults. The essence of much of his work is satire. A good example of his humor with a serious intent is his story "Der Verkäufer und der Elch" from his work* Kontakt mit der Zeit *(1981).*

What view of successful merchandising does the factory owner in this story represent?

Der Verkäufer und der Elch
Eine Geschichte mit 128 deutschen Wörtern
Franz Hohler

Kennen Sie das Sprichwort° „Dem Elch° eine Gasmaske verkaufen?" Das sagt man bei uns von jemandem°, der sehr tüchtig° ist, und ich möchte jetzt erzählen, wie es zu diesem Sprichwort gekommen ist.

Es gab einmal einen Verkäufer, der war dafür berühmt°, daß er allen alles
5 verkaufen konnte.

Er hatte schon einem Zahnarzt eine Zahnbürste° verkauft, einem Bäcker ein Brot und einem Blinden einen Fernsehapparat.

„Ein wirklich guter Verkäufer bist du aber erst", sagten seine Freunde zu ihm, „wenn du einem Elch eine Gasmaske verkaufst."
10 Da ging der Verkäufer so weit nach Norden, bis er in einen Wald kam, in dem nur Elche wohnten.

proverb / moose
someone / capable

famous

toothbrush

„Guten Tag", sagte er zum ersten Elch, den er traf, „Sie brauchen bestimmt eine Gasmaske."

what for   „Wozu°?" fragte der Elch. „Die Luft ist gut hier."

nowadays   15   „Alle haben heutzutage° eine Gasmaske", sagte der Verkäufer.

„Es tut mir leid", sagte der Elch, „aber ich brauche keine."

„Warten Sie nur", sagte der Verkäufer, „Sie brauchen schon noch eine."

in the middle   Und wenig später begann er mitten° in dem Wald, in dem nur Elche wohnten, eine Fabrik zu bauen.

crazy   20   „Bist du wahnsinnig°?" fragten seine Freunde.

„Nein", sagte er, „ich will nur dem Elch eine Gasmaske verkaufen." Als
rose / poisonous /   die Fabrik fertig war, stiegen° soviel giftige° Abgase aus dem Schornstein°,
smokestack   daß der Elch bald zum Verkäufer kam und zu ihm sagte: „Jetzt brauche ich eine Gasmaske."

immediately   25   „Das habe ich gedacht", sagte der Verkäufer und verkaufte ihm sofort° eine. „Qualitätsware!" sagte er lustig.

„Die anderen Elche", sagte der Elch, „brauchen jetzt auch Gasmasken.
polite form   Hast du noch mehr?" (Elche kennen die Höflichkeitsform° mit „Sie" nicht.)

„Da habt ihr Glück", sagte der Verkäufer, „ich habe noch Tausende."

by the way   30   „Übrigens°", sagte der Elch, „was machst du in deiner Fabrik?"

„Gasmasken", sagte der Verkäufer.

P.S. Ich weiß doch nicht genau, ob es ein schweizerisches oder ein schwedi-
werden verwechselt: *are*   sches Sprichwort ist, aber die beiden Länder werden ja oft verwechselt°.
confused

Fragen

1. Welche Beispiele zeigen, dass der Verkäufer ein guter Verkäufer ist?
2. Was muss ein „sehr guter" Verkäufer verkaufen können?
3. Warum glaubt der Elch, dass er keine Gasmaske braucht?
4. Warum kann der Verkäufer Gasmasken an alle Elche verkaufen?

Fragen zur Diskussion

1. Glauben Sie, dass die Worte **„Dem Elch eine Gasmaske verkaufen"** wirklich ein Sprichwort sind? Warum (nicht)?
develops / necessity   2. Der Autor entwickelt° eine Situation, in der die Notwendigkeit° eines Pro-
arises   duktes entsteht°, damit Menschen es wollen oder brauchen. An was für
happened   Beispiele können Sie aus Ihrem eigenen Leben denken, wo dies geschehen°
ist?
3. Wo sehen Sie Beispiele von Ironie in dieser Geschichte?

LERNZIELE

Sprechintentionen
Talking about future plans
Talking about cultural events
Making suggestions
Discussing post-graduation plans
Discussing who invented, wrote, or
  discovered something

Lesestück
Wo ist mein Zuhause?

Land und Leute
Other nationalities in Germany

Grammatik
Future time: present tense
Future time: future tense
Relative clauses
Relative pronouns
Passive voice
Summary of uses of **werden**

Die multikulturelle Gesellschaft

*Diese jungen Leute
treffen sich in der
Fußgängerzone in
Hannover.*

BAUSTEINE FÜR GESPRÄCHE

Rockfans gegen Ausländerhass

MONIKA: Peter, hast du Lust am Wochenende zu dem Open-Air-Konzert in Frankfurt zu gehen?

PETER: Ich weiß nicht. Ich fliege in zwei Wochen nach Amerika zurück und wollte mir noch Freiburg ansehen.

MONIKA: Ach, komm' doch. Nach Freiburg kannst du auch nächstes Wochenende noch fahren.

PETER: Aber ich kenne keinen einzigen von den Rockmusikern, die da spielen werden!

MONIKA: Es geht ja gar nicht nur um die Musik. Das Motto ist „Heute die! Morgen du!" – Mit dem Konzert demonstrieren wir gegen Rassismus und Ausländerhass.

PETER: Glaubst du denn, dass da viele Leute kommen werden?

MONIKA: Oh ja! Stell' dir vor, man erwartet ungefähr 150.000 Menschen.

PETER: Gut, dann lass uns gehen und auch demonstrieren!

Brauchbares

1. **Frankfurt,** with a population of 653,000, is Germany's fifth largest city after **Berlin,** 3,471,000; **Hamburg,** 1,708,900; **München,** 1,321,500; **Köln,** 1,011,500. **Frankfurt** is an industrial city and banking center.

2. **Freiburg** is a popular tourist town because of its location at the foot of the Black Forest **(Schwarzwald)** mountains. There are numerous ski slopes, mountain trails for hiking, and lakes for boating, windsurfing and swimming. **Freiburg** has a famous cathedral and an excellent university, which many Americans attend.

3. **Demonstrieren:** In the 1990's Germany has been the scene of many events that give people the chance to voice their opposition to the hostility toward foreigners expressed by groups such as skinheads. These events have included rock concerts, each attended by as many as 150,000 people, as well as **Lichterketten** (chains of people holding candles) with as many as 300,000 participants each.

4. **Lass uns:** The phrase **lass uns** is equivalent to English *let's (do something)*. The verb **lassen** is like the modals in that it takes an infinitive without **zu: lass uns gehen.**

Fragen

1. Warum wollte Peter zuerst nicht zu dem Open-Air-Konzert gehen?
2. Für Monika geht es nicht um die Musik. Worum geht es ihr?
3. Wie viele Leute erwartet man zu dem Konzert?

1. Nächste Woche.   Fragen Sie drei Kursteilnehmerinnen/Kursteilnehmer, was sie nächste Woche machen wollen.

Talking about future plans

S1:
Was machst du nächste Woche?

S2:
Ich fahre nach [Freiburg].
Ich fliege nach [Europa].
Ich fange einen neuen Job an.
Ich bereite ein Referat vor.

2. Kennst du das?   Spielen Sie zusammen mit Ihrer Partnerin/Ihrem Partner die Rolle von zwei Personen, die über kulturelle Veranstaltungen° sprechen.

events

Talking about cultural events

S1:
Kennst du

> **die Rockband, die heute [in der Stadt] spielt?**
> den Film, der diese Woche im [Odeon] spielt?
> die Oper, die heute Abend im Fernsehen kommt?
> den neuen Roman, den ich lesen sollte?

S2:
Ja, sehr gut sogar.
Ja, aber das interessiert mich nicht.
Nein, leider nicht.
Nein, warum fragst du?

3. Lass uns ins Konzert gehen.   Sprechen Sie in einer Gruppe darüber, was Sie machen wollen. Jedes Gruppenmitglied schlägt etwas anderes vor°.

schlägt vor: suggests

Making suggestions

➤➤ *Lass uns ...*

essen gehen ☐ unsere Freunde anrufen ☐ unseren Freunden helfen ☐ Tennis oder Fußball spielen ☐ joggen gehen ☐ den ganzen Tag faulenzen

Diese Gymnasiasten diskutieren in ihrer Arbeitsgruppe.

Vokabeln

Substantive

der **Ausländerhass**   xenophobia,
  hatred of foreigners
der **Fan, -s**   fan; supporter (sport)
der **Hass**   hate
das **Motto, -s**   motto

der **Rassismus**   racism
der **Rockfan, -s**   rock fan
der **Rockmusiker, -/die**
  Rockmusikerin, -nen   rock
  musician

Verben

an·sehen (sieht an), sah an,
  angesehen   to look at; **ich sehe**
  es mir an   I'm having a look at it
demonstrieren   to demonstrate
lassen (lässt), ließ, gelassen   to
  leave behind; to let, permit; **lass**
  uns gehen   let's go

sich (*dat.*) **vor·stellen**   to imagine;
  stell dir vor/stellen Sie sich
  vor   just imagine
zurück·fliegen, flog zurück, ist
  zurückgeflogen   to fly back

Andere Wörter

einzig   only, sole, single

Besondere Ausdrücke

es geht nicht nur um [die
  Musik]   it's not just about [the
  music]

WO IST MEIN ZUHAUSE?

Vorbereitung auf das Lesen[*]

influence

Sie lesen in diesem Text von Ausländern in Deutschland, ihrem Einfluss° auf die
deutsche Kultur° und ihren Problemen.

■ *Vor dem Lesen*

complete
connect

1. Die Kultur jedes Landes zeigt Elemente von anderen Ländern und Kulturen.
   Versuchen Sie in Gruppenarbeit die folgende Tabelle zu ergänzen°. Mit
   welcher Kultur oder welchem Land verbinden° Sie diese Dinge oder Ideen?

---

[*]Remember, words that appear with a raised degree mark (°) but for which no definition
is given in the margin are active words you should learn and be able to use. Their
definitions appear in the **Vokabeln** section that most closely follows the word.

Idee/Ding	Wo findet man sie/es?	Woher kommt sie/es?
Jeans	fast überall	Amerika
Kartoffeln		
Kaffee		
Football		
Fußball		
Demokratie		
Papier		
Kindergarten		

2. Listen Sie fünf Elemente Ihrer Kultur auf°. Wissen Sie, woher sie kommen?   **listen auf:** list

⫸ Jazz   Der Jazz kommt aus Amerika.

3. Sehen Sie sich die Tabelle unten an und schreiben Sie drei Sätze über die Tabelle.

⫸ Mehr Ausländer kommen aus Italien als aus Griechenland.

4. Was für Probleme könnten Ausländer in einer fremden Kultur haben? Machen Sie in Gruppenarbeit eine Liste von vier oder mehr Problemen.

■ *Beim Lesen*

1. Schreiben Sie für jeden Absatz° einen Titel.   paragraph
2. Markieren Sie die Zeilen°, wo man die folgende Information findet.   lines

    a. _____ Asylbewerber aus Osteuropa

    b. _____ Asylgesetze in Deutschland

    c. _____ Ausländerhass

    d. _____ ausländische Kinder und Jugendliche

    e. _____ Demonstrationen gegen Intoleranz

    f. _____ Prozent von Ausländern in Deutschland

Ausländer in Deutschland
7,37 Millionen Anfang 1998
Die zehn größten Nationalitätengruppen sind: Türken   2.107.000 Jugoslawen (Serben)   721.000 Italiener   608.000 Griechen   363.000 Polen   283.000 Kroaten   207.000 Österreicher   185.000 Portugiesen   132.000 Spanier   132.000 Bosnier   90.000

P eter kommt aus Chicago und ist seit fast einem Jahr Austauschstudent in Mainz. Heute Abend möchte er mit seinen Freunden Monika und Stefan essen gehen und sie sprechen gerade darüber, in welches Restaurant sie gehen wollen. „Wohin möchtest du gern gehen, Peter?" fragen

5 sie ihn. „Ich habe heute Lust, türkisch oder griechisch zu essen. Was meint ihr?" „Ich weiß nicht", sagt Stefan, „ich esse fast alles gern." „Ich würde lieber spanisch essen gehen", antwortet Monika. „Im Don Quichotte ist das Essen gut und da gibt es Flamenco-Musik." Während die drei essen, sprechen sie über die multikulturellen Aspekte Deutschlands.

im Ganzen: altogether

10   Im Ganzen° wohnen über 7,3 Millionen Ausländer in Deutschland. Das sind etwa neun Prozent der Einwohner Deutschlands. Zwischen 1955 und 1973 brauchte Westdeutschland Arbeiter, die es vor allem aus Italien, Spanien, Griechenland und der Türkei rekrutierte. Zuerst wollten die Auslän-der nur ein paar Jahre in Deutschland bleiben, um genug Geld für sich und

stay

15   ihre Familien zu Hause zu verdienen. Als ihr Aufenthalt° immer länger wurde, brachten die meisten nach eingen Jahren auch ihre Familie nach Deutschland. Seit Ende 1998 gibt es in Deutschland eine neue Regierung*, deren Ziel es ist, es Ausländern leichter zu machen, deutsche Staatsbürger zu werden. Seit dem Fall der kommunistischen Regierungen in Osteuropa Ende

applicants for political asylum /
  in addition / **nahm auf:** accepted

laws governing political
  asylum / political refugees

20   der achtziger Jahre kamen zu den ausländischen Arbeitnehmern auch viele Asylbewerber° hinzu°. Deutschland nahm die meisten auf°, denn es hatte neben seinem hohen Lebensstandard bis 1993 auch die liberalsten Asylge-setze° Europas.

im Allgemeinen: in general

fifth
familiar

Ob Asylanten° oder ausländische Arbeitnehmer – kulturelle Unterschiede

25   machen den Ausländern die Integration in die deutsche Gesellschaft nicht immer leicht. Im Allgemeinen° funktioniert die Integration von Ausländern unter Kindern und Jugendlichen viel besser als unter Erwachsenen. Da heute ein Fünftel° von allen ausländischen Kindern in Deutschland geboren sind, sprechen sie perfekt Deutsch, sind mit der Kultur vertraut° und tragen meis-

30   tens auch die gleiche Kleidung wie ihre Schulfreunde. Die jungen Leute wer-den in Deutschland bleiben, denn das Land ihrer Eltern ist ihnen oft fremd.

keep
victim
minority
out
commit / acts of violence

Schwieriger ist es für Ausländer, die weniger gut Deutsch sprechen oder auch in Deutschland die Kultur und Tradition ihrer Heimat beibehalten° wollen. Sie werden leicht das Opfer° von Ausländerhass.

35   Denn auch in Deutschland gibt es eine Minderheit° von Einwohnern, die gegen alles Ausländische ist. Ihr Motto ist „Ausländer raus°" und sie verüben° sogar Gewalttätigkeiten° gegen Ausländer. Viel mehr Deutsche protestieren jedoch gegen die Intoleranz und stehen auf der Seite der Aus-länder. Die Regierung, die Kirchen, die Medien, die Gewerkschaften und

hostility toward foreigners

40   auch große Rock- und Sportstars sprechen immer wieder offen gegen Aus-länderfeindlichkeit°. Seit 1992 haben in mehreren deutschen Städten hun-derttausende von Einwohnern gegen Intoleranz und Fremdenhass demonstriert.

owner

Peter, Monika und Stefan sind inzwischen mit dem Essen fertig und un-

45   terhalten sich mit dem Besitzer° des Lokals. In den sechziger Jahren war er aus Spanien gekommen, um bei Opel in Rüsselsheim zu arbeiten. Vor ein paar Jahren hat er dann das Restaurant aufgemacht. „Natürlich bin ich Spanier", sagt er stolz, „aber Mainz ist jetzt mein Zuhause." Nur seine Kinder machen ihm Sorgen, denn ihr Spanisch ist nicht so gut und Spanien

50   ist für sie ein fremdes Land.

Essen aus vielen Ländern gibt es auf diesem internationalen Volksfest in Berlin.

Brauchbares

1. **Don Quichotte** (l. 7) is the German for Don Quixote, the protagonist of a novel by Miguel de Cervantes (1547–1616) and one of the most famous characters in Spanish literature. The German word is pronounced [dõki'chŏt]. The English word *quixotic* is related to this character (Don Quixote).
2. **Flamenco-Musik** (l. 8), along with flamenco dancing, is a popular entertainment form. Flamenco dancing is characterized by colorful costumes, stomping of the feet, and clapping of the hands.

Nach dem Lesen*

1. Fragen zum Lesestück

1. Wer ist Peter?
2. Wozu hat Peter heute Lust?
3. In was für ein Restaurant gehen die drei?
4. Worüber sprechen die drei beim Essen?
5. Wann kamen die ersten ausländischen Arbeitnehmer nach Deutschland?
6. Warum waren die ersten ausländischen Arbeitnehmer sehr willkommen?
7. Warum kamen so viele Asylbewerber nach Deutschland?
8. Warum ist es leichter für Jugendliche sich in die deutsche Kultur zu integrieren?
9. Was machen einige Deutsche, die gegen Ausländer sind?
10. Wie zeigen viele Deutsche, dass sie gegen die Intoleranz sind?

---

*A coalition of Social Democrats (**SPD**) and the Greens (**die Grünen**) replaced the government of Christian Democrats (**CDU**)/Christian Union (**CSU**) who had been in power for 16 years.

2. Einige Themen. Lesen Sie den Text noch einmal°. Machen Sie eine Liste von Stichwörtern° zu den folgenden Themen.

1. Geschichte der Ausländer in Deutschland
2. Probleme der Ausländer in Deutschland
3. Deutschland: eine internationale Gesellschaft

3. Zur Diskussion. Machen Sie eine Liste: Was sollte eine Ausländerin/ein Ausländer von der deutschen Kultur wissen? Was sollte eine Ausländerin/ein Ausländer von Ihrer Kultur wissen?

4. Erzählen wir.

1. Stellen Sie sich vor, dass Sie als Ausländerin/Ausländer in Deutschland leben. Erzählen Sie etwas von sich. Woher kommen Sie? Warum sind Sie nach Deutschland gekommen? Wie gefällt es Ihnen in Deutschland?
2. **Rollenspiel.** Eine Reporterin/Ein Reporter interviewt eine ausländische Arbeitnehmerin/einen ausländischen Arbeitnehmer in Ihrem Land.

Vokabeln

Substantive

der **Arbeiter, -**/die **Arbeiterin, -nen** worker
der **Arbeitnehmer, -**/die **Arbeitnehmerin, -nen** employee, worker
der/die **Erwachsene** (*noun decl. like adj.*) adult
die **Gesellschaft, -en** society; company
die **Gewerkschaft, -en** labor union
die **Heimat** native country
die **Intoleranz** intolerance

der/die **Jugendliche** (*noun decl. like adj.*) young person
die **Kirche, -n** church
der **Klub, -s** club
die **Kultur, -en** culture
das **Lokal, -e** restaurant; bar
die **Möglichkeit, -en** possibility
die **Seite, -n** side; page
das **Spiel, -e** game
die **Tradition, -en** tradition
das **Vorurteil, -e** prejudice

Verben

auf·machen to open
geboren: ist geboren was born

lachen to laugh

Andere Wörter

denen (*dat. pl. of relative pronoun*) them; which
fremd foreign, strange; **das ist mir fremd** (*dat.*) that is strange to me
gerade just; straight
inzwischen in the meantime, meanwhile
kulturell culture, culturally

mehrere several; various
multikulturell multicultural
noch einmal again, once more
schwierig difficult
stolz proud; **stolz auf** (+ *acc.*) proud of
während (*sub. conj.*) while
wenigstens at least

Besondere Ausdrücke

die **[sechziger/achtziger] Jahre** the [1960s/1980s]

GRAMMATIK UND ÜBUNGEN

1. Future time: present tense

Ich **helfe** dir morgen bestimmt.

> *I'll help* you tomorrow for sure.
> *I'm going to help* you tomorrow for sure.

Arbeitest du heute Abend?

> *Are you working* tonight?
> *Are you going to work* tonight?

German generally uses the present tense (e.g., **ich helfe, arbeitest du?**) to express future time. English expresses future time by the future tense (e.g., *I'll help*), with a form of *go* (e.g., *I'm going to help*), or with the present progressive tense *(are you working?)*.

1. Was für Pläne hast du? Erzähl mal! Sie sprechen mit einer Freundin/einem Freund über Ihre Pläne. Geben Sie die Sätze auf Deutsch wieder. Benutzen Sie Präsens, um das Futur auszudrücken°.

to express

1. Are you going to watch TV tonight?
2. No, I'm going to the movies.
3. What are you going to do tomorrow?
4. My vacation starts tomorrow.
5. Are you going to Zürich again?
6. No, we'll go there next summer.

2. Future time: future tense°

das Futur

Wir **werden** unsere Freunde **einladen.**
Jutta **wird** es allein **machen.**

We *will invite* our friends.
Jutta *will do* it alone.

German, like English, does have a future tense, although in German it is not used as often as the present tense to express future time. The future tense in German may be used to express intention.

Katrin **wird** wohl zu Hause **sein.**
Das **wird** sicher falsch **sein.**

Katrin *is probably* at home.
That's *most likely* wrong.

In addition to expressing intention, the future tense may be used to express an assumption (present probability) when it is used with adverbs such as **wohl, sicher,** or **schon.** These adverbs all mean *probably* in English.

ich **werde** es sicher **finden**	wir **werden** es sicher **finden**
du **wirst** es sicher **finden**	ihr **werdet** es sicher **finden**
er/es/sie **wird** es sicher **finden**	sie **werden** es sicher **finden**
Sie **werden** es sicher **finden**	

In both English and German, the future tense is a compound tense. In English, the future tense is a verb phrase consisting of *will* or *shall* plus the main verb. In German, the future tense is also a verb phrase and consists of a form of **werden** plus an infinitive in final position.

Go to the
Deutsch heute Web Site at
www.hmco.com/college

Ausländische Mitbürger

Germany is home to more than 7.3 million foreigners. Just over 2 million are from Turkey, around 1 million are from the former Yugoslavia, and many have come from Italy, Greece, and Poland.

In the 1960s, West Germany sought many "guest workers" (**Gastarbeiter**) to relieve the labor shortage of the post-war economic boom, especially in the construction and steel industries. The early workers came from Italy, Greece, Spain, and Turkey. In 1961 there were 700,000 foreigners living in Germany; by 1970 there were 2.6 million. Even though many of the foreign workers (**ausländische Arbeitnehmer**) returned to their home countries, many others have stayed and raised their children in Germany. Today foreign workers are still an important factor in the German economy. In spite of this, German laws make it difficult for resident foreigners (**ausländische Mitbürger**) to obtain citizenship. However, foreigners are eligible to receive all social benefits and in some cities they have obtained the right to vote and to run for local office.

In the late 1980s and early 1990s, the number of ethnic German resettlers (**Aussiedler**) coming from the former Soviet Union and Eastern Europe increased dramatically. During the Cold War the **Aussiedler** were considered courageous people who had escaped a totalitarian regime. During the time of economic recession in the years after unification in 1990, the **Aussiedler** were seen as competition for jobs, housing, and social benefits. At the same time, a large number of refugees seeking political asylum arrived in Germany. Between 1989 and 1992 more than 1 million people applied for political asylum. Asylum seekers (**Asylanten**) receive financial aid while waiting for their cases to be heard and further benefits to help get started if asylum is granted. A 1993 amendment to the asylum law (**Asylgesetz**) reduced the number of people granted asylum.

In the first half of the 1990s radical groups such as the neo-Nazis and skinheads gave vent to a virulent xenophobia (**Ausländerhass**) and committed numerous hate crimes against them. A large segment of the public protested against these acts of violence. While xenophobia and "excessive population" of foreigners (**Überfremdung**) remain issues, there has been increasing public debate about how Germany

Türkischer Ladenbesitzer in Frankfurt.

can become a true multicultural society (**multikulturelle Gesellschaft**) and how to revise German citizenship requirements so that foreigners can more easily become German citizens.

Diskussion

One of the major hindrances to complete integration of foreigners into Germany was the difficulty of becoming a German citizen. According to traditional German law, German citizens were people whose parents were German. As a result, many people born in Germany were not citizens, while others like the **Aussiedler** were citizens, although they had never lived in Germany. Another difficulty was that unlike most European countries, Germany did not recognize dual citizenship, and many residents of Germany did not want to renounce their homeland to become German citizens. Discuss what characteristics you think are important for a person to be a citizen of a country. Do you think that dual citizenship should be recognized by countries?

---

2. Kein Streik.   Der Gewerkschaftsführer° erklärt, was die Gewerkschaft mit dem Management besprechen wird. Sagen Sie die Sätze noch einmal im Futur.

union leader

>> Wir verdienen bestimmt mehr.   *Wir werden bestimmt mehr verdienen.*

1. Wir arbeiten wohl 38 Stunden die Woche.
2. Bei Krankheit zahlt die Firma ja weiter.
3. Wir bekommen ja sechs Wochen bezahlten Urlaub.
4. Der Arbeitstag fängt wohl um halb acht an.
5. Das Arbeitsklima wird doch besser.
6. Wir streiken bestimmt nicht.

Michael weiß nicht, ob Ursel ihn **besuchen wird.**	Michael doesn't know whether Ursel *will visit* him.
Hans sagt, dass sie sicher **kommen wird.**	Hans says she*'ll come* for sure.

The auxiliary **werden** is in final position in a dependent clause because it is the finite verb. It follows the infinitive.

3. Ein tolles Wochenende.   Erik erzählt, was seine Freunde wahrscheinlich am Wochenende machen werden. Beginnen Sie jeden Satz mit **Erik sagt, dass _____.**

>> Inge wird wohl mit Gülay Hausaufgaben machen.
Erik sagt, dass Inge wohl mit Gülay Hausaufgaben machen wird.

1. Erkan wird wohl seinem Vater im Geschäft helfen.
2. Am Sonntag werden alle drei wohl aufs Schulfest gehen.
3. In der Schulband wird Erkan wohl Gitarre spielen.
4. Hinterher° werden sie wohl in ein türkisches Lokal gehen.
5. Sie werden dort wohl andere Freunde treffen.

afterward

cues

☞ **4. Was für Pläne hast du für die Zeit nach dem Studium?**   Bilden Sie eine kleine Gruppe und fragen Sie die anderen Gruppenmitglieder nach ihren Plänen nach dem Studium. Benutzen Sie die Sprechhilfen°.

Discussing post-graduation plans

S1: Weißt du schon, was du nach dem Studium machen wirst?
S2: Ich werde wohl bei einer Computer-Firma arbeiten. Und du?

ein Jahr ins Ausland gehen
bei einer [spanischen/deutschen/großen/kleinen/Computer-/Auto-] Firma
 arbeiten
mit meinem italienischen Freund ein Lokal aufmachen
eine Stelle in [Brüssel/Straßburg/Berlin] suchen
in die Politik gehen
weiterstudieren

research lab

bei einem Forschungslaboratorium° arbeiten
erst mal nichts tun

3. Relative clauses

Ist das **der Mann, den** Sie meinen?

Is that *the man (whom)* you mean?

Das ist **das Auto, das** du kaufen möchtest.

That's *the car (that)* you'd like to buy.

Wer ist **die Frau, die** gerade hereinkommt?

Who is *the woman (who* is) just coming in?

A relative clause provides additional information about a previously mentioned noun or pronoun. The clause is introduced by a relative pronoun (e.g., **den, das, die**) that refers back to the noun, which is the antecedent (e.g., **Mann, Auto, Frau**). Since a relative clause is a dependent clause, the finite verb (e.g., **meinen, möchtest, hereinkommt**) stands in last position.

In English, the relative pronoun may or may not be stated. In German, the relative pronoun must always be stated. In written German, relative clauses are set off from main clauses by commas.

Wer die Welt verstehen will, der muß sie lesen.
DIE ⊕ WELT

4. Relative pronouns°

	Masculine	Neuter	Feminine	Plural
Nominative	der	das	die	die
Accusative	den	das	die	die
Dative	dem	dem	der	denen
Genitive	**dessen**	**dessen**	**deren**	**deren**

The forms of the relative pronoun are the same as the forms of the definite articles, except for the dative plural and all genitive forms.

Masculine	Das ist der Mann, **der** uns gefragt hat.
Neuter	Das ist das Kind, **das** uns gefragt hat.
Feminine	Das ist die Frau, **die** uns gefragt hat.
Plural	Das sind die Leute, **die** uns gefragt haben.

The *gender* (masculine, neuter, or feminine) of the relative pronoun depends on the gender of the noun to which it refers. In the examples above, **der** is masculine because it refers to **der Mann** and **die** is feminine because it refers to **die Frau**. Whether a pronoun is singular or plural also depends on the noun to which it refers. The pronoun **die** that refers to **die Leute** is plural and therefore requires the plural verb **haben**.

Nominative	Ist das der Mann, **der** hier war?
Accusative	Ist das der Mann, **den** Sie meinen?
Dative	Ist das der Mann, **dem** Sie es gesagt haben?
Genitive	Ist das der Mann, **dessen** Auto Sie gekauft haben?

The *case* (nominative, accusative, dative, or genitive) of a relative pronoun depends on its grammatical function in the relative clause. In the examples above, **der** is nominative because it is the subject of its clause; **den** is accusative because it is the direct object of the verb **meinen** in that clause; **dem** is dative because it is an indirect object in the clause; and **dessen** is genitive because it shows possession.

Wie heißt die Frau, **für die** Sie arbeiten?	What is the name of the woman *for whom* you work?
Wo ist die Firma, **bei der** Sie arbeiten?	Where is the firm *(that)* you work *for?*

A relative clause can also be introduced by a preposition followed by a relative pronoun. The case of the relative pronoun then depends on what case the preposition takes. In **für die, die** is accusative because of **für**; in **bei der, der** is dative because of **bei.**

In German, whenever a relative pronoun is the object of a preposition, the preposition precedes the pronoun. In colloquial English the preposition is usually in last position [*(that) you work for*].

case
bezieht sich: refers to

ändert sich: changes

Bankrott machen: go bankrupt

solve

appliances, equipment

5. Die deutsche Wirtschaft.   Lesen Sie die Sätze über die deutsche Wirtschaft. Identifizieren Sie die Relativpronomen darin und erklären Sie, in welchem Fall° jedes Pronomen ist und worauf es sich bezieht°.

⟫   Die Regierung arbeitet für einen Welthandel, der wirklich frei ist.
der = nominative, subject, Welthandel

1. Ein Land wie Deutschland, das wenig Rohstoffe hat, lebt vom Handel.
2. Die Produkte, die man produziert, müssen von bester Qualität sein.
3. Denn es gibt mehrere Länder, mit denen Deutschland konkurrieren muss.
4. In der Zukunft ändert sich° wohl der Markt, für den Deutschland produzieren muss.
5. Einige Firmen, die Dinge produzieren, die man nicht mehr kauft, werden Bankrott machen°.
6. Das bedeutet, dass die Arbeiter, deren Firmen bankrott sind, arbeitslos werden.
7. Die Arbeitslosigkeit ist ein Problem, das nur schwer zu lösen° ist.

6. Die sind doch gar nicht kaputt.   Ihr Freund repariert gern elektrische Geräte°. Er sagt, welche Geräte er reparieren wird. Sagen Sie ihm, dass die Dinge, die er für Sie reparieren will, gar nicht kaputt sind. Benutzen Sie den Nominativ des Relativpronomens.

S2: Ich repariere jetzt diesen Computer, ja?
S1: Das ist doch nicht der Computer, der kaputt ist.

1.   2.   3.

4.   5. *

---

*Note that you need a plural construction: **Das sind doch nicht die ...**

7. Die Sachen sind toll.   Gabi hat neue Kleidung. Fragen Sie Gabi, ob sie die Kleidung zum Geburtstag bekommen hat. Benutzen Sie den Akkusativ der Relativpronomen.

➤➤ Wie gefällt dir diese Jacke?
   Toll. Ist das die Jacke, die du zum Geburtstag bekommen hast?

1. Wie gefällt dir diese Hose?
2. Wie gefällt dir dieses Hemd?
3. Wie gefällt dir dieser Rock?
4. Wie gefällt dir dieser Pulli?
5. Wie gefallen dir diese Jeans?
6. Wie gefallen dir diese Schuhe?

8. Peter schreibt über die Ausländer.   Peter schreibt seinem Freund Thomas über die Situation der Ausländer in Deutschland. Ergänzen Sie die Sätze mit den passenden Relativpronomen.

1. In dem Brief, _____ Peter an seinen Freund Thomas schreibt, berichtet er

   über die Ausländer.

2. In Deutschland sind viele Ausländer, _____ in den großen Industriestädten

   leben.

3. In manchen Vierteln°, in _____ die Ausländer wohnen, wohnen nur wenige   quarters, sections (of a city)

   Deutsche.

4. Dort gibt es Läden, in _____ die Ausländer die Lebensmittel kaufen können,

   _____ sie von ihrer Heimat her kennen.

5. Es sind meistens die Kinder, _____ es in dem fremden Land ganz gut

   gefällt.

6. Die Kinder lernen Deutsch, _____ sie dann oft besser sprechen als die

   Eltern.

7. Die Ausländer, _____ die Deutschen bei der Integration im Allgemeinen°   **im Allgemeinen:** in general

   wenig helfen, bleiben oft unter sich.

Mein Freund ist Ausländer

9. Wer sind diese Leute? Sie, Ihre Freundin Katie und Ihr Freund Jens sind auf einer Party. Katie kennt niemanden. Jens sagt etwas über die Leute. Da Katie kein Deutsch spricht, übersetzen Sie die Sätze für sie ins Englische.

➤➤ Frau Meier, deren Sohn in Marburg studiert, ist Rechtsanwältin.
Mrs. Meier, whose son is studying in Marburg, is a lawyer.

1. Herr Schnell, dessen Tochter bei Volkswagen arbeitet, fährt einen Golf.
2. Herr und Frau Gescheit, deren Kinder gut Englisch können, haben ein großes Haus.
3. Der alte Herr, dessen Sohn arbeitslos ist, hat vor ein paar Wochen Bankrott gemacht.
4. Herr Ettel, dessen Frau Chefärztin ist, studiert noch.
5. Diese junge Frau, deren Vater ein bekannter Rechtsanwalt ist, hat letzte Woche geheiratet.
6. Und dieser junge Mann, dessen Eltern sehr reich sind, ist der Glückliche.

10. Frage-Ecke. Fragen Sie Ihre Partnerin/Ihren Partner, wer die ver-schiedenen° Leute sind. Ihre Partnerin/Ihr Partner fragt Sie auch. Es ist möglich, dass Sie beide die Leute unterschiedlich° beschreiben.

various
differently

S1: Wer ist Herr Rot?
S2: Das ist der Journalist, der für die *Times* arbeitet. Und wer ist Frau ... ?
S1: Das ist ...

funny

Frau Blau	der Professor	Sie/Er schreibt an einem Roman.
Herr Klein	die Studentin	Sie/Er trägt immer komische° Hüte.
Herr Rot	der Ingenieur	Alle mögen sie/ihn.
Dr. Kühler	der Journalist	Ihr Mann ruft sie jeden Tag an.
Herr Hamburger	die Sekretärin	Ihr/Ihm gefällt es gut hier.
Frau König	der Arzt	Sie/Er arbeitet für die *Times*.
Frau Kaiser	der Musiker	Sie/Ihn sieht man nur mit der Zeitung unterm Arm.
Herr Bass	die Lehrerin	Sie/Er lächelt immer so viel.

groups of three

11. Erzähl mal. Bilden Sie Dreiergruppen° und beenden Sie die Sätze.

➤➤ Wien ist eine Stadt, ... [*die sehr alt ist*].
[*die ich besuchen möchte*].
[*in der ich leben möchte*].

1. Die Schweiz ist ein Land, ...
2. Österreich ist ein Land, ...
3. Volkswagen ist eine Firma, ...
4. Ich hätte gern eine Präsidentin/einen Präsidenten, ...
5. Ich habe einen Freund, ...
6. Ich habe eine Freundin, ...
7. Ich habe eine Professorin/einen Professor, ...
8. Der Juli ist ein Monat, ...

5. The passive voice°

das Passiv

| Active voice | **Stefan** fragt mich fast jeden Tag. | *Stefan* asks me almost every day. |
| Passive voice | **Ich** werde fast jeden Tag gefragt. | *I'm* asked almost every day. |

In the active voice, the subject is "active": the subject is the agent that performs the action expressed by the verb. Active voice focuses attention on the agent. The attention in the active sentence above is focused on Stefan, who asks me almost every day.

In the passive voice, the subject is "passive": the subject is acted upon by an expressed or unexpressed agent. Passive voice focuses attention on the receiver of the action. The attention in the passive sentence above is focused on me who is asked almost every day.

The subject (e.g., **ich**) of a passive sentence corresponds to the object of an active sentence (e.g., **mich**).

In everyday conversation, speakers of German use the active voice much more often than the passive voice. The passive is used in instructions, recipes, and technical and scientific manuals, where, just as in English, an impersonal style is preferred.

6. Passive voice: present tense and simple-past tense

| Present | Ich **werde gefragt.** | I *am asked.* |
| Simple past | Ich **wurde gefragt.** | I *was asked.* |

In English, a passive verb phrase consists of a form of the auxiliary verb *to be* and the past participle of the verb (e.g., *asked*). In German, the passive verb phrase consists of a form of the auxiliary **werden** and the past participle of the main verb (e.g., **gefragt**). The tenses you will encounter most frequently in passive voice are the present and simple past.

12. Was wird heute gemacht?   Es ist Samstag und es gibt viel zu tun. Sagen sie, was heute alles bei Monika gemacht wird.

➤➤ Brot / kaufen   *Brot wird gekauft.*

1. die Wäsche / waschen
2. das Haus / sauber machen
3. das Auto / waschen
4. die Gartenarbeit / machen
5. das Essen / kochen
6. die Garage / aufräumen

7. *Von* + agent

Without agent	Die Gartenarbeit wird gemacht.	The yard work is being done.
With agent	Die Gartenarbeit wird **von meiner Schwester** gemacht.	The yard work is done *by my sister.*

In the passive voice, the agent is often omitted. If the agent (e.g., **Schwester**) is expressed, in most passive sentences it is the object of the preposition **von** and thus in the dative case.

Discussing who invented, wrote, or discovered something

13. Wer war das? Sie und Ihre Partnerin/Ihr Partner fragen einander, was von wem gemacht wurde.* Benutzen Sie die Stichwörter und bilden Sie Sätze im Passiv.

invented

S1: Von wem wurde das Telefon erfunden°?
S2: Das Telefon wurde von Alexander Graham Bell erfunden.

der Film *Titanic*	gebaut	Carl Friedrich Benz
Mickey Mouse	geschrieben	James Cameron
die Brooklyn Bridge	gemacht	Christopher Columbus
Hamlet	entdeckt°	Walt Disney
die amerikanische Verfassung	erfunden	Alexandre Eiffel
der Eiffelturm		Albert Einstein
die Röntgen-Strahlen°		Thomas Jefferson
Amerika		Robert Koch
der Tuberkelbazillus°		Johann Roebling
das erste deutsche Auto		Wilhelm Conrad Röntgen
die Relativitätstheorie		William Shakespeare

discovered

X-rays

tuberculosis bacillus

14. Ausländer in Deutschland. Der Austauschstudent, David, spricht mit Gisela über Ausländer in Deutschland. Geben Sie das Gespräch auf Englisch wieder.

DAVID: Gisela, ich sehe hier in Deutschland so viele ausländische Geschäfte – türkische, griechische, italienische, spanische.

GISELA: Ja, das stimmt°. Es gibt in Deutschland über 7 Millionen Ausländer. Zwischen 1955 und 1978 wurden Arbeiter in Westdeutschland gebraucht. Sie kamen vor allem aus Italien, Griechenland, Spanien und der Türkei.

das stimmt: that's right

DAVID: Wurden sie gut akzeptiert?

GISELA: Nicht alle. Wegen der größeren kulturellen Unterschiede wurden zum Beispiel Türken nicht so leicht in die deutsche Gesellschaft integriert wie Italiener.

DAVID: Und heute?

MONIKA: In der Zeitung wird oft von Problemen berichtet. Aber in den letzten Jahren wird immer mehr gegen Ausländerhass protestiert.

---

*Antworten: der Film *Titanic*: James Cameron; Mickey Mouse: Walt Disney; die Brooklyn Bridge: Johann Roebling; *Hamlet*: William Shakespeare; die amerikanische Verfassung: Thomas Jefferson; der Eiffelturm: Alexandre Eiffel: die Röntgen-Strahlen: Wilhelm Conrad Röntgen; Amerika: Christopher Columbus; der Tuberkelbazillus: Robert Koch; das erste deutsche Auto: Carl Friedrich Benz; die Relativitätstheorie: Albert Einstein

8. Impersonal passive construction

Samstags **wird** schwer **gearbeitet.**   On Saturdays people *work* hard.
Sonntags **wird** nicht **gearbeitet.**   No one *works* on Sundays.

In German it is possible to use passive without having a subject or an agent. Such a construction is called an impersonal passive construction.

Es wird jetzt gearbeitet.   ⎰ There is work going on now.
⎱ People are working now.

The pronoun **es** begins an impersonal passive construction if no other words precede the verb. **Es** is a dummy subject. An English equivalent of the impersonal passive often uses an introductory phrase such as *there is* or *there are*.

15. Was wird hier gemacht?   In diesem Wohnhaus ist viel los. Sprechen Sie mit Ihrer Partnerin/Ihrem Partner darüber, was in jeder Wohnung gemacht wird.

S1: Was wird in Wohnung Nummer 2 gemacht?
S2: In Wohnung Nummer 2 wird gespielt *or* Es wird gespielt.

9. Summary of the uses of *werden*

■ *Active voice: main verb*

Herr Heller **wird** alt.   Mr. Heller *is growing* old.
Die Kinder **wurden** müde.   The children *were getting* tired.
Frau Ullmann **ist** Chefin der   Ms. Ullmann *has become* head
   Firma **geworden.**   of the company.

Werden as a main verb is equivalent to English *to grow, get,* or *become.*

■ *Auxiliary verb in future tense*

Matthias **wird** hoffentlich mehr **arbeiten.**   I hope Matthias *will work* more.
Du **wirst** das wohl **wissen.**   You *probably know* that.

Werden is used with a dependent infinitive to form the future tense.

■ *Passive voice: auxiliary verb*

Viele Geschäfte **wurden** von Ausländern **aufgemacht.**   Many businesses *were opened* by foreigners.
Die Gäste **werden** oft von ethnischen Musikgruppen **unterhalten.**   The guests *are* often *entertained* by ethnic music groups.

Werden is used with a past participle to form the passive voice. The passive voice can occur in any tense.

16. Die deutsche Wirtschaft.   Eine deutsche Geschäftsfrau spricht mit ausländischen Journalisten über die wirtschaftliche Situation in Deutschland. Stellen° Sie fest, wie **werden** benutzt wird. Dann geben Sie die Sätze auf Englisch wieder. Sagen Sie, ob **werden** (a) Hauptverb im Aktiv ist (geben Sie die Zeit° an), (b) als Futur benutzt wird oder (c) als Passiv-Konstruktion benutzt wird (geben Sie die Zeit an).

stellen fest: determine
tense

>> Viele alte Fabriken werden modernisiert.
   werden modernisiert / *present passive*
   Many old factories are being modernized.

  1. Hier wird noch viel gemacht.
  2. Die Situation wird im nächsten Jahr sicher besser.
  3. Der Export wird langsam weniger.
  4. Wer wird dem Land helfen?
  5. Werden die Waren auf dem Weltmarkt eine Zukunft haben?
  6. Man meint, dass das Land immer weniger Rohstoffe haben wird.
  7. Das Leben wurde in letzter Zeit teurer.
  8. Die Industrie wird sich wohl neue Märkte suchen.
  9. Manche Arbeiter wollen einfach nicht arbeiten. Was soll aus ihnen werden?
 10. Die Situation wird hoffentlich in den nächsten Jahren besser.

WIEDERHOLUNG

1. Eine bekannte Autorin.   Lesen Sie den folgenden Bericht über Kirsten Elsners Karriere als Autorin. Beantworten Sie dann die Fragen dazu.

cared

Herr Elsner bekam eine neue Stelle in einer anderen Stadt. Weil Frau Elsner dort keine Arbeit fand, blieb sie zu Hause und sorgte° für die Kinder. Am Anfang machte sie alles gern. Sie kochte, putzte, ging einkaufen und half den Kindern bei den Schulaufgaben. Um etwas für die Kinder zu tun, fing sie an, kurze Geschichten für sie zu schreiben. Sie wurde durch die Kindergeschichten bald bekannt. Jetzt nennt man sie nicht mehr Kirsten Elsner, die Frau von Herrn Elsner. Jetzt heißt sie Kirsten Wiener, und Herr Elsner ist der Mann von der bekannten Autorin.

1. Warum wohnten Elsners in einer neuen Stadt?
2. Warum blieb Frau Elsner zu Hause?
3. Was machte sie zu Hause?
4. Warum fing sie an Kindergeschichten zu schreiben?
5. Wie nennt man Herrn Elsner jetzt?

2. Über Politik. Gisela erzählt über Professor Lange. Ergänzen Sie ihre Sätze im Passiv mit dem passenden Verb.

besuchen □ diskutieren □ halten □ lesen □ schreiben □ sprechen

⋙ An der Universität _____ oft über Politik _____ .
⋙ An der Universität wird oft über Politik gesprochen.

1. Die interessantesten Vorlesungen _____ von Professor Lange _____ .

2. Diese Vorlesungen _____ von den Studenten gut _____ .

3. Sein Buch *Die neue Politik* _____ nicht nur von Studenten _____ .

4. Im Fernsehen _____ auch über Politik _____ .

5. In der Zeitung _____ darüber _____ .

3. Ein Student an der Uni. Bernd möchte wissen, wie es Phillip an der Universität geht. Sagen Sie ihm, dass es nicht so gut geht, aber dass es Phillip nichts auszumachen scheint°. Beenden Sie die Sätze mit den passenden Adjektivendungen, wo sie notwendig° sind. Dann beantworten Sie die Fragen negativ mit Adjektiven aus der Liste von Antonymen.

°seems
°necessary

alt □ dumm □ faul □ groß □ lustig □ leicht □ schlecht □ teuer

⋙ Studiert Peter an einer klein _____ Universität?   *Studiert Peter an einer kleinen Universität? Nein, an einer großen.*

1. Ist er ein fleißig_____ Student?

2. Ist er intelligent_____ ?

3. Liest er gern ernst_____ Geschichten?

4. Wohnt er in einer modern_____ Wohnung?

5. Wohnt er in einem klein_____ Zimmer?

6. Hat er ein schwer_____ Leben?

7. Hat er einen gut_____ Studentenjob?

8. Findet er Wohnen und Essen billig_____ ?

4. Markus schreibt über Frauen.   Ergänzen Sie die Kommentare von Markus über die Situation der Frauen in Deutschland mit den passenden Relativpronomen.

1. Viele Frauen sind mit dem Frauenbild, _____ in vielen Schulbüchern noch zu finden ist, unzufrieden°.

   dissatisfied

2. In diesen Büchern ist es immer ein Junge, _____ etwas baut oder Fußball spielt.

3. Und es ist immer ein Mädchen, _____ zusieht° und weniger gefährliche° Sachen macht.

   watches / dangerous

4. Die Frauen, _____ Berufe wie Elektrikerin und Mechanikerin gelernt haben, haben es besonders schwer.

5. Man nennt eine Frau, _____ wegen der Arbeit vier Tage von zu Hause weg ist, eine Rabenmutter°.

unfit mother

6. Ein Mann, _____ dieselbe Arbeit macht, ist aber kein Rabenvater°.

unfit father

7. Es gibt also noch traditionelle Rollen, von _____ Männer und Frauen sich emanzipieren müssen.

5. Ihre Meinung.   Beantworten Sie die folgenden Fragen und fragen Sie dann Ihre Partnerin/Ihren Partner, was ihre/seine Meinung ist.

1. Möchten Sie in einem anderen Land studieren? Warum (nicht)?
2. Möchten Sie während des Sommers in einem anderen Land arbeiten? Warum (nicht)?
3. Möchten Sie in einem anderen Land leben? In welchem Land? Warum?
4. Möchten Sie in einem Land leben, dessen Sprache Sie nicht können? Warum (nicht)?
5. Würden Sie in einem anderen Land für weniger Geld als in Amerika arbeiten? Warum (nicht)?

6. Erzählen Sie mal.   Diskutieren Sie die folgenden Themen in kleinen Gruppen.

1. Erzählen Sie mal von einem Buch, das Sie gern kaufen würden.
2. Erzählen Sie mal von einer Reise, die Sie gern machen würden.
3. Erzählen Sie mal von Ferien, die Sie gern machen würden.
4. Erzählen Sie mal von Politikern, die Sie gern reden hören würden.
5. Erzählen Sie mal von einem Film, den Sie gern sehen würden.
6. Erzählen Sie mal von einer Rockband, die Sie gern hören würden.

7. Zum Schreiben

1. Beschreiben Sie entweder° was für eine Familie oder was für eine Welt Sie gern hätten. Benutzen Sie mindestens° zwei Relativpronomen in Ihrem Absatz°.

entweder ... oder: either ... or / at least
paragraph

2. Machen Sie eine Liste mit Problemen, die ausländische Arbeitnehmer oder Minderheiten° in einem Land haben können. Diskutieren Sie in kleinen Gruppen über Ihre Listen. Stellen Sie dann eine Liste zusammen, mit der alle übereinstimmen°, und nummerieren Sie die Probleme. Beginnen Sie mit „1" für das wichtigste Problem. Wenn Sie fertig sind, stellen° Sie Ihre Liste den Kursteilnehmern vor.

minorities

agree with
stellen vor: present

3. Was meinen Sie zu der folgenden Aussage°: „Kinder, die in zwei Sprachen und zwei Kulturen aufwachsen°, haben viele Vorteile°." Schreiben Sie einen kurzen Absatz°, in dem Sie der Aussage zustimmen° oder dagegen argumentieren.

comment
grow up / advantages
paragraph / agree with

Hinweise: In a relative clause the finite verb is in final position. The gender of the relative pronoun depends on the gender of the noun to which it refers. Its case depends on its function in the clause.

GRAMMATIK: ZUSAMMENFASSUNG

The future tense

ich **werde** es **machen**	wir **werden** es **machen**
du **wirst** es **machen**	ihr **werdet** es **machen**
er/es/sie **wird** es **machen**	sie **werden** es **machen**
	Sie **werden** es **machen**

The German future tense consists of the auxiliary **werden** plus an infinitive in final position.

Erika sagt, dass sie es sicher **machen wird.**

In a dependent clause, the auxiliary **werden** is in final position because it is the finite verb.

Future time: present tense

Ich **komme** morgen bestimmt.
Fahren Sie nächstes Jahr nach Deutschland?

I'll come tomorrow for sure.
Are you going to Germany next year?

German uses the future tense less frequently than English. German generally uses the present tense if the context clearly indicates future time.

Uses of the future tense

Future time	Frank **wird** mir **helfen.**	Frank *will help* me.
Intention	Frank **wird** mir **helfen.**	Frank will (*intends to*) *help* me.

Future tense is used to express intention or future time if the context doesn't make it clear that the events will take place in the future.

Assumption	Anna **wird** uns sicher **glauben.**	Anna *probably believes* us.
	Das **wird** wohl **stimmen.**	That *is probably correct.*

The future tense may also be used to express an assumption (present probability) when it is used with adverbs such as **sicher, schon,** and **wohl.**

Freie und
Hansestadt
Hamburg

Hessen

Mecklenburg-
Vorpommern

Saarland

Sachsen-
Anhalt

Freistaat
Sachsen

Niedersachsen

Freie
Hansestadt
Bremen

Rheinland-
Pfalz

Schleswig-
Holstein

Freistaat
Thüringen

Baden-
Württemberg

Freistaat
Bayern

Berlin

Brandenburg

Nordrhein-
Westfalen

Relative clauses

Wie teuer ist **der Fernseher, den** du kaufen willst?

Wie alt ist **das Auto, das** du verkaufen möchtest?

Ist das **die CD, die** du gestern gekauft hast?

How expensive is *the television (that)* you want to buy?

How old is *the car (that)* you want to sell?

Is that *the CD (that)* you bought yesterday?

A relative clause provides additional information about a previously mentioned noun or pronoun. The clause is introduced by a relative pronoun, which refers back to the noun or pronoun (called an antecedent). A relative clause is a dependent clause, and thus the verb is in final position.

Relative pronouns

	Masculine	Neuter	Feminine	Plural
Nominative	der	das	die	die
Accusative	den	das	die	die
Dative	dem	dem	der	**denen**
Genitive	**dessen**	**dessen**	**deren**	**deren**

Nominative	Ist das der Mann, **der** immer so viel fragt?
Accusative	Ist das der Mann, **den** Sie meinen?
	für den Sie arbeiten?
Dative	Ist das der Mann, **dem** Sie oft helfen?
	von dem Sie erzählt haben?
Genitive	Ist das der Mann, **dessen** Auto Sie gekauft haben?

The *gender* (masculine, neuter, or feminine) and *number* (singular or plural) of the relative pronoun are determined by its antecedent, i.e., the noun to which it refers. The *case* (nominative, accusative, dative, or genitive) of the relative pronoun is determined by its function within its clause (subject, direct object, object of a preposition, etc.).

Present and simple past tenses in the passive voice

Present	Der Brief **wird geschrieben.**	The letter *is being written.*
Simple past	Der Brief **wurde geschrieben.**	The letter *was being written.*

Von + agent

Das Geld wurde **von den Arbeitern** verdient.	The money was earned *by the workers.*

In passive voice the agent is the object of the preposition **von** and thus in the dative case. The agent may be omitted. **(Viel Geld wurde verdient.)**

EINE KURZGESCHICHTE

Helga Novak was born in 1935 in Berlin. She studied philosophy and journalism in Leipzig and worked in various types of places: factories, a laboratory, and a bookstore. In 1961 she moved to Iceland and returned to Germany in 1967 to live in Frankfurt as a writer. In 1980, the New Literary Society in Hamburg gave her an award for her novel Die Eisheiligen, *as the best first novel by a German speaker. Novak is also recognized as an outstanding poet. In 1997 she was awarded the Literary Prize of Brandenburg* **(Brandenburgischer Literaturpreis)** *for her most recent volume of poems,* Silvatica *(Songs of the Forest).*

In her stories, Helga Novak deals with ordinary people in everyday situations. Through the use of simple sentences and a dry, unemotional style, she suggests much more about human relationships than she actually says. In "Schlittenfahren," taken from her work Geselliges Beisammensein (1968), *the father does not communicate with his children but simply leaves his retreat long enough to shout the same sentences in their direction, sentences devoid of meaning for them and him. However, the repetition of "kommt rein" at the end of the story takes on a new and possibly serious dimension and reveals the problem of using language just to be saying something.*

In what sense do the private home **(Eigenheim)** *and the garden represent two separate and unrelated scenes of activity? What do the father's actions say about his relationship with the children?*

Schlittenfahren
Helga M. Novak

Das Eigenheim° steht in einem Garten. Der Garten ist groß. Durch den Garten fließt° ein Bach°. Im Garten stehen zwei Kinder. Das eine der Kinder kann noch nicht sprechen. Das andere Kind ist größer. Sie sitzen auf einem Schlitten°. Das kleinere Kind weint. Das größere

5 sagt, gib den Schlitten her. Das kleinere weint. Es schreit°.

Aus dem Haus tritt° ein Mann. Er sagt, wer brüllt°, kommt rein°. Er geht in das Haus zurück. Die Tür fällt hinter ihm zu.

Das kleinere Kind schreit.

Der Mann erscheint wieder in der Haustür. Er sagt, komm rein. Na° wirds

10 bald. Du kommst rein. Nix°. Wer brüllt, kommt rein. Komm rein.

Der Mann geht hinein. Die Tür klappt°.

Das kleinere Kind hält° die Schnur° des Schlittens fest. Es schluchzt°.

Der Mann öffnet die Haustür. Er sagt, du darfst Schlitten fahren, aber nicht brüllen. Wer brüllt, kommt rein. Ja. Ja. Jaaa. Schluß° jetzt.

15 Das größere Kind sagt, Andreas will immer allein fahren.

Der Mann sagt, wer brüllt, kommt rein. Ob er nun Andreas heißt oder sonstwie°.

Er macht die Tür zu.

Das größere Kind nimmt dem kleineren den Schlitten weg. Das kleinere

20 Kind schluchzt, quietscht°, jault°, quengelt°.

Glosses (margin):

- private home
- flows / brook
- sled
- screams
- steps / bawls / **rein = herein:** in
- **Na ... bald:** hurry up
- **Nix = nichts**
- slams
- **hält fest:** holds tight / rope / sobs
- **Schluß jetzt:** that's enough
- otherwise
- squeals / howls / whines

Der Mann tritt aus dem Haus. Das größere Kind gibt dem kleineren den Schlitten zurück. Das kleinere Kind setzt sich auf den Schlitten. Es rodelt°.   sleds

25   Der Mann sieht in den Himmel°. Der Himmel ist blau. Die Sonne ist   sky
groß und rot. Es ist kalt.

Der Mann pfeift° laut. Er geht wieder ins Haus zurück. Er macht die Tür   whistles
hinter sich zu.

Das größere Kind ruft°, Vati, Vati, Vati, Andreas gibt den Schlitten nicht   calls
mehr her.

Die Haustür geht auf. Der Mann steckt den Kopf heraus. Er sagt, wer
30   brüllt, kommt rein. Die Tür geht zu.

Das größere Kind ruft, Vati, Vativativati, Vaaatiii, jetzt ist Andreas in den
Bach gefallen.

Die Haustür öffnet sich einen Spalt° breit°. Eine Männerstimme° ruft, wie   crack / wide / man's voice
oft soll ich das noch sagen, wer brüllt, kommt rein.

Fragen

1. In was für einem Haus wohnt die Familie?
2. Was wissen Sie über den Garten?
3. Was wissen Sie über die Kinder?
4. Warum weint das kleinere Kind?
5. Warum kommt der Mann aus dem Haus? Was sagt er?
6. Wie ist das Wetter?
7. Wer fährt am Ende mit dem Schlitten?
8. Warum ruft das ältere Kind am Ende den Vater?
9. Was antwortet der Vater?

Fragen zur Diskussion

1. Der Mann kommt mehrere Male zur Tür. Welche Sätze beschreiben das? Was sagen diese Sätze über den Mann?
2. Der Mann geht mehrere Male ins Haus. Welche Sätze beschreiben das? Was ist damit gesagt?
3. Welchen Satz sagt der Mann immer wieder? Welchen Effekt hat das auf die Kinder? Auf den Leser?
4. Was wird über Jahreszeit und Wetter gesagt? Welche Rolle spielt das?
5. Warum benutzt die Autorin immer wieder das Wort „der Mann"? Welches andere Wort könnte sie benutzen?
6. Wie meint der Mann den letzten Satz? Wie verstehen Sie ihn?

Reference Section

Contents

Bausteine: English Equivalents

Note that the English version of the dialogues are equivalents rather than literal translations.

Einführung

Wie heißt du?

Vorm schwarzen Brett

ALEX: Hallo! Ich heiße Alex. Und du?
GISELA: Grüß dich. Ich heiße Gisela.
ALEX: Willst du auch nach Florenz?
GISELA: Ja.
ALEX: Toll! Du, hier ist meine Telefonnummer: 791 20 97. (Sieben, einundneunzig, zwanzig, siebenundneunzig.)
GISELA: Danke – und meine Telefonnummer ist 791 23 44. (Sieben, einundneunzig, dreiundzwanzig, vierundvierzig.)
ALEX: Wie bitte?
GISELA: 791 23 44.
ALEX: O.K. Also, bis bald! Tschüs.

What is your name?

In front of the bulletin board

Hi. My name is Alex. How about you?
Hi. My name is Gisela.
Are you also planning to go to Florence?
Yes.
Great. Hey, here is my telephone number: 791 20 97.

Thanks—and my telephone number is 791 23 44.

I beg your pardon?
791 23 44.
Ok. Well, see you later. So long.

Wie heißen Sie?

Im Büro

FRAU KLUGE: Bitte? Wie heißen Sie?
GISELA: Gisela Riedholt.
FRAU KLUGE: Wie schreibt man das?
GISELA: R-i-e-d-h-o-l-t.
FRAU KLUGE: Und Ihre Adresse?
GISELA: Meine Semesteradresse oder meine Heimatadresse?
FRAU KLUGE: Ihre Semesteradresse, bitte.
GISELA: Lepsiusstraße 27 (siebenundzwanzig), 12163 (zwölf, eins, sechs, drei) Berlin.
FRAU KLUGE: Danke, Frau Riedholt.
GISELA: Bitte.

What is your name?

In the office

Can I help you? What is your name?
Gisela Riedholt.
How do you spell (write) that?
R-i-e-d-h-o-l-t.
And your address?
My school address or my home address?

Your school address, please.
27 Lepsius Street, 12163 Berlin.

Thank you, Ms. Riedholt.
You're welcome.

Kapitel 1

Wie geht's?

In der Bibliothek

PROFESOR LANGE: Guten Morgen, Frau Riedholt. Wie geht es Ihnen?
GISELA: Guten Morgen, Professor Lange. Gut, danke. Und Ihnen?
PROFESSOR LANGE: Danke, ganz gut.

How are you?

In the library

Good morning, Ms. Riedholt. How are you?

Good morning, Professor Lange. Fine, thanks. And you?

Thanks, not bad.

Im Hörsaal

ALEX: Hallo, Gisela.
GISELA: Grüß dich, Alex. Wie geht's?
ALEX: Ach, nicht so gut.
GISELA: Was ist los? Bist du krank?
ALEX: Nein, ich bin nur furchtbar müde.

Was machst du gern?

MICHAEL: Was machst du heute Abend?
GISELA: Nichts Besonderes. Musik hören oder so. Vielleicht gehe ich ins Kino.
MICHAEL: Hmm. Spielst du gern Schach?
GISELA: Schach? Ja. Aber nicht so gut.
MICHAEL: Ach komm, wir spielen zusammen, ja?
GISELA: Na gut! Wann?
MICHAEL: Um sieben?
GISELA: O.K. Bis dann.

In the lecture hall

Hi, Gisela.
Hello, Alex. How are you?
Oh, not so well.
What's wrong? Are you sick?
No, I'm just terribly tired.

What do you like to do?

What are you doing tonight?
Nothing special. Listening to music or something like that. Maybe I'll go to the movies.
Hmm. Do you like to play chess?
Chess? Yes. But not very well.
Oh come on, we'll play together, OK?
All right. When?
At seven?
OK. See you then.

Kapitel 2

Wie ist das Wetter?

Im Sommer

FRAU KLUGE: Schönes Wetter, nicht wahr, Professor Lange?
PROFESSOR LANGE: Ja, aber es ist zu heiß und trocken.
FRAU KLUGE: Vielleicht regnet es morgen ja.
PROFESSOR LANGE: Na, hoffentlich!

Im Herbst

MICHAEL: Heute ist es wirklich kalt, nicht?
GISELA: Ja, sehr, und gestern war es noch so schön.
MICHAEL: Jetzt bleibt es bestimmt kalt.
GISELA: Leider.

Im Winter

STEFAN: Was für ein Wetter!
MONIKA: Der Wind ist furchtbar kalt. Ich glaube, es schneit bald.
STEFAN: Wie viel Grad ist es?
MONIKA: Es ist zwei Grad.

How's the weather?

In the summer

Nice weather, isn't it, Professor Lange?
Yes, but it's too hot and dry.
Maybe it'll rain tomorrow after all.
Well, I hope so.

In the fall

It's really cold today, isn't it?
Yes, very much so. And it was still so nice yesterday.
Now it'll stay cold for sure.
Unfortunately.

In the winter

What weather!
The wind is awfully cold. I think it's going to snow soon.

What's the temperature?
It's two degrees.

Kapitel 3

Was brauchst du?

DIANE: Sag mal, Stefan, gibt es hier eine Apotheke?
STEFAN: Ja, was brauchst du denn?
DIANE: Ich brauche etwas gegen Kopfschmerzen.
STEFAN: Nimmst du Aspirin? Ich habe eins.

What do you need?

Tell me Stefan, is there a pharmacy (around) here?
Yes, what do you need?
I need something for a headache.
Do you take aspirin? I have one.

Gehst du heute einkaufen?

MONIKA: Stefan, gehst du heute nicht einkaufen?
STEFAN: Doch. Warum fragst du?
MONIKA: Wir haben keinen Kaffee mehr.
STEFAN: Ein Pfund ist genug, nicht? Möchtest du sonst noch etwas?
MONIKA: Ja, bitte ein Brot. Kauf das doch bei Rischart. Da ist das Brot besser.

Are you going shopping today?

Stefan, aren't you going shopping today?
Yes, I am. Why do you ask?
We don't have any more coffee.
One pound is enough, right? Would you like anything else?
Yes, a loaf of bread, please. But buy that at Rischart's. The bread is better there.

Kapitel 4

Notizen für die Klausur

GISELA: Hallo, Michael. Kannst du mir bitte deine Notizen leihen?
MICHAEL: Ja, gern.
GISELA: Das ist nett. Für die Klausur muss ich noch viel arbeiten.
MICHAEL: Klar, hier hast du sie. Kannst du sie morgen wieder mitbringen?

Notes for the test

Hi, Michael. Can you please lend me your notes?

Yes, glad to.
That's nice [of you]. I still have to study a lot for this test.

Of course, here they are. Can you bring them back tomorrow?

Ist das dein Hauptfach?

MICHAEL: Grüß dich. Seit wann gehst du denn in eine Literatur-Vorlesung? Studierst du nicht Geschichte?
MELANIE: Nein, nicht mehr. Ich mache jetzt Germanistik.
MICHAEL: Ah ja? Als Nebenfach?
MELANIE: Nein, als Hauptfach.
MICHAEL: Ach, wirklich? Du, möchtest du nachher Kaffee trinken gehen?
MELANIE: Ich kann leider nicht, muss noch etwas lesen. Morgen habe ich ein Referat und bin nicht besonders gut vorbereitet.

Is that your major?

Hi! Since when have you been taking a literature course? Aren't you studying history?
No, not any more. I'm taking German now.
Oh yes? As a minor?
No, as a major.
Oh, really? Aha. Say, would you like to go out for coffee afterwards?
Unfortunately I can't. I still have to read something. Tomorrow I have an oral report and I'm not especially well prepared.

Kapitel 5

Fährst du morgen zur Uni?

UWE: Fährst du morgen mit dem Auto zur Uni?
CLAUDIA: Ja. Willst du mitfahren?
UWE: Ja, gern. Ich hab' so viele Bücher für die Bibliothek. Kannst du mich vielleicht abholen?
CLAUDIA: Ja, kein Problem. Ich komme dann um halb neun bei dir vorbei. Geht das?
UWE: Ja, klar. Ich warte dann unten.

Are you driving to the university tomorrow?

Are you going by car to the university tomorrow?
Yes. Do you want to come along?
Yes, I'd like to. I've got so many library books. Can you pick me up maybe?
Yes, no problem. I'll come by your place at eight-thirty. Is that OK?
Yes, of course. I'll be waiting downstairs then.

In den Ferien

MICHAEL: Was machst du in den Ferien?
MELANIE: Ich fahre nach Österreich.
MICHAEL: Fährst du allein?
MELANIE: Nein, ich fahre mit meiner Freundin. Die kennt Österreich ziemlich gut.
MICHAEL: Fahrt ihr mit dem Auto?

On vacation

What are you doing on vacation?
I'm going to Austria.
Are you going alone?
No, I'm going with my friend. She knows Austria rather well.
Are you going by car?

MELANIE: Nein, mit der Bahn. Wir wollen vor allem wandern.

MICHAEL: Und wo übernachtet ihr?

MELANIE: In Wien schlafen wir bei Freunden. Und sonst zelten wir.

No, by train. Above all we want to hike.

And where are you staying?

In Vienna we're sleeping at our friends' house. And otherwise we're camping.

Kapitel 6

Was habt ihr vor?

UWE: Sagt mal, was macht ihr am Wochenende?

MELANIE: Keine Ahnung.

MICHAEL: Ich habe am Freitag Probe mit der Band. Am Samstag spielen wir in der Musikfabrik.

UWE: Du, Melanie, da können wir doch zusammen hingehen, oder?

MELANIE: Gute Idee. Das ist super. Vielleicht geht auch Alex mit?

MICHAEL: Der kann nicht. Er muss fürs Examen arbeiten.

UWE: Also, Melanie, ich hole dich um acht ab. In Ordnung?

What are your plans?

Say, what are you doing on the weekend?

No idea.

I've got a rehearsal with the band on Friday. On Saturday we're playing at the Musikfabrik.

Hey, you know, Melanie, we can go there together, right?

Good idea. That's great. Maybe Alex will go along too?

He can't. He has to study for his comprehensives.

All right then, Melanie, I'll pick you up at eight. Is that all right?

Es hat geschmeckt.

ALEX: Wo warst du gestern Abend?

GISELA: Warum?

ALEX: Ich habe bei dir angerufen, aber da war niemand da. Ich wollte mit dir ins Kino gehen.

GISELA: Gestern war ich mit Claudia im Café an der Uni. Sie hat mich eingeladen.

ALEX: Ah, das Café ist gut. Die haben tolle Salate.

GISELA: Ja, genau, wir haben Fischsalat gegessen.

ALEX: Hör auf, ich kriege gleich Hunger!

It tasted good.

Where were you last night?

Why?

I called, but there was no one there. I wanted to go to the movies with you.

I was with Claudia at the Café an der Uni yesterday. She treated me.

Ah, the Café is good. They have great salads.

Yes, that's right. We had fish salad.

Stop, I'm getting hungry!

Kapitel 7

Was machst du nach dem Kurs?

PETER: Was machst du nach dem Kurs? Gehst du in die Bibliothek?

MONIKA: Nein, ich treffe Anna im Alstadtcafé.

PETER: In der Fußgängerzone?

MONIKA: Ja, gehst du mit?

PETER: Nein, danke, ins Alstadtcafé gehe ich nicht so gern. Da ist immer so schlechte Luft. Alles ist voll Rauch.

MONIKA: Gehst du vielleicht mit in einen Biergarten? Im Waldgarten sitzt man schön draußen.

PETER: Aber du, ich bin pleite.

MONIKA: Macht nichts. Ich lade dich ein.

What are you doing after class?

What are you doing after class? Are you going to the library?

No, I'm meeting Anna in the Altstadtcafé.

In the pedestrian mall?

Yes, are you coming?

No, thanks, I don't like going to the Altstadtcafé. The air is always so bad there. Everything is full of smoke.

Maybe you'll go along to a beer garden? You can sit outside at the Waldgarten.

But, hey, I'm broke.

Doesn't matter. I'm treating you.

Vorbereitungen für ein Fest

MONIKA: Sag, willst du nicht endlich mal das Wohnzimmer aufräumen? Da liegen überall deine Bücher herum.

STEFAN: Muss das sein?

MONIKA: Klar, wir müssen das Essen vorbereiten und den Tisch decken. In einer Stunde kommen die Leute.

STEFAN: Was? Schon in einer Stunde? Du meine Güte! Und wir müssen noch Staub saugen, Staub wischen, abwaschen, abtrocknen, die Küche sieht aus wie . . .

MONIKA: Jetzt red nicht lange, sondern mach schnell. Ich helf' dir ja.

Preparations for a party

Say, don't you want to straighten up the living room, finally? Your books are lying around everywhere.

Do I have to?

Of course, we have to prepare the food and set the table. People are coming in an hour.

What? In an hour? Good heavens! And we still have to vacuum, dust, do the dishes, dry them, the kitchen looks like . . .

Now stop talking so much and hurry up. You know I'm going to help you.

Kapitel 8

Ein Ferienjob

PERSONALCHEFIN: Herr Ohrdorf, Sie studieren jetzt im achten Semester Informatik und wollen zwei Monate bei uns arbeiten.

UWE: Ja, richtig.

PERSONALCHEFIN: Wie ich sehe, haben Sie schon als Informatiker gearbeitet.

UWE: Ja, ich habe letztes Jahr auch einen Ferienjob gehabt und da habe ich ganz gute praktische Erfahrungen gesammelt.

PERSONALCHEFIN: Und was wollen Sie später damit machen?

UWE: Ich möchte eine Stelle bei einer Bank, eine Aufgabe mit viel Verantwortung, hoffe ich.

A summer job

Mr. Ohrdorf, you're now in your eighth semester of computer science and want to work here for two months.

Yes, that's right.

From what I can see, you have already worked as a computer specialist.

Yes, I also had a summer job last year and I got some good practical experience there.

And what do you want to do with it later on?

I would like a position with a bank, an assignment with lots of responsibility, I hope.

Kapitel 9

Hast du dich erkältet?

CLAUDIA: Hallo, Uwe! Was ist los? Du hustest ja fürchterlich.

UWE: Ja, ich habe mich erkältet. Der Hals tut mir furchtbar weh.

CLAUDIA: Hast du auch Fieber?

UWE: Ja, ein bisschen – 38.

CLAUDIA: Du Armer! Du siehst auch ganz blass aus!

UWE: Ich fühle mich auch wirklich krank. Vielleicht gehe ich lieber zum Arzt.

CLAUDIA: Na, das würde ich aber auch sagen! Vergiss nicht, dass wir ab Samstag eine Woche lang mit Gisela und Alex in Zermatt Ski laufen wollen!

(Drei Tage später)

Have you caught a cold?

Hi, Uwe! What's wrong? You're coughing terribly.

Yes, I've caught a cold. My throat's hurting a lot.

Do you have a fever?

Yes, a little—38 [= 100.4°F].

You poor fellow! You also look pretty pale!

I do feel pretty sick. Perhaps I'd better go to the doctor.

Well, I would certainly say that, too. Don't forget that beginning Saturday we want to go skiing with Gisela and Alex in Zermatt for a week.

(Three days later)

Wie fühlst du dich heute?

CLAUDIA: Wie fühlst du dich heute? Bist du gestern zum Arzt gegangen?

UWE: Ja, ich war in der Uni-Klinik. Die Ärztin hat mir was verschrieben und es geht mir jetzt schon wesentlich besser. Das Fieber ist weg.

How do you feel today?

How do you feel today? Did you go to the doctor yesterday?

Yes, I was in the university clinic. The doctor prescribed something and I already feel significantly better. The fever is gone.

CLAUDIA: Willst du immer noch am Samstag mit in die Schweiz fahren?

UWE: Aber klar doch! Den Urlaub haben wir doch schon seit Monaten geplant.

CLAUDIA: Das Wetter soll nächste Woche toll sein. Vergiss nicht deine Sonnenbrille mitzubringen.

Do you still want to go to Switzerland on Saturday?

Of course. After all, we've planned this vacation for months.

The weather is supposed to be great next week. Don't forget to bring your sunglasses along.

Kapitel 10

Wie war's?

MICHAEL: Wo warst du gestern Abend?

GISELA: Ich war mit Alex im Theater, im Berliner Ensemble.

MICHAEL: Ah, und was gab es? Wie war es?

GISELA: Man spielte ein Brecht-Stück, *Leben des Galilei.* Es war sehr interessant.

MICHAEL: Hattet ihr gute Plätze?

GISELA: Ja, wir hatten ganz prima Plätze. Wir hatten sogar Studentenkarten. Die kosteten nur zehn Mark, und wir konnten wirklich gut sehen.

MICHAEL: Würdest du das Stück empfehlen?

GISELA: Ja, unbedingt. Ich wollte es zuerst gar nicht sehen, aber dann fand ich es absolut toll.

MICHAEL: In der Zeitung stand ja eine gute Kritik.

GISELA: Naja, und danach gingen wir noch in die Wunder-Bar, tranken etwas und unterhielten uns lange über das Stück.

MICHAEL: Du, ich habe Karten für die Oper nächste Woche. Hättest du Lust mitzugehen?

How was it?

Where were you last night?

I was with Alex at the theater, at the Berliner Ensemble.

Ah, what were they playing? How was it?

They performed a play by Brecht, *Galileo.* It was very interesting.

Did you have good seats?

Yes, we had really first-rate seats. We even had student tickets. They cost only 10 marks, and we could really see well.

Would you recommend the play?

Yes, without reservation. At first I didn't want to see it, but then I found it absolutely great.

There was a good review in the paper.

Yes, well, and afterwards we went to the Wunder-Bar, drank something and talked a long time about the play.

Hey, I have tickets for the opera next week. Would you like to come along?

Kapitel 11

Stellenanzeigen

ALEX: Na, was gibt's Neues in der Zeitung?

UWE: Ich weiß nicht. Ich hab' bis jetzt nur die Anzeigen durchgesehen.

ALEX: Welche? Die Heiratsanzeigen?

UWE: Quatsch. Die Stellenanzeigen! Ich suche Arbeit. Ich hätte gern einen interessanten Job, wo man gut verdient.

ALEX: Ja, das wäre toll. Du suchst ja schon eine ganze Weile. Viel Glück!

Want ads

Well, what's new in the newspaper?

I don't know. Up to now I have only looked through the classified ads.

Which ones? The ones for marriage partners?

Nonsense. The want ads! I'm looking for work. I would like an interesting job where you can earn a lot of money.

Yes, that would be great. You've been looking a long time already. Lots of luck!

Ein Termin

UWE: Guten Tag. Ohrdorf ist mein Name, Uwe Ohrdorf. Ich würde gern Frau Dr. Ziegler sprechen. Ich habe einen Termin bei ihr.

SEKRETÄRIN: Guten Tag, Herr Ohrdorf. Ja bitte, gehen Sie doch gleich hinein. Sie erwartet Sie schon.

An appointment

Hello. My name is Ohrdorf, Uwe Ohrdorf. I would like to speak to Dr. Ziegler. I have an appointment with her.

Hello, Mr. Ohrdorf. Yes, please go right in. She's expecting you.

Kapitel 12

Rockfans gegen Ausländerhass

MONIKA: Peter, hast du Lust am Wochenende zu dem Open-Air-Konzert in Frankfurt zu gehen?

PETER: Ich weiß nicht. Ich fliege in zwei Wochen nach Amerika zurück und wollte mir noch Freiburg ansehen.

MONIKA: Ach, komm' doch. Nach Freiburg kannst du auch nächstes Wochenende noch fahren.

PETER: Aber ich kenne keinen einzigen von den Rockmusikern, die da spielen werden!

MONIKA: Es geht ja gar nicht nur um die Musik. Das Motto ist „Heute die! Morgen du!" – Mit dem Konzert demonstrieren wir gegen Rassismus und Ausländerhass.

PETER: Glaubst du denn, dass da viele Leute kommen werden?

MONIKA: Oh ja! Stell' dir vor, man erwartet ungefähr 150.000 Menschen.

PETER: Gut, dann lass uns gehen und auch demonstrieren!

Rock fans against xenophobia

Do you feel like going to the outdoor concert in Frankfurt on the weekend?

I don't know. I'm flying back to America in two weeks and I still wanted to have a look at Freiburg.

Oh, come on. You can still go to Freiburg next weekend.

But I don't know a single one of the rock musicians who are going to play there!

It's not only about the music, of course. The slogan is "Today them! Tomorrow you!"—With the concert we're demonstrating against racism and xenophobia.

Do you think that many people will come?

Oh yes! Just imagine, about 150,000 people are expected.

OK, then let's go and demonstrate also.

Supplementary Word Sets

The following word lists will help you to increase the number of things you can say and write.

Audio-visual equipment

die **Boxen** (*pl.*)   speakers
die **Compact Disk**   compact disk
der **Farbfernseher**   color television
der **Kassettenrecorder**   cassette recorder
der **Kopfhörer**   headphone
der **Lautsprecher**   loudspeaker
das **Mikrofon**   microphone
der **Plattenspieler**   record player
der **Radiorecorder**   cassette radio
der **Schwarzweißfernseher**   black-and-white television
die **Stereoanlage**   stereo system
das **Tonband,** das **Band**   tape
das **Tonbandgerät**   (reel-to-reel) tape recorder
der **Tuner**   tuner
der **Verstärker**   amplifier
der **Videorecorder**   video recorder (VCR)

Body care and hygiene

die **Haarbürste**   hair brush
der **Haartrockner,** der **Föhn**   hair dryer
das **Handtuch**   hand towel
das **Make-up**   makeup
der **Rasierapparat**   razor
die **Schere**   scissors
die **Seife**   soap
der **Spiegel**   mirror
das **Taschentuch**   handkerchief
die **(elektrische) Zahnbürste**   (electric) toothbrush
die **Zahnpasta**   toothpaste

Buildings and other landmarks

die **Autobahnauffahrt (-ausfahrt)**   expressway on-ramp (off-ramp)
die **Bahnlinie**   railroad line
der **Bauernhof**   farm
die **Brücke**   bridge
die **Bundesstraße**   federal highway
die **Burg**   fortress
das **Denkmal**   monument
die **Fabrik**   factory
der **Fernsehturm**   TV tower
der **Friedhof**   cemetery
der **Funkturm**   radio and TV tower
der **Fußweg**   footpath
die **Kapelle**   chapel
die **Kirche**/der **Dom**/das **Münster**   church/cathedral
das **Kloster**   monastery
die **Mühle**   mill

das **Museum**   museum
das **Parkhaus**   parking garage
die **Polizei**   police
die **Post**   post office
die **Ruine**   ruin
das **Schloss**   castle
die **Tiefgarage**   underground garage
der **Tunnel**   tunnel

Chores

(das) **Abendessen vorbereiten, machen**   to prepare supper
Fenster putzen   to clean windows
den **Hund**/die **Katze füttern**   to feed the dog/cat
(die) **Wäsche bügeln**   to iron the wash, laundry
Wäsche, Kleider flicken   to mend clothes

(die) **Bäume beschneiden/pflanzen/fällen**   to prune/to plant/to cut down trees
das **Haus**/den **Zaun**/das **Boot streichen**   to paint the house/the fence/the boat
die **Hecke schneiden**   to trim the hedge
(das) **Holz sägen/spalten/hacken**   to saw/to split/to chop wood
das **Laub harken**   to rake leaves
(den) **Rasen mähen**   to mow the lawn
(den) **Schnee fegen, kehren/schippen**   to sweep/to shovel snow
(das) **Unkraut jäten**   to pull out weeds

Classroom objects

der **Filzstift**   felt-tip pen
die **Folie**   transparency
das **Klassenzimmer**   classroom
die **Kreide**   chalk
die **Landkarte;** die **Wandkarte**   map; wall map
der **Overheadprojektor**   overhead projector
der **Papierkorb**   wastebasket
das **Ringbuch**   loose-leaf binder
der **Schwamm**   sponge
das **Sprachlabor**   language lab
die **Videokassette**   videocassette
der **Videorecorder**   video recorder (VCR)
die **(Wand)tafel**   chalkboard

Clothing

das **Abendkleid**   evening dress/gown
der **Anorak**   jacket with hood, parka
der **Blazer**   blazer

die **Daunenjacke**   down jacket
der **Hosenrock**   culottes
die **Kniestrümpfe** (*pl.*)   knee socks
das **Kostüm**   woman's suit
die **Latzhose**   bib overalls
der **Mantel**   coat
der **Overall**   jumpsuit
der **Parka**   parka
das **Polohemd**   polo shirt
der **Regenmantel**   raincoat
der **Rollkragenpullover**   turtleneck
die **Sandalen** (*pl.*)   sandals
die **Schal**   scarf
der **Schlafanzug**   pajamas
die **Sportschuhe** (*pl.*)   athletic shoes
die **Strickjacke**   (cardigan) sweater
das **Sweatshirt**   sweatshirt
das **Trägerkleid**   jumper
der **Trainingsanzug**   sweat suit
die **Turnschuhe** (*pl.*)   fitness/workout shoes
die **Weste**   vest
der **Wintermantel**   winter coat

Collectibles

sammeln   to collect
alte Flaschen   old bottles
Briefmarken   stamps
Glas   glass
das **Kuscheltier**   stuffed animal
Münzen   coins
Pflanzen (getrocknet)   plants (dried)
Puppen   dolls
Silber   silver
Streichholzschachteln   matchboxes
Zinn   pewter

College majors

Amerikanistik   American studies
Anglistik   English language and literature
Betriebswirtschaft   business administration
Biologie   biology
Chemie   chemistry
Chinesisch   Chinese
Englisch   English
Französisch   French
Germanistik   German language and literature
Informatik   computer science
Ingenieurwesen   engineering
Italienisch   Italian
Japanisch   Japanese
Jura   law
Kommunikationswissenschaft   communications
Kunstgeschichte   art history
Marketing   marketing
Medizin   medicine

Pädagogik/Erziehungswissenschaften   education
Philosophie   philosophy
Physik   physics
Politik   political science
Psychologie   psychology
Publizistik   journalism
Religionswissenschaft/Theologie   religion
Rechnungswesen   accounting
Romanistik   Romance languages and literature
Russisch   Russian
Sozialkunde   social studies
Sozialwissenschaften/Soziologie   sociology
Spanisch   Spanish
Sprachwissenschaft/Linguistik   linguistics
Theaterwissenschaft   theater studies
Volkswirtschaft   economics

Colors

dunkel[blau]   dark [blue]
hell[blau]   light [blue]
lila   lilac
orange   orange
purpur   purple
rosa   pink

Computer terminology

der **Anwender**   program user
anwenderfreundlich   user friendly
anzeigen   to display
mit dem Computer arbeiten   to work on the computer
auswählen   to select a program
der **Bildschirm**   screen
die **CD-ROM**   CD-ROM
der **Personalcomputer**   personal computer
das **Diskettenlaufwerk**   diskette drive
der **Drucker**   printer
der **Laserdrucker**   laser printer
der **Matrixdrucker**   matrix printer
der **Tintenstrahldrucker**   ink jet printer
der **Typendrucker**   letter-quality printer
die **e-Mail**   e-mail; **eine Mail schicken**   to send email
die **Festplatte**   hard disk
die **Floppy-Disk**   floppy disk
das **Internet**   Internet
laden   to load
ein **Programm laufen lassen**   to run a program
der **Monitor**   monitor
das **Netz**   network
das **Passwort**   password
der **Positionsanzeiger**   cursor
programmieren   to program
die **Programmiersprache**   computer language
die **Software;** das **Softwarepaket**   software; software package

speichern to store; **auf Diskette speichern** to store on diskette
ein **Gbyte(GB)–Speicher** a gigabyte memory
die **Tastatur** keyboard
die **Taste;** die **Funktionstaste** key; function key
das **Textverarbeitungsprogramm** word processing program

Directions

Asking directions

Wo ist [der Bahnhof]? Where is the [train station]?
Wie weit ist es [zum Bahnhof]? How far is it [to the train station]?
Wie komme ich am schnellsten [zum Bahnhof]? What is the quickest way [to the train station]?
Wo ist hier in der Nähe [ein Café]? Is there [a café] around here?
Wissen Sie den Weg nach [Obersdorf]? Do you know the way to [Obersdorf]?
Wir wollen nach [Stuttgart]. Wie fahren wir am besten? We're going to [Stuttgart]. What is the best route?

Giving directions

Da fahren Sie am besten mit [der U-Bahn]. It's best if you go by [subway].
Fahren Sie mit dem [Dreier]; Nehmen Sie den [Dreier]. Take number [3] [bus].
Fahren Sie mit der [Drei]; Nehmen Sie die [Drei]. Take number [3] [subway or streetcar].
[Dort/An der Ecke/An der Kreuzung] ist die Haltestelle. [Over there/on the corner/at the intersection] is the [bus]stop.
An der [ersten] Kreuzung gehen Sie [rechts]. At the [first] intersection turn [right].
Gehen Sie die [erste] Straße [links]. Take the [first] street [to the left].
Gehen Sie geradeaus. Go straight ahead.
Bei der Ampel biegen Sie [rechts] ab. At the traffic light turn [right].

Family

der **Enkel** grandson
die **Enkelin** granddaughter
das **Enkelkind** grandchild
der **Halbbruder** half brother
die **Halbschwester** half sister
die **Schwiegermutter** mother-in-law
der **Schwiegervater** father-in-law
der **Schwager** brother-in-law
die **Schwägerin** sister-in-law

geschieden divorced
ledig single
verheiratet married

Farewells and greetings

Adé. 'Bye. (*used in southern Germany and Austria*)
Auf Wiederhören. Good-bye. (*on the telephone*)
Bis dann! See you later.
Ciao. So long.
Grüezi. Hello. (*used in Switzerland*)
Grüß Gott. Good-bye. Hello. (*used in southern Germany and Austria*)
Mach's gut. Take it easy.
Servus. Good-bye! Hello! (*used in southern Germany and Austria among friends*)

Film

der **Abenteuerfilm** adventure movie
der **Actionfilm** action movie
der **Horrorfilm** horror film
der **Liebesfilm** romance
der **Science-Fiction-Film** science fiction movie
die **Außenaufnahme** location shot
das **Drehbuch** (film) script
die **Filmfestspiele** (*pl.*) film festival
die **Filmkomödie** comedy film
die **Filmkritik** movie criticism
die **(Film)leinwand** (movie) screen
der **Filmemacher**/die **Filmemacherin** filmmaker
der **(Film)schauspieler**/die **(Film)schauspielerin** movie actor/actress
die **(Film)szene** (movie) scene
das **(Film)studio** (movie) studio
der **Kameramann**/die **Kamerafrau** cameraman/ camerawoman
der **Regisseur**/die **Regisseurin** director

Foods

Breakfast

das **Ei (weich gekocht)** egg (soft-boiled)
das **Graubrot** light rye bread
der **Honig** honey
der **Joghurt** yogurt
der **Kakao** cocoa
die **Marmelade** jam, marmalade
der **Pumpernickel** pumpernickel bread
die **Schokolade** hot chocolate
das **Schwarzbrot** dark rye break
der **Tomatensaft** tomato juice
das **Vollkornbrot** coarse, whole-grain bread
das **Weißbrot** white bread

Main meal

die **Suppe** soup
der **gemischte Salat** vegetable salad plate
der **grüne Salat** tossed (green) salad

der **Braten** roast
das **Kalbfleisch** veal

das **Kotelett**   chop
das **Rindfleisch**   beef
die **Roulade**   roulade
das **Schnitzel**   cutlet
das **Schweinefleisch**   pork
der **Speck**   bacon
der **Truthahn**   turkey

die **Bohnen** (*pl.*)   beans
der **Champignon**   mushroom
die **Erbsen** (*pl.*)   peas
die **Karotten, gelbe Rüben** (*pl.*)   carrots
der **Kohl**   cabbage
der **Mais**   corn
die **(gefüllte) Paprikaschote**   (stuffed) pepper
die **Pilze** (*pl.*)   mushrooms
der **Reis**   rice
das **Sauerkraut**   sauerkraut
der **Spargel**   asparagus
die **Zwiebel**   onion

das **Salz**   salt
der **Pfeffer**   pepper
der **Zucker**   sugar

Lunch/supper

die **(saure) Gurke**   (half-sour) pickle
das **Spiegelei**   fried egg
der **Thunfisch**   tuna fish
die **Wurst**/der **Aufschnitt**   sausage/cold cuts

Desserts and fruit

das **Eis**   ice cream
der **Karamelpudding**   caramel custard
das **Kompott**   stewed fruit
die **Schokoladencreme**   chocolate mousse
der **Vanillepudding**   vanilla pudding

die **Sahne**   cream
die **Schlagsahne**   whipped cream

die **Ananas**   pinapple
die **Erdbeeren** (*pl.*)   strawberries
die **Himbeeren** (*pl.*)   raspberries
die **Orange, Apfelsine**   orange
der **Pfirsich**   peach
die **Pflaume**   plum
der **Rhabarber**   rhubarb
die **Zitrone**   lemon
die **Zwetsch(g)e**   plum

Food preparation

backen   to bake
braten   to fry; to roast

grillen   to grill
kochen   to cook

Free time

angeln   to fish
ausgehen   to go out
basteln   do-it-yourself projects
Blumen (z.B. Rosen, Dahlien, Lilien, Nelken)   flowers
   (e.g., roses, dahlias, lilies, carnations)
campen   to go camping
zum Fitnesstraining gehen   to go for a workout
fotografieren   to photograph
Freunde treffen   to meet friends
die **Gartenarbeit**   gardening
im Internet surfen   to surf the Internet
Konzert/Theater besuchen   to attend concerts/plays
malen   to paint
reisen   to travel
schreiben (Gedichte, Geschichten, Romane, Dramen)   to write (poems, stories, novels, plays)
Video-, Computerspiele   video/computer games
Videofilme ansehen   to watch videotapes
zeichnen   to draw

Geographic terms

die **Anhöhe;** der **Hügel**   hill
der **Atlantik**   Atlantic (Ocean)
der **Bach**   brook
das **(Bundes)land**   (federal) state in Germany and Austria
der **(Bundes)staat**   (federal) state in the U.S.A.
die **Ebbe**/die **Flut**   low tide/high tide
der **Fluss**   river
das **Gebirge**   mountain range
die **Gezeiten** (*pl.*)   tides
der **Gipfel**   peak
der **Gletscher**   glacier
die **Insel**   island
der **Kanal**   canal; channel
der **Kanton**   canton (*Switzerland*)
die **Küste**   coast
das **Meer**   sea
der **Pazifik**   Pacific (Ocean)
der **See**   lake
die **See**   sea
der **Strand**   beach
das **Tal**   valley
der **Teich**   pond
das **Ufer**   shore
der **Wald**   woods
die **Wiese**   meadow
die **Wüste**   desert

Household

der **Backofen**   oven
die **Badewanne**   bathtub

die **Dusche**   shower
das **Mikrowellengerät**   microwave
das **Spülbecken**/die **Spüle**   kitchen sink
der **Trockner**/der **Wäschetrockner**   clothes dryer
das **Waschbecken**   washbasin

Jewelry

das **Armband**   bracelet
die **Halskette**   necklace
die **Kette**   chain
die **Ohrringe** (*pl.*)   earrings
der **Ring**   ring

Literature

die **Anthologie**   anthology
das **Drama**   drama, play
das **Gedicht**   poem
die **Kurzgeschichte**   short story
der **Roman**   novel
die **Zeitschrift**   magazine
die **Illustrierte**   illustrated magazine

der **Autor**/die **Autorin**   author
der **Dichter**/die **Dichterin**   poet
der **Dramatiker**/die **Dramatikerin**   dramatist
der **Schriftsteller**/die **Schriftstellerin**   writer

Music and theater

das **Theaterstück;** die **Tragödie;** die **Komödie;** der
    Einakter   play; tragedy; comedy; one-act play
das **Musical**   musical comedy
die **Oper**   opera
die **Operette**   operette

der **Dirigent**/die **Dirigentin**   conductor
der **Regisseur**/die **Regisseurin**   director
der **Sänger**/die **Sängerin**   singer
der **Schauspieler**/die **Schauspielerin**   actor/actress
der **Zuschauer**/die **Zuschauerin**   spectator

der **Beifall,** der **Applaus**   applause
die **Bühne**   stage
das **Foyer**   hallway, lobby
die **Inszenierung**   mounting of a production
das **Orchester**   orchestra
die **Pause**   intermission
das **Programmheft**   program
die **Vorstellung**   performance

dirigieren   to conduct
proben   to rehearse
singen   to sing
üben   to practice

Musical instruments

das **Akkordeon**   accordion
die **Blockflöte**   recorder
die **Bratsche**   viola
das **Cello**   cello
das **Fagott**   bassoon
die **Flöte**   flute
die **Geige, Violine**   violin
die **Gitarre**   guitar
die **Harfe**   harp
die **Klarinette**   clarinet
das **Klavier**   piano
der **Kontrabass**   double bass
die **Oboe**   oboe
die **Orgel**   organ
die **Posaune (+ blasen)**   trombone (to play)
die **Pauke**   kettle drum
das **Saxophon**   saxophone
das **Schlagzeug**   percussion (instrument)
die **Trommel**   drum
die **Trompete (+ blasen)**   trumpet (to play)
die **Tuba (+ blasen)**   tuba (to play)
das **(Wald)horn (+ blasen)**   French horn (to play)

Personal qualities and characteristics
Adjectives for mood or personality

ausgezeichnet   excellent
elend   miserable
erstklassig   first-rate
fantastisch   fantastic
furchtbar   horrible
kaputt   worn out, tired
klasse   terrific
miserabel   miserable
nervös   nervous
prima   excellent
schrecklich   dreadful
toll   great
traurig   sad

Adjectives for personality

fies   disgusting; unfair
klug   smart
lahm   slow, sluggish
langsam   slow
praktisch   practical
schlau   clever, smart
verrückt   crazy

Physical description of people

blond   blond
dick   fat
dunkel   brunette

fett   fat
gut aussehend   handsome
hässlich   ugly
hübsch   pretty
mager   thin, skinny
normal   normal
schwach   weak
stark   strong
vollschlank   full-figured

Professions

ein **Angestellter**/eine **Angestellte**   white-collar worker
der **Apotheker**/die **Apothekerin**   pharmacist
der **Arzt**/die **Ärztin**   physician
der **Betriebswirt**/die **Betriebswirtin**   manager
der **Dolmetscher**/die **Dolmetscherin**   interpreter
der **Elektriker**/die **Elektrikerin**   electrician
der **Flugbegleiter**/die **Flugbegleiterin**   flight attendant
der **Hochschullehrer**/die **Hochschullehrerin**   college/ university professor
der **Ingenieur**/die **Ingenieurin**   engineer
der **Journalist**/die **Journalistin**   journalist
der **Krankenpfleger**/die **Krankenschwester**   nurse
der **Lehrer**/die **Lehrerin**   teacher
der **Mechaniker**/die **Mechanikerin**   mechanic
der **Musiker**/die **Musikerin**   musician
der **Pfarrer**/die **Pfarrerin**   clergyperson
der **Physiotherapeut**/die **Physiotherapeutin**   physical therapist
der **Rechtsanwalt**/die **Rechtsanwältin**   lawyer
der **Sekretär**/die **Sekretärin**   secretary
der **Sozialarbeiter**/die **Sozialarbeiterin**   social worker
der **Sozialpädagoge**/die **Sozialpädagogin**   social worker (with college degree)
der **Tierarzt**/die **Tierärztin**   veterinarian
der **Verkäufer**/die **Verkäuferin**   salesperson
der **Volkswirt**/die **Volkswirtin**   economist
der **Wissenschaftler**/die **Wissenschaftlerin**   scientist
der **Zahnarzt**/die **Zahnärztin**   dentist

Specialty shops

das **Blumengeschäft**   florist shop
die **chemische Reinigung**   dry cleaning shop
das **Eisenwarengeschäft**   hardware store
das **Elektrogeschäft**   appliance store
das **Feinkostgeschäft**   delicatessen
das **Fotogeschäft**   camera store
der **Juwelier**   jeweler's; jewelry store
das **Kaffeegeschäft**   store selling coffee
der **Kiosk**   kiosk, stand
der **Klempner**   plumber's shop
die **Konditorei**   coffee and pastry shop
das **Möbelgeschäft**   furniture store
der **Optiker**   optician's shop
das **Schreibwarengeschäft**   stationery store

das **Schuhgeschäft**   shoe store
der **Schuhmacher**; der **Schuster**   shoe repair (shop)
das **Sportgeschäft**; die **Sportausrüstungen**   sporting goods store; sporting goods
der **Waschsalon**   laundromat

Sports and games

das **Ballonfahren**   ballooning
das **Billard**   billiards
das **Bodybuilding**   bodybuilding
die **Dame**   checkers
das **Drachenfliegen**   hang gliding
das **Eishockey**   hockey
das **Fallschirmspringen**   parachute jumping
der **Federball**   badminton
das **Fitnesstraining**   working out
der **Flipper**   pinball machine; **ich flippere**   I play the pinball machine
die **Gymnastik**   calisthenics
der **Handball, Hallenhandball**   handball
das **Hockey**   field hockey
auf dem **Hometrainer/Heimtrainer fahren**   to ride an exercise bike
das **Inline-Skaten**   inline skating
das **Krafttraining**   power training
die **Leichtathletik**   track and field
das **Mountainbiking**   to go mountain biking
der **Radsport**, das **Radfahren**   bicycling
das **Rollerblading (gehen)**   (to go) in-line skating, rollerblading
das **Rollschuhlaufen**   roller skating
das **Schlittschuhlaufen**   ice skating
das **Segelfliegen**   glider flying
das **Skateboardfahren**   skateboarding
der **Skilanglauf**   cross-country skiing
das **Snowboarding**   snow boarding
das **Turnen**   gymnastics
der **Wasserball**   water polo
das **Windsurfen**   windsurfing

boxen   to box
fechten   to fence
jagen   to hunt
kegeln   to bowl
ringen   to wrestle
rudern   to row
schießen   to shoot
(hart) trainieren   to have a (good) workout

Table setting

die **Butterdose**   butter dish
der **Eierbecher**   egg cup
der **Esslöffel**   tablespoon
das **Gedeck**   table setting
das **Gericht**   dish (food)

die **Kaffeekanne**/die **Teekanne**   coffeepot/teapot
das **Milchkännchen**   creamer (small pitcher for cream or milk)
die **Schüssel**   bowl
die **Serviette**   napkin
die **Speise**   dish (food)
der **Teelöffel**   teaspoon
der **Teller**   plate
die **Untertasse**   saucer
die **Zuckerdose**   sugar bowl

Transportation

die **Kutsche**   carriage
der **Pferdewagen**   horse-drawn wagon
der **LKW (= Lastkraftwagen)**/der **Laster**   truck
der **PKW (= Personenkraftwagen)**   passenger car
der **Anhänger**   trailer
der **Campingwagen,** der **Wohnwagen**   camper (pulled by a car)
der **Caravan**   camper (recreational vehicle)
der **Combi**   station wagon

die **Bergbahn**   mountain railway; cable car
die **Eisenbahn**   train, railway
der **Güterzug**   freight train

das **Boot**   boat
das **Containerschiff**   container ship
die **Fähre**   ferry
der **Frachter**   freighter
das **Kanu**   canoe
das **Motorboot**   motorboat
der **Passagierdampfer**   passenger ship
das **Ruderboot**   rowboat
das **Segelboot**   sailboat
das **Segelschiff**   sailing ship
der **Tanker**   tanker

der **Hubschrauber**   helicopter
der **Jet**   jet
der **Jumbojet**   jumbo jet
das **(Propeller)flugzeug**   propeller plane
das **Raumschiff**   spaceship
das **Segelflugzeug**   glider; sailplane

TV programs

das **Familiendrama**   soap opera
die **Fernsehkomödie**   sitcom (situation comedy)
die **Fernsehserie**   series

die **Fernsehshow,** die **Unterhaltungsshow**   game show
der **Krimi**   detective or crime drama
die **Nachrichten** (*pl.*)   news
die **Quizsendung,** das **Fernsehquiz**   quiz show
die **Seifenoper**   soap opera
der **Spielfilm**   feature (film)
die **Sportschau**   sports program
der **Zeichentrickfilm**   cartoon

Weather expressions

der **Blitz**   lightning
Celsius   centigrade
der **Donner**   thunder
das **Gewitter**   thunderstorm
der **Hagel**   hail
das **Hoch**   high-pressure system
die **Kaltfront**   cold front
der **Landregen**   all-day rain
der **Luftdruck**   air pressure
der **Nebel**   fog
der **Niederschlag**   precipitation
der **Nieselregen**   drizzle
der **Schauer**   shower
der **Schneefall**   snowfall
der **Sprühregen**   drizzle
der **Tau**   dew
die **Temperatur**   temperature
das **Tief**   low-pressure system
die **Warmfront**   warm front
der **Wetterbericht**   weather report; **Was steht im Wetterbericht?** What's the weather report?
die **Wettervorhersage**   weather forecast
die **Windrichtung**   wind direction

bedeckt   overcast
bewölkt   cloudy; **stark bewölkt**   very cloudy
eisig   icy cold
heiter   fair
klar   clear, cloudless
neb(e)lig   foggy
schwül   humid
stürmisch   stormy
wolkenlos   cloudless
wolkig   cloudy

Es gießt (in Strömen).   It's pouring.
Es regnet Bindfäden.   It's raining cats and dogs.
Es ist nasskalt.   It's damp and cold.

Supplementary Expressions

1. Expressing skepticism

Ist das dein Ernst?   Are you serious?
Meinst du? Wirklich? Meinst du das wirklich?   Do you think so? Really? Do you really mean that?
Das ist ja komisch/eigenartig/merkwürdig.   That's funny/strange.
Irgendetwas stimmt hier nicht.   Something's wrong here.
Ist das wahr?   Is that true?
Woher weißt du das? Wo/Von wem hast du das gehört?   How do you know that? Where/From whom did you hear that?

2. Expressing insecurity or doubt

Das ist unwahrscheinlich.   That's unlikely.
Das glaub' ich nicht.   I don't believe that.
Das ist zweifelhaft.   That's doubtful.
Das kann nicht sein.   That can't be.

3. Expressing annoyance

Quatsch! / Unsinn! / Blödsinn!   Nonsense!
Hör mal.   Listen.
Geh.   Go on.
(Das ist doch) nicht zu glauben.   (That is) not to be believed.
(Das ist) unerhört/unglaublich.   (That is) unheard of/unbelievable.
Das tut/sagt man nicht.   One doesn't do/say such a thing.
Das kannst du doch nicht machen/sagen.   You can't do/say that.
Frechheit!   The nerve!; She's/He's/You've got some nerve!
Also komm.   Come on.

4. Stalling for time

Also./ Na ja./Ja nun.   Well./Well, of course./Well, now.
hmmmmmmmmmm   hmmmmmmmmmm
Lass mich mal nachdenken.   Let me think about it.
Das kann ich so (auch) nicht sagen.   I can't say that (either).
Da muss ich erst mal überlegen.   Let me think.

5. Being noncommital

(Das ist ja) interessant.   (That is) interesting.
hmmmmmmmmmm   hmmmmmmmmmm

Wirklich?   Really?
Ach ja?   Oh really?
So so.   Oh yes, I see.

6. Expressing good wishes

Gesundheit!   Bless you!
Guten Appetit.   Enjoy your meal.
Prost! / Auf Ihr Wohl! / Zum Wohl!   Cheers! / To your health!
Herzlichen Glückwunsch!   Congratulations!
Herzlichen Glückwunsch zum Geburtstag!   Happy birthday!
Gute Besserung.   Get well soon.
Viel Glück!   Good luck!
Viel Vergnügen/Spaß!   Have fun!
Alles Gute!   All the best! Best wishes!

7. Courtesy expressions

Bitte (sehr/schön).   Please.
Danke (sehr/schön).   Thanks (very much).

8. Saying "you're welcome"

Bitte (sehr/schön).   You're (very) welcome.
Gern geschehen.   Glad to do it.
Nichts zu danken.   Don't mention it.

9. Expressing surprise

Ach nein!   Oh no!
(Wie) ist das (nur) möglich!   (How) is that possible?
Das hätte ich nicht gedacht.   I wouldn't have thought that.
Das ist ja prima/toll/klasse/stark/Wahnsinn!   That's great/fantastic/terrific, etc.!
(Das ist ja) nicht zu glauben!   (That's) unbelievable!
Kaum zu glauben.   Hard to believe.
Um Himmels willen!   For heaven's sake!
Sag' bloß.   You don't say.

10. Expressing agreement (and disagreement)

Natürlich (nicht)! / Selbstverbständlich (nicht)!   Naturally, of course (not)!
Klar.   Sure.
Warum denn nicht?   Why not?
Das kann (nicht) sein.   That can(not) be.
(Das) stimmt (nicht).   (That's) (not) right.
Richtig. / Falsch.   Right. / Wrong.

Das finde ich auch/nicht.   I think so, too./I don't think so.

Genau. / Eben.   Exactly. / That's right.

Du hast Recht.   You're right.

11. Responding to requests

Bitte. / Selbstverständlich. / Natürlich. / Klar.   Glad to. / Of course. / Naturally.

Gern. / Machen wir. / Mit Vergnügen.   Glad to. / We'll do it. / With pleasure.

(Es tut mir Leid, aber) das geht nicht.   (I'm sorry but) that won't work.

12. Expressing regret

(Das) tut mir Leid.   I'm sorry.

(Es) tut mir Leid, dass [ich nicht kommen kann].   I'm sorry [I can't come].

Leider [kann ich morgen nicht].   Unfortunately [I can't tomorrow].

(Es) geht leider nicht.   That won't work, unfortunately.

Schade.   That's a shame. / Too bad.

(So ein) Pech.   That's tough luck.

13. Excusing oneself

Bitte entschuldigen Sie mich.   Please excuse me. / I beg your pardon.

Entschuldigung. / Verzeihung. / Entschuldigen Sie.   Excuse (pardon) me.

14. Expressing indifference

(Das) ist mir egal.   That's all the same to me.

Das macht mir nichts aus.   It doesn't matter to me.

Das ist nicht meine Sorge.   That's not my problem.

Macht nichts.   Doesn't matter.

Das ist mir Wurscht.   I couldn't care less.

Ich habe nichts dagegen. / Meinetwegen.   I have nothing against it.

15. Expressing admiration

Ach, wie schön! / Klasse!   Oh, how nice! / Great! / Terrific!

Fantastisch! / Toll! / Super! / Stark! / Irre! / Einsame Spitze!   Fantastic!/ Great! / Super! / Incredible! / Really great!, etc.

Erstklassig! / Ausgezeichnet!   First-rate! / Excellent!

Das ist aber nett [von Ihnen/dir].   That's really nice [of you].

16. Expressing rejection

(Das ist) schrecklich!   (That is) awful!

Das ärgert mich.   That annoys me.

Der/Das/Die gefällt mir (gar) nicht.   I don't like him/that/her (at all).

Ich mag sie/ihn nicht.   I don't like her/him.

Ich kann sie/ihn nicht leiden.   I don't like her/him.

Ich finde das schlecht/langweilig.   I think that is bad/boring.

Ich finde sie/ihn nicht sympathisch/nett.   I don't find her/him likeable/nice.

17. Expressing joy and pleasure

Wir freuen uns auf [seinen Besuch/die Ferien].   We're looking forward to [his visit/our vacation].

Wir sind froh (darüber), dass [er wieder arbeitet].   We're happy (about the fact) that [he's working again].

Es freut mich, dass [sie gekommen ist].   I'm happy that [she has come].

Das tun/kochen/essen wir gern.   We like to do/cook/eat that.

Das macht mir/uns Spaß.   I/We enjoy that. / That's fun.

18. Expressing sadness

Ach (nein)!   Oh (no)!

Wie schrecklich!   How awful/horrible.

Mein Gott! / O je!   My God!

Ich bin sehr traurig darüber.   I am very unhappy about that.

Ich bin deprimiert/frustriert.   I am depressed/frustrated.

19. Making requests

Hättest du/Hätten Sie Lust [mitzukommen]?   Would you like [to come along]?

Hättest du/Hätten Sie Zeit [uns zu besuchen]?   Would you have time [to come see us]?

Ich hätte gern [ein Pfund Äpfel].   I'd like [a pound of apples].

Könntest du/Könnten Sie [mein Auto reparieren]?   Could you [repair my car]?

Würdest du/Würden Sie mir bitte helfen?   Would you please help me?

Hättest du/Hätten Sie etwas dagegen?   Would you mind?

Dürfte ich [ein Stück Kuchen haben]?   May I/Is it OK if I [have a piece of cake]?

Macht es dir/Ihnen etwas aus?   Do you mind?

Sei/Seien Sie so gut.   Be so kind.

Ist es dir/Ihnen recht?   Is it OK with you?

20. Asking for favors

Könntest du/Könnten Sie mir einen Gefallen tun und [mich mitnehmen]?   Could you do me a favor and [take me along]?

Ich hätte eine Bitte: könntest/würdest du (könnten/würden Sie) [mich mitnehmen]?   I have a request: could/would you [take me along]?

21. Making surmises

Ich glaube schon. / Ich denke ja.   I think so.

Das dürfte/könnte wahr/richtig sein.   That might/could be true/right.

Wahrscheinlich [stimmt das].   Probably [that's right].

Ich bin ziemlich sicher, dass [er das gesagt hat].   I'm quite sure that [he said that].

Ich nehme an, dass [das stimmt].   I assume that [that's right].

Das scheint [nicht zu stimmen].   That appears [not to be right].

22. Expressing expectation

Hoffentlich. / Hoffentlich [kommt sie].   I hope. / I hope [she comes].

Ich hoffe (es) (sehr).   I hope (so) (very much).

Ich freue mich auf [die Ferien].   I'm looking forward to [my vacation].

Ich kann es kaum erwarten.   I can hardly wait.

23. Expressing fears

Ich befürchte/Ich fürchte, dass [sie nicht kommt].   I'm afraid [she's not coming].

Ich habe Angst [nach Hause zu gehen].   I'm afraid [to go home].

Ich habe Angst vor [dem Hund].   I'm afraid of [the dog].

Das ist mir unheimlich.   It scares me.

24. Giving advice

Ich schlage vor, dass [wir um acht anfangen].   I suggest that [we begin at eight].

Das würde ich dir/Ihnen (nicht) raten.   I would (not) advise that.

Das würde ich (nicht) machen/sagen.   I would (not) do/say that.

An [deiner/ihrer/seiner] Stelle würde ich [zu Hause bleiben].   If I were [you/her/him], I'd [stay home].

25. Correcting misunderstandings

Das habe ich nicht so gemeint.   I didn't mean it that way.

Das habe ich nur aus Spaß gesagt.   I only said that in fun/jest. I was only kidding.

Das war nicht mein Ernst.   I wasn't serious.

Vocabulary for Authentic Text Activities

Kapitel 2

Geburtsanzeige

Ammersee the name of a lake in Bavaria
die **Eltern** (*pl.*) parents
die **Geburtsanzeige** birth announcement
ist gekommen has arrived
das **Gewicht** weight
die **Größe** *here:* length
die **Schwester** sister
überglücklich overjoyed
die **Welt** world

Kapitel 3

Krone

ab as of
Achtung attention
können can
die **Öffnungszeiten** store hours
seit for
stressfreier with less stress

Preisring-Markt

Edamer type of Dutch cheese
Fanta the name of a popular soft drink
griech. (= griechisch) Greek
holl. (= holländisch) Dutch
Mailänder Milanese
3er Packung pack of three
das **Rindergulasch** beef for stew
Sarotti the name of a brand of chocolate
die **Schokolade** chocolate
der **Sekt** champagne
Söhnlein Brillant the name of a brand of champagne
das **Sonderangebot** special
die **Theke** counter

Kapitel 4

Fernseh-Programm

ab 4 from age 4
das **Abenteuer** adventure
der **Beruf** profession
dt. (= deutsch) German
fliegend flying
das **Glücksrad** Wheel of Fortune
Info (= Information) information
Jede Menge Leben Full House
das **Krankenhaus** hospital

die **Nachrichten** news
namenlos nameless
polit (= politisch) political
die **Presseschau** current issues in the press
ran come on!
das **Revier** district
die **Reiter** (*pl.*) cavalry
Riskier' was! Take a Chance.
SAT 1 (= Satellit 1) cable station 1
die **Schlagzeile** headline
die **Schwarzwaldklinik** The Black Forest Clinic
die **Serie** series
die **Tagesschau** daily news
trickreich tricky
die **Umwelt** environment
die **Volksmusik** folk music
volkstümlich traditional
die **Vorschau** preview
das **Wunschkonzert** request concert
ZDF (= Zweites Deutsches Fernsehen) TV channel 2
der **Zeichentrickfilm** cartoon

Kapitel 5

Restop Altea Motel

die **Ausflugsfahrt** excursion
der **Ausgangspunkt** starting point
äußerst extremely
der **Badestrand** beach
Bergsteigen mountain climbing
bzw. (= beziehungsweise) respectively
einladen to invite
die **Erholung** relaxation
erreichbar accessible
die **Fahrtrichtung** direction
hoteleigen private (hotel's own)
die **Kulturstätte** place of cultural interest (e.g., castle, museum)
die **Lage** site, location
das **Loch** hole
Mondsee the name of a lake and a town on the lake in Austria, about 30 km east of Salzburg
Salzkammergut an area in Austria, famous for its many lakes and alpine landscape
die **Schiffsrundfahrt** boat excursion
überraschen to surprise
die **Umgebung** environs, the area
die **Veranstaltung** event (e.g., concert)
das **Vergnügen** fun

3 Tage Budapest

die **Ankunft**   arrival
das **Bad**   bath
ca. (= circa)   approximately
die **Dusche**   shower
die **Ecke**   corner
der **Einbettzuschlag**   additional charge for single room
die **Halbpension**   halfboard, i.e., including breakfast and one other meal
inbegriffen   included
die **Leistung**   service
lt. (= laut)   according to
die **Nächtigung**   overnight stay
der **Pauschalpreis**   all-inclusive price
die **Reiseleitung**   tour guide
die **Stadtrundfahrt**   city tour
der **Stornoschutz**   cancellation insurance
Verfügung: zur freien Verfügung   free time
das **WC**   toilet

Kapitel 6

Café an der Uni

die **Ananas**   pineapple
die **Beilage**   side dish
der **Champignon**   mushroom
Fanta   the name of a popular soft drink
Fass: vom Fass   on tap
das **Gebäck**   cake and pastries
gebrühter Tee   brewed tea
das **Gericht**   dish (food)
geöffnet   open
die **Johannisbeere**   currant
die **Kugel**   scoop of ice cream
der **Pilz**   mushroom
die **Preiselbeere**   cranberry
die **Remoulade**   tartar sauce
die **Sahne**   cream
die **Schlagsahne**   whipped cream
das **Schnitzel**   slice, cutlet
die **Schüssel**   bowl
das **Spiegelei**   fried egg
die **Speise**   dish (food)
der **Thunfisch**   tuna
der **Truthahn**   turkey
Wahl: nach Wahl   of your choice
Wiener Art   Viennese style
Bitte treffen Sie an unserer Schauvitrine Ihre Wahl, und bestellen Sie bei Ihrer Bedienung!   Please make your selection at the display case and order it from your server.
Alle Preise sind Inklusivpreise und enthalten Bedienungsgeld und Mehrwertsteuer.   All prices include service charge and value added tax.

Jule Neigel Band

das **Olympiastadion**   Olympic stadium

Oly Disco

der **Einlaß**   entry
der **Eintritt**   admittance
m (= Meter)   meter
das **Olympiazentrum**   the name of a subway station
der **Studentenausweis**   student I.D.
U3 (= U-Bahnlinie 3)   the subway line 3

Staatstheater am Gärtnerplatz

das **Dach**   roof
der **Fiedler**   fiddler
der **Vorverkauf**   advance ticket sale

Konen

die **Baumwolle**   cotton
bügelfrei   no-iron
ein- und zweireihig   single and double-breasted
frech   snazzy
das **Leinen**   linen
das **Markenfabrikat**   brand name
pflegeleicht   easy care
rein   pure
schmal   trim
Single   sleeveless shirt
das **Sonderangebot**   special
der **Streifen**   stripe
uni   plain (one color)
die **Viskose**   viscose
vorwiegend   predominantly
weit   roomy

Kapitel 8

*Stellenangebote **or** Stellenanzeigen*

ab sofort   beginning immediately
aufgeschlossen   outgoing
die **Ausbildung**   training
die **Aushilfe**   temporary job
die **Bewerbung**   application
Elektroinstallateur/in   electrician
f. = für
der **Festfahrer**   permanent employee (driver)
das **Fotofachlabor**   photo lab
Fotolaborant/in   photo lab technician
die **Gräfin**   countess
jhr. (= -jährig)   year-old
der **Kundenbereich**   customer service
der **Lebenslauf**   a short biography in narrative form
od. = oder
der **Raum**   area

der **Schichtdienst**   shift work
der **Schnellkurs**   crash course
selbständig   independent
Sprachkenntnisse   proficiency in a foreign language
das **Stellenangebot**   job offer
su. = suchen
tätig zu werden   to work
tüchtig   capable and hard-working
u. = und *or* **unter**
Wunsch: auf Wunsch   as you wish (your choice)
Zeugnisse   references
Zuschr. (= Zuschriften)   replies
Zwillingsmädchen   twin girls

Kapitel 9

Occasion unique à Yverdon

Occasion unique à Yverdon (*French*)   Unique
   opportunity in Yverdon
A luxury villa, early 19th century, including adjoining
   property of 16,317 square meters, as well as a farm
   requiring renovation. Unmatched view overlooking
   Neuchatel and lake, two minutes by car from center of
   city.
For more information, write: 22-120-5843, Est Vaudois.
   1820 Montreux.

Bootsgarage am Luganersee

der **Anteil**   share
der **Aufzug**   hoist
das **Außenbad**   outdoor pool
Cheminée (*French*)   fireplace
die **Einstellhalle**   parking garage
das **Hallenbad**   indoor pool
inkl. (= inklusive)   inclusive
der **Lift**   elevator
Luganersee   Lake Lugano
die **Pergola** (*Italian*)   arbor
die **Zahlung**   payment

Pian San Giacomo

For sale: Chalet, consisting of 1 apartment with large
   living room, fireplace, 3 bedrooms, bathroom, large
   terrace.
1 apartment with living room, bedroom, bathroom, wood
   storage, laundry room, electric heating.

Beautiful garden with granite table, parking space, serene
   and sunny, open view, completely furnished.
5 minutes from the S. Bernardino racetrack. 40 minute
   drive on the expressway N13 from Lugano or Locarno.
Price: 395,000 francs. Call during evening hours (091)
   54 20 21

Kapitel 11

Heiraten/Bekanntschaften

die **Bekanntschaft**   acquaintance
Bildzuschr. (= Bildzuschriften)   picture included with
   replies
ca. (= circa)   approximately
cm (= Zentimeter)   centimeter
die **Erscheinung**   appearance
freundl. = freundlich
gebildet   educated, cultured
gemeinsam   joint, together
großzügig   generous
Handeln   acting
das **Herz**   heart
das **Hirn**   brain; *here:* brains (*colloq.*), mind
Küchenhilfe   kitchen help
J. = Jahre
jugendl. (= jugendlich)   youthful
liebenswert   lovable, amiable
m. = mit
mögl. (= möglichst)   if at all possible
das **Niveau**   class
Nr. (= Nummer)   number
reiselustig   fond of travel
schlk. (= schlank)   slim, slender
schüchtern   shy
selbständig   independent
symp. (= sympathisch)   likeable
Tel.-Ang. (= Telefonangabe)   telephone
der **Tierliebhaber**   a person fond of animals
treu   loyal, faithful
u. = und *or* **unter**
unt. = unter
verbringen   to spend (time)
Verlieben: zum Verlieben   to fall in love with
verwitwet   widowed
Zuschr. (= Zuschriften)   replies

Pronunciation and Writing Guide

The best way to learn to pronounce German is to imitate speakers of German, as completely and accurately as you can. Some of the sounds of German are just like those of English and will cause you no trouble. Others may sound strange to you at first and be more difficult for you to pronounce. With practice, you will be able to master the unfamiliar sounds as well as the familiar ones.

Though imitation is the one indispensable way of learning to pronounce any language, there are two things that should help you in your practice. First, you should learn how to manipulate your vocal organs so as to produce distinctly different sounds. Second, you should learn to distinguish German sounds from the English sounds that you might be tempted to substitute for them.

As you learn to pronounce German, you will also start to read and write it. Here a word of caution is in order. The writing system of German (or any language) was designed for people who already know the language. No ordinary writing system was ever designed to meet the needs of people who are learning a language. Writing is a method of reminding us on paper of things that we already know how to say; it is not a set of directions telling us how a language should be pronounced.

This Pronunciation and Writing Guide will give you some help with the German sound system. Further practice with specific sounds will be given in the Lab Manual section of the *Arbeitsheft.*

Stress

Nearly all native German words are stressed on the "stem syllable," that is, the first syllable of the word, or the first syllable that follows an unstressed prefix.

Without prefix		*With unstressed prefix*	
den'ken	to think	**beden'ken**	to think over
kom'men	to come	**entkom'men**	to escape

In the end vocabulary of this book, words that are not stressed on the first syllable are marked. A stress mark follows the stressed syllable.

German Vowels

German has short vowels, long vowels, and diphthongs. The short vowels are clipped, and are never "drawled" as they often are in English. The long vowels are monophthongs ("steady-state" vowels) and not diphthongs (vowels that "glide" from one vowel sound toward another). The diphthongs are similar to English diphthongs except that they, like short vowels, are never drawled. Compare the English and German vowels in the words below.

English (with off-glide)	*German (without off-glide)*
bait	Beet
vein	wen
tone	Ton
boat	Boot

Spelling as a reminder of vowel length

By and large, the German spelling system clearly indicates the difference between long and short vowels. German uses the following types of signals:

1. A vowel is long if it is followed by an **h** (unpronounced): **ihn, stahlen, Wahn.**
2. A vowel is long if it is double: **Beet, Saat, Boot.**
3. A vowel is generally long if it is followed by one consonant: **den, kam, Ofen, Hut.**
4. A vowel is generally short if it is followed by two or more consonants: **denn, Sack, offen, Busch, dick.**

Pronunciation of vowels

Long and short a

Long [ā] = **aa, ah, a (Saat, Bahn, kam, Haken):** like English *a* in *spa,* but with wide-open mouth and no off-glide.
Short [a] = **a (satt, Bann, Kamm, Hacken):** between English *o* in *hot* and *u* in *hut.*

Long and short e

Long [ē] = **e, ee, eh, ä, äh (wen, Beet, fehlen, gähnt):** like *ay* in English *say,* but with exaggeratedly spread lips and no off-glide.
Short [e] = **e, ä (wenn, Bett, fällen, Gent):** Like *e* in English *bet,* but more clipped.

Unstressed [ə] *and* [ər]

Unstressed [ə] = **e (bitte, endet, gegessen):** like English *e* in *begin, pocket.*
Unstressed [ər] = **er (bitter, ändert, vergessen):** When the sequence [ər] stands at the end of a word, before a consonant, or in an unstressed prefix, it sounds much like the final -*a* in English *sofa;* the **-r** is not pronounced.

Long and short i

Long [ī] = **ih, ie (ihn, Miete, liest):** like *ee* in *see,* but with exaggeratedly spread lips and no off-glide.
Short [i] = **(in, Mitte, List):** like *i* in *mitt,* but more clipped.

Long and short o

Long [ō] = **oh, o, oo (Sohne, Ofen, Tone, Moos):** like English *o* in *so,* but with exaggeratedly rounded lips and no off-glide.
Short [o] = **o (Most, Tonne, offen, Sonne):** like English *o* often heard in the word *gonna.*

Long and short u

Long [ū] = **uh, u (Huhne, schuf, Buße, Mus):** like English *oo* in *too,* but with more lip rounding and no off-glide.
Short [u] = **u (Hunne, Schuft, Busse, muss):** like English *u* in *bush,* but more clipped.

Diphthongs

[ai] = **ei, ai, ay (nein, Kaiser, Meyer, Bayern):** like English *ai* in *aisle,* but clipped and not drawled.
[oi] = **eu, äu (neun, Häuser):** like English *oi* in *coin,* but clipped and not drawled.
[au] = **au (laut, Bauer):** like English *ou* in *house,* but clipped and not drawled.

Long and short ü

Long [ǖ] = **üh, ü (Bühne, kühl, lügen):** To pronounce long [ǖ], keep your tongue in the same position as for long [ī], but round your lips as for long [ū].

Short [ü] = **ü (Küste, müssen, Bünde):** To pronounce short [ü], keep your tongue in the same position as for short [i], but round your lips as for short [u].

Long and short **ö**

Long [ö] = **ö, öh (Höfe, Löhne, Flöhe):** To pronounce long [ö], keep your tongue in the same position as for long [ē], but round your lips as for long [ō].
Short [ö] = **ö (gönnt, Hölle, Knöpfe):** To pronounce short [ö], keep your tongue in the same position as for short [e], but round your lips as for short [o].

Consonants

Most of the German consonant sounds are similar to English consonant sounds. There are four major differences.

1. German has two consonant sounds without an English equivalent: [x] and [ç]. Both are spelled **ch.**
2. The German pronunciation of [l] and [r] differs from the English pronunciation.
3. German uses sounds familiar to English speakers in unfamiliar combinations, such as [ts] in an initial position: **zu.**
4. German uses unfamiliar spellings of familiar sounds.

The letters **b, d,** *and* **g**

The letters **b, d,** and **g** generally represent the same consonant sounds as in English. German **g** is usually pronounced like English *g* in *go*. When the letters **b, d,** and **g** occur at the end of a syllable, or before an **s** or **t,** they are pronounced like [p], [t], and [k] respectively.

b = [b] **(Diebe, gaben)**	b = [p] **Dieb, Diebs, gab, gabt**
d = [d] **(Lieder, laden)**	d = [t] **Lied, Lieds, lud, lädt**
g = [g] **(Tage, sagen)**	g = [k] **Tag, Tags, sag, sagt**

The letter **j**

The letter **j (ja, jung)** represents the sound *y* as in English *yes.*

The letter **l**

English [l] typically has a "hollow" sound to it. When an American pronounces [l], the tongue is usually "spoon-shaped": It is high at the front (with the tongue tip pressed against the gum ridge above the upper teeth), hollowed out in the middle, and high again at the back. German [l] **(viel, Bild, laut)** never has the "hollow" quality. It is pronounced with the tongue tip against the gum ridge, as in English, but with the tongue kept flat from front to back. Many Americans use this "flat" [l] in such words as *million, billion,* and *William.*

The letter **r**

German [r] can be pronounced in two different ways. Some German speakers use a "tongue-trilled [r]," in which the tip of the tongue vibrates against the gum ridge above the upper teeth—like the *rrr* that children often use in imitation of a telephone bell or police whistle. Most German speakers, however, use a "uvular [r]," in which the back of the tongue is raised toward the uvula, the little droplet of skin hanging down in the back of the mouth.

You will probably find it easiest to pronounce the uvular [r] if you make a gargling sound before the sound [a]: ra. Keep the tip of your tongue down and out of the way; the tip of the tongue plays no role in the pronunciation of the gargled German [r].

r = [r] + vowel **(Preis, Jahre, Rose):** When German [r] is followed by a vowel, it has the full "gargled" sound.

r = vocalized [r] **(Tier, Uhr, Tür):** When German [r] is followed by a vowel, it tends to become "vocalized," that is, pronounced like the vowel-like glide found in the final syllable of British English *hee-uh* (here), *thay-uh* (there).

The letters s, ss, ß

s = [s̱] **(sehen, lesen, Gänse):** Before a vowel, the letter **s** represents the sound [s̱], like English *z* in *zoo*.

s = [s] **(das, Hals, fast):** In most other positions, the letter **s** represents the sound [s], like English [s] in *so*.

[s] = **ss, ß (wissen, Flüsse, weiß, beißen, Füße):** The letters **ss** and **ß** (called **ess-tsett**) are both pronounced [s]. When they are written between vowels, the double letters **ss** signal the fact that the preceding vowel is short, and the single letter **ß** signals the fact that the preceding vowel is long (or a diphthong).

The letter v

v = [f] **(Vater, viel):** The letter **v** is generally pronounced like English [f] as in *father*.

v = [v] **(Vase, November):** In words of foreign origin, the letter **v** is pronounced [v].

The letter w

w = [v] **(Wein, Wagen, wann):** Many centuries ago, German **w** (as in **Wein**) represented the sound [w], like English *w* in *wine*. Over the centuries, German **w** gradually changed from [w] to [v], so that today the **w** of German **Wein** represents the sound [v], like the *v* of English *vine*. German no longer has the sound [w]. The letter **w** always represents the sound [v].

The letter z

z = final and initial [ts] **(Kranz, Salz, Zahn, zu):** The letter **z** is pronounced [ts], as in English *rats*. In English, the [ts] sound occurs only at the end of a syllable; in German, [ts] occurs at the beginning as well as at the end of a syllable.

The consonant clusters gn, kn, pf, qu

To pronounce the consonant clusters **gn, kn, pf, qu** correctly, you need to use familiar sounds in unfamiliar ways.

gn: pronunciation is [gn]   **pf:** pronunciation is [pf]
kn: pronunciation is [kn]   **qu:** pronunciation is [kv]

gn = [gn-] **(Gnade, Gnom)**
kn = [kn-] **(Knie, Knoten)**
pf = [pf-] **(Pfanne, Pflanze)**
qu = [kv-] **(quälen, Quarz, quitt)**

The combination ng

ng = [ŋ] **(Finger, Sänger, Ding):** The combination **ng** is pronounced [ŋ], as in English *singer*. It does not contain the sound [g] that is used in English *finger*.

The combinations sch, sp, and st

sch = [š] **(Schiff, waschen, Fisch)**
sp = [šp] **(Spaten, spinnen, Sport)**
st = [št] **(Stein, Start, stehlen)**

Many centuries ago, both German and English had the combinations **sp, st, sk,** pronounced [sp], [st], [sk]. Then two changes took place. First, in both languages, [sk] changed to [š], as in English *ship, fish,* and German **Schiff, Fisch.**

Second, in German only, word-initial [sp-] and [st-] changed to [šp-] and [št-]. The *sp* in English *spin* is pronounced [sp-], but in German **spinnen** it is pronounced [šp-]. The *st* in English *still* is pronounced [st-], but in German **still** it is pronounced [št-]. Today, German **sch** always represents [š] (like English *sh*, but with more rounded lips); **sp-** and **st-** at the beginning of German words or word stems represent [šp-] and [št-].

The letters ch

The letters **ch** are usually pronounced either [x] or [ç]. The [x] sound is made in the back of the mouth where [k] is produced.

If you have ever heard a Scotsman talk about "Lo*ch* Lomond," you have heard the sound [x]. The sound [x] is produced by forcing air through a narrow opening between the back of the tongue and the back of the roof of the mouth (the soft palate). Notice the difference between [k], where the breath stream is stopped in this position and [x], where the breath stream is forced through a narrow opening in this position.

To practice the [x] sound, keep the tongue below the lower front teeth and produce a gentle gargling sound, without moving the tongue or lips. Be careful not to substitute the [k] sound for the [x] sound.

ck, k = [k] (Sack, pauken, Pocken, buk)
ch = [x] (Sache, hauchen, pochen, Buch)

The [ç] sound is similar to that used by many Americans for the *h* in such words as *hue, huge, human.* It is produced by forcing air through a narrow opening between the front of the tongue and the front of the roof of the mouth (the hard palate). Notice the difference between [š], where the breath stream is forced through a wide opening in this position and the lips are rounded, and [ç], where the breath stream is forced through a narrow opening in this position and the lips are spread.

To practice the [ç] sound, round, your lips for [š], then use a slit-shaped opening and spread your lips. Be careful not to substitute the [š] sound for [ç].

sch = [š] (misch, fischt, Kirsche, Welsch, Menschen)
ch = [ç] (mich, ficht, Kirche, welch, München)

Note two additional points about the pronunciation of **ch:**

1. **ch = [x]** occurs only after the vowels **a, o, u, au.**
2. **ch = [ç]** occurs only after the other vowels and **n, l,** and **r.**

The combination chs

chs = [ks] (sechs, Fuchs, Weichsel)
chs = [xs] or [çs] (des Brauchs, du rauchst, des Teichs)

The fixed combination **chs** is pronounced [ks] in words such as **sechs, Fuchs,** and **Ochse.** Today, **chs** is pronounced [xs] or [çs] only when the **s** is an ending or part of an ending **(ich rauche, du rauchst; der Teich, des Teichs).**

The suffix -ig

-ig = [iç] (Pfennig, König, schuldig): In final position, the suffix **-ig** is pronounced [iç] as in German **ich.**
-ig = [ig] (Pfennige, Könige, schuldige): In all other positions, the **g** in **-ig** has the sound [g] as in English *go.*

The glottal stop

English uses the glottal stop as a device to avoid running together words and parts of words; it occurs only before vowels. Compare the pairs of words below. The glottal stop is indicated with an *.

an *ice man	a nice man
not *at *all	not a tall
an *ape	a nape

German also uses the glottal stop before vowels to avoid running together words and parts of words.

Wie *alt *ist *er?
be*antworten

The glottal stop is produced by closing the glottis (the space between the vocal cords), letting air pressure build up from below, and then suddenly opening the glottis, resulting in a slight explosion of air. Say the word *uh-uh,* and you will notice a glottal stop between the first and second *uh.*

The Writing System

German punctuation

Punctuation marks in German are generally used as in English. Note the following major differences.

1. In German, dependent clauses are set off by commas.
   German Der Mann, der hier wohnt, ist alt.
   English The man who lives here is old.

2. In German, independent clauses, with two exceptions, are set off by commas. Clauses joined by **und** (*and*) or **oder** (*or*) need not be set off by commas, unless the writer so chooses for the sake of clarity.
   German Robert singt und Karin tanzt. *or* Robert singt, und Karin tanzt.
   English Robert is singing and Karin is dancing.

3. In German, a comma is not used in front of **und** in a series as is often done in English.
   German Robert, Ilse und Karin singen.
   English Robert, Ilse, and Karin are singing.

4. In German, opening quotation marks are placed below the line.
   German Er fragte: „Wie heißt du?"
   English He asked, "What is your name?"
   Note that a colon is used in German before a direct quotation.

5. In German, commas stand outside of quotation marks.
   German „Meyer", antwortete sie.
   English "Meyer," she answered.

German capitalization

1. In German, all nouns are capitalized.
   German Wie alt ist der Mann?
   English How old is the man?

2. Adjectives are not capitalized, even if they denote nationality.
   German Ist das ein amerikanisches Auto?
   English Is that an American car?

3. The pronoun **ich** is not capitalized, unlike its English counterpart *I.*
   German Morgen spiele ich um zwei Uhr Tennis.
   English Tomorrow I am playing tennis at two o'clock.

Grammatical Tables

1. Personal pronouns

Nominative	ich	du	er	es	sie	wir	ihr	sie	Sie
Accusative	mich	dich	ihn	es	sie	uns	euch	sie	Sie
Dative	mir	dir	ihm	ihm	ihr	uns	euch	ihnen	Ihnen

2. Reflexive pronouns

	ich	du	er/es/sie	wir	ihr	sie	Sie
Accusative	mich	dich	sich	uns	euch	sich	sich
Dative	mir	dir	sich	uns	euch	sich	sich

3. Interrogative pronouns

Nominative	wer	was
Accusative	wen	was
Dative	wem	
Genitive	wessen	

4. Relative and demonstrative pronouns

	Masculine	Neuter	Feminine	Plural
Nominative	der	das	die	die
Accusative	den	das	die	die
Dative	dem	dem	der	denen
Genitive	dessen	dessen	deren	deren

5. Definite articles

	Masculine	Neuter	Feminine	Plural
Nominative	der	das	die	die
Accusative	den	das	die	die
Dative	dem	dem	der	den
Genitive	des	des	der	der

6. *Der*-words

	Masculine	Neuter	Feminine	Plural
Nominative	dieser	dieses	diese	diese
Accusative	diesen	dieses	diese	diese
Dative	diesem	diesem	dieser	diesen
Genitive	dieses	dieses	dieser	dieser

Common **der-**words are **dieser, jeder, mancher, solcher,** and **welcher.**

7. Indefinite articles and *ein*-words

	Masculine	Neuter	Feminine	Plural
Nominative	ein	ein	eine	keine
Accusative	einen	ein	eine	keine
Dative	einem	einem	einer	keinen
Genitive	eines	eines	einer	keiner

The **ein-**words include **kein** and the possessive adjectives: **mein, dein, sein, ihr, unser, euer, ihr,** and **Ihr.**

8. Plural of nouns

Type	Plural signal	Singular	Plural	Notes
1	∅ (no change)	das Zimmer	**die Zimmer**	Masculine and neuter nouns
	¨ (umlaut)	der Garten	**die Gärten**	ending in **el, -en, -er**
2	-e	der Tisch	**die Tische**	
	¨e	der Stuhl	**die Stühle**	
3	-er	das Bild	**die Bilder**	Stem vowel **e** or **i** cannot take umlaut
	¨er	das Buch	**die Bücher**	Stem vowel **a, o, u** takes umlaut
4	-en	die Uhr	**die Uhren**	
	-n	die Lampe	**die Lampen**	
	-nen	die Freundin	**die Freundinnen**	
5	-s	das Radio	**die Radios**	Mostly foreign words

9. Masculine *N*-nouns

	Singular	Plural
Nominative	der Herr	die Herren
Accusative	den Herrn	die Herren
Dative	dem Herrn	den Herren
Genitive	des Herrn	der Herren

Some other masculine **N-**nouns are **der Journalist, der Junge, der Komponist, der Kollege, der Mensch, der Nachbar, der Pilot, der Präsident, der Soldat, der Student, der Tourist.**

A few masculine **N-**nouns add **-ns** in the genitive; **der Name > des Namens.**

10. Preceded adjectives

	Singular Masculine	Neuter	Feminine	Plural
Nom.	der **alte** Tisch ein **alter** Tisch	das **alte** Buch ein **altes** Buch	die **alte** Uhr eine **alte** Uhr	die **alten** Bilder keine **alten** Bilder
Acc.	den **alten** Tisch einen **alten** Tisch	das **alte** Buch ein **altes** Buch	die **alte** Uhr eine **alte** Uhr	die **alten** Bilder keine **alten** Bilder
Dat.	dem **alten** Tisch einem **alten** Tisch	dem **alten** Buch einem **alten** Buch	der **alten** Uhr einer **alten** Uhr	den **alten** Bildern keinen **alten** Bildern
Gen.	des **alten** Tisches eines **alten** Tisches	des **alten** Buches eines **alten** Buches	der **alten** Uhr einer **alten** Uhr	der **alten** Bilder keiner **alten** Bilder

11. Unpreceded adjectives

	Masculine	Neuter	Feminine	Plural
Nominative	kalter Wein	kaltes Bier	kalte Milch	alte Leute
Accusative	kalten Wein	kaltes Bier	kalte Milch	alte Leute
Dative	kaltem Wein	kaltem Bier	kalter Milch	alten Leuten
Genitive	kalten Weines	kalten Bieres	kalter Milch	alter Leute

12. Nouns declined like adjectives

■ *Nouns preceded by definite articles or* **der**-*words*

	Masculine	Neuter	Feminine	Plural
Nominative	der Deutsche	das Gute	die Deutsche	die Deutschen
Accusative	den Deutschen	das Gute	die Deutsche	die Deutschen
Dative	dem Deutschen	dem Guten	der Deutschen	den Deutschen
Genitive	des Deutschen	des Guten	der Deutschen	der Deutschen

■ *Nouns preceded by indefinite article or* **ein**-*words*

	Masculine	Neuter	Feminine	Plural
Nominative	ein Deutscher	ein Gutes	eine Deutsche	keine Deutschen
Accusative	einen Deutschen	ein Gutes	eine Deutsche	keine Deutschen
Dative	einem Deutschen	einem Guten	einer Deutschen	keinen Deutschen
Genitive	eines Deutschen	—	einer Deutschen	keiner Deutschen

Other nouns declined like adjectives are **der/die Bekannte, Erwachsene, Fremde, Jugendliche, Verwandte.**

13. Irregular comparatives and superlatives

Base form	bald	gern	gut	hoch	nah	viel
Comparative	eher	lieber	besser	höher	näher	mehr
Superlative	ehest-	liebst-	best-	höchst-	nächst-	meist-

14. Adjectives and adverbs taking umlaut in the comparative and superlative

alt	jung	oft
arm	kalt	rot
blass (blasser *or* blässer)	krank	schwach
dumm	kurz	schwarz
gesund (gesünder *or* gesunder)	lang	stark
groß	nass (nässer *or* nasser)	warm

15. Prepositions

With accusative	With dative	With either accusative or dative	With genitive
bis	aus	an	(an)statt
durch	außer	auf	trotz
für	bei	hinter	während
gegen	mit	in	wegen
ohne	nach	neben	
um	seit	über	
	von	unter	
	zu	vor	
		zwischen	

16. Verbs and prepositions with special meanings

abhängen von
anfangen mit
anrufen bei
antworten auf (+ *acc.*)
arbeiten bei (*at a company*)
aufhören mit
beginnen mit
sich beschäftigen mit
danken für
denken an (+ *acc.*)
sich erinnern an (+ *acc.*)
erzählen von
fahren mit (*by a vehicle*)
fragen nach
sich freuen auf (+ *acc.*)
sich freuen über (+ *acc.*)
sich fürchten vor (+ *dat.*)
halten von
helfen bei

hoffen auf (+ *acc.*)
sich interessieren für
lächeln über (+ *acc.*)
lachen über (+ *acc.*)
reden über (+ *acc.*) *or* von
riechen nach
schreiben an (+ *acc.*)
schreiben über (+ *acc.*)
sprechen über (+ *acc.*), von, *or* mit
sterben an (+ *dat.*)
studieren an *or* auf (+ *dat.*)
suchen nach
sich vorbereiten auf (+ *acc.*)
warnen vor (+ *dat.*)
warten auf (+ *acc.*)
wissen über (+ *acc.*) *or* von
wohnen bei
zeigen auf (+ *acc.*)

17. Dative verbs

antworten
danken
fehlen
gefallen
gehören
glauben
helfen
Leid tun
passieren
schmecken
weh·tun

The verb **glauben** may take an impersonal accusative object: **ich glaube es.**

18. Present tense

	lernen[1]	arbeiten[2]	tanzen[3]	geben[4]	lesen[5]	fahren[6]	laufen[7]	auf·stehen[8]
ich	lerne	arbeite	tanze	gebe	lese	fahre	laufe	stehe ... auf
du	lernst	arbeitest	tanzt	gibst	liest	fährst	läufst	stehst ... auf
er/es/sie	lernt	arbeitet	tanzt	gibt	liest	fährt	läuft	steht ... auf
wir	lernen	arbeiten	tanzen	geben	lesen	fahren	laufen	stehen ... auf
ihr	lernt	arbeitet	tanzt	gebt	lest	fahrt	lauft	steht ... auf
sie	lernen	arbeiten	tanzen	geben	lesen	fahren	laufen	stehen ... auf
Sie	lernen	arbeiten	tanzen	geben	lesen	fahren	laufen	stehen ... auf
Imper. sg.	lern(e)	arbeite	tanz(e)	gib	lies	fahr(e)	lauf(e)	steh(e) ... auf

1. The endings are used for all verbs except the modals, **wissen, werden,** and **sein.**
2. A verb with a stem ending in **-d** or **-t** has an **e** before the **-st** and **-t** endings. A verb with a stem ending in **-m** or **-n** preceded by another consonant has an **e** before the **-st** and **-t** endings, e.g., **atmen > du atmest, er/es/sie atmet; regnen > es regnet.** Exception: If the stem of the verb ends in **-m** or **-n** preceded by **-l** or **-r,** the **-st** and **-t** do not expand, e.g., **lernen > du lernst, er/es/sie lernt.**
3. The **-st** ending of the **du**-form contracts to **-t** when the verb stem ends in a sibilant (**-s, -ss, -ß, -z,** or **-tz).** Thus the **du-** and **er/es/sie**-forms are identical.
4. Some strong verbs have a stem-vowel change **e > i** in the **du-** and **er/es/sie**-forms and the imperative singular.
5. Some strong verbs have a stem-vowel change **e > ie** in the **du-** and **er/es/sie**-forms and the imperative singular. The strong verbs **gehen** and **stehen** do not change their stem vowel.
6. Some strong verbs have a stem-vowel change **a > ä** in the **du-** and **er/es/sie**-forms.
7. Some strong verbs have a stem-vowel change **au > äu** in the **du-** and **er/es/sie**-forms.
8. In the present tense, separable prefixes are separated from the verbs and are in last position.

19. Simple past tense

	Weak verbs *lernen*[1]	*arbeiten*[2]	**Strong verbs** *geben*[3]
ich	lernte	arbeitete	gab
du	lerntest	arbeitetest	gabst
er/es/sie	lernte	arbeitete	gab
wir	lernten	arbeiteten	gaben
ihr	lerntet	arbeitetet	gabt
sie	lernten	arbeiteten	gaben
Sie	lernten	arbeiteten	gaben

1. Weak verbs have a past-tense marker **-te** + endings.
2. A weak verb with a stem ending in **-d** or **-t** has a past-tense marker **-ete** + endings. A weak verb with a stem ending in **-m** or **-n** preceded by another consonant has a past-stem marker **-ete** plus endings, e.g., **er/es/sie atmete; es regnete.** Exception: If the stem of the verb ends in **-m** or **-n** preceded by **-l** or **-r,** the **-te** past-tense marker does not expand, e.g., **lernte.**
3. Strong verbs have a stem-vowel change + endings.

20. Auxiliaries *haben, sein, werden*

ich	habe	bin	werde
du	hast	bist	wirst
er/es/sie	hat	ist	wird
wir	haben	sind	werden
ihr	habt	seid	werdet
sie	haben	sind	werden
Sie	haben	sind	werden

21. Modal auxiliaries: present, simple past, and past participle

	dürfen	**können**	**müssen**	**sollen**	**wollen**	**mögen**	**(möchte)**
ich	darf	kann	muss	soll	will	mag	(möchte)
du	darfst	kannst	musst	sollst	willst	magst	(möchtest)
er/es/sie	darf	kann	muss	soll	will	mag	(möchte)
wir	dürfen	können	müssen	sollen	wollen	mögen	(möchten)
ihr	dürft	könnt	müsst	sollt	wollt	mögt	(möchtet)
sie	dürfen	können	müssen	sollen	wollen	mögen	(möchten)
Sie	dürfen	können	müssen	sollen	wollen	mögen	(möchten)
Simple past	durfte	konnte	musste	sollte	wollte	mochte	
Past participle	gedurft	gekonnt	gemusst	gesollt	gewollt	gemocht	

22. Verb conjugations: strong verbs *sehen* and *gehen*

■ *Indicative*

	Present		Simple past	
ich	sehe	gehe	sah	ging
du	siehst	gehst	sahst	gingst
er/es/sie	sieht	geht	sah	ging
wir	sehen	gehen	sahen	gingen
ihr	seht	geht	saht	gingt
sie	sehen	gehen	sahen	gingen
Sie	sehen	gehen	sahen	gingen

	Present perfect				Past perfect			
ich	habe		bin		hatte		war	
du	hast		bist		hattest		warst	
er/es/sie	hat		ist		hatte		war	
wir	haben	gesehen	sind	gegangen	hatten	gesehen	waren	gegangen
ihr	habt		seid		hattet		wart	
sie	haben		sind		hatten		waren	
Sie	haben		sind		hatten		waren	

	Future			
ich	werde		werde	
du	wirst		wirst	
er/es/sie	wird		wird	
wir	werden	sehen	werden	gehen
ihr	werdet		werdet	
sie	werden		werden	
Sie	werden		werden	

■ *Imperative*

	Imperative	
Familiar singular	sieh	geh(e)
Familiar plural	seht	geht
Formal	sehen Sie	gehen Sie

■ *Subjunctive*

	Present-time subjunctive	
ich	sähe	ginge
du	sähest	gingest
er/es/sie	sähe	ginge
wir	sähen	gingen
ihr	sähet	ginget
sie	sähen	gingen
Sie	sähen	gingen

Past-time subjunctive					
ich	hätte			wäre	
du	hättest			wärest	
er/es/sie	hätte			wäre	
wir	hätten	gesehen		wären	gegangen
ihr	hättet			wäret	
sie	hätten			wären	
Sie	hätten			wären	

■ *Passive voice*

	Present passive		Past passive	
ich	werde		wurde	
du	wirst		wurdest	
er/es/sie	wird		wurde	
wir	werden	gesehen	wurden	gesehen
ihr	werdet		wurdet	
sie	werden		wurden	
Sie	werden		wurden	

23. Principal parts of strong and irregular weak verbs

The following list includes all the strong and irregular verbs from the **Vokabeln** lists. Compounds verbs like **herumliegen** and **hinausgehen** are not included, since the principal parts of compound verbs are identical to the basic forms: **liegen** and **gehen.** Separable-prefix verbs like **einladen** are included only when the basic verb **(laden)** is not listed elsewhere in the table. Basic English meanings are given for all verbs in this list. For additional meanings, consult the German-English vocabulary on pages R-37–R-57. The number indicates the chapter in which the verb was introduced.

Infinitive	Present-tense vowel change	Simple past	Past participle	Subjunctive	Meaning
anfangen	fängt an	fing an	angefangen	finge an	to begin 10
anrufen		rief an	angerufen	riefe an	to telephone 6
sich anziehen		zog an	angezogen	zöge an	to get dressed 9
sich ausziehen		zog aus	ausgezogen	zöge aus	to get undressed 9
beginnen		begann	begonnen	begönne or begänne	to begin 9
bleiben		blieb	ist geblieben	bliebe	to stay 2
bringen		brachte	gebracht	brächte	to bring 4
denken		dachte	gedacht	dächte	to think 2
einladen	lädt ein	lud ein	eingeladen	lüde ein	to invite; to treat 6
empfehlen	empfiehlt	empfahl	empfohlen	empföhle	to recommend 10
essen	isst	aß	gegessen	äße	to eat 3
fahren	fährt	fuhr	ist gefahren	führe	to drive, travel 5
fallen	fällt	fiel	ist gefallen	fiele	to fall 10
finden		fand	gefunden	fände	to find 2
fliegen		flog	ist geflogen	flöge	to fly 5
geben	gibt	gab	gegeben	gäbe	to give 3
gefallen	gefällt	gefiel	gefallen	gefiele	to please 5
gehen		ging	ist gegangen	ginge	to go 1
gewinnen		gewann	gewonnen	gewönne or gewänne	to win 5
haben	hat	hatte	gehabt	hätte	to have 2
halten	hält	hielt	gehalten	hielte	to hold; to stop 6
hängen		hing	gehangen	hinge	to be hanging 7
heißen		hieß	geheißen	hieße	to be called, named E
helfen	hilft	half	geholfen	hülfe or hälfe	to help 7
kennen		kannte	gekannt	kennte	to know 3
kommen		kam	ist gekommen	käme	to come 1
lassen	lässt	ließ	gelassen	ließe	to let, allow 12
laufen	läuft	lief	ist gelaufen	liefe	to run 5
leihen		lieh	geliehen	liehe	to lend 4
lesen	liest	las	gelesen	läse	to read 4
liegen		lag	gelegen	läge	to lie 2
nehmen	nimmt	nahm	genommen	nähme	to take 3
nennen		nannte	genannt	nennte	to name 8

Infinitive	Present-tense vowel change	Simple past	Past participle	Subjunctive	Meaning
riechen		roch	gerochen	röche	*to smell* 3
scheinen		schien	geschienen	schiene	*to shine; to seem* 2
schlafen	schläft	schlief	geschlafen	schliefe	*to sleep* 5
schließen		schloss	geschlossen	schlösse	*to close* 3
schreiben		schrieb	geschrieben	schriebe	*to write* E
schwimmen		schwamm	ist geschwommen	schwömme *or* schwämme	*to swim* 1
sehen	sieht	sah	gesehen	sähe	*to see* 4
sein	ist	war	ist gewesen	wäre	*to be* 1
sitzen		saß	gesessen	säße	*to sit* 5
sprechen	spricht	sprach	gesprochen	spräche	*to speak* 5
stehen		stand	gestanden	stände *or* stünde	*to stand* 7
sterben	stirbt	starb	ist gestorben	stürbe	*to die* 10
tragen	trägt	trug	getragen	trüge	*to wear; to carry* 6
treffen	trifft	traf	getroffen	träfe	*to meet; to hit* 5
treiben		trieb	getrieben	triebe	*to engage in* 1
trinken		trank	getrunken	tränke	*to drink* 3
tun		tat	getan	täte	*to do* 6
vergessen	vergisst	vergaß	vergessen	vergäße	*to forget* 5
verlieren		verlor	verloren	verlöre	*to lose* 11
waschen	wäscht	wusch	gewaschen	wüsche	*to wash* 7
werden	wird	wurde	ist geworden	würde	*to become* 4
wissen	weiß	wusste	gewusst	wüsste	*to know* 4
zwingen		zwang	gezwungen	zwänge	*to compel* 10

German-English Vocabulary

This vocabulary includes all the words used in **Deutsch heute** except numbers. The definitions given are generally limited to the context in which the words are used in this book. Chapter numbers are given for all words and expressions occurring in the chapter vocabularies and in the *Erweiterung des Wortschatzes* sections to indicate where a word or expression is first used. Recognition vocabulary does not have a chapter reference. The symbol ~ indicates repetition of the key word (minus the definite article, if any).

Nouns are listed with their plural forms: **der Abend, -e.** No plural entry is given if the plural is rarely used or nonexistent. If two entries follow a noun, the first one indicates the genitive and the second one indicates the plural: **der Herr, -n, -en.**

Strong and irregular weak verbs are listed with their principal parts. Vowel changes in the present tense are noted in parentheses, followed by simple-past and past-participle forms. All verbs take **haben** in the past participle unless indicated with **sein.** For example: **fahren (ä), fuhr, ist gefahren.** Separable-prefix verbs are indicated with a raised dot: **auf·stehen.**

Adjectives and adverbs that require an umlaut in the comparative and superlative forms are noted as follows: **warm (ä).** Stress marks are given for all words that are not accented on the first syllable. The stress mark follows the accented syllable: **Amerika'ner.** In some words, either of the two syllables may be stressed.

The following abbreviations are used:

abbr	abbreviation	*dat.*	dative	*p.p.*	past participle
acc.	accusative	*decl.*	declined	*part.*	participle
adj.	adjective	*f.*	feminine	*pl.*	plural
adv.	adverb	*fam.*	familiar	*sg.*	singular
colloq.	colloquial	*gen.*	genitive	*sub.*	subordinate
comp.	comparative	*m.*	masculine	*subj.*	subjunctive
conj.	conjunction	*n.*	neuter	*sup.*	superlative

A

ab (*prep. + dat.*) after, from a certain point on; away 9; **~heute** from today on 9; **~und zu** now and then

der Abend, -e evening 1; **gestern ~** last night 6; **Guten ~.** Good evening. 1; **heute ~** tonight, this evening 6; **zu ~ essen** to have (eat) dinner/supper 6

das Abendessen, - dinner, supper 3; **zum ~** for dinner 3; **Was gibt's zum ~?** What's for dinner? 3

das Abendkleid, -er evening dress

abends evenings, in the evening 3

aber (*conj.*) but 1

ab·fahren (fährt ab), fuhr ab, ist abgefahren to depart (by vehicle) 7

die Abfahrt, -en departure

ab·holen to pick up 5

das Abitur' diploma from college-track high school (**Gymnasium**) 4

der Absatz, ⸚e paragraph

der Abschnitt, -e passage; paragraph

absolut' absolutely, completely 10

ab·trocknen to dry dishes; to wipe dry 7

ab·waschen (wäscht ab), wusch ab, abgewaschen to do dishes

ach oh E

achten to pay attention

Achtung! (*exclamation*) Pay attention!; Look out!

die Adres'se, -n address E; **Wie ist deine/Ihre ~?** What is your address? E

das Aero'bic aerobics 1; **~ machen** to do aerobics 1

ähnlich similar 9

die Ahnung, -en hunch, idea 6; **Keine ~!** No idea! 6

akade'misch academic; **akademischer Beruf** profession requiring university education

die Aktivität', -en activity

alle all 4

allein' alone 5

allein'stehend single

allem: vor ~ above all 5

allerdings of course 8

alles everything 2; all 3; **Alles Gute.** Best wishes.

allgemein' general; **im Allgemeinen** in general

die Alliier'ten (*pl.*) Allies (WW II)

der Alltag everyday life

die Alpen (*pl.*) Alps 5

als (*after a comp.*)   than 2; as; (*sub. conj.*)   when 10

also   well E; therefore, so 2

alt (ä)   old E; **Wie ~ bist du/sind Sie?**   How old are you? E; **Ich bin [19] Jahre ~.**   I'm [19] years old. E

das **Alter**   age

am: **~ Freitag/Montag**   on Friday/Monday E

(das) **Ame′rika**   America 2

der **Amerika′ner, -**/die **Amerika′nerin, -nen**   American person 2

amerika′nisch   American (*adj.*) 4

an (+ *acc./dat.*)   at; to 4; on 7

andere   other 2

(sich) ändern   to change; to alter

anders   different(ly) 2

der **Anfang, ¨e**   beginning 9

an·fangen (fängt an), fing an, angefangen   to begin 10; **mit [der Arbeit] ~**   to begin [the work]

an·geben (gibt an), gab an, angegeben   to give; name, cite

angegeben   cued

der/die **Angestellte** (*noun decl. like adj.*)   salaried employee, white-collar worker 11

die **Anglis′tik**   English studies (language and literature) 4

die **Angst, ¨e**   fear 7; **~ haben (vor** + *dat.*)   to be afraid (of) 7

der **Anhang, ¨e**   appendix, reference section

an·kommen, kam an, ist angekommen (in + *dat.*)   to arrive (in) 7

die **Ankunft, ¨e**   arrival

an·rufen, rief an, angerufen   to phone 6; **bei [dir] ~**   to call [you] at home 6

an·schauen   to look at; to watch 7

(sich) (dat.) an·sehen (sieht an), sah an, angesehen   to look at; **Ich sehe es mir an.**   I'm having a look at it. 12

(an)statt′ (+ *gen.*)   instead of 8

die **Antwort, -en**   answer 6

antworten (+ *dat.*)   to answer (*as in* **Ich antworte der Frau.**   I answer the woman.) 11; **antworten auf** (+ *acc.*)   to answer (*as in* **Ich antworte auf**

die **Frage.**   I answer the question.) 11

die **Anzeige, -n**   announcement; ad 11

sich (*acc.*) **an·ziehen, zog an, angezogen**   to get dressed 9; **Ich ziehe mich an.**   I get dressed.; **sich** (*dat.*) **an·ziehen**   to put on 9; **Ich ziehe [mir die Schuhe] an.**   I put on [my shoes].

der **Anzug, ¨e**   man's suit 6

der **Apfel, ¨**   apple 3

der **Apfelsaft**   apple juice 3

die **Apothe′ke, -n**   pharmacy 3; **in die ~**   to the pharmacy 3

der **Apothe′ker, -**/die **Apothe′kerin, -nen**   pharmacist

der **Apparat′, -e**   apparatus, appliance 9

der **Appetit′**   appetite; **Guten ~!**   Enjoy your meal.

der **April′**   April 2

das **Äquivalent′, -e**   equivalent; **äquivalent** (*adj.*)   equivalent

die **Arbeit**   work; die **Arbeit, -en** (school or academic) paper; piece of work 4

arbeiten   to work; to study 1; **am Computer ~**   to work at the computer 6; **bei einer [Firma]~**   to work at a [company] 8; **mit dem Computer ~**   to do work on a computer 8; **mit Textverarbeitungsprogrammen** to do word processing 8

der **Arbeiter, -**/die **Arbeiterin, -nen** worker 12

der **Arbeitgeber, -**/die **Arbeit-geberin, -nen**   employer

der **Arbeitnehmer, -**/die **Arbeit-nehmerin, -nen**   employee, worker 12

die **Arbeitsgruppe, -n**   study group

arbeitslos   unemployed, out of work 11

der **Arbeitsplatz, ¨e**   job, position; workplace 8

die **Arbeitssuche**   job search

der **Architekt′, -en, -en**/die **Architek′tin, -nen**   architect 8

die **Architektur′**   architecture

argumentie′ren   to argue

arm (ä)   poor 9; **Du Armer.**   Poor fellow. 9

der **Arm, -e**   arm 9

die **Armbanduhr, -en**   wristwatch

die **Art, -en**   type, kind; manner; **auf diese ~ und Weise**   in this way

der **Arti′kel, -**   article 4

der **Arzt, ¨e**/die **Ärztin, -nen** (medical) doctor, physician 6

das **Aspirin′**   aspirin 3

der **Asylant′, -en, -en**/die **Asylan′tin, -nen**   refugee

der **Asyl′bewerber, -**/die **Asyl′bewerberin, -nen** applicant for asylum

das **Asyl′bewerberheim**   home for people seeking political refuge

das **Asyl′gesetz, -e**   law governing refugees

atmen   to breathe

auch   also 1

auf (+ *acc./dat.*)   on top of; to; on 7; **~ dem Weg**   on the way 3; **~ den Markt**   to the market 3; **~[Deutsch]**   in [German] 9; **~ Wiedersehen.**   Good-bye. 1

der **Aufenthalt, -e**   stay

die **Aufgabe, -n**   assignment; task, set of duties 8; die **Hausaufgabe, -n**   homework 8; **Hausaufgaben machen**   to do homework 10

auf·geben (gibt auf), gab auf, aufgegeben   to give up 8

auf·hören   to stop (an activity) 6

auf·listen   to list

auf·machen   to open 12

auf·nehmen (nimmt auf), nahm auf, aufgenommen   to accept

auf·passen   to watch out 8; **~ auf** (+ *acc.*)   to take care of 8

auf·räumen   to straighten up (a room) 7

auf·schreiben, schrieb auf, aufgeschrieben   to write down 10

auf·stehen, stand auf, ist aufgestanden   to get up; to stand up 6

auf·teilen (in + *acc.*)   to split up (into) 10

auf·wachen, ist aufgewacht   to wake up 9

auf·wachsen (wächst auf), wuchs auf, ist aufgewachsen   to grow up

das **Auge, -n**   eye 9

der **August′**   August 2

aus (+ *dat.*)   out of 5; to come/be from (be a native of) 2; **Ich komme ~ [Kanada].**   I come from [Canada]. 2

die **Ausbildung**   training, education

der **Ausdruck,** ⸚e   expression

auseinan'der   apart, away from each other

aus·gehen, ging aus, ist ausgegangen   to go out 6

ausgenommen   except for

ausgesprochen   really, very, exceptionally

das **Ausland** (*no pl.*)   foreign countries 7; **im ~**   abroad 7

der **Ausländer, -/**die **Ausländerin, -nen**   foreigner 4

die **Ausländerfeindlichkeit**   hostility toward foreigners

der **Ausländerhass**   xenophobia 12

ausländisch   foreign

aus·leihen, lieh aus, ausgeliehen   to rent (video); to check out (book) 4

aus·machen   to matter; **Es macht [mir] nichts aus.**   It doesn't matter to [me]. 11

die **Ausnahme, -n**   exception

aus·räumen   to empty the [dishwasher] 7

die **Aussage, -n**   comment

aus·sehen (sieht aus), sah aus, ausgesehen   to appear, look like, seem 6

der **Außenhandel**   foreign trade 11

außer (+ *dat.*)   besides; except for 15

außerdem   besides, in addition, as well 6

der **Aussiedler, -/**die **Aussiedlerin, -nen**   emigrant

aus·suchen   to select, choose

der **Austauschstudent, -en, -en/**die **Austauschstudentin, -nen**   exchange student 7

aus·wählen   to choose, select

aus·wandern, ist ausgewandert   to emigrate 9

der **Ausweis, -e**   identification card

sich (*acc.*) **aus·ziehen, zog aus, ausgezogen**   to get undressed; **Ich ziehe mich aus.**   I get undressed. 9; **sich** (*dat.*) **aus·ziehen**   to take off; **Ich ziehe [mir die Schuhe] aus.**   I take off [my shoes]. 9

der/die **Auszubildende** (*noun decl. like adj.*)   trainee, apprentice

das **Auto, -s**   automobile, car 5

die **Autobahn, -en**   freeway, expressway 7

der **Autor,** *pl.* **Auto'ren/**die **Auto'rin, -nen**   author

B

der **Bäcker, -/**die **Bäckerin, -nen**   baker 3; **beim ~**   at the baker's/bakery 3; **zum ~**   to the baker's/bakery 3

die **Bäckerei', -en**   bakery 3

das **Bad,** ⸚er   bath; bathroom 7

der **Badeanzug,** ⸚e   swimming suit 6

die **Badehose, -n**   swimming trunks 6

baden   to bathe 9; to swim

das **Badezimmer,-**   bathroom

das **BAföG** (= das **Bundesausbil-dungsförderungsgesetz**)   national law that mandates financial support for students

die **Bahn, -en**   train; railroad 5

der **Bahnhof,** ⸚e   train station 7

bald   soon 2; **Bis ~.**   See you later. E

die **Bana'ne, -n**   banana 3

die **Band, -s**   band (musical) 6

die **Bank,** ⸚e   bench

die **Bank, -en**   bank 8

die **Bar, -s**   bar, pub, nightclub 10

die **Barock'architektur**   baroque architecture

der **Basketball**   basketball 1

der **Bau**   construction

der **Bauch,** *pl.* **Bäuche**   abdomen; belly 9

bauen   to build 10

der **Bauer, -n, -n/**die **Bäuerin, -nen**   farmer

der **Baum,** ⸚e   tree

der **Baustein, -e**   building block

der **Beam'te** (*noun decl. like adj.*)/die **Beam'tin, -nen**   official, civil servant

beant'worten   to answer (a question, a letter) 5

bedeu'ten   to mean 11; **Was bedeutet das?**   What does that mean? 11

die **Bedeu'tung, -en**   significance; meaning

die **Bedie'nung**   service (in a restaurant)

beein'flussen   to influence 2

been'den   to finish, complete

begin'nen, begann, begonnen   to begin 9; **mit [der Arbeit] ~**   to begin [(the) work]

behaup'ten   to claim

der/die **Behin'derte** (*noun decl. like adj.*)   handicapped person

bei (+ *dat.*)   at 3; near, in the proximity of 5; while, during (*indicates a situation*); **~ der Uni**   near the university 5; **~ [dir]**   at [your] place/house/home 5; **~ [Ingrid]**   at [Ingrid's] 3; **beim Bäcker**   at the baker's/bakery 3; **beim Fernsehen**   while watching TV; **~ [mir] vorbei-kommen**   to stop by [my] place 5; **~ uns**   at our house; in our country

bei·behalten (behält bei), behielt bei), beibehalten   to retain

beide   both 7

das **Bein, -e**   leg 9

das **Beispiel, -e**   example 2; **zum Beispiel** (*abbrev.* z.B.)   for example 2

bekannt'   known, famous 5; **Das ist mir ~.**   I'm familiar with that.

der/die **Bekann'te** (*noun declined like adj.*)   acquaintance 9

bekom'men, bekam, bekommen   to receive 3; **Kinder ~**   to have children

bemer'ken   to notice; to remark

die **Bemer'kung, -en**   remark; observation

benut'zen   to use 7

beob'achten   to observe 7

bequem'   comfortable

bereit'   ready; prepared; willing 5

der **Berg, -e**   mountain 5; **in die Berge fahren**   to go to the mountains

der **Bericht', -e**   report

berich'ten   to report 10

der **Beruf', -e**   profession, occupation 8

beruf'lich   career related; professional

berufs'tätig   working 8

die **Berufs'wahl**   choice of profession

berühmt' famous 5

beschäf'tigen to occupy, keep busy 11; **sich beschäftigen (mit)** to be occupied (with) 11; **beschäftigt sein** to be busy 11

beschrei'ben, beschrieb, beschrieben to describe 6

beset'zen to occupy

der **Besit'zer, -/**die **Besit'zerin, -nen** owner

beson'der special; **(nichts) Besonderes** (nothing) special 1; **besonders** especially, particularly 3

besprech'en (i), besprach, besprochen to discuss

besser (*comp. of* **gut**) better 3

(die) **Besserung: Ich wünsche dir gute ~.** I wish you a speedy recovery./Get well soon.

best- (-er, -es, -e) best 8

beste'hen to exist; **~ aus** to consist of

bestel'len to order

bestimmt' certain(ly), for sure 2

der **Besuch', -e** visit 3; **~ haben** to have company 3; **zu ~** for a visit

besu'chen to visit 5; to attend (e.g., a seminar) 5

der **Besu'cher, -/**die **Besu'cherin, -nen** visitor

betref'fen (i), betraf, betroffen to deal with, concern

das **Bett, -en** bed E; **zu (ins) ~ gehen** to go to bed

die **Bettdecke, -n** blanket 7

die **Bevöl'kerung, -en** population

bevor' (*sub. conj.*) before 5

die **Bewe'gung, -en** movement; progress

die **Bewer'bung, -en** application

bezah'len to pay (for) 3; **das Essen ~** to pay for the meal 3

die **Bibliothek', -en** library 1; **in der ~** in/at the library 1

das **Bier, -e** beer 3

der **Biergarten, ⸚** beer garden 7

das **Bild, -er** picture; photograph E; image

bilden to form

die **Bildgeschichte, -n** picture story

die **Bildung** education; die **Bildungskosten** (*pl.*) education costs

billig cheap 3

bin am E

die **Biographie', -n** biography 4

die **Biologie'** biology 4

bis (+ *acc.*) until, til 1; **~ auf** (+ *acc.*) except for; **~ bald.** See you later. E **~ dann.** See you then. 1

bisschen: ein ~ a little 1

bitte (*after* **danke**) You're welcome. E; please E; **~?** May I help you? E; **~ schön.** You're welcome.; **~ sehr.** (*said when handing someone something*) Here you are.; **Wie ~?** (I beg your) pardon? E

bitten, bat, gebeten (**um** + *acc.*) to request, ask (for) something

blass pale 9

blau blue E

bleiben, blieb, ist geblieben to stay, to remain 2

der **Bleistift, -e** pencil E

der **Blick, -e** view

blond blond 9

bloß mere(ly) only

die **Blume, -n** flower 3

der **Blumenmarkt, ⸚e** flower market

die **Bluse, -n** blouse 6

der **Boden, ⸚** floor 7; ground

der **Bodensee** Lake Constance

borgen to borrow

böse (**auf** + *acc.*) angry (at) 7; bad, mean; **Sei [mir] nicht ~.** Don't be mad at [me]. 7

brauchbar usable; **Brauchbares** something usable

brauchen to need 3

braun brown E; **hell~** light brown 9

das **Brett, -er** board; shelf; das **schwarze ~** bulletin board

der **Brief, -e** letter 5

der **Brieffreund, -e/**die **Brief-freundin, -nen** pen pal 9

der **Briefträger, -/**die **Briefträgerin, -nen** letter carrier

die **Brille, -n** eyeglasses 6; **Tragen Sie eine ~?** Do you wear glasses? 6

bringen, brachte, gebracht to bring 4

buchstabie'ren to spell

das **Brot, -e** bread; sandwich 3

das **Brötchen,-** bread roll 3

die **Brücke, -n** bridge 10

der **Bruder, ⸚** brother 4

das **Buch, ⸚er** book E

das **Bücherregal, -e** bookcase E

die **Büchertasche, -n** book bag E

die **Buchhandlung, -en** bookstore 3

das **Bundesland, ⸚er** federal state

die **Bundesrepublik Deutschland (BRD)** Federal Republic of Germany (FRG) (*the official name of Germany*) 10

der **Bundesstaat, -en** federal state (in the U.S.A.)

der **Bundestag** lower house of the German parliament

der **Bürger, -/**die **Bürgerin, -nen** citizen

das **Büro', -s** office

der **Bus, -se** bus 5

die **Butter** butter 3

bzw. (= bezie'hungsweise) or; respectively

C

das **Café, -s** café 5

der **Campingplatz, ⸚e** camp site

der **CD-Spieler, -** (*also der* **CD-Player, -**) CD player E

das **Chaos** chaos

der **Chef, -s/**die **Chefin, -nen** boss 8

die **Chemie'** chemistry 4

(das) **China** China

circa (*abbr.* **ca.**) approximately

die **Cola, -s** cola drink 6

die **Comics** (*pl.*) comics 11

der **Compu'ter,-** computer E; **am ~ arbeiten** to work at the computer 6; **mit dem ~ arbeiten** to do work on the computer 8

das **Compu'terspiel, -e** computer game 1

der **Couchtisch, -e** coffee table 7

der **Cousin', -s** cousin (m.) (*pronounced* **kuzē'**)

D

da there E; (*sub. conj.*) since, because 9

dabei' and yet, with it; here (with me)

dage'gen against it; on the other hand

daher therefore, for that reason 4

das **da-Kompositum** da-compound

die **Dame, -n** lady 5

danach' after it; afterwards 10

der **Dank** thanks 5; **Vielen ~.** Many thanks. 5

danke Thanks E; **~ sehr.** Thank you very much.

danken (+ *dat.*) to thank 5

dann then E; **Bis ~.** See you then. 1

das the (*n.*); that E

dass (*sub. conj.*) that 5

das **Datum,** *pl.* **Daten** date

dauern to last; to require time 11

dazu' to it, to that; in addition

decken to cover 7; **den Tisch ~** to set the table 7

dein your (*fam. sg.*) E

die **Demonstration', -en** demonstration 10

demonstrie'ren to demonstrate 12

denen (*dat. pl. of demonstrative and relative pronoun*) them; which 12

denken, dachte, gedacht to think, believe 2; **~ an** (+ *acc.*) to think of/about 7

denn (*conj.*) because, for 3; (*flavoring particle adding emphasis to questions*) 3

deprimiert' depressed

der the (*m.*) E

deshalb therefore, for that reason 4

das **Dessert', -s** dessert

deswegen therefore, for this reason 9

deutsch German (*adj.*) 2

(das) **Deutsch** German class E; German (language) 1; **~ machen** to do German (homework) 1; **auf Deutsch** in German 9

der/die **Deutsche** (*noun declined like adj.*) German person 2

die **Deutsche Demokra'tische Republik' (DDR)** German Democratic Republic (GDR)

der **Deutschkurs, -e** German class or course

(das) **Deutschland** Germany 2

der **Dezem'ber** December 2

der **Dialekt', -e** dialect 9

der **Dialog', -e** dialogue

der **Dichter, -**/die **Dichterin, -nen** poet 9

dick fat 9; thick

die the (*f.*) E

der **Dieb, -e**/die **Diebin, -nen** thief

die **Diele, -n** entrance hall

der **Dienstag** Tuesday E

dies (-er, -es, -e) this, these 4

diesmal this time 11

das **Ding, -e** thing 9

dir (*dat.*) (to or for) you 5; **Und ~?** And you? (How about you?) (*as part of response to* **Wie geht's?**) 1

die **Disco, -s** dance club 6

die **Disket'te, -n** disk, diskette 4

die **Diskussion', -en** discussion; debate

diskutie'ren to discuss

doch (*flavoring particle*) really, after all, indeed 3; Yes, of course; on the contrary (*response to negative statement or question*) 3; but still, nevertheless, however, yet 5; **Geh ~ zum ...** Well then, go to . . . 3

der **Dom, -e** cathedral 7

die **Donau** Danube

der **Donnerstag** Thursday E

doppelt double, doubly

dort there 3

dorthin' (to) there

die **Dose, -n** can, tin; box

der **Dozent', -en, -en**/die **Dozen'tin, -nen** lecturer at a university

dran: ich bin ~ it's my turn 11

draußen outside 7

dritt- (-er, -es, -e) third 8

die **Drogerie', -n** drugstore 3

der **Drogerie'markt, ¨e** self-service drugstore

der **Drogist', -en, -en**/die **Drogis'tin, -nen** druggist

du you (*fam. sg.*) E; **~!** Hey! E; **~ meine Güte!** My heavens! 7

dumm (ü) dumb, stupid

dunkel dark 9

dünn thin 9

durch (+ *acc.*) through 3; divided by E; by (means of which)

durch·arbeiten to work through; to study 4

durch·sehen (sieht durch), sah durch, durchgesehen to look through; to glance over; to examine 11

dürfen (darf), durfte, gedurft to be permitted, be allowed to; may 4

der **Durst** thirst 6; **~ haben** to be thirsty 6

(sich) duschen to shower 9

duzen to address someone with the familiar **du**-form

E

eben just, simply 6; even, smooth; (*flavoring particle*) *used to support a previous statement, express agreement; made as a final statement it implies the speaker has no desire to discuss a point further*

ebenso likewise

echt genuine; **~?** (*slang*) Really?

die **Ecke, -n** corner 7

die **Ehefrau, -en** wife

ehemalig former

der **Ehemann, ¨er** husband

das **Ei, -er** egg 3; **Rühr~** scrambled egg; **Spiegel~** fried egg; **weich gekochtes ~** soft-boiled egg

die **Eidgenossenschaft, -en** confederation

eigen own 10

eigentlich actually 7

der **Eigentümer, -**/die **Eigentümerin, -nen** owner

die **Eigentumswohnung, -en** condominium

ein(e) a, an E

einan'der one another, each other 7; **mit~** with each other 7

eindeutig unambiguous

der **Eindruck, ¨e** impression

einfach simple; simply 6

das **Einfami'lienhaus, ¨er** single-family house

der **Einfluss,** *pl.* **Einflüsse** influence

die **Einführung, -en** introduction

die **Einheit** unity; **Der Tag der deutschen Einheit** The Day of German Unity (*celebrated on October 3*)

einige some, several; **einiges** something

ein·kaufen to shop 3; **~ gehen** to go shopping 3

die **Einkaufsstraße, -n** shopping street

die **Einkaufstasche, -n** shopping bag 3

das **Einkommen, -** income

ein·laden (lädt ein), lud ein, eingeladen to invite; to treat 6 die **Einladung, -en** invitation

einmal once, one time; **noch ~** again, once more 12

ein·räumen to place or put in; to load the dishwasher 7; **Geschirr in die Spülmachine ~** to put dishes into the [dishwasher]

ein·setzen to insert, fill in

der **Einwohner, -/**die **Einwohnerin, -nen** inhabitant 2

einzeln single, singly, individual(ly)

einzig- (-er, -es, -e) only, sole 12

das **Eis** ice; ice cream

die **Eisenbahn, -en** railroad

eisern iron; **der Eiserne Vorhang** Iron Curtain

der **Elch, -e** moose

elegant' elegant

die **Eltern** (*pl.*) parents 4

die **E-Mail, -s** e-mail

der **Empfangs'chef, -s/**die **Empfangs'chefin, -nen** hotel receptionist

empfeh'len (ie), empfahl, empfohlen to recommend 10

das **Ende, -n** end, conclusion 4; **am ~** (in) the end 4; **zu ~** over, finished 10

endgültig final; definite

endlich finally 7

die **Endung, -en** ending

die **Energie'** energy

(das) **Englisch** English (language); (academic subject) 1; **auf Englisch** in English

der **Enkel, -/**die **Enkelin, -nen** grandson/granddaughter

das **Enkelkind, -er** grandchild

entde'cken to discover

(sich) entschei'den, entschied, entschieden to decide

(sich) entschul'digen to excuse (oneself); **Entschuldigen Sie!** Excuse me!

die **Entschul'digung, -en** apology

die **Entspan'nung, -en** relaxation; **zur ~** for relaxation

entste'hen, entstand, ist entstanden to come about

entweder ... oder (*conj.*) either . . . or

die **Entwick'lung, -en** development

er he, it E

das **Erd'geschoss** the ground floor of a building

das **Ereig'nis, -se** occasion, event

die **Erfah'rung, -en** experience 8

erfin'den, erfand, erfunden to invent

der **Erfolg', -e** success 8

erfolg'reich successful

ergän'zen to complete

das **Ergeb'nis, -se** result

sich erin'nern (an + *acc.***)** to remember

sich erkäl'ten to catch a cold 9; **erkältet: ich bin ~** I have a cold 9

die **Erkäl'tung, -en** cold (illness) 9; **Was macht deine ~?** How's your cold? 9

erklä'ren to explain 3

erlau'ben (+ *dat. with persons***)** to permit, allow

ernst serious 1

errei'chen to reach, achieve

erschei'nen, erschien, ist erschienen to appear, seem

erst (*adv.*) not until, only, just 9; (*adj.*) first 9; **~ einmal** first of all

erstaunt' to be astonished, astounded

erstens first of all

der/die **Erwach'sene** (*noun decl. like adj.*) adult 12

erwar'ten to expect 8

die **Erwei'terung, -en** expansion, extension

erzäh'len (über + *acc.***/von)** to tell (about) 1

der **Erzie'hungsurlaub** leave of absence for child rearing

es it E; **~ gibt (+** *acc.***)** there is, there are 3

die **Essecke, -n** dining area

das **Essen, -** meal; prepared food 3

essen (isst), aß, gegessen to eat 3; **zu Abend ~** to have (eat) dinner 6

das **Esszimmer, -** dinning room 7

das **Etikett', -e** label

etwa approximately, about 2

etwas something 3; some, somewhat 3; **noch ~** something else (in addition) 3

euch: bei~ in your country

euer your (*pl. fam.*) 2

(das) **Euro'pa** Europe 2

die **Europä'ische Union'** European Union

ewig forever, eternally 6

das **Exa'men, -** comprehensive exam, finals 4; **~ machen** to graduate from the university 4

F

die **Fabrik', -en** factory

das **Fach, ¨er** (academic) subject; field 4

das **Fachgeschäft, -e** specialty shop

das **Fachwerkhaus, -häuser** half-timbered house

fahren (ä), fuhr, ist gefahren to drive; to travel 5; **mit [dem Auto] ~** to go by [car] 5

der **Fahrplan, ¨e** train schedule

das **Fahrrad, ¨er** bicycle 5

der **Fahrradweg, -e** bicycle path

die **Fahrschule, -n** driving school

der **Fall, ¨e** case, situation; fall, demise

fallen (ä), fiel, ist gefallen to fall 10

falsch wrong, false 9

die **Fami'lie, -n** family 4

der **Fan, -s** fan; supporter (sports) 12

fände (*subj. of finden*) would find 11

die **Farbe, -n** color E; **Welche ~ hat ... ?** What color is . . . ? E

fast almost 7

faul lazy 1

faulenzen to lounge around, be idle 6

der **Februar** February 2

fehlen (+ *dat.***)** to be lacking, missing

fehlend missing

feiern to celebrate 6

der **Feiertag, -e** holiday

das **Fenster, -** window E

die **Ferien** (*pl.*) vacation 4; **in den ~** on/during vacation 5; **in die ~ gehen/fahren** to go on vacation; **Semes'terferien** semester break 4

die **Ferienreise, -n** vacation trip 7

der **Fernsehbericht, -e** TV report

das **Fernsehen** television (the industry) 4

fern·sehen (sieht fern), sah fern, ferngesehen to watch TV 4

der **Fernseher, -** television set E

die **Fernsehsendung, -en** television program 10

fertig finished; ready 4

fest firm(ly)

das **Fest, -e** party; celebration; feast 5; **auf dem ~** at the party; **ein ~ geben** to give a party 5

die **Feststimmung** festive atmosphere

fett gedruckt in boldface

das **Fieber** fever 9

der **Film, -e** film 4

der **Filmregisseur, -e**/die **Filmregisseurin, -nen** movie director

finden, fand, gefunden to find; to think, 2; **Sie finden die Brötchen gut.** They like the rolls. 3; **Wie findest du das?** What do you think of that?

der **Finger, -** finger 9

die **Firma,** *pl.* **Firmen** company 5; **bei einer ~ arbeiten** to work for a company 8

der **Fisch, -e** fish 3

der **Fischmann, ̈er**/die **Fischfrau, -en** fishmonger

fit fit

das **Fitnesstraining** fitness training 1; **~ machen** to work out

die **Flasche, -n** bottle; **eine ~ Mineral'wasser** a bottle of mineral water 5

das **Fleisch** meat 3

fleißig industrious, hard-working 1

fliegen, flog, ist geflogen to fly 5

der **Flug, ̈e** flight

der **Flugbegleiter, -**/die **Flugbegleiterin, -nen** flight attendant

der **Flughafen, ̈** airport 10

das **Flugzeug, -e** airplane 5

der **Flur, -e** entrance hall, hallway

der **Fluss, ̈e** river

föhnen to blow-dry; **ich föhne mir die Haare** I blow-dry my hair

folgen, ist gefolgt (+ *dat.*) to follow

folgend following

die **Forschung** research

der **Fotograf', -en, -en**/die **Fotogra'fin, -nen** photographer

die **Fotografie', -n** photograph; photography

fotografie'ren to photograph 6

die **Frage, -n** question 1; **eine ~**

stellen to ask a question; **eine ~ an** (+ *acc.*) **stellen** to ask someone a question 9; **Sie stellt eine Frage an ihn.** She asks him a question; *also* (+ *dat.*) **eine ~ stellen** to ask someone a question; **Sie stellt ihm eine Frage.** She asks him a question. 9

fragen to ask, to question 3; **~ nach** to inquire about

fraglich questionable

der **Franken** frank; **Schweizer Franken (sFr.)** Swiss unit of currency

(das) **Frankreich** France

der **Franzo'se, -n, -n**/die **Französin, -nen** French person

franzö'sisch French (*adj.*)

(das) **Franzö'sisch** French (language)

die **Frau, -en** woman; wife E; **Frau ...** Mrs. . . . ; Ms. . . . (*term of address for all adult women*) E

die **Frauenpolitik** federal policy concerning women

frei free 4; **~ haben** to be off work 6; **~ sein** to be unoccupied 6

die **Freiheit, -en** freedom 8

der **Freitag** Friday E

die **Freizeit** free time 6

die **Freizeitbeschäftigung, -en** leisure activity

fremd foreign; strange 12; **das ist mir ~** (*dat.*) that is strange to me 12

der **Fremdarbeiter, -**/die **Fremdarbeiterin, -nen** foreign worker

das **Fremdenverkehrsbüro, -s** tourist office

die **Freude, -n** pleasure; **~ machen** to give pleasure 8

sich freuen (**auf** + *acc.*) to look forward (to); **~** (**über** + *acc.*) to be pleased (about/with) 9

der **Freund, -e**/die **Freundin, -nen** friend 1; boyfriend/girlfriend

freundlich friendly 1

die **Freundlichkeit** friendliness

der **Frieden** peace 10

friedlich peaceful

frisch fresh 3

froh happy 1

früh early 5

der **Frühling** spring 2

das **Frühstück, -e** breakfast 3; **zum ~** for breakfast 3

sich fühlen to feel (ill, well, etc.) 9

führen to lead, carry in stock, have for sale; **ein Gespräch ~** to conduct a conversation

der **Führerschein, -e** driver's license 6

funktionie'ren to function, work

für (+ *acc.*) for 2

furchtbar terrible, horrible; very 1

fürchten to fear 9; **sich fürchten** (**vor** + *dat.*) to fear, be afraid (of) 9

fürchterlich horrible, horribly 9

der **Fuß, ̈e** foot 5; **zu ~** on foot 5

der **Fußball** soccer 1

der **Fußballverein, -e** soccer club

die **Fußgängerzone, -n** pedestrian zone 7

G

die **Gabel, -n** fork 7

ganz complete(ly), whole; very 1; **~ gut** not bad, OK 1; **~ schön** really quite 9; **~ schön [blass]** pretty [pale] 9; **im Ganzen** altogether

gar: ~ nicht not at all 7

die **Gardi'nen** (*pl.*) curtains

der **Garten, ̈** garden E

der **Gast, ̈e** guest 5

der **Gastgeber, -**/die **Gastgeberin, -nen** host, hostess

das **Gebäck'** pastries

das **Gebäu'de, -** building

geben (gibt), gab, gegeben to give 3; **es gibt** (+ *acc.*) there is, there are 3; **Was gibt's zum [Abendessen]?** What's for [dinner]? 3; **Was gibt's/gab es?** What is/was playing? 10; **Was gibt's Neues?** What's new? 11

gebo'ren, ist geboren born 12

gebrau'chen to use 6

der **Geburts'tag, -e** birthday 2; **Ich habe im [Mai] ~.** My birthday is in May. 2; **Wann hast du ~?** When is your birthday? 2; **zum ~** for one's birthday; **Alles Gute zum ~.** Happy birthday.

die **Gefahr', -en** danger 10

gefähr'lich dangerous

gefal′len (gefällt), gefiel, gefallen (+ *dat.*) to please, be pleasing (to) 5; **Es gefällt [mir].** [I] like it. 5

das Gefühl′, -e feeling

gegen (+ *acc.*) against 3; **~ [sechs] Uhr** around/about [six] o'clock 5

gegenseitig in turn; one another

gegenü′ber (+ *dat.*) opposite; across from there; in opposition to

das Gehalt′, ¨er salary 11

gehen, ging, ist gegangen to go 1; **Es geht (nicht).** It will (won't) do./It's (not) OK/It's (not) possible. 1; **Es geht nicht nur um [die Musik].** It's not just about [the music]. 12; **Geht das?** Is that OK? 5; **Mir geht es gut.** I'm fine 9; **Wie geht es Ihnen?** How are you? (*formal*) 1; **Wie geht's?** How are you? (*informal*) 1; **zu Fuß ~** to walk 5

gehö′ren (+ *dat.*) to belong to 5

gelb yellow 3

das Geld money 3; **es geht um ~** it revolves around money 12

gelernt′ trained

das Gemü′se, - vegetable 3

gemüt′lich comfortable, informal 5

genau′ exact(ly) 6; **Genau!** That's right! 6

genau′so exactly the same 7

die Generation′, -en generation

genug′ enough 3

geöf′fnet open 13

gera′de just; straight 12

das Gerät′, -e apparatus; tool; instrument

gera′ten, geriet, ist geraten get into a state; **in eine [Panik]~** to get in a [panic]

die Germanis′tik German studies (language and literature) 4

gern gladly, willingly; used with verbs to indicate liking, as in **Ich spiele gern Tennis.** I like to play tennis. 1; **~ haben** to like, as in **Ich habe sie ~.** I like her.

das Geschäft′, -e store; business 8

die Geschäfts′frau, -en businesswoman 8

der Geschäfts′mann, -leute businessman 8

die Geschäfts′zeit, -en business hours

das Geschenk′, -e present, gift

die Geschich′te, -n story; history 4

das Geschirr′ dishes 7; **~ spülen** to wash dishes 7

der Geschirr′spüler dishwasher

die Geschwin′digkeitsbegrenzung speed limit

die Geschwis′ter (*pl.*) siblings 4

die Gesell′schaft, -en society; company 12

das Gesetz′, -e law

das Gesicht′, -er face 9

gespannt′ curious; eager

das Gespräch′, -e conversation; **ein ~ führen** to conduct a conversation

der Gesprächs′partner,-/die Gesprächs′partnerin, -nen conversation partner

gestern yesterday 2; **~ Abend** last night 6

gesund′ (ü) healthy 6

die Gesund′heit health

geteilt′ durch divided by (in division) E

das Getränk′, -e beverage 3

die Gewalt′tätigkeit, -en act of violence; violence

die Gewerk′schaft, -en labor union 12

die Gewich′te (*pl.*) weights; **~ heben** to lift weights 1

das Gewicht′heben weightlifting 1

gewin′nen, gewann, gewonnen to win 5

die Gitar′re, -n guitar E

das Glas, ¨er glass 3

glauben (+ *dat. when used with a person*) to believe 1; **Ich glaube ja.** I think so. 1; **Ich glaube nicht.** I don't think so. 1

gleich immediately; in a minute; same; similar 6

gleichberechtigt entitled to equal rights 8

die Gleichberechtigung, -en equal rights 8

gleichzeitig at the same time

das Glück luck 8; happiness; **Viel ~!** Good luck! 11; **zum ~** fortunately 8

glücklich happy; lucky 1

Glückwunsch: Herzlichen ~ (zum Geburtstag)! Happy birthday!

gnädig gracious; **gnädige Frau** Madam

das Golf golf 1

der Grad degree 2; **Es ist minus [10] ~.** It's minus [10] degrees. 2; **Wie viel ~ ist es?** What's the temperature? 2

das Gramm (*abbr.* **g**) gram (1 ounce = 28.35g) 3

grau gray E

die Grenze, -n border, boundary; limit 10

(das) Griechenland Greece

das Grillfest, -e barbecue party

der Groschen, - 1/100 of the Austrian **Schilling**

groß (ö) large, big; tall (people) E

(das) Großbritan′nien Great Britain

die Größe, -n size

die Großeltern (*pl.*) grandparents 4

die Großmutter, ¨ grandmother 4

die Großstadt, ¨e city

der Großvater, ¨ grandfather 4

grün green E

der Grund, ¨e reason 11

das Grundgesetz constitution of Germany

die Grundschule, -n primary school (grades 1–4)

die Grünen (*pl.*) environmentalist political party

die Gruppe, -n group

gruppie′ren to group, organize

der Gruß, ¨e greeting; (*closing of a letter*) **viele Grüße** best regards 1; (*closing of a letter*) **liebe/herzliche Grüße** best regards 9

Grüß dich! (*fam.*) Hi! E

gültig valid

günstig favorable; reasonable (price)

die Gurke, -n cucumber 3

gut good, well; fine 1; **Mir geht es ~.** I'm fine. 9; **Na ~!** All right. 1

Güte: Du meine ~! Good heavens! 7

der Gymnasiast′, -en, -en/die Gymnasias′tin, -nen student in a **Gymnasium**

das Gymna′sium, *pl.* **Gymnasien** college-track secondary school 4

die Gymnas′tik calisthenics

H

das **Haar, -e** hair 9

haben (hat), hatte, gehabt to have 2; **Angst ~ vor** (+ *dat.*) to be afraid of 7; **Besuch ~** to have company 3; **Was hast du?** What is wrong with you?, What's the matter? 9

das **Hähnchen, -** chicken 3

halb half 1; **~ [zwei]** half past [one] 1; **~ so groß** half as large 2

der **Halbbruder, ¨** half brother

die **Halbschwester, -n** half sister

Hallo! Hello., Hi E

der **Hals, ¨e** throat, neck 9

halten (hält), hielt, gehalten to hold 6; **~ von** to think of, have an opinion about 6; **eine Vorlesung ~** to give a lecture 4

die **Haltestelle, -n** stop (for bus, streetcar, subway)

die **Hand, ¨e** hand 9

der **Handel** trade 11

der **Handschuh, -e** glove 6

die **Handtasche, -n** handbag, purse 6

das **Handy, -s** cellular phone 5

hängen, hängte, gehängt to hang something, put 7

hängen, hing, gehangen to be hanging, be suspended 7

hart hard; difficult 8

der **Hass** hatred 12

hässlich ugly; hideous

hast has E

hat has E

hätte (*subj. of* **haben**) would have 11

der **Hauptbahnhof** main train station

das **Hauptfach, ¨er** major (subject) 4

das **Hauptgericht, -e** main course, entrée

die **Hauptschule, -n** classes 1–9, meant for students intending to learn a trade

die **Hauptspeise, -n** main course, entrée

die **Hauptstadt, ¨e** capital 2

das **Hauptverb, -en** main verb

das **Haus,** *pl.* **Häuser** house 3; **nach Hause** (to go) home 3; **zu**

Hause (to be) at home 3

die **Hausarbeit** housework; chore 7

die **Hausaufgabe, -n** homework 10; **Hausaufgaben machen** to do homework

die **Hausfrau, -en** housewife 8

der **Haushalt** household; **den ~ machen** to take care of the house; to do the chores 8

der **Hausmeister, -/die Hausmeisterin, -nen** building superintendent

He! Hey!

heben: Gewichte ~ to lift weights 1

das **Heft, -e** notebook E

die **Heimat** native country 12

die **Heimatadresse, -n** home address E

die **Heirat** marriage 11

heiraten to marry, to get married 11

die **Heiratsanzeige, -n** ad for marriage partner

heiß hot 2

heißen, hieß, geheißen to be named, be called E; **Wie heißt du?** What is your name? (*informal*); **Wie heißen Sie?** What is your name? (*formal*) E; **Du heißt [Mark], nicht?** Your name is [Mark], isn't it? E; **das heißt (d.h.)** that means, that is (i.e.) 8; **es heißt** it says 8

die **Heizung** heating

helfen (i), half, geholfen to help 7; **~ bei** to help with 7; **Hilfe!** Help!

hell light; bright 9; **~braun** light brown 9

das **Hemd, -en** shirt 6

her (*prefix*) (*indicates motion toward speaker*) 7

herauf' up here

heraus'·finden, fand heraus, herausgefunden to find out

heraus'·suchen to pick out

der **Herbst** autumn, fall 2; **im ~** in the fall 2

der **Herd, -e** cooking range 7

der **Herr, -n, -en** gentleman E; **Herr ...** Mr. . . . (*term of address*) E; **~ Ober** (*term of address for a waiter*)

her·stellen to produce; to manufacture 11

herum' around 7

herum'·liegen, lag herum, herumgelegen to lie around 7

das **Herz, -ens, -en** heart

heute today E; **~ Abend** this evening 1; **~ Morgen** this morning 1; **~ Nachmittag** this afternoon 1

heutzutage nowadays

hier here 2

die **Hilfe** help

hin (*prefix*) (*indicates motion away from speaker*) 7

hinein' into, in 11

hinein'·gehen, ging hinein, hineingegangen to go in 11

hinter (+ *acc./dat.*) behind, in back of 7

hinterher' afterwards

der **Hinweis, -e** tip, hint

hmm hmm 2

das **Hobby, -s** hobby 6

hoch (höher, höchst-) high 4; **hoh-** *before nouns, as in* **ein hoher Lebensstandard** a high standard of living

das **Hochdeutsch** High German, standard German

das **Hochhaus, -häuser** high-rise

die **Hochschule, -n** institution of higher education (e.g., university)

der **Hochschullehrer, -/die Hochschullehrerin, -nen** teacher at a university or college

hoffen to hope 5

hoffentlich (*colloq.*) hopefully; I hope so. 2

höflich polite

hoh- (-er, -es, -e) high (*the form of* **hoch** *used before nouns, as in* **hohe Berge** high mountains) 5

der/die **Homosexuel'le** (*noun decl. like adj.*) homosexual (person)

hören to hear; to listen to 1; **Musik ~** listening to music 1

der **Hörsaal, -säle** lecture hall 1

die **Hose, -n** pants, trousers 6; **ein Paar Hosen** a pair of pants; **die kurzen Hosen** shorts 6

der **Hund, -e** dog 7

der **Hunger** hunger 6; **~ haben** to be hungry 6

husten to cough 9

der **Hut, ¨e** hat 6

I

ich I E; **~ auch** me, too
die **Idee', -n** idea 6
identifizie'ren to identify
Ihnen (*dat. of* **Sie**) (to) you; **Und Ihnen?** And you? (*as part of response to* **Wie geht es Ihnen?**) 1
ihr (*pron.*) you (*familiar pl.*) 1; (*poss. adj.*) her, their 2
Ihr (*poss. adj.*) your (*formal*) E
illuso'risch illusory
illustrie'ren to illustrate
die **Immatrikulation'** matriculation
immer always 3; **~ mehr** more and more 8; **noch ~** still 10; **wie ~** as always 11; **~ wieder** again and again 5
die **Immunologie'** immunology
in (+ *acc./dat.*) in 2; into; to 3
die **Industrie', -n** industry 8
die **Informa'tik** computer science 4
der **Informa'tiker, -/**die **Informa'tikerin, -nen** computer scientist 8
die **Information', -en** information 4
der **Ingenieur', -e/**die **Ingenieu'rin, -nen** engineer 4
der **Inline-Skater, -/**die **Inline -Skaterin, -nen** inline skater
das **Institut', -e** institute
das **Instrument', -e** instrument 9
intelligent' intelligent, smart 1
interessant' interesting 1
das **Interes'se, -n** interest
interessie'ren to interest 6; **sich interessieren (für)** to be interested (in) 9
interessiert' sein (an + *dat.*) to be interested (in)
international' international
das **Internet** Internet; **im Internet surfen** to surf the Internet
das **Interview, -s** interview 6
interviewen to interview
der **Interviewer, -/**die **Interviewerin, -nen** interviewer 12
die **Intoleranz'** intolerance 12
die **Investition', -en** investment
inzwi'schen in the meantime 12
irgendwann sometime, at some point
isolie'ren insulate
ist is E
(das) **Ita'lien** Italy
italie'nisch Italian (*adj.*)

J

ja yes E; (*flavoring particle*) indeed, of course; **na ~** well now
die **Jacke, -n** jacket 6
das **Jackett', -s** (pronounced /zhakĕt'/) a man's suit jacket; sport coat 6
das **Jahr, -e** year E; **Ich bin [19] Jahre alt** I'm [19] years old. F; **die [sechziger/achtziger] Jahre** the [1960s/1980s] 12; **vor [10] Jahren** [10] years ago
die **Jahreszeit, -en** season 2
das **Jahrhun'dert, -e** century 9
jährlich yearly, annually
das **Jahrzehnt', -e** decade
der **Januar** January 2
je ... desto ... the ... the ... (*with comp.*); **je größer desto besser** the bigger the better
die **Jeans** (*pl.*) jeans 6
jed- (-er, -es, -e) each, every 4; **jeder** everyone 4
jedenfalls at any rate
jedoch' (*conj. or adv.*) however, nonetheless 8
jemand (-en, -em) someone
jetzt now 2
der **Job, -s** job 4
jobben to have a temporary job (e.g., a summar job) (*colloq.*) 4
joggen to jog 1
das **Jogging** jogging 1; **~ gehen** to go jogging 1
der **Journalist', -en, -en/**die **Journalis'tin, -nen** journalist 8
der **Jude, -n, -n/**die **Jüdin, -nen** Jew
jüdisch Jewish
die **Jugendherberge, -n** youth hostel
der/die **Jugendliche** (*noun decl. like adj.*) young person 12
der **Juli** July 3
jung (ü) young 4
der **Junge, -n -n** boy E
der **Juni** June 2
der **Juraprofessor, en/**die **Juraprofessorin, -nen** law professor

K

der **Kabarettist', -en, -en/**die **Kabarettis'tin, -nen** cabaret artist

der **Kaffee** coffee 3
das **Kaffeehaus, -häuser** café (in Austria); coffeehouse
der **Kalen'der, -** calendar
kalt (ä) cold 2; **es wird ~** it is getting cold 6
die **Kamera, -s** camera
der **Kamm, ¨e** comb 3
(sich) kämmen to comb 9; **Ich kämme mich./Ich kämme mir die Haare.** I comb my hair. 9
(das) **Kanada** Canada 2
der **Kana'dier, -/**die **Kana'dierin, -nen** Canadian (person) 1
kana'disch Canadian (*adj.*) 4
der **Kanton', -e** canton (a Swiss state)
kaputt' broken; exhausted (*slang*) 5
die **Karot'te, -n** carrot 3
die **Karte, -n** card; postcard 1; ticket 6; die **Karten** (*pl.*) playing cards 1
die **Kartof'fel, -n** potato 3
der **Käse** cheese 3
die **Kasset'te, -n** cassette
das **Kasset'tendeck, -s** cassette deck E
die **Kategorie', -n** category
die **Katze, -n** cat 7
kaufen to buy 3
die **Kauffrau, -en** merchant (*f.*)
das **Kaufhaus, -häuser** department store 3
der **Kaufmann, -leute,** also ¨**er** merchant (*m.*)
kaum hardly
kein not a, not any 3; **~ ... mehr** no more ... 3
der **Keks, -e** cookie
der **Keller, -** cellar, basement
kennen, kannte, gekannt to know, be acquainted with [people, places, or things] 3; **~ lernen** to get to know; to make the acquaintance of
die **Kettenerzählung, -en** chain story
das **Kilo(gramm)** (*abbr.* **kg**) kilo(gram) (= 2.2 pounds) 3
der **Kilometer -** (*abbr.* **km**) kilometer (= .062 miles) 2
das **Kind, -er** child E
der **Kindergarten, ¨** nursery school; kindergarten 8
das **Kindergeld** government's cash contribution to families with children, child allowance

die **Kindheit** childhood
das **Kinn, -e** chin 9
das **Kino, -s** movie theater 1; **ins ~
gehen** to go to the movies 1
die **Kirche, -n** church 12
das **Kissen, -** pillow 7
die **Klammer, -n** parenthesis
klar clear; (*interj.*) of course,
naturally 4
die **Klasse, -n** class 4; die **erste ~**
first grade
der **Klassiker, -**/die **Klassikerin,
-nen** author of a classical work
klassisch classic(al)
die **Klausur', en** test 4; **eine ~
schreiben** to take a test 4
das **Klavier' -e** piano 10; das
~konzert piano concerto; piano
concert 10
das **Kleid, -er** dress 6
die **Kleidung** clothing 6; das
Kleidungsstück, -e article of
clothing
klein small; short (*of people*) E
klettern, ist geklettert to climb
das **Klima** climate 2
klingeln to ring 11
die **Klinik, -en** clinic 9
das **Klischee', -s** cliché 5
das **Kloster,** convent; monastery
der **Klub, -s** club 12
die **Kneipe, -n** bar, pub 6
das **Knie, -** (*pl. pronounced* /Kni ə/)
knee 9
der **Koch, -e**/die **Köchin, -nen** cook
kochen to cook 6
der **Kochtopf, -e** pot for cooking;
am ~ stehen to stand at the
stove
der **Kolle'ge, -n, -n**/die **Kolle'gin,
-nen** colleague 8
Köln Cologne
kombinie'ren to combine
komisch funny; strange
kommen, kam, ist gekommen
to come 1; **~ aus ...** to be
from ... ; **Woher kommst du?**
Where are you from?/Where do
you come from? 2; **Ich komme
aus ...** I come/am from ... 2
der **Kommentar', -e** comment;
commentary
die **Kommo'de, -n** chest
of drawers 7
der **Kommunis'mus** communism

kompliziert' complicated 8
die **Komponen'te, -n** component
der **Komponist', -en -en**/die
Komponis'tin, -nen composer 5
der **Kompromiss', -e** compromise
die **Konditorei', -en** pastry shop
die **Konjunktion', -en** conjunction
die **Konkurrenz', -en** competition
konkurrie'ren to compete 11
können (kann), konnte, gekonnt
to be able to; can 4
könnte (*subj. of* **können**) would be
able to 4
die **Kontakt'linse, -n** contact lens;
die ~ einsetzen to put in the
lens
das **Konzentrations'lager, -** concentration camp
das **Konzert', -e** concert 6; **ins ~
gehen** to go to a concert 6
der **Kopf, -e** head 9; **etwas geht
[mir] durch den ~** [I'm] thinking
about something
die **Kopfschmerzen** (*pl.*) headache 3
der **Kopie'rer** copier
der **Körper, -** body 9
korrigie'ren to correct
kosten to cost 4
das **Kostüm', -e** costume; ladies' suit
krank sick, ill 1
das **Krankenhaus, -häuser** hospital 6
die **Krankenkasse** health insurance
der **Krankenpfleger, -**/die **Krankenpflegerin, -nen** nurse
die **Krankenschwester, -n** female
nurse 7
die **Krankenversicherung** health
insurance
die **Krankheit, -en** illness 9
kränklich sickly
die **Krawat'te, -n** necktie 6
die **Kredit'karte, -n** credit card 9
der **Krieg, -e** war 5
kriegen to get 6
der **Krimi, -s** mystery (novel or
film) 4
die **Krise, -n** crisis
die **Kritik'** criticism; review 10
kritisch critical 1
die **Küche, -n** kitchen 3
der **Kuchen, -** cake 3
das **Küchengerät, -e** kitchen
appliance
die **Küchenmaschine, -n** mixer
(*also used for* food processor)

der **Kugelschreiber, -** ballpoint
pen E
kühl cool 2
der **Kühlschrank, -e** refrigerator 7
der **Kuli, -s** (*colloq. for* **Kugelschreiber**) ballpoint pen E
kulminie'ren to culminate
die **Kultur', -en** culture 12
kulturell' culture, culturally 12
der **Kunde, -n, -n**/die **Kundin, -nen**
customer, client 11
die **Kündigung, -en** dismissal
die **Kunst, -e** art; skill
die **Kunstgeschichte** art history 4
der **Künstler, -**/die **Künstlerin, -nen**
artist 5
der **Kurs, -e** course, class 4
der **Kursteilnehmer, -**/die
Kursteilnehmerin, -nen
member of a class or course
kurz short, brief 5; die **kurzen
Hosen** shorts 6
die **Kurzgeschichte, -n** short story
die **Kusi'ne, -n** cousin (*f.*) 4

L

lächeln to smile 7; **~ über** (+ *acc.*)
to smile about
lachen to laugh 12; **~ über** (+ *acc.*)
to laugh about
der **Laden,** store 3
die **Lampe, -n** lamp E
das **Land, -er** country, land 2; **aufs
~ fahren** to go to the country
landen to land
die **Landkarte, -n** map 5
lang (ä) long 4
lange (*adv.*) for a long time 5
langsam slow(ly) 9
langweilig boring 6
lassen (lässt), ließ, gelassen to
leave; to let, permit; to have
something done 12; **Lass uns
gehen.** Let's go. 12
laufen (läuft), lief, ist gelaufen to
run; to go on foot, to walk 5
laut (*adj.*) loud; noisy 2; (*prep. +
gen. or dat.*) according to
das **Leben** life 7
leben to live 5
die **Lebensmittel** (*pl.*) food;
groceries 3

der **Lebensstandard** standard of living 9

leer empty 11

legen to lay or put something in a horizontal position 7

lehren to teach 8

der **Lehrer, -**/die **Lehrerin, -nen** teacher 8

leicht light; easy 8

die **Leichtathletik** track and field

Leid: Es tut mir ~. I'm sorry. 4

leider unfortunately 2

leihen, lieh, geliehen to lend; to borrow 4

lernen to learn; to study 4

lesen (ie), las, gelesen to read 4

das **Lesestück, -e** reading selection

letzt last 5

die **Leute** (*pl.*) people 3

das **Licht, -er** light

lieb (*adj.*) dear; **Liebe [Barbara].** **Lieber [Paul] ...** Dear [Barbara], Dear [Paul] . . . (*used at the beginning of a letter*) 1

die **Liebe** love 4

lieben to love

lieber (*comp. of gern*) preferably, rather 7; **ich sitze ~ draußen** I prefer to sit outside 7

der **Liebesroman, -e** romance (novel) 4

der **Liebling, -e** favorite 3; darling; **Lieblings-** (*prefix*) favorite: das **Lieblingsgetränk** favorite drink 3

liebsten: am ~ best liked most of all 9

(das) **Liechtenstein** Liechtenstein

liegen, lag, gelegen to lie; to be situated, be located 2

die **Limona'de** carbonated, fruit-flavored drink; lemonade

links on/to the left 11

die **Lippe, -n** lip 9

die **Liste, -n** list

der **Liter,-** (*abbr.* **1**) liter (= 1.056 U.S. quarts) 3

die **Literatur'** literature 4

der **Löffel, -** spoon 7

logisch logical

das **Lokal', -e** restaurant; bar 12

los loose; **Was ist ~?** What's wrong? What's going on? 1

lösen to solve

die **Luft** air 7

die **Luftbrücke** airlift

die **Lust** desire; enjoyment 10; **~ haben** (+ **zu** + *inf.*) to be in the mood, to feel like doing something 10

lustig funny; merry; cheerful 1

M

machen to do; to make 1; **Deutsch ~** to do/study German (homework) 1; **Examen ~** to graduate from the university 4; **(Es) macht nichts.** (It) doesn't matter. 7; **Mach schnell!** Hurry up! 7

das **Mädchen, -** girl E

der **Magen, ¨** stomach 9; die **~schmerzen** (*pl.*) stomachache 9

die **Mahlzeit, -en** meal; **~!** Enjoy your meal.

der **Mai** May 2

mal time; times (in multiplication) E; **drei~** three times; **mal (= einmal)** once, sometime; (*flavoring particle that softens a command and leaves the time indefinite*) **Sag ~ ...** Tell me . . . 3; **Moment ~!** Just a minute! 11

die **Mama** mom 4

man one, people, (*impersonal*) you E

manch (-er, -es, -e) many a (*sg.*); some (*pl.*) 4

manchmal sometimes 3

der **Mann, ¨er** man E; husband

der **Mantel, ¨** outer coat 6

die **Margari'ne** margarine 3

die **Mark** mark; die **Deutsche ~ (DM)** (basic monetary unit in Germany) 3

markie'ren to check

der **Markt, ¨e** market 3; **auf den ~** to the market 3

die **Marmela'de** marmalade, jam 3

der **März** March 2

die **Maschi'ne, -n** machine 8

Maschi'neschreiben, schrieb Maschine, Maschine geschrieben to type

die **Mathe** (*short for* **Mathematik**) math 4

die **Mathematik'** mathematics 4

die **Mauer, -n** (exterior) wall 10

mehr (*comp. of viel*) more 2;

immer ~ more and more 8; **~ oder weniger** more or less; **kein ... ~** no more . . . 3; **nicht ~** no longer, not anymore 4

mehrere several; various 12

mein my E

meinen to mean; to think, have an opinion 7; **Was meinst du?** What do you think?

die **Meinung, -en** opinion; **meiner ~ nach** in my opinion

meist (*superlative of viel*) most 4; die **meisten (Leute)** most of (the people) 4

meistens most of the time, mostly 5

die **Mensa, -s** university cafeteria

der **Mensch, -en, -en** person, human being 1; **~!** Man!/Wow!

merken to notice; to realize 11; **sich** (*dat.*) **~** to note down

das **Messer, -** knife 7

der **Meter, -** (*abbr.* **m**) meter (= 39.37 inches)

der **Metzger,-** butcher 3; **beim ~** at the butcher's 3; **zum ~** to the butcher's 3

die **Metzgerei', -en** butcher shop, meat market 3

(das) **Mexiko** Mexico

mieten to rent

die **Mietwohnung, -en** rental apartment

der **Mikrowellenherd, -e** microwave (oven)

die **Milch** milk 3

die **Million', -en** million 2

die **Minderheit, -en** minority

mindestens at least

das **Mineral'wasser** mineral water 3

minus minus 2

die **Minu'te, -n** minute 1

mit (+ *dat.*) with 3; **~ dem [Auto] fahren** to go by [car] 5

der **Mitarbeiter, -**/die **Mitarbeiterin, -nen** employee 11

die **Mitbestimmung** co-determination

der **Mitbewohner, -**/die **Mitbewohnerin, -nen** roommate

mit·bringen, brachte mit, mitgebracht to bring along 4

der **Mitbürger, -**/die **Mitbürgerin, -nen** fellow citizen

miteinan'der with each other 7

mit·fahren (fährt mit), fuhr mit, ist mitgefahren to drive/ride along 5

mit·gehen, ging mit, ist mitgegangen to go along 6; **er geht mit in einen Biergarten** he's going along to a beer garden 7

das **Mitglied, -er** member 9

die **Mitgliedschaft** membership

mit·kommen, kam mit, ist mitgekommen to come along

das **Mittagessen** midday meal 3; **zum ~** for the midday meal, for lunch 3

die **Mittagspause** lunch break; the time during which a store closes for lunchtime

mitten: ~ in ... in the middle of . . .

der **Mittwoch** Wednesday E

die **Möbel** (*pl.*) furniture 7

das **Möbelstück, ⁻e** piece of furniture 7

möchte (*subj. of* **mögen**) would like 3

modern' modern 4

mögen (mag), mochte, gemocht to like 4

möglich possible 6

die **Möglichkeit, -en** possibility 2

der **Moment', -e** moment 11; **im ~** at the moment 11; **~ mal!** Just a minute! 11

der **Monat, -e** month 2

der **Montag** Monday E; **am ~** on Monday E; **~ in acht Tagen** a week from Monday

morgen tomorrow 2

der **Morgen** morning 1; **Guten ~.** Good morning. 1

morgens mornings, every morning 3

das **Motorrad, ⁻er** motorcycle 5

das **Motto, -s** motto 12

das **Mountainbike, -s** mountain bike 6

müde tired 1

multikulturell' multicultural 12

der **Mund, ⁻er** mouth 9

die **Münze, -n** coin

das **Musical, -s** musical 6

die **Musik'** music 1; **~ hören** listening to music 1

musika'lisch musical 1

der **Mu'siker, -/die Mu'sikerin, -nen** musician 8

müssen (muss), musste, gemusst to have to; must 4

müsste (*subj. of* **müssen**) would have to 11

die **Mutter, ⁻** mother 4

die **Muttersprache, -n** native language

die **Mutti, -s** mom 4

die **Mütze, -n** cap 6

N

na: ~ gut! All right. 1; well (*interjection*); **na ja** well now

nach (+ *dat.*) after 1; to (*with cities and countries used without an article,* e.g., **nach Berlin; nach Deutschland**) 2; **~ Hause** (to go) home 3; **fragen ~** to ask about

der **Nachbar, -n, -n/die Nachbarin, -nen** neighbor 1

das **Nachbarland, ⁻er** neighboring country 2

nachdem' (*conj.*) after

nach·denken, dachte nach, nachgedacht (über) (+ *acc.*) to think (about), reflect (on)

nachher afterwards 4

der **Nachmittag, -e** afternoon 1

der **Nachname, -ns, -n** last name

die **Nachricht, -en** message; **Nachrichten** (*pl.*) newscast

nach·schlagen (schlägt nach), schlug nach, nachgeschlagen to look up

nach·sehen (sieht), sah nach, nachgesehen to look up

die **Nachspeise, -n** dessert

nächst next 7

die **Nacht, ⁻e** night 1; **Gute ~.** Good night. 1

der **Nachtisch, -e** dessert

der **Nachttisch, -e** bedside table 7

die **Nähe** nearness, proximity; vicinity; **in der ~** near at hand

der **Name, -ns, -n** name

nämlich after all; that is (to say); you know; you see 7

die **Nase, -n** nose 9

nass (nasser or **nässer)** wet 2

der **National'rat** National Council (*Switzerland*)

natür'lich natural(ly) 1; of course

die **Natür'lichkeit** naturalness

der **Natur'wissenschaftler, -/die Natur'wissenschaftlerin, -nen** (natural) scientist

neben (+ *acc./dat.*) beside, next to, besides 7

nebenan' next door

das **Nebenfach, ⁻er** minor (subject) 4

der **Neffe, -n -n** nephew 4

negativ negative

nehmen (nimmt), nahm, genommen to take 3

nein no E

nennen, nannte, genannt to name 8

nervös' nervous

nett nice 1

neu new E; **Was gibt's Neues?** What's new? 11

neugierig curious

der **Neuschnee** newly fallen snow

(das) **Neuschott'land** Nova Scotia

neutral' neutral 9

die **Neutralität'** neutrality

nicht not 1; **~?** (*tag question*) don't you?; isn't it? E; **Du heißt [Monika], ~?** Your name is Monika, isn't it? E; **~ mehr** no longer, not anymore 4; **~ nur ... sondern auch** not only . . . but also 5; **~ so [kalt]** not as [cold] 2; **~ wahr?** isn't that so? 1; **noch ~** not yet 2

die **Nichte, -n** niece 4

der **Nichtraucher, -/die Nicht- raucherin, -nen** non-smoker

nichts nothing 1; **~ Beson'deres** nothing special 1; **(Es) macht ~!** (It) doesn't matter. 7

nie never 10

(das) **Niederdeutsch** Low German (term for dialects spoken in northern Germany)

(die) **Niederlande** (*pl.*) the Netherlands

niedrig low 11

niemand no one 6

noch still; in addition 2; **~ ein ...** another . . . 3; **~ einmal** again, once more 12; **~ immer** still 10; **~ nicht** not yet 2; **Sonst ~ einen Wunsch?** Anything else? 3; **sonst ~ etwas** something else 3; **was ~** what else? 7

der **Norden** north 3

nördlich   to the north 2
(das) Norwegen   Norway
der **Notdienst**   emergency service
die **Note, -n**   grade; note 4
(sich) notie'ren   to make a note of
die **Notiz', -en**   note 4
der **Novem'ber**   November 2
die **Nudeln** (*pl.*)   noodles 3
der **Numerus clausus**   limited number of university positions for study in certain subjects
die **Nummer, -n**   number E
nummerie'ren   to number
das **Nummernschild, -er**   license plate
nur   only 1
nützlich   useful

O

ob (*sub. conj.*)   whether, if 7
oben   above
oberflächlich   superficial 7
das **Obst**   fruit 3
obwohl' (*sub. conj.*)   although 5
oder   or 1; **~?**   Or don't you agree? 6; **Du kommst doch, ~?** You're coming, aren't you?
offen   open 3; frank
öffentlich   public 7
öffnen   to open 10
oft   often 1
ohne (+ *acc.*)   without 3
das **Ohr, -en**   ear 9
O.K.   okay, OK 1
der **Okto'ber**   October 2
die **Oma, -s**   grandma 4
der **Onkel,-**   uncle 4
der **Opa, -s**   grandpa 4
das **Open-Air-Konzert**   outdoor concert 10
die **Oper, -n**   opera 10; **in die ~ gehen**   to go to the opera 10
die **Oran'ge, -n**   orange 3
der **Oran'gensaft**   orange juice 3
die **Ordnung**   order; **in ~**   that is all right, OK 6
organisie'ren   to organize
der **Ort, -e**   place (geographical) 9
der **Ostblock**   the eastern block
der **Osten**   east 2
(das) Österreich   Austria 2
der **Österreicher, -/die Österrei-cherin, -nen**   Austrian person 2
österreichisch   Austrian (*adj.*) 5

östlich   eastern
der **Ozean, -e**   ocean 2

P

paar; ein ~   a few 3; **alle ~ Minuten**   every few minutes
der **Papa, -s**   dad 4
das **Papier', -e**   paper E
der **Park, -s**   park 7
parken   to park
das **Parterre'**   the ground floor of a building
die **Partnerschaft, -en**   partnership
die **Party, -s**   party 3; **auf eine ~**   to a party; **auf einer ~**   at a party
der **Passagier', -e/die Passagie'rin, -nen**   passenger
passen (passt) (+ *dat.*)   to fit; to be appropriate
passend   appropriate; suitable
passie'ren, ist passiert (+ *dat.*)   to happen 7; **Was ist dir passiert?**   What happened to you? 7
passiv   passive(ly) 6
die **Pause, -n**   break, rest; intermission
die **Person', -en**   person
der **Personal'chef, -s/die Personal'chefin, -nen**   head of the human resources (personnel) department 8
persön'lich   personal(ly)
die **Persön'lichkeit, -en**   personality; personage
der **Pfennig, -e**   1/100 of the German Mark
die **Pflanze, -n**   plant E
das **Pfund, -e** (*abbrev.* **Pfd.**)   pound (= 1.1 U.S. pounds) 3
die **Philosophie'**   philosophy 4
die **Physik'**   physics 4
der **Phy'siker, -/die Phy'sikerin, -nen**   physicist 8
das **Picknick, -s**   picnic 4; **~ machen**   to have a picnic 4
die **Pizza, -s**, also **Pizzen**   pizza 6
der **Plan, ⁻e**   plan 5; schedule
planen   to plan
der **Platz, ⁻e**   place; seat; space; square 4; **~ nehmen**   to take a seat 13
pleite   broke, out of money 7
plötzlich   suddenly

die **Politik'**   politics; political science 11
der **Poli'tiker, -/die Poli'tikerin, -nen**   politician 8
poli'tisch   political(ly) 10
die **Polizei'**   police
das **Polohemd, -en**   polo shirt 6
die **Pommes frites** (*pl.*)   French fries 6
das **Popkonzert, -e**   pop concert 10
das **Porträt, -s**   portrait 5
positiv   positive
die **Post**   mail; post office 11
das *or* der **Poster, -**   poster E
die **Postleitzahl, -en**   postal code
der **Praktikant', -en, en/die Praktikan'tin, -nen**   intern
praktisch   practical(ly); for all practical purposes 1
der **Präsident', -en, -en/die Präsiden'tin, -nen**   president 10
die **Praxis**   (a professional) practice
präzis'   precise(ly)
der **Preis, -e**   price 11
prima   fantastic, great (**prima** *takes no adj. endings*) 10
privat'   private 4
pro   per
die **Probe, -n**   rehearsal 6
proben   to rehearse
probie'ren   to try; to (put to the) test; (*food*) to taste
das **Problem', -e**   problem 5
das **Produkt', -e**   product 5
produzie'ren   to produce
der **Profes'sor,** *pl.* **Professo'ren/die Professo'rin, -nen**   professor E
das **Prozent'**   percent 4
der **Prozent'satz**   percentage
die **Prüfung, -en**   test, examination 4
die **Psychologie'**   psychology 4
der **Pulli, -s**   sweater 6
der **Punkt, -e**   dot, spot, point; period 8
pünktlich   punctual 7
putzen   to clean 7; **Ich putze mir die Zähne**   I'm brushing my teeth 9

Q

die **Qualität', -en**   quality 9
der **Quatsch**   nonsense; **~!**   Nonsense! 11

R

das **Rad, -̈er** (*short for* **Fahrrad**) bike, bicycle 5; wheel; **Rad fahren (fährt Rad), fuhr Rad, ist Rad gefahren** to (ride a) bicycle, to bike 6

der **Radfahrer, -/die Radfahrerin, -nen** cyclist, bike rider

das **Radio, -s** radio E

die **Radtour, -en** bicycle trip

der **Rappen, -** 1/100 of the Swiss Frank

(sich) rasie'ren to shave 9

der **Rassis'mus** racism 12

der **Ratschlag, -schläge** advice, piece of advice

der **Rauch** smoke 7

rauchen to smoke

der **Raucher, -/die Raucherin, -nen** smoker

der **Raum, -̈e** room; space

raus (*contraction of* **heraus**) out

reagie'ren (auf + *acc.*) to react (to)

die **Real'schule, -n** school from 5th to 10th grade that prepares students for careers in business, health fields, etc.

rechnen to calculate; ~ **mit** to count on

das **Recht, -e** right; law; ~ **auf** + *acc.* right to; **Recht haben** to be right; **Du hast Recht.** You're right. 7

rechts on/to the right 11

der **Rechtsanwalt, -anwälte/die Rechtsanwältin, -nen** lawyer 8

die **Rechtswissenschaft** (study of) law

die **Rede, -n** speech

reden (über + *acc.*) to talk/speak (about) 7

das **Referat', -e** report; seminar paper 4

die **Regel, -n** rule

regelmäßig regular(ly)

die **Regelstudienzeit** limit on time to complete university studies

der **Regen** rain 2

der **Regenmantel, -̈** raincoat 6

der **Regenschirm, -e** umbrella 5

regie'ren to govern

die **Regie'rung, -en** government 10

die **Regie'rungsform** form of government

das **Regie'rungsgebäude, -** government building

regnen to rain 2; **es regnet** it's raining 2

reich rich 5

das **Reich** empire; das **Dritte ~** the Third Reich

das **Reichstagsgebäude** German parliament building in Berlin

reif ripe

die **Reinigung** cleaning

die **Reise, -n** trip, journey 7

reisen, ist gereist to travel

der/die **Reisende** (*noun decl. like adj.*) traveler, passenger

der **Reisepass, -̈e** passport

relativ' relative 2

renovie'ren to renovate

reparie'ren to repair

der **Repor'ter, -/die Repor'terin, -nen** reporter 6

der **Rest, -e** rest, remaining part 6

das **Restaurant' -s** restaurant 7

das **Rezept', -e** prescription; recipe

richtig correct, right; proper 6

riechen, roch, gerochen to smell 3

der **Rinderbraten** roast beef 3

der **Rock, -̈e** skirt 6

die **Rockband, -s** rock band 10

der **Rockfan, -s** rock fan 12

die **Rockmusik** rock (music) 6

der **Rockmusiker, -/die Rockmusikerin, -nen** rock musician 12

der **Roggen** rye

der **Rohstoff, -e** raw material 9

der **Rollladen, -läden** window shutters that unroll vertically

die **Rolle, -n** role; **eine ~ spielen** to play a role

das **Rollenspiel, -e** role play

das **Rollerblading** rollerblading; ~ **gehen** to go rollerblading 1

der **Roman', -e** novel 4

die **Rosi'ne, -n** raisin

rot red E

der **Rotwein, -e** red wine 3

der **Rücken, -** back 9; die **Rückenschmerzen** (*pl.*) backache 9

die **Rückmeldung** registration subsequent to the first one (university)

die **Rückreise, -n** return trip

der **Rucksack, -säcke** backpack E

die **Ruhe** peace and quiet

der **Ruhetag, -e** the day on which a restaurant is closed

ruhig calm, easygoing; quiet 1

das **Rührei, -er** scrambled egg

(das) **Rumä'nien** Rumania

der **Russe, -n, -n/die Russin, -nen** Russian person

(das) **Russland** Russia

S

die **Sache, -n** thing 6; affair, concern; (*pl.*) clothes 6

der **Saft, -̈e** juice 3

sagen to say; tell 2; **sag mal** tell me 3

der **Salat', -e** lettuce; salad 3

sammeln to collect 8

der **Samstag** (*in southern Germany*) Saturday E

samstags Saturdays, every Saturday 3

der **Satz, -̈e** sentence 11

sauber clean 7

sauber machen to clean 7

das **Schach** chess 1

schade that's too bad, a pity, a shame 9

schaden (+ *dat.*) to harm

der **Schaffner, -/die Schaffnerin, -nen** conductor (on a train or streetcar)

die **Schallplatte, -n** (phonograph) record

der **Schauplatz, -̈e** scene

der **Schein, -e** glow; (*type of official document*) **der Geldschein** bill; **der Seminarschein** certificate of attendance for one semester of a course

scheinen, schien, geschienen to shine 2; to appear, seem

schenken to give (as a gift) 5

das **Schiff, -e** ship 5

der **Schilling, -e** shilling; **österreichischer ~ (öS)** Austrian unit of currency

der **Schinken, -** ham 3

der **Schirm, -e** umbrella 6

schlafen (ä), schlief, geschlafen to sleep 5; **bei jemandem ~** to sleep at someone's house

das **Schlafzimmer, -** bedroom 7

schlagen (ä), schlug, geschlagen to hit, beat; to whip

das **Schlagobers** (*Austrian*) whipped cream

die **Schlagsahne** whipped cream

die **Schlange** snake; line ~ **stehen** to stand in line

schlank slender 8

schlecht bad, badly 1; **Mir ist ~.** I feel nauseated. 9

schließen, schloss, geschlossen to close 3

schließlich finally, after all 9

das **Schloss, ¨er** castle, palace; lock

schmecken (+ *dat.*) to taste 6; **Es schmeckt [mir].** It tastes good to [me]. 6; **Hat es geschmeckt?** Did it taste good? 6

der **Schmerz, -en** pain 9

(sich) schminken to put on makeup; **ich schminke mich** I put on makeup; **Ich schminke mir die Augen.** I put on eye make-up. 9

schmutzig dirty

der **Schnee** snow 2

schneien to snow 2; **es schneit** it's snowing 2

schnell fast, quickly 6; **Mach ~!** Hurry up! 7

schon already 3

schön nice, beautiful 2; **ganz ~** really quite 9

die **Schönheit** beauty

der **Schornstein, -e** smokestack

der **Schrank, ¨e** wardrobe 7

schreiben, schrieb, geschrieben to write E; ~ **an** (+ *acc.*) to write to; ~ **über** (+ *acc.*) to write about 7; ~ **von** (+ *dat.*) to write about; **Wie schreibt man das?** How do you spell that? E

die **Schreibmaschine, -n** typewriter; ~ **schreiben** to type

der **Schreibtisch, -e** desk 7

der **Schriftsteller, -/die Schriftstellerin, -nen** writer 5

der **Schuh, -e** shoe 6

die **Schule, -n** school 4

die **Schulklasse, -n** (school) class

schützen to protect 10

schwach (ä) weak 9

die **Schwangerschaft** pregnancy; der **Schwangerschaftsurlaub** maternity leave

schwarz black E

schwätzen to talk, gossip

(das) **Schweden** Sweden

schweigen to be silent

die **Schweiz** Switzerland 2

der **Schweizer, -/die Schweizerin, -nen** Swiss person 2

Schweizer Swiss (*adj.*) 9

(das) **Schweizerdeutsch** Swiss German

schwer hard, difficult; heavy 4

die **Schwester, -n** sister 4

Schwieger- (*prefix meaning* in-law); **~tochter** daughter-in-law

schwierig difficult 12

schwimmen, schwamm, ist geschwommen to swim 1

schwül humid 2

der **See, -n** lake

die **See, -n** sea

segeln to sail

sehen (ie), sah, gesehen to see 4

sehr very (much) 1

sei (**du**-*imperative of* **sein**) 3; ~ **[mir] nicht böse.** Don't be mad [at me]. 7

die **Seife** soap

die **Seifenoper, -n** soap opera

sein his; its 1

sein (ist), war, ist gewesen to be 1

seit (+ *dat.*) since (*time or date*) 4; for (*time period*) 4; ~ **wann** since when, (for) how long 4; ~ **kurzer Zeit** recently

seitdem since then

die **Seite, -n** side; page 12

der **Sekretär, -e/die Sekretärin, -nen** secretary

selber oneself, myself, itself, etc.

selbst oneself, myself, itself, etc. 7

selbstverständlich of course, it goes without saying

selten seldom 9

das **Semester, -** semester 4

die **Semesteradresse, -n** school address E

die **Semesterferien** (*pl.*) semester break 4

das **Seminar, -e** seminar 4

die **Seminararbeit, -en** seminar paper 4

der **Seminarschein, -e** certificate of attendance for one semester of a course

die **Semmel, -n** bread roll

die **Sendung, -en** TV or radio program 10

der **September** September 2

der **Sessel, -** easy chair 7

setzen to set or put something down 7; **sich setzen** to take/have a seat 9

das **Shampoo, -s** shampoo

die **Shorts** (*pl.*) shorts 6

sicher safe; secure; certain(ly) 8

die **Sicherheit** safety, security

sie she, it E; they 1

Sie you (*formal*) E

siezen to address someone with the formal **Sie**-form

sind are E

der **Sinn** meaning, purpose

die **Situation, -en** situation 9

der **Sitz, -e** headquarters, seat

sitzen, saß, gesessen to sit 5

die **Sitzung, -en** session

der **Ski, -er** (**Ski** *is pronounced* **Schi**) ski 5; **Ski laufen** (*also* **Ski fahren**) to ski 5; **zum Skilaufen gehen** to go skiing

der **Skiläufer, -/die Skiläuferin, -nen** skier 5

so so, thus, this way E, ~ **... wie** as . . . as 2; ~**?** Is that so? Really? 4

sobald (*sub. conj.*) as soon as 8

die **Socke, -n** sock 6

das **Sofa, -s** soda 7

sofort immediately

sogar even 10

der **Sohn, ¨e** son 4

solch (-er, -es, -e) such a (*sg.*); such (*pl.*) 4

der **Soldat, -en, -en/die Soldatin, -nen** soldier 10

sollen (soll), sollte, gesollt to be supposed to; to be said to 4

der **Sommer** summer 2

das **Sonderangebot, -e** special offer

sondern (*conj.*) but, on the contrary 5; **nicht nur ... ~ auch** not only . . . but also 5

der **Sonnabend** (*in northern Germany*) Saturday E

die **Sonne** sun 2

die **Sonnenbrille, -n** sun glasses 6

sonnig sunny 2

der **Sonntag** Sunday E

sonst otherwise 3; ~ **noch etwas?** Anything else? 3; ~ **noch einen Wunsch?** Would you like anything else? 3

die **Sorge, -n** care, worry 11; **sich Sorgen machen (um)** to worry (about) 11

sorgen für to take care of

die **Sorte, -n** type, kind

sowie' (*conj.*) as well as

sozial' social; **das sozia'le Netz** social "safety net," social legislation

die **Sozial'hilfe** social welfare

die **Spaghet'ti** *pl.* spaghetti 3

(das) **Spanien** Spain

spanisch Spanish (*adj.*)

die **Spannung, -en** tension

sparen to save (e.g., money, time) 11

der **Spaß** enjoyment; fun 8; **an der Arbeit ~ haben** to enjoy one's work 8; **Es/Das macht ~** It/That is fun. 8; **Viel ~.** Have fun. 8; der **Spaß, ̈e** joke 8; **Er hat nur ~ gemacht.** He was only joking. 8

spät late 1; **Wie ~ ist es?** What time is it? 1; **später** later 1

spazie'ren fahren (ä), fuhr spazieren, ist spazieren gefahren to go for a drive 6

spazie'ren gehen, ging spazieren, ist spazieren gegangen to go for a walk 4

der **Spazier'gang, -gänge** walk, stroll

der **Spiegel, -** mirror 7

das **Spiegelei, -er** fried egg

das **Spiel, -e** game 12

spielen to play 1

der **Spielfilm, -e** feature film

der **Sport** sport(s) 1; **~ treiben** to engage in sports 1

sportlich athletic 1

der **Sportverein, -e** sports club

die **Sprache, -n** language 9

sprachlich with regard to language, linguistically

sprechen (i), sprach, gesprochen to speak 5; **~ mit** to speak to/with (someone); **~ über** (+ *acc.*) to speak about 7; **~ von** (+ *dat.*) to speak about/of 7

spülen to rinse; to wash 7; **Geschirr ~** to wash dishes 7

die **Spülmaschine, -n** dishwasher 7

der **Staat, -en** state; country 4

staatlich (*abbrev.* **staatl.**) public, government-owned 4

der **Staatsbürger, -/die Staatsbürgerin, -nen** citizen 5

die **Stadt, ̈e** city 2; **das ~ viertel** city district

der **Stammbaum, -bäume** family tree

stark (ä) strong 9

starr motionless

statt (+ *gen.*) instead of 9

der **Staub** dust 7; **~ wischen** to dust 7; **ich wische ~** I'm dusting; **~ saugen** to vacuum 7

das **Steak, -s** steak 6

stecken to stick, put or insert something into something else 7

stehen, stand, gestanden to stand; to be located 7; **es stand in der Zeitung ...** it said in the newspaper . . . 10; **stehen bleiben, blieb stehen, ist stehen geblieben** to stop

stehlen (ie), stahl, gestohlen to steal

steigen, stieg, ist gestiegen to rise, climb

die **Stelle, -n** job; position; place, spot 8

stellen to stand, place, put something (upright) 8; **eine Frage ~ + dat.** to ask someone a question 9; **eine Frage an + acc. ~** to ask someone a question 9

das **Stellenangebot, -e** job offer (ad)

die **Stellenanzeige, -n** want ad

sterben (i), starb, ist gestorben to die 10

die **Stereoanlage, -n** stereo system

das **Stichwort, ̈er** key word, cue

der **Stiefel,-** boot 6

die **Stiefmutter, ̈** stepmother 4

der **Stiefvater, ̈** stepfather 4

stimmen to be correct; **Das stimmt.** That's right.

das **Stipen'dium,** *pl.* **Stipendien** scholarship, grant 4

der **Stock,** *pl.* **Stockwerke** floor/story (above ground level) of a building

stolz (auf + acc.) proud (of) 12

der **Strand, ̈e** beach

die **Strandkleidung** beach clothes

die **Straße, -n** street E

die **Straßenbahn, -en** streetcar 5

der **Streik, -s** strike 11

streng strict

stressen to stress; **gestresst** stressed

die **Strumpfhose, -n** pantyhose 6

das **Stück, -e** piece 3; piece (of music); play (theater) 6

der **Student', -en, -en/die Studen'tin, -nen** student E

der **Studen'tenausweis, -e** student identification card

das **Studen'tenheim, -e** dormitory 4

das **Studienbuch** book in which courses one has attended are entered

das **Studienfach, ̈er** college major

der **Studiengang, -gänge** course of study

die **Studiengebühren** (*pl.*) administrative fees at the university; tuition

der **Studienplatz, ̈e** opening for student in a particular course of study at a university

studie'ren to study; to go to college 1; **~ an/auf** (+ *dat.*) to study at (a college) 7

das **Studium** studies 4

der **Stuhl, ̈e** chair E

die **Stunde, -n** hour 6; lesson; class; **die Klavier~** piano lesson

das **Substantiv, -e** noun

suchen to look for 3

der **Süden** south 2

südlich to the south 2

super super, great 6

der **Supermarkt, ̈e** supermarket 3; **in den ~** to the supermarket 3

surfen to surf

süß sweet; nice

sympa'thisch likeable, agreeable 1; **er ist mir ~** I like him

T

die **Tabel'le, -n** chart; table

die **Tablet'te, -n** tablet, pill 3

der **Tag, -e** day E; **Guten ~./~.** Hello.; Hi. 1; **eines Tages** one day; **[Montag] in acht Tagen** a week from Monday

das **Tagebuch, ̈er** diary

tagen to be in session, to meet

der **Tagesplan, ̈e** daily schedule

die **Tagesreise** a day's journey
täglich daily
tagsüber during the day
der **Tagtraum, -̈e** daydream
der **Tankwart, -e**/die **Tankwartin, -nen** gas station attendant
die **Tante, -n** aunt 4
der **Tante-Emma-Laden, -̈** mom-and-pop store
tanzen to dance 1
die **Tasche, -n** bag; pocket 3; handbag, purse 6
das **Taschenbuch, -̈er** paperback book 5
die **Tasse, -n** cup 3
die **Technologie', -n** technology
der **Tee** tea 3
der **Teil, -e** part 10
teilen to divide (up) 10; (*math*) ~ **durch** to divide by
die **Teilzeitarbeit** part-time work 11
die **Teilzeitbeschäftigung, -en** part-time work
das **Te'lefon, -e** telephone E
telefonie'ren (mit jemandem) to telephone (someone) 11
die **Telefon'nummer, -n** telephone number E; **Wie ist deine/Ihre ~?** What's your telephone number? E; **Wie ist die ~ von ... ?** What is the telephone number of . . . ? E
die **Telefon'zelle, -n** telephone booth
das **Tempolimit** speed limit
das **Tennis** tennis 1
der **Teppich, -e** rug, carpet 7
der **Termin', -e** appointment; **einen ~ bei jemandem haben** to have an appointment with someone 11
der **Termin'kalender, -** appointment calendar
teuer expensive 4
das **Textverarbeitungsprogramm, -e** word processing program; **mit Textverarbeitungsprogram-men arbeiten** to do word processing 8
das **Thea'ter, -** theater 6; **ins ~ gehen** to go to the theater 6; die **~karte, -n** theater ticket 6; das **~stück** play 6
das **Thema,** *pl.* **Themen** theme, topic 6
tippen to type 8

der **Tisch, -e** table E; **den ~ decken** to set the table 7
das **Tischtennis** table tennis, Ping-Pong 1
die **Tochter, -̈** daughter 4
die **Toilette, -n** toilet; men's/ladies' room
tolerant' tolerant 1
toll great, fantastic E
die **Toma'te, -n** tomato 3
das **Tor, -e** gate
die **Torte, -n** layered-cake with a cream or fruit filling 3
der **Tourist', -en, -en**/die **Touris'tin, -nen** tourist
die **Tradition', -en** tradition 12
tragen (ä), trug, getragen to carry; to wear 6
die **Traube, -n** grape 3
der **Traum,** *pl.* **Träume** dream
träumen (+ von) to dream (of)
traurig sad 1
(sich) treffen (i), traf, getroffen to meet 5; **Ich treffe mich mit Freunden,** I'm meeting friends.
der **Treffpunkt, -e** meeting place; rendezvous
treiben, trieb, getrieben to drive; to engage in 1
die **Treppe, -n** staircase
trinken, trank, getrunken to drink 3
das **Trinkgeld** tip
trocken dry 2
trotz (+ *gen.*) in spite of 8
trotzdem nevertheless 8
tschüs so long, good-bye (*informal*) E
das **T-Shirt, -s** T-shirt 6
tun, tat, getan to do 6; **Es tut mir Leid** I'm sorry 4
die **Tür, -en** door E
der **Türke, -n, -n**/die **Türkin, -nen** Turk
die **Türkei'** Turkey
turnen to do gymnastics
typisch typical

U

die **U-Bahn, -en** (*abbr. for* **Untergrundbahn**) subway 5
über (+ *acc./dat.*) about 3; over, above; across 7

überall everywhere 5
überglücklich ecstatic
überhaupt' altogether, in general; **~ nicht** not at all
übernach'ten to spend the night, to stay (in hotel or with friends) 5
überset'zen to translate
übrig remaining, leftover
übrigens by the way
die **Uhr, -en** clock E; **Wie viel ~ ist es?** What time is it? 1; **um [zehn] ~** at [ten] o'clock 1; **Um wie viel ~?** At what time? 1
um (+ *acc.*) at 1; around 3; **~ [zehn] Uhr** at [ten]o'clock 1; **~ wie viel Uhr?** At what time? 1; **Er ging ~ die Ecke.** He went around the corner.; **~ ... zu** (+ *inf.*) (in order) to 9; **Es geht nicht nur ~ [die Musik].** It's not just about [the music]. 12
die **Umfrage, -n** opinion poll, survey
der **Umstand, -̈e** circumstance, situation; **unter Umständen** perhaps, maybe
die **Umwelt** environment
unbedingt without reservation, absolutely 10
und and E; plus (*in addition*) E; **~ dir/Ihnen?** And you? (How about you?) 1
der **Unfall, -̈e** accident
unfreundlich unfriendly 1
(das) **Ungarn** Hungary
ungefähr approximately 5
unglaub'lich unbelievable, unbelievably 7
ungleich different
unglücklich unhappy 1
die **Uni, -s** (*colloq. for* Universität) 1
die **Universität', -en** university 1
unmusikalisch unmusical 1
uns us 3
unser our 2
unsicher insecure; unsafe 11
unsympathisch unpleasant, unappealing, disagreeable 1
unten downstairs; below 5
unter (+ *acc./dat.*) under, beneath; among 7; **~ anderem** among other things
unterbre'chen (unterbricht), unterbrach, unterbrochen to interrupt

unterhal'ten (unterhält), unterhielt, unterhalten to entertain; **sich unterhalten** to converse 10; **~ über** (+ *acc.*) to converse about 10

der **Unterschied, -e** difference 7

unzufrieden dissatisfied

die **Urgroßeltern** (*pl.*) great-grandparents

der **Urlaub** vacation 9; **in** *or* **im** *or* **auf ~ sein** to be on vacation 9; **in ~ fahren** to go on vacation 9

die **USA** (*pl.*) U.S.A. 2

usw. (= **und so weiter**) and so forth

V

variie'ren to vary

die **Vase, -n** vase 7

der **Vater, ⁚** father 4

der **Vati, -s** dad 4

(sich) verän'dern to change

die **Verän'derung, -en** change

verant'wortlich (für) responsible (for) 10

die **Verant'wortung, -en** responsibility 8

das **Verb, -en** verb

verbin'den, verband, verbunden to combine

verbrin'gen, verbrachte, verbracht to spend (time)

verdie'nen to earn 4

der **Verein', -e** club

die **Verei'nigung** unification

vereint' unified

die **Verfas'sung, -en** constitution 8

verfol'gen to pursue; to follow; to persecute

verges'sen (vergisst), vergaß, vergessen to forget 5

verglei'chen, verglich, verglichen to compare

die **Vergnü'gung, -en** pleasure

verhasst' hated

verhei'ratet married 8

verkau'fen to sell 11

der **Verkäu'fer, -**/die **Verkäu'ferin, -nen** salesperson

der **Verkehr'** traffic

das **Verkehrs'mittel, -** means of transportation 7

verlas'sen (verlässt), verließ, verlassen to leave, abandon 10

verlet'zen to injure, hurt 9; **Ich habe mir den Arm verletzt.** I've hurt my arm. 9; **Ich habe mich verletzt.** I hurt myself. 9

verlie'ren, verlor, verloren to lose 11

vermie'ten to rent (out)

der **Vermie'ter, -**/die **Vermie'terin, -nen** landlord/landlady

vermis'sen to miss someone or something

verrückt' crazy

verschie'den various

verschrei'ben, verschrieb, verschrieben to prescribe 9

verständ'lich understandable

versteh'en, verstand, verstanden to understand 8

versu'chen to try 5

verur'sachen to cause

verwandt' related

der/die **Verwand'te** (*noun declined like adj.*) relative 9

verwech'seln to confuse or mistake something or someone for something or someone else

der **Vetter, -n** cousin (*m.*) 4

das **Video, -s** video 4

der **Videorecorder, -** VCR, video cassette recorder 7

das **Videospiel, -e** video game 1

viel (mehr, meist-) much 1; **viele** many 3; **Viel Glück!** Good luck! 11; **viele Grüße** (*closing in a personal letter*) regards 1

vielleicht' maybe, perhaps 1

das **Viertel, -** a fourth, quarter 1; district of a city; **~ vor [zwei]** quarter to [two]; **~ nach [zwei]** quarter past [two] 1

der **Viktua'lienmarkt** an outdoor market in Munich

die **Vitamin'tablette, -n** vitamin pill

die **Voka'bel, -n** vocabulary word

voll full 7

der **Volleyball** volleyball 1

von (+ *dat.*) of E; from 2; by [the person doing something]

vor (+ *acc./dat.*) before 1; in front of 7; **~ allem** above all 5; **~ [zehn] Jahren** [ten] years ago

vorbei' over; gone 10

vorbei'·kommen, kam vorbei, ist vorbeigekommen to come by 5; **bei [mir] ~** to come by [my] place 5

vor·bereiten to prepare 4; **sich ~ (auf** + *acc.*) to prepare oneself (for) 11

vorbereitet prepared; **Ich bin (nicht) gut vorbereitet.** I'm (not) well prepared. 4

die **Vorbereitung, -en** preparation 7

vor·haben to intend, have in mind 6

der **Vorhang, ⁚e** drape; curtain; der **Eiserne ~** the Iron Curtain

vorher previously; beforehand

vorig last, previous; **voriges Jahr** last year

die **Vorlesung, -en** lecture 4; **eine ~ halten** to give a lecture

der **Vorname, -ns, -n** first name 7

die **Vorspeise, -n** appetizer

sich (*dat.*) **vor·stellen** to imagine 12; **Ich stelle mir das so vor, ...** I imagine that like this . . . 12

die **Vorstellung, -en** concept; notion; performance

der **Vorteil, -e** advantage

das **Vorurteil, -e** prejudice 12

die **Vorwahl, -en** area code

W

der **Wagen, -** car; wagon 5

die **Wahl** vote; choice, selection

wählen to choose; to elect

wahnsinnig crazy

wahr true 5; **nicht ~?** isn't that so? 5

während (*prep.*) (+ *gen.*) during 8; (*conj.*) while 12

wahrschein'lich (*adj.*) probable; (*adv.*) probably 5

der **Wald, ⁚er** forest 7

der **Walkman, -s** personal stereo 5

die **Wand, ⁚e** (interior) wall E

der **Wanderer, -**/die **Wanderin, -nen** hiker

wandern, ist gewandert to hike; **~ gehen** to go walking/hiking 1

die **Wanderung, -en** hike; **eine ~ machen** to go on a hike

wann when E; **seit ~** since when, (for) how long 4

war (*past tense of* **sein**) was 2

die **Ware, -n** wares, merchandise, goods 11

wäre (*subj. of* **sein**) would be 11

warm warm 2; **schön ~** nice and warm 2

warten (**auf** + *acc.*) to wait (for) 5

warum' why 3

was what 1; **~ für (ein)** ... what kind of (a) . . . 1; **~ für ein Wetter!** Such weather! 2; **~ gab es?** What was playing? 10; **~ gibt's Neues?** What's new? 11; **~ gibt's zum [Abendessen]?** What's for [dinner]? 3; **~ hast du?** What's wrong? 9; **~ ist los?** What's wrong? 1; **~ noch?** What else? 7

die **Wäsche** laundry 7; **~ waschen** to do the laundry

waschen (ä) wusch, gewaschen to wash 7; **sich ~** to wash oneself 9; **Ich wasche [mir] die Hände.** I'm washing [my] hands. 9

die **Waschmaschine, -n** washing machine

das **Wasser** water 3; **ein ~** a bottle/glass of mineral water 6

der **Wasserski, -er** water ski 5; **Wasserski fahren** to waterski 5

das **WC** toilet

wechseln to change 8

weg away; off; gone 9

der **Weg, -e** way 3; **auf dem ~** on the way 3

wegen (+ *gen.*) on account of, because of 8

weg·fahren (fährt), fuhr weg, ist weggefahren to drive away; to leave

weh·tun (+ *dat.*) to hurt 9; **Die Füße tun mir weh.** My feet hurt. 9

weich soft

weil (*sub. conj.*) because 5

die **Weile** while; **eine ganze ~** a long time 11

der **Wein, -e** wine 3

das **Weingeschäft, -e** wine shop

weiß white E

der **Weißwein, -e** white wine 3

weit far 7

weiter farther, further 2; additional

welch (-er, -es, e) which E; **Welche Farbe hat ...?** What color is . . .

? E; **Welcher Tag ist heute?** What day is today? E

die **Welt, -en** world 5

der **Weltkrieg, -e** world war 5

wem (*dat. of* **wer**) (to or for) whom 5

wen (*acc. of* **wer**) whom 3

wenig little 4; **ein ~** a little 4; **wenige** few 4

weniger minus (*in subtraction*) E; less

wenigstens at least 12

wenn (*sub. conj.*) when, whenever 3; if 4

wer who 1

der **Werbespot, -s** ad on TV or radio

die **Werbung** advertising

werden (wird), wurde, ist geworden to become 4; will (*auxiliary verb of the fut. tense*): **Das wird sie sicher finden.** She will certainly find it.

werfen (i), warf, geworfen to throw

das **Werkzeug, -e** tool

wesentlich essential; substantial; in the main 9

wessen (*gen. of* **wer**) whose 8

der **Westen** west 2

westlich western 10

das **Wetter** weather 2; **Was für ein ~!** Such weather! 2; **Wie ist das ~?** How's the weather? 2

wichtig important 5

die **Wichtigkeit** importance

wie how E; as 2; **~ alt bist du?** How old are you?; **~ bitte?** I beg your pardon? E; **~ geht es Ihnen?** How are you? 1; **~ geht's?** How are you? 1; **~ immer** as always 11; **~ ist das Wetter?** How is the weather? 2; **~ ist deine Telefonnummer?** What is your telephone number? E; **~ lange** for how long; **~ schreibt man das?** How do you spell that? E; **~ spät ist es?** What time is it? 1; **~ viel** how much E; **~ viel Grad ist es?** What's the temperature? 2; **~ viel macht das?** How much/What does that come to? 3; **~ viele** how many? E **~ wär's mit ... ?** How about . . . ?

wieder again 2; **immer ~** again and again 5

wieder·geben (gibt), gab wieder, wiedergegeben to reproduce, render

die **Wiederho'lung, -en** review; repetition

Wiedersehen: Auf ~. Good-bye. 1

wiederum in turn; on the other hand

die **Wiedervereinigung** reunification 10

Wien Vienna

wie viel' how much E; **~ Grad ist es?** What's the temperature? 2; **~ macht das?** How much/What does that come to? 3; **wie viele** how many? E

das **Willkom'men** welcome

der **Wind** wind 6

windig windy 2

windsurfen to windsurf; **~ gehen** to go windsurfing 6

der **Winter** winter 2

wir we 1

wirklich really 2

die **Wirklichkeit** reality 8

die **Wirtschaft** economy 5

wirtschaftlich economically 5

der **Wirtschaftsminister, -/die Wirtschaftsministerin, -nen** minister for economic affairs

die **Wirtschaftswissenschaft** economics

wissen (weiß), wusste, gewusst to know (a fact) 4

die **Wissenschaft, -en** science 8

der **Wissenschaftler, -/die Wissenschaftlerin, -nen** scientist 5

wo where 2

die **Woche, -n** week E

das **Wochenende, -n** weekend 1; **am ~** on the weekend 1; **Schönes ~!** Have a nice weekend! 3

woher where from 2; **~ kommst du?** Where are you from? 2

wohin where (to) 5

wohl probably; indeed; well 9

wohnen to live, reside 2; **bei jemandem ~** to live at someone else's residence das **Wohnhaus, -häuser** residential building; apartment building

die **Wohnung, -en** dwelling; apartment 7

das **Wohnzimmer, -** living room 7

wollen (will), wollte, gewollt to want to; intend to 4

wollte (*subj. of* **wollen**) would want 11

das **Wort, ⁀er** word E; **Worte** words (in context)

die **Wortverbindung, -en** phrase; expression

der **Wortschatz** vocabulary

wozu' what for, to what purpose, why

der **Wunsch, ⁀e** wish 3; **Sonst noch einen ~?** Anything else? 3

wünschen to wish 9

würde (*subj. of* **werden**) would 9; **Ich ~ das auch sagen** I would also say that 9

die **Wurst, ⁀e** sausage 3; lunch meat

das **Würstchen, -** frankfurter 3

die **Würze, -n** spice

Z

z.B. (*abbr. for* **zum Beispiel**) e.g. (for example) 4

die **Zahl, -en** number, numeral E

zahlen to pay 4; **~, bitte.** I'd like to pay, please (*in a restaurant*).

die **Zahlung, -en** payment; **in ~ nehmen** to take in trade

der **Zahn, ⁀e** tooth 9

der **Zahnarzt, ⁀e**/die **Zahnärztin, -nen** dentist 8

die **Zahnbürste, -n** toothbrush

die **Zahnpaste/Zahnpasta** toothpaste

die **Zahnschmerzen** (*pl.*) toothache 9

zeigen to show 8

die **Zeile, -n** line

die **Zeit, -en** time 4; **zur ~** at the moment 11

der **Zeitausdruck, ⁀e** time expression

die **Zeit lang: eine** a while

die **Zeitschrift, -en** magazine; journal

die **Zeitung, -en** newpaper 3; **Es stand in der ~.** It said in the newspaper. 10

das **Zelt, -e** tent

zelten to camp in a tent 5

das **Zentral'institut** department or school in university

das **Zentrum,** (*pl.*) **Zentren** center

zerstö'ren to destroy 10

ziehen, zog, ist gezogen to move

das **Ziel, -e** goal 9

ziemlich quite, rather, fairly 2

der **Zigeu'ner, -**/die **Zigeu'nerin, -nen** gypsy

das **Zimmer, -** room E

zu (+ *dat.*) (*prep.*) to (*with people and some places*) 3; **~ Abend essen** to eat dinner 6; **~ Besuch** for a visit; **~ Ende** over, finished 10; **~ Fuß gehen** to walk, 5; **~ Hause** (to be) at home 3; **um ... ~** (+ *inf.*) (in order) to 9; **zur Zeit** at the moment 11

zu too 2; **zu viel'** too much 4

zueinan'der to each other

zuerst' first of all; at first 6

zufrie'den satisfied, content

der **Zug, ⁀e** train 5

das **Zuhau'se** home

die **Zukunft** future 11

zum (*contraction of* **zu dem**) to or for the

zumin'dest at least

zunächst' at first

zurück' back, in return 4

zurück'·bringen, brachte zurück, zurückgebracht to bring back

zurück'·fliegen, flog zurück, ist zurückgeflogen to fly back 12

zurück'·zahlen to pay back 4

zusam'men together 1

der **Zusam'menhang, ⁀e** connection

die **Zutaten** (*pl.*) ingredients; toppings (pizza) 6

zwar to be sure, it's true, indeed 7

der **Zweifel, -** doubt

zweit- second 8

zwingen, zwang, gezwungen to force, compel 10

zwischen (+ *acc./dat.*) between, among 7

English-German Vocabulary

The English-German end vocabulary contains the words included in the active vocabulary lists and the *Erweiterung des Wortschatzes* section of the chapters. Not included from the active lists are numbers, articles and pronouns. The plural forms of nouns are given. Strong and irregular weak verbs are indicated with a raised degree mark (°). Their principal parts can be found in the Reference Section. Separable-prefix verbs are indicated with a raised dot: **mit·bringen.**

A

abdomen der Bauch, ¨e
able: to be ~ to können°
about über
above all vor allem
abroad im Ausland
absent: to be ~ fehlen
absolute(ly) absolut; unbedingt; ~ **great** ganz/wirklich toll
accident der Unfall, ¨e
account: on ~ of wegen
acquaintance der/die Bekannte (*noun decl. like adj.*); **to make the ~ of** kennen lernen
actually eigentlich
addition: in ~ noch, dazu
address die Adresse, -n; **What is your ~?** Wie ist deine/Ihre Adresse?
adult der/die Erwachsene (*noun decl. like adj.*)
advertisement die Reklame, -n; die Anzeige, -n
aerobics das Aerobic
afraid: to be ~ (of) Angst haben (vor + *dat.*), (sich) fürchten (vor + *dat.*)
after nach (*prep.*); nachdem (*conj.*) ~ **all** schließlich
afternoon der Nachmittag, -e; **this ~** heute Nachmittag
afternoons nachmittags
afterwards nachher
again wieder; noch einmal
against gegen
ago: [ten years] ~ vor [zehn Jahren]
air die Luft
airplane das Flugzeug, -e
airport der Flughafen, ¨e
all alle; **at ~** überhaupt; ~ **day** den ganzen Tag

allowed: to be ~ to dürfen°
almost fast
alone allein
Alps die Alpen (*pl.*)
already schon
also auch
although obwohl
always immer
America (das) Amerika
American (*adj.*) amerikanisch; ~ **(person)** der Amerikaner, -/ die Amerikanerin, -nen
among unter
and und; ~ **so on** und so weiter
angry böse; **Don't be ~ with me.** Sei mir nicht böse; **to feel ~** sich ärgern
another noch ein
answer die Antwort, -en; to ~ **[the woman]** [der Frau] antworten; **to ~ the question** auf die Frage antworten, die Frage beantworten
any einige; etwas; **I don't have any . . .** Ich habe kein ...
anyone jemand
anything: ~ else? Sonst noch etwas?
apartment die Wohnung, -en
apology die Entschuldigung, -en
apparatus der Apparat, -e
appear scheinen°; erscheinen°
apple der Apfel, ¨ ~ **juice** der Apfelsaft
appliance das Gerät, -e
appointment der Termin, -e
approximately ungefähr
April der April
architect der Architekt, -en, -en/die Architektin, -nen
arm der Arm, -e
arrive an·kommen°

art die Kunst, ¨e; ~ **history** die Kunstgeschichte
article der Artikel, -
artificial künstlich
as als; wie; ~ **. . . ~** so ... wie; ~ **always** wie immer
ask fragen; ~ **for** bitten° um; **to ~ him a question** ihm/an ihn eine Frage stellen
aspirin das Aspirin
assignment die Aufgabe, -n
astonished erstaunt
at an; auf; ~ **(a place)** bei; ~ **[seven]** um [sieben]
attic der Dachboden
August der August
aunt die Tante, -n
Austria (das) Österreich
Austrian österreichisch (*adj.*) ~ **(person)** der Österreicher, -/ die Österreicherin, -nen
author der Autor, -en/die Autorin, -nen
automobile das Auto, -s
autumn der Herbst
awareness das Bewusstsein
away weg; ab

B

back der Rücken, -; **~ache** die Rückenschmerzen (*pl.*); (*adv.*) zurück
bad schlecht; schlimm; böse; **not ~** ganz gut; **too ~** schade
badly schlecht
bag die Tasche, -n
bake backen°
baker der Bäcker, -/die Bäckerin, -nen

bakery die Bäckerei, -en; **at the ~** beim Bäcker; **to the ~** zum Bäcker

balcony der Balkon, -s

ballpoint pen der Kugelschreiber, - [der Kuli, -s (*colloq.*)]

banana die Banane, -n

band die Band, -s

bank die Bank, -en

bar die Bar, -s; die Kneipe, -n

basement der Keller, -

basketball der Basketball

bath das Bad, ̈er

bathe baden

bathing: ~ suit der Badeanzug, ̈e; **~ trunks** die Badehose, -n

bathroom das Bad, ̈er; die Toilette, -n

be sein°; **~ so kind.** Sei/Seien Sie so gut.

beautiful schön

because weil; denn; **~ of** wegen

become werden°

bed das Bett, -en; **to make the ~** das Bett machen

bedroom das Schlafzimmer, -

beer das Bier; **~ garden** (der Biergarten, ̈

before vor; vorher; bevor

begin an·fangen°; beginnen°; **~ the work** mit der Arbeit anfangen

beginning der Anfang, ̈e

behind hinter

believe glauben; **I ~ so.** Ich glaube schon/ja.

belong to gehören

beside (bei; neben; außer; außerhalb

besides außerdem; außer

best best; **~ of all** am besten

better besser

between zwischen

bicycle das Fahrrad, ̈er; **to ride a ~** mit dem Fahrrad fahren; Rad fahren

big groß

bike das Rad, ̈er; **~ trip** die Radtour, -en

biology die Biologie

birthday der Geburtstag, -e; **When is your ~?** Wann hast du Geburtstag?; **for one's ~** zum Geburtstag

black schwarz

blond blond

blouse die Bluse, -n

blue blau

body der Körper, -

book das Buch, ̈er

book bag die Büchertasche, -n

bookcase das Bücherregal, -e

bookstore die Buchhandlung, -en

boot der Stiefel, -

border die Grenze, -n

boring langweilig

born geboren; **I was born in 1982.** Ich bin 1982 geboren.

borrow leihen; borgen

boss der Chef, -s/die Chefin, -nen

both beide; beides

bother stören

bottle die Flasche, -n

boy der Junge, -n, -n; **~ friend** der Freund, -e

bread das Brot, -e

breakfast das Frühstück; **for ~** zum Frühstück; **to eat ~** frühstücken

breathe atmen

bridge die Brücke, -n

bright hell

bring bringen°; **~ along** mit·bringen°

broke (out of money) pleite

broken: ~ down kaputt

brother der Bruder, ̈; **brothers and sisters** die Geschwister (*pl.*)

brown braun

brush: to ~ [my] teeth [mir] die Zähne putzen

build bauen

bus der Bus, -se

business das Geschäft, -e

businessman der Geschäftsmann, pl. Geschäftsleute

businesspeople die Geschäftsleute

businesswoman die Geschäftsfrau, -en

busy: to be ~ beschäftigt sein; **to keep ~** (sich) beschäftigen

but aber; sondern

butcher der Metzger, -/die Metzgerin, -nen

butcher shop die Metzgerei, -en; **at the ~** beim Metzger; **to the ~** zum Metzger

butter die Butter

buy kaufen

by (close to) bei, an (*+ dat.*), neben (*+ dat.*); **~ [car]** mit [dem Auto]

C

café das Café, -s

cafeteria (university) die Mensa, -s *or* Mensen

cake der Kuchen, -; die Torte, -n

call nennen°; an·rufen°; **to ~ [your] home** bei [dir] anrufen

called: it's ~ (es) heißt

calm ruhig

camera der Fotoapparat, -e; die Kamera, -s

camp campen; **to ~ in a tent** zelten

can können°

can die Dose, -n

Canada (das) Kanada

Canadian (person) der Kanadier, -/die Kanadierin, -nen

cap die Mütze, -n

capital die Hauptstadt, ̈e

car das Auto, -s; der Wagen, -

card die Karte, -n; **(playing) cards** die Karten (*pl.*)

cardboard die Pappe

care die Sorge, -n; **to ~ for** sorgen für; **to take ~ of something** auf etwas auf·passen

carpet der Teppich, -e

carrot die Karotte, -n

carry tragen°

cassette die Kassette, -n

cassette deck das Kassettendeck, -s

castle das Schloss, *pl.* Schlösser

cat die Katze, -n

CD player der CD-Spieler, -; der CD-Player, -

celebration die Feier, -n; das Fest, -e

cellar der Keller, -

century das Jahrhundert, -e

certain(ly) bestimmt; sicher

chair der Stuhl, ̈e; **easy ~** der Sessel, -

change wechseln

cheap billig

check: The ~, please. Zahlen, bitte.

cheerful lustig

cheese der Käse

chemistry die Chemie

chess das Schach; **~ game** das Schachspiel

chest of drawers die Kommode, -n

chicken das Hähnchen, -

child das Kind, -er

chin das Kinn

chocolate die Schokolade, -n
chore die Pflicht, -en; **household chores** die Hausarbeit; **to do the chores** den Haushalt machen
Christmas das Weihnachten; **Merry ~!** Frohe or Fröhliche Weihnachten!
church die Kirche, -n
cigarette die Zigarette, -n
circle der Kreis, -e
city die Stadt, ⸚e; **old part of the ~** die Altstadt; **~ hall** das Rathaus, ⸚er
class die Klasse, -n; **German ~** die Deutschstunde
classical klassisch
clean sauber; **to ~** putzen; auf·räumen; sauber machen
clear klar
client der Kunde, -n, n/die Kundin, -nen
climate das Klima
clock die Uhr, -en
close eng; nah(e)
close: to ~ schließen°; zu·machen
clothing die Kleidung; **article of ~** das Kleidungsstück, -e
coat der Mantel, ⸚; **sport ~** das Jackett, -s; der Sakko, -s
coffee der Kaffee; **for (afternoon) ~** zum Kaffee; **to go for ~** Kaffee trinken gehen; **~house** das Kaffeehaus, ⸚er; **~ table** der Couchtisch, -e
cola drink die Cola
cold kalt; die Erkältung, -en; **to catch a ~** sich erkälten
colleague der Kollege, -n, -n/die Kollegin, -nen
collect sammeln
college das College, -s; **to go to ~** studieren; auf/an die Universität gehen
color die Farbe, -n; **What ~ is . . . ?** Welche Farbe hat ... ?
comb der Kamm, ⸚e; **to ~ (one's hair)** (sich) kämmen
come kommen°; **to ~ along** mit·kommen°; **to ~ by** vorbei·kommen°
commercial (TV or radio) der Werbespot, -s; die Reklame, -n
compact disc die Compact Disc, -s; die CD, -s

company die Gesellschaft, -en; die Firma, *pl.* Firmen; **to have ~** Besuch haben
compete konkurrieren
complete(ly) ganz; voll
compromise der Kompromiss, -e
computer der Computer, -; **~ game** das Computerspiel, -e; **~ science** die Informatik; **~ language** die Programmiersprache, -n
concept die Vorstellung, -en
concert das Konzert, -e
concerto das Konzert, -e
condition der Zustand, ⸚e
consciousness das Bewusstsein
constitution die Verfassung, -en
contrary: on the ~ sondern; doch
cook kochen
cool kühl
corner die Ecke, -n
correct richtig
cost kosten
cough husten
could könnte
country das Land, ⸚er; der Staat; **in our ~** bei uns; **in the ~** auf dem Land(e); **out into the ~** ins Grüne; **to the ~** aufs Land
course der Kurs, -e; die Vorlesung, -en; die Veranstaltung, -en
course: of ~ natürlich; klar; selbstverständlich
courtyard der Hof, ⸚e
cousin (*female*) die Kusine, -n; **~** (*male*) der Vetter, -n
cover decken
cozy gemütlich
crazy verrückt
create schaffen°
criticism die Kritik, -en
crooked schief
cucumber die Gurke, -n
cultural(ly) kulturell
culture die Kultur, -en
curious neugierig; gespannt
customer der Kunde, -n, -n/die Kundin, -nen
cyber cafe das Internetcafé, -s

D

dad der Vati, -s
daily täglich
dance: to ~ tanzen

dance club die Disco, -s
dancing: I'm going ~. Ich gehe tanzen.
danger die Gefahr, -en
dangerous gefährlich
dark dunkel
darling der Liebling, -e
data die Tatsachen (*pl.*)
date das Datum; **What's the ~ today?** Den Wievielten haben wir heute?; Der Wievielte ist heute?
daughter die Tochter, ⸚
day der Tag, -e; **one/some ~** eines Tages; **all ~** den ganzen Tag; **days of the week** die Wochentage (*pl.*); **every ~** jeden Tag; **What ~ is today?** Welcher Tag ist heute?
dear lieb (-er, -e, -es)
December der Dezember
decide (sich) entscheiden°; beschließen°; **to make a decision (after reflecting on it)** sich entscheiden
deed die Tat, -en
degree der Grad
demonstrate demonstrieren
demonstration die Demonstration, -en
dentist der Zahnarzt, ⸚e/die Zahnärztin, -nen
depart ab·fahren°
department store das Kaufhaus, -häuser
depend on ab·hängen° von
describe beschreiben°
desire die Lust
desk der Schreibtisch, -e
dessert der Nachtisch, -e
destroy zerstören
develop (sich) entwickeln
development die Entwicklung, -en
dialect der Dialekt, -e
die sterben°
difference der Unterschied, -e
different verschieden; anders; **something ~** (et)was anderes
difficult schwer; schwierig
difficulty die Schwierigkeit, -en
dining room das Esszimmer, -
dinner das Abendessen, -; **for ~** zum Abendessen; **to eat ~** zu Abend essen
discussion die Diskussion, -en

dishes   das Geschirr
dishwasher   die Spülmaschine, -n; der Geschirrspüler, -; **to empty the ~**   die Spülmaschine ausräumen; **to load the ~**   die Spülmaschine einräumen
diskette   die Diskette, -n
distorted   schief
district   das Viertel, -; **city ~**   das Stadtviertel, -
disturb   stören
divide   teilen; auf·teilen (in + *acc.*)
divided by [in mathematics]   geteilt durch
do   machen; tun°; **to ~ a task**   eine Arbeit machen; **to ~ chores**   den Haushalt machen
doctor   der Arzt, ¨e/die Ärztin, -nen; **to go to the ~**   zum Arzt gehen
doesn't he (she)   nicht? nicht wahr?
dog   der Hund, -e
doll   die Puppe, -n
done   fertig; **to have something ~**   etwas machen lassen
door   die Tür, -en
dormitory   das Studentenheim, -e
downstairs   unten
dream: to ~ of   träumen (von)
dress   das Kleid, -er; **to ~**   (sich) an·ziehen°; **I get dressed.**   Ich ziehe mich an.
drink   das Getränk, -e; **to ~**   trinken°
drive   fahren°; **to ~ along**   mit·fahren; **to ~ away**   weg·fahren°; **to go for a ~**   spazieren fahren°
driver   der Fahrer, -/die Fahrerin, -nen
dry   trocken; **to ~ (dishes)**   ab·trocknen
dumb   dumm; **something ~**   etwas Dummes
during   während
dust   der Staub; **to , ~**   Staub wischen
duty   die Pflicht, -en
dwelling   die Wohnung, -en

E

each   jed- (-er, -es, -e)
ear   das Ohr, -en

early   früh
earn   verdienen
east   der Osten
easy   leicht
easygoing   ruhig
eat   essen°
economic   wirtschaftlich
economy   die Wirtschaft
educate   aus·bilden
education   die Erziehung; die Ausbildung; das Schulwesen
egg   das Ei, -er
else: what ~?   was noch?; **something ~?**   sonst noch etwas?
employed   berufstätig
employee   der Arbeitnehmer, -/die Arbeitnehmerin, -nen; der Mitarbeiter, -/die Mitarbeiterin, -nen
employer   der Arbeitgeber, -/die Arbeitgeberin, -nen
empty   leer
end   das Ende, -n; **in/at the ~**   am Ende
energy   die Energie
engage: to ~ in sports   Sport treiben
engineer   der Ingenieur, -e/die Ingenieurin, -nen
England   (das) England
English (*adj.*)   englisch; **~ language**   (das) Englisch
enjoy: to ~ something   Spaß an einer Sache haben
enjoyment   die Lust; das Vergnügen; der Spaß
enough   genug
entrance hall   der Flur, -e
environment   die Umwelt; **environment-friendly**   umweltfreundlich
especially   besonders
etc.   usw.
eternal(ly)   ewig
even   sogar; **~ if**   auch wenn
evening   der Abend, -e; **Good ~.**   Guten Abend.; **this ~**   heute Abend
evenings   abends
every   jed- (-er, -es, -e); **~ day**   jeden Tag
everyone   jeder
everything   alles
everywhere   überall

exactly   genau; **~ the same**   genauso
exam   die Klausur, -en
examination   die Klausur, -en; die Prüfung, -en; **comprehensive ~**   das Examen, -; **to take an ~**   eine Klauser schreiben
examine   durch·sehen°; prüfen
example   das Beispiel, -e; **for ~**   zum Beispiel (z.B.)
excellent(ly)   ausgezeichnet
except   außer
excuse   die Entschuldigung, -en; **~ me!**   Entschuldigung!
expect   erwarten
expensive   teuer
experience   die Erfahrung, -en
explain   erklären
explanation   die Erklärung, -en
expressway   die Autobahn, -en
eye   das Auge, -n

F

face   das Gesicht, -er
fact   die Tatsache, -n
factory   die Fabrik, -en
fairly   ganz; ziemlich
fall   der Herbst; **to ~**   fallen°
false   falsch
familiar   bekannt
family   die Familie, -n
famous   bekannt; berühmt
fantastic   fantastisch; toll; prima
far   weit
farmer   der Bauer, -n, -n/die Bäuerin, -nen
farmhouse   das Bauernhaus, -häuser
farther   weiter
fast   schnell
fat   dick
father   der Vater, ¨
favorite   Lieblings-; **~ (program)**   (die) Lieblings(sendung)
fear   die Angst, ¨e, **to ~**   sich fürchten (vor + *dat.*); **to ~ for**   Angst haben um
feast   das Fest, -e
February   der Februar
Federal Republic of Germany   die Bundesrepublik Deutschland (BRD)
feel   sich fühlen; **to ~ like**   Lust haben; **I don't ~ like working.**

Ich habe keine Lust zu arbeiten.; **I don't ~ like it.**   Dazu habe ich keine Lust.

feeling   das Gefühl, -e
fence   der Zaun, ̈e
fever   das Fieber
few   wenig(e); **a ~**   ein paar
fight   kämpfen
film   der Film, -e
finally   endlich, schließlich
find   finden°
fine   fein; gut; **I'm ~.**   Es geht mir gut.
finger   der Finger, -
finished   fertig; zu Ende
first   erst; **at ~**   zuerst; **~ of all**   erst einmal, erstens
first name   der Vorname, -ns, -n
first-rate   klasse, spitze, ausgezeichnet
fish   der Fisch, -e
fit   passen
flatware   das Besteck, -e
floor   der Boden, ̈; **~ (of a building)**   der Stock, *pl.* Stockwerke; **first ~**   das Erdgeschoss
flower   die Blume, -n
fluent(ly)   fließend
fly   fliegen°
food   das Essen; die Lebensmittel (*pl.*)
foot   der Fuß, ̈e; **to go on ~**   zu Fuß gehen°; laufen°
for   für *(prep.)*; denn *(conj.)*; **(time)** seit; **~ a year**   seit einem Jahr
force   zwingen°
foreign   fremd
foreigner   der Ausländer, -/die Ausländerin, -nen
forest   der Wald, ̈er
forever   ewig
forget   vergessen°
forgetful   vergesslich
fork   die Gabel, -n
(the) former   jen- (-er, -es, -e); ehemalig
formerly   früher
fortunately   zum Glück
fourth   das Viertel, -
France   (das) Frankreich
frank(ly)   offen
free   frei; **for ~**   umsonst, gratis
freeway   die Autobahn, -en
freezer   der Gefrierschrank, ̈e

French (adj.)   französisch; **~ (language)**   (das) Französisch
French fries   die Pommes frites (*pl.*)
fresh   frisch
Friday   der Freitag
friend   der Freund, -e/die Freundin, -nen
friendliness   die Freundlichkeit
friendly   freundlich
from   von; , **(native of)**   aus; **Where do you come ~?**   Woher kommst du?
fruit   das Obst
full   voll
fun   das Vergnügen; der Spaß; **That's ~.**   Es macht Spaß.; **to have lots of ~**   viel Spaß haben
funny   lustig
furnished   möbliert
furniture   die Möbel (*pl.*); **piece of ~**   das Möbelstück, -e
further   weiter
future   die Zukunft

G

game   das Spiel, -e
garage   die Garage, -n
garbage   der Müll
garden   der Garten, ̈
gasoline   das Benzin
general: in ~   überhaupt, allgemein
gentleman   der Herr, -n, -en
genuine   echt
German (*adj.*)   deutsch; **~ (person)**   der/die Deutsche (*noun decl. like adj.*); **~ (language)**   (das) Deutsch; **to do ~ (homework)**   Deutsch machen; **I'm doing ~.**   Ich mache Deutsch.; **~ Mark**   die D-Mark; **~ studies (language and literature)**   die Germanistik
German Democratic Republic   die Deutsche Demokratische Republik (DDR)
Germany   (das) Deutschland
get   bekommen°; kriegen; holen; **to ~ up**   auf·stehen°; **to ~ together**   zusammen·kriegen, sich treffen°
girl   das Mädchen, -; **~ friend**   die Freundin, -nen
give   geben°; **to ~ (as a gift)**   schenken; **to ~ up**   auf·geben°

glad   froh; **~ to**   gern
gladly   gern
glove   der Handschuh, -e
go   gehen°; **to ~ along**   mit·gehen; **to ~ along with [you]**   mit [dir] mitgehen; **to ~ by [car]**   mit [dem Auto] fahren°; **to ~ for coffee**   Kaffee trinken gehen
goal   das Ziel, -e
golf   das Golf
gone   weg
good   gut; **~ Gracious/Heavens!**   Du meine Güte!
good-bye   Auf Wiedersehen.; Tschüs. (*colloq.*)
government   die Regierung, -en
grade   die Note, -n; **[seventh] ~**   [die siebte] Klasse
grandfather   der Großvater, ̈
grandmother   die Großmutter, ̈
grandparents   die Großeltern (*pl.*)
grape   die Traube, -n
gray   grau
great   toll, ausgezeichnet, prima; **absolutely ~**   ganz/wirklich toll
green   grün
greeting   der Gruß, ̈e
groceries   die Lebensmittel (*pl.*)
group   die Gruppe, -n
grow   wachsen°
guest   der Gast, ̈e; der Besucher, -/die Besucherin, -nen
guilty   schuldig; **not ~**   unschuldig
guitar   die Gitarre, -n

H

hair   das Haar, -e
half   die Hälfte, -n; halb
hall   der Flur, -e
hand   die Hand, ̈e
handbag   die (Hand)tasche, -n
hang   hängen°
happen   passieren°; **What happened to you?**   Was ist dir passiert?
happy   froh, glücklich
hard   hart; schwer
hardly   kaum
hard-working   fleißig
has   hat
hat   der Hut, ̈e
hatred   der Hass; **~ of foreigners**   der Ausländerhass

have haben°; **to ~ to** müssen°;
  to ~ something done etwas
  machen lassen°; **~ some cake.**
  Nehmen Sie etwas Kuchen.
head der Kopf, ⁻e
headache die Kopfschmerzen (*pl.*)
healthy gesund
hear hören
heavy schwer
hello Guten Tag.; Grüß dich.; Hallo.
  (*informal*)
help helfen°; **to ~ with [work]**
  bei [der Arbeit] helfen; **~!** Hilfe!; **~
  me!** Hilf mir!
here hier, da; **~ [toward the
  speaker]** her; **~ you are** bitte
  sehr
Hey! Du!; He!
Hi! Tag! Hallo!
high hoch
hike die Wanderung, -en; **to ~**
  wandern
history die Geschichte
hobby das Hobby, -s
hold halten°
holiday der Feiertag, -e
home: at ~ zu Hause; **(to go) ~**
  nach Hause; **at the ~ of** bei
homeland die Heimat
homework die Hausaufgaben (*pl.*);
  to do ~ die Hausaufgaben
  machen
homosexual der/die Homosexuelle
  (*noun decl. like adj.*)
hope die Hoffnung, -en; **to ~**
  hoffen; **to ~ for** hoffen auf (+
  acc.); **I ~** hoffentlich
horrible furchtbar; fürchterlich;
  schrecklich
horribly furchtbar; fürchterlich;
  schrecklich
hospital das Krankenhaus, ⁻er
hot heiß
hour die Stunde, -n
house das Haus, ⁻er
household der Haushalt
housework die Hausarbeit
how wie; **~ are you?** Wie geht es
  Ihnen?/Wie geht's?
however aber
human being der Mensch, -en, -en
hunch die Ahnung, -en
hunger der Hunger
hungry: to be ~ Hunger haben; to
  get ~ Hunger bekommen/kriegen

hurt weh·tun°, verletzen
husband der (Ehe)mann, ⁻er

I

ice das Eis
ice cream das Eis
idea die Idee, -n; die Vorstellung,
  -en; die Ahnung; **No ~!** Keine
  Ahnung!
idle: be ~ faulenzen
if wenn; ob; **even ~** wenn auch
ill krank
illegible unleserlich
illness die Krankheit, -en
image das Bild, -er; die Vorstellung,
  -en
imagine sich (*dat.*) vor·stellen; **~
  that!** Stell dir das vor!
immediately gleich
important wichtig; **to be ~** eine
  Rolle spielen
impression der Eindruck, ⁻e
improve verbessern
in(to) in; hinein
indeed in der Tat
independent unabhängig
individual einzeln
industrious fleißig
industry die Industrie, -n
inflation die Inflation
influence beeinflussen°
inhabitant der Einwohner, -/die
  Einwohnerin, -nen
injure verletzen
innocent(ly) unschuldig
in order to um … zu
insecure unsicher
insert stecken
in spite of trotz
instead of (an)statt
instrument das Instrument, -e
intelligent intelligent
intend to vor·haben°; wollen
interested: to be ~ (in) (sich)
  interessieren (für)
interesting interessant
international international
intolerance die Intoleranz
invite ein·laden°
is ist; **isn't it?** nicht?; nicht wahr?
  (*tag question*); **Your name is
  [Sandra], isn't it?** Du heißt
  [Sandra], nicht?

J

jacket die Jacke, -n
January der Januar
jeans die Jeans (*pl.*)
job der Beruf, -e; der Job, -s; die
  Stelle, -n; **to have a ~**
  berufstätig sein; **to have a
  temporary ~** jobben
jog joggen
jogging das Jogging
join in mit·machen (bei + *dat.*)
journalist der Journalist, -en,
  -en/die Journalistin, -nen
juice der Saft, ⁻e
July der Juli
June der Juni
just eben; erst; gerade

K

key der Schlüssel, -
kilogram das Kilo(gramm)
kilometer der Kilometer, -
kind gut, nett; **be so ~** sei/seien
  Sie so gut/nett; **what ~ of person**
  was für ein Mensch
kindergarten der Kindergarten
kitchen die Küche, -n; **~ appliance**
  das Küchengerät, -e; **~ range**
  der Herd, -e
knee das Knie, -
knife das Messer, -
know (a fact) wissen°; **to ~ (be
  acquainted)** kennen°; **to get to
  ~** kennen lernen; **to ~ [German]**
  Deutsch können

L

lack fehlen
lake der See, -n
lamp die Lampe, -n
land das Land, ⁻e
language die Sprache, -n
large groß
last letzt; **~ night** gestern Abend;
  to ~ dauern
late spät
later später; **until ~/see you ~** bis
  später, tschüs, bis dann, bis bald
laugh lachen
laundry die Wäsche
law das Gesetz, -e; **~ (field of
  study)** Jura (*no article*)

lawyer der Jurist, -en, -en/die Juristin, -nen; der Rechtsanwalt, ¨e/die Rechtsanwältin, -nen
lay legen
lazy faul
lead führen
learn lernen
least: at ~ wenigstens
leave lassen°; weg·fahren°; ab·fahren°
lecture die Vorlesung, -en
left: on/to the ~ links
leg das Bein, -e
leisure time die Freizeit
lend leihen°
lesson die Stunde, -n; **piano ~** die Klavierstunde, -n
let lassen°
letter der Brief, -e
lettuce der (Kopf)salat, -e
library die Bibliothek, -en
lie liegen°
life das Leben, -
light (*adj.*) leicht; **~ (in color)** hell
like: would ~to möchte; **to ~** gern haben; mögen; gefallen°; **What do you ~ to do?** Was machst du gern? **I ~ to swim.** Ich schwimme gern. **How do you ~ the cheese?** Wie findest du den Käse?; **would you ~ to** hättest du Lust
likewise ebenso; auch
lip die Lippe, -n
listen: to ~ to music Musik hören
literature die Literatur
little klein; wenig; **a ~** ein bisschen, ein wenig
live leben; wohnen
living room das Wohnzimmer, -
living standard der Lebensstandard
located: to be ~ liegen°
lock das Schloss, ¨er
long lang; lange; **a ~ time** lange
longer: no ~ nicht mehr
look: to ~ at an·sehen°, an·schauen; **to ~ like ...** wie ... aus·sehen°; **to ~ for** suchen; **to ~ forward to** sich freuen auf (+ *acc.*)
lose verlieren°
lot: a ~ viel
lots of viel
loud laut

lounge around faulenzen
love die Liebe; **to ~** lieben; **in ~** verliebt
low niedrig
luck das Glück; **Good ~!** Viel Glück!; **to be lucky** Glück haben
lunch das Mittagessen; **for ~** zum Mittagessen; **to have ~** zu Mittag essen°
lunch meat die Wurst, ¨e

M

machine die Maschine, -n
magazine die Zeitschrift, -en
major subject das Hauptfach, ¨er
mail die Post
main Haupt-; **~ train station** der Hauptbahnhof, ¨e
make machen
mama die Mama
man der Mann, ¨er; **~!** Mensch!
manner die Art
many viele; **how ~** wie viele; **too ~** zu viele
map die Landkarte, -n
March der März
margarine die Margarine
market der Markt, ¨e
marmalade die Marmelade
marriage die Heirat, -en
married verheiratet
marry heiraten
math die Mathe
mathematics die Mathematik
matter aus·machen; **it doesn't ~** (es) macht nichts; **it doesn't ~ to [me]** es macht [mir] nichts aus
May der Mai
may dürfen°; **that ~ well be** das mag wohl sein
maybe vielleicht
meal das Essen
mean meinen; bedeuten; **What does that ~?** Was bedeutet das?
meaning die Bedeutung, -en
meanwhile inzwischen
meat das Fleisch
meat market die Metzgerei, -en
medicine das Medikament, -e
meet (sich) treffen°; kennen lernen; **I'm meeting friends.** Ich treffe mich mit Freunden.

member das Mitglied, -er
merchandise die Ware, -n
merchant der Kaufmann, ¨er/die Kauffrau, -en; (*pl.*) die Kaufleute
mere(ly) bloß
merry lustig
microwave oven der Mikrowellenherd, -e
milk die Milch
million die Million, -en
mind: to have in ~ vor·haben°
mineral water das Mineralwasser
minor subject das Nebenfach, ¨er
minute die Minute, -n; **Just a ~, please!** Einen Moment, bitte!
mirror der Spiegel, -
Miss Fräulein
missing: to be ~ fehlen
mixer (food processor) die Küchenmaschine, -n
modern modern
mom die Mutti, -s; die Mama
moment der Moment, -e; **at the ~** im Moment, zur Zeit
Monday der Montag
Mondays montags
money das Geld
month der Monat, -e; **a ~ ago** vor einem Monat; **every ~** jeden Monat
more mehr; **no ~ ...** kein ... mehr; **~ and ~** immer mehr; **~ or less** mehr oder weniger
morning der Morgen; **Good ~.** Guten Morgen.; **this ~** heute Morgen
mornings morgens
most of the time meistens
mostly meistens
mother die Mutter, ¨
motorcycle das Motorrad, ¨er
motto das Motto, -s
mountain der Berg, -e
mouth der Mund, ¨er
movie der Film, -e; **~ theater** das Kino, -s
movies das Kino, -s; **to the ~** ins Kino
Mr. Herr
Mrs. Frau
Ms. Frau
much viel; **how ~** wie viel; **too ~** zu viel
multicultural multikulturell
music die Musik

music lesson die Musikstunde, -n
musical das Musical, -s
musical instrument das Musik-instrument, -e
musician der Musiker, -/die Musikerin, -nen
must müssen°
mystery (novel or film) der Krimi, -s

N

name Name, -ns, -n; **first ~** der Vorname, -ns, -n; **last ~** der Nachname, -ns, -n; **What is your ~?** Wie heißen Sie?; **to ~** nennen°; **Your ~ is [Mark], isn't it?** Du heißt [Mark], nicht?
named: to be ~ heißen°
napkin die Serviette, -n
narrow eng
natural(ly) klar; natürlich; selbst-verständlich
nature die Natur
near bei; **~by** in der Nähe, nah(e)
neck der Hals, ̈e
need brauchen
neighbor der Nachbar, -n, -n/die Nachbarin, -nen
neighboring country das Nachbarland, ̈er
nephew der Neffe, -n, -n
nervous nervös
never nie
nevertheless trotzdem
new neu; **What's ~?** Was gibt's Neues?
newspaper die Zeitung, -en
next nächst
nice nett; schön
niece die Nichte, -n
night die Nacht, ̈e, **last ~** gestern Abend; **Good ~.** Gute Nacht.
no nein; kein; nicht; **~ longer** nicht mehr; **~ more . . .** kein . . . mehr
noodles die Nudeln (*pl.*)
no one niemand
nonsense der Quatsch
north der Norden
nose die Nase, -n
not nicht; **isn't that so?** nicht?; **~ at all** gar nicht; **~ any, no** kein; **~ only . . . but also . . .** nicht nur … sondern auch …

note die Notiz, -en
notebook das Heft, -e
nothing nichts; **~ special** nichts Besonderes
notice bemerken, merken
novel der Roman, -e
November der November
now jetzt; nun; **~ and then** ab und zu
number die Zahl, -en; die Nummer, -n; **phone ~** die Telefonnummer
numeral die Zahl, -en
nurse der Krankenpfleger, -/die Krankenpflegerin, -nen; **~ (female only)** die Kranken-schwester, -n
nursery school der Kindergarten, ̈

O

observe beobachten
obtain bekommen°; kriegen
occupied: to be ~ beschäftigt sein
occupy beschäftigen
occur (to come into one's mind) einfallen°
ocean der Ozean, -e
October der Oktober
of von
offer an·bieten°
office das Büro, -s
often oft
oh ach, ah; **~ I see** ach so; **~ my** o je; **~ well** na ja
OK okay (O.K.); ganz gut; **It's (not) ~.** Es geht (nicht).
old alt; **I'm [19] years ~.** Ich bin [19] Jahre alt. **How ~ are you?** Wie alt bist du?
on an; auf; **~ account of** wegen
once einmal; mal; **~ more** noch einmal
one (*pronoun*) man; **~ another** einander
oneself selbst, selber
only nur; erst; bloß
open offen, geöffnet; **to ~** auf·machen; öffnen
opera die Oper, -n
opinion die Meinung, -en; **What's your ~?** Was hältst du davon?
or oder
orange die Orange, -n; **~ juice** der Orangensaft

orchestra das Orchester, -
order die Ordnung; **in ~** in Ordnung; **to ~** bestellen
organization die Organisation, -en
organize organisieren
other ander- (-er, -es, -e)
otherwise sonst; anders
out of aus
outside draußen
over (time) vorbei; **~ (task)** fertig; **~ (position)** über
own (*adj.*) eigen; (*verb*) besitzen°

P

page die Seite, -n
pain der Schmerz, -en
paint malen; streichen
pale blass
pants die Hosen, -n
pantyhose die Strumpfhose, -n
paper das Papier; **~ (theme, essay)** die Arbeit, -en; **~ plate** der Pappteller, -
paperback das Taschenbuch, ̈er
pardon: I beg your ~? Wie bitte?
parents die Eltern (*pl.*)
park der Park, -s
part der Teil, -e; **in ~** zum Teil; **to play a ~** eine Rolle spielen
participate (in) mit·machen (bei); **I ~ in a game.** Ich mache bei einem Spiel mit.
particular besonder-
particularly besonders
party die Party, -s; die Feier, -n; das Fest, -e; die Fete, -n; **at a ~** auf einem Fest; **to give a ~** ein Fest geben; **to go to a ~** auf ein Fest gehen
passive passiv
patio die Terrasse, -n
pay: to ~ for bezahlen; zahlen; **to ~ back** zurück·zahlen
peace der Frieden
pedestrian der Fußgänger, -/die Fußgängerin, -nen; **~ zone** die Fußgängerzone, -n
pen der Kugelschreiber, - [der Kuli, -s (*colloq.*)]
pencil der Bleistift, -e
people die Leute (*pl.*); die Menschen (*pl.*); die Einwohner (*pl.*); man
per pro

percent　das Prozent
perhaps　vielleicht
period　der Punkt, -e
permit　lassen°
permitted: to be ~　dürfen°
person　der Mensch, -en, -en; die
　Person, -en
pharmacy　die Apotheke, -n;
　to the ~　in die Apotheke
philosophy　die Philosophie
phone　das Telefon, -e; **~ number**
　die Telefonnummer, -n
photograph　das Bild, das Foto; **to ~**
　fotografieren
physics　die Physik
piano　das Klavier, -e; **~ lesson**
　die Klavierstunde, -n
pick up　ab·holen
picnic　das Picknick, -s
picture　das Bild, -er
piece　das Stück, -e
Ping-Pong　das Tischtennis
pity: what a ~　schade
place　der Platz, ¨e; die Stelle, -n;
　der Ort, -e; **to my ~**　zu mir; **at
　my ~**　bei mir
plan　der Plan, ¨e; **to ~**
　vor·haben°; planen
plant　die Pflanze, -n; **to ~**
　pflanzen
plastic　das Plastik
play　das Theaterstück, -e; **to ~**
　spielen
please　bitte; **to ~**　gefallen°
pleased: to be ~ (about)　sich
　freuen (über + acc.)
pleasure　die Freude, -n; die Lust;
　das Vergnügen
pocket　die Tasche, -n
point　der Punkt, -e
police　die Polizei
political(ly)　politisch
politician　der Politiker, -/die
　Politikerin, -nen
portion　der Teil -e
position　die Stelle, -n
possible　möglich; **It's (not) ~.**　Es
　geht (nicht).; **That would (not)
　be ~.**　Das ginge (nicht).
post office　die Post; **to go to the ~**
　auf die *or* zur Post gehen
postal code　die Postleitzahl, -en
postcard　die Postkarte, -n
poster　das/der Poster, -
potato　die Kartoffel, -n

pound　das Pfund, -e
practical(ly)　praktisch
prefer: I ~ to work.　Ich arbeite
　lieber.
prejudice　das Vorurteil, -e
preparation　die Vorbereitung, -en
prepare (for)　(sich) vor·bereiten
　(auf + *acc.*)
present　das Geschenk, -e
president　der Präsident, -en,
　-en/die Präsidentin, -nen
pretty　schön; **~ pale**　ganz schön
　blass
price　der Preis, -e
private(ly)　privat
probably　wahrscheinlich
produce　her·stellen, produzieren
product　das Produkt, -e
profession　der Beruf, -e
professor　der Professor, -en/die
　Professorin, -nen
program　das Programm, -e; **TV** *or*
　radio ~　die Sendung, -en
programmer　der Programmierer,
　-/die Programmiererin, -nen
promise　versprechen°
protect　schützen
proud(ly)　stolz
psychology　die Psychologie
pub　die Kneipe, -n; die Gaststätte,
　-n; die Wirtschaft, -en
public　öffentlich; staatlich
pullover　der Pulli, -s; der Pullover, -
punctual(ly)　pünktlich
pure　rein
purse　die Handtasche, -n
put　legen; stellen; stecken; setzen;
　hängen

Q

quality　die Qualität, -en
quarter　das Viertel, -
question　die Frage, -n
questionable　fraglich
quick　schnell
quiet　ruhig; still
quite　ziemlich

R

racism　der Rassismus
radio　das Radio, -s
railroad　die Bahn, -en

rain　der Regen; **to ~**　regnen
raincoat　der Regenmantel, ¨
range (kitchen)　der Herd, -e
rare(ly)　selten
rather　ziemlich; **~ than**　lieber als
raw material　der Rohstoff, -e
reach　erreichen
read　lesen°
ready　fertig
real　echt; richtig
reality　die Wirklichkeit
really　wirklich; richtig; echt (*slang*);
　~ neat　echt toll
reason　der Grund, ¨e; **for that ~**
　daher; darum; deshalb; deswegen;
　aus diesem Grund
reasonable (price)　günstig
receive　bekommen°
recently　vor kurzem; neulich; seit
　kurzer Zeit
recommend　empfehlen°
record　die Platte, -n
record player　der Plattenspieler, -
recover (from)　sich erholen (von)
recuperate　sich erholen
recycle　recyceln
recycling　das Recycling
red　rot
refrigerator　der Kühlschrank, ¨e
rehearsal　die Probe, -n
related　verwandt
relative　der/die Verwandte (*noun
　decl. like adj.*)
remain　bleiben°
remaining　übrig
remember (someone/something)
　sich erinnern (an + jemand/
　etwas)
rent　die Miete, -n; **to ~**　mieten;
　vermieten
repair　reparieren
report　der Bericht, -e; das Referat,
　-e; **to ~**　berichten
reporter　der Reporter, -/die
　Reporterin, -nen
request　bitten° (+ um)
reservation: without ~　unbedingt
responsibility　die Verantwortung,
　-en
responsible　verantwortlich
rest　der Rest, -e; **to ~**　sich
　aus·ruhen
restaurant　das Restaurant, -s; die
　Gaststätte, -n; **town hall ~**　der
　Ratskeller, -

return zurück·fahren°; zurück·ge-hen°; zurück·kommen°; **to ~ (something)** (etwas) zurück·geben

reunification die Wiederver-einigung

rich reich

ride: to ~ a bike mit dem Fahrrad fahren°, Rad fahren°

right das Recht, -e; **Is it all ~ with you?** Ist es dir recht?; **to be ~** Recht haben; **you're ~** du hast Recht; **that's ~** genau; richtig; **~ to** Recht (auf + *acc.*); **equal rights** die Gleichberechtigung; **on/to the ~** rechts

ring klingeln

rinse spülen

river der Fluss, ⸚e

roast beef der Rinderbraten

rock: ~ music die Rockmusik; **~ musician** der Rockmusiker, -/die Rockmusikerin, -nen

role die Rolle, -n

roll das Brötchen, -

romance (novel) der Liebes-roman, -e

room das Zimmer, -

rug der Teppich, -e

run laufen°

running das Jogging

S

sad traurig

safe sicher

sail: to ~ segeln

salary das Gehalt, ⸚er

same gleich; **It's all the ~ to me.** Das ist mir egal.

sandwich das [Wurst]Brot, -e

satisfied zufrieden

Saturday der Samstag; der Sonnabend; **on ~** am Samstag

Saturdays samstags

sausage die Wurst, ⸚e

save (time, money, etc.) sparen

say sagen

schedule der Stundenplan, ⸚e

school die Schule, -n

science die Wissenschaft, -en; die Naturwissenschaft, -en

scientist der Wissenschaftler, -/die Wissenschaftlerin, -nen

season die Jahreszeit, -en

seat der Platz, ⸚e; **Is this ~ taken?** Ist hier frei?; **to ~ oneself** sich setzen°

secretary der Sekretär, -e/die Sekretärin, -nen

see sehen°

seem scheinen°

seldom selten

self: oneself, myself, itself, etc. selbst, selber

sell verkaufen

semester das Semester, -

seminar das Seminar, -e; **~ room** das Seminar, -e; **~ report** die Seminararbeit, -en

send schicken

sentence der Satz, ⸚e

separate: to ~ trennen

September der September

serious ernst; **Are you ~?** Ist das dein Ernst?

serve dienen

set setzen; **to ~ the table** den Tisch decken

several einige; mehrere

shampoo das Shampoo

shave (sich) rasieren

shine scheinen°

ship das Schiff, -e

shirt das Hemd, -en

shoe der Schuh, -e

shop das Geschäft, -e; der Laden, ⸚; **to ~** ein·kaufen

shopping: to go ~ ein·kaufen gehen

shopping bag die Einkaufstasche, -n

short kurz; **~ (people)** klein

shorts die Shorts (*pl.*), die kurzen Hosen

show zeigen

shower die Dusche, -n; **to ~** (sich) duschen

sick krank

side die Seite, -n

significance die Bedeutung

similar ähnlich; gleich

simple einfach

simply einfach

since seit (*prep.*); da (*conj.* = because); **~ when** seit wann

sing singen°

singer der Sänger, -/die Sängerin, -nen

single einzeln

single-family home das Einfamilienhaus, ⸚er

sister die Schwester, -n

sit sitzen°; **to ~ down** sich setzen

situated: to be ~ liegen°

situation die Situation, -en

ski der Ski, -er; **to ~** Ski laufen°, Ski fahren°

skirt der Rock, ⸚e

sleep schlafen°; **to ~ at [a friend's] house** bei [einem Freund] schlafen

slow(ly) langsam

small klein

smart intelligent

smell riechen°

smile (about) lächeln (über + acc.)

smog der Smog

smoke der Rauch; **to ~** rauchen

snow der Schnee; **to ~** schneien

so so; also; **Isn't that ~?** Nicht?; **~ that** damit; **~ long.** Tschüs; **I believe ~.** Ich glaube schon/ja.

soap die Seife

soccer der Fußball

society die Gesellschaft, -en

sock die Socke, -n

sofa das Sofa, -s

soft drink die Limonade, -n

software die Software

soldier der Soldat, -en, -en/die Soldatin, -nen

solution die Lösung, -en

solve lösen

some etwas; einige; manch (-er, -es, -e); **at ~ point** irgendwann

someone jemand

something etwas/was; **~ like that** so was

sometime irgendwann

sometimes manchmal

somewhat etwas

son der Sohn, ⸚e

song das Lied, -er

soon bald; **as ~ as** sobald

sorry: I'm ~ (es) tut mir Leid

south der Süden

space der Platz, ⸚e

spaghetti die Spaghetti (*pl.*)

Spanish (language) (das) Spanisch

speak sprechen°

speechless sprachlos

spell buchstabieren; **How do you ~ that?** Wie schreibt man das?

spend (money) aus·geben°; **to ~ (time)** verbringen°; **to ~ the night** übernachten
spite: in ~ of trotz
splendid großartig
spoon der Löffel, -
sport der Sport; **to engage in sports** Sport treiben°
spring der Frühling
stairs die Treppe, -n
stand stehen°; **to ~ up** auf·stehen°; **to ~/put upright** stellen
standard German (das) Hochdeutsch
state (in Germany) das Land, ¨er; **~ (in the U.S.A.)** der Staat, -en
state-owned staatlich
stay bleiben°; **to ~ at a hotel** im Hotel übernachten
steak das Steak, -s
step der Schritt, -e; die Stufe, -n
stepfather der Stiefvater, ¨
stepmother die Stiefmutter, ¨
steps die Treppe, -n
stereo system die Stereoanlage, -n
still noch; immer noch; noch immer
stomach der Magen
stomachache die Magenschmerzen (*pl.*)
stop auf·hören (mit); halten°; stehen bleiben°
store das Geschäft, -e; der Laden, ¨
story die Geschichte, -n
straight gerade
straighten up auf·räumen
strange merkwürdig
street die Straße, -n; **~ car** die Straßenbahn, -en
stress der Stress
strict(ly) streng
strike der Streik, -s; **to ~** streiken
stroll spazieren gehen
strong stark
student der Student, -en, -en/die Studentin, -nen
studies das Studium
study studieren; lernen; arbeiten; durch·arbeiten; **to ~ for a test** für eine Klausur lernen
stupid dumm
subject (academic) das Fach, ¨er
subway die U-Bahn
such solch (-er, -es, -e); **~ a** so ein

suddenly plötzlich
suit (man's) der Anzug, ¨e; **(woman's) ~** das Kostüm, -e; **to ~** passen
summer der Sommer
sun die Sonne, -n
sunglasses die Sonnenbrille, -n
Sunday der Sonntag
Sundays sonntags
superficial oberflächlich
supermarket der Supermarkt, ¨e **to the ~** in den Supermarkt; **at the ~** im Supermarkt
supper das Abendessen; **for ~** zum Abendessen; **to have ~** zu Abend essen
supposed: to be ~ to sollen°
sure sicher; bestimmt; **(agreement) ~ !** Natürlich!
surf surfen
surprise überraschen
suspense: to be in ~ gespannt sein
sweater der Pulli, -s; der Pullover, -
swim schwimmen°
swimming: to go ~ schwimmen gehen° ;**~ suit** der Badeanzug, ¨e; **~ trunks** die Badehose, -n
Swiss (*adj.*) Schweizer; **~ (person)** der Schweizer, -/die Schweizerin, -nen
switch (to change) wechseln
Switzerland die Schweiz

T

table der Tisch, -e; **bedside ~** der Nachttisch, -e
table tennis das Tischtennis
take nehmen°; **~ along** mit·nehmen°
take care of (someone) auf·passen (auf + *acc.*)
take off sich (*dat.*) [etwas] aus·ziehen°; **I take off my shoes** Ich ziehe mir die Schuhe aus.
talk sich unterhalten°; **to ~ (about)** reden (über); sprechen° (über +*acc.*/von)
tall (people) groß
talk die Aufgabe, -n
taste schmecken; probieren
tasty lecker
tax die Steuer, -n
teacher der Lehrer, -/die Lehrerin, -nen

telephone das Telefon, -e; **to ~** telefonieren; an·rufen°
telephone number die Telefonnummer, -n; **What is your ~?** Wie ist deine/Ihre Telefonnummer?
television das Fernsehen; **~ set** der Fernseher, -; **color ~** der Farbfernseher; **~ program** die Fernsehsendung, -en; **to watch ~** fern·sehen°
tell sagen; erzählen; **to ~ (about)** erzählen (über + *acc.*/von)
tennis das Tennis
terrace die Terrasse, -n
terrible schlimm; furchtbar; schrecklich
test die Klausur, -en; **to take a ~** eine Klausur schreiben°; **to study for a ~** für eine Klausur lernen
than als (*after a comparison*)
thank danken; **~ you very much** danke sehr/schön
thanks danke; der Dank; **~ a lot, many ~** vielen Dank
that dass; jen- (er, -es, -e)
theater das Theater, -; **to go to the ~** ins Theater gehen; **~ play** das Theaterstück, -e; **movie ~** das Kino, -s
then dann; da
there da; dort; dahin; **~ is/are** es gibt
thereby dadurch
therefore also; deshalb; daher; darum; deswegen
these diese
thin dünn, schlank
thing das Ding, -e; die Sache, -n
think denken°; meinen; **What do you ~?** Was meinst du? **What do you ~ of the cake?** Was hältst du von dem Kuchen?; **I don't ~ so.** Ich glaube nicht.
third das Drittel, -
thirst der Durst
thirsty: to be ~ Durst haben°
this dies (-er, -es, -e); **~ afternoon** heute Nachmittag
throat der Hals, ¨e
throw werfen°; **to ~ away** weg·werfen°
Thursday der Donnerstag
thus also
ticket die Karte -n; **entrance ~**

die Eintrittskarte; **train/bus ~** die Fahrkarte

tie: neck ~   die Krawatte, -n; **to ~** binden°

tight   eng

time   die Zeit, -en; das Mal, -e; mal; **at this ~**   zur Zeit; **at that ~** damals; **at the same ~**   zur gleichen Zeit; **for a long ~** lange; **a short ~ ago**   vor kurzem, neulich; **What ~ is it?** Wie viel Uhr ist es?/Wie spät ist es?; **At what ~?**   Um wie viel Uhr?; **Have a good ~!**   Viel Vergnügen!

times   mal; **[three] ~**   [drei] mal

tinker   basteln

tired   müde; kaputt

to   an; auf, in; nach; zu

today   heute; **What day is it ~?** Welcher Tag ist heute?

together   zusammen

tolerant   tolerant

tomato   die Tomate, -n

tomorrow   morgen; **day after ~** übermorgen

tonight   heute Abend

too   zu; **me ~**   ich auch; **~ little** zu wenig; **~ much**   zu viel

tool   das Gerät, -e; das Werkzeug, -e

tooth   der Zahn, ¨e; **to brush [my] teeth**   [mir] die Zähne putzen

toothache   die Zahnschmerzen (*pl.*)

tour   die Tour, -en

tourist   der Tourist, -en, -en/die Touristin, -nen

town hall restaurant   der Ratskeller, -

trade   der Handel; **foreign ~**   der Außenhandel

tradition   die Tradition, -en

traffic   der Verkehr

train   der Zug, ¨e; die Bahn; **~ station**   der Bahnhof, ¨e; **to go by ~**   mit dem Zug/der Bahn fahren

translation   die Übersetzung, -en

transportation: means of ~   das Verkehrsmittel, -

travel   fahren°; reisen; **to ~ by train** mit dem Zug fahren

tree   der Baum, ¨e

treat   ein·laden°

trip   die Reise, -n, die Fahrt, -en; die Tour, -en; **bike ~**   die Radtour, -en

trousers   die Hose, -n

truck   der Lastwagen, -

true   wahr

try   versuchen; probieren

T-shirt   das T-Shirt, -s

Tuesday   der Dienstag

Tuesdays   dienstags

turn: to have one's ~   dran sein; **it's your ~**   du bist dran

TV   das Fernsehen; **~ set**   der Fernseher, -; **~ program**   die Fernsehsendung, -en

type: to ~   tippen; **to be able to ~** Schreibmaschine schreiben können

typewriter   die Schreibmaschine, -n

U

umbrella   der Regenschirm, -e; der Schirm, -e

unbelievable   unglaublich

uncle   der Onkel, -

under   unter

understand   verstehen°

undress   (sich) aus·ziehen°; **I get undressed.**   Ich ziehe mich aus.

unemployed   arbeitslos

unfortunately   leider

unification   die Vereinigung

unified   vereinigt; vereint

union   die Gewerkschaft, -en

university   die Universität, -en; die Uni, -s; **to attend a ~**   an/auf die Universität gehen; **at the ~** an/auf der Universität

unsafe   unsicher

until   bis; **~ now**   bisher; **~ later** bis später; tschüs; bis dann; bis bald

up to   bis zu

U.S.A.   die USA (*pl.*); **to the ~**   in die USA

use   benutzen; gebrauchen; **to ~ up** verbrauchen

utensil   das Gerät, -e

V

vacation   der Urlaub; die Ferien (*pl.*); **~ trip**   die Ferienreise, -n; **on/during ~**   in Urlaub/in den

Ferien; **to go on ~**   in Urlaub/in die Ferien fahren°; **to be on ~** in Urlaub/in den Ferien sein°

vacuum   der Staubsauger, -; **to ~** Staub saugen

vain: in ~   umsonst

vase   die Vase, -n

VCR   der Videorecorder, -

vegetable   das Gemüse, -

very   sehr; ganz

vicinity: in the ~   in der Nähe

video   das Video, -s

video camera   die Videokamera, -s

video game   das Videospiel, -e

video recorder   der Videorecorder, -

village   das Dorf, ¨er

visit   der Besuch; **to ~**   besuchen

visitor   der Besucher, -/die Besucherin, -nen

volleyball   der Volleyball

W

wait (for)   warten (auf)

walk   der Spaziergang, ¨e; **to take a ~**   einen Spaziergang machen; **to go for a ~**   spazieren gehen°

walking: to go ~   wandern/ spazieren gehen°

wall   die Wand, ¨e; die Mauer, -n

want (to)   wollen°

war   der Krieg, -e; **world ~**   der Weltkrieg, -e

warm   warm

was   war

wash   die Wäsche; **to ~**   (sich) waschen°; **to ~ dishes** ab·waschen°; Geschirr spülen

washing machine   die Waschmaschine, -n

watch   die (Armband)uhr, -en; **to ~** an·sehen°; **to ~ TV**   fern·sehen°; **to ~ out**   auf·passen

water   das Wasser

water ski   der Wasserki, -er; **to ~** Wasserski fahren°

way   der Weg, -e; **on the ~**   auf dem Weg; die Art; **this ~**   so; auf diese Weise

weak   schwach

wear   tragen°

weather   das Wetter; **~ report**   der Wetterbericht, -e

Wednesday   der Mittwoch

week die Woche, -n; **a ~ from
[Monday]** [Montag] in acht
Tagen; **a ~ ago** vor einer Woche

weekend das Wochenende; **on the
~** am Wochenende; **over the ~**
übers Wochenende

weightlifting das Gewichtheben

welcome: you're ~ bitte (sehr)

well gut; wohl; **I'm not ~.** Mir
geht's schlecht; **~ (interjection)**
na!, nun!; **~ now, oh ~** na

well known bekannt

west der Westen

wet nass

what was; **~ kind (of), ~ a** was
für (ein)

when wann; wenn; als

where wo; **~ (to)** wohin; **~ do
you come from?** Woher
kommst du?

whether ob

which welch (-er, -es, -e)

while während

white weiß

who wer

whole ganz

whom wen (*acc. of* wer); wem (*dat.
of* wer)

whose wessen

why warum

willingly gern

wind der Wind

window das Fenster, -

windsurfing: to go ~ windsurfen
gehen°

wine der Wein, -e

winter der Winter

wish wünschen; **I ~ I had . . .**
Ich wollte, ich hätte …

with mit; **~ it** damit; **~ me** mit
mir; **to live ~ a family** bei einer
Familie wohnen

woman die Frau, -en

wonder: to ~ about gespannt sein

woods der Wald, ¨er

word das Wort, ¨er

word processing die
Textverarbeitung; **~ program**
das Textverarbeitungsprogramm;
to do ~ mit Textverarbeitungsprogrammen arbeiten

work die Arbeit; **to do the ~** die
Arbeit machen; arbeiten; **to ~
through** durch·arbeiten; **to ~
out** trainieren; **It doesn't ~.** Es
geht nicht.; **It works.** Es geht.

worker der Arbeiter, -/die Arbeiterin, -nen; der Arbeitnehmer,
-/die Arbeitnehmerin, -nen

workplace der Arbeitsplatz, ¨e

world die Welt, -en; **~ war** der
Weltkrieg, -e

worry die Sorge, -n; **to ~ about**
sich Sorgen machen (um); sich
kümmern um

worth wert

worthwhile wert; **to be ~** sich
lohnen

would würde; **~ like** möchte;
How ~ it be? Wie wär's?; **~ you
like to** hättest du Lust

wow Mensch!

write schreiben°; **to ~ to someone**
jemandem/an jemanden
schreiben; **to ~ down**
auf·schreiben

writer der Schriftsteller, -/die
Schriftstellerin, -nen

wrong falsch; **What's ~?** Was ist
los?; **What is ~ with you?** Was
hast du?

X

xenophobia der Ausländerhass

Y

year das Jahr, -e; **a ~ ago** vor
einem Jahr

yearly jährlich

yellow gelb

yes ja

yesterday gestern

yet noch; schon; **not ~** noch nicht

young jung

youth die Jugend; der/die
Jugendliche (*noun decl. like adj.*)

Z

zip code die Postleitzahl, -en

Index

Permissions and Credits

Texts

Pages 280–281: Reprinted by permission of the author, Dr. Ulla Fölsing.

pp. 379–380: Adaptation of Garner, Guido, "Die Kündigung, nur noch drei Tage." In *Kultur-Chronik,* April 1994, pp. 27–29.

pp. 405–406: Hohler, Franz, "Der Verkäufer und der Elch." In *Kontakt mit der Zeit, Texte mit deutschen Wörtern,* Hg. Dieter Stöpfgeschoff, Sveriges Radios förlag, Stockholm, 1976.

p. 316: Mani Mattcr, "Heidi," from *Us emer lääre Gygechaschte,* Zürich· © Benziger Verlag, AG, 1972 and LP Zyt, *I han ese Zündhölzli azünd,* Produktion & Copyright: Zytglogge Verlag, Gumligen.

pp. 432–433: Helga M. Novak, "Schlittenfahren," from *Palisaden Erzählungen,* © 1980 by Luchterhand Literaturverlag, Darmstadt and Neuwied.

Realia

Page 7: Deutsche Bahn AG; p. 14: Bertelsmann Club; p. 25: *Konjugation* by Rudolf Steinmetz, *Anspiel: Konkrete Poesie im Unterricht Deutsch als Fremdsprache,* Krusche/Krechel, © Inter Nationes, Bonn; p. 30: PZ, 6/98, Universum Verlagsanstalt, Wiesbaden; p. 39: *Berliner Zeitung;* p. 63: Partner für Berlin-Gesellschaft für Hauptstadt Marketing mbH; p. 74: *Der Standard;* p. 81: Bertelsmann Club; p. 93: *Die Zeit;* p. 103: courtesy Preisring-Markt; p. 105: Dussmann–das KulturKaufhaus; p. 108: Bundesministerium der Finanzen, Referat Öffentlichkeitsarbeit; p. 109: AOL; p. 114: Berliner Universitätsbuchhandlung; p. 133: *Deutschland,* Nr. 3, Juni 1997; p. 139: debitel; p. 145: Brockhaus; p. 170: Salzburger Sportwelt Amadé; p. 179: courtesy Restop Altea; p. 196: Austrian Tourist Office; p. 205: courtesy Staatl. Mineralbrunnen Siemens Erben, Mainz; p. 206: "Jule Neigel Band," in *Live in Concert,* 4/95 & Studenten im Olympiazentrum e.V., Geschäftsleitung Discothek, Helen-Meyer-Ring 9, 80809 München; p. 211: AMICA; p. 219: mediadesign akademie; p. 221: Modehaus Konen, München; p. 227: Deutsche Bahn AG; p. 240: Haus am Walde, Bremen; p. 255: Verband der privaten Krankenversicherung e. V., Köln; p. 264: Daimler-Benz Aerospace; p. 267: Siemens; p. 274: Hannes Keller AG Computerzentrum Zürich; p. 295: top, *Focus,* 2/1998, Quelle: DataConcept; bottom, *Brigitte,* 11/99; p. 305: courtesy EMS; p. 311: Schweizer Bank Verein/Swiss Bank Corporation, Basel; p. 330: courtesy ZDF; p. 344: Berliner Ensemble; p. 351: *Spiegel;* p. 353: Haus der Geschichte; p. 355: *Deutsche Welle Plus,* 5/99; pp. 374 & 381: *Focus,* 2/1998, Quelle: DataConcept; p. 384: Expo2000 Hannover; pp. 388 & 402: *Hörzu,* 7/8/98; p. 418: courtesy *Die Welt;* p. 423: © Manfred Papan; p. 427: courtesy Foyer; p. 428: Deutsche Bahn AG.

Photos

Page 2: Beryl Goldberg; p. 6: David R. Frazier Photolibrary; p. 10, top: Stuart Cohen; p. 10, bottom & p. 11: Beryl Goldberg; p. 13: David R. Frazier Photolibrary; p. 23: Beryl Goldberg; pp. 25 & 30: David R. Frazier Photolibrary; p. 34: Beryl Goldberg; pp. 40 & 41: Ulrike Welsch; p. 45: Stuart Cohen; p. 50: David R. Frazier Photolibrary; p. 55; Beryl Goldberg; p. 63: Stuart Cohen; p. 64: Ulrike Welsch; p. 66: Beryl Goldberg; p. 67: Kathy Squires; p. 72: Ulrike Welsch; p. 77: Bildarchiv Foto Marburg/Art Resource; p. 88: Beryl Goldberg; p. 91, top: Ulrike Welsch; bottom: David R. Frazier Photolibrary; p. 95: David R. Frazier Photolibrary; p. 98: Ulrike Welsch; p. 100: David R. Frazier Photolibrary; p. 102: Beryl Goldberg; p. 106: Ulrike Welsch; p. 108: Stuart Cohen; p. 111: David R. Frazier Photolibrary; p. 113: Ulrike Welsch; p. 126: Beryl Goldberg; pp. 128, 130 & 132: Ulrike Welsch; p. 137: Kathy Squires; p. 138: Ulrike Welsch; p. 143: Ulrike Welsch; p. 156: David R. Frazier Photolibrary; p. 159: Beryl Goldberg; pp. 163 & 165: Kathy Squires; p. 167: David R. Frazier Photolibrary; p. 169: Kathy Squires; pp. 171, 175 & 177: David R. Frazier Photolibrary; p. 191: Stuart Cohen; p. 199: Beryl Goldberg; p. 202: Kathy Squires; pp. 204 & 207: David R. Frazier Photolibrary; p. 208: Musik + Show/A. Keuchel; p. 210: David R. Frazier Photolibrary; p. 216: Beryl Goldberg; p. 220: Bildarchiv Huber; p. 231: Bildarchiv Engelmeier; p. 233: Beryl Goldberg; p. 235: Kathy Squires; p. 237: Beryl Goldberg; p. 239: Stuart Cohen; p. 241: Ulrike Welsch; p. 245: David R. Frazier Photolibrary; p. 246: Engraving of the Francis Daniel Pastorius homestead, Germantown, PA, by Max Zeitler, 1908. Reproduced from Marion D. Learned, *The Life of Francis Daniel Pastorius* (Philadelphia: Wm. J. Campbell, 1908), courtesy of The Balch Institute for Ethnic Studies Library; pp. 249 & 253: Beryl Goldberg; pp. 256 & 260: Ulrike Welsch; p. 273: Beryl Goldberg; p. 275: Kathy Squires; p. 277: Bildarchiv Engelmeier; p. 285: Beryl Goldberg; p. 288: David R. Frazier Photolibrary; p. 289: Ulrike Welsch; p. 298: dpa/ipol; p. 304: Beryl Goldberg; p. 306: Swiss National Tourist Office; p. 314: The Picture Cube/Steven Saks; p. 316: Keystone Press AG Archiv; p. 319: The Stock Market/G. Anderson; p. 320: The Stock Market/Robin Prange; p. 324: Keystone Press AG Archiv; p. 339: Beryl Goldberg; p. 343, top: German Information Center; bottom: Kathy Squires; p. 346: Corbis/Bettmann; p. 349: Sipa Press; p. 352: Beryl Goldberg; p. 361: dpa/ipol; p. 367: Beryl Goldberg; p. 373: Beryl Goldberg; p. 377: Ulrike Welsch; p. 380: Stuart Cohen; p. 382: dpa/ipol; p. 385: Beryl Goldberg; p. 390: Ulrike Welsch; p. 398: David R. Frazier Photolibrary; p. 407: Beryl Goldberg; p. 409: Ulrike Welsch; pp. 413 & 416: Beryl Goldberg.

Illustrations

All illustrations by Anna Veltfort, except illustrations on pp. 168 & 394 by Penny Carter.